MAKING EQUALITY RIGHTS REAL

MAKING EQUALITY
RIGHTS REAL
Securing Substantive Equality under the Charter

Edited by
Fay Faraday, Margaret Denike, and M. Kate Stephenson

Making Equality Rights Real: Securing Substantive Equality under the *Charter*
© Irwin Law Inc., 2006

Published in 2006 by

Irwin Law
14 Duncan Street
Suite 206
Toronto, Ontario
M5H 3G8

www.irwinlaw.com

ISBN-10: 1-55221-118-5   ISBN-13: 978-155221-118-2

Sophia Moreau, "The Wrongs of Unequal Treatment," is reprinted by permission of the University of Toronto Press Inc. (www.utpjournals.com).

Denise G. Réaume, "Discrimination and Dignity," is reprinted by permission of the *Louisiana Law Review*.

Library and Archives Canada Cataloguing in Publication

Making equality rights real : securing substantive equality under the Charter / edited by Fay Faraday, Margaret Denike and M. Kate Stephenson.

Includes bibliographical references and index.
ISBN 1-55221-118-5

1. Canada. Canadian Charter of Rights and Freedoms. 2. Equality before the law—Canada. 3. Civil rights—Canada. 4. Discrimination—Law and legislation—Canada. I. Faraday, Fay, 1966– II. Denike, Margaret, 1961– III. Stephenson, M. Kate

KE4381.5.M33 2006   342.7108'5   C2006-902146-5
KF4483.C56M33 2006

The publisher acknowledges the financial support of the Government of Canada through the Book Publishing Industry Development Program (BPIDP) for its publishing activities.

We acknowledge the assistance of the OMDC Book Fund, an initiative of Ontario Media Development Corporation.

Printed and bound in Canada.

1 2 3 4 5   10 09 08 07 06

Contents

Acknowledgments

Section 15 of the *Canadian Charter of Rights and Freedoms* — our constitutional equality rights guarantee — came into force on 17 April 1985. Marking the twentieth anniversary of section 15, this book celebrates both a generation of constitutional protection for equality rights and also the generations of equality-seekers and advocates who have helped to build the foundation for substantive equality in Canada.

On the same day in April 1985 that section 15 came into force, the Women's Legal Education and Action Fund Inc./Fonds D'Action et D'Éducation Juridiques pour les Femmes (LEAF/FAEJ) was founded as a national, federally incorporated, non-profit advocacy organization to secure equal rights for women in Canada as guaranteed by the *Charter*. To this end, LEAF engages in equality rights litigation, research, and public education. Commencing with the Supreme Court of Canada's landmark case in *Andrews v. Law Society of British Columbia*, [1989] 1 S.C.R. 143, LEAF has contributed to the development of equality rights jurisprudence and the meaning of substantive equality in Canada. LEAF has developed and advocated equality rights arguments in contexts where sex inequality is compounded by other dynamics of discrimination such as race, class, aboriginal status, sexual orientation, and disability. LEAF is a leader in developing legal theory and litigation strategies that recognize women's diversity, and that address the ways in which inequality manifests itself in women's lives. We hope that this book will build on that legacy and contribute to the next generation of advocacy for substantive equality and public education on equality law.

This book grew out of a group initiative by LEAF's National Legal Committee to study the impact and future implications to equality jurisprudence of the Supreme Court of Canada's 1999 ruling in *Law v. Canada*. Colloquially referred to as "The *Law* Project," this initiative has truly been a collective effort which could not have been realized without the contributions of many dedicated volunteers. Special thanks are given to the LEAF Foundation for its financial support of the *Law* Project, the national consultation, and two national colloquia at which the papers in this collection were initially presented and workshopped. Thanks are also offered to the Court Challenges Program for its financial support to hold the national consultation in February 2004 and to the Women's Program/Status of Women Canada who supported LEAF Staff and the National Office on this project. We thank the Elementary Teachers' Federation of Ontario for its financial support which has enabled us to develop the colloquium papers into a published collection. We also thank the thousands of individuals who support LEAF annually and who make all of LEAF's work possible.

Many women contributed their ideas and energy to this project. In particular we acknowledge the contributions of LEAF Staff Fiona Sampson, Marian Ali, and Marina Browning; the many dedicated women who volunteered with us on LEAF's National Legal Committee and who contributed to the development of the substantive ideas that informed both the *Law* Project and this book (Kim Bernhardt, Gillian Calder, May Chui, Jennifer Koshan, Veronica Jackson, and Celeste McKay); LEAF's Board of Directors; and all who participated at the consultation and colloquia. We are particularly grateful to Diana Majury who served on the National Legal Committee, generously contributed her ideas and energy, and assisted us in coordinating this project through its early stages and through the colloquia.

Fay Faraday was responsible for the lion's share of the work involved in making this project happen. Margaret Denike and Kate Stephenson wish to thank her personally, and we all thank her law firm, Cavalluzzo Hayes Shilton McIntyre & Cornish LLP, for providing Fay with time and resources to work on the project. Fay gives particular thanks to Elizabeth Shilton, Mary Cornish, and Karen Schucher for being remarkable mentors in equality rights litigation, and to Wendy Balaban and Lucy Liegghio for their invaluable assistance. Fay offers love and gratitude to Jim, Robbie, and Alexander for all their support. Margaret Denike would like to thank Sal Renshaw for her generosity and support.

LEAF FAEJ

Introductory Materials

Preface

The Honourable Claire L'Heureux-Dubé

The year 2005 marks the twentieth anniversary of section 15 of the *Charter*. It celebrates a generation of constitutional protection for equality rights in Canada. In this time, the *Charter* has become deeply engrained in the Canadian consciousness and identity. It provides a language for and expresses aspirations for how Canadians view their relationships with the state and with each other. It fundamentally shapes the meaning of Canadian democracy.

At this point in the *Charter*'s history, it is important to reflect on what it means to have guaranteed equality as a bedrock principle of Canada's Constitution. It is important to examine the evolution of our conception of equality and to assess the challenges that remain in order for future generations to secure the full and concrete realization of true equality in the lives of Canadians.

This book makes a significant contribution to this endeavour. It provides a timely critical assessment of equality rights in Canada and provides invaluable insights into the considerations that will advance equality in the future.

An important part of the struggle for equality over the past twenty years has been to develop a more complete and sophisticated conception of what "equality" means. It has been necessary to move beyond the narrow formalistic understanding of equality that was ill-equipped to examine or restrain dynamics of discrimination under the *Bill of Rights*.

To this end, section 15 of the *Charter* deliberately ushered in important changes by broadening the measure and reach of equality rights with the aim of promoting and achieving *substantive* equality in Canada. It moved beyond formal equality "before the law" and introduced a stronger, more comprehensive guarantee of equality before and under the law, as well as, importantly, the right to equal protection and equal benefit of the law without discrimination. In this way, section 15 has enabled courts to move from requiring that laws treat similarly situated individuals identically to requiring that laws treat individuals as substantive equals, recognizing and accommodating their underlying differences.

Through this evolution, it is clear that we have only begun to learn the language and nuance of equality. We continue to modify and expand the vocabulary of equality, and to articulate the values and principles that enable equality to speak to the multiple and varied manifestations and dynamics of inequality and the nature and effects of discriminatory laws and practices. This book is part of the project of articulating the substantive meaning of equality and of ensuring that this meaning reflects our deepest values and aspirations for what it means to be human beings, as individuals and in relation to one another, equally capable and deserving of respect and concern.

The importance of the equality guarantees and the analytical frameworks and approaches that give them meaning cannot be understated. The paradigm of equality extends beyond traditional human rights, as it gives shape to all other rights. It informs the way we understand and approach the areas and applications of family law, employment law, tax law, and criminal law, among others. It affects how we view a wide range of issues and aspects that shape our lives such as sexual orientation, sexual violence, poverty, and disability. It has guided our recognition of the responsibilities of individuals and institutions in society, and the obligations of governments to address and eradicate the effects of discrimination and to ameliorate the symptoms and impacts of systemic inequality and pre-existing conditions of disadvantage.

The past twenty years have made evident that while some approaches to equality have been effective in challenging prejudice and oppression in some contexts, they may well reinforce and perpetuate them in others. Through dialogue and debate about what the guarantee of equality means, we have developed the language and analysis of substantive equality. Substantive equality is grounded in the understanding that true equality requires a critical examination of unspoken assumptions, traditions, and myths; instead of simple formalistic likes-treated-alike, substantive equality can require substantive change that will ensure the accommodation of differences. The essays in this volume collectively map the movement toward such understanding and scrutinize the obstacles we continue to face in making equality a reality for all.

The Canadian approach to substantive equality was adopted by the Supreme Court of Canada in 1989 with *Andrews v. Law Society of British Columbia*, the first case to interpret section 15 of the *Charter*. As Sheila McIntyre writes in her essay in this volume, this approach "offered significant direction, and laid indispensable foundations for a substantive approach to application of section 15" by rejecting a formalistic similarly situated analysis, calling for a contextual approach to evaluating equality claims, and clarifying that the purpose of section 15 is to protect disadvantaged groups. In making the link between equality and discrimination in *Andrews*, Justices Bertha Wilson and William McIntyre made it clear that the purpose of section 15 was to protect and promote "substantive equality" and that the *Charter*'s equality guarantee had a "large remedial component" that required the legislature to take positive measures to improve the status of disadvantaged groups. As I commented in *Egan v. Canada*:

> Treating historically vulnerable, disadvantaged or marginalized groups in the same manner as groups which do not generally suffer from such vulnerability may not accommodate, or even contemplate, those differences. In fact, ignoring such differences may compound them, by making access to s. 15 relief most difficult for those groups that are the most disadvantaged of all in Canadian society.

By critically assessing the equality approaches that have subsequently applied this language of substantive equality, the chapters in this book look to the ways in which we still have a long way to go to fulfill this vision of equality, to affirm such differences, and to make section 15 meaningful to all who are disempowered.

Of central interest and concern to these authors is the impact of the Supreme Court of Canada's subsequent clarification and unification of the approach to the equality which was set out a decade after *Andrews* in the case of *Law v. Canada*. This case located the principle of human dignity at the heart of equality and it clarified the purpose of the equality guarantees. In *Law v. Canada*, the two-fold purpose of section 15 was described as being to "prevent the violation of human dignity and freedom through the imposition of disadvantage, stereotyping, or political or social prejudice" and "to promote a society in which all persons enjoy equal recognition at law as human beings or as members of Canadian society, equally capable and equally deserving of concern, respect and consideration." This approach explicitly articulated the underlying principles of substantive equality in terms of equal human dignity and full membership in society. In this sense, it emphasizes the link between equality and discrimination to help determine the values that are offended in and by discriminatory laws, policies, and practices. It also lays emphasis on the commitment and obligation to "promote" equality.

As we seek to define and characterize the underlying values of substantive equality, by way of concepts such as human dignity, we face yet another new challenge — that of expanding and clarifying the language of these values, so as to make them more than empty abstractions. As Denise Réaume has aptly emphasized, "Giving that concept [of human dignity] some meaningful content stands as perhaps the most significant challenge facing the Court in the coming years." She observes that

> It is out of the close reflection on the political, historical and social contexts within which distinctions between groups arise that we will develop an increasingly rich concept of dignity.... Asking whether legislation affects membership in society in a basic way or denies participation in important social institutions suggests that these forms of participation are crucial in their own right to a life with dignity.

Our ability to articulate a vision of equality that resonates domestically and internationally to enable full participation and membership of citizens in all societies is particularly pressing in our increasingly interconnected global community. National appellate courts throughout the world are increasingly looking to the judgments of other jurisdictions, particularly when making decisions about human rights issues such as equality to guide their decisions. Deciding on applicable legal principles and solutions increasingly involves a consideration of the approaches that have been adopted to similar legal problems elsewhere. So too, as various authors in this collection point out, Canadian courts are increasingly looking to the role of international human rights norms in shaping the next generation of *Charter* jurisprudence. In drawing on these norms and in sharing models and experiences with other jurisdictions, we face the responsibility for both our past and our future.

In their thorough examination of equality and human dignity, the authors in this collection make significant contributions to mapping the concerns and considerations that will mark the next generation of evolution in equality rights in Canada. It will be crucial for women — and for all groups who have experienced oppression and disadvantage — to participate in the analyses and conversations that clarify the values and reality of substantive equality. The Canadian experience suggests that when groups who experience discrimination help to forge and shape the development of constitutional guarantees of equality, these norms have the potential to provide one of the most powerful means available for making equality a reality for all. Taking hope and inspiration from this experience, we must therefore re-dedicate ourselves to achieving equality in all aspects of the law. For it is my firm belief that justice without equality is no justice at all.

In Pursuit of Substantive Equality

Fay Faraday, Margaret Denike, & M. Kate Stephenson

A. INTRODUCTION

> Every individual is equal before and under the law and has the right to the equal protection and equal benefit of the law without discrimination and, in particular, without discrimination based on race, national or ethnic origin, colour, religion, sex, age or mental or physical disability.

With these words, the right to equality is guaranteed to all individuals as a constitutional right in section 15 of the *Canadian Charter of Rights and Freedoms*. Section 15 of the *Charter* came into effect in April 1985. In the two decades since then, the right to equality has been one of the most hotly contested *Charter* rights, being disputed in over 350 reported court cases across Canada. It is a right that in very short order has become deeply engrained in Canadian legal, political, and social discourse. It has become a bedrock value, fundamentally reflecting and shaping how Canadians view themselves and their society.

The *Charter* right to equality is at once one of the most cherished and most controversial rights. And this is as it should be because the goal of equality is transformative. As Sheila McIntyre writes, "[w]hen equality claims are really substantive, they should challenge privileged understandings of the world and privileged players' understandings of themselves."[1] More than any other constitutional right, the right to equality is a redistributive right. It calls into scrutiny the quality of the relationships we forge with others in society. It questions the justice of the distribution of rights, privileges, burdens, power, and material resources in society and the basis for that distribution. It requires us to articulate and critically examine previously unspoken assumptions and norms and how these norms are embedded in the laws that structure our relationships. Most significantly, it requires us to transform those legal structures to secure substantive equality.

Not surprisingly, this is not an uncontroversial undertaking. Justices Cory and Iacobucci addressed this tension between the goal of equality and the persistent reality of inequality in *Vriend v. Alberta* as follows:

> The rights enshrined in s. 15(1) of the *Charter* are fundamental to Canada. They reflect the fondest dreams, the highest hopes and finest aspirations of Canadian society....
>
> ... It is easy to praise these concepts as providing the foundation for a just society which permits every individual to live in dignity and in harmony with all. The difficulty lies in giving real effect to equality. Difficult as the goal of equality may be it is worth the arduous struggle to attain. It is only when equality is a reality that fraternity and harmony will be achieved. It is then that individuals will truly live in dignity.[2]

Similarly, in *Law v. Canada*, Justice Iacobucci wrote that section 15 "is perhaps the *Charter*'s most conceptually difficult provision." While the "quest for equality expresses some of humanity's highest ideals and aspirations," the challenge is "to transform these ideals and aspirations into practice in a manner which is meaningful for Canadians."[3]

This is the terrain examined in this collection of essays. In the chapters that follow, the authors critically assess the state of equality jurisprudence from many angles and seek to build bridges from the aspirations to the reality of substantive equality. Collectively, the essays attempt to craft a more secure footing for substantive equality as section 15 of the *Charter* moves into its second generation. The essays in this book are divided into three parts, which examine fundamental aspects of the project to secure substantive equality:

- Part One addresses the theme of "What Does Equality Mean?" The five essays in this section address the substantive content and goals of equality rights, and the extent to which jurisprudence under the *Charter* either facilitates or restricts the achievement of these goals.

They articulate with precision what we mean by equality and the harms of inequality, question whether comparison is fundamental to equality, and explore the governmental obligation to promote equality. They critically examine the concept of human dignity as it relates to substantive equality, the enduring tension between formal equality and substantive equality, and the challenge of building equality principles into remedies for *Charter* breaches.

- Part Two addresses "Equality Claims in Context." From the outset, section 15 jurisprudence has insisted that equality claims must be examined contextually. The five essays in this section look at this concept critically, interrogating what it means to look at equality in context, what context matters to equality claimants, in what ways context is resisted by the courts, and what challenges and obstacles are presented as equality claimants seek to have their reality and experience of discrimination recognized and rectified.

- Part Three addresses "Shifting and Blending Paradigms: The *Charter*, Statutory Human Rights, and International Human Rights." While from the earliest section 15 jurisprudence there has been a degree of cross-pollination between understandings of discrimination under the *Charter* and statutory human rights in Canada, the evolution of constitutional, statutory, and international human rights have diverged in significant ways. The papers in this section examine the differences in these streams of equality/anti-discrimination law, both to articulate ways in which the strands should remain distinct and to identify ways in which understandings of equality developed under statutory human rights and in international law can enrich equality jurisprudence under section 15 in the years ahead.

The dominant framework for assessing equality rights under the *Charter* is what has become known as "the *Law* test." Articulated by the Supreme Court of Canada in the appeal of *Law v. Canada* in 1999 as a set of guidelines which synthesized the various principles that had been developed to that point, the *Law* test has been the most critical development in equality jurisprudence since *Andrews v. Law Society of British Columbia*[4] first addressed section 15 rights. Before examining the themes of this book in more detail, we turn first to look briefly at how we have arrived at the *Law* test so that we can more fully explore its potential for securing substantive equality.

B. GETTING TO *LAW*: THE CRITICAL FOUNDATION FOR SUBSTANTIVE EQUALITY

The foundation for substantive equality rights under the *Charter* is built both on the language of section 15 itself and on the Supreme Court of Canada's first section 15 ruling in *Andrews*. While the 1989 ruling in *Andrews* was crucial in setting the direction for future equality jurisprudence, in the early 1990s the Supreme Court entered a period of discord in which multiple legal tests were articulated and no clear consensus prevailed on how to identify unconstitutional discrimination. It is out of this discord that the *Law* test emerged as an attempt to restore consensus on what equality means under the *Charter*. The history of how we got to *Law* is important for understanding both the significance of that decision and the importance of identifying some of the tensions that continue to rumble below the surface of the *Law* test.

When section 15 of the *Charter* first came into effect in April 1985, it brought with it a promise to broaden and strengthen equality rights for Canadians. As equality rights were constitutionalized for the first time, feminists and other equality-seeking groups had high hopes that section 15 would be a vehicle for achieving substantive equality for disadvantaged groups in Canada. During the constitutional consultations on the wording of the proposed equality provisions, they lobbied extensively to ensure that the wording of section 15 was significantly broader than the anti-discrimination provisions of the *Canadian Bill of Rights*. They ensured that section 15 enshrined not just equal treatment before the law but equal protection and equal benefit of the law as well.

In 1989, the Supreme Court's ruling in *Andrews* bolstered the hopes of equality advocates as the Court unanimously adopted a number of important principles which underscored that section 15 aimed to have substantive rather than formal effect. First, the Court confirmed that the equality analysis must focus on the *effects* of a law, not just its purpose. Second, relying on the broad language in section 15 itself, the Court rejected the "similarly situated" test which had plagued the *Bill of Rights*. Under that earlier formal equality analysis, the only goal of equality law was to "treat likes alike" while ignoring the ways in which different groups in society experience systemic disadvantage. Third, instead of formal equality, the Court recognized that the goal of section 15 is substantive equality, which requires that the differences between groups and individuals be recognized and accommodated so that a law secures equality in its effect. Fourth, the Court rejected the notion that all distinctions are discriminatory and adopted an "analogous grounds" approach under which the key factor identifying instances of discrimination was the context of the affected group, and in particular its historical disadvantage and relative powerlessness in society. Fifth, the Court confirmed that justifications for discrimination should be addressed under section 1 of the *Charter* where the government bears the onus of proof rather than under section 15. Finally, and very significantly, the Court confirmed that section 15 has two purposes: to protect against discriminatory laws and to promote equality in our society.

The unanimity of the Court in *Andrews* broke down in a trilogy of cases — *Egan, Miron,* and *Thibaudeau* — in 1995.[5] Members of the Court were at odds with each other over crucial questions such as how to identify if a distinction was discriminatory and how a law's purpose should be factored into an assessment of discrimination. Four judges (McLachlin, Sopinka, Cory, and Iacobucci JJ.) continued to apply the *Andrews* test although they articulated it slightly differently. While McLachlin J. (as she then was) emphasized stereotypical assumptions as being at the heart of discrimination, Cory and Iacobucci JJ. stressed that discrimination could be affected by dynamics other than stereotype. Four judges (Lamer C.J.C., LaForest, Gonthier, and Major JJ.) focused on the ground of distinction and whether it was relevant to the "functional values underlying the legislation." This approach was sharply criticized by the other members of the Court as being tautological, importing section 1 justifications into an analysis of section 15, and allowing a narrow focus on the ground of distinction to omit an analysis of the discriminatory impact of that distinction. Finally, writing for herself, L'Heureux-Dubé J. emphasized that the nature of the group affected and the interest affected were the key considerations in the discrimination inquiry and that the purpose of the law had no place until section 1.

C. THE *LAW* TEST: THE CURRENT PLATFORM FOR EQUALITY RIGHTS

In 1999 the Supreme Court of Canada decided the appeal in *Law v. Canada*. The case involved a widow's claim that her equality rights were violated when she was denied a Canada Pension Plan spousal survivor's pension because she was under the age of thirty-five. As the claim was brought by a relatively privileged woman seeking benefits historically provided to economically dependent and elderly women, no equality seeking groups intervened in the appeal and no one predicted that the appeal would be the one to usher in a new framework for assessing equality claims. Yet that is what happened. In its unanimous decision, the Court used the case as an opportunity to synthesize and consolidate its section 15 equality analysis. In its revised and unified analysis, the Court laid down a new set of "guidelines" that tried to mend the fractiousness that had arisen in the trilogy. As such, *Law* is the most important *Charter* equality decision since *Andrews*. The analytical framework from *Law* has established the current platform for assessing equality rights that is regularly applied by parties and courts across the country.

The broad outline of the Supreme Court's approach in *Law* is not new or surprising. The members of the Court all agreed that the purpose of section 15 was "... to prevent the violation of essential human dignity and freedom through the imposition of disadvantage, stereotyping, or political or social prejudice, and to promote a society in which all persons enjoy equal recognition at law as human beings or as members of Canadian society, equally capable and equally deserving of concern, respect and consideration."[6] They also agreed that section 15 claims would be approached by focusing on three central issues:

1. whether the law imposes differential treatment between the claimant or others in purpose or effect;
2. whether one or more enumerated or analogous grounds of discrimination are the basis for the differential treatment; and
3. whether the law in question has a purpose or effect that is discriminatory within the meaning of the equality guarantee.[7]

These inquiries are in keeping with the prior approach of the Court, and particularly that which was inaugurated in *Andrews*.

The novel and controversial aspects of the *Law* approach concern how the court should go about answering the third inquiry; that is, how to determine when differential treatment constitutes discrimination. What makes particular treatment qualitatively discriminatory? The controversial developments in *Law* relate to the ways in which context is assessed to identify discrimination and to how the Court has linked discrimination to the question of "human dignity."

Rather than clarifying or resolving the dispute underlying the different approaches in the trilogy, the *Law* test incorporates aspects of all the divergent approaches. The fact that these different approaches could often lead to conflicting results was avoided in *Law* itself by describing the various considerations as "contextual factors" that may or may not be significant in identifying discrimination in any given case, depending on the circumstances, but the tensions persist and have produced deeply conflicting reasons in subsequent cases.[8] The contextual factors identified by the Court include:

1. whether the group or individual at issue experiences pre-existing disadvantage, stereotyping, prejudice, or vulnerability;
2. whether there is correspondence between the ground on which the claim is based and the actual need, capacity, or circumstances of the claimant;
3. whether the legislation has an ameliorative purpose or effect for a group which has been historically disadvantaged in the context of the legislation; and
4. what is the nature of the interest affected by the legislation.

Although Iacobucci J. cautioned that this list of contextual factors is not closed, and that there is no specific formula to be applied in every case, the four enumerated factors quickly became a test that has been applied mechanically in subsequent cases, in aid of determining whether an impugned law violates the purpose of section 15 by causing an "injury to dignity."

The concept of dignity has become at once the touchstone and shorthand for identifying unconstitutional discrimination. The "turn towards dignity," as Denise Réaume describes it, has met with extensive criticism by feminist and other equality theorists. Numerous authors have critiqued *Law* as imposing an additional hurdle on equality claimants. They note that not only do claimants have to establish that they are treated differently, based on one of the enumerated or analogous grounds of protection, they now also have to establish that this treatment violates human dignity. Moreover, dignity as a concept has been considered too vague and malleable to anchor section 15.[9] As Sheilah Martin has observed, dignity has been used by the courts to define many *Charter* rights, including sections 2(a) (freedom of conscience and religion); 2(b) (freedom of thought, belief, opinion, and expression); 2(d) (freedom of association); 3 (the right to vote); 6 (mobility rights); 7 (the right to life, liberty, and security of the person); 8 (the right to be secure against unreasonable search and seizure); 11(c) (the right not to be compelled to testify in proceedings against oneself); 11(d) (the right to be presumed innocent until proven guilty); and 12 (the right not to be subject to cruel and unusual punishment).[10] The Supreme Court of Canada has itself observed that "The *Charter* and the rights it guarantees are inextricably bound to concepts of human dignity. Indeed, notions of human dignity underlie almost every right guaranteed by the *Charter*."[11] In post-*Law* cases, courts have turned dignity into a shorthand for equality itself, truncating the equality analysis into a single question of whether a reasonable person in the claimant's position would legitimately feel that her dignity was demeaned by the law in question.

The problems with this shorthand are glaring. First, it reduces equality to a question of "feelings," rather than focusing on the social relations and power dynamics that inhere in a given instance of differential treatment. In other words, it locates inequality in individuals rather than in the social relations *structured by law* that have material impacts on an individual. Second, the shorthand of dignity requires an assessment of the "reasonableness" and "legitimacy" of the feelings expressed by the equality claimant, inviting her feelings or experience to be rejected if a judge deems them to be unwarranted. Moreover, as Fiona Sampson notes in her chapter in this volume, the equality claimant must posit herself as a victim, whether or not she wants to do so, and then must wait to see if this victim status is objectively acceptable in relation to an un-named standard (such as the white able-bodied male). The "reasonable person" analysis, she observes, "inevitably incorporates elements of the decision-maker's perspective and value system" which may or may not be divorced from the dominant norm.[12] Third, the dignity requirement permits (and even requires) judges to assess the claimant's feelings by reference to the purpose of the legislation, since it is presumed that the feelings of a "reasonable" person would take into account the beneficial purposes of the legislation. Again, rather than questioning the underlying social relations that create the differential treatment and give meaning to the material experience of inequality, those social relations are reified as the justification for the differential treatment.

Supreme Court decisions since *Law* reveal that the hoped-for consensus on the meaning and application of section 15 that *Law* was intended to herald has not materialized. Outcomes in equality cases have been unpredictable and inconsistent. At the same time, various trends have emerged in the jurisprudence that obfuscate rather than illuminate the path to substantive equality. An increasingly narrow and rigid focus on identifying the "appropriate comparator group"[13] reintroduces the formalism of identifying which likes should be treated alike while eroding the substantive equality goal of eliminating discriminatory effects and accommodating differences in order to achieve equality. The mechanical application of the four contextual factors provides only a superficial analysis which fails to capture the true context of experiences of discrimination and fails to acknowledge the different goals of equality that are served by the individual factors. And the central focus on human dignity erodes the recognition of the material harms of inequality in favour of abstract and subjective feelings of insult. It shifts the focus from structural and contextual implications of inequality to formalist ones that individualize the claim of inequality, isolate the claim from the broader social context which gives them meaning, and reinforce the social/power dynamics and distinctions that give rise to inequality.

The project of this book, then, is to re-examine the gap between the aspirations for substantive equality enshrined in our *Charter* and the failure to implement them in practice. The essays in this book seek to critically examine both the limitations and potential of the *Law* framework to secure the ultimate goal of substantive equality and to develop analyses that will assist in the next generation of equality jurisprudence under the *Charter*.

D. PART ONE: WHAT DOES EQUALITY MEAN?

Articulating and providing nuance to what we understand equality to mean and what we want equality rights to accomplish is crucial to securing a firm foundation for substantive equality. Equality advocates would generally agree with the dual purpose that has been ascribed to section 15: on one hand it protects against laws which violate equality; on the other hand, it promises that law will promote equality. But it is not enough to assume, as the Supreme Court did in *Vriend*, that "the concept and principle of equality is almost intuitively understood ... by all."[14] We must in fact say what we mean by equality so that we can do what we say. We must be precise so there is no slippage between aspiration and application.

The authors of the essays in Part One of this book aim to address that difficult issue. Drawing on both philosophy and law, Sophia Moreau identifies four distinct goals that the guarantee of substantive equality serves,[15] identifies the specific harms that arise when those substantive equality goals are denied, and examines the degree to which the four contextual factors from *Law* are and are not meaningful in relation to specific equality goals. She exposes the flaws of being imprecise. The *Law* test's failure to separate out the distinct equality goals prevents it from recognizing substantive harms and results in the mechanical application of contextual factors that may have no relationship to the specific harm caused by a given discriminatory law.

Beverley Baines examines the questions of whether comparison is fundamental to interpreting the *Charter*'s equality guarantee and whether a comparative analysis can move beyond formal equality. Drawing on critiques developed in American anti-discrimination theory, she analyses the structure of section 15 jurisprudence in relation to the four concepts of equality, comparison, discrimination, and status. She concludes that comparison is essential to dismantling status hierarchies that subordinate women. Instead of the dignity principle adopted in *Law*, she proposes a comparative analysis that focuses on "status" or "anti-subordination" which defines equality in terms of power. She invokes a constitutive comparison that keeps the focus on the sociological group seeking equality, that measures the degree to which laws have the effect of perpetuating subordination of sociological groups, and that recognizes that securing substantive equality requires an interrogation of and levelling down of institutions that support privilege and status hierarchies.

In examining what we mean by substantive equality, Sheila McIntyre calls on all of us and the courts to squarely examine and confront the reality that inequality exists because it rewards dominant groups. She calls for us to eschew formalist abstraction and the privileged innocence it fosters by insisting that a finding of discrimination turn upon a critical examination of who benefits from inequality, of the agency of the dominant, and of how unequal treatment shores up historic and existing relations of domination. By collectively ignoring the underlying systems and structures of power that perpetuate domination in favour of general abstractions, courts have allowed formalism to continue to dominate our equality jurisprudence.

Denise Réaume takes up an analysis of the concept of "dignity" that looks less to its limitations than to its potential as a touchstone for substantive equality. While acknowledging that dignity has been widely criticized by feminist and equality advocates for being too vague and malleable, she writes that "the process of giving that concept some meaningful content stands as perhaps the most significant challenge facing the Court in the coming years." She argues that a dignity-based analysis can give equality rights real substance by, for example, relating behaviour based on prejudice and stereotype to the impairment of fundamental human aspirations such as self-determination, personal fulfilment, and autonomy. In addition, she examines the potential of recognizing "dignity-constituting benefits." By acknowledging that a life with dignity includes participation in important social institutions, violations of dignity and equality are evidenced when legislation affects membership or denies participation in these social institutions.

Melina Buckley in her chapter describes the project of achieving substantive equality as being "transformative" in nature. Substantive equality, she writes, "entails changes at all levels of society: individual behaviour, perceptions, and attitudes; ideas and ideology; community and culture; institutions and institutional practices; and, deeper structures of social and economic power."[16] Looking at section 15's dual purpose, she examines the courts' reluctance to hold governments accountable to the positive obligation to *promote* equality. She proposes that the equality analysis developed by the Supreme Court in *Meiorin* in the statutory human rights context is better suited to judicial review of governmental responsibility to promote equality and outlines a principled basis for determining the content of the government's positive obligations, drawing on the lessons of *Meiorin*.

E. PART TWO: EQUALITY CLAIMS IN CONTEXT

While it is in some respects trite law to say that equality claims must be assessed contextually, this issue of "context" is also perhaps one of the greatest hurdles to transforming aspirations of substantive equality into reality. The five authors in this section of the book provide critical analyses of how the comparative analysis and contextual factors in the *Law* test have been applied, but they also ask much more fundamental questions such as: What does and what should count as context? and why? What does it really mean to look at an equality claim *in context*? Does the platform for analysis provided in *Law* enable the courts to adequately engage with that context in a manner that illuminates the true experiences of inequality? Where the contexts of true inequality are multi-layered and multi-dimensional, how can they be rendered as justiciable legal claims?

In order to ensure that equality rights are achieved in practice, it is necessary for equality jurisprudence to recognize the complexity of the dynamics of oppression. It is necessary for equality jurisprudence to encompass and comprehend the broad context that gives meaning to a particular legal manifestation of inequality. To determine whether equality jurisprudence is equipped to do this, it is valuable to measure the *Law* test against real and multi-dimensional circumstances of women's lived experience. What emerges from the analyses in this section is that the four contextual factors from *Law* are not employed in a manner that captures the true context of inequality. The contextual factors instead fail to take context seriously and to examine it deeply.

The four "contextual factors" were introduced in *Law* as a series of considerations, any one of which might assist in determining whether differential treatment is qualitatively discriminatory. However, as discussed in Sophia Moreau's chapter these contextual factors are only of assistance if and to the extent that they actually relate to the specific kinds of harm occasioned by a particular dynamic of unequal and unfair treatment. The jurisprudence has not yet embraced this nuance. Rather, in post-*Law* cases the contextual factors have been treated as a series of steps, all of which might be an occasion for an equality claim to fail. As Judith Keene notes in her chapter, one of the primary problems with applications of the *Law* framework has been the "majority's practice of disaggregating the elements of the test set out in *Law* and giving each meticulous but separate consideration, with the result that there is never a focus on the larger, substantive picture: the effect of the impugned government action on the claimant."[17]

While the contextual factors have been construed as distinct additional inquiries and hurdles that equality claimants must overcome, much of the criticism of these factors has focused on the second contextual factor: whether there is a correspondence between the ground on which a claim is based and the actual need, capacity, or circumstance of the claimant. In practice, this factor has been used to reanimate the relevance/functional values type of analysis that was rejected by a majority of the Court in the pre-*Law* trilogy. Under the second contextual factor, courts have imported an examination of the legislation's purpose and the relevance of the differentiating personal characteristic into an analysis of whether there is discrimination. The question has been framed by the Court in terms of whether the differential treatment at issue is somehow *relevant* to the purpose of the law; if the answer is yes, the conclusion is that dignity is not harmed. Equality rights are seen to be violated only where there is no "relevant" difference between the two groups involved (that is, where the claimant and the "comparator group" are similarly situated) *vis-à-vis* the purpose of the legislation, and is not violated where the two groups are different in a way that is relevant to the purpose of the legislation. This is the similarly situated test — formal equality — that was rejected in *Andrews*.

Bruce Ryder's 2004 study of equality cases in the five years post-*Law* confirms that "the correspondence factor has thus far proved to be the most important factor in determining whether or not the Court finds a difference in treatment on a prohibited ground to be discriminatory."[18] He finds that there is a direct correlation between the Court's finding on whether the correspondence factor is satisfied and whether the equality claim fails; it "has aligned with the outcome of the discrimination inquiry in all section 15 cases" since *Law*.[19] Ryder finds that historical disadvantage, far from being the most compelling factor, as Iacobucci J. in *Law* suggested it would be, has played a secondary role; the part played by the remaining two contextual factors has been minimal in determining the outcomes of equality claims.

Apart from reducing an examination of "context" to the four corners of the impugned legislation, this invocation of legislative purpose is also problematic in both doctrinal and practical terms because it imports section 1 considerations (justifications of discriminatory treatment) into the discrimination analysis and significantly shifts the burden of proof off of the government and onto the equality claimant.

In addressing "Equality Claims in Context," the authors in Part Two of the book aim to envision more complex constructions of context that are able to keep the focus on the dynamics of oppression and the substantive effect of inequality on the claimant group.

Diana Majury, in her chapter, discusses the implications of the courts' use of the liberal language of choice to justify existing inequalities and to support a finding that legislative distinctions and differential treatment enhance a claimant's dignity by affirming the consequences of individual choice. By conflating concepts of choice, dignity, and equality, courts assume that if we have choice we have equality. Courts fail, she argues, to look behind or beyond the choice *simpliciter* to the structural relations that inform and constrain such choice or to look at the inequalities that such choice produces. Such an "individualized approach to choice depoliticizes the choices that are made and the context within which they are made." What is missing from the assertion that choice is *per se* a good thing are the contexts of power and inequality that underlie and circumscribe any particular choice, the ranges of choices, the cost of choice, and whether context in fact coerces "choice" or renders a choice in effect unchoosable.

Fiona Sampson deals with the failures of the *Law* test in the context of gendered disability claims. With attention to the difficulties posed by comparator group analysis and the injury to dignity analysis, she provides a critique of the *Law* test from a gendered disability perspective. She uses the case of *Auton* to expose and assess the constraints of *Law*. The subjectivity of the "injury to dignity" test is particularly problematic in this context because the "reasonable person" inquiry inevitably incorporates elements of the decision-maker's perspective and value system and thus privileges the perspective of the person for whom the experience of contextualized discrimination is alien: "Because the experience of gendered disability is so far removed from the dominant norm, the circumstances of a woman with a disability as an equality claimant may be impossible to assess from the perspective of a 'reasonable' person."

Melanie Randall discusses the limitations of equality jurisprudence as articulated under the *Charter* for addressing the concrete inequalities and gender subordination in the context of male violence against women in intimate relationships. She notes that section 15 has barely been engaged in the struggle to end intimate violence against women, in part because the approaches taken by the Supreme Court of Canada have narrowed "the possibilities for capturing the nature and complexities of discrimination and inequality." While she questions whether the restrictive scope of *Charter* rights can adequately examine "the nature of the specific problem of intimate gendered violence and abuse in women's lives, its complexity and its vastness (implicating so many institutions and social relations at the macro and micro levels)," she also examines the promise of section 15's purpose of *promoting* equality and the government's obligations that should be engaged by that purpose.

Judith Keene demonstrates the limitations of the *Law* analytical framework through an analysis of the Supreme Court of Canada's decision in *Gosselin v. Québec (Attorney General)*[20] with attention to the Court's narrow reading of the contextual factors and the malleable nature of the concept of human dignity. By disaggregating the four contextual factors, the Court loses sight of the substantive harm of discrimination. Further, because any person's understanding of the concept of dignity "is heavily class- and culture-bound," the average judge "who is still a white, affluent, able-bodied man, may be unable to appreciate what factors negatively affect the dignity of someone of whose life he can have little real understanding." From a position of privilege, a person may also maintain a double standard that conceives of some types of indignity as simply part of life for other people, particularly in cases of adverse-effect discrimination which by definition involve norms that are unquestioned by the majority and in cases of access to government benefits of which the majority have no need.

Gwen Brodsky and Shelagh Day analyse why poverty is an urgent equality issue for women and why the denial of the means of subsistence is an equality rights violation. Building on an analysis of the *Gosselin* case,[21] they demonstrate that stereotyping is not a sufficient basis for understanding what counts as discrimination. Discrimination and human dignity have other dimensions — such as a concern with protecting physical and psychological integrity — that must be more fully considered and developed. The right to substantive equality must encompass a basic right to income security because without that security, profound deprivations of personal autonomy and of physical and psychological integrity, which are incompatible with equality, result. Brodsky and Day argue that poverty must be dealt with as an aspect of sex, race, and disability discrimination because a central cause of poverty is entrenched patterns of systemic discrimination. At the same time, poverty exacerbates the impact of discriminatory measures. Looking at poverty through this group-based equality lens shows the qualitatively different impact of discrimination on different groups and reveals how poverty is one of the conditions that impedes equal participation in society.

F. PART THREE: SHIFTING AND BLENDING PARADIGMS: THE *CHARTER*, STATUTORY HUMAN RIGHTS, AND INTERNATIONAL HUMAN RIGHTS

Equality jurisprudence under the *Charter* has often drawn on concepts of discrimination that were developed earlier under statutory human rights codes. *Charter* jurisprudence is also increasingly drawing upon understandings of fundamental human rights enshrined in international human rights covenants and instruments that Canada has ratified to interpret the meaning of *Charter* rights. A strong theme that is echoed by numerous authors in this volume is the difference between the courts' treatment and record on *Charter* equality claims as compared with statutory human rights claims. It is widely recognized, as Judith Keene notes, that "most decisions of courts and tribunals construing human rights legislation display a deeper understanding of the dynamics of substantive discrimination and of the disadvantaged position of persons protected by that legislation than do those of courts and tribunals construing section 15 of the *Charter*."[22] Similarly, there is increasing discussion of the distance between the human rights norms which Canada has endorsed on the international stage and the realization of those norms domestically and increased questioning of what significance international rights have to domestic constitutional standards.

The three essays in Part Three of this book examine emerging questions that relate to the shifting and blending that is happening across these distinctive paradigms. Leslie Reaume examines the fundamental — and necessary — differences between analyses of discrimination under statutory human rights instruments and the *Charter*. She critically examines the emerging trend in which statutory human rights tribunals have begun to apply the *Law* test developed under section 15 of the *Charter* to supplant the concept of the *prima facie* case and the shifting burden of proof established more than twenty years ago by *O'Malley v. Simpson Sears Ltd.*[23] as the bedrock of the statutory human rights framework. She argues that allowing the imported *Charter* test to dominate an analysis that should be driven by the principles of statutory interpretation and the jurisprudence developed in the specific regulatory context of statutory human rights poses a danger to the development of substantive equality theory and practice in the statutory human rights context.

Andrea Wright critically examines a second emerging trend in statutory human rights law by which human rights tribunals and reviewing courts are frequently neglecting or displacing the broad and adaptable *O'Malley* test in favour of restricting and rigid comparator-group analyses and reductive tests that require comparative evidence in order to meet the *prima facie* case of discrimination. She argues that the comparator-group test requires artificial and precarious comparisons with "others," which look and operate like formal equality analyses, lead to poor choices of "comparator groups," and efface the gravamen of the discrimination complaint, de-contextualizing the complainant's experience and resulting in the denial of substantive equality. She questions the *Charter* proposition that equality is necessarily comparative, urges a steadfast application of the *O'Malley* test in statutory human rights contexts, and emphasizes the need for a conceptualization of equality as the attainment of particularized ideals, not comparative ones.

Jennifer Koshan examines the impact of international law on equality jurisprudence in Canada with attention to its strategic potential for enhancing equality rights claims. The principle of protecting human dignity is enshrined in several international human rights instruments, as are provisions to prevent discrimination and promote equality. To evaluate their utility in the Canadian context, she conducts a review of Supreme Court decisions that refer to international law, particularly in equality rights cases. She cautions that, to the extent that the Court has drawn on sources of international law, it has done so without any apparent consistency, and more often than not it has done so to support a finding that there was no discrimination or to narrow the interpretation of Canadian equality provisions.

G. CONCLUSIONS

Each of the papers in this collection aims to envision ways in which we can deepen our understandings of the dynamics of inequality and oppression and so produce a richer, more nuanced legal framework for eradicating discrimination and promoting substantive equality. With only two decades' experience with *Charter* equality litigation, the project to secure substantive equality remains a work in progress. However sophisticated our analyses, we remain challenged to put the substantive equality aspirations of the *Charter* into practice in a way that resists backsliding into formal equality paradigms.

To do this, we need to be rigorous in our assessments of how domination and discrimination function systemically and structurally, and we need to stay open to developing new approaches to addressing inequalities at their fundamental and pervasive levels of operation in society. The past generation has taught us that we cannot rely on formulaic and mechanistic schemes and tests to address and remedy existing inequalities; rather, we need to seek ways of thinking and talking about equality that give primacy to the rich narratives of lived experience, and that ground our analysis in this lived experience.

Rather than approaching equality claims by inquiring whether an individual has experienced differential treatment, inquiries instead need to begin from the standpoint of experience and focus on whether claimants have been subjected to forms of marginalization, oppression, disadvantage, or devaluation. As Fiona Sampson notes, this entails shifting the focus from the comparator groups, typically defined through a dominant norm, to the effects of the impugned treatment and the inequality experienced by the claimant. It also entails, as Sheila McIntyre states, that equality litigators insist that discrimination "turn not on arguing dignitary harm to those adversely treated by law, but on a showing of how unequal treatment shores up historic and existing relations of domination."

The struggle to make equality rights real is grounded in the reality of people's lived experience. As we continue this struggle, we must, in law and politics, hold governments accountable to take seriously the obligation to promote equality through the law — to build equality in at the front end — in order to build a more truly inclusive and substantively just society.

ENDNOTES

1 Sheila McIntyre, "Answering the Siren Call of Abstract Formalism with the Subjects and Verbs of Domination" at 108.

2 *Vriend v. Canada*, [1998] 1 S.C.R. 493 at paras. 67–68.

3 *Law v. Canada*, [1999] 1 S.C.R. 497 at para. 2.

4 [1989] 1 S.C.R. 143.

5 *Egan v. Canada*, [1995] 2 S.C.R. 513; *Miron v. Trudel*, [1995] 2 S.C.R. 418; *Thibaudeau v. Canada*, [1995] 2 S.C.R. 627.

6 *Law v. Canada*, above note 3 at para. 51.

7 *Ibid.* at para. 88.

8 See, in particular, *Lavoie v. Canada*, [2002] 1 S.C.R. 769 and Sheila McIntyre's analysis of that case in note 23 of her chapter, "Answering the Siren Call of Abstract Formalism with the Subjects and Verbs of Domination."

9 See Peter W. Hogg, *Constitutional Law of Canada*, looseleaf (Toronto: Thomson Carswell, 2004) vol. 2 at 52-27; Christopher Bredt & Adam Dodek, "Breaking the Law's Grip on Equality: A New Paradigm for Section 15" (2003) 20 Sup. Ct. L. Rev. (2d) 33 at 47; Sheilah Martin, "Balancing Individual Rights to Equality and Social Goals" (2001) 80 Can. Bar Rev. 299 at 329–32; Dianne Pothier, "Connecting Grounds of Discrimination to Real People's Real Experiences" (2001) 13 C.J.W.L. 37 at 56; B. Baines, "*Law v. Canada:* Formatting Equality" (2000) 11:3 Const. Forum 65 at 68.

10 See Sheilah Martin, "Court: Challenges: *Law*" (Winnipeg: Court Challenges Program, 2002).

11 *Blencoe v. British Columbia (Human Rights Commission)*, [2000] 2 S.C.R. 307 at paras. 76–78.

12 Fiona Sampson, "The *Law* Test for Discrimination and Gendered Disability Inequality" at 259.

13 In *Auton v. British Columbia (Attorney General)*, [2004] 3 S.C.R. 657 at para. 53, this was expressed as requiring that the comparator group "mirror the characteristics of the claimant or claimant group relevant to the benefit or advantage sought, except for the personal characteristic related to the enumerated or analogous ground raised as the basis for the discrimination.... The comparator must align with both the benefit and the 'universe of people potentially entitled' to it and the alleged ground of discrimination."

14 *Vriend v. Canada*, above note 2 at para. 68.

15 In distinguishing the substantive goals of equality conceptions, Professor Moreau writes that unequal treatment wrongs individuals when (a) it is based upon prejudice or stereotyping; (b) it perpetuates oppressive power relations; (c) it leaves some individuals without access to basic goods; and (d) it diminishes individuals' feelings of self-worth.

16 Melina Buckley, "*Law v. Meiorin*: Exploring the Governmental Responsibility to Promote Equality under Section 15 of the *Charter*" at 180.

17 Judith Keene, "The Supreme Court, the *Law* Decision, and Social Programs: The Substantive Equality Deficit" at 358.

18 Bruce Ryder, "What's *Law* Good For? An Empirical Overview of *Charter* Equality Rights Decisions" (2004) 24 Sup. Ct. L. Rev. (2d) 103.

19 *Ibid.* at 217.

20 [2002] 4 S.C.R. 429.

21 *Ibid.*

22 Judith Keene, above note 17 at 363.

23 [1985] 2 S.C.R. 536.

WHAT DOES EQUALITY MEAN?

one

The Wrongs of Unequal Treatment

Sophia Moreau[1]

A. INTRODUCTION

Over the past twenty years, analytic philosophers in the United States and England have devoted extensive thought to the different reasons we have for valuing equality — and, relatedly, to the different ways in which we can conceptualize the wrong or wrongs done to individuals when the state does not treat them as equals.[2] However, neither Canadian legal academics nor Canadian courts have made extensive use of this literature in interpreting the equality provisions of the *Canadian Charter of Rights and Freedoms*.[3] There are a number of good reasons why one might expect this philosophical literature to remain somewhat remote from Canadian legal debates.

One reason is that philosophers have tended to approach the question of what kind of equality matters as an inquiry into which system of general principles for the distribution of resources should guide legislatures in the design of particular policies. Since a court cannot unproblematically assume that it is either institutionally competent to make judgments about the most appropriate general distributive principles, or possessed of the institutional mandate to do so, these philosophical discussions can seem of little relevance to a court's task of interpreting constitutionalized equality rights. Furthermore, philosophers have tended to focus on the distribution of goods that can be privately owned, such as income and real property. Although this is usually done only for ease of illustration, the result has been that their work often lacks explicit discussion of claims for the equal availability of goods that are not privately appropriable — for instance, access to public spaces that have been designed in such a way that everyone can move easily through them, or the freedom to present one's relationship in public as involving the most extensive kind of commitment that our society recognizes. Yet it is very often these sorts of goods that claimants in equality rights cases have been denied. Finally, and most importantly, philosophical discussions have tended to assume — either implicitly or, as in the case of Ronald Dworkin, quite explicitly — that questions concerning the just distribution of resources can be pursued without broaching questions about the just distribution of political and social power.[4] Consequently, prior to the work of Elizabeth Anderson, and more recently, Samuel Scheffler, most philosophers did not concern themselves directly with inequalities in the distribution of political or social power, or with how to conceptualize the wrong that is done by institutional structures and policies that stigmatize individuals, marginalize them, or perpetuate their domination by others.[5]

The latter question is of course of particular relevance to Canadian equality jurisprudence, given that the Supreme Court of Canada has construed the protection offered by section 15 of the *Charter* as limited to those forms of unequal treatment that involve "discrimination."[6] Indeed, for this reason, it might be thought that any more general discussion of inequality could have only limited relevance, if any, to Canadian equality jurisprudence. However, if we are to define discrimination broadly enough to include not only intentional discrimination[7] but also what has come to be called "adverse effects discrimination" — that is, discrimination that merits the name not because some have deliberately been denied a benefit out of malice or prejudice but because, under the circumstances, even the unintended effect of depriving these people of this particular benefit is unfair to them — then it seems we must understand discrimination, quite generally, as "depriving some of a benefit available to others, in circumstances where this treatment is unfair to them."[8] But, of course, this is just the most general characterization that philosophers defending some form of equality would give of the kind of unequal treatment that they hold to be objectionable.[9] No plausible theory of equality maintains that what is objectionable about unequal treatment is the mere fact that some individuals end up with more or less than others. Rather, such theories hold that unequal treatment is objectionable when, and to the extent that, this treatment is unfair. Hence, the real question for philosophers writing on equality has been, when unequal treatment is unfair, what makes it so? Or, as we might otherwise put it, what is the nature of the wrong or wrongs done to individuals when they are unfairly treated unequally? This is precisely the question that courts and legal academics face, in interpreting the equality rights contained in section 15.

As I hope this paper will show, the philosophical literature on equality can help us answer this question, in spite of the differences in focus and context noted above. We can learn, in particular, from some of the conceptual distinctions that have been drawn in the philosophical literature between various ways of understanding the wrong that is done to individuals when the state unfairly treats them unequally. I shall begin by separating out one abstract conception of this wrong and four more specific, substantive conceptions of the wrong, and I shall suggest that all of them can be found in Canadian equality jurisprudence. As my discussion will suggest, these different conceptions of the wrong are not reducible to a single, unifying explanation; that is, there is no one factor that all of them can be understood as invoking as the source of the wrong. Assuming that all of them are plausible conceptions of the wrong, it follows that there is no single type of wrong present in all cases of unfairly unequal treatment. There is, rather, a variety of wrongs, each irreducible to the others. But a given case may involve more than one of these wrongs.

With this theoretical basis in place, I shall turn to consideration of the test laid down by the Supreme Court in *Law v. Canada* for violations of section 15(1).[10] I shall argue that, at least in its current form, this test fails to separate out these different conceptions of the wrong, and that this has rendered it both conceptually problematic and less able to recognize as discriminatory certain instances in which the claimant has indeed suffered one or more of the wrongs I have discussed. In conclusion, I shall explore several ways in which *Law* nevertheless leaves us room to maneuver in seeking a new approach to section 15, one that would acknowledge the distinctness of the various ways in which unequal treatment can wrong individuals, and would therefore place courts in a better position both to identify these wrongs and to decide whether section 15 is indeed rightly construed as offering protection against all of them.

B. AN ABSTRACT CONCEPTION OF THE WRONG

Regardless of how we conceive of the wrong that is done to individuals by unfair unequal treatment (for brevity's sake, I shall presuppose the qualification "unfair" from now on, and shall simply refer to "the wrong(s) of unequal treatment"), we can see it as the violation of a certain abstract ideal of how citizens ought to be treated by the state. Before we turn to various substantive conceptions of the wrong of unequal treatment, it will help to distinguish them from this more abstract ideal. It is the ideal of respect for the equal dignity of all. Dworkin described this abstract ideal in a particularly clear way in his 1978 paper, "What Rights Do We Have?" He proposed there that "[g]overnment must not only treat people with concern and respect, but with equal concern and respect. It must not distribute goods or opportunities unequally on the ground that some citizens are entitled to more because they are worthy of more concern."[11] Echoing this language, Justice McIntyre described the purpose of section 15 in *Andrews v. Law Society of Upper Canada* as that of ensuring that all individuals "are recognized at law as human beings equally deserving of concern, respect and consideration."[12] Neither of these statements explicitly appeals to the ideal of dignity. But both do so implicitly, for they imply that the reason why governments must treat all individuals with equal concern and respect is that governments must proceed on the assumption that all individuals possess supreme worth in and of themselves, under all conditions. "Dignity," on a Kantian understanding, is precisely the concept of this unchanging, supreme value that inheres in every human being. It is, as Kant wrote, the idea of a human being's "unconditional and incomparable worth."[13] Because this worth is unconditional — that is to say, is independent of the individual's circumstances or the extent to which she is actually shown respect by others — it cannot be diminished by others' disregard for it. So even if an individual is marginalized or stigmatized in her society, this cannot diminish her dignity in the objective sense we are considering. She always has a claim to concern and respect for her intrinsic worth. And because all individuals have this same intrinsic worth, all are entitled to an equal degree of concern and respect.[14]

I shall have more to say presently about this objective understanding of dignity; for it is often conflated — and conflated in the jurisprudence — with a quite different, subjective concept of dignity, that identifies a person's dignity with her own *feelings* of self-worth. For the present, however, all that is necessary for our purposes is to note that, on its own, this objective conception of dignity does not have sufficient content to explain the precise nature of the wrongs that are done to individuals who are not treated with equal concern and respect. That is because the mere idea that all human beings have unconditional worth does not tell us what kinds of treatment fail to show proper consideration for that worth. The abstract ideal of equal concern and respect for the dignity of all must be therefore given content by a substantial conception of what kinds of treatment violate human dignity. Each of the more specific conceptions of the wrong of unequal treatment that I shall now consider may be seen as an attempt to give content to this abstract ideal.[15] However, as we shall see, in the case of each specific, substantive conception, it is generally the particular features of certain forms of unequal treatment that drive the analysis and provide the explanation of why the treatment is wrong. In only one case does the concept of dignity itself play a substantial explanatory role. This does not, of course, show that the ideal of dignity is unhelpful, or that it should be abandoned. On the contrary, it provides a useful way of indicating that individuals cannot be treated in certain ways by the state. But *what* ways these are, in almost all cases, must be determined by factors other than the ideal of dignity itself. And if my arguments are correct, these factors are diverse in nature.

C. SUBSTANTIVE CONCEPTIONS OF THE WRONG: UNEQUAL TREATMENT WRONGS INDIVIDUALS WHEN ...

1) It Is Based upon Prejudice or Stereotyping

One of the most common reasons for thinking that a certain denial of a benefit or imposition of a burden[16] wrongs an individual is that it is based upon prejudice or stereotyping. By "based upon," I mean either "motivated by" or "publicly justified in terms of." Given our shared public sense of the inappropriateness of allowing prejudice to determine who receives a benefit, prejudice functions most often simply as a motive and not as part of the public justification for a particular policy. Stereotyping, however, functions both as a factor in motivation and as a factor in public justification (in some cases, by providing a convenient rationalization for treatment that was in fact motivated by prejudice).

Of the cases in which the Supreme Court has found a section 15 violation, many have involved unequal treatment which the Court has found to have been based upon a stereotype.[17] But what exactly is it about denying individuals a benefit on the basis of a prejudice or stereotype that makes it unfair? Why does it wrong them?

To arrive at an answer, we need to consider in more detail what it is for something to be a stereotype, and what it is to act out of prejudice.[18] Consider stereotypes first. On one understanding, a stereotype is simply any generalization or classification that one group of people treats as though it captured an essential feature of certain other individuals, and which is taken to render unnecessary any individualized consideration of their characteristics or circumstances.[19] On this view it is not necessary, for a generalization to qualify as a stereotype, that it carry negative connotations. What is essential to a stereotype is, rather, that it is used as a way of avoiding an individualized investigation into a particular person's abilities or circumstances. And it is also essential, on this view, that the generalizations that amount to stereotypes have been adopted by one group as a description of other individuals, rather than derived from these individuals' own attempts at self-definition. If these are the essential features of stereotypes, then we can notice at least two reasons why denying an individual a benefit on the basis of a stereotype may amount to a wrong.

First, the generalization may fail to describe this individual accurately. When it fails to do so, she is denied a benefit on the basis of a consideration that does not apply to her. And so, from her perspective, the denial is arbitrary, in the sense that it does not correspond to her actual situation.[20] One might be tempted to think that this is, on its own, a full and complete explanation of why it is wrong to deny someone a benefit on the basis of a stereotype. But it is worth pausing here to note that we do not think, in other contexts, that every arbitrary denial of a benefit amounts to a wrong against individuals by the state, simply by virtue of its arbitrariness. Section 7 of the *Charter,* for instance, protects individuals against arbitrary deprivations of liberty and security interests by requiring that such deprivations be in accordance with "principles of fundamental justice." But it does not protect against just any arbitrary deprivations of a liberty or security interest; it only protects against *some* arbitrary deprivations — namely, deprivations of certain core liberty or security interests. Likewise, in the context of equality rights, our jurisprudence does not treat every arbitrary denial of a benefit on the basis of a stereotype as an instance of unfair treatment. It restricts recognition of unfair treatment to those cases in which the stereotype pertains to one of the "grounds" of discrimination that is either enumerated in the *Charter* itself or analogous to those enumerated there.[21] One explanation for this approach is that mere arbitrariness is not, on its own, sufficient to constitute unfair treatment.[22] Perhaps a further factor must also be present.

What might this further factor be, in cases involving stereotypes? This question brings us to the second reason for thinking that denial of a benefit on the basis of a stereotype wrongs an individual. Someone who has been denied a benefit on the basis of a stereotype has been publicly defined by another group's image of him. Rather than being allowed to present himself and his circumstances as he understands them, he has been presented in the manner of another's choosing. And in certain circumstances, this will lessen his autonomy. That is, it will limit his power to define and direct his life in important ways — to shape his own identity, and to determine for himself which groups he belongs to and how these groups are to be characterized in public. Of course, it is only in certain circumstances that being publicly defined by another's image of oneself will detract from one's autonomy. Not every instance in which the state applies another group's generalization to me, rather than using some characterization of my choosing, will substantially reduce my powers of self-direction. In some cases, this will be necessary as an expedient and will have no significant effects on me; in other cases, it will be necessary to ensure the accuracy of the image of me that is presented in public, because my own perception of this particular aspect of myself is mistaken.

We can, I believe, see the appeal to enumerated and analogous grounds as an attempt to distinguish those circumstances in which the individual's autonomy is indeed lessened from those in which it is not — in other words, to mark out the situations in which denial of a benefit on the basis of a stereotype is not only potentially arbitrary, in the sense that it does not correspond to the individual's actual situation, but also such as to affect the individual's autonomy and, hence, such as to amount to a *wrong* against her. Stereotypes that pertain to recognized grounds such as race, gender, and sexual orientation, for instance, seem much more likely to lessen one's autonomy than would a stereotype such as "owners of red cars drive dangerously," when used as the basis for denying certain individuals reduced auto-insurance premiums. Although the latter stereotype is likely to result in the denial of a lower premium to some car owners who do not drive dangerously, and this denial will therefore be arbitrary from the perspective of these car owners, they do not seem thereby to have been legally wronged. And this may be because they have not suffered the second, and necessary, component of the wrong—that is, harm to their power to define and direct their lives in important ways.[23]

Thus far, we have been considering a view of stereotypes according to which it is not essential that they carry negative connotations. Some, however, do carry such connotations. They imply that the subjects of the generalization are inferior to those to whom the generalization does not apply—most often, inferior in some respect that is quite specific to the benefit in question (less capable at performing this job, less able to take advantage of that benefit), but occasionally, in the case of the most insidious stereotypes, inferior *tout court*, as human beings. These negative connotations enable the stereotype to rationalize the denial of the benefit in a further respect: in addition to giving us reasons for thinking that the benefit is not relevant to the individual, the stereotype now implies that the individual is not *deserving* of the benefit.

Although some scholars view negative connotations as essential to stereotypes and to the wrongs done by them, negative connotations do not seem essential to all of the generalizations that we find unacceptable as a basis for differential treatment.[24] There are, for instance, those generalizations that treat one feature as a proxy for another, based on relatively reliable statistical evidence. Many of these generalizations do not carry connotations of inferiority, and are used simply because separate consideration of each individual's actual traits would be difficult.[25] For this reason, it seems preferable to treat negative connotations, not as a necessary part of any stereotype, but as a factor that adds an additional dimension to the wrong we have already described, in those cases where it is present.

The presence of negative connotations may add to the wrong in several respects. First, it may render the denial of the benefit arbitrary in a further way, in those cases where the negative connotations concern the individuals' worth as human beings. For in these cases, the individuals will have been denied a benefit on the basis of an assumption that the government should not have accepted as relevant; namely, an assumption of the lesser intrinsic worth of certain individuals.[26] Moreover, in proceeding on the basis of this assumption, the government is violating its obligation to treat these individuals as if they had supreme intrinsic worth, or dignity.

In these explanations, of course, the ideal of concern and respect for dignity does play a substantive explanatory role. But there is also a further way in which the presence of negative connotations adds to the wrong of unequal treatment, which does not depend on the ideal of concern and respect for dignity — though it can be understood as giving content to it. When an individual is denied a benefit and the public justification for this denial appeals to a characteristic that carries connotations of inferiority of any sort, that individual is publicly proclaimed to be inferior. This will not amount to a wrong in all circumstances. If the assumed inferiority is relative to specific abilities or traits, rather than to the individual's worth as a human being, it may simply be an accurate description of her. But if it is not an accurate description of some specific ability, or if it presents her as being of less than supreme worth as a human being, then its public proclamation will impose limits on what she can do that were not already imposed by her own abilities, and it may also weaken her own sense of what it is possible for her to accomplish. In both of these ways, it will harm her autonomy.

We have been considering unequal treatment based upon stereotype. But what about those cases in which it is motivated by prejudice? If we understand "prejudice" simply as a belief in the inferiority of a certain individual that leads him to be seen as unworthy of the benefit, then the wrong here will seem the same as the wrong in cases of stereotypes carrying negative connotations. In some cases, however, prejudice involves more than a belief in a person's inferiority: it involves a malicious desire to use the occasion to cause harm to him.[27] In such cases, there seems to be a further aspect to the wrong. Rather than simply failing to show due concern for the individual's actual identity and circumstances, the government has actively set out to harm him. It has, one might say, abused its power over him: it has used this power in the service of a malicious purpose, rather than a legitimate one. So the wrong suffered by such individuals has a further dimension: they have been the victims of an abuse of government power.

I want now to note two implications of the above conception of the wrong of unequal treatment that will prove significant for our purposes. First, so understood, this wrong is not fundamentally a relational or comparative one. Of course, it is true that those who are denied a benefit on the basis of a stereotype are denied a benefit that others have received. And it is also true that they are denied this benefit on the basis of assumptions made about them by *other* groups. But the reason why this treatment amounts to a wrong, on the conception outlined above, is not given by any comparative fact — that is, any fact that depends on a comparison between the situation of these individuals and that of the groups who have received the benefit. Rather, it depends only on the fact that, considered in and of themselves, these individuals have been treated in an unacceptable way by the government: they have been denied a benefit in a manner that lessens their autonomy, that may have been arbitrary, that may have involved the unacceptable assumption that they lack intrinsic worth, and that, if motivated by prejudice, amounted to an abuse of government power. In order to ascertain whether their treatment by the government had these features, we do not need to compare the situation of these individuals with that of others. Hence, when the wrong of unequal treatment is understood as based upon stereotype or prejudice, it is incorrect to suppose that the assessment of an individual's claim requires the establishment of a "comparator group."

Second, and relatedly, because the wrong, so understood, is not relative to the situation of other individuals, it cannot ever be eliminated by the fact that the law that imposes the differential treatment aims to improve the position of another group that is worse off in terms of resources or power, or even worse off in terms of the stereotypical treatment it has received in the past. A stereotype is no less a stereotype because the law that employs it also works to improve the plight of others; this fact about their situation does not make the denial of the benefit any less arbitrary from the perspective of those who are stereotyped, nor any less of a threat to their autonomy. And this means that the presence of an "ameliorative purpose," which courts currently treat as weighing against a finding that the unequal treatment has been unfair, does *not* weigh against it when the wrong is understood as based upon stereotype or prejudice.

2) It Perpetuates Oppressive Power Relations

A different reason that unequal treatment may wrong individuals, one that has been discussed extensively by Anderson and Scheffler, is that it may perpetuate oppressive power relations.[28] It may, that is, have the effect of further entrenching or reinforcing power imbalances that are unacceptably large and that leave certain individuals without sufficient social or political influence. What amounts to an "unacceptably large" imbalance or a "sufficient" influence in this context is, of course, a question that different theorists have answered in different ways; but, as my arguments need not presuppose one answer or another, I shall leave the question open.[29]

It may seem that any conception of the wrong of unequal treatment that locates it in the perpetuation of oppressive power relations could not be significantly different from the conception we have just considered. When the denial of a certain benefit perpetuates oppressive power relations, is this not precisely *because* the denial was based upon a stereotype or a prejudice? Not necessarily. It need not involve prejudicial motives because, as recent literature on systemic discrimination has taught us, oppressive power relations are often the indirect effect of institutional structures — structures that were not designed deliberately to harm the individuals in question, or express contempt for them, but nevertheless perpetuate the social or political domination of certain groups. Nor does oppression always involve stereotyping. As Amartya Sen has noted, it is sometimes a sign of extreme oppression that the oppressed person or group has come to fit the image that has been defined for them by the dominant social group, and has come to lack all motivation for a change in their identity.[30] In such cases, the generalization that we make about these individuals may in fact be accurate; and the oppressed individuals may have adopted the generalization for themselves, as an accurate depiction of themselves. So the generalization will not be a "stereotype" in the sense we considered above: it will not be inaccurate, and the individuals to whom it is applied would indeed themselves assent to it, as a description of themselves. But this does not mean that the denial of a certain benefit to the individuals to whom this generalization applies does not have the effect of perpetuating objectionable forms of domination. Moreover, even in cases where there is no such extreme oppression, the denial of the benefit may not involve the application of a generalization at all, but may simply result from an omission in a certain scheme of protection or a policy with unforeseen side effects on a particular group. Hence, there can be denials of benefits that perpetuate oppressive power relations without involving stereotypes or prejudices.

An example of such a case might help to make this point more forcefully. Consider the treatment received by the claimant in *Vriend v. Alberta*.[31] Delwin Vriend was barred from bringing a complaint of discrimination on the basis of sexual orientation against his employer under Alberta's *Individual's Rights Protection Act* (IRPA),[32] because at the time it did not include "sexual orientation" among its list of prohibited grounds. The Alberta legislature had omitted this ground simply because it believed the issue was "too controversial." It seems implausible to suggest that members of the legislature could not have believed that the controversial nature of this ground was a good reason for omitting it from the legislation unless motivated by prejudice or by stereotypes about homosexuals. It seems more likely that they simply made a judgment about which decision would yield the most popular support. Yet it is clear that the denial of this benefit to Vriend perpetuated oppressive power relations — in particular, between homosexuals as a group and those who disparaged their sexual orientation.

One might suggest, however, that even if stereotyping and prejudice are not present in such cases, nevertheless what *makes* the perpetuation of oppression wrong is essentially the same as one of the elements — indeed, the main element — that made unequal treatment on the basis of stereotyping and prejudice wrong; namely, harm to the victim's autonomy. This certainly seems to be part of the reason that oppressive power relations are objectionable: if other individuals exert significant control over me, I will be less able to shape my own life in accordance with my choices. But I am not certain that this is the heart of the wrong that is done through the perpetuation of oppression. When some individuals are oppressed by others, certain goods are denied to them — such as the opportunity to participate as equals in public political argument, the opportunity to have equal influence in certain social contexts, and the opportunity to contribute to a genuinely collective self-determination. These goods have value in and of themselves, quite apart from their instrumental value in promoting individual autonomy. So it seems plausible to hold that, merely by virtue of being deprived of these goods, the individual has been wronged, quite apart from whether this has also lessened his autonomy.

Unlike the good of autonomy, the goods listed above are all relational: they concern the individual's standing and opportunities in relation to those of others, and they can be assessed only through a comparison of the individual with others. This leads to one important difference between the wrong of being denied a benefit where this perpetuates oppressive power relations and the wrong of being denied a benefit on the basis of stereotype or prejudice. We saw above that the latter wrong is not essentially relational: the wrong of being denied a benefit on the basis of a stereotype or prejudice is dependent solely upon facts about this individual's treatment and its effects upon her, considered quite apart from others. By contrast, one must engage in comparative judgments to ascertain whether differential treatment in fact perpetuates oppressive power relations. And when it does, this amounts to a wrong largely because it denies the individual access to certain relational goods.

This wrong, then, is essentially comparative. It is important to note, however, that the relevant comparator group is not the group that has been given the benefit in question but the group or groups who exercise oppressive amounts of power over those who have been denied the benefit. This is because, in order to ascertain whether the denial of a benefit genuinely perpetuates oppressive power relations, one needs to focus, not on the group that has been given the benefit but, rather, on whether or not there is indeed some group that exercises an undue amount of power over those who are denied the benefit and on whether the denial of the benefit will perpetuate these unacceptable power relations. The group that dominates may indeed be coextensive with the class of people who have been given the benefit. But it will not always be so. Certainly in *Vriend*, the benefits of the IRPA in an employment context were obtained mainly by employees, whereas the group that exercised undue amounts of power over individuals such as Vriend consisted of some, but not all, employees and some employers — namely, any who disparaged homosexuals as unworthy of human rights protection. And even in cases where the group that receives the benefit is indeed coextensive with the group that exercises unacceptable domination over those denied the benefit, what is relevant about the comparator group is not their receipt of the benefit but their oppression of those who have been denied it.

A further implication of this conception of the wrong is that, although it is relational, the wrong is not lessened or eliminated by the fact that the law resulting in the denial of the benefit has an ameliorative purpose. Even if a law aims to eliminate the *oppression* of some other group — perhaps a group that, in absolute terms, was much worse off than those denied the benefit — this does not eliminate or diminish the oppression of those to whom the benefit is denied.

This is not to say that the fact that a law has an ameliorative purpose is of no relevance at all. The presence of an ameliorative purpose may indeed be relevant to the question of whether the law is justified, all things considered (in legal terms, this is the question asked in section 1 analysis). But because it does not lessen the oppression of those who are denied the benefit, it seems implausible to treat it as relevant to whether the unequal treatment that these individuals have received is unfair to them, or amounts to a wrong to them, in the sense relevant to section 15 analysis. And indeed, *Vriend* is a good illustration of this. Anti-discrimination legislation is inherently remedial: the IRPA was specifically designed by the Alberta legislature to try to eliminate the oppression of other groups — for instance, working women, and various ethnic minorities. Yet the fact that the legislation had this purpose was quite properly not treated by the Court as a factor weighing against the conclusion that Vriend had been treated unfairly.

3) It Leaves Some Individuals without Access to Basic Goods

Much of the recent philosophical work on equality has aimed to show that, in many cases, our concern over unequal treatment is not ultimately a concern that some people have unfairly been given less than others but, rather, a concern that these people do not have *enough*, when their situation is considered on its own, in absolute terms. Harry Frankfurt, for instance, has argued that inequalities are morally problematic only when they result in certain people having less than what is "sufficient."[33] He writes that:

> When we consider people who are substantially worse off than ourselves, we do very commonly find that we are morally disturbed by their circumstances. What directly touches us in cases of this kind, however, is not a quantitative discrepancy but a qualitative condition....[34]

That is to say, what is of moral importance to us, in Frankfurt's view, is not the relative difference between those who have more and those who have less, but the absolute condition of those who are worse off. It is whether those who are worse off lack sufficient goods. (What amounts to "sufficient goods" depends on what, in a moral context, one takes to be morally relevant, or, in a legal context, legally relevant. It may be "goods sufficient to maintain one's life"; or "goods sufficient for a life in which one has time to do more than stay alive"; or it may be a set of goods that is important not because of their contribution to the individual's own well-being, but because they are "goods necessary for the individual to function as an equal in society." I shall consider these alternatives presently.) Derek Parfit has drawn a similar distinction between a concern for eliminating inequalities *per se* and the aim of giving priority to those who are "worse off." And he, too, has suggested that perhaps the moral value of equality may not inhere entirely in the aim of improving the situation of those who are worse off — not because it matters that they are worse off than others but simply because it matters that, in absolute terms, they are so badly off.[35]

For a variety of reasons, one might think that although this concern for the situation of those who are badly off may ground some of our moral objections to inequality, it cannot be the basis for a legal complaint about unequal treatment — or, at least, cannot be the basis for a section 15 challenge. First, one might hold that our concern for those who lack access to basic goods can only be interpreted as the view that the government is under a positive duty to provide certain basic goods to all citizens, and one might doubt whether any section of the *Charter* can plausibly be construed as imposing such a positive duty. Second, and alternatively, one might maintain, as Justice Arbour did in *Gosselin*, that although there *can* be a positive duty on the government to ensure that individuals have access to certain basic goods, the proper way to understand this positive duty is as an implication of the section 7 right not to be deprived of "security of the person" except in accordance with principles of fundamental justice.[36] This duty is best understood in terms of section 7, one might claim, because our concern that all individuals have access to basic goods is ultimately a concern for their physical and psychological *security*. Moreover, one might argue, unlike section 7, section 15 protects only against wrongs that are inherently *comparative* in nature. And the wrong of being deprived of access to basic goods is clearly not comparative. So if any section of the *Charter* protects against this wrong, it must be section 7; it cannot be section 15.

However, each of these lines of reasoning can be questioned. First, it is not clear that our concern here must be construed as an insistence that the government is under a positive duty to provide certain basic goods to all. Some theories of the nature and justification of the *Charter* and the rights it guarantees imply that it cannot impose positive duties on governments to provide certain benefits; similarly, certain theories of the appropriate roles of the courts and the legislatures imply that courts simply do not have the institutional mandate to interpret the *Charter* as imposing positive duties on governments.[37] My aim here is not to take a stand on the adequacy of these theories. It is, rather, to suggest that the claims that these theories make about the indefensibility of positive rights under the *Charter could* quite coherently limit, and help to give shape to, our concern for the absolute level of those who are badly off. Rather than treating this concern as giving rise to what Raz has called a "closure principle" (that is, a principle stating that where this consideration is present, nothing else counts in determining whether a particular government action is justified), we might treat it as a concern that is itself limited by the need to defer to the government's choice of whether or not to legislate in a particular area and to provide particular benefits to the public.[38] If we treat it in this way, our concern will take the form of an objection to the way in which the government sometimes acts, *once* it has chosen to legislate in a certain area. The objection will be that if the government chooses to make a certain benefit available to the public — for instance, government pensions, unemployment insurance, or a certain level of welfare payment that it deems sufficient for basic survival — then it wrongs individuals if it denies them these benefits and this denial leaves them without access to a relevant basic good. Hence *if* the government wishes to legislate over a certain matter and to provide certain benefits, it must do so in a way that does not leave the most disadvantaged groups in our society without access to the relevant basic goods. But it may also choose not to legislate over these areas, and in this case, even those who are very badly off can have no equality-based objection.[39]

One might contend, however, that even if the *Charter* can plausibly be interpreted as imposing a positive duty on the government to ensure that individuals have access to certain basic goods, this duty is not best understood in terms of section 15 equality rights. Rather, the proper way to understand this duty is as an implication of the section 7 right not to be deprived of "security of the person" except in accordance with principles of fundamental justice. Recall that one consideration advanced in support of this suggestion was that section 15 protects only against wrongs that are inherently comparative in nature. This claim has already been shown to be incorrect by our discussion of the wrong of differential treatment that is based upon stereotyping or prejudice. We saw there that this wrong is not essentially comparative. It pertains only to these individuals' situations and, most notably, to the effects upon their autonomy; and these can be ascertained without drawing comparisons with another group. Since the wrong of denying individuals a benefit because of prejudice or stereotyping is clearly at the heart of section 15, it cannot be said that section 15 protects only against wrongs that are inherently comparative.

But one further reason was given above for thinking that our concern for those who lack access to basic goods is best understood in terms of section 7 rights to security of the person; that this concern is essentially a concern for the *security* of those who are worse off — that is, a concern to ensure that they have all of the goods necessary for basic health and survival. This is certainly one way of understanding the concern. But there are other ways. It may be a concern that they be given goods sufficient for a life that includes more than simply working to survive. Or it may be the concern that Anderson foregrounds — namely, that each individual have sufficient resources to be able to participate in and enjoy the goods of society and to participate in democratic self-government.[40] We need not decide this issue here. What is important for our purposes is to note that there are other, equally plausible ways of understanding the concern. We need not see it as the type of concern that can be adequately addressed through section 7.

I have now tried to counter various arguments purporting to show that it is inappropriate to consider section 15 as protecting against the wrong of denying individuals a benefit in a manner that leaves them without access to basic goods. I want now to argue, further, that in a number of section 15 cases, this is the most plausible way of making sense of the wrong that was alleged by the claimants, and recognized as a wrong by at least some members of the Supreme Court. Consider first the case of *Eldridge v. British Columbia (A.G.)*.[41] The case concerned the failure of the British Columbia government to provide funding for sign language interpreters for individuals requiring medical services. The Supreme Court held that this did constitute a violation of the claimants' equality rights. Their reasoning was that effective communication with one's medical practitioners is an essential, not an ancillary, part of medical service; and the British Columbia government had chosen to fund essential medical services. In other words, the denial of this benefit left deaf persons lacking in a basic good that was relevant to the area in which the government had chosen to legislate.

The Court's objection to the treatment of deaf persons in *Eldridge* is, I believe, misconstrued if construed simply as an objection to the *difference* between the effective communication available to hearing persons and the difficulties experienced by deaf persons in the absence of interpreters. If it were simply an objection to this difference, then it would be adequately met by eliminating the difference in the levels of communication with medical personnel enjoyed by hearing persons and by deaf persons. But it would not matter, for the purposes of section 15, *how* this difference was eliminated — and, in particular, it would not matter whether the government eliminated the difference by raising the level of communicative efficacy enjoyed by the deaf or simply by lowering the level enjoyed by the hearing. Suppose, fancifully, that the government had attempted to eliminate the difference in this case by "leveling down" and ensuring that hearing persons found communication with medical staff just as difficult as deaf persons. (Imagine, for example, that the government required medical staff to address hearing persons only in languages other than their own.) This would hardly remove the unfairness to deaf persons, even though it would eliminate the difference between their situation and that of those with normal hearing. It would also, of course, result in an irrational legislative agenda: choosing to provide funding for essential medical services and yet denying all individuals the effective communication that they must have if they are to take full advantage of these services. But that is a separate objection. What is relevant for our purposes is simply that, in such a situation, the original objection of deaf persons would remain: whatever other objections could be made to this new scheme, they could still object that they were treated unfairly by the government. They were denied access to a relevant basic good, even though the government had chosen to legislate in this area.

Two more recent cases in which this is a plausible way of construing one of the main wrongs alleged by the claimant are *Gosselin* and *Canadian Foundation for Children, Youth and the Law v. Canada (A.G.)*, or the "Spanking Case."[42] Louise Gosselin's complaint pertained to Quebec's social assistance scheme, which for a time set the base welfare payment for those under age thirty at one-third of the amount, viewed by the government as the basic survival amount, that was payable to those aged thirty and above. The scheme stipulated that under-thirties could receive an amount comparable to that received by those aged thirty and above only if they participated in designated work activity or education programmes. One aspect of the wrong alleged by Gosselin pertained to the stereotypes that she viewed as underlying the restrictions on the amount payable to those under thirty: she held that they were based upon an inaccurate view of young persons as better able to find employment than people older than thirty, as less needy, and as able to rely upon parents for additional support. But only part of her objection was to the unfairness of being denied the full benefit on the basis of a stereotype. Her complaint was also that she was not, under the scheme, given *enough* to live on: the amount she received left her unable to pay for adequate shelter, food, and clothing. And this aspect of her complaint seems best understood in terms of the wrong of being denied access to a basic good relevant to the area in which the government had chosen to legislate. Similarly, part of the complaint of the Canadian Foundation for Children, Youth, and the Law was that the exclusion from the crime of assault of "reasonable" force exerted "by way of correction" left children without a basic good — namely, protection against intentional physical force. As Mr Binnie wrote in dissent, quoting Peter Newell, "Children are people, and hitting people is wrong."[43] What is objectionable is not the mere difference between the treatment received by adults and the treatment received by children, but, rather, the fact that, as a result of the exemption for reasonable corrective force, children were left without access to the basic good of protection from intentional infliction of physical force.

I have now tried to show that this way of construing the wrong of unequal treatment has some plausibility. Before we move on, we should note two implications of this conception. First, as we have seen, this conception of the wrong renders it non-comparative. Consequently, when a claimant is alleging this type of wrong, there is no need to locate a relevant comparator group; we need only ask whether the government has legislated in the area in question and whether the denial of a benefit to these individuals results in their lacking access to a relevant basic good. Second, it is once again irrelevant whether the law in question aims to ameliorate the position of some other group. For recall that the claim of those who have been denied the benefit is not, on this conception of the wrong, dependent on their being the worst-off of any group in society; it simply depends on the fact that they lack access to a relevant basic good, and this fact is not changed by the way in which the legislation affects others.

4) It Diminishes Individuals' Feelings of Self-Worth

A further way of understanding the wrong of unequal treatment is in terms of injury to a person's sense of self-worth.[44] This way of understanding the wrong appeals to a subjective conception of dignity. That is, it is concerned not with the objective idea of individual worth that we earlier saw was central to the abstract ideal of equal concern and respect for dignity, but with the individual's own *perception* of her self-worth — with whether the individual believes herself to have worth as a human being or feels as though she is worthless. This subjective conception of dignity is essentially a conception of self-respect. Hence, this way of understanding the wrong of unequal treatment is as an injury to the individual's self-respect. The individual has been made to feel as though she is worthless.

As Scanlon has argued, however, many quite legitimate policies that recognize and reward some individuals' initiative or labour will make others feel that they are of lesser worth. For instance, a law firm's policy of giving bonuses to lawyers who bill over and above the target hours will inevitably result in certain other lawyers feeling as though they are of lesser worth, even if the policy is applied in a manner that seems wholly fair and unobjectionable. The feelings of inferiority generated in the lawyers who do not receive the bonus will seem to us simply an unfortunate side-effect of the policy, and not grounds for thinking that it wrongs these individuals.

What examples like this suggest is that the mere fact that unequal treatment decreases the self-respect of those who are denied the benefit is not sufficient to render that treatment unfair. It follows, therefore, that this way of understanding the wrong of unequal treatment cannot stand on its own as a complete explanation of why certain forms of differential treatment are objectionable. We will deem a person's feelings of inferiority an appropriate object of redress, as a matter of equality rights, only if we have *already* determined that the differential treatment of this person was *unfair,* or amounted to a wrong, in light of one of the other conceptions of the wrong that is done by unequal treatment. It may be that, once the differential treatment has been shown to amount to a wrong of one or another of the types examined above, then the claimant can show that he has suffered a *further* wrong by losing his sense of self-worth as a result. But merely having one's sense of self-respect injured cannot, on its own, render unequal treatment unfair.

As we shall see, this has significant implications. For it suggests that, to the extent that the *Law* test reduces "dignity" to an experiential good (albeit one that is assessed from the perspective of a reasonable person in the claimant's position), it mistakenly tries to treat what can be at most one of the wrongs involved in discrimination as a full and complete account of these wrongs. And it thereby conceals the more important work that is done by the explanation of why the differential treatment is unfair in the first place — an explanation that cannot itself be provided by an appeal to the way in which the treatment has affected the claimant's feelings of self-respect.

5) Conclusion

I have now canvassed four substantive conceptions of the wrong of unequal treatment. I do not mean to imply that they constitute an exclusive list; only that all seem represented in the case law, and all seem to offer plausible accounts of this wrong. As I have tried to suggest, each conception appeals to distinct kinds of facts about the unequal treatment, or distinct kinds of facts about the effects of this unequal treatment upon the individual. Hence, each locates the wrongness of unequal treatment in a somewhat different combination of factors. If I am right to think that each is a plausible explanation of why unequal treatment wrongs individuals, then it follows that we cannot give a single, unified explanation of these wrongs — that is, an explanation that traces the wrong in each case back to the same factor. This is not a problem. It simply reflects the fact that our objections to unequal treatment stem from many different considerations. Rather than referring to "the wrong" of unequal treatment, then, we should recognize that there are multiple "wrongs" that can be involved.

It must be emphasized that this result does not call into question the usefulness of appealing to the abstract ideal of concern and respect for human dignity as a way of indicating that there are certain ways in which individuals may not legitimately be treated by the state. All that it does is suggest that we cannot *derive* our conclusions about which forms of treatment these are, and about why exactly they are impermissible, from a single ideal, such as the ideal of concern and respect for dignity.[45] As we saw when discussing stereotyping and prejudice, the ideal of concern and respect for a person's intrinsic dignity does play an explanatory role in cases where the stereotype or prejudice involves the assumption that certain individuals lack incomparable worth: for it is evident that if *any* treatment at all is to violate the ideal of concern and respect for human dignity, legislation based on the assumption that some individuals lack dignity must do so. In other cases, however — that is, in cases of unequal treatment based upon stereotypes that do not involve assumptions about the lesser worth of individuals, or cases of unequal treatment that perpetuates oppressive power relations or that denies certain individuals access to basic goods, or that lowers individuals' self-respect — we must look to considerations other than dignity for a detailed explanation of why the treatment wrongs these individuals.

D. RESPONSES TO OBJECTIONS

Before turning to consider the implications of my analysis of equality for the *Law* test for violations of section 15, I want to respond to two objections that might be made to my analysis.

First, one might object that there is indeed a common thread that runs through the various conceptions of the wrong of unequal treatment that I have discussed. All are instances of some individuals being *arbitrarily* denied a certain benefit — that is, denied it for no legitimate legal reason. Does not the notion of arbitrariness, then, provide us with a unified explanation of these apparently different wrongs?

In considering this objection, it is important to note at the outset that the sense of "arbitrariness" at issue here is very different from the sense that I considered earlier, when discussing the wrong of denying individuals a benefit on the basis of stereotypes or prejudice. We saw earlier that such treatment may be arbitrary in the sense that the benefit is denied for reasons that do not correspond to the particular situation of the individual. But we also saw that this does not make this treatment arbitrary in the stronger sense that there is no legitimate legal reason for it: as we noted, the use of informed statistical generalizations is often a necessary legislative expedient, and not one that seems to us to impugn the legislative act as discriminatory. Indeed, I suggested that this was precisely why our jurisprudence recognizes as "discriminatory" only those instances of stereotyping that occur on enumerated or analogous grounds. Only these are "arbitrary" in the further sense that there is no legitimate legal reason for them.

The sense of arbitrariness at issue now, then, concerns the justifiability of the denial of the benefit. Is there a legitimate legal reason for it? My hypothetical objector's contention is that this consideration alone is sufficient to account for, and to provide an explanatory unity to, the different conceptions of the wrong that I have discussed.

This contention faces two related problems. The first is that, at least in Canadian jurisprudence, we separate the question of whether or not a particular instance of unequal treatment is unfair — which we take to determine whether or not section 15 has been violated — from the question of whether it is nevertheless justified, all things considered — which we reserve for the further stage of assessing whether it is saved by section 1 of the *Charter*. And this means that if the contention that the unfairness of unequal treatment is always a matter of arbitrariness is to accord with our jurisprudence, we cannot read "arbitrariness" in the strong, unqualified manner suggested above. We cannot, that is, read it as "the absence of any legitimate reason for the denial of the benefit." For whether there is, all things considered, a legitimate reason for the denial of the benefit is a further and broader question than the question that these conceptions of the wrong of unequal treatment attempt to address. They aim simply to explain when and why unequal treatment is unfair *to the claimant,* quite apart from whether other social goals may ultimately render it justifiable. Hence, we need to modify the contention so that "arbitrariness" is understood as referring to "the absence of a legitimate legal reason pertaining to the *fairness to the claimant* of denying her a benefit."

This modification, however, makes even clearer a problem that was already present in the unmodified contention — and this is the second, and decisive, problem that I want to discuss. It is that the notion of arbitrariness does not itself provide us with any further explanatory power, beyond that provided by the various substantive conceptions of the wrong that I have examined. For what does all of the explanatory work in the suggestion that these are instances in which there is no "legitimate legal reason" for a particular denial of a benefit (or no legitimate legal reason pertaining to its fairness to the claimant) is the appeal to "legitimate" legal reasons. It is true that each of the substantive conceptions of the wrong that I have discussed can be seen as fleshing out a different reason for thinking that the denial of a benefit is supported by no legitimate legal reasons. However, what explains *why* there are no legitimate legal reasons in such cases — or, to put it differently, what determines what constitutes a "legitimate" reason under the circumstances — are the diverse considerations that I have discussed, such as the fact that denial of a certain benefit on the basis of a stereotype harms an individual's autonomy, or the fact that denial of certain benefits perpetuates oppressive power relations. We do not add anything to these explanations by noting that, in such cases, there are no legitimate legal reasons for denying the benefit. So although it is true that these diverse conceptions of the wrong all involve a type of "arbitrariness," this notion does not itself have any independent explanatory power. Consequently, it cannot provide explanatory unity.

The second objection to my analysis that I wish to discuss concerns the sense in which the idea of "equality" really continues to play a role in these diverse conceptions of why unequal treatment is unfair. One might object that if, as I have argued, none of these conceptions locate the wrong in the difference between what is had by those individuals who receive the benefit and what is had by those who lack it, then paradoxically, what is wrong with "unequal" treatment seems, on my view, to have little to do with "equality." Indeed, if all that matters in such cases is the type of treatment that the claimant himself has received and it is irrelevant how he compares with the group that receives the benefit, then it seems that it is immaterial whether there has been any differential or "unequal" treatment in the first place. What matters is simply whether this particular claimant has been treated *unfairly* by the government. It so happens that the particular types of unfair treatment that ground our concerns over inequality arise in a context in which some individuals receive a benefit and those who are treated unfairly do not; but this differential treatment is not essential to their claim. If this is correct, however, then how are these conceptions of the wrong of unequal treatment really explanations of the wrong or wrongs of *unfair* treatment?

This objection is correct in assuming that, on the conceptions I have discussed, it is never the difference between those who have been denied a benefit and those who have received it that helps to explain why unequal treatment is unfair. But it does not follow that the conceptions fail as an account of why "unequal" treatment is wrong because they give no role to the notion of "equality." Nor does it follow that the requirement that we establish differential treatment before asking whether the individual has been treated unfairly serves no function. I shall try to explain each of these points in turn.

When we speak of "equality," we often think simply of what might be called "horizontal" relations — or relations between citizens, all of whom are potential recipients of a particular distributive scheme of the government. However, as I noted at the beginning of this article, whether the government has treated individuals "equally" through a particular scheme never depends only on the horizontal relations that it creates between them. That is, it never depends simply on how much each is given, relative to others. For, as I noted earlier, no plausible theory of equality holds that a particular distributive scheme wrongs individuals simply because it gives them less than others. This is why the question with which we began was: What in particular makes *some* unequal distributions of the government unfair to those individuals who receive less? The conceptions of the wrong of unequal treatment that I have discussed all locate the unfairness primarily in what we can call "vertical" relations — that is, relations between the government and the individuals who are denied the benefit. For all of these conceptions point to particular facts about the way in which the government has treated these individuals that render this treatment unfair *to them*. Most of these conceptions concern only vertical relations, although cases of "perpetuation of oppressive power relations" are special in that the reason why the denial of a benefit in such cases amounts to an unacceptable vertical relation is that the government has allowed certain horizontal relations to persist in society. So this particular conception of the wrong combines vertical and horizontal relations.

My analysis suggests, then, that although we tend to associate "equality" with horizontal relations, it is vertical relations that are determinative in most cases. This does not mean that the notion of "equality" drops out of my analysis, which is still an analysis of when and why certain forms of unequal treatment are unfair to individuals, or amount to wrongs toward them. The fact that it explains these wrongs in terms that do not make reference to horizontal relations between citizens does not mean that it is no longer an analysis of why certain forms of unequal treatment are unfair to individuals. Nor is it any less an analysis of unequal treatment simply because it implies that some of the wrongs done by unequal treatment could also be done by treatment that is not unequal — that is, could also be done in a context in which there was no comparator group that has received the benefit denied to the claimant.

But this brings us to the second point, which concerns the question of whether there is, on this analysis, any reason to require claimants to point to a comparator group that has received the benefit they have been denied, and thereby demonstrate that they have received differential treatment. This requirement can, I believe, still serve a valuable evidentiary function. For what the presence of differential treatment tells us is that the government has chosen to put in place a particular distributive scheme; and the kinds of unfair treatment identified by the various conceptions of the wrong that I have discussed all have in common the fact that they arise in the context of the government's having chosen to distribute a particular benefit (or burden). They are all, we might say, forms of unfairness in the context of distribution. It will almost always be true that, if the government has set up a certain distributive scheme, some group will have received a benefit. So the requirement that the claimant point to such a group serves as a way of confirming that the context we are dealing with is one of distribution. It is therefore a useful device, even though the mere difference between the claimant and the group that has received the benefit does not, on my analysis, play any role in explaining why the treatment of the claimant is unfair.

E. PROBLEMS WITH THE *LAW* TEST

My analysis of the wrongs of unequal treatment implies that there are a number of respects in which the *Law* test is problematic. In this section of the article, I shall lay out these problems. In the subsequent and final section, I shall try to show that it is nevertheless possible to use the basic framework of the *Law* test to move forward and to develop an approach that eliminates these problems.

The problems that I shall discuss all stem from a conflation of the different conceptions of the wrong of unequal treatment. In at least three respects, the test laid down in *Law* seems to conflate different conceptions of this wrong. This conflation creates certain conceptual problems within the test. Moreover, it has the effect of rendering the test unable to register certain instances of unfair unequal treatment — that is, unable to recognize that they are indeed unfair and should be treated as violations of section 15.

The *Law* test involves three stages of analysis. First, the claimant must establish that she has received differential treatment; that is, she has been denied a benefit that others have received. Second, she must show that the differential treatment occurred on an enumerated or analogous ground. Third, she must show that this unequal treatment was unfair, or amounted to discrimination — which, according to the Court in *Law,* involves showing that her dignity was infringed, in the sense that a reasonable person in her position would have been made to feel inferior.

The first problematic conflation in this test occurs in the use that the test makes of the concept of "dignity." As we have seen, one way of understanding the concept of dignity is as the concept of an objective worth possessed by all human beings: the Kantian concept of "incomparable worth." The *Law* test quite properly takes this concept as the starting point for its analysis of section 15: when Mr Justice Iacobucci speaks of the essential purpose of section 15 as being "to prevent the violation of essential human dignity," it is this objective conception of dignity that he is invoking.[46] He seems, in fact, to be invoking the abstract ideal that the state ought to treat individuals with concern and respect for the dignity of all. However, when proceeding to discuss dignity, Iacobucci J. then identifies it with "whether an individual or group feels self-respect and self-worth" and with "physical and psychological integrity and empowerment."[47] This is clearly the different, subjective concept of dignity that we considered when we looked at the last of the substantive conceptions of the wrong of unequal treatment: it is the concept, not of objective worth, but of how a person *feels* when treated in a certain way. And the precise approach that Iacobucci J. then proceeds to lay down for the third stage of the *Law* test seems to draw upon this subjective concept of dignity, rather than offering a comprehensive and explicit analysis of the kinds of treatment that amount to a violation of dignity in the objective sense. For the approach is, Iacobucci J. states, to measure "the manner in which a person legitimately *feels* when confronted by a particular law."[48] The court is to ask: Has he been made to feel inferior, and is this feeling legitimate under the circumstances?

As the qualifier "legitimately" indicates, Mr Justice Iacobucci was quite aware that not every decrease in one's sense of self-worth amounts to a wrong. He rightly attempted to restrict the test to those feelings of inferiority that have been generated by unequal treatment that is *unfair*. This is, in my view, the real rationale for the requirement that the test must be applied from the perspective of a reasonable person in the position of the claimant: the aim is to ensure that courts assess not just whether the claimant has come to feel inferior and to feel as though others regard him as inferior, but whether he has come to feel this as a result of *unfair* treatment. But — and this is where the test becomes problematic — although the test thus purports to be about the feelings of the claimant, the question on which it really turns is whether or not the treatment received by the claimant was unfair. And this question must, as we noted earlier, be answered by appeal to some *other* substantive conception of what makes unequal treatment into a wrong against the individual: unfairness is not shown simply by pointing to the individual's feelings. Nor, for the reasons given above, can the unfairness of the treatment be assessed simply by appealing to the objective concept of dignity. Rather, courts must invoke some substantive conception of why individuals are wronged by unequal treatment. They must appeal, for instance, to the fact that the differential treatment was based upon stereotyping and prejudice; to the fact that it perpetuates oppressive power relations; or to the fact that it leaves the claimant lacking access to basic goods. And this means that the *Law* test ultimately relies upon conceptions of the wrong that are not explicitly discussed in this case itself and that have not subsequently received explicit discussion because the *Law* test obscures the fact that they must be invoked.

The problem with the *Law* test's use of "dignity," then, is that in moving from the objective concept of dignity to the subjective concept, and in supposing that the subjective concept (combined with an idea of reasonableness) provides a complete explanation of the wrong of unequal treatment, the test hides all the real work that must be done in the test by *other* substantive conceptions of the wrong. It is these other substantive conceptions that must tacitly be invoked by courts in determining whether or not a certain claimant's feelings of inferiority were reasonable. These conceptions do the real work in determining whether a particular instance of unequal treatment amounts to discrimination.

It would be preferable, then, if the *Law* test simply retained the original objective concept of dignity with which it began. Rather than asking whether a reasonable person in the claimant's position would *feel* inferior, courts could look directly to various substantive conceptions of the wrong of unequal treatment to determine whether or not the treatment was, in fact, unfair. If the treatment is found to be unfair, then it will follow that it violates the abstract ideal of equal concern and respect for dignity. But this conclusion will be driven by the various substantive conceptions of what makes unequal treatment unfair.

The *Law* test also conflates different conceptions of the wrong of unequal treatment in requiring that every claimant establish a comparator group. The test demands that claimants initially identify a group that received the benefit that she, the claimant, was denied. But it then requires courts to conduct the subsequent analysis of whether the treatment of the claimants was indeed unfair in light of this same comparator group. As I argued earlier, the requirement that claimants be able to point to another group that received the benefit may serve a useful evidentiary function, confirming that we are indeed dealing with a context in which the government has undertaken a certain distributive scheme. However, as we have seen, it is often not appropriate to take a comparative approach to the subsequent question of whether or not the treatment was unfair to, or wronged, the claimant. Moreover, even where the wrong is a relative one that requires comparisons to be made between the claimant and others — such as in cases involving the perpetuation of oppressive power relations — the relevant comparator group is not, at this later stage, the group of individuals who have received the benefit; rather, it is the group, or groups, that unduly dominate those who have been denied the benefit.

It follows that more of a distinction must be made between the first stage of the *Law* test, in which we inquire whether or not the treatment was differential, and the third stage, in which we inquire whether or not the differential treatment was unfair.[49] Comparing the claimant with those who have received the benefit may serve a useful function at the first stage. But such comparison is highly misleading if extended to the stage in which we ask whether or not the treatment was unfair. For even in cases where the wrong is relational, it will not be the group of individuals who were given the benefit who form the relevant comparator group.

There is also a third respect in which the *Law* test conflates different conceptions of the wrong of unequal treatment. It concerns the four "contextual factors" that the test deems relevant to whether a particular instance of differential treatment amounts to unfair treatment, or discrimination. These are (i) whether the claimant is part of a group that has suffered from past disadvantage or stereotyping; (ii) whether the ground of discrimination corresponds to the claimant's real needs and circumstances; (iii) whether the law in question improves the situation of a group that is worse off than the claimant; and (iv) the significance of the interest affected, both to the claimant and in constitutional or societal terms. Although the Supreme Court has repeatedly acknowledged that not all of these factors are necessarily relevant in a particular case, both it and the lower courts nevertheless tend to proceed in each case by examining each factor in turn and then engaging in a kind of weighing and balancing exercise to determine whether the combination of those that are present is strong enough to amount to discrimination. In this balancing exercise, the second factor — the actual correspondence between the ground of discrimination and the claimant's needs or circumstances — is often taken as weighing heavily, if not decisively, in favour of a finding that no discrimination has occurred.[50]

My suggestion in what follows will be that this is a problematic way of approaching the question of whether the differential treatment is discriminatory. As I shall try to demonstrate, not all of these contextual factors are relevant to each of the substantive conceptions of the wrong of unequal treatment. Some are relevant to some conceptions; others are relevant to others. And one, the ameliorative purpose, does not lessen the wrong of unequal treatment on any of these conceptions. In any given case, it is inappropriate to weigh in the balance those factors that are irrelevant to the kind of wrong that has occurred: the presence of an irrelevant factor should not weigh in favour of the conclusion that certain treatment is discriminatory, nor should the absence of an irrelevant factor be counted against the claimant. Instead of considering all of the contextual factors in any given case, courts must first clarify which type of wrong is at issue in the case at bar. They should then look only to those contextual factors that are relevant in determining whether or not this type of wrong has occurred and, hence, whether the unequal treatment was unfair.

Why is it that not every contextual factor is relevant to each of the four substantive conceptions of the wrong considered in Section C? I shall try briefly to explain why, focusing on each of these conceptions in turn. Since I have already tried to demonstrate that the ameliorative purpose factor is not relevant to most of these conceptions, I shall omit it from consideration here, except when discussing the wrong of unfairly being deprived of one's sense of self-worth.

Let us turn first to the wrong of being denied a benefit on the basis of a stereotype or prejudice. Whether or not the claimant is a member of a historically disadvantaged group may indeed be relevant to this wrong. For if a particular instance of stereotyping or prejudice is not an isolated occurrence but part of an ongoing pattern, or if it is applied to a group that already faces considerable social or economic barriers, this will likely increase the severity of its impact on the individual's autonomy. However, it will not always do so — and, in particular, will not do so where the denial of the benefit affects the individual only in minor ways. Hence, the relevance of this first factor in any given case seems to be directly bound up with the strength of the fourth factor, the importance of the interest affected. If the benefit is less valued by the individual, or affects him in ways that are only peripheral to his conception of what makes his life worth living, then it will, for those reasons, have much less of an impact on his autonomy — even if he is a member of a disadvantaged group. The second contextual factor, "correspondence of the ground of discrimination to the claimant's actual situation" is also relevant to this wrong, though it matters how we understand it. Treatment based upon prejudice may indeed take into account the claimant's actual circumstances; it is objectionable because it attaches negative value to them or aims to harm the claimant through them. Hence Iacobucci J.'s qualifying phrase "in a manner that respects his or her value as a human being" is crucial here.[51] Moreover, given that, as we have seen, mere arbitrariness is not on its own sufficient to ground this wrong, this second contextual factor must be supplemented by a direct inquiry into whether the prejudicial or stereotyped treatment harms the individual's autonomy.

Consider next the wrong of being denied a benefit in circumstances where this perpetuates oppressive power relations. Whether the claimant is a member of a historically disadvantaged group has direct bearing on this wrong, as does the importance of the interest of hers that is affected. However, the fact that the ground of discrimination corresponds to the claimant's actual situation does not in any way weigh against the conclusion that this wrong has occurred, for this wrong concerns the oppressive effects of the differential treatment, and not whether the treatment was based upon stereotyping or inaccurate generalizations.

What about the wrong of being denied a benefit where this leaves one lacking in access to basic goods? Pre-existing disadvantage may be relevant here, depending which goods are viewed as "basic." If this category includes goods beyond what is necessary for survival, then it may indeed be possible for individuals not to be members of historically disadvantaged groups and yet to lack the good in question. The importance of the interest affected is likewise clearly relevant, since, however we define "basic goods," they will include only goods that affect certain important interests. Once again, however, whether there is correspondence between the ground of discrimination and the claimant's circumstances is irrelevant: this wrong simply depends upon whether or not the claimant lacks certain goods (assuming, of course, that the government has chosen to legislate in the relevant area).

Finally, what of the wrong of unfairly being deprived of one's self-respect? This seems to be the only substantive conception of the wrong of unequal treatment to which all four of the contextual factors are relevant. All of them may make a difference to whether an individual comes to feel inferior to others as a result of experiencing unfair treatment. However, as I have argued, this fourth conception of the wrong of unequal treatment cannot stand alone, as a complete explanation of why certain inequalities are objectionable. A person's loss of self-respect will seem to be an appropriate object of redress, as a matter of equality rights, only where the unequal treatment that led to this loss of self-respect can be seen as unfair in light of one of the *other* substantive conceptions of the wrong. And not all of the four contextual factors are relevant to these other conceptions.

Given that not every contextual factor is relevant to every way of understanding the wrong of unequal treatment, it is crucial that courts first establish which conceptions of the wrong are at issue in a given case. Only then will they be in a position to know which contextual factors are relevant to determining whether or not the unequal treatment in that case was indeed unfair. If they simply inquire into the presence or absence of each of the factors and conduct a general weighing and balancing, they risk taking as determinative the absence of a contextual factor that is irrelevant to the wrong — or one of the wrongs, if there is more than one — that the claimant alleges to have suffered. This is arguably what occurred in the majority judgment in *Gosselin*.[52] The majority conducted a detailed analysis of the various contextual factors in this case. Their judgment seemed to turn, however, on the combination of the ameliorative purpose which the government declared the legislation to have (namely, encouraging young people to find employment and assisting them in acquiring the necessary skills) and the fact that, in the majority's view, the legislation did not rely upon stereotypes and in fact "was calibrated to address the particular needs and circumstances of young adults requiring social assistance."[53] Part of Louise Gosselin's claim did seem to turn on the wrong of being denied a benefit on the basis of stereotypes — namely, the assumption that young people are more employable and less needy than those thirty and above. Even if we accept the majority's contention that this was not in fact a stereotype but an accurate description of the circumstances of young people, however, their reasoning seems problematic. This is partly because, as we have seen, the presence of an ameliorative purpose does not negate the wrong on any of the conceptions we examined. But it is also partly because Gosselin seems to have been claiming that she suffered a further wrong, one unconnected to issues of stereotyping. She objected in part to the fact that, as a result of being denied the full welfare payment received by those over thirty, she was left without enough to live on — that is, was left lacking in what is by any standard a "basic good." The government had chosen to enact welfare legislation, yet it denied her what it had itself determined to be the basic survival amount, and this denial left her without access to certain basic goods. If this is how we understand one of the wrongs that Gosselin claimed to have suffered, then it will seem irrelevant whether or not there was a correspondence between her circumstances and the assumptions made by the government about the situation of young people. In other words, even if we accept the majority's assessment of the issue of stereotyping, there is still a further issue that could have been addressed. Had the majority separated out the different wrongs that were contained in Gosselin's claims, and had they applied in each case only the contextual factors relevant to determining whether or not that wrong had occurred, they might have reached a different conclusion about whether the treatment she received was discriminatory.

Of course, they might also have simply rejected the idea that section 15 protects against the wrong of leaving certain individuals without access to basic goods in an area in which one has chosen to legislate. But because the *Law* test hides the real work that is done by such substantive conceptions of the wrong of unequal treatment, the majority never engaged in explicit consideration of this question.

F. USING *LAW* TO MOVE FORWARD

In conclusion, I want to mention several ways in which the *Law* test nevertheless leaves us room to maneuver in seeking an alternative approach to section 15, one that allows courts to distinguish between different conceptions of the wrong of unequal treatment and that encourages open and explicit discussion of which conceptions are indeed relevant to section 15, and which underlie the complaints in particular section 15 challenges.

First, the fact that the *Law* test has its roots in the abstract ideal of equal respect for the dignity of all, and that this ideal can be given content by any of the substantive goals of equality rights that I have considered, suggests that we can begin to move away from the narrower, subjective conception of dignity employed in the *Law* test without doing violence to the essential thrust of the discussion in *Law*. The test for whether or not discrimination has occurred could still be understood as a test that is undertaken from the position of a reasonable person in the claimant's position. But the purpose of the test must be understood not as that of determining whether or not a reasonable person in the claimant's position would *feel* inferior as a result of unequal treatment but, simply, as determining whether or not a reasonable person in the claimant's position would judge that the treatment really was *unfair*. That is, did it really amount to a *wrong*, in light of one of the other substantive conceptions of the wrong of unequal treatment?

Second, although we can continue to follow the approach of initially asking whether there was a group that received the benefit which the claimant was denied, we should treat this inquiry purely as instrumental in determining whether or not the legislature is engaged in a certain distributive scheme. And we should not automatically carry this comparison over into the later stages of the analysis. Rather, when we arrive at the stage of determining whether or not the treatment was indeed unfair, we need to ask whether or not a comparative approach to this question is appropriate and, if so, what the appropriate comparator group is. Our answer will depend upon whether the wrong alleged by the claimant is relational — as, for instance, is the wrong of being denied a benefit where this perpetuates oppressive power relations — or not relational.

Finally, courts must, in the determination of whether the treatment of a given claimant is indeed unfair, look only to the contextual factors relevant to the particular wrongs that this claimant is alleging. This more limited appeal to the contextual factors is quite consistent with the guiding ideas behind the *Law* test. For Iacobucci J. indicated there, and the Supreme Court has repeatedly emphasized, that the four contextual factors are merely *indicia* of discrimination and not elements that must be made out in all cases. We can be true to the underlying purpose of the *Law* test, then, and yet narrow our focus to those contextual factors that are relevant to the wrong or wrongs in the case at bar.

Of course, all this depends on a clearer understanding of the wrongs that section 15 protects against. I have tried, in this article, to outline four substantive ways of understanding the wrong of unequal treatment, as well as one more abstract way. It may be that not all of them are relevant to section 15, or that other conceptions that I have not discussed make better sense of the purposes of this section. These are questions to be resolved through public and judicial discussion. My hope is that, in recognizing at least the possibility of a diversity of explanations of why unequal treatment is wrong and in moving away from a version of the *Law* test that hides the real work done by tacitly invoked conceptions of what makes unequal treatment unfair, we will be more likely to make progress in these discussions.

ENDNOTES

1   For extremely helpful comments on earlier drafts of this paper, I am grateful to Alan Brudner, Justice Kathryn Feldman, Andrew Green, Robert Leckey, Stephen Moreau, Denise Réaume, Arthur Ripstein, Lorne Sossin, Ernest Weinrib, and audiences at the University of Toronto and at LEAF's 2003 Colloquium "In Pursuit of Substantive Equality."

2   For seminal pieces see Elizabeth S. Anderson, "What Is the Point of Equality?" (1999) 109 Ethics 287 ["What Is the Point"]; Richard J. Arneson, "Equality and Equal Opportunity for Welfare" (1989) 56 Phil. Stud. 77; Arneson, "Equality of Opportunity for Welfare Defended and Recanted" (1999) 7. J. Pol. Phil. 488; G.A. Cohen, "On the Currency of Egalitarian Justice" (1989) 99 Ethics 906; Ronald Dworkin, *Sovereign Virtue: The Theory and Practice of Equality* (Cambridge, MA: Harvard University Press, 2000) [*Sovereign Virtue*]; Ronald Dworkin, "Sovereign Virtue Revisited" (2002) 113 Ethics 55; Thomas Nagel, *Equality and Partiality* (New York: Oxford University Press, 1991); Thomas M. Scanlon, "The Diversity of Objections to Inequality" (Lindley Lecture, University of Kansas, 22 February 1996) (Lawrence, KS: Department of Philosophy, University of Kansas, 1997) ["Diversity of Objections"]; Amartya Sen, *Inequality Reexamined* (Cambridge, MA: Harvard University Press, 1992).

3   Part I of the *Constitution Act, 1982,* being Schedule B to the *Canada Act 1982* (U.K.), 1982, c.11 [the *Charter*].

4   See Dworkin, *Sovereign Virtue*, above note 2 at 12. Dworkin provides no defence of this position, except to say that a full theory of equality is best approached "by accepting initial, even though somewhat arbitrary, distinctions among these issues." Although this claim is certainly compatible with recognizing that inequalities in the distribution of resources are *influenced by* inequalities in the distribution of political and social power, and although it leaves open the possibility that, in developing a full theory of equality, we may later come to *modify* our conclusions about the best principles for the distribution of resources in light of our conclusions about the appropriate distribution of political power, Dworkin never suggests any such modifications. Nor does he explore whether part of what is objectionable, from the standpoint of justice, about some inequalities in the distribution of resources is precisely the fact that they perpetuate inequalities in political and social power.

5   See Anderson, "What Is the Point," above note 2, and Samuel Scheffler, "What Is Egalitarianism?" (2003) 31.1 Phil. & Public Aff. 5. In this respect, the philosophical debates concerning equality contrast sharply with the discussions of equality that have occurred amongst political theorists, many of whom have inquired into the importance of social recognition and the distribution of social power, and who have explicitly problematized the relation between these questions and questions of distributive justice. See, for instance, Iris Marion Young, *Justice and the Politics of Difference* (Princeton, NJ: Princeton University Press, 1990) [*Justice & Politics*]; Iris Marion Young, "Equality of Whom? Social Groups and Judgments of Injustice" (2001) 9.1 J. Pol. Phil. 1; Nancy Fraser, "From Redistribution to Recognition?

Dilemmas of Justice in a 'Post-Socialist' Age" (1995) 212 New Left Rev. 69 ["From Redistribution"]; "Culture, Political Economy, and Difference: On Iris Young's Justice and the Politics of Difference" (1995) 3 J. Pol. Phil. 166 ["Culture"]; Nancy Fraser, "A Rejoinder to Iris Young" (1997) 223 New Left Rev. 126 ["Rejoinder"].

6   See *Andrews v. Law Society of British Columbia*, [1989] 1 S.C.R. 143 at para. 35 [*Andrews*].

7   Interestingly, many of the philosophers who have written on discrimination have simply defined it as "intentional discrimination"; for the most recent example of this, see Matt Cavanagh, *Against Equality of Opportunity* (Oxford: Oxford University Press, 2002). One of the few philosophers who does not do this is Lawrence A. Alexander, "What Makes Wrongful Discrimination Wrong? Biases, Preferences, Stereotypes, and Proxies" (1992) 141 U. Pa. L. Rev. 149. However, Alexander simply assumes the truth of utilitarianism and offers a utilitarian account of the wrongness of discrimination. Hence, his account lacks wide appeal even amongst moral philosophers, and it is of limited usefulness for any legal argument that aims not to presuppose the truth of a general moral theory.

8   Note that this definition does not imply that discrimination can never be justified, all things considered. It simply stipulates that discrimination always involves an element of unfairness *to the particular individuals* who have been discriminated against — or, as I prefer to put it, a "wrong" against these individuals. Hence, this definition allows, as the Supreme Court did in *Andrews,* both that discriminatory treatment always involves an element of unfairness, and that it may nevertheless turn out to be justified, all things considered, in light of other social goals.

9   One might here object that discrimination is a narrower idea, and is concerned with a quite particular *kind* of unfairness — namely, unfairness resulting from the use of a prejudice or a stereotype. I argue against this narrow interpretation of discrimination below.

10   [1999] 1 S.C.R. 497 [*Law*].

11   Ronald Dworkin, "What Rights Do We Have?" in Ronald Dworkin, *Taking Rights Seriously* (Cambridge, MA: Harvard University Press, 1977) 266 at 272–73. Equal concern, on Dworkin's view, involves equal attentiveness to our "capacity for suffering," and presumably, therefore, to our basic needs; equal respect involves equal attentiveness to our capacity for self-direction and hence, presumably, to the basic liberties necessary for its exercise.

12   *Andrews*, above note 6 at 180–81.

13   See Immanuel Kant, *Groundwork for the Metaphysics of Morals*, trans. James W. Ellington (Indianapolis: Hackett, 1993) at s. II, 436.

14   Notice that the term "equal" does very little independent work here. That is, Dworkin's ideal is really an ideal of "concern and respect," based on an assumption of the supreme worth of each human being: it is an ideal that pertains to the relationship between the government and the citizen in question, not one that depends on any comparison between citizens. So although it is true that all citizens deserve "equal" concern and respect, this is simply a consequence of the fact that each deserves a certain level of concern and respect, and the harm that is done when any particular

individual is not treated with equal concern and respect is reducible to the harm that is done by the fact that this individual has not received the concern and respect that is owing *to her*. One therefore might think — as Joseph Raz has suggested, in a comment on Dworkin's abstract ideal of equal concern and respect — that this is not, then, really an ideal of equality at all, and that any account of the wrongs of unequal treatment that purports to flesh out this ideal will not be an account of equality. I shall consider this objection in detail, in a more generalized form, in Section D. For Raz's analysis of Dworkin's ideal of equal concern and respect, see Joseph Raz, *The Morality of Freedom* (Oxford: Clarendon Press, 1986) at 220–21.

15   Samuel Scheffler has recently contested this claim: "What Is Egalitarianism," above note 5. He argues that it is misleading to treat the correct substantive account of why certain inequalities are objectionable as an attempt to flesh out Dworkin's ideal of governments treating citizens with equal concern and respect. Dworkin's ideal, Scheffler claims, imports an objectionable hierarchy into our thought about equality: it suggests that the government somehow stands over and above citizens, handing out resources to them, rather than focusing us on relations between citizens, as co-governors. I believe Scheffler's objection is mistaken: it seems to conflate a claim about a certain way in which Dworkin's mode of presenting his ideal may mislead his readers with a claim about what this ideal *logically implies*. The latter claim is not defended by Scheffler, nor does it seem defensible: it is difficult to see how Dworkin's ideal could be incompatible with treating the government as a government *by* the citizens. For Dworkin's own response, see "Equality, Luck and Hierarchy" (2003) 31 Phil. & Public Aff. 190; for Scheffler's rejoinder, see Samuel Scheffler, "Equality as the Virtue of Sovereigns: A Reply to Ronald Dworkin" (2003) 31 Phil. & Public Aff. 199.

16   For brevity's sake, I shall refer hereafter simply to "denial of a benefit." But this should not be taken to imply that the imposition of a burden is equivalent to the denial of a benefit. These may be equivalent on some views; but those theories of equality that foreground equality of *welfare* may identify "imposition of a burden" with a *decrease* in well-being, while identifying "denial of a benefit" with the mere *lack of an increase* in well-being. On such views, therefore, the two would not be equivalent.

17   Indeed, the Supreme Court seems increasingly to be regarding stereotyping as a crucial factor, the absence of which makes it much more difficult for claimants to succeed in s. 15 challenges. For some recent examples of cases in which the majority's decision that the differential treatment was not unfair seems to have been crucially influenced by their perception that there was no stereotyping, see *Gosselin v. Quebec (A.G.)*, [2002] 4 S.C.R. 429 [*Gosselin*]; *Nova Scotia (A.G.) v. Walsh*, [2002] 4 S.C.R. 325 [*Walsh*]. In *Gosselin*, the claimant alleged, among other things, that the differential treatment she received (a significantly reduced welfare stipend) was based on the stereotype that persons under age thirty were better able to find jobs than those older, and could rely upon parental support. One of the main factors driving the majority's rejection of her s. 15 challenge seems to have been their belief that this was not, in fact, a stereotype but an accurate description of the circumstances of those under thirty. In *Walsh,* the claimant argued that the differential treatment she had received (she had been denied the presumption of equal property division given to hetero-

sexual married cohabitants) was based upon the false assumption that all unmarried cohabitants have made a *choice* to avoid the obligations imposed by marriage. Again, the majority seems to have rejected the claim in large part because it accepted this as an accurate description of the choices made by those in the claimant's circumstances.

18   For one explanation, and an attempt to distinguish the wrong done here from the wrong done by other forms of unequal treatment, see Scanlon, "The Diversity of Objections," above note 2 at 3. For an attempt to subsume the wrong done by stereotyping under a more general conception of the wrong done by all forms of equal treatment, see Anderson, "What Is the Point," above note 2.

19   For this conception of stereotypes, see John Hart Ely, *Democracy and Distrust* (Cambridge, MA: Harvard University Press, 1980) at 155; and, for discussion of both this conception and the conception I later mention, Sujit Choudhry, "Distribution vs. Recognition: The Case for Anti-Discrimination Laws" (2000) 9 Geo. Mason U.L. Rev. 145 at 152–59.

20   Notice that, even if the denial is arbitrary in this sense, it does not follow that the denial is "arbitrary" in the stronger sense that it is not supported by any legitimate legal reasons or reflects only the mere whims of the legislator. There may be very good reasons for appealing to a certain statistically informed generalization, rather than engaging in individualized assessments — even where this results in some individuals being denied a benefit on the basis of factors that do not apply to them. For a general discussion of whether this stronger notion of arbitrariness can capture all of the wrongs of unequal treatment, see Section D.

21   See *Andrews*, above note 6.

22   However, for a defence of the view that the unfairness of unequal treatment lies only in its arbitrariness, see David M. Beatty, "The Canadian Conception of Equality" (1996) 46 U.T.L.J. 349 at 369.

23   This explanation of the function of grounds of discrimination may not be complete. Indeed, it will not be complete if, as I shall go on to argue, there are other substantive conceptions of the wrong of unequal treatment that are irreducible to this first one. But it may still be part of any explanation of their function *in those cases* where the denial of a benefit has been based upon a stereotype.

24   However, for two discussions that take negative connotations to be central to all stereotypes, see Denise R éaume, "Discrimination and Dignity," below Chapter 4, and Scanlon, "Diversity of Objections," above note 2 at 3.

25   Consider, for instance, the "spouse in the house" rule challenged in *Falkiner v. Director, Income Maintenance Branch* (2002), 59 O.R. (3d) 481, which treated cohabitation and certain financial arrangements as a proxy for having a partner who provides enough support that one does not require social assistance. Although this proxy may have been based in part on the stereotypical assumption that women are supported by the men they cohabit with, it was not based on any assumptions about women's inferiority as human beings or their lack of ability to earn. The problem was, rather, (i) that the proxy itself was inaccurate: it caught many women who were not in fact in a spousal relationship, and its use denied them consideration of their actual circumstances, and (ii) that the stereotypical assumption that women are sup-

ported by the men they cohabit with worked to undermine these women's autonomy. And a further type of wrong suffered by these women is that they were denied the basic good of being free to choose whom they live with without sacrificing their own financial independence. I discuss this different type of wrong at a later point in this section of the article, under the heading of denying individuals access to basic goods.

I acknowledge that, apart from such cases of "proxy discrimination," it is difficult to think of stereotypes that are neutral or laudatory. Some may initially appear so; but on further consideration, seem to import assumptions of inferiority. Consider, for instance, the stereotype of "the hard-working immigrant." While apparently laudatory, this stereotype has the tacit derogatory implications that (i) immigrants need to be hard-working because they have no valuable skills to offer, and (ii) immigrants need to prove that they are decent people by showing that they are hard-working, whereas the rest of us do not.

26 There are two different explanations of why the government should not accept an assumption of inferior human worth as relevant to its decisions. It may be that it should treat it as irrelevant because it is false: no individual is, in fact, of less than incomparable worth. On the other hand, it may be that it should treat it as irrelevant simply because a government owes it to individuals to treat them *as if* they were each of incomparable worth. The former explanation treats truth as the standard of correctness in public political argument; the latter appeals instead to something like Rawls' notion of a "political" conception of the citizen, which does not make a claim to truth but is simply adopted as a basic assumption in the political domain. See John Rawls, "Justice as Fairness: Political Not Metaphysical" (1985) 14.3 Phil. & Public Aff. 223, repr. in John Rawls, *Collected Papers*, ed. S. Freeman (Cambridge: Harvard University Press, 1999); John Rawls, *Justice as Fairness: A Restatement*, ed. E. Kelly (Cambridge, MA: Harvard University Press, 2001).

27 It is difficult to locate cases that can definitively be said to be of this type. This is partly because such actions are so obviously unacceptable that governments usually try to justify the denial of the benefit as in some way appropriate to the situation or needs of the individuals in question; this can make it very difficult to tell whether the case also involved malicious motives. But it is also because assumptions about the inferiority of certain individuals can lead a government to believe that it is not in fact harming members of that group by denying them certain benefits but is, rather, simply giving them the treatment that is appropriate for them, given their lesser abilities or worth. (This is one way of understanding the Jim Crow laws passed in United States between 1865 and 1967, which legalized many forms of segregation of African Americans. Although certain members of the legislatures that passed these laws undoubtedly desired to harm African Americans, many simply believed that African Americans were not harmed by this differential treatment but, rather, were being treated in a manner appropriate to their needs and situation. This belief was certainly morally culpable; but it does not amount to malice in the sense that I use here.)

One case of discrimination that clearly did involve a malicious desire to harm an individual, however, is provided by the facts of *Roncarelli v. Duplessis*, [1959] S.C.R.

121. The premier of Quebec had revoked the liquor license of Frank Roncarelli, a restaurant proprietor who was a Jehovah's Witness, simply out of a desire "to punish the appellant [Roncarelli]" for his membership in this religious group and to punish him for the role that the premier believed he had played in encouraging proselytizing by other Jehovah's Witnesses. Although this case was argued as a torts case based upon abuse of public office, it is a good example of discrimination that is based upon a desire to harm or punish an individual and not simply upon the misguided belief that such individuals, being inferior, are not in fact harmed by being denied the benefits in question.

28   See Anderson, "What Is the Point," above note 2; Elizabeth Anderson, Symposium: Reply (22 December 1999), online: Brown Electronic Article Review Service, www. brown/edu/Departments/Philosophy/bears/homepage.html. See also Scheffler, "What Is Egalitarianism?" above note 5. Both of these accounts differ from mine, however, in that they treat this as a complete account of the wrong of unequal treatment.

29   For seminal discussions of the nature of oppression see Young, *Justice & Politics,* above note 5; Fraser, "From Redistribution," "Culture," and "Rejoinder," above note 5.

30   This is what Sen calls the phenomenon of "adaptive preference" formation. See Sen, *Inequality Reexamined,* above note 2; Amartya Sen, *Rationality and Freedom* (Cambridge, MA: Harvard University Press, 2002).

31   [1998] 1 S.C.R. 493 [*Vriend*].

32   R.S.A. 1980, c. I-2 [IRPA].

33   Harry Frankfurt, "Equality as a Moral Ideal" in Harry Frankfurt, *The Importance of What We Care About* (Cambridge: Cambridge University Press, 1988) 134 at 146–48.

34   *Ibid.* at 134.

35   Derek Parfit, "Equality or Priority?" (The Lindley Lecture, University of Kansas, 21 November 1991) (Lawrence, KS: Department of Philosophy, University of Kansas, 1991) 1. See also the discussion of equality by Raz, *The Morality of Freedom,* above note 14 at 217–44.

36   Above note 17 at paras. 319–58.

37   See, for example, Patrick Monaghan, *Politics and the Constitution: The Charter, Federalism and the Supreme Court of Canada* (Toronto: Carswell, 1987).

38   See Raz, *The Morality of Freedom,* above note 14 at 220.

39   We can think of such duties on the government as having a form similar to the tort law "duty of easy rescue" recognized in some jurisdictions. Whether someone is under a duty of easy rescue depends on such contingent factors as whether he is sufficiently physically close to the plaintiff to be able to save him and whether he can do so at relatively little cost to himself. But although the duty's existence is in this way contingent, when the duty does exist, it imposes a categorical requirement on the defendant: he must act, even if he does not desire to. The same is true of the duty not to leave individuals without access to basic goods in an area in which one has chosen

to legislate. Although this duty is contingent upon a government's having decided to legislate in a certain area and to provide some benefits to some individuals, once a government makes this decision, it is under a categorical requirement to ensure that all individuals have access to those basic goods that are relevant to this area. And this requirement is not contingent upon the government's wishing specifically to provide these particular basic goods.

40　See Anderson, "What Is the Point," above note 2 at 315.

41　[1997] 3 S.C.R. 624 [*Eldridge*].

42　[2004] 1 S.C.R. 76 [*Canadian Foundation for Children*].

43　*Ibid.* at para. 108.

44　For discussion of this way of understanding the wrong of unequal treatment, see Scanlon, "Diversity of Objections," above note 2 at 10.

45　For a theory that does take the idea of dignity to be explanatorily basic, see Réaume, "Discrimination and Dignity," above note 24.

46　*Law,* above note 10 at para. 51.

47　*Ibid.* at para. 53.

48　*Ibid.* [Emphasis added].

49　The second stage of the test involves determining whether the differential treatment has occurred on an enumerated or analogous ground. I shall not discuss this stage explicitly, since it seems that some rationale for it can be found on each conception of the wrong of unequal treatment. The grounds can be seen as linked by virtue of the fact that stereotypes or prejudices relating to them tend to undermine autonomy; that they tend to be bound up with oppressive power relations; such that denials of benefits on these bases tend to perpetuate such power relations; or that denials of benefits on these bases tend to result in those who are worse off lacking certain basic goods. That the grounds simultaneously serve these diverse functions is not, I think, problematic, although it does mean that when courts recognize certain grounds as analogous, they are doing so, not once and for all, but in the context of the *type of wrong* at issue in that case.

50　As is noted, and criticized, by Binnie J. in *Canadian Foundation for Children,* above note 42 at paras. 97–98.

51　*Law,* above note 10 at para. 88.

52　Above note 17. The majority included McLachlin C.J.C. and Gonthier, Iacobucci, Major, and Binnie JJ.

53　*Ibid.* at para. 70.

two

Equality, Comparison, Discrimination, Status

Beverley Baines

A. INTRODUCTION

Is comparison fundamental to interpreting the equality guarantee in section 15 of the *Charter*?[1] Jurists and feminists disagree about the answer to this question. On the one side, the Supreme Court of Canada subscribes unequivocally to comparison, to the point of relying on it to deny an equality claim.[2] On the other side, feminist legal theorists such as Diana Majury have asked "whether because it is a comparative concept, equality can ultimately only mean formal equality, albeit in forms more sophisticated than treating *x* and *y* identically."[3] Since feminists have strong reservations about formal equality, Majury was speaking for those who criticize the Court's reliance on comparison. In this paper, I intend to examine this controversy. I propose to argue that comparison is essential to dismantling gender status hierarchies that subordinate women. The remainder of this introduction briefly outlines the four concepts that I will rely on to make this argument: equality, comparison, discrimination, and status.

First, equality: the Court's approach to equality is founded on distinguishing substantive from formal equality. Notwithstanding their differences, the Court and its critics may not be so far apart. Given the Court's penchant for asserting that "equality is a substantive concept,"[4] the Justices may intend to attribute comparison only to substantive equality. If so, their approach would narrow the focus of their disagreement with feminists. Instead of debating the larger question of whether comparison is essential to equality, jurists and feminists would differ over a more focused issue; namely, which concept of equality — formal or substantive — does comparison serve? Furthermore, since both sides have yet to explain the meaning of comparison, this lacuna gives them a common starting point.

Next, comparison: recently Elisa Holmes advanced a new theory of comparison in an article entitled "Anti-Discrimination Rights Without Equality."[5] As her title suggests, Holmes challenged the prevailing assumption of "some kind of relationship between anti-discrimination rights and equality."[6] Her argument is at once novel and complex. Its novelty lies in using comparison to differentiate equality from anti-discrimination; its complexity arises from treating comparison as if it informs both sides of this distinction. Effectively, Holmes argued for alternative approaches to comparison, referring to one as constitutive and to the other as instrumental. She then attributed constitutive comparison to equality analysis while maintaining anti-discrimination analysis uses instrumental comparison. Ultimately, she concluded that the distinction between constitutive and instrumental comparison sustained "the possibility that in fact anti-discrimination principles are not egalitarian in any significant way."[7]

Third, discrimination: like Holmes, I invoke discrimination, albeit not to distinguish it from equality. Rather, I treat discrimination as a principle that facilitates applying Holmes' theory of comparison to the Court's distinction between formal and substantive equality. Unfortunately, Holmes precluded applying her theory directly to the Court's approach to equality when she dismissed the distinction between formal and substantive equality, claiming they blur into each other in the context of rights claims.[8] Fortunately, the Court has not only distinguished substantive from formal equality but also justified this distinction by evoking the American anti-discrimination principle.[9] However, it is not clear that the Court understood the main features of this principle, which were set out by Yale law professor Owen Fiss in a seminal article written in the 1970s.[10] Not only is one of these features consistent with instrumental comparison,[11] but Fiss also explained why anti-discrimination is the principle that informs formal equality.[12] Contrary to the Court's opinion, in other words, discrimination (as anti-discrimination is known in section 15 jurisprudence) operates as the principle that links instrumental comparison with formal equality. What remains, therefore, is to discover whether a distinctive principle is consistent with constitutive comparison and substantive equality.

Finally, status: although the Court dismissed the relevance of status to equality,[13] I argue to the contrary. More specifically, I invoke constitutive comparison, explaining that it operates in a way that is consistent with targeting status harms. My argument follows that of Fiss who long ago contrasted status harms with the harms of discrimination.[14] Rejecting the latter as formal equality, he proffered the former as the real challenge for the equal protection clause of the American Fourteenth Amendment. Although Fiss named the principle that redresses status harms as the "group-disadvantaging" principle,[15] this label quickly fell into disuse. Instead, contemporary American legal theorists who subscribe to his approach refer to it more appropriately as the "anti-subordination" principle.[16] To summarize, my argument is that constitutive (but not instrumental) comparison targets status (but not discrimination) harms by invoking the anti-subordination (but not anti-discrimination) principle. Thus, I have identified a distinctive principle, anti-subordination, that is available to link constitutive comparison with substantive (but not formal) equality.

In concluding, I explore the limitations of using Holmes' theory of comparison to distinguish formal and substantive equality by applying it to three of the equality cases that women lost at the Supreme Court of Canada: *Symes*, *Trociuk*, and *Law*.[17] However, I also acknowledge that foremost among the limitations is the fact that my argument is at a very preliminary stage. Clearly, it raises more questions than it resolves. Thus, I put it forward tentatively, hoping others will take up the issues that it raises.

B. EQUALITY

In this section, I explain that the Supreme Court of Canada's approach to equality is founded on distinguishing substantive from formal equality. This distinction appeared in the Court's first section 15(1) decision, although no mention was made of substantive equality. Rather, Justice McIntyre made a distinction between formal equality and "true equality."[18] During the ensuing decade, there appeared "differences of opinion among the members of this Court as to the appropriate interpretation of section 15(1)."[19] However, in the course of rendering the Court's unanimous opinion in *Law*, Justice Iacobucci approved the distinction. In effect, his contribution was to rename "true equality" as substantive equality.[20] Thus, the distinction remains the same today as when Justice McIntyre originally formulated it.

Justice McIntyre began *Andrews* by qualifying the application of section 15(1), stating it "is not a general guarantee of equality."[21] He elaborated that "it does not provide for equality between individuals or groups within society in a general or abstract sense, nor does it impose on individuals or groups an obligation to accord equal treatment to others."[22] Rather, when the guarantee of equality in section 15(1) is compared with the anti-discrimination provisions in federal and provincial human rights legislation, we can see that section 15(1) is limited to "the application or operation of law, whereas the Human Rights Acts apply also to private activities."[23] Under these circumstances, it is surprising that he did not pursue the distinction between equality and discrimination, as Elisa Holmes subsequently did.

Instead, Justice McIntyre opted to make a distinction between formal equality and "true equality."[24] Formal equality obtains when persons who are similarly situated are treated similarly, leaving persons who are differently situated to be treated differently.[25] Continuing, he added that this "similarly situated test would have justified the formalistic separate but equal doctrine of *Plessy v. Fergusson*."[26] In other words, formal equality evokes the separate but equal doctrine as well as the similarly situated test. Accordingly, formal equality addresses only the claims of similarly situated equality seekers seeking identical treatment; all other claims are simply regarded as already consistent with the separate but equal doctrine.

Justice McIntyre criticized this approach as "seriously deficient,"[27] in part because it mandated identical treatment and partly because of its categorical dismissal of difference. "It must be recognized," he wrote, "that every difference in treatment between individuals under the law will not necessarily result in inequality and, as well, that identical treatment may frequently produce serious inequality."[28] Formal equality's unresponsiveness led Justice McIntyre to design a new approach, one that he labeled "true equality."[29] He described "the essence of true equality" as "the accommodation of differences," predicting under this new approach "it will frequently be necessary to make distinctions."[30] The value of "true equality" lies, therefore, in its capacity to remedy the deficiencies of formal equality.

In spite of distinguishing "true equality" from formal equality, Justice McIntyre left unanswered the question of whether formal equality remained viable. It did not matter in *Andrews* because the Court decided that section 15(1) was infringed by the Canadian citizenship requirement for admission to the legal profession in British Columbia. In contrast, in *Law* when Justice Iacobucci upheld the age requirements for Canada Pension Plan survivor's benefits, the outcome was consistent with the separate but equal doctrine and hence with formal equality. However, Justice Iacobucci echoed Justice McIntyre's words about equality being a "substantive concept";[31] and he distinguished substantive equality, his new name for "true equality," from formal equality.[32] In other words he did not subscribe to the separate but equal doctrine; nor did he advocate formal equality. Thus, the contradictory outcomes in *Andrews* and *Law* seem unlikely to portend the revival of formal equality.

Rather, what these contradictory outcomes call for is making the distinction between formal and substantive equality more intelligible. Since Justice Iacobucci confirmed Justice McIntyre's assertion that equality is a "comparative concept,"[33] this paper focuses on whether comparison serves to distinguish substantive from formal equality. As a preliminary matter, however, we must also recognize that feminists such as Diana Majury argue that comparison serves formal equality. In other words, we must first resolve this controversy over whether to attribute comparison to substantive equality, as the Justices maintain, or to formal equality as feminists argue. Accordingly, I explore the concept of comparison in the next section.

C. COMPARISON

One reason for turning to comparison is that the Court is committed to it. In *Andrews*, Justice McIntyre stated equality "is a comparative concept, the condition of which may only be attained or discerned by comparison with the condition of others in the social and political setting in which the question arises."[34] The strength of this assertion is also its weakness. On the one hand, Justice McIntyre's conceptualization is not necessarily confined to those to whom the law applies as obtains under the similarly situated test. On the other hand, it could be so limited given that his reference to "the social and political setting in which the question arises" is ambiguous, and especially absent any authority to the contrary. Indeed, his failure to cite any authority is surprising in view of Justice McIntyre's reputation as "Paladin of Common Law."[35] After all, the common law invariably relies on reasoning from precedent.

In *Law*, Justice Iacobucci addressed Justice McIntyre's assertion about equality being "a comparative concept"[36] by elaborating three features that he attributed to this concept. According to Justice Iacobucci, comparison is: (i) the first step in a three-stage process of analyzing section 15(1);[37] (ii) assigned to claimants, although courts could "refine" it;[38] and (iii) implemented by "[l]ocating the appropriate comparator,"[39] which involved considering a "variety of factors" that included not only the "purpose and effect of the legislation," but also relevant "biological, historical, and sociological similarities and dissimilarities."[40] As this third feature makes clear, his conceptualization extends well beyond comparing only those to whom the law applies. Accordingly, Justice Iacobucci distinguished comparison from what prevailed under the similarly situated test.

In *Hodge*,[41] Justice Binnie varied all three of the features that Justice Iacobucci had identified. According to Justice Binnie, comparison is: (i) in many cases "only developed ... at the third stage";[42] (ii) assigned to the courts which must "step in and measure the claim to equality rights in the proper context and against the proper standard";[43] and (iii) implemented by identifying "a 'comparator group' with whom the claimant shares the characteristics *relevant* to qualification for the benefit or burden in question apart from the *personal* characteristic that is said to be the ground of the wrongful discrimination."[44] Again this third feature defines comparison. Unlike Justice Iacobucci, however, Justice Binnie made a distinction between relevant and personal characteristics, expressing a clear preference for the former. Since his preference limits comparison to relevant characteristics, it follows that he restricted comparison to those to whom the law already applies. In effect, Justice Binnie's conceptualization of comparison represents a reversion to the similarly situated test.

The outcome in *Hodge* illustrates this reversion. Justice Binnie used marital status to deny a Canada Pension Plan (CPP) survivor's pension to Betty Hodge. He maintained that because she had left a common law relationship (she had been abused) four months before her partner died, she was a former rather than a separated spouse.[45] In other words, he held that a separation period is unknown to common law relationships. As a former spouse, therefore, her comparator group was divorced spouses who are not eligible for CPP survivor's pensions, rather than separated married spouses who are eligible. In sum, the Court ruled that separation (the personal characteristic) did not raise the issue of marital status discrimination (the relevant characteristic) because not all common law relationships end with a separation period. This ruling directly parallels the Court's decision in *Bliss* that pregnancy (the personal characteristic) did not raise the issue of sex discrimination (the relevant characteristic) because not all women become pregnant — a decision that Justice McIntyre criticized precisely because of its application of the similarly situated test.[46]

While *Hodge* exemplifies comparison with a vengeance, my main concern is to identify what is missing from the Court's approach to this concept. I suggest the Justices treat comparison as if its meaning is self-evident. Comparison is satisfied by identifying who should be compared to whom. As I have already demonstrated, one danger of such a simplistic approach is the ever-present risk of slipping backwards into the ostensibly unacceptable, but ridiculously seductive, clutches of the similarly situated test. More troublingly, however, identifying who should be compared tells us nothing about how the activity of comparison operates. Even assuming we could convincingly identify who should be compared, what does it mean to "compare" people? For instance, is there more than one way to carry out the activity of comparison?

Elisa Holmes' work may assist in answering these questions because she offered a theory of comparison.[47] More specifically, she identified two approaches to comparison. One sets out a comparator or standard against which the comparison is to be made. Put analytically, to compare is to mirror. In Holmes' words, this approach "uses a comparison heuristically"; "the comparator may be imaginary rather than real"; and "the comparison itself is not of the essence."[48] Labeling this approach as "instrumental" comparison, she described it normatively as the analysis that applies if we aspire to equalize something of value by ensuring "that everyone has some."[49] As such, Holmes concluded that instrumental comparison serves anti-discrimination law (for reasons that will become evident in the next section).

In contrast, the second approach does not value a comparison as heuristic. Rather, it treats comparison as intrinsic.[50] Expressed normatively, this approach to comparison applies when "the independently valuable thing might be something which it is important to an egalitarian to have *equalized* whether or not it is important for everyone to have: if anyone is to have it, it should be had in equal measure."[51] Moreover, in an affirmation of its value Holmes aligned this approach with equality law. And finally, she named it as "constitutive" comparison.[52]

Two features are unique to constitutive comparison. The first is balancing. Since "there is value in a particular other value being had in *equal measure*, not just in having the other value"[53] constitutive comparison extends beyond identifying a comparator to balancing what the equality seeker and comparator have. To understand the difference between the balancing approach of constitutive comparison and the mirroring approach of instrumental comparison, imagine an old fashioned weigh scale where the weights are moved from one side to the other. Now, put the equality seeker on one side of the scale and the comparator on the other. If they mirror each other, nothing more is required. If not, however, then the sides are unbalanced. To achieve a balance something must be moved from one side to the other. In other words, a change in value for one necessarily results in a change in value for the other. Thus, balancing connotes a relationship of reciprocity between equality seeker and comparator.

The second unique feature of constitutive comparison follows from the first. If balancing is to occur, it is virtually inevitable that one side will be faced with leveling-down. However, the same cannot be said of instrumental comparison. Leveling-down is neither necessary nor even valuable to proponents of instrumental comparison (who may even reject it) because this approach "is not comparative in other than a heuristic sense."[54] Under these circumstances, it is only proponents of constitutive comparison who must confront what Holmes adverted to as the "leveling-down objection."[55]

According to this objection, constitutive comparison holds that "whatever level of that other value is had, it is valuable to have it equally, even if it is equalized by lowering the total level of that value, and by increasing no-one's share of that value."[56] Or again, "if a detriment is to occur to someone, there is value in imposing the detriment on everyone, even though such an action is good for no-one."[57] However, this objection rests on seriously flawed contradictory assumptions. On the one hand, it denies there is any value in improving the share of equality seekers, that is, in leveling-up their side, unless their comparator's side also improves. On the other hand, it assumes improving the share of equality seekers necessarily lowers the total level of that value, rather than simply lowering the level of the value held by their comparators. Ultimately, both assumptions blatantly equate comparators' values with the totality of values.

In reality, the "leveling-down objection" is the self-interested expression of the haves (the comparators) wanting to keep what they have. They desperately want to deter adherence to constitutive comparison because, in a world of scarcity, they would have less than they do now if the have-nots (the equality seekers) were to strive for equality with them. They consistently underplay, ignore, and even deny the value of the leveling-up that necessarily complements any leveling-down. In other words, while comparators (the haves) have no reason to fear instrumental comparison because it always respects their values, they have every reason to avoid constitutive comparison which may well harm what they most value. Like Holmes, therefore, I suggest equality seekers (the have-nots) should be wary of discrediting the leveling-down feature of constitutive comparison.

What remains is to apply Holmes' theory of comparison to the Supreme Court of Canada's approach to equality. Unfortunately this application is not straightforward. Not only did Holmes use instrumental and constitutive comparison to make a distinction that the Court has never made between anti-discrimination and equality rights, but she also precluded applying her theory of comparison directly to the distinction the Court actually made between formal and substantive equality, explaining that this distinction collapses in the context of rights claims. "All egalitarian principles have a form," she wrote, adding: "Each also needs some substance."[58] Without more, therefore, we cannot assume that Holmes' theory of comparison applies to the Court's approach to equality.

To complicate matters further, the Court and its feminist critics differ over how comparative analysis, albeit defined singularly by them, serves equality jurisprudence. The Court has steadfastly defined equality as a substantive concept and a comparative concept, by implication linking substantive equality with comparison. However, feminist critics question this connection.[59] As Diana Majury put it, we must ask "whether because it is a comparative concept, equality can ultimately only mean formal equality, albeit in forms more sophisticated than treating x and y identically."[60] Thus, we cannot simply assume that comparison distinguishes substantive from formal equality.

The foregoing complexities notwithstanding, in the next two sections I pursue the possibility of a relationship between comparison and equality. In Section D, I invoke the anti-discrimination principle which Holmes maintained was informed by instrumental comparison, and I explain its consistency with equality, albeit only with formal equality. Given that constitutive comparison remains unaligned, I argue in Section E that a novel principle — status — could not only illuminate it but also inform substantive equality. That is, status and discrimination can serve respectively to differentiate constitutive from instrumental comparison as well as distinguishing substantive from formal equality. Accordingly, with the intervention of these two principles, Holmes' theory of comparison can be applied to the Court's approach to equality.

D. DISCRIMINATION

The only issue raised in this section is whether the discrimination principle should be aligned with formal equality or with substantive equality. Resolving this issue would also explain the connection between equality and comparison, given the relationship that Holmes established between discrimination and instrumental comparison. What follows, therefore, is an analysis of the discrimination principle that is subject to two caveats. One involves recognizing that, unlike equality and comparison which remain open to interpretation, discrimination is a well-established legal principle with a lengthy history and identifiable structural features that cannot be ignored. The other caveat accepts Holmes' conclusion that the distinction between direct and indirect discrimination is irrelevant to explaining the relationship between discrimination and equality.[61]

Clearly, discrimination is fundamental to the Supreme Court of Canada's equality jurisprudence. Justice McIntyre first invoked this principle in *Andrews*, employing it to define the equality guarantee in section 15(1);[62] and Justice Iacobucci acknowledged its same relevance in *Law*.[63] Further, the Justices have continued to rely on it, most recently to found a violation of section 15(1) in the *Newfoundland and Labrador Association of Public and Private Employees* case.[64] Since the Court also relied on substantive equality to decide these section 15(1) cases, by implication the Justices treat these two principles — discrimination and substantive equality — as consistent.

Not everyone accepts the Court's alignment, however. Foremost among the dissenters is Yale law professor Owen Fiss who published a seminal analysis of the American anti-discrimination principle in 1976.[65] Fiss condemned this principle as consistent with formal equality, contending that it was by no means an inevitable feature of American equal protection jurisprudence.[66] Since the American anti-discrimination principle served as the precedent for its Canadian counterpart,[67] I intend to assess its contemporary relevance to Canadian equality jurisprudence by setting out the three structural features — substance, procedure, and beneficiaries — that Fiss identified in order to determine whether they apply to the Court's reasoning in *Andrews* and *Law*. The more similarities there are between the structural features of the American and Canadian principles, the greater the likelihood that the latter is as consistent with formal equality as is the former.

The first structural feature of the American anti-discrimination principle that Fiss identified was its substance. By substance he meant its definition of equality. According to Fiss, the American principle defined equality as prohibiting discrimination.[68] While there are other ways of defining equality, as Holmes argued and as I suggest in Section E, nevertheless Canadian proponents of the discrimination principle define it in the same way as Fiss did. In *Andrews*, Justice McIntyre referred to discrimination as the "evil,"[69] and he described the relevant query in terms of asking whether the legislation imposed "disadvantages" or withheld "advantages."[70] Similarly, in *Law*, Justice Iacobucci adverted to "fighting the evil of discrimination,"[71] although he diverged somewhat by describing the relevant inquiry as encompassing not just one but four contextual factors; that is, not only disadvantage[72] but also actual needs,[73] ameliorative purposes or effects,[74] and affected interests.[75] Irrespective of which or how many of these contextual factors evidence it, however, the Canadian principle still defines equality in terms of prohibiting discrimination. Consequently, the Canadian discrimination principle shares the same substantive structural feature as its American counterpart.

The second structural feature that Fiss attributed to the American antidiscrimination principle pertained to its procedure or, more accurately, to its test for inequalities. Dubbing this test "means[/]end rationality," he explained that it measures the "fit" between the criterion (means) and the purpose (end) of the impugned legislation.[76] More specifically, fit measures the inclusiveness of legislation. When a legislative criterion is "overinclusive (it picked out more persons than it should), or underinclusive (it excluded persons that it should not)," the result is "ill-fit" or discrimination.[77] Moreover, given that the process of measuring fit or ill-fit consists of setting out a standard (the legislative purpose or end) against which the comparison (the legislative criterion or means) is made, the means/end rationality test clearly functions just like instrumental comparison.[78] That the means/end rationality test (as Fiss identified it) and instrumental comparison (as Holmes described it) are fungible simply reinforces Holmes' conclusion that instrumental comparison informs discrimination.

Whether identified as instrumental comparison or means/end rationality, the procedural structure of the American principle is also discernible in the Justices' reasoning about the Canadian discrimination principle. In *Andrews*, Justice McIntyre signalled his adherence to instrumental comparison (or the means/end rationality test) by considering whether Canadian citizenship (the means) was an over- or under-inclusive criterion for achieving the legislative purpose of an independent legal profession (the end).[79]

Similarly, Justice Iacobucci subscribed to instrumental comparison (or the means/end rationality test) in *Law* when he questioned whether mature age (the means) was an over- or under-inclusive criterion for promoting the legislative purpose of independent spousal survivors (the end).[80] Thus, the Canadian discrimination principle and its American counterpart evince the same procedural structure when they employ instrumental comparison (or means/end rationality) to test for inequalities.

The final structural feature focused on the beneficiaries of the American anti-discrimination principle, by which Fiss meant who qualifies as equality seekers. In fact, the main purpose of his article was to establish that the American equal protection clause guarantees equality to "groups not just individuals."[81] According to Fiss, there are two classes of groups: natural and artificial. Natural classes are social groups "that have an identity and existence wholly apart from the challenged state statute or practice."[82] But the anti-discrimination principle nowhere acknowledges social groups.[83] "It knows," Fiss maintained, "only criteria or classifications."[84] That is, "the triggering mechanism and the object of inquiry"[85] of the anti-discrimination principle is legislative classification. And classification yields artificial groups that "do not have an independent social identity and existence, or if they do, the condition of interdependence is lacking."[86] Moreover, their artificiality makes it "difficult, if not impossible, to make an assessment of their socioeconomic status or of their political power (other than that they have just lost a legislative battle)."[87] In sum, Fiss identified artificial classes — the classifications created by legislation — as the groups that the anti-discrimination principle benefits.

Andrews was inconclusive about this third structural feature; Justice McIntyre did not define the beneficiaries of section 15(1) in terms of groups, whether natural or artificial. Instead he imported the notion of "grounds" into his analysis of this section, characterizing the list of prohibited categories — "race, national or ethnic origin, colour, religion, sex age or mental or physical disability" — as the "enumerated grounds," and insisting other "analogous grounds" might also be included.[88] Although he decided that citizenship constituted an analogous ground, and that permanent residents who were refused admission to the practice of law were denied equality, he never canvassed the question of whether they constituted a social group.[89] However, since permanent residents are creatures of legislative definition, by implication Justice McIntyre was prepared to recognize an artificial group as a beneficiary of the Canadian discrimination principle.

Nor did Justice Iacobucci hesitate to attribute this approach to Justice McIntyre and then to confirm it as his own.[90] More specifically, in designing his three-step approach to section 15(1), Justice Iacobucci identified legislative classification as the first step.[91] A section 15(1) claim must begin by asking whether the impugned law draws a formal distinction or has the effect of making a distinction based on one or more personal characteristics.[92] The best way to understand the significance of this first step is to recognize what it does not ask, and then compare that omission with the approach the Court took to analyzing a freedom of expression claim under section 2(b) of the *Charter*.

Using the discrimination principle, the Court's analysis of section 15(1) does not begin by asking who the equality seeker is, let alone by inquiring about the social group this claimant represents. By comparison the first step in the analysis of a *Charter* section 2(b) freedom of expression claim focuses directly on the claimant's activity or conduct.[93] Does the claimant's activity convey meaning?[94] If so then the next step, one still within the confines of the section 2(b) test, is to ask whether the claimant's activity or conduct has been restricted by the government's action.[95] In other words, both steps take their definition from the claimant, not from the legislation. Thus, the contrast between the approach to section 2(b) and to section 15(1) is striking.

Since the discrimination principle focuses on the legislative classification and not the claimant's social experience, thereby defining the beneficiaries of the equality guarantee as artificial groups, it is consistent with the last of the three structural features that constitute the American anti-discrimination principle. In sum, irrespective of whether they are regarded individually or collectively, the structural similarities between the Canadian and American principles point irresistibly to the conclusion that these principles are synonymous. They differ in only two respects. One, and it seems insignificant, is that Canadians use the discourse of discrimination rather than anti-discrimination. The other is more troubling because it concerns the difference between attributing the anti-discrimination principle to formal equality as Fiss did and treating it as consistent with substantive equality as the Court does (by implication) with its Canadian counterpart.

While the Court was silent about the reasoning that underlies this relationship, Fiss explained how he arrived at his conclusion. According to Fiss, the anti-discrimination principle is limited to the legislative domain, testing for inequalities by using the purpose (or end) of the impugned legislation as the standard against which to measure the legislative classification (or means) that the equality seekers invoke. Effectively, this principle concentrates on legal phenomena. A legalist's dream, in other words, it ignores Judith Shklar's injunction about the relevance of social considerations.[96] Absent these considerations, therefore, it is little wonder Fiss concluded that the anti-discrimination principle is "conducive to ... the ideals of 'mechanical jurisprudence'... at the expense of substantive results."[97] That is, it functions consistently with formal equality.

Under these circumstances, the concordance between the structural features of the American and Canadian principles suggests that the latter is as likely to be consistent with formal equality as the former. Accordingly, the Supreme Court of Canada must decide either to subscribe to the discrimination principle and hence formal equality, or to renew the commitment to substantive equality by finding a principle other than discrimination to structure it. In the next section, I argue for the availability of such a principle, depicting it as distinctive from discrimination because it focuses on social (not artificial) groups and tests for inequalities by relying on constitutive (not instrumental) comparison. This principle is status.

E. STATUS

Assuming that the Court is right to distinguish substantive from formal equality, and that Fiss is persuasive about the discrimination principle yielding formal equality, what remains is to identify a principle other than discrimination that could define substantive equality. Two possibilities come immediately to mind. One is dignity; the other, status. The Court invoked the former; while various American legal scholars, beginning with Fiss, proposed the latter. Accordingly, in what follows, first I dismiss dignity and then I argue for status, using the three structural features that Fiss attributed to the discrimination principle to sustain both contentions.

I dismiss the dignity principle because its structural features are indistinguishable from those of the discrimination principle. First, dignity defines equality as prohibiting the violations of human dignity that arise from "unfair treatment" or "when individuals and groups are marginalized, ignored, or devalued,"[98] meaning that its definition proscribes the same harms as the discrimination principle. Second, dignity and discrimination also share the same procedural structure which begins and ends with "locating the appropriate comparator"[99] (or standard) and hence relies on instrumental comparison (or means/end rationality) as the test for inequality. Finally, since dignity-seekers do not have "to establish membership in a sociologically recognized group,"[100] they are as likely to be members of artificial classes as are the groups that seek the benefit of the discrimination principle. In sum, their structural similarities are sufficient to sustain the conclusion that the dignity principle, like the discrimination principle, is consistent with formal equality. Furthermore, Justice Iacobucci confirmed dignity's formalism, albeit in a different context, when he held that violations of human dignity could be determined "on the basis of judicial notice and logical reasoning alone," without the necessity of recourse to "social science data."[101]

What does status have to recommend it? I argue that all three structural features of status distinguish it from discrimination (and dignity). First, status defines equality in terms of power, making it directly relevant to identifying women's inequalities. Second, it is ideally suited to invoking constitutive comparison to measure the inequalities that women face arising from power imbalances. And third, status deeply distrusts artificial classifications on the ground that they contribute all too frequently to the women's disempowerment. Not surprisingly, of course, each of these structural features has a downside: status is unknown to jurisprudence; it can adduce no reason to benefit men; and it is unacceptable to women who do not choose to identify as women. After assessing all of these features, however, I conclude that status is responsive to the quest for a principle that could inform substantive equality.

To explain how status and its corollary, status harm, define equality, Fiss began with the situation of black Americans, whom he described as "America's perpetual underclass."[102] The two main characteristics of this depiction — "the relative position of the group and the duration of the position" — "make efforts to improve the status of the group defensible."[103] The history of black Americans reveals, moreover, that political status even more than socioeconomic status "explains their special position in equal protection theory."[104] Fiss elaborated that the political power of blacks is "severely limited," indeed for the last two centuries it was "circumscribed in most direct fashion — disenfranchisement."[105] Their political powerlessness means rectification must turn "not ... on whether the law embodies a classification, racial or otherwise" but rather on whether the "law simply has the *effect* of hurting blacks."[106] Put differently, a negative effect (or status harm) continues their "subordination," leading Fiss to conclude that the "political status of the group justifies the institutional allocations" that courts should impose.[107] When status is used to interpret the Equal Protection clause in the American *Constitution*, therefore, it defines equality as "dismantling unjust status hierarchies."[108]

This approach is also apposite to women in Canada given their status is that of a perpetually subordinated class. At Confederation, women were denied civil, political, and social rights; only men could enter into contracts, receive remuneration for employment, vote, hold political office, and control marital and familial relations. While some changes occurred, at the middle of the twentieth-century, gender-biased policies and laws continued to govern domestic labour, matrimonial property, child custody, domestic violence, statutory rape, social assistance, child care tax deductions, survivor's pension benefits, medical services, employment benefits, un/employment insurance, etc. In 1970, the Royal Commission on the Status of Women made 167 recommendations to improve the status of Canadian women in nine contexts: culture, economy, education, family, taxation, poverty, public life, immigration and citizenship, and criminal law.[109] Little had changed a decade later as evidenced by the arguments of the women who lobbied the federal and provincial governments to strengthen the equality guarantee in the *Charter*.[110] And, as recently as 2004 in a book aptly entitled *Gendering the Vertical Mosaic*, Roberta Hamilton concluded that the social meanings that privilege masculinity over femininity still permeate our existence.[111]

Assuming status structures the definition of equality in terms of dismantling status hierarchies, it must also distinctively structure the test for inequality. In other words, unlike the discrimination principle which tests for instrumental comparison (or means/end rationality), status must use the constitutive approach to comparison. Moreover, the essence of constitutive comparison is reciprocal balancing, which means that any increase in favour of equality seekers must be accompanied by a corresponding decrease (or leveling-down) of the comparators. Is status up to this challenge? The answer depends on which concept of status — legal or sociological — is invoked.

The legal concept of status differs significantly from its sociological counterpart; the former concentrates on individuals and their legal relationships, whereas the latter emphasizes social collectivities and their comparative social evaluation.[112] More specifically, legal status is "a special condition of a continuous and institutional nature, differing from the legal position of the normal person, which is conferred by law and not purely by the act of the parties, whenever a person occupies a position of which the creation, continuance or relinquishment and the incidents are a matter of sufficient social or public concern."[113] Since legal status is "primarily concerned with legal meanings and legal consequences,"[114] the identity of individuals and groups who are defined by their legal status stands alone.

In contrast, "sociological status is usually tied to a system of social hierarchy" in which "one group receives relatively positive associations and another, correspondingly negative associations."[115] Consequently, the identities of the groups within any particular status hierarchy "are not freestanding."[116] To the contrary, any "change in the meanings attributed to one will affect not only its own social identity, but the identity of the other group."[117] Unlike its legal status, in other words, the sociological status of a group cannot increase "without decreasing the status of another."[118] Thus, sociological status operates consistently with the reciprocal balancing approach of constitutive comparison.

Radha Jhappan provided a vivid illustration of the significance of the reciprocity that defines both the sociological concept of status and constitutive comparison when she concluded that section 15 litigation "has seemingly packed the winners' circle with those already privileged by their structural positions, their socioeconomic, racial, gender, heterosexual, and able-bodied statuses."[119] Jhappan clearly recognized this litigation has consequences not only for the equality seekers who lose but also for their comparator groups who gain and/or retain the privileges of power. However, lawyers who understand legal status as freestanding would mistake her reference to privileged comparators as winners as a misinterpretation of the outcome of litigation. That is, these lawyers would characterize the privileged comparators as beyond the reach of the legal system because, after all, they had not actually been parties to the litigation. Yet, Jhappan's conclusion would make perfect sense to sociologists who understand that the identities of "antagonistic groups are not independent of each other."[120]

The third structural feature that distinguishes status from discrimination concerns their respective equality seekers. Unlike the discrimination principle which opts for the artificial groups (or classifications) defined by the impugned legislation, status is unambiguously committed to treating natural (or social) groups as the beneficiaries of equality laws. Social status involves prestige and honour, attaching to individuals because they are members of a group. Status arises from competitions over material resources or over symbolic things, and it results in the existence of status groups. These groups which are organized around distinctive identities or common styles of life give rise, in turn, to status hierarchies. Various traits serve to distinguish status hierarchies, with the most common ones being race, sex, religion, and national or ethnic origin.

However, not every group in the ordinary sense of that word, nor even every interest group in the political science sense, is a status group in an ongoing status hierarchy.[121] Groups such as "[g]amblers, sluggards, gossips, opticians, and MTV watchers ... are not groups who suffer overlapping and reinforcing forms of subordination and social disadvantage due to their place in [a] social hierarchy."[122] While any number of social traits could organize a group, the appropriate question is "whether there has been a history of using the trait to create a system of social meanings, or define a social hierarchy, that helps dominate and oppress people."[123]

What about women, do we qualify as a status group? Since the trait of being female as opposed to being male is a central feature of our social existence and affects many spheres of our lives, the response is yes: being a woman constitutes a status identity.[124] By focusing on sex/gender, however, I do not mean to suggest that women have no other status identities. Indeed, we have racial, lesbian, and religious status identities, to name a few. Thus sex/gender is a potential focal point, but not to be construed as a limitation.

In sum, applying the three structural features to status reveals that it defines equality as power (or more accurately as dismantling unjust social hierarchies), operates consistently with constitutive comparison, and depicts equality seekers as natural (or social) groups. Status could serve, in other words, as a distinctive principle available to inform substantive equality. Not surprisingly, recent scholarship has acknowledged its significance by renaming it as the anti-subordination principle.[125]

Like the discrimination principle, however, status (or the anti-subordination principle) has its critics. They maintain that status is unknown to jurisprudence; that it can adduce no reason to benefit men; and that it is unacceptable to women who do not choose to identify as women. The first critique may be a consequence of the pervasive influence of the "from status to contract" movement of the nineteenth century which led most lawyers to believe status hierarchies had disappeared, replaced by juridical persons who are equal in capacity and entitlement. Similarly, the second critique results not from conceptualizing status but rather from the prevalence of patriarchy and the laudable impulse of constitutive comparison to make the existence of patriarchy transparent. Finally, the third critique would be very troubling if it were shown that requiring equality seekers to belong to social, rather than artificial, groups militates against women's claims of intersectionality. Still, in the absence of evidence sustaining this third critique I contend we should take status seriously, pursuing the possibility that it offers to define substantive equality.

F. CONCLUSION

I have argued that it would be easier to understand how the Court distinguishes between formal and substantive equality if we were to follow Holmes in conceptualizing two approaches to comparison — instrumental and constitutive — that could respectively sustain the two mediating principles that Fiss identified: discrimination and status. However, this exercise remains academic unless it can be shown that status (or constitutive comparison) might have achieved substantive equality for women in cases that we lost because the Court applied the discrimination principle (or instrumental comparison). To illustrate my contention that the Court applied the discrimination principle to cases that could have yielded substantive equality for women using status (or the anti-subordination principle), I draw on *Symes*, *Trociuk*, and *Law*.[126]

Symes is one of five sex equality cases litigated by women and decided by the Supreme Court of Canada.[127] Women lost all five appeals. In *Symes*, a woman lawyer contended that disallowing child care as a business expense deduction was more disadvantageous to women who aspired to entrepreneurial activities than to similarly-minded men.[128] However, since the impugned provision of the *Income Tax Act* was facially (or sex) neutral, Symes made no effort to claim that men could do something (deduct child care as a business expense) that women were excluded from doing; rather, she argued that the policy exacerbated the already disadvantaged entrepreneurial status of women. Although she did not rely on the means/end rationality test of under-inclusiveness, the Court held that she had failed to establish under-inclusiveness, the more so because she could avail herself of the personal deduction for child care.[129] More specifically, the male majority relied on the discrimination principle to deny Symes' equality claim and the women on the Court — Justices L'Heureux-Dubé and McLachlin — dissented. In effect, Justice L'Heureux-Dubé wrote about section 15(1) as if it should be defined in terms of dismantling unjust status hierarchies.

The Supreme Court of Canada has also decided five sex equality cases litigated by men, deciding in favour of the men's section 15(1) argument in every case.[130] In *Trociuk*, the Court struck down vital statistics legislation that protected birth mothers from being forced to acknowledge biological fathers in the birth registration process. Justice Deschamps decided that the impugned provision was under-inclusive and hence discriminatory because it denied these unacknowledged fathers the opportunity to affirm their biological ties and familial bonds across the generations.[131] However, she ignored the parallel aspirations of mothers, including the birth mother in *Trociuk*, Reni Ernst, who had deposed: "I felt there was no reason why the children should bear the last name of somebody I was not married to and had no plans to set up life with."[132] In other words, the remedial purpose of the legislation — empowering women who chose to counter centuries of male control over children — was irrelevant. Far from confirming its dismantlement, therefore, *Trociuk* represented a regression to an earlier unjust status hierarchy, all neatly obscured by the Court's reliance on the means/end rationality of the discrimination principle.

Finally, *Law* is one of four section 15(1) cases litigated on grounds other than sex that women lost.[133] *Law* is significant not because thirty-year-old Nancy Law relied on the means/end rationality test for discrimination, arguing unsuccessfully that the Canada Pension Plan was under-inclusive because it denied immediate survivor benefits to youthful spouses; they had to survive to retirement age to collect these benefits. Rather, *Law*'s significance lies in how the age-based classifications in the legislation structured the claim for equality. Put differently, the legislation was perceived as sex neutral; its impact on the social group, women, was never considered. Yet, surely statistical evidence would show that proportionately more young women marry and then survive older men than vice versa. In other words, why were differential survivors' benefits not treated as impacting more heavily on women and hence as another indication of the subordinate status of women? The answer would appear to be that the pressure for classification — that is, for relying on the legislatively defined category of age — is irresistible under the discrimination principle. Therefore, in every case we should ask if the prevailing legal principle discourages or deters women from seeking equality on the ground of sex.

In sum, we should also ask the larger question, namely: why does the unjust status hierarchy organized around gender continue in the face of the constitutional demand for equality? Why is section 15(1) of the *Charter* not defined in terms of power and the dismantling of unjust status hierarchies? One reason may be the Court's obsession with legalism, which takes

the form of insisting that section 15(1) analysis begin and end with the impugned legislation, unlike section 2(b) analysis which takes its lead from
social realities. And, the second reason may be comparison — more specifically, constitutive comparision — which may be too threatening for the
current Court. After all, if adopted, constitutive comparison would force
the Court to honour its commitment to treat section 15(1) as remedial[134] by
recognizing the necessity of leveling-down privileged groups such as men.

ENDNOTES

1   *Canadian Charter of Rights and Freedoms,* Part I of the *Constitution Act, 1982,* being Schedule B to the *Canada Act 1982* (U.K.), 1982, c. 11 [*Charter*], s. 15, which provides:

> 15. (1) Every individual is equal before and under the law and has the right to the equal protection and equal benefit of the law without discrimination and, in particular, without discrimination based on race, national or ethnic origin, colour, religion, sex, age or mental or physical disability.

> 15. (2) Subsection (1) does not preclude any law, program or activity that has as its object the amelioration of conditions of disadvantaged individuals or groups including those that are disadvantaged because of race, national or ethnic origin, colour, religion, sex, age or mental or physical disability.

2   *Hodge v. Canada,* [2004] 3 S.C.R. 357, 2004 SCC 65 [*Hodge*].

3   Diana Majury, "The Charter, Equality Rights, and Women: Equivocation and Celebration" (2002) 40 Osgoode Hall L.J. 297 at 306.

4   *Law v. Canada (Minister of Employment and Immigration),* [1999] 1 S.C.R. 497 [*Law*].

5   Elisa Holmes, "Anti-Discrimination Rights Without Equality" (2005) 68 (2) Mod. L. Rev. 175.

6   *Ibid.*

7   *Ibid.*

8   *Ibid.* at 178–79. Holmes also dismissed the distinctions between direct and indirect discrimination, equality of opportunity and equality of results, and equality of welfare and equality of resources.

9   *Law Society of British Columbia v. Andrews,* [1989] 1 S.C.R. 143 at para. 37 [*Andrews*], McIntyre J. cited his own decision in *Ontario Human Rights Commission and O'Malley v. Simpsons-Sears Ltd.,* [1985] 2 S.C.R. 536 at 551 [*Simpsons-Sears*], where he relied on *Griggs v. Duke Power Co.,* 401 U.S. 424 (1971) [*Griggs*] as the source of his definition of discrimination.

10   Owen M. Fiss, "Groups and the Equal Protection Clause" (1976) 5 Phil. & Pub. Affairs 107.

11   *Ibid.* at 111.

12   *Ibid.* at 108.

13   *Law,* above note 4 at para. 53.

14   Fiss, above note 10 at 157.

15   *Ibid.* at 108.

16   Jack M. Balkin & Reva B. Siegel, "The American Civil Rights Tradition: Anticlassification or Antisubordination" in Robert Post, ed., *The Origins and Fate of Antisubordination Theory: A Symposium on Owen Fiss's "Groups and the Equal Protection Clause"* (August 2002) online: www.bepress.com/ils/iss2 (accessed 15 June 2003).

17   *Symes v. Canada,* [1993] 4 S.C.R. 695 [*Symes*]; *Trociuk v. British Columbia (Attorney General),* [2003] 1 S.C.R. 835, 2003 S.C.C. 34 [*Trociuk*]; *Law,* above note 4.

18   *Andrews,* above note 9 at para. 31.

19 *Law,* above note 4 at para. 5.

20 *Ibid.* at para. 46.

21 *Andrews,* above note 9 at para. 25.

22 *Ibid.*

23 *Ibid.* at para. 38.

24 *Ibid.* at para. 31.

25 *Ibid.* at para. 27.

26 *Ibid.* at para. 28.

27 *Ibid.*

28 *Ibid.* at para. 26.

29 *Ibid.* at para. 31.

30 *Ibid.*

31 *Law,* above note 4 at para. 25.

32 *Ibid.* at para. 46.

33 *Ibid.* at paras. 24 & 56.

34 *Andrews,* above note 9 at para. 26.

35 W.H. McConnell, *William R. McIntyre: Paladin of Common Law* (Montreal & Kingston: McGill-Queen's University Press, 2000).

36 *Law,* above note 4 at paras. 24 & 56.

37 *Ibid.* at para. 24.

38 *Ibid.* at para. 58.

39 *Ibid.* at para. 56.

40 *Ibid.* at paras. 56 & 57.

41 *Hodge,* above note 2.

42 *Ibid.* at para. 17.

43 *Ibid.* at para. 22.

44 *Ibid.* at para. 1 (emphasis in original).

45 *Ibid.* at para. 2.

46 *Andrews,* above note 9 at para. 29, citing *Bliss v. Attorney General of Canada,* [1979] 1 S.C.R. 183.

47 Holmes, above note 5.

48 *Ibid.* at 186.

49 *Ibid.*

50 *Ibid.* at 187.

51 *Ibid.*

52 *Ibid.* at 186.

53 *Ibid.*

54 *Ibid.*

55 *Ibid.*

56 *Ibid.*

57 *Ibid.*

58 *Ibid.* "Even Aristotle," Holmes added, "who is often said to have espoused a principle of formal equality, did no such thing. Noticing that some substance *has* to be added,

he wrote: 'Equals are entitled to equal things. But here we are met by the important question: Equals and unequals *in what*? This is the difficult problem.'"

59   For example, Mary Jane Mossman, "Achieving Gender Equality: Legal Principles and Social Arrangements" (1998) 32 Kobe U.L.R. 21; Patricia Hughes, "Recognizing Substantive Equality as a Foundational Constitutional Principle" (1999) 22 Dal. L.J. 5; Donna Greschner, "The Purpose of Canadian Equality Rights" (2002) 6 R. Const. Studies 291; Diana Majury, above note 3; Denise G. Réaume, "Discrimination and Dignity" (2003) 63 Louisiana L.R. 645, reprinted in this volume; Daphne Gilbert, "Time to Regroup: Rethinking Section 15 of the *Charter*" (2003) 48 McGill L.J. 627.

60   Majury, above note 3 at 306.

61   Holmes, above note 5 at 178 included the difference between direct and indirect discrimination amongst other distinctions about which she explained: "But these differences are not conceptual. They are differences among normative principles all of which are (or might be) *egalitarian* in the same sense."

62   *Andrews,* above note 9 at paras. 35–39.

63   *Law,* above note 4 at para. 39.

64   *Newfoundland (Treasury Board) v. NAPE,* [2004] 3 S.C.R. 381, 2004 S.C.C. 66 [*NAPE*], wherein the equality seekers lost at the s. 1 stage.

65   Fiss, above note 10.

66   *Ibid.* at 108.

67   In *Andrews,* above note 9 at para. 37, McIntyre J. cited his own decision in *Simpsons-Sears,* above note 9 at 549, wherein he relied on *Griggs,* above note 9 and *Dennis v. United States,* 339 U.S. 162 (1950) as the sources for his definition of discrimination.

68   Fiss, above note 10 at 108.

69   *Andrews,* above note 9 at para. 35.

70   *Ibid.* at para 37.

71   *Law,* above note 4 at para. 23.

72   *Ibid.* at paras. 63–68.

73   *Ibid.* at paras. 69–71.

74   *Ibid.* at para. 72–73.

75   *Ibid.* at para. 74–75.

76   Fiss, above note 10 at 111.

77   *Ibid.*

78   See text at notes 47 & 48.

79   *Andrews,* above note 9 at para. 55.

80   *Law,* above note 4 at para. 101.

81   Fiss, above note 10 at 136.

82   *Ibid.* at 148.

83   *Ibid.* at 129.

84   *Ibid.*

85   *Ibid.* at 126.

86   *Ibid.* at 156.

87   *Ibid.*

88   *Andrews*, above note 9 at para. 38.

89 *Ibid.* at paras. 48–49.

90 *Law,* above note 4 at para. 23.

91 *Ibid.* at para. 39.

92 *Ibid.*

93 *Irwin Toy Ltd. v. Quebec (Attorney General),* [1989] 1 S.C.R. 927 at 967–71.

94 *Ibid.* at 968.

95 *Ibid.* at 971.

96 Judith N. Shklar, *Legalism: Law, Morals, and Political Trials* (Cambridge: Harvard University Press, 1964).

97 Fiss, above note 10 at 175.

98 *Law,* above note 4 at para. 53.

99 *Ibid.* at para. 56.

100 *Ibid.* at paras. 65–66.

101 *Ibid.* at para. 77.

102 Fiss, above note 10 at 150.

103 *Ibid.*

104 *Ibid.* at 151.

105 *Ibid.* at 152.

106 *Ibid.* at 153.

107 *Ibid.,* continuing: "The socioeconomic status of the group supplies an additional reason for the judicial activism and also determines the content of the intervention — improvement of the status of that group."

108 Jack M. Balkin, "The Constitution of Status" (1997), 106 Yale L.J. 2313 at 2345.

109 Canada, *Report of the Royal Commission on the Status of Women* (Ottawa: Information Canada, 1970).

110 Alexandra Dobrowolsky, *The Politics of Pragmatism: Women, Representation, and Constitutionalism in Canada* (Oxford: Oxford University Press, 2000); Penney Kome, *The Taking of Twenty-Eight: Women Challenge the Constitution* (Toronto: Women's Educational Press, 1983); Sherene Razack, *Canadian Feminism and the Law: The Women's Legal Education and Action Fund and the Pursuit of Equality* (Toronto: Second Story Press, 1991); Mary Eberts, "Sex-based Discrimination and the *Charter*" in Anne F. Bayefsky & Mary Eberts, eds., *Equality Rights and the Canadian Charter of Rights and Freedoms* (Toronto: Carswell, 1985); Katherine J. de Jong, "Sexual Equality: Interpreting Section 28" in Bayefsky & Eberts; Beverley Baines, "Law Gender Equality" in Sandra Burt, Lorraine Code, & Lindsay Dorney, eds., *Changing Patterns: Women in Canada* (Toronto: McClelland & Stewart, 1993); Mary Jane Mossman, "The Paradox of Feminist Engagement with Law" in Nancy Mandell, ed., *Feminist Issues: Race, Class and Sexuality,* 2d ed. (Toronto: Prentice Hall, 1997).

111 Roberta Hamilton, *Gendering the Vertical Mosaic: Feminist Perspectives on Canadian Society,* 2d ed. (Toronto: Pearson Prentice Hall, 2004).

112 Balkin, above note 108 at 2325.

113 R.H. Graveson, *Status in the Common Law* (London: University of London, Athlone Press, 1953) at 2.

114 Balkin, above note 108 at 2323.

115 *Ibid.*

116 *Ibid.*

117 *Ibid.*

118 *Ibid.*

119 Radha Jhappan, "Introduction: Feminist Adventures in Law" in Radha Jhappan, ed., *Women's Legal Strategies in Canada* (Toronto: University of Toronto Press, 2002) at 3.

120 Balkin, above note 108 at 2329.

121 *Ibid.* at 2359.

122 *Ibid.*

123 *Ibid.* at 2366.

124 *Ibid.* at 2360.

125 Balkin & Siegel, above note 16.

126 *Symes*, above note 17; *Trociuk*, above note 17; *Law*, above note 4.

127 *Symes, ibid.*; *Native Women's Association of Canada v. Canada*, [1994] 3 S.C.R. 627; *Thibaudeau v. Canada*, [1995] 2 S.C.R. 627; *Vancouver Society of Immigrant and Visible Minority Women v. Canada*, [1999] 1 S.C.R. 10; and *NAPE*, above note 64.

128 *Symes, ibid.* at 763.

129 *Ibid.* at 761.

130 Men initiated and won s. 15(1) arguments in: *R. v. Hess, R. v. Nguyen*, [1990] 2 S.C.R. 906; *Schachter v. Canada*, [1992] 2 S.C.R. 679; *Weatherall v. Canada*, [1993] 2 S.C.R. 872; *Benner v. Canada*, [1997] 1 S.C.R. 358; and *Trociuk*, above note 17. However, the Canadian government successfully invoked s. 1 in *Hess* and *Weatherall*.

131 *Trociuk, ibid.* at paras. 16–17.

132 *Trociuk v. British Columbia (Attorney General)* (2001), 200 D.L.R. (4th) 685 (C.A.) at 741 (Newbury J.A.).

133 *Law*, above note 4; *Nova Scotia v. Walsh*, [2002] 4 S.C.R. 325; *Gosselin v. Quebec*, [2002] 4 S.C.R. 429; *Hodge*, above note 2.

134 *Andrews,* above note 9 at para. 34.

three

Answering the Siren Call of Abstract Formalism with the Subjects and Verbs of Domination

Sheila McIntyre

A. INTRODUCTION

Recent *Charter*[1] equality jurisprudence reveals a steady shift away from the substantive equality analysis the Supreme Court purports to have embraced with *Andrews*.[2] Because I am not persuaded that the Supreme Court's purchase on substantive analysis was ever firm, I do not believe that this shift flows from the test set by the Supreme Court of Canada in the case of *Law v. Canada*.[3] Although the *Law* test does create additional hurdles beyond those previously understood as the *Andrews* test, I favour the new third leg in particular, and a high threshold to make out a section 15 claim generally.[4] I think narrowing the coverage of section 15(1) should make it much more difficult for governments to urge, or for courts to adopt, a deferential approach to section 1[5] or to remedies, and it may disrupt the tendency of governments, timid courts, and the Right to reconstruct (in)equality claims as policy debates about line-drawing best left to legislatures rather than to "activist" judges.

In this paper, I review what most equality-seeking groups considered the strengths of *Andrews* (and what *Charter* critics from the Right have most deplored)[6] to highlight both what I believe is worth preserving and what has left openings congenial to formalist habits of thinking ever since. I argue that to the extent members of the Supreme Court understand what it means to have adopted a substantive approach to the equality guarantees, and to the extent they are sincere in rejecting formalism, the Court has consistently shown failure of nerve in articulating and applying the substantivism they have repeatedly endorsed. In the result, the Court has produced an inconsistent and incoherent jurisprudence that supplies too little guidance to lower courts, too much scope for the re-emergence of formalism in section 15 determinations, and too much ammunition to formalists who seek to discredit outcomes consistent with *Andrews* as illegitimate "judicial activism." I then offer some ideas on why the grip of formalism remains so enduring. I argue that formalism's idealization of blindfolded justice encourages and legitimates in members of dominant groups studied ignorance and privileged innocence of their(our) personal implication in maintaining and benefiting from systemic inequality. It also renders supremacist thinking and habits invisible, or merely normal, to advocates and judges. I suggest why and how equality advocates like LEAF might disrupt judicial embrace of substantive rhetoric and formalist practice by speaking substantivism boldly enough to confront the dominant with the hard facts of their(our) stake in oppression.

B. *ANDREWS*

Read as a whole, *Andrews* offered significant direction, and laid indispensable foundations for a substantive approach to application of section 15. The Court explicitly rejected a purely formalist approach to section 15 that would require the same treatment of those deemed by the legislature or the court and/or the dominant to be the same, and allowing differential treatment of those accordingly deemed "different." The Court also rejected the softer, "similarly situated" test. It acknowledged that identical treatment of formally equal citizens may exacerbate the inequality of social, political, or economic unequals; and that recognition and accommodation of social, political, and economic differences among citizens are "the essence" of equality. Consistent with endorsing a substantive approach to equality rights, the majority also called for a contextual approach to applying section 15, rather than the abstract, blindfolded justice approach that is seen to be the virtue of formalism.[7] Wilson's short judgment is most explicit in calling for an examination of "the context of the impugned law as well as the context of the place of the [complainant] group in the entire social, political and legal fabric of our society."[8] The Court followed human rights jurisprudence in making clear that proof of discriminatory intent would not be required to make out an infringement of section 15. In the result, the Court decisively rejected two formalist approaches to the guarantee: Peter Hogg's purely formalist model,[9] by which every legal distinction drawn on an enumerated ground would require justification under section 1; and the similarly situated analysis adopted by Justice McLachlin,[10] then of the BC Court of Appeal, which would require only "unreasonable" — that is, irrationally drawn or prejudiced — distinctions to need section 1 justification. McIntyre J. reasoned that because all laws draw direct or indirect distinctions among citizens, mere line-drawing in government-authored prohibitions, burdens, entitlements, benefits, or privileges was insufficient to infringe section 15. Only government-authored distinctions that "discriminate" within the meaning of section 15 would infringe the equality guarantee and require justification. Once "discrimination" was made out by the claimant, questions as to its reasonableness or other policy justification were properly addressed under section 1 where the onus would be on the state to meet what, for the *Andrews* majority, was a relatively rigorous threshold of justification.[11]

Had *Andrews* established no more than this, it would have warranted celebration. But it went some distance further. Wilson J. stated clearly that the purpose of section 15 was "to protect those groups who suffer social, political and legal disadvantage in our society."[12] In attempting to identify what constitutes an analogous ground, the judgments of McIntyre, Wilson, and La Forest — not least because of LEAF's intervention[13] — offered such indicators as: minority status marked by the presence of stereotyping, historic disadvantage and vulnerability to political or social prejudice; exclusion from the mainstream of society; being defined by ascribed stereotypical attributes rather than individual merits; lacking political power and being overlooked or marginalised in the political process.[14] A linkage between these "indicia of disadvantage" and what became known as the "*Andrews* test" has never clearly and consistently been made by a majority of the Court. In fact, it was obscured by McIntyre's tautological definition of "discrimination" as a legal *distinction* that *differentiates* in its allocation of benefits or burdens among citizens:

> ... discrimination may be described as a distinction, whether intentional or not but based on grounds relating to personal characteristics of the individual or group, which has the effect of imposing burdens, obligations, or disadvantages on such individual or group not imposed on others, or which withholds or limits access to opportunities, benefits and advantages available to other members of society.[15]

Although subsequent cases offered hints about what it was that converted a legal distinction into "discrimination,"[16] I think La Forest J. was quite correct in his *Egan*[17] judgment in remarking that McIntyre J.'s definition was "not of great assistance." "Ordinarily," La Forest wrote, governmental decisions which make distinctions "do result in advantages or disadvantages to individuals...."[18] In my view, it is in exiting this tautology that the third leg of the *Law* framework marks an improvement upon *Andrews*. The third leg conditions an infringement on a finding that a state-authored distinction (direct or indirect) drawn on an enumerated or analogous ground imposes a burden upon or withholds a benefit from the claimant *in a manner that reflects stereotypes or that has the effect of perpetuating or promoting second class status*.[19] Regrettably, this requirement that a distinction reflect (and hence reinforce) negative stereotypes of the Other, or result in subordination, has been shorthanded to a requirement that the complainant prove that a government-authored or -condoned[20] distinction violates "essential human dignity." Leave aside, for the moment, the perils of a concept as abstract and malleable as "dignity" as the measure of equality,[21] and a concept as slight as "indignity" for such harms of discrimination as hunger, homelessness, cultural genocide, pervasive targeting for sexual abuse, systemic under- and unemployment and unequal pay, and forced sterilization and eugenic pre-natal screening based on sex, race, sexual orientation, poverty, and/or disability. Unless what converts a government-authored distinction into discrimination is only particular adverse effects such as reflecting and reinforcing pre-existing disadvantage, including stereotyping, section 15 will largely be applied in formalist ways, no matter how often the Supreme Court labels its approach "substantive."[22]

While *Andrews* remains an important landmark for abjuring formalism, embracing a purposive and contextual analysis, and focusing on effects that bear some undefined relation to social, political, or legal disadvantage, its murkiness about what converts a legal distinction on a prohibited ground into "discrimination" has left ample room for the pull of formalism in subsequent case law. I am not sure whether this murkiness was intentional and amounted to soft-peddling the significance of a substantive approach, or bespeaks intellectual ambivalence on the Supreme Court reflecting some disjunction between the adoption of substantive principles and the judges' formalist socialization. I can identify what is soft-pedalled or shied away from and its affinities with a formalist orientation. In explaining the adoption of the "analogous grounds" approach over the Hogg or McLachlin approaches, *Andrews* speaks generically of groups lacking political power, "disadvantaged groups," groups subject to "stereotyping" or "stigmatization," groups "excluded from the mainstream." It speaks, in other words, in the passive voice, and weakly. Its focus is on the Other. There is no overt indication of who does the disempowering, stigmatizing, or marginalizing, of who enjoys entrenched political power, of how disadvantage and the inferiorizing stereotypes that legitimate second class status come about and whose hold on privileged entitlement such stereotypes shore up.

There are stronger and more politically accurate umbrella terms than "disadvantaged" for the situations of the groups in question: dispossessed, disempowered, demonized, dehumanized, degraded, debased, demeaned, discredited. If a single generic is required, I propose "oppressed." These more starkly violative verbs evoke an active subject and invite critical judgment, not pious abstractions about concern, respect, and dignity, far less condescending pity about "the disadvantaged." They imply wrongdoing against the targets of discrimination, and leave little room for disagreement over whether the target should "feel" injured. The focus shifts from debates about appropriate comparators to analysis of relations between excluders and excluded, stigmatizers and stigmatized, expropriator and dispossessed.

What *Andrews* and its progeny shy away from enables what formalists most idealize: application of law with one's eyes shut. Whether intentional or due to the unconscious worldview of privilege, the Court's shying away from the substantively transformative implications of embracing a substantive equality approach generates further failures of nerve. The refusal to be boldly substantive in linking an impugned law to the relations of domination which perpetuate and rationalize the systemic inequality of specific historically and currently subordinated groups, allows section 15(1) analysis to regress into the malleable terrain of similarly situated reasoning. Interveners and the parties strategize over selection of comparators to persuade courts to reject the place at which, or the policy reasons underlying why, government has drawn lines of entitlement or obligation among citizens in a particular place. Because reasonable people can and do disagree about the correct comparator chosen or the point at, or bases upon which, benefit cut-offs become markers of second class status, outcomes will be wildly unpredictable and inconsistent from case to case.[23] The problem with this focus is not primarily one of increasing the onus on the claimant to prove that distinctions have been made irrationally instead of requiring government to prove that subordinating distinctions are "reasonable limits" under section 1.[24] The problem is the legitimacy of judicial review that amounts to little more than apparently subjective and inconsistent opinions about the credibility of complainants' claims to injured dignity and about the rationality of legislative judgment calls by an unelected, unrepresentative, and unaccountable elite. The legitimacy problem doesn't diminish when the judicial punch-line is that eligibility or disqualification for state benefits is or is not an injury to "dignity" rather than "discrimination."

So long as the Supreme Court evades analytic and discursive clarity about what converts a distinction into discrimination, equality analysis reduces to some form of debate about line-drawing — about which comparators to keep in the analytic frame;[25] about what distinguishes empirically sound generalizations about "actual need" from stereotypes tracking institutionalized inequality;[26] about when individual or group exclusion is just hard luck and when it is reasonably construed as an affront to human dignity.[27] Arguments for deference by the unelected, unrepresentative, and unaccountable judiciary to the legislature become difficult to refute. Most *Charter* watchers seem to agree that the Supreme Court is becoming generally more deferential to the legislature in its *Charter* judgements[28] even as Right wing attacks on illegitimate "judicial activism" continue to escalate. Although Sheilah Martin has shown that the Supreme Court has not been inclined to deference at the section 1 stage in section 15 claims, this may be because the majority of equality claims never get to section 1.[29] The finding that a distinction is not "discriminatory" or not an injury to basic human dignity, nonetheless, often appears the product of deferential reasoning about the rationality of government line-drawing. Accordingly, although I concede that pushing the court to be bolder at the section 15(1) stage is no small order, I also think deference will be, and will appear to be, profoundly misplaced once a law has been found to have the effect of reflecting, reinforcing, or perpetuating men's oppression of women, or white supremacy, or heterosexual homophobia, or ablist dehumanization of people with disabilities.[30] Recasting infringements of section 15(1) as instances of oppression of dispossessed groups might also overcome judicial timidity about ordering substantive remedies appropriate to the equality infringement alleged. I think remedying oppression requires less nerve than ordering lines to be drawn anew.

C. THE CALL OF FORMALISM

I am arguing that failures of nerve in articulating the meaning of, and in applying a substantive equality approach to, section 15 create space for the re-emergence of formalist thinking in the adjudication of equality claims. Although formalist logic may appear at any stage in the *Charter* analysis,[31] it most often appears at the section 15 or section 1 stage where it not only works to defeat discrimination claims, but where — because it appears erratically in different judges at different times and in different types of legal claims — it does the most harm to the coherent development of the jurisprudence. Why, though, does formalism re-emerge, whether in the explicitly discredited logic of *Bliss*,[32] or the "relevance" version of the similarly situated test which appeared with the 1995 trilogy[33] and which continues to permeate some post-*Law* analyses,[34] and in application of the "dignity" standard?[35]

The formalist approach to equality, as I am using the term, entails the privileging of abstract principles over material facts, and idealizing disembodied reason as the distinguishing feature of legal (as opposed to political, sociological, or moral) reasoning and of adjudication (as opposed to policy formation). Formalists prefer rules over standards, and incline toward the articulation and application of "canons" and "tests" and checklists of "factors" to reduce at least the appearance of subjectivism and discretion in the adjudicative process. Put differently, formalism aspires to the decontextualized application of objectified rules and definitions by impartial adjudicators. Formalists do not ask questions about the genesis of the rules that their idealized model requires to be applied equally to all, about the context in which they will be applied, or about the interests, assumptions, and values of the adjudicators who will assess similarity of situation and choose whom to compare when ensuring that likes are treated alike. Law and Economics scholar Richard Epstein has put it this way:

> common law rules in their ideal form make legal entitlements among strangers without reference to personal status. Legal rules do not refer to flesh-and-blood individuals, but to those lifeless abstractions, A and B, about whom nothing else is known or — more to the point — is relevant. ... Stating propositions in general form is, moreover, a powerful antidote to abuse and favoritism.[36]

Formalists' abstraction of material inequality from their equality analyses enables their explicit denial of the existence of systemic inequality or their insistence on its irrelevance to rules application.[37]

I don't think anyone has unpacked the linkages between these formalist norms and ideals and the rationalization of structures of domination better than Catharine MacKinnon.[38] I want to simply introduce a few riffs on MacKinnon's analysis because I think we need to grapple with why formal equality retains such a significant pull on the courts in the face of over fifteen years of substantive equality analysis, much of it explicitly named as such, in the Supreme Court's human rights and section 15 jurisprudence.

First, exposure to substantive equality theory and jurisprudence postdates the formal professional training of many litigators and judges. Even judges who mean to decide cases consistent with substantive norms may fall back on formalism as a kind of default position when faced with novel cases or claims that are particularly challenging to their personal values or their conception of the appropriate judicial role. The way legal professionals are initially taught to think of equality has staying power.

Second, outside of legal circles and, in particular, in the mainstream media, formal equality thinking is dominant ideology in two senses of that term: it is the prevailing understanding of "equality," not least because the dominant so insist; and it is overwhelmingly the ideology of dominant groups, not least because its premises and outcomes correlate perfectly with the interests of members of dominant groups.[39]

At a material level, adoption and application of the abstraction, false symmetries, and decontextualized facts that a formal equality model dictates, as MacKinnon points out, "ensures that law will most reinforce existing distributions of power when it most closely adheres to its own ideal of fairness" such that "what counts as reason is that which corresponds to the way things are. Practical rationality in this approach, means that which can be done without changing anything."[40] This decontextualized and abstract method allows formalists to outlaw as so-called "reverse discrimination" any state action designed to remedy the accrued harms of historically lawful forms of discrimination, and allows them to characterize a government's refusal to prohibit sexual orientation discrimination as "neutral," "even-handed" and, hence, equal treatment of heterosexuals and non-heterosexuals under provincial human rights law.[41] Finally, it renders predictable that judicial attention to context and material inequality will be denounced as "judicial activism" inconsistent with the appropriate role of courts in our constitutional order.

I think very few equality claims since 1985 have seriously threatened to mandate significant redistribution of resources from dominant groups to the communities they have dispossessed.[42] So aside from tax challenges which would have had significant price tags to taxpayers generally,[43] I don't think that the pull of formalism can be attributed to the material self-interest of the privileged. Rather, I think the appeal and pull of formal equality principles lie primarily in protecting the insular worldview of the dominant and in shoring up presumptions essential to guiltless, and even smug, enjoyment of the fruits of their institutionalized privilege. I mean the presumptions of social, moral, and intellectual superiority over the systemically subordinated, and of superior entitlement to resources, power, credibility, security, and recognition. I also mean the presumption of personal non-complicity in maintaining, benefiting from or trading on systemic inequalities. This systemically inflated self-regard of the dominant thrives in a formal equality regime and is at risk when substantive equality rights are actually, rather than rhetorically, applied in constitutional law.

Under conditions of systemic sexual, racial, and economic inequality and of pervasive ablism, heterosexism, and colonialism, we are all gendered, raced, and classed, all socialized to heterosexist, ablist, and imperialist norms. Within each of these *relations* of inequality, the dominant and subordinated do not *relate* as equals. Subordinating treatment of members of systemically oppressed groups by members of dominant groups is not occasional, aberrant, irrational, or random; not the province of misfit, ignorant, or ill-educated bigots; not the marker of anti-social, counter-cultural, or uncivilized individuals. Presuming the superiority and, thus, the superior entitlements of the dominant is the rational result of acculturation as a member of one or more dominant groups in our civil society. I want to call this worldview and the deeply ingrained but mostly unreflective habits of privilege which dominant status teaches the systemically empowered and the systemically disempowered alike, "supremacism." The supremacist attitudes and behaviours of dominant group members are continuously re-inscribed in their relations with other dominant group members and with members of systemically dispossessed groups.

Supremacism is learned behaviour, so normalized as to be openly expressed and deemed simple common sense by dominant groups. I would describe the judgment of La Forest J. in *Egan* as a paradigm of supremacism.[44] Roughly translated, his section 15 holding was that legislation designed to promote the dominance of the heterosexual family is fundamental to preserving its dominance, and to that end it is relevant to take citizens' sexual orientation into account so as to withhold state benefits from couples who do not conform to and reinforce the dominant order. Although the five judges who found a section 15(1) infringement in *Egan* did articulate several criticisms of La Forest's reasoning, they answered at the level of logic,[45] rather than confronting its explicitly supremacist nature.[46]

As Patricia Williams has observed of the formalist approach to the equal protection guarantees of the US Constitution,

> The rules may be color-blind, but people are not. The question remains, therefore, whether the law can truly exist apart from the color-conscious society in which it exists, as a skeleton devoid of flesh; or whether law is the embodiment of society, the reflection of a particular citizenry's arranged complexity of relations.... The real issue is precisely the canonized status of any one group's control. Black individuality is subsumed in a social circumstance — an idea, a stereotype — that pins us to the underside of this society and keeps us there, out of sight/out of mind, out of the knowledge of mind which is law.[47]

Formalism doesn't simply codify supremacist norms as neutral, universal, even-handed rules; it rewards intellectual and political complacency. Because supremacist habits and conventions are learned, they need to be unlearned. Formalism requires them to be unseen and unthought and, thereby, disavowed. When equality claims are really substantive, they should challenge privileged understandings of the world and privileged players' understandings of themselves. Formalist discourse and formalist principle conveniently secure the opposite result.

Embrace of formal equality not only allows, but gives respectability to, dissociation by members of dominant groups from their implication in relations of dominance. Epstein's idealized model of liberal law makes a virtue of disregarding the race or gender or class of both party A and party B in the adjudication of legal disputes, as well as of the adjudicator.[48] But as Williams notes, whatever formal equality law purports to be doing bears no relation to what and who real people actually see and unsee, regard and disregard. Under conditions of systemic inequality, Otherness is marked; dominant status is not. Otherness is marked as deviant, defective, un(der)developed, and inferior by comparison with the unstated norms associated with the dominant and seen to justify their supremacy. Members of dominant groups do not for a minute unsee the race, gender, sexuality, disability, or nationality of non-dominant groups. They do, however, unsee their own. Formalism construes as principled, rather than self-serving, such wilful blindness. It facilitates in members of dominant groups what Sherene Razack and Mary Louise Fellows have termed "the race to innocence"[49] and what I have elsewhere analyzed as "studied ignorance and privileged innocence."[50]

The systemically normalized and reinforced superiority of the dominant generates and rationalizes a sense of superior entitlement to social, economic, and political opportunities, resources, and instruments of power. It also breeds inflated self-esteem and arrogant self-regard, imperious habits, and a sense of privileged standing to pronounce on almost anything as well as to dominate discussion. It cultivates expectations of credibility and validation and of deference from "Others."[51] These deformations of privilege account for the disproportionate outrage and wounded egos which have followed the release of every "chilly climate" report with which I am familiar. They also explain arch-formalist Mr. Justice McClung's extraordinary response to having his sexist views named as such in the *Ewanchuk* decision.[52]

Schooled as they(we) are to presumptions of superiority and of superiority of entitlement and the inflated self-regard they inculcate, the privileged react badly to any criticism, especially from those culturally deemed their inferiors. Schooled as they(we) are to dissociate from the cause and effect of acculturation to supremacism and the routine, unreflective manifestation of discriminatory beliefs and postures, and urged as they(we) are to view "racists" or "homophobes" and other "bigots" as ignorant, aberrant Others, the privileged construe having their(our) views, postures, and conduct named discriminatory as a personal attack amounting to a deep reputational harm. Privileged presumptions of superiority and superiority of entitlement pose serious dangers if the judicial recognition of dignitary injury remains the measure of what converts a legal distinction into discrimination. I think (privileged) judges will validate what amount to reverse discrimination claims as "dignitary" harms to privileged complainants. Likewise, I think judges will be slow to uphold equality challenges to laws that privilege privileged interests where they see no dignitary harm in lines of entitlement they consider natural or deserved.[53]

Denise Réaume has acknowledged the "dilemma" of framing legal claims around a dignity standard. She observes that the harms caused by demeaning and humiliating behaviour to the dignity of marginalised groups "are precisely the harms that the courts are least likely to see."[54] I would add a corollary: naming unreflective habits of privilege will be deemed outrageous assaults on the over-inflated dignity of those who like to presume themselves unraced, engendered, and so on.

Réaume argues that litigators will have to confront this dilemma head-on. Speaking of a tort claim for "intentional outrage to dignity," she argues that litigators advocating on behalf of members of marginalised groups will have to take on the task of educating the judiciary. Although there is no guarantee that judges will "get it" initially, she posits that "we are more likely to make progress if we identify the central issue for what it is, rather than ignoring it or masking it."[55] On this we agree. Concretely, I think we disagree on the terminology needed to effect such education.

D. SPEAKING SUBSTANTIVELY

Former Justice L'Heureux-Dubé has suggested that we regard substantive equality "as a language like every other"; that is, as "an embodiment of the norms, attitudes, and culture" that are expressed through equality's rules of grammar and syntax, nuances, exceptions and dialects."[56] She notes that we lack fluency in this new language — in part, because it does not fit easily with the traditions and norms of law's first (formal) equality language, but also because most legal professionals have only a "working knowledge" of its basic vocabulary and rules and speak substantive equality so little that they(we) haven't reached the stage where they(we) have begun to think in this second language. I think this is a fruitful way of understanding the disjuncture between the reiteration of substantive catchphrases[57] and the more-or-less formalist reasoning that appears in many equality judgments. It is helpful to view formal equality as most adjudicators' first language, and substantive equality as a second language that judges have only just begun to speak haltingly.

Because formal equality is the first language and the cultural backdrop of the analysis of most legal advocates and adjudicators, timid, soft-peddling, or vague articulations of substantive principles and their application creates space for a range of mixed results, by which I mean different mixes of both equality languages. Sometimes this faint-heartedness produces the equivalent of "Franglais," the adoption of formalist idioms into substantive discourse. I would describe the 1995 trilogy's adoption of the "relevance" test this way. Sometimes it yields linguistic inventions that only the dominant understand, somewhat like giving English words a French accent without knowing that the term means something quite different in French. I view the tax cases like *Symes*[58] and *Thibaudeau* this way. The male majority thinks formalistically, invents distinctions, manipulates comparators and coins abstractions like "the post-divorce family unit" to defeat the claim, while purporting to apply substantive precedent. Sometimes formalists just raise their voices as if substantivists have a hearing problem. The most dramatic examples, the Court of Appeal majority judgments in *Eldridge* and *Vriend*,[59] were answered in clear, substantivist terms by the Supreme Court,[60] but not without failures of nerve and, in the case of *Vriend*, undue defensiveness.[61] My personal view is that more, rather than less, boldness in both judgments, especially in *Vriend*, might have altered and made less dishonest the public debate that followed release of both decisions. Instead, easy cases like *Eldridge* and *Vriend*, both of them illustrations of the virtues of entrenched minority rights and of judicial review, became metaphors for extreme "judicial activism."[62]

In my view, what is needed, and has always been needed, is bolder judicial elaboration of the *Andrews* skeleton and the flesh *Law* put on that skeleton, to banish the comfortable abstractions that permit the court to focus on "differences" and on feelings such as self-worth, concern, and dignity rather than on the concrete and attitudinal relations of inequality that generate and rationalize discriminatory acts, policies, and laws. I don't believe the Court will explicitly reverse *Andrews* or expressly rehabilitate formal equality or similarly situated analysis. But neither do I believe they will begin to think in what they claim is Canada's official equality language until our advocacy confronts the studied ignorance and privileged innocence that formalist ideology not only permits, but elevates and idealizes as principle.

Many LEAF facta do a wonderful job documenting and unpacking the linkages between the facts of women's inequality and laws which reflect or reinforce that inequality. The facta, for instance, highlight the sexist or racist or ablist underpinnings of, say, rape evidence rules,[63] or of state-authored and judicially approved involuntary confinement of a drug-addicted, poor, aboriginal woman.[64] They expose the disparate impacts on already disadvantaged women of under-inclusive state benefits or stereotype-based and -reinforcing penalties.[65] Consistent with substantive equality analysis, feminist litigation focuses on inequality of results. Sadly, this remains necessary educative work in face of formalist fictions about the equality of the sexes and/or about mounting sex discrimination against men. However, too often, we pose no challenge to the formalist habit of focusing attention exclusively on the Other without addressing the effects of relations of inequality on the dominant. We translate only one side of the relevant relations of equality. We have lapsed into the abstractions provided by precedent, such as "disadvantaged" and "marginalised"; or we engage with courts in their arm's length speculation about whether the ordinary similarly situated person would or should feel demeaned by being excluded from X state benefits or denied Y state protections. Focus remains on the Other; entitlement to judge the reasonableness of the Other's experience of exclusion, dispossession, deprivation, and/or objectification, resides — unremarked — with the privileged. This methodology and stance, Sherene Razack has observed, suggests

> ... that with a little practice and the right information, we can all be innocent subjects, standing outside hierarchical social relations, who are not accountable for the past or implicated in the present. It is not our ableism, racism, sexism, or heterosexism that gets in the way ... but *their* difference, *their* biology, or *their* lifestyle. In sum, the ... differences approach reinforces an important epistemological cornerstone of imperialism: the colonized possess a series of knowable characteristics and can be studied, known, and managed accordingly by the colonizers whose own complicity remains masked.[66]

Preventing the re-entry of formalist logic requires far more educative work, I think, to disrupt the privileged innocence and unreflectively supremacist habits that formalism authorizes. Some of this is simply a matter of rhetoric. Let us stop talking in the passive voice of "disadvantaged" groups. Let us choose more active descriptors — disenfranchised, disempowered, dehumanized — which invite questions of authorship. Choose the explanatory language of the *Law* decision which has been reduced to manipulable shorthand such as "actual need," "ameliorative purpose," "dignity." Iacobucci J.'s explanations of the factors and his efforts at explaining second class status are far more concrete than what has been made of them.

I think LEAF should intervene whenever decisions in the courts below have incorporated formalist logic. We should appeal to other interveners to abjure similarly situate arguments, even when they hold out the prospect of succeeding. Failing that, LEAF should be prepared to counter formal equality interventions with substantive arguments and not only remind all levels of courts that the Supreme Court has decisively repudiated a formal equality approach to section 15, but explain what that means in the particular case. Among other things, I think LEAF should seek cases that would allow us to argue why enumerated grounds should presumptively apply only to those who have been subordinated on that ground.[67] Men, for instance, would only have standing to make a claim on the ground of sex, if they can establish how a sex-based assignment of benefits or penalties shores up male (or race or ageist or heterosexist) domination.

Most importantly, our advocacy practice must illuminate how particular discriminatory effects on particular dispossessed/disempowered communities reinforce the power, resources, and systemically ascribed superiority of particular, named dominant groups. As well, we must anticipate and prepare to deconstruct supremacist thinking and expend as much effort and intelligence illuminating unequal laws' benefits to the dominant as we do explaining their inequality reinforcing effects on oppressed communities.

This approach has implications for other strategic advocacy issues. I would not depart from a focus on grounds. We need the grounds to illuminate who oppresses whom systematically.[68] The focus should be on how a law reinforces structural inequalities in two directions, by further dispossessing those already deprived by specific relations of oppression — male domination, white supremacy, ablism, heterosexism, etc. — while increasing the unjust enrichment of the oppressor group(s). I would urge that a deference approach at the section 1 stage is never appropriate once a law has been shown to worsen the inequality of any disempowered community in a way that furthers enforced supremacy of the corresponding dominant group(s). In my view, resisting advocacy and adjudication air-brushed by abstraction for the bluntest, most discomforting subjects and verbs of domination holds the only promise of unseating privileged innocence and/or privileged evasions of the substantivism the Court purports to espouse on the bench.

ENDNOTES

1 *Canadian Charter of Rights and Freedoms*, Part I of the *Constitution Act, 1982*, being Schedule B to the *Canada Act 1982* (UK), 1982, c.11.

2 *Andrews v. Law Society of British Columbia*, [1989] 1 S.C.R. 143 [*Andrews*]. The Court has specifically described its approach to s. 15 as "substantive" in *Eldridge v. A.G.B.C.*, [1997] 3 S.C.R. 624 at paras. 60–61 [*Eldridge*], and *Vriend v. Alberta*, [1998] 1 S.C.R. 493 at para. 83 [*Vriend*].

3 *Law v. Canada (Minister of Employment and Immigration)*, [1999] 1 S.C.R. 497 [*Law*].

4 In this respect I agree with Donna Greschner, "Does *Law* Advance the Cause of Equality?" (2001) 27 Queen's L. J. 299 at 306: "the mere possibility of shrinkage in the scope of s. 15 cannot by itself justify rejecting the *Law* approach." A substantive approach is necessarily narrowing by contrast with a formal equality approach which would require all differential treatment to be justified under s. 1.

5 Arbour J. offers this view of the inappropriateness of deference to state justifications of infringements of s. 15 articulated in *Lavoie v. Canada*, [2002] 1 S.C.R. 769 at paras. 90 and 91 [*Lavoie*].

6 See Frederick Lee Morton & Rainer Knopff, *The Charter Revolution and the Court Party* (Peterborough: Broadview Press, 2000); Anthony Peacock, "Strange Brew: Toqueville, Rights, and the Technology of Equality" and Karen Selick, "Rights and Wrongs in the Canadian Charter" in Anthony Peacock, ed., *Rethinking the Constitution: Perspectives on Constitutional Reform, Interpretation, and Theory* (Toronto: Oxford University Press, 1995); and Patrick James, Donald Abelson, & Michael Lusztig, "Introduction: The Myth of the Sacred in the Canadian Constitutional Order" and Anthony Peacock, "Judicial Rationalism and the Therapeutic Constitution: The Supreme Court's Reconstruction of Equality and Democratic Process under the Charter of Rights and Freedoms," both in Patrick James *et al.*, *The Myth of the Sacred: The Charter, The Courts and the Politics of the Constitution in Canada* (Montreal & Kingston: McGill-Queen's University Press, 2002).

7 *Andrews*, above note 2, judgment of McIntyre J. at 164–69.

8 *Ibid.* at 152. McIntyre J. also urged an examination of context without using that term at 168: "Consideration must be given to the content of the law, to its purpose, and its impact upon those to whom it applies, and also upon those whom it excludes from its application."

9 *Ibid.* at 178–79.

10 See (1986), 27 D.L.R. (4th) 600 at 605 & 610, quoted and rejected by McIntyre J. in *Andrews, ibid.*, at 179.

11 *Andrews, ibid.* at 177–78. By limiting s. 15(1) to cover discriminatory distinctions only, *Andrews* narrowed the scope of the guarantee and increased the burden on claimants at the threshold level to prove substantive discrimination, not merely distinction-drawing. At the same time, although it prevented the state from having to defend every legal distinction some citizen decides to challenge, it also made satisfaction of the s. 1 onus more challenging. *Canadian Bill of Rights* precedent had established that no more than a rational basis would be required to justify ordi-

nary statutory line-drawing among citizens. Where "discrimination" means more than mere distinction, and is associated with adverse effects on grounds which, as McIntyre J. phrased it, "reflect the most common and probably the most socially destructive and historically practised bases of discrimination" (*Andrews* at 175), more stringent judicial scrutiny of government line-drawing will follow — so long as the definition of "discrimination" conforms to the substantive approach. I think this is a good thing.

12   *Ibid.* at 154. McIntyre J. offered the more abstract statement of purpose that continues to be cited in post-*Law* judgments at 171: the purpose of s. 15 is "the promotion of a society in which all are secure in the knowledge that they are recognized at law as human beings equally deserving of concern, respect and consideration."

13   See the intervention Factum of the Women's Legal Education and Action Fund (LEAF) for the *Andrews* appeal in Women's Legal Education and Action Fund, *Equality and the Charter: Ten Years of Feminist Advocacy Before the Supreme Court of Canada* (Toronto: Emond Montgomery, 1996) at paras. 23, 33–35, 50, 51, & 55. LEAF argued that the history of the *Charter*'s equality guarantees shows that:

> they were intended to benefit individuals and groups which historically have had unequal access to social and economic resources, either because of overt discrimination or because of the adverse effects of apparently neutral forms of social organization premised on the subordination of certain groups and the dominance of others. In this factum, we refer to these intended beneficiaries as the powerless, the excluded, the disadvantaged.

As I argue below, I would urge non-passive language that links powerlessness, exclusion, and disadvantage to acts, policies, and systems by and in the interests of specific dominant groups.

14   *Andrews*, above note 2, McIntyre J. at 180, Wilson J. at 152, and La Forest J. at 195.

15   *Ibid.* at 174.

16   See the observation of Wilson J. in both *McKinney v. University of Guelph,* [1990] 3 S.C.R. 229 at 392–93 and *R. v. Turpin,* [1989] 1 S.C.R. 1296 at 1331–32 that a determination of whether identical treatment or differential treatment is discrimination requires a search for disadvantage that exists apart from the legal distinction being challenged. See also Lamer J.'s analysis in *R. v. Swain,* [1991] 1 S.C.R. 933 at 992 stating that the purpose of s. 15 is "to remedy or prevent discrimination against groups subject to stereotyping, historical disadvantage and political and social prejudice in Canadian society."

17   *Egan v. Canada,* [1995] 2 S.C.R. 513 [*Egan*].

18   *Ibid.* at para. 11. Donna Greschner has pointed out a similar weakness in the third contextual factor of the *Law* test. Competent counsel can construe most (non-penal) statutes to have an ameliorative purpose for someone. See above note 4 at 311.

19   *Law*, above note 3 at para. 88.

20   In *Vriend*, above note 2 at paras. 99–100, the Court held that state inaction that resulted in denying gay and lesbian targets of discrimination the protection of otherwise comprehensive human rights legislation sends "a strong and sinister message"

tantamount "to condoning or even encouraging discrimination against lesbians and gay men."

21 As Debra McAllister sums it up, "The more subjective the [s. 15] test is, the more unpredictable litigation becomes. Further, the pre-existing case law becomes less helpful as a roadmap for future litigation.... Human dignity, it seems, is very much in the eye of the beholder, and therefore may be of little assistance in identifying discrimination." See "Section 15: The Unpredictability of the *Law* Test" (2003) 15 N.J.C.L. 35 at 36–37. Greschner, above note 4 at 312–13, is more blunt: "Dignity becomes an assertion, not an analysis. To ask whether a law offends 'dignity' gives precious little guidance to litigators and judges; conclusions about dignity become masks for the exercise of judicial discretion." For other cautions about the vagueness and malleability of human dignity as the measure of whether a legal distinction infringes s. 15, see Sheilah Martin, "Balancing Individual Rights to Equality and Social Goals" (2001) 80 Can. Bar Rev. 299 at 329; Sonia Lawrence, "Harsh, Perhaps Even Misguided: Developments in *Law*, 2002" (2003) 20 S.C.L.R (2d) 93 at 96–100; Christopher Bredt & Adam Dodek, "Breaking *Law*'s Grip on Equality: A New Paradigm for Section 15" (2003) 20 S.C.L.R. (2d) 33 at 45–47; and Michelle Boivin, "Le besoin urgent d'un nouveau cadre conceptual en matière de droits à l'égalité (2004) 45 C. de D. 327 at 335.

22 On this point, I believe June Ross and I disagree. See "A Flawed Synthesis of the Law" (2000) 11:3 Const. Forum 74.

23 *Lavoie v. Canada*, [2002] 1 S.C.R. 769 is surely the most dramatic example of the incoherence of post-*Law* equality jurisprudence. Four judges (Bastarache, Gonthier, Iacobucci, and Major JJ.) held that slightly preferential treatment of Canadian citizens over non-citizens in access to certain federal public service jobs made non-citizens *feel* slighted and so infringed s. 15(1), but was constitutionally defensible as a reasonable means of enhancing the significance of citizenship as a unifying bond for Canadians and of promoting naturalization by permanent residents. Three judges (McLachlin, L'Heureux-Dubé, and Binnie JJ.) held the preference to be clear discrimination that could not be justified. In their view it bore no rational connection to its two purposes: "... we fail to see how the value of Canadian citizenship can in any way be enhanced by a law that the majority concedes discriminates against non-citizens.... The notion that a trivial advantage, secured at the cost of violating s. 15(1)'s equality guarantee, could enhance citizenship, is difficult for us to fathom" (para. 11). Arbour J. found no infringement of s. 15 on the basis that the reasonable non-citizen would not consider her essential human dignity diminished by a preference adopted in many western democracies. However, having urged a high threshold for a finding of discrimination, Arbour J. then noted that the burden on government to justify equality infringements should also be high. She emphasized in *obiter* that had she found the distinction between citizens and non-citizens discriminatory, she would not have found it justified for the reasons advanced by the government. LeBel J. showed a degree of disdain for the complainant's discrimination claim, and, *obiter*, insisted that had he found an infringement, he would have adopted the deferential stance of the Bastarache quartet at the s. 1 stage, not Arbour's far more

rigorous scrutiny. In sum, the judgment offers four completely distinct appraisals of the preference ranging from LeBel (not remotely discriminatory, and, anyway, easily justified) to Arbour (not discriminatory, but once found discriminatory, hard to justify), to the Bastarache group (barely discriminatory, but easily justified), to the McLachlin group (seriously discriminatory and impossible to justify). Sonia Lawrence has observed that *Lavoie* exposes the "deep divisions" on the Court about "the proper application of the section 15 analysis as set out in *Law*, the correct approach to section 1, and the appropriate relation between the two." See "Section 15(1) at the Supreme Court 2001–2002: Caution and Conflict in Defining 'The Most Difficult Right'" (2002) 16 S.C.L.R. 103 at 115.

24 The claimant will have to persuade the court of the irrelevance or irrationality or disproportionately adverse effects of the lines drawn either at s. 15(1) or s. 1. Precedent suggests that the outcome is not going to turn on who prevails in the event the arguments for and against the government produce a tie such that the onus of proof determines the matter.

25 *Corbiére v. Canada (Minister of Indian and Northern Affairs)*, [1998] 2 S.C.R. 203.

26 In *Gosselin v. Quebec*, [2002] 4 S.C.R. 429 [*Gosselin*], the majority, in my view, complacently ignored empirical data on actual need and embraced pernicious stereotypes about undeserving welfare and about (poor) persons with disabilities. Four dissenting judges and most commentators on the decision share my view. See, for example, Natasha Kim & Tina Piper, "*Gosselin v. Quebec*: Back to the Poorhouse" (2003) McGill L.J. 749.

27 I would argue, for instance, that eligibility criteria challenged by Nancy Law did not infringe s. 15. Assisting older or disabled widows and widows with dependent children through survivor benefits unavailable to a thirty-year-old, able-bodied, and childless widow does not strike me as an injury to the latter's human dignity. Nor do I view the generalizations about labour force opportunities underlying the benefits to have been premised on or reinforcing of negative stereotypes about young, able-bodied, childless women. Professor Baines would disagree. See "*Law v. Canada*: Formatting Equality" (2000) 11:3 Const. Forum 65.

28 For empirical demonstrations, see James Kelly, "The *Charter of Rights and Freedoms* and the Rebalancing of Liberal Constitutionalism in Canada, 1982–1997" (1999) 37 Osg. Hall L.J. 625, and Sujit Choudhry & Claire Hunter, "Measuring Judicial Activism on the Supreme Court of Canada: A Comment on *Newfoundland (Treasury Board) v. NAPE*" (2003) 48 McGill L.J. 525. For a critique of the way that the "doctrine" of deference is deployed in *Charter* cases, see Guy Davidov, "The Paradox of Judicial Deference" (2001) 12 N.J.C.L. 133 arguing that a review of the cases reveals that "[t]here is no way of telling when deference will be used, nor what impact it will have in a given case. It is an open-ended doctrine used by the courts to justify any decision whatsoever" (at 163).

29 Martin, above note 21 at 347–61. Martin analyzed forty-two cases decided by the year 2000. No s. 15(1) breach was found in thirty-one cases. Of the eleven cases where an infringement of s. 15(1) was found, the breach was saved under s. 1 in only three cases (all three upheld mandatory retirement provisions). Of the twelve cases

decided since Martin's article, no infringement of s. 15 was found in seven, and two of the five infringements were found justified under s. 1. For a dispiriting analysis of where s. 15 claims founder, especially since the *Law* decision, see Bruce Ryder, Cidalia Faria, & Emily Lawrence, "What's *Law* Good For? An Empirical Overview of Charter Equality Rights Decisions" (2004) 24 S.C.L.R. (2d) 103. It should be noted that *Newfoundland v. NAPE*, [2004] 3 S.C.R. 381 [*NAPE*], adopts deference in determining that Newfoundland could justify unilateral revocation of pay equity payments undertaken to remedy its discriminatory wage practices.

30 Justice Arbour takes this view in *Lavoie*, above note 5.

31 Dianne Pothier has helpfully illuminated this in the context of under-inclusive legislation in "The Sounds of Silence: *Charter* Application when the Legislature Declines to Speak" (1996) 7:4 Const. Forum 114.

32 The classic formalism of *Bliss v. Canada (AG)*, [1979] 1 S.C.R. 183 was explicitly repudiated by the Supreme Court of Canada in *Andrews*, above note 2 at 166–67. It re-emerged in the majority decisions of the BC Court of Appeal in *Eldridge v. B.C.* (1995), 125 D.L.R. (4th) 323 and of the Alberta Court of Appeal in *Vriend v. Alberta* (1996), 132 D.L.R. (4th) 604, and was, again, explicitly repudiated: see *Eldridge*, and *Vriend,* both above note 2. It has now re-emerged in *Trociuk v. B.C.*, [2003] 1 S.C.R. 835.

33 *Egan*, above note 17; *Thibaudeau v. Canada*, [1995] 2 S.C.R. 627 [*Thibaudeau*]; and *Miron v. Trudel*, [1995] 2 S.C.R. 418.

34 For instance, in Justice Gonthier's s. 15 analysis in *M. v. H.*, [1999] 2 S.C.R. 3, and in Chief Justice McLachlin's decision in *Gosselin*, above note 26. For a sharp criticism of the latter, see Lawrence, above note 21, at 100–4.

35 See, for example, *Gosselin, ibid.*; *Hodge v. Canada*, [2004] 3 S.C.R. 357; and *NAPE*, above note 29.

36 Richard Epstein, "A Common Law for Labor Relations: A Critique of the New Deal Labor Legislation" (1983) 92 Yale L.J. 1357.

37 Arch-formalists like Ted Morton and Rainer Knopff, for instance, describe systemic inequality as a "theory" popular among feminists, and refer to the substantive equality jurisprudence launched with the *Andrews* decision as "the feminist version" of s. 15. See *The Charter Revolution and the Court Party,* above note 6 at 68 and 126–27.

38 See Catharine McKinnon, "Difference and Dominance" in *Feminism Unmodified: Discourses on Life and Law* (Cambridge: Harvard University Press, 1987) at 32–45 and *Toward a Feminist Theory of the State* (Cambridge: Harvard University Press, 1989) at 157–70. MacKinnon was part of the LEAF National Legal Committee that conceptualized and drafted LEAF's *Andrews* factum.

39 See Sheila McIntyre, "Backlash against Equality: The 'Tyranny' of the 'Politically Correct'" (1993) 38 McGill L.J. 1 at 26–35.

40 Catharine MacKinnon, *Toward a Feminist Theory of the State*, above note 38 at 163 & 162.

41 See *Vriend v. Alberta* (1996), above note 32.

42 *Thibaudeau*, above note 33, may be an exception. All aboriginal claims pose a much more direct threat of court-ordered reparations for wrongful expropriation. The outcry from non-aboriginal people when such claims succeed exemplifies the worst

of formalist and supremacist logic. See for example the outcry that followed *R. v. Marshall*, [1999] 3 S.C.R. 456. See also *R. v. Kapp*, [2004] B.C.J. No. 1440 (S.C.) reviewing history of legal challenges by non-aboriginal fishing interests of legal recognition of aboriginal fishing rights and rejecting characterization of such rights as racially discriminatory against white fishers.

43 To the extent income inequality correlates with membership in one or more subordinated groups, a remedy producing higher taxes would be redistributive but not as obviously as, say, workplace hiring quotas or restitution for lands and resources wrongfully expropriated from Canada's First Nations.

44 *Egan*, above note 17 (Lamer, Gonthier, & Major JJ. concurring). The same supremacism permeates Justice La Forest's opinion in *Canada v. Mossop*, [1993] 1 S.C.R. 554 (Lamer, Sopinka, & Iacobucci JJ. concurring). Yet La Forest J. exposed the ablism of the formalist logic of the BC Court of Appeal in *Eldridge,* above note 2, while Iacobucci J. split from La Forest J., Lamer J., and Sopinka J. in *Egan.* This is to say that a given privileged individual may be inconsistent in manifesting supremacist reasoning and values

45 La Forest J. rationalizes the denial of old-age poverty relief to same-sex couples as a measure designed to promote heterosexual marriage which, "from time immemorial" in "our" legal, philosophical, and religious traditions has been of "fundamental importance" as a social institution due to the biological and social realities that heterosexual couples have the "unique" ability to procreate and produce and nurture most [of our] children. The s. 15 majority contests the empirical accuracy of these claims. They also contest the analytic incoherence of injecting the first two legs of the s. 1 analysis into s. 15.

46 Justice Cory's s. 15 analysis does not engage Justice La Forest's s. 15 reasoning at all. Only Justice L'Heureux Dubé's solo concurrence criticizes the potential of the "relevance" test to enable intentionally discriminatory state purposes to be found not to infringe s. 15(1). See *Egan,* above note 17 at paras. 43–45.

47 Williams, *The Alchemy of Race and Rights: Diary of a Law Professor* (Cambridge: Harvard University Press, 1991) at 120–21.

48 See quote in text at note 36 above.

49 Mary Louise Fellows & Sherene Razack, "The Race to Innocence: Confronting Hierarchical Relations Among Women" (1998) 1 J. of Gender, Race & Justice 335. See also Sherene Razack, *Looking White People in the Eye: Gender, Race, and Culture in Courtrooms and Clasrooms* (Toronto: University of Toronto Press, 1998) at 3–22.

50 Sheila McIntyre, "Studied Ignorance and Privileged Innocence: Keeping Equity Academic" (2000) 12 C.J.W.L. 147.

51 *Ibid.* at 170–74, for the parallel deformations generated by systemic devaluation and deprivation and by systemic validation and entitlement.

52 *R. v. Ewanchuk*, [1999] 1 S.C.R. 330. See Constance Backhouse, "The Chilly Climate for Women Judges: Reflections on the Backlash from the *Ewanchuk* Case" (2003) 15 C.J.W.L. 167; Hester Lessard, "Farce or Tragedy? Judicial Backlash and Justice McClung" (1999) 10 Const. Forum 65; and Sheila McIntyre, "Personalizing the Political and Politicizing the Personal: Understanding Justice McClung and His

Defenders" in Elizabeth Sheehy, ed., *Adding Feminism to Law: The Contributions of Justice Claire L'Heureux-Dubé* (Toronto: Irwin Law Inc., 2004) at 309.

53 The *Gosselin* decision seems to bear this out. See Shelagh Day & Gwen Brodsky, "The Denial of the Means of Subsistence as an Equality Violation" in this volume. See, too, Natasha Kim & Tina Piper, above note 26, particularly at 767–68.

54 Denise Réaume, "Indignities: Making a Place for Dignity in Modern Legal Thought" (2002) 28 Queen's L.J. 61 at ¶44.

55 *Ibid.* at ¶45.

56 Claire L'Heureux-Dubé, "Conversations on Equality" (1999) 26 Man. L.J. 273 at §23.

57 I mean phrases like "sometimes identical treatment will produce inequality" and "the essence of true equality is accommodation of difference" and "mere distinction does not amount to discrimination."

58 *Symes v. Canada*, [1993] 4 S.C.R. 695.

59 See note 32, above.

60 See note 2, above.

61 In my view, the Court's decision in *Eldridge*, was not nearly critical enough of the cravenness of the discriminatory conduct of the BC agencies responsible for delivery of medical services. It is not simply that the government refused to provide a relatively tiny amount of funding for a medical service necessary to deaf citizens, it is that they did so, in part, to forestall the risks of a more costly discrimination claim by non-English speaking groups. La Forest J. had nothing harsher to say about this calculating discrimination than that it should be rejected as "conjectural," and then ordered a fairly deferential remedy (figure out how best to deliver sign interpretation services and implement them within six months). The *Vriend* decision refused to pronounce on whether Alberta had intentionally discriminated; refused to repudiate the s. 1 arguments offered by Alberta as both dishonest and discriminatory; disregarded Alberta's remedies arguments to the effect that the Court should not assume the province would prefer sexual orientation be read in than that the entire human rights act be struck down; and refused the invitation of the Canadian Association of Human Rights Agencies to censure Justice McClung's homophobic and anti-egalitarian outbursts in the Alberta Court of Appeal. The Court also engaged Alberta's state's rights arguments and Justice McClung's attacks on judicial activism as if they were sincere, rather than metaphors for indulging heterosexist and anti-substantivist ideology. In the result, the escalation of state-sanctioned gay and lesbian bashing was legitimated as a defence of provincial rights and judicial neutrality. Justice McClung's homophobic remarks were ultimately criticized by the Canadian Judicial Council. See Canadian Judicial Council, "Panel expresses strong disapproval of McClung conduct," News release and reasons in relation to complaints against Justice McClung, May 21, 1999, online: www.cjc-ccm.gc.ca/english/news_releases/1999_05_21.htm.

62 See for example F.L. Morton, "Canada's Judge Bork: Has the Counter-Revolution Begun?" (1996) 7:4 Const. Forum 121 (praising Justice McClung's "attacks on Canada's new imperial judiciary" in the Alberta Court of Appeal decision against Vriend's equality claim); Morton & Knopff, above note 6, at 15–19, 68; Anthony Peacock,

"Judicial Rationalism," above note 6; and Kent Roach, *The Supreme Court on Trial: Judicial Activism or Democratic Dialogue* (Toronto: Irwin Law, 2001) 85–88, 195–96, 202.

63 See Factum for *Seaboyer and Gayme v. The Queen,* in *Equality and the Charter,* above note 13 at 190.

64 See Factum for *Winnipeg Child and Family Services v. G.(D.F.),* online: www.leaf. ca/legal-facta.html.

65 See Facta for *Auton v. B.C.* and *Falkiner v. Ontario* at LEAF website, *ibid.*

66 Sherene Razack, *Looking White People in the Eye,* above note 49 at 10.

67 This would entail challenging some of the *dicta* in *Trociuk,* above note 32.

68 I share Dianne Pothier's views on this point. See Pothier, "Connecting Grounds of Discrimination to Real People's [*sic*] Real Experiences" (2001) 13 C.J.W.L. 37.

four

Discrimination and Dignity

Denise G. Réaume[1]

A. INTRODUCTION

Canadian equality jurisprudence in the *Charter*[2] era has been marked from the beginning by its rejection of a formal equality approach in favour of the pursuit of substantive equality. However, it has turned out to be easier to avoid a pure formal equality approach than to articulate the substance of substantive equality. If the guarantee of equality is to go beyond the Dicean objective of ensuring that all those covered by the terms of a rule receive the benefit of inclusion, there must be criteria determining when statutory distinctions between persons are legitimate and when they are not. The development of these criteria presents not only significant conceptual difficulties but, perhaps more importantly, moral and political ones. Equality should not be an empty ideal, but if we expect the courts to supervise the various distributive tasks that occupy the modern state, how should *they* distribute benefits and burdens?

The right to equality[3] is not like other constitutional rights. With the right to vote, to free expression, to a fair trial, or to freedom from unreasonable search, we can readily identify a human interest or cluster of interests that lies at the heart of the right which guides judicial interpretation of its contours. This is not to say that there is no controversy about the understanding and scope of these interests, but at least the participants in the debate are working from the same map. By contrast, it is not clear that we have any handle on what human interest underlies the right to equality.

Without one, Dicey's pull is likely to be strong, and equality protections will do little more than correct glaring deviations from the terms of statutory rules themselves. Developing a conception of such an interest should help in formulating appropriate obligations to impose on government to secure that interest.

In this article, I examine the recent efforts of the Supreme Court of Canada to develop a substantive conception of equality through the invocation of the value of human dignity. The process of naming dignity as the touchstone of equality analysis has been laborious. The process of giving that concept some meaningful content stands as perhaps the most significant challenge facing the Court in the coming years. This turn toward dignity in Canadian equality jurisprudence has come in for a great deal of criticism.[4] Dignity is said to be vague to the point of vacuous and, therefore, too easily useable to dress up decisions based on nothing more than conservative gut reaction or excessive deference to Parliament. Recent cases[5] might be thought to bear out this criticism. There is no doubt that dignity can be used as an empty place-holder for other less presentable reasons for finding or refusing to find a violation of equality. But since I shall argue that *some* substantive interest or value must underpin section 15 if it is to have any critical bite at all, the job of articulating that interest cannot be avoided.[6] Although a great deal of work needs to be done in fleshing out a concept of dignity capable of filling this role, the Court is on the right track in latching onto dignity as the substantive concept informing equality rights. Rather than join the critics, I propose to work with what has already been said about what dignity means to see what constructive work it might do.[7]

B. PUTTING THE "SUBSTANCE" IN SUBSTANTIVE EQUALITY

The disappointing results of adjudication under the equal rights clause of the *Canadian Bill of Rights*[8] led to a concerted push after 1982 and the enactment of the *Charter of Rights and Freedoms* to convince the Supreme Court to abandon a formal equality approach in favour of "substantive equality."[9] But what exactly is the substance in substantive equality? To get a handle on this we must go back to the basics. Equality rights are a means of challenging the existing distribution of some benefit or burden.[10] The point of a claim is to make an argument that some other principle of entitlement, wider in at least some respect than that used by the legislature, is the appropriate criterion for distribution of the benefit at issue.[11] Every distribution requires the setting of criteria that govern that distribution. Defining criteria in a rule automatically gives rise to a form of equality — anyone who has not received the benefit but fulfills the criteria has not been treated equally.[12] In this sense, equality is a side-effect or by-product of the proper application of any rule, whatever that rule is. The disappointment in the *Canadian Bill of Rights* jurisprudence arose out of the Supreme Court's tendency fairly automatically to accept as justified the criteria provided by the legislation under challenge — equality was conceived of as a matter of treating likes alike and the legislation itself was allowed to determine what counted as alike for its purposes. This idea is what has been labeled "formal equality" — it is received wisdom in Canada now that this is not good enough as an approach to section 15.[13]

If the legislature's criteria for distribution are unsatisfactory, what should replace them? What would a vision of substantive equality require? Substantive equality pays attention to the actual conditions of life of members of disadvantaged groups — rules creating, or exacerbating, or perhaps simply not correcting background inequalities should be changed,[14] even if they distribute some benefit equally within their own four corners. Such an approach requires a theory as to which background conditions of inequality require attention in our society, which in turn requires an account of the respects in which people should be equal. In other words, we need to know what underlying universal entitlements there are — what goods or benefits each person is entitled to share in. Once these are known, equality inheres in applying the principles that govern those entitlements. If every person is entitled to the satisfaction of her needs, then someone whose needs are not satisfied has not been treated equally; if every person is entitled to the means of subsistence, then someone who is lacking those means is not being treated equally, etc. More concrete rules providing access to pension benefits or medical attention, for instance, can be assessed according to whether they are conducive to the satisfaction of needs or the provision of the means of subsistence, etc. Thus, substantive equality appeals to some set of underlying principles specifying a range of benefits that are properly distributed universally.[15] Its conception of equality is just as formal as that which flows from accepting the legislature's criteria at face value; it simply relies on different criteria for allocation of specific benefits — criteria ultimately justified by reference to underlying universal entitlements.

Indeed, any approach to the adjudication of equality rights that does not simply insist on the application of the challenged legislation according to its own terms must ultimately rely on an argument that an alternative criterion of distribution is better than the one provided by the legislature. This is true even of approaches that focus exclusively on assessing the adequacy of the legislative distinction as a means of achieving legislative objectives.[16] In the first instance, this approach hinges on determining the legislative objective, a matter that can itself be a matter of controversy and which is merely an oblique way of prescribing criteria for the distribution of the benefit in issue. An objective of alleviating poverty will carry different implications for the distribution of social assistance than an objective of encouraging self-sufficiency. Furthermore, if there is to be any room to challenge the legitimacy of the legislative objective (without which we are back to Dicey), these will hinge on some argument that there is some universal principle of entitlement, some respect in which people are entitled to be treated equally, which is not satisfied by the actual objective.

In other words, the truly substantive question in the context of how to distribute various goods is that of determining the proper criteria for each benefit likely to come up for distribution in a modern society, taking into account the need to redress existing inequalities. The task is a daunting one, considered comprehensively, quickly leading us into debates about whether it is the proper province of the judiciary. While dramatic redistribution in various ways is undoubtedly called for in our society, it remains intensely controversial what is the best comprehensive theory of distributive justice.[17] Grappling with this question is the central concern of government. To make sense of *Charter* equality provisions, we must articulate a role for the courts in assessing distributive criteria that allows for critically assessing existing criteria, but does not simply shift full responsibility for such distributive questions from the legislature to the courts.

Thus, a substantive equality approach to the adjudication of constitutional equality claims must be a principled approach to determining when the legislature has mistaken the principle of entitlement appropriate to some benefit, an approach that provides a reason for widening the criteria of entitlement at least somewhat. I am not sure this yields a different conception of equality — that is, a "substantive" one — but it does suggest that we look for a substantive foundation for equality analysis — a set of values or human interests that can tell us when and why entitlement criteria are too narrow, given the benefit in issue. We do not have ready to hand a comprehensive theory of the interests that ground universal entitlements. We should expect, then, that courts will proceed cautiously in assessing the adequacy of existing criteria for distribution of benefits. As they deal with cases, one by one, they should be feeling their way toward the articulation of universal entitlements which can be regarded as foundational and against which legislation can be assessed.

The survey of Canadian equality jurisprudence sketched in the next section shows the Supreme Court gradually coming to the realization that if legislative criteria cannot be accepted at face value, there must be some substantive value capable of telling us which criteria are illegitimate, why, and what they should be replaced with. The jurisprudence has finally settled on the interest in dignity as the underlying value. The identification of human dignity as a value operates as the basis for the articulation of a universal entitlement to respect for that dignity. The distribution of concrete benefits can therefore be judged according to whether they are consistent with the respect each is equally owed. This allows the courts to begin to develop a more comprehensive theory of equality suitable to enforcement through constitutional rights protections. In some measure, virtually everyone will agree that the dignity of each person should be respected. Through grappling with the specific issues raised by the cases, we can hope that the concept of dignity will grow organically in accordance with our best critically reflective judgments about what is most important to people, as individuals, as members of communities, and as participants in society. In participating in this process, courts will be contributing to the ongoing debate about the role of equality in our political culture.

C. FUMBLING TOWARD DIGNITY: THE FIRST DECADE OF EQUALITY JURISPRUDENCE

Even in *Andrews v. Law Society of British Columbia*,[18] the Supreme Court's first attempt to provide a test for the violation of section 15(1), some implicit grasp of the need for a substantive foundation for equality rights is only dimly apparent. *Andrews* struck down a provision restricting access to the British Columbia Bar to Canadian citizens. Andrews was a British subject who had immigrated to Canada and was faced with a three-year hiatus in his legal career while he waited for his residency period to pass before he was eligible to become a Canadian citizen. In quickly pointing out that not every legislative distinction is discriminatory, requiring justification under section 1 to be upheld,[19] the Court gestured toward the need for criteria to distinguish discriminatory distinctions from non-discriminatory ones.

In one move apparently designed to respond to this need, the Court declared that courts should have regard to the *impact* of legislation on those affected in determining whether there is discrimination. This assertion was hailed as a major victory by those desperate to ensure that section 15 jurisprudence not collapse into the aridity of formal equality.[20] However, since every piece of legislation has some impact which leaves some better off than others (just as all legislation distinguishes between classes of persons), an injunction to have regard to impact merely pushes the inquiry back one level — what kind of impact discriminates, or inflicts a "real" disadvantage, and what kind does not?

The Court's initial answer to this question focused on whether the distinction used is based on a "special characteristic" of the claimant. This close attention to the basis of the legislative distinction, labeled the "grounds approach," suggests that tying a burden to certain personal characteristics itself constitutes the sort of impact about which section 15 is concerned. An approach of this sort is straightforward as long as the personal characteristics whose use is illegitimate are clear. Section 15 lists several such characteristics, but in *Andrews* itself the Court decided that this list is not exhaustive — other discriminatory grounds could be added on the basis of their analogous character. Treating the list as open-ended requires some means of determining what makes an unlisted characteristic analogous. To provide a deeper foundation for this approach, we need a theory about why some grounds are enumerated in the *Charter* as potentially problematic bases for legislative distinctions or effects, which can, in turn, provide a basis for declaring other, unmentioned grounds to be analogous. The need for a substantive foundation was not initially widely realized. Instead, many seemed to assume that necessary and sufficient conditions for the recognition of analogous grounds could be produced through a purely conceptual analysis of the common features of the grounds listed in section 15.[21] That has turned out to be a false hope, as the search for conceptual solutions to normative questions usually is.

For a brief moment in the wake of *Andrews*, without a great deal of thought having been given to what makes a new ground analogous, it looked as though the Court was going to define equality rights exclusively in terms of an expandable list of "special characteristics" which were to be treated simply as prohibited bases for legislative distinction. The rule coming out of *Andrews*, and evidently relied on soon after in *McKinney v. University of Guelph*,[22] has typically been summarized as holding that a claimant may

establish discrimination by showing disadvantage based on a ground enumerated in section 15 or analogous thereto, whether by explicit design or in
effect.[23] It soon became clear, though, that the Court not only did not want
to render every legislative distinction unconstitutional (subject to section 1
rescue), it did not even want to rule out every distinction *explicitly* relying
on an enumerated ground.[24] Thus some further argument is needed to determine when use of a characteristic is justified even though it is on the list
of protected characteristics. In other words, the Court quickly settled into
the view that only those distinctions that are based on an enumerated or
analogous ground *and are discriminatory* are prohibited by section 15. This
takes us back to the search for particular kinds of effects, as yet still unidentified and explained, that violate equality as distinguished from those that
do not, however negative their consequences.

It is frequently argued that this development in the jurisprudence has
reduced the scope of equality rights.[25] But if purely conceptual conditions
for recognizing analogous grounds are unavailable, a requirement that a
distinction be discriminatory is the natural consequence of the need for a
substantive foundation to explain when new analogous grounds should be
recognized.[26] Whatever value explains why a new ground should be added
may also provide a reason for thinking that some uses of listed grounds
do not actually conflict with that value. We cannot test this until we have
identified and fleshed out that value, a task ultimately to be carried out
using the interest in human dignity. For now, suffice it to say that the introduction of the requirement of discrimination may be less a new threshold requirement of section 15 than a matter of making explicit a condition
already present.

The two points in the analysis of section 15 at which controversy tends
to collect — which personal characteristics are illegitimate bases for legislative distinctions, and what kinds of deprivations or disadvantaging impacts constitute discrimination — mark the points at which a substantive
foundation for equality analysis is needed. We might refer to them as the
"type of distinction" lens and the "type of impact" lens for analyzing what
constitutes discrimination.[27] These two lenses will often seem two sides of
the same coin — two perspectives from which to go about deciding what
is the difference between a discriminatory and a non-discriminatory rule.
The use of a certain type of distinction constitutes a certain kind of harm;
the presence of a certain kind of harm leads us to classify certain distinctions as impermissible. As the case law has developed, the key factors in the

cases determining whether section 15 has been violated can be related to one or both of these aspects of the analysis of an equality issue. A dignity-based analysis has emerged as their ground.

In *Andrews*, a small start is made in providing the necessary substantive foundation for equality analysis. The argument operates through the lens of considering whether citizenship is a personal characteristic whose use is discriminatory. This analysis is dominated by the question of whether the exclusion based on citizenship is based on stereotype or prejudice.[28] However, the notion of stereotype is left undeveloped and does not seem to inform the analysis of why restricting citizens' access to the legal profession violates the right to equal protection and benefit of the law. Indeed, the main section 15 analysis, penned by McIntyre J., has a rather antiseptic and imprecise air.[29] There is no close examination of the stereotype detected in the legislation, nor any analysis of what makes it so wrong.[30] The judgments of Wilson and La Forest JJ. add a few more clues. Wilson J. focuses on characteristics that identify groups who "suffer social, political and legal disadvantage in our society"[31] as picking out means of classification that violate section 15. Disadvantage or vulnerability can be indicated by a group's status as a "discrete and insular minority."[32] This analysis seems to rely on an instinctive grasp of the sorts of group disadvantage that mark our society, and also assumes that these instincts are widely shared. However, we need to spell out what is meant by social, political, and legal disadvantage to make this test meaningful. As long as we are talking about blatant restrictions meant to keep people of colour or women out of certain spheres, the disadvantage may seem too clear to need much analysis. But once we move into deciding whether conditioning certain benefits on marital status, or sexual orientation, or age threatens to "bring about or reinforce ... disadvantage" in the relevant sense, different judges' intuition tends to lead them in different directions.

La Forest J. articulates a number of additional factors that help determine whether a distinction violates "fundamental values."[33] He points out that citizenship is often at least temporarily beyond the control of the individual. Although one can choose whether or not to become a citizen, the residency requirement prevents that choice from having immediate effect. Second, La Forest J. notes the close historical connection between citizenship and race, or national or ethnic origin, as bases on which myriad professions and livelihoods have in the past been denied to generations of immigrants in a clear effort to reserve the best jobs for the native-born. His depiction of the "intolerance"[34] demonstrated in earlier efforts to marginal-ize immigrants gives some life and substance to the reference to stereotype and prejudice in McIntyre J.'s judgment. Finally, he points out that citi-zenship is irrelevant to the qualifications for admission to the bar. These factors lead him to conclude that such a basis for distinction would under-mine a resident's faith in social and political institutions and confidence that "[one] can freely and without obstruction by the state pursue [one's] and [one's] families' hopes and expectations of vocational and personal de-velopment."[35] These last remarks point to "personal development," or self-fulfillment, as a human good that equality rights are designed to protect. This gives us a start in thinking about what counts as a disadvantage arising out of legislation that should attract constitutional attention. But, the state cannot be charged with the task of ensuring that all its members achieve self-fulfillment. So it is the irrelevance of the criterion used in the statute, together with its relative immutability and its use as a tool of exclusion in times past that makes this an unacceptable obstacle to self-fulfillment.[36]

The upshot of the early equality cases can be described as follows: there is something about the use of some kinds of personal characteristics that can make their use in legislative line-drawing objectionable, but it is not necessarily the case that every use of even a characteristic explicitly flagged in section 15 is discriminatory. This tells us to look for an account of what it is about the use of certain personal characteristics that constitutes discrimi-nation, or of what kinds of consequences of using such characteristics are discriminatory ones. As provided by *Andrews*, the starting point for such an account is an analysis of the consequences of prejudice and stereotype. In the early cases, disagreement tended to express itself more through the anal-ysis of whether a distinction could be justified under section 1 rather than whether it was discriminatory, with agreement on section 1 justification occasionally papering over the emergence of diverging opinions on what counts as discrimination.[37] However, this period of relative consensus about the interpretation of section 15 did not last long. Deep disagreement about the missing magic ingredient necessary to convert a characteristic into an analogous ground or to make the use of an existing ground actually dis-criminatory was needed to push the Court to further develop the possible competing accounts of the substantive value underlying equality rights.

Such disagreement surged to the surface in two cases decided on the tenth anniversary of the coming into force of section 15 in 1995:[38] *Miron v. Trudel*[39] and *Egan v. A-G. Canada*.[40] *Miron* involved a challenge to a provision of the Ontario *Insurance Act* setting out a standard term in automobile insurance contracts which entitled the spouse of a policy holder to collect under the policy for income loss due to a car accident caused by the driver of an uninsured vehicle. The legislative history of the provision made it clear that "spouse" meant married spouse, excluding common law relationships. Miron challenged this as a denial of equality. *Egan* concerned a challenge to provisions of the *Canada Pension Act* confining certain benefits to opposite sex couples (whether married or common law). Egan would otherwise have qualified for the benefit designed to top up the family income of elderly couples of whom one had retired and the other was in low-income employment, but was excluded on the basis that he and his partner were the same sex. He challenged the provision as discriminatory on the basis of sexual orientation. Neither marital status nor sexual orientation is a ground actually listed in section 15.

In both cases, the Court split three ways — four, four, and one. A bare majority found each of the provisions to be a violation of section 15,[41] with L'Heureux-Dubé J. offering separate reasons for that conclusion.[42] Within the majority on the section 15 issue, then, there were two different approaches taken in analyzing discrimination. A minority of four[43] in each case decided that the legislation was not discriminatory, adding a third approach. The judgments thereby reveal both the type of distinction lens and the type of impact lens. The minority judgment of Gonthier J. in *Miron* appeals to relevance to determine whether marital status is an analogous ground and therefore potentially discriminatory. In *Egan*, given the Attorney General's concession that sexual orientation is an analogous ground, the section 15 minority uses irrelevance directly to indicate discriminatory impact for purposes of section 15. The disagreement between the McLachlin approach and the L'Heureux-Dubé approach in favour of a finding of a section 15 violation might be described as a dispute over which of these two questions — what kinds of distinctions are discriminatory, and what kinds of effects constitute discrimination — should be the focus of analysis. In the end, both approaches appeal clearly to dignity for the first time[44] as some sort of touchstone for answering these questions.

In contrast, judgments finding no discrimination make no reference to dignity; rather, they argue that legislation violates section 15 only when the distinction used is irrelevant to the legislative objective. Working backwards from the characteristics flagged in section 15 as potentially discriminatory, Gonthier J. characterizes them as ones commonly used to make distinctions that have little or no rational connection with the subject matter and as generally reflecting stereotypes.[45] This approach claims that we can identify distinctions as discriminatory by whether the characteristic used is relevant to the statutory purpose. However, Gonthier J.'s use of the test of relevance begs the question rather than answering it. It is trite to observe that an examination of relevance is meaningless without a determination of the "functional values underlying the legislation,"[46] or more simply, the legislative objective. After all, the concept of relevance refers to the assessment of a means/ends relationship. We cannot assess whether the means are good ones without knowing what the end is. Relevance is therefore not an independent criterion for diagnosing discrimination or anything else. The relevance of a criterion for distribution will simply follow from the characterization of the end. This puts all the weight on the formulation of the legislative objective; when the statement of the objective itself is informed by discriminatory attitudes, the distinction used by the legislature is bound to pass a relevance test but still be objectionable.[47]

This is exactly what happens in Gonthier J.'s opinion in *Miron* and La Forest J.'s in *Egan*. That marriages, or at least heterosexual unions, are foundational to "civilization" is endorsed by both judges, and the legislation in both cases is taken to be a recognition of this "fundamental value."[48] A legislative distinction designed to foster, indeed to construct, a form of relationship deemed essential to civilization is, by definition, relevant to that end.[49] Although Gonthier J. explicitly recognizes that the legislature's objective may itself be discriminatory,[50] he cannot get past his own conviction that the state is entitled to foster the traditional marriage relationship long enough to consider whether that conviction might itself be grounded in prejudice against alternative family forms. He cannot see that the undoubted value of the traditional family cannot by itself justify treating other family forms as less worthy.[51] Thus, the discussion of relevance begs the central question: is it a denial of equality to bestow a legal "seal of approval" on one particular form of family? Four members of the court evidently think not, but it is not exactly clear why. An appeal to relevance alone cannot provide an answer.

This question of the proper statement of the legislature's objective is simply the issue, from a different angle, of the appropriate criteria of access to the relevant insurance and pension benefits. Some sense of the correct principle of entitlement to that benefit will flow from the characterization of the objective of distribution. The outcome of this debate will usually determine whether the distinction used in the legislation is relevant to the objectives envisioned.[52] This should remind us that the section 15 test must include reference to a substantive value capable of informing the characterization of the legislative objective in a principled manner. In other words, we need a test for when a legislative objective itself denies equality.

McLachlin J.'s judgment for four members of the majority in *Miron* approaches the question through the type of distinction lens. Her description of the purpose of section 15 as "prevent[ing] the violation of human dignity and freedom by imposing limitations, disadvantages or burdens through the stereotypical application of presumed group characteristics rather than on the basis of individual merit, capacity, or circumstance"[53] links the prohibited grounds of differentiation to dignity. This suggests that the grounds listed in section 15 were chosen because they have some connection to stereotypes falsely attributing negative attributes to members of groups identified by these characteristics, and this, in turn, violates dignity. To deny benefits on such a basis is to discriminate. To expand the list, we should look for other personal characteristics that are used to stereotype.[54] Four factors already recognized in the case law as bases for the recognition of an analogous ground are then linked to the idea of the violation of dignity: (1) the historically disadvantaged status of a group, (2) its minority status, (3) the personal nature of the characteristic relied on by the legislature, and (4) its immutable nature. These factors are not necessary and sufficient conditions for the recognition of an analogous ground, but merely indicate the larger "unifying principle"[55] of preventing the violation of human dignity. However, the link between dignity and these four factors is described only very vaguely. The "theme" of violation of dignity, she says, is "reflected in" these four qualities useful in identifying new grounds.[56] Nor does her analysis of the case at hand help draw out the link. She concludes that marital status is an analogous ground because it exhibits three of the four factors identified as markers of analogous grounds. First, the choice whether to marry or not is an important personal freedom, making married or unmarried status an important aspect of the person. Second, she notes that conjugal relationships outside of marriage have traditionally been disapproved of and therefore excluded from a host of benefits attached to marriage, giving common law couples the status of an historically disadvantaged group. Interestingly, she ties this disapproval to religious attitudes, thus suggesting that the underlying motivation is based on prejudice, but this theme is not very well developed. Finally, she notes that the option of marrying may not be open to a particular couple or may be beyond the control of any one party within a couple, lessening the mutability of the status of marriage. Having found these features applicable to the situation of being in a conjugal relationship outside of marriage, she concludes rather summarily that "[t]he essential elements necessary to engage the overarching purpose of section 15(1) — violation of dignity and freedom, an historical group disadvantage, and the danger of stereotypical group-based decision-making — are present and discrimination is made out."[57]

Thus, McLachlin J. first suggests that it is the use of stereotype that violates dignity, but then focuses on the four factors that have developed as a means of identifying analogous grounds and declares marital status to be an analogous ground based on the applicability to it of some of those factors. There is no direct analysis of how these four factors are related to the problem of stereotyping, nor how, if at all, the exclusion of common law couples in this case was grounded in stereotype. Instead, the conclusion that the legislation is discriminatory is mediated by the application of the four factors that determine whether a new ground is sufficiently analogous; they are used as a proxy for stereotyping without the connection being articulated.[58] In fact, her analysis seems to turn less on a finding that the legislature inaccurately attributed unfavourable characteristics to common law couples and more on the suggestion that the traditional disapproval of common law relationships is grounded in a religious belief that all other forms of conjugal relationship are immoral.[59] Of course, one could say that the attribution of immorality to such relationships is "inaccurate," but this just seems an oblique way of describing prejudice. Perhaps because the actual case does not turn on stereotype, as such, she does little to spell out the connection she sees between stereotype and violation of dignity.[60] The suggestion of a connection between the sorts of characteristics whose use is potentially discriminatory, the use of stereotypes, and the violation of dignity gestures toward an analysis of the grounds of discrimination in terms of a specific kind of harm done through their use, but the analysis is incomplete.[61]

L'Heureux-Dubé J. approaches the question of which distinctions constitute discrimination by trying to identify the *harm* of discrimination,[62] explicitly arguing that a focus on what characterizes the enumerated grounds and therefore identifies appropriately analogous ones obscures the central issue.[63] In *Egan* she goes so far as to treat investigating the ground of discrimination within the section 15 analysis as merely an instrument — a means of detecting discrimination as an effect rather than an independent element in the analysis.[64] Thus, she repeatedly states that discrimination is to be identified by its effects. The question is: what kinds of effects are discriminatory ones? We have already established that this cannot be answered by reference to the effect of the denial of the specific statutory benefit without making all legislative distinctions discriminatory. Although there is some slippage on this point in L'Heureux-Dubé J.'s analysis, in the final analysis she does identify some further harm marking a distinction as discriminatory in noting that the economic consequences of the legislative distinction are merely symptomatic of the crucial effect — the offence to dignity.[65] From the outset, she points to section 15's role in giving effect to the place of "inherent human dignity" at the heart of individual rights.[66]

> Equality ... means nothing if it does not represent a commitment to recognizing each person's equal worth as a human being, regardless of individual differences. Equality means that our society cannot tolerate legislative distinctions that treat certain people as second-class citizens, that demean them, that treat them as less capable for no good reason, or that otherwise offend fundamental human dignity.[67]

She goes on to cash this out in terms of an entitlement to equal concern and respect,[68] using this language repeatedly throughout her judgments on section 15.

L'Heureux-Dubé J. suggests her own two-part framework for the analysis of section 15 cases — both the nature of the group affected by the legislation and the particular interests affected should be examined. The various factors flagged elsewhere in the case law — minority status, history of bias against a group, vulnerability, constructive immutability — are relevant to deciding whether a group is at risk of having its dignity violated.[69] The nature of the concrete disadvantage imposed by the legislation is examined to see whether it is significant enough to constitute a violation of dignity. Thus, she ultimately brings together the two points in the *Andrews* analysis at which substantive grounding is needed, and ties both to the concept of dignity. The examination of the nature of the group is an effort to articulate why characteristics that mark group identity are problematic bases for legislative distinctions. The exploration of the interest affected is the means of deciding what sorts of disadvantages or burdens count as discriminatory. Ultimately, however, the important interest is respect for one's dignity, rather than interest in the specific benefit at issue, and the characteristics that are picked out as problematic are the ones whose use violates dignity.

In both *Egan* and *Miron*, the gist of L'Heureux-Dubé J.'s argument is that the restriction of the benefits at issue to opposite sex couples and married couples treats other family forms as less valuable. In *Miron* she argues that the explicit choice of marriage is one way people form intimate relationships of great personal significance to them, emotionally, socially, and economically; but, such relationships can be formed in other ways. Commitment can be expressed otherwise than through the observance of formalities, even through the gradual cumulative effect of a series of smaller decisions binding two lives. These other forms of commitment deserve equal respect from the legal system. In *Egan*, she concludes that excluding same-sex couples from the pension benefit sends the message "essentially that society considers such relationships to be less worthy of respect, concern and consideration than relationships involving members of the opposite sex."[70] In ultimately tying the interest affected to the importance of having one's significant intimate relationships recognized as legitimate, L'Heureux-Dubé J. comes closer than the rest of the Court to identifying the crux of the matter. If the benefit being distributed by the legislation is that recognition, rather than the money payable under the policy, it is hard to see how the exclusion of common law and same sex couples could be read other than as a denial of the equal worth of such relationships.

Although declining to go along with L'Heureux-Dubé J.'s simplified two-part analysis, Cory J.'s analysis in *Egan* nevertheless shares much of her essential reasoning. Cory J. appeals to dignity at two points. First, dignity is invoked to decide that denial of recognition of same sex relationships can be a denial of the equal benefit of the law even if this particular couple would not have benefited economically from being included in the pension plan provision.[71] Such denial "may have a serious detrimental impact upon the sense of self-worth and dignity of members of a group because it stigmatizes them."[72] It attributes inferiority to the excluded group and treats them as less deserving of benefits. Dignity comes up the second time to ground the argument for treating sexual orientation as an analogous ground.[73] At this stage, Cory J.'s analysis draws on some of the factors that had been relied on in past cases, but not as mechanically as McLachlin J.'s analysis does in *Miron*. Cory J. is very clear that the factors pointing to an analogous ground are not important in their own right, but are only meant to aid in determining whether the right sort of interest is at stake — the interest in dignity. Thus, like L'Heureux-Dubé J., he canvasses both the type of impact and type of distinction lenses and grounds both in dignity.[74] He outlines the various ways in which gays and lesbians have been stigmatized, harassed, and victimized in the past, including the way their intimate relationships have been stigmatized, in order to decide that they constitute a historically disadvantaged group. He then argues that the challenged provision is grounded in the stereotype that "homosexuals ... cannot and do not form lasting, caring, mutually supportive relationships with economic interdependence in the same manner as heterosexual couples."[75] Given these conclusions, it is no surprise that he holds that the exclusion of same sex couples from the pension benefit participates in the stigmatization of same sex relationships that has long characterized our society in violation of human dignity.

D. THE CRYSTALLIZATION OF DIGNITY AS THE SUBSTANTIVE FOUNDATION OF EQUALITY RIGHTS

With the decision in *Law v. Canada (Minister of Employment and Immigration)*[76] in 1999, the Supreme Court united around the identification of the missing ingredient in a successful section 15 challenge — a showing that legislation violates the human dignity of those negatively affected by its operation.[77] In reviewing the case law up to this point, Iacobucci J. highlights and ratifies the previous efforts to connect equality and dignity by McLachlin J., Cory J., and L'Heureux-Dubé J. as follows:

> the purpose of s. 15(1) is to prevent the violation of essential human dignity and freedom through the imposition of disadvantage, stereotyping, or political or social prejudice, and to promote a society in which all persons enjoy equal recognition at law as human beings or as members of Canadian society, equally capable and equally deserving of concern, respect and consideration. Legislation which effects differential treatment between individuals or groups will violate this fundamental purpose where those who are subject to differential treatment fall within one or more enumerated or analogous grounds, and where the differential treatment reflects the stereotypical application of presumed group or personal characteristics, or otherwise has the effect of perpetuating or promoting the view that the individual is less capable, or less worthy of recognition or value as a human being or as a member of Canadian society.[78]

On the meaning of dignity, Iacobucci J. has this to say:

What is human dignity? There can be different conceptions of what human dignity means .... [T]he equality guarantee in s. 15(1) is concerned with the realization of personal autonomy and self-determination. Human dignity means that an individual or group feels self-respect and self-worth. It is concerned with physical and psychological integrity and empowerment. Human dignity is harmed by unfair treatment premised upon personal traits or circumstances which do not relate to individual needs, capacities, or merits. It is enhanced by laws which are sensitive to the needs, capacities, and merits of different individuals, taking into account the context underlying their differences. Human dignity is harmed when individuals and groups are marginalized, ignored, or devalued, and is enhanced when laws recognize the full place of all individuals and groups within Canadian society. Human dignity within the meaning of the equality guarantee does not relate to the status or position of an individual in society *per se*, but rather concerns the manner in which a person legitimately feels when confronted with a particular law. Does the law treat him or her unfairly, taking into account all of the circumstances regarding the individuals affected and excluded by the law?[79]

On the basis of his survey of the past case law, Iacobucci J. reformulates the section 15 test as follows:[80]

a court that is called upon to determine a discrimination claim under s. 15(1) should make the following three broad inquiries:

(A) Does the impugned law (a) draw a formal distinction between the claimant and others on the basis of one or more personal characteristics, or (b) fail to take into account the claimant's already disadvantaged position within Canadian society resulting in substantively differential treatment between the claimant and others on the basis of one or more personal characteristics,

(B) Is the claimant subject to differential treatment based on one or more enumerated and analogous grounds, and

(C) Does the differential treatment discriminate, by imposing a burden upon or withholding a benefit from the claimant in a manner which reflects the stereotypical application of presumed group or personal characteristics, or which otherwise has the effect of perpetuating or promoting the view that the individual is less capable or worthy of recognition or value as a human being or as a member of Canadian society, equally deserving of concern, respect, and consideration?[81]

Most of the work of an equality rights analysis will be performed at the third stage of this test. Iacobucci J. collects from the past case law four categories of "contextual factors" helpful in distinguishing discriminatory from non-discriminatory legislation through demonstrating whether a legislative distinction or impact has the effect of demeaning dignity. The first of these is "pre-existing disadvantage, vulnerability, stereotyping, or prejudice experienced by the individual or group."[82] The fact that the claimant belongs to a historically disadvantaged group may indicate a longstanding failure by the legal system or social mores to extend equal concern and respect which the challenged law may perpetuate or further promote.[83] Pre-existing disadvantage is also said to be linked to stereotyping — the use of inaccurate assumptions about the merits, capabilities, and worth of an individual or group which stigmatize members of a group.[84]

The second contextual factor capable of indicating a violation of dignity asks whether the legislative distinction properly reflects the actual needs, merits and circumstances of the members of the group affected by it.[85] This factor is used to admonish Parliament not to overlook actual circumstances by laying down "one size fits all" rules that unfairly exclude vulnerable groups.[86] The third factor identified by Iacobucci J. is that of whether the legislation seeks to ameliorate the situation of a more disadvantaged group. In such circumstances, the distinction used is unlikely to be found to violate dignity.[87] Finally, Iacobucci J. adopts L'Heureux-Dubé J.'s idea, articulated in *Egan*, that a crucial factor in finding harm to dignity is an analysis of the nature of the interest affected by the legislation. This makes it clear that it is not the actual, concrete effect of the legislation that matters — not the dollars and cents or the specific opportunity, benefit, or service denied — but rather whether imposing such a cost on the individual or group implicates dignity.[88] The social and constitutional significance of the cost to the individual must be taken into account to make this decision — does it affect membership in a basic way, deny participation, or constitute a complete failure to recognize members of a particular group?[89]

These factors are all presented as indicators of when a legislative distinction violates human dignity,[90] yet the analysis of how each is related to dignity remains underdeveloped. Similarly, the four factors are said not to be either necessary or sufficient conditions for the violation of dignity, yet in subsequent cases the factors have tended to be somewhat mechanically applied. Without the relationship between the factors and dignity being fully explained, it is the factors themselves that the Court has tended to rely upon to determine the outcome of cases.

The decision in *Law* hinged on whether the use of age in determining entitlement to the survivor benefits is based on accurate generalizations. Crucial to this determination is the decision that the point of survivor benefits is to respond to the long-term income needs of surviving spouses. This leads the Court to give its stamp of approval to Parliament's assumption that surviving spouses over the age of forty-five or over thirty-five if raising children or if disabled will have a harder time making up for the loss of their spouse's income than younger and less encumbered people, and that this handicap is unlikely to diminish over time. By contrast, although a younger or less encumbered person may well experience short-term economic dislocation after a spouse's death, this is likely to diminish with time. "The challenged legislation simply reflects the fact that people in the appellant's position are more able to overcome long-term need because of the nature of a human being's life cycle."[91] Therefore, no stigma attaches to those temporarily denied the survivor benefit;[92] there is no implication that they are less worthy of concern.[93]

Law was a fairly easy case on its facts, making it possible for the Court to unite around the abstract idea that dignity is the substantive touchstone for equality analysis. Since *Law*, dignity has been used more often than not by a majority of the judges to deny equality claims,[94] giving rise to the fear amongst equality advocates that its very introduction signals a conservative turn in the jurisprudence. It bears pointing out, however, that if some substantive concept is needed to ground equality rights, that concept must be at the forefront of the analysis in any case in which a claim is to be rejected; it will be the reason why claims fail when they do. However, it should not be forgotten that it is also the reason why claims succeed. While the Court has perhaps tended to pay more attention to the concept of dignity when it is needed to deny a claim than when it serves to explain why one is upheld, its role on both sides of the argument must be fully considered in any assessment of its value in equality jurisprudence. A full analysis of whether dignity is necessarily a conservative force in equality jurisprudence would require a close analysis of its use in all the cases since *Law*. I will not undertake that analysis here, partly for the sake of brevity, but partly because I think the Court has been less than helpful in articulating the concept in such a way as to explain how it functions to justify the denial of claims. Instead, I propose to start from first principles, constructing a concept that I think is sound and grows out of the central considerations that the Court has relied on over the years to guide its decision-making. Although this concept may not take equality law as far as some might wish, it is far from an inherently conservative idea.

E. DEFINING DIGNITY

Many of the indicators of discrimination identified in the case law probe the issue through asking whether the personal characteristic used by the legislation is an acceptable basis for distinction. This, in turn, opens up the question of what sorts of harm or deprivation section 15 seeks to prevent, and that question has now been answered by saying that it is the harm of violating human dignity that section 15 protects against. It is an understanding of this harm that must drive the recognition of analogous grounds; it is equally crucial to distinguishing discriminatory uses of enumerated characteristics from non-discriminatory ones; that is, the kinds of impact on people's lives capable of grounding a section 15 claim. Harm to dignity becomes itself a kind of harm, independent of the denial of the specific benefit distributed by the legislation. We are looking, then, for distinctions and deprivations that constitute this harm. What, then, is dignity and how is it violated?

In trying to define discrimination, the early cases repeatedly returned to several themes or factors which are consciously brought together and attached to the concept of dignity in the decision in *Law*. However, the connections between dignity and the developing list of factors that indicate its violation remain elusive. I will not try, systematically, to explain or criticize all of the Canadian case law in terms of my explication of the concept of dignity. Instead, I will attempt to provide a plausible reconstruction of the most important features of the Court's analysis of equality. My aim is to show that a dignity-based analysis has the potential to give equality rights law some real substance. I do not claim that this potential has always been lived up to in the decisions to date. It follows from the analysis I propose that discerning the meaning of a legislative distinction always relies on a close analysis of the context of the specific legislation, the benefit involved, and the group deprived. Thus, a complete analysis of the concept of dignity requires a detailed exploration of all the cases to see how carefully the contextual factors have been read. The exercise here is designed to set up that larger task.

1) The Jurisprudence Reconfigured: Three Forms of Indignity

The central insight in a dignity-based account is that valuing human dignity means acknowledging the inherent worth of human beings; therefore, violating dignity involves conveying the message that some are of lesser worth than others. The Supreme Court has, so far, concentrated on elaborating a list of apparently independent, though overlapping, contextual factors said to be capable of revealing violations of dignity. I argue that we can detect in these factors three forms of indignity or denial of worth that can be inflicted by a legislature or state actor. The first two are fairly obvious and explain most of the case law decided so far: the grounding of legislation in prejudice and the use of stereotype. A third form of indignity is only slowly emerging: it involves exclusion from benefits or opportunities that are particularly significant because access to them constitutes part of the minimum conditions for a life with dignity. In this case, it is the nature of the benefit itself that makes its denial a violation of dignity. When prejudice or stereotype motivates the exclusion from such benefits and opportunities, the indignity is exacerbated. Our prejudice and stereotype detectors may be more sensitive to more minor instances of tainted legislation in such cases.

Any of the three forms can be inflicted through the explicit use of a characteristic important to personal and group identity, or through the adoption of uniform, facially neutral standards that fail to take account of the diverse circumstances of various groups. In asking how the legislature can convey a message of lesser worth, the various factors commonly referred to in the cases then fall into place as interpretive guides or diagnostic tools for discerning whether one of these forms is present. This account draws the conceptual map of equal protection law differently than the Supreme Court's three-part test plus four contextual factors, but I hope that it enables the development of a more meaningful concept of dignity.

So far, the Court has dealt most often with the first two forms of denial of worth, and hence, the factors identified as markers of the violation of dignity have tended to be ones that should alert us to the presence of prejudice or stereotype, in society and as reflected in legislation, or help us to contextualize the harm they do. They are relevant not in their own right, but because they help us sniff out prejudice and stereotype. This explains why the Court has repeatedly stated that the various relevant factors are neither necessary nor sufficient conditions of a finding of discrimination.[95] The presence of these features of context do not constitute discrimination; they simply help us read the implicit meaning of legislative distinctions imposing burdens or denying benefits to see whether it connotes the inferiority of a group. Exhibiting prejudice and stereotype are core cases of impugning the moral worth of others. I argue, however, that the Canadian approach understands what it means to treat another as less valuable not as a subjective attitude and corresponding psychological consequences, but as an objective meaning or import arising out of certain forms of legislative classification.

Further, from the beginning, a link has been made between stereotyping and its tendency to undermine its victims' "personal development."[96] This points in the direction of self-fulfillment as a human good that equality rights are designed to protect, and suggests a connection between dignity and autonomy. Respect for dignity includes respect for agency as a fundamental characteristic of humanity. References to the importance of self-determination or personal fulfillment recognize human beings as choosers and planners, as beings with projects and dreams who make commitments and attachments and at least partly measure their own sense of worth according to their ability to exercise their capacities and realize their dreams. Behaviour based in prejudice or stereotype often impairs autonomy. However, there are ways of restricting self-fulfillment that are themselves sufficiently harmful to constitute a violation of dignity, even absent an underpinning in prejudice or stereotype. The launching pad for the further development of this line of thinking is the inclusion of the nature of the interest affected by the legislation on the list of contextual factors, a factor first suggested as relevant by L'Heureux-Dubé J. The idea that we should ask whether legislation affects membership in society in a basic way or denies participation in important social institutions suggests that these forms of participation are crucial in their own right to a life with dignity.

2) Dignity as Inherent Worth

In some shape or form the concept of dignity has been part of the foundation of most major modern political and moral theories since the Enlightenment.[97] In its modern guise, its role has been to give an egalitarian twist to notions of worth that had previously been defined by hierarchical understandings of relations between people.[98] Before the Enlightenment, worth was identified with honour, which cannot be equally distributed without destroying its meaning. Those honoured were the social superiors of those not. The introduction of the concept of dignity democratized or universalized the idea of human worth. Dignity refers to a somewhat ineffable quality that we ascribe equally to all human beings in virtue of which we accord them a special kind of worth. One might say this involves a sort of "leveling up," raising common people up to the moral status previously enjoyed only by the aristocracy.

It is commonly said that dignity refers both to a set of empirical qualities or characteristics and to a moral quality of persons as such.[99] When we think of dignity as an empirical attribute, we think, as Aurel Kolnai suggests, of a range of characteristics having to do with composure, self-control, invulnerability, and self-assuredness.[100] As an empirical matter, these are characteristics that individuals exhibit in greater or lesser abundance, but they point us in the direction of a characterization of dignity as a moral quality, as an entitlement we can all claim. For they are all character or behavioural side-effects of an underlying sense of self that we associate with dignity. They describe a person who is a self-conscious being with a secure sense of his or her worth and place in the world, in command of his or her life and under no one's thumb. To enjoy this sense of worth requires that a person be secure in his or her identity as an individual, including as a member of those communities with which he or she identifies. He or she must feel a sense of belonging in his or her society,[101] entitled to participate in its institutions and endeavours. Thus, a secure sense of self requires both confidence in one's identity and the ability to participate in society. This sense of self-worth *can* describe an empirical state of affairs, yet we know that not every human being is fortunate enough to actually enjoy such a healthy self-image. We nevertheless think something like this sense of self is every person's birth right. We therefore ascribe dignity, in this aspirational sense, in the sense of what each individual is entitled to, to all human beings.

To ascribe dignity to human beings not as an empirical matter, but as a moral matter — that is, to treat it as an inherent aspect of humanity — is to treat human beings as creatures of intrinsic, incomparable, and indelible worth, simply as human beings; no further qualifications are necessary.[102] In this basic sense, dignity is ascribed to human beings independently of their particular accomplishments or merits or praiseworthiness. It refers to a kind of worth that is not contingent on being useful, or attractive, or pleasant, or otherwise serving the ends of others. Dignity means worthiness, but not in the sense of pointing to some *other* form of value that makes one worthy. Kolnai nicely captures the non-derivative nature of this kind of worth:

> Dignity means "being worthy of …", the completion that most aptly suggests itself would seem to be "worthy of being appreciatively acknowledged *as* worthy to be thus acknowledged and appreciated," *sans plus*.[103]

Of course, some may be able to jump higher than others, or knit faster, or may be kinder to their neighbours; nevertheless, there is a basic respect in which worth is attributed to human beings automatically, not as a matter of degree, but rather equally to all persons. Just as it need not be earned, it also cannot be lost. This deep sense of moral worth is simply part of our conception of the person. The possession of dignity calls for a particular moral response: respect for the intrinsic worth it signifies. "Humanity," as Thomas Hill puts it, "should be honored and respected or at least not mocked, dishonored, or degraded."[104] Out of this can be developed prescriptions about how to treat others in such a way as to show respect for their dignity.

As something inherently "possessed" by human beings, dignity cannot be taken away. It can, however, be dishonoured through a failure to show respect, through the treatment of others as less than creatures of inherent worth. Thus dignity is violated by such a failure of respect, whatever the empirical consequences of that failure for those affected. Harm to dignity need not be contingent upon a showing of other specific effects, whether psychological or material. At the same time, violations of dignity do often have psychological and material consequences, which in turn have implications for the subsequent ability of people to live in dignity. Dignity may be an inherent quality of human beings, but a subjective sense of self-worth is an empirical psychological and emotional state that has enormous implications for the quality of life. And a person's subjective sense of self as someone of worth is crucially tied to how she is treated by others.[105] We may not be able to guarantee that people actually *feel* the sense of worth to which they are entitled, but we can aspire to a state in which empirical realities strive to match inherent moral entitlements, in which at least it is not state policy that presents the obstacle to people enjoying the subjective sense of self characteristic of those whose dignity is respected. To protect dignity, we must be attentive to the ways in which our treatment of others diminishes self-respect. These two sides of the equation — how one treats others and the response that treatment provokes — must both shape our examination of what the protection of dignity requires.

What it is in the human person that grounds the attribution of worth associated with the concept of dignity is, of course, an issue of enormous philosophical dispute, which cannot be finally resolved here. Nor should it be necessary to have a complete philosophical account of dignity in hand in order to say something useful about how the concept can illuminate equality jurisprudence. We are at the beginning of what should be a continuous process of debate about and refinement of the concept. The brief account presented here draws upon several themes in the common currency of thought about dignity to develop a concept that is attractive and that finds significant resonance in the key elements of the Canadian jurisprudence.

This account highlights two aspects of human personality in virtue of which human beings are valued and are to be treated as worthy of respect. These are not necessarily the only relevant aspects, simply the two that seem to me most helpful in illuminating the equality jurisprudence so far.[106] First, human beings are capable of having a conception of the self. This makes respect for identity crucial to respect for dignity. Second, humans are capable of formulating and revising a conception of the good. This makes respect for people's plans and projects relevant to protecting dignity. These two aspects of personality are connected, since one develops an identity partly through the life one creates for oneself, and a conception of the good partly in the context of one's sense of who one is. Both aspects of personality can be understood as abstract capacities that all human beings have, but respect for the capacity requires some measure of respect for its use as well; people must be given some scope to be who they are and conduct their lives as they see fit. Some limits on this freedom are inevitable, since it is obviously possible for people to adopt conceptions of the self and projects and plans that are unworthy of the approbation or even tolerance of others. For now, it is enough to note that these limits will eventually need to be negotiated.

The integration of the exercise of human capacities into the concept of dignity is meant to ward off an overly abstract conceptualization whose failure to make room for the particularities of human experiences of identity and life projects would make respect for dignity a homogenizing force.[107] Highlighting these two key aspects of human personality also avoids an excessively individualistic account. Both identity development and formulation of a conception of the good are undertaken by individuals, but they are undertaken in large part with and through relationships with others.[108] For this reason, involvement in communities of various sizes and scopes can be crucial to the individual enjoyment of self-worth. That dependency must be recognized by any account of what respect for the dignity of others requires.

3) Dignity and Equality

It is easy to see how a concept of dignity along the lines sketched above would be relevant to a range of human rights — how it might help explain our sense of the inviolability of the physical person, or the importance of certain freedoms.[109] Can it also help explain equality rights?[110] Remember that equality claims arise in a context in which the legislature has distributed some benefit and a plaintiff contests the basis for that distribution. In order to be able to challenge the chosen distributive criteria, one must be able to point to some wrong that distribution commits, independent of the denial of the concrete benefit itself — some independent right that the exclusion infringes which is best corrected by redistributing the concrete benefit at issue. To treat dignity as a quality of human beings grounds a principle of entitlement to respect that is fully universal and which therefore is owed to each equally. In virtue of having dignity, each person is owed respect as a creature of inherent worth. This approach does not give us a comprehensive set of correct principles of entitlement against which directly to judge every specific benefit distributed through legislation, but rather identifies an underlying good — respect for dignity — that is properly distributed in equal shares. In order, then, to find violations of section 15, we should look for distributive criteria which, in distributing the concrete benefit with which they are concerned in a particular way, thereby fail to accord equal respect to all persons as bearers of dignity, as persons of equal moral status. Legislation that conveys the implication that the members of a particular group are of lesser worth, not full members of society, violates dignity.

a) Prejudice

Let us start with an examination of prejudice to begin an account of what constitutes a violation of dignity and why. To treat state reliance on prejudice as wrongful implies that there is some harm in prejudice. The idea of violation of dignity attempts to capture this harm. A legislative distinction based on prejudice denies a class of persons a benefit out of *animus* or contempt. It directly connotes a belief in their inferiority, a denial of equal moral status. Legislated prejudice denies a benefit for the sake of causing harm to those denied. It thus treats members of a group as *loci* of intrinsic negative value, rather than intrinsic moral worth. Such treatment not only deprives them of the concrete benefit at issue, but also, through doing so, treats them as unworthy of basic human respect. It thus constitutes an insult to their humanity or their dignity as persons. Distinctions that make an important aspect of human identity the target of stigmatization, humiliation, and the excuse for deprivation violate dignity in this way.

Prejudice works through the attribution of negative worth to personal characteristics that are important aspects of identity; it thus constitutes an assault on the sense of self of its victims. Personal identity has both an individual and a social dimension. The kinds of characteristics that people regard as important to their sense of self tend to be, at the same time, characteristics by which they define themselves as individuals and through which they identify as members of a group.[111] This group affiliation is as important to human identity as any purely individual understanding of the self. We develop a sense of self only through our interactions with others, and our most intimate and formative interactions are frequently with people who share a cultural or ethnic identity that distinguishes them from other such clusters of people in society. And we know from our social and political history that it has tended to be precisely this aspect of identity that has often been targeted for contempt — *individuals* have been denied respect through use of a characteristic identifying them as part of a *group* that is devalued.

This explains the grounds listed in section 15 whose use is a likely indicator of discrimination, and supports the use of a group-based focus in discerning discrimination. Race, national or ethnic origin, color, religion, and sex are all aspects of personal identity that are socially understood as aspects of self in which people are entitled to take pride, but have nevertheless been used to classify groups as unworthy.[112] Age and mental or physical disability are characteristics that have been unfairly used to characterize the whole person to the exclusion of other attributes and capacities, thus reducing the person to one aspect of his or her identity. Our knowledge of how this has been done in the past can guide our reading of current legislative treatment to see if past practices and attitudes are being reinforced, and can enable us to detect other, non-enumerated, ways of categorizing that threaten to subject members of a group to contempt in a similar way. The sorts of factors often relied upon to determine whether a new ground should be recognized as analogous to those listed in section 15 operate as more concrete signposts. Thus, the characteristics that are important to one's sense of self are typically actually or constructively immutable. Long-term disadvantage is taken as an indicator, and result, of past prejudices previously translated into legal disabilities. Status as a chronic minority is a warning signal because it renders a group vulnerable to such prejudice.

So far, this description of the wrong of prejudice locates it in the subjective attitudes of the actor. It is the intended imputation of inferior moral status that makes action on that basis wrong. If this was all there were to dignity, ascertaining whether a particular legislative distinction was constitutional would require an assessment of what was going on in the minds of the legislators who enacted it — what *they* meant by the use of the distinction. There is no doubt that such subjective intentions to subordinate fellow human beings constitute a denial of dignity, but this is only a start. Violation of dignity has meaning not only subjectively, from the legislator's point of view, but according to the objective or social meaning of certain forms of behavior, including the use of particular legislative distinctions. Prejudice makes vivid a specific social meaning of contempt and therefore a kind of harm not fully recognized before — being treated as unworthy. Recognizing this should alert us to be on the lookout for other ways in which lack of respect for human dignity can be conveyed, including ways in which this can be done unwittingly. Entrenched prejudice can unleash social forces that devalue members of particular groups even when those acting within the practices shaped by those social forces have no subjective desire to show contempt. The sorts of distinctions and denials that constitute an infringement on dignity are, then, a matter of social construction. To understand the violation of dignity in its entirety, we must look to the meaning of government action, which is always something that must be socially constructed rather than merely treated as a matter of one-sidedly plumbing the content of the actor's mind. Seeing dignity and its violation as socially constructed allows for the inclusion of stereotype under the umbrella of discrimination.

b) Stereotype
Stereotypes are inaccurate generalizations about the characteristics or attributes of members of a group that can usually be traced back to a time when

social relations were based more overtly on contempt for the moral worth of the group. Stereotypes partly stem from backhanded recognition that acting on prejudice is a violation of human dignity. Negative characteristics, such as lack of intelligence, laziness, being fit for some pursuits rather than others, predisposition to criminality, avarice, vice, etc., which are in fact distributed throughout the human race, are falsely attributed predominantly to members of a particular group. It is then the negative characteristic that becomes the focus of contempt. Nevertheless, inaccurate assumptions and stereotypes about the capacities, needs, or desires of members of a particular group can carry forward ancient connotations of second-class status, even if the legislators did not intend that meaning. The overt hostility may have come to be washed out of the picture with the passage of time or the "normalization" of such attitudes, but the implication that those to whom the stereotype applies are less worthy than others remains.

Once this construction of a group has set in, others are likely to treat members of that group disadvantageously out of an honest belief that this merely reflects their just deserts or even simply because that is how everyone treats them, without ever thinking about the insult involved. They may even understand their conduct, as with certain traditional sexist practices, as a positive effort to accommodate the "natural weaknesses" of the stereotyped group. However, neither the absence of contempt as a subjective matter nor well-meaning paternalism prevents the use of stereotype from violating dignity. To be denied access to benefits or opportunities available to others on the basis of the false view that because of certain attributes members of one's group are less worthy of those benefits or less capable of taking up those opportunities can scarcely fail to be experienced as demeaning because it *is* demeaning. The message such legislation sends is that members of this group are inferior or less capable, and such a message is likely, in turn, to reinforce social attitudes attributing false inferiority to the group. Legislative distinctions which are best understood as grounded in stereotype simply do violate dignity, however well-meaning the legislators may have been.[113]

Given that negative stereotyping *means* the attribution of inferiority, if legislation is grounded on and stands to reinforce false stereotypes, to leave it in force would itself reinforce its discriminatory social meaning. Antecedent good intentions cannot wash that negative meaning away.[114] In other words, government action, certainly action in the form of lawmaking, should not be regarded as a series of discrete acts to be assessed at the time of the action, that is, the passing of particular legislation. Legislators may not have been consciously aware of the stereotypical assumptions grounding their conduct in enacting legislation to begin with, but once these assumptions are brought to the surface through litigation, the issue becomes what message is sent by *continuing* to enforce such legislation.

Inaccurate assumptions about the attributes or capacities of a group are the stuff of stereotype. Such inaccuracy may, in turn, render use of a particular characteristic irrelevant to the legislative objective at hand (assuming to begin with that the objective is a valid one). This explains why so many of the cases turn on an assessment, within the section 15 analysis, of the relationship between the criterion used and the purported legislative objective. If the proffered objective is not itself discriminatory, but the criteria used to distribute the statute's benefit do not serve it very well, it is a signal that the use of that criterion may well indicate the implicit acceptance of derogatory stereotypes.

Treating violations of dignity as a matter of the social meaning of certain distinctions also makes it clear that the harm involved is not primarily a matter of harm to the feelings of those affected by a distinction. Prejudice and stereotype stigmatize and often humiliate. The connection between prejudice and the humiliation it often causes makes it easy to slip into treating the harm to be protected against as a kind of emotional harm — the bad feelings typically aroused in the victims of prejudice and stereotype. But this would be to subjectivize the nature of the interest at issue. Instead, the harm should be understood to inhere in the denial of respect *per se*. In other words, harm to dignity is better understood as an independent, objective harm, not a matter of hurt feelings. Feelings of worthlessness may be a common symptom of being treated with disrespect, and may be relevant diagnostically, but the evil to be prevented or remedied is conveying the implication of worthlessness.

This account is roughly consistent with the Supreme Court's characterization of the appropriate perspective from which to judge the impact of legislation as "subjective-objective": "the reasonably held view of one who is possessed of similar characteristics [to those affected by the legislation], under similar circumstances, and who is dispassionate and fully apprised of the circumstances."[115] The viewpoint of those affected by the use of a distinction to deny benefits must be taken into account and the Court must try to put itself in the shoes of members of this group rather than simply adopting the perspective of the legislator. At the same time, more than the affected group's say-so is required. The Court must be satisfied that their interpretation captures the legislation's real meaning, that its import is to attribute lesser worth to some group. However, I would register one note of caution: the Court occasionally slips into the language of "feelings" to describe the appropriate standard — whether the legislation might reasonably make members of a group "feel" demeaned or devalued.[116] Indeed, one might argue that the device of adopting the perspective of those affected by the legislation, albeit an objective version thereof, pulls the analysis inevitably in the direction of ascertaining their feelings and then assessing their reasonableness. This undoubtedly has the laudable objective of forcing the Court to take into account the perspective of vulnerable groups, and this is crucial when the task is to assess whether the import of legislation is to impugn the dignity of a possibly oppressed minority. However, unless judges are careful, it risks reducing the question of the relevant impact of legislation to its psychological effects rather than keeping the Court focused on the meaning of dignity and its impairment.

In the final analysis, the question of what constitutes a violation of dignity is a normative question, not an empirical one about psychological effects. It is the Court's responsibility to make the normative judgments about the meaning of certain forms of treatment, not implicitly put the onus on claimants to have "reasonable" reactions to their treatment. Especially in the case when a claim is rejected, it seems to me more constructive, or at least less loaded, for the Court to tell a claimant that he or she is wrong about the social meaning of the challenged legislation than to imply that the claimant's feelings are unwarranted or unreasonable. At the same time, it bears repeating that a court must always be sensitive to the meaning legislation has for those negatively affected by it in order to have any hope of avoiding simply ratifying dominant, potentially oppressive, understandings of social relations. The project of constructing the concept of dignity is actively normative, requiring critical reflection on existing social relations. It cannot be reduced either to a question of the legislature's intentions or to a sampling of popular opinion.[117]

The search for the social meaning of legislation for violations of dignity requires an interpretive exercise that takes account of the entire social context within which the challenged legislation operates. Indeed, we must consider the whole social context because, once we eschew reliance on the legislator's subjective understanding, it is the whole context that determines the social meaning of particular legislative conduct. Neither prejudice nor stereotype typically operates in discrete, isolated circumstances. Instead the wholesale classification of a group as unworthy of full moral status, when it is in force, operates to subordinate members of the group in ways that stand to affect every corner of their lives, infect every attitude and predisposition toward them. The web of restrictions and exclusions created subjects members of the group to the pervasive message that the social meaning of the most intimate aspects of their personality is one of inferiority. The social relations that ensue give birth to the stereotypes that feed the next round of putative justifications for continued exclusion. The effects of such pervasive and long term cramping of the lives of the members of such a group is not easily undone; the social meaning of imposed inferiority is not easily eradicated. Even once the most egregious exclusions have been remedied, the fact of having been associated with a wide array of negative meanings in the past makes the group more vulnerable to continued devaluation even as a result of fairly minor exclusions. Pockets of negative meaning may remain here and there in the law long after the central institutions of discrimination have been removed.

This seems to me to be the insight lying behind La Forest J.'s nuanced analysis in *Andrews* of the ways that immigrants have been systematically excluded from the best employment opportunities throughout much of our past. It is against this backdrop that the apparently isolated use of citizenship as a criterion for admission to the legal profession must be read, and against this history it inevitably takes on connotations of attributing lesser worth to the non-citizen, even though this sort of use of citizenship has largely faded from the scene.[118] L'Heureux-Dubé J. has shown herself to be especially attuned to the importance of context and past history in revealing continuing prejudicial implications of rules excluding women, gays and lesbians, and other long subordinated groups. Her judgments have carefully examined the import of current distinctions against past practices of exclusion. On the other hand, bases for distinction that do not have such a monolithically negative track record of being used to subordinate, such as age, do not as easily attract such a meaning.

The explicit use of the characteristics enumerated in section 15 or ones analogous to them is not the only way that prejudice or stereotype can manifest itself in legislation. Rejecting the adoption of the legislature's subjective viewpoint in interpreting the meaning of legislation allows us to see how prejudice and stereotype can operate even in facially neutral legislation. Thus, some adverse impact claims can ground valid discrimination complaints as instances of the violation of dignity through the use of stereotype or prejudice. While not every distinction that has a disproportionate impact on an identifiable group is ultimately grounded in stereotype or prejudice, some are. Many adverse impact claims involve situations in which a facially neutral rule is in fact informed by traditional assumptions about who is qualified for certain benefits, which assumptions themselves may be grounded in old prejudices or stereotypes.[119] The qualification may be stated without reference to a criterion like race or sex and yet be linked to it through using attributes more common in one group than another. This implicit use of the attributes of a dominant group in setting criteria for distribution can often be traced back to an understanding of the enterprise being regulated that more openly excluded certain groups or simply assumed they were unfit to participate, even if there is no current conscious intent to continue past exclusionary practices. In other words, rules that implicitly appeal to attributes of the dominant group to define who gets access to benefits can carry forward the meaning of lesser worth rooted in prejudice or stereotype.[120]

c) Dignity-Constituting Benefits

More significantly, facially neutral rules that simply overlook the circumstances of particular groups can also imply their lesser worth. If a good case cannot be made for the relevance of the qualification used, to uphold its use itself potentially sends out a message that the well-being, the life chances, the opportunities and aspirations of those excluded do not count for much. They are allowed to be outweighed by minor concerns such as the convenience of maintaining habitual practices. Public institutions and programs built, even unwittingly, in the image of a dominant group convey the message that others are not equally entitled to participate in society and its enterprises, and are not equally members of its institutions. This kind of indignity depends in part on the significance of the benefit denied. Every facially neutral rule excludes some group from its benefit. If the exclusive effect cannot be tied back to prejudice and consequent stereotypes, it is wrongful only if the benefit at stake is important to a life of dignity.

Again, the point in time to properly assess the social meaning of the legislation is not the point of enactment, but the point at which its consequences for the dignity of those it affects have been tested and recognized. Once the courts have authoritatively decided that the legislation unjustifiably excludes members of a group from benefits or opportunities that are constitutive of dignity in our society, the government cannot seek to uphold the legislation merely because those consequences were unanticipated or unintended without thereby cementing the indignity.

The leading Supreme Court decision dealing with an indirect discrimination claim illustrates how the fact of being left out, even through mere oversight rather than as the ultimate product of prejudice or stereotype, can violate dignity. In *Eldridge v. British Columbia Attorney-General*,[121] the failure to provide sign language interpreters for the deaf in hospitals was held to be a violation of section 15. The relevant legislation and regulations did not specifically exclude medicare coverage for sign language interpreters; it simply neglected to include the service. Specifically noting that the Court "has staked out a different path than the United States Supreme Court,"[122] La Forest J. proclaimed, "A legal distinction need not be motivated by a desire to disadvantage an individual or group in order to violate section 15(1). It is sufficient if the effect of the legislation is to deny someone the equal protection or benefit of the law."[123] Although noting that the disabled have frequently been subjected to prejudice and stereotyping, La Forest J. recognizes that we do not require such an explanation of how their needs have come to be ignored in order to see how that failure creates obstacles to their participation in society. It is the failure to accommodate their special needs and the consequences of that failure for full participation that constitute the discrimination. He borrows the following statement of the position from Sopinka J. in *Eaton v. Brant County Board of Education*:[124]

> Exclusion from the mainstream of society results from the construction of a society based solely on "mainstream" attributes to which disabled persons will never be able to gain access. Whether it is the impossibility of success at a written test for a blind person, or the need for ramp access to a library, the discrimination does not lie in the attribution of untrue characteristics to the disabled individual. The blind person cannot see and the person in a wheelchair needs a ramp. Rather it is the failure to make reasonable accommodation, to fine-tune society so that its structure and assumptions do not result in the relegation and banishment of disabled persons from participation, which results in discrimination against them.[125]

This locates the indignity in the denial of participation in social life itself, bringing to the surface the third form that a violation of dignity can take.

The argument depends on the idea that there are some benefits or opportunities, some institutions or enterprises, which are so important that denying participation in them implies the lesser worth of those excluded. La Forest J. argues that interpreters are necessary to give deaf patients the same quality of care that hearing patients receive.[126] The quality of medical care is certainly important, but this underplays the violation of dignity involved in this situation. More fundamental is that without interpreters, deaf patients are denied one of the core rights of personhood — the right to decide what will and what will not be done to their body. The idea that people have the right to grant or refuse consent to medical treatment is fundamental to our concept of dignity. To deny deaf patients the means of understanding what medical treatment is being proposed denies them the very possibility of meaningful consent, and therefore treats them like children, lacking capacity to decide where their best interests lie.[127] The insult to dignity is profound, and it is not mitigated by the fact that the decision-makers may not have thought about it this way. What matters is that when we do think about it, we can see that it is simply unacceptable to treat deaf patients as though their consent to medical treatment does not matter. It is the participation in the exercise of the power to give or refuse consent that is the important institution to which access is denied by the failure to provide sign interpreters as much as the receipt of adequate medical treatment.

This point about the importance of participation in key institutions or access to significant benefits and opportunities can be generalized. Our conception of human dignity includes the idea that individuals should have at least a fighting chance of crafting a life for themselves. Respect for autonomy is part of respect for the inherent worth of persons. Control over the major determinants of how one's life goes is part of what gives one's existence meaning and value. When denial of autonomy is combined with prejudice or stereotype, the indignity is exacerbated, so that this form of indignity can flavour the analysis in a case even when, strictly speaking, it is not necessary to the result. Cutting off significant opportunities because of prejudice or inaccurate assumptions about those persons being denied undermines the ambition to make one's own life. It says that some people are incompetent to shape the character of their life, but rather should have it dictated to them by others. This is one way to read the result in *Andrews*. Work is of fundamental importance to most people. Choice of occupation is an important part of each person's definition of his or her life. Access to a particular occupation, especially one as socially and politically significant as law, should not be categorically denied on the basis of characteristics that have nothing to do with one's ability to undertake the responsibilities of the profession. Treating people according to a stereotyped view of who they are not only mistakenly underestimates their qualifications; it participates in a social practice that confines them to a way of life not of their making, one whose social meaning is bound up with markers of inferiority. It is hard to see how people who have been so denied can see themselves and be seen otherwise than as second-class citizens, especially if such exclusion has been a systemic feature of their experience. Their lives will reflect a lower level of accomplishment and worth than they were capable and desirous of, and this shortcoming is likely to be falsely attributed to them rather than to the conditions to which they are subjected. This will create a feedback loop that is likely to lead to future treatment reinforcing a status of lesser worth.

Even absent prejudice, sometimes the importance of specific opportunities or benefits to the ability to craft one's own life means that denying access itself implies the lesser worth of those denied. The specific benefit distributed by the legislation is seen as a means to the underlying benefit of autonomy. To the extent that our conception of humanity incorporates notions of autonomy, we will be disposed towards the view that our law should at least aim at its equal distribution. It is clear that equal opportunity to craft a life is denied when the rules are designed, however unwittingly, in ways that prevent the participation of some people in institutions of major significance to the quality of life. While it may not be possible for the courts to police this in any very finely grained way, they may nevertheless respond to the categorical denial of opportunity as a violation of equality.

Findings of the violation of dignity on this ground may be more open to contest than ones grounded in prejudice or stereotype. It may not always be easy to detect prejudice or stereotype, but once it is acknowledged, the insult in the legislation incorporating it is clear. The issue of which social institutions and opportunities are important enough to be regarded as constituting dignity involves still more delicate interpretive questions. That may be why, in identifying the nature of the interest affected as one of the factors to be considered in finding discrimination, the Court has tended to pinpoint as problematic legislation that "restricts access to a fundamental social institution," or affects "a basic aspect of full membership in Canadian society," or "constitute[s] a complete non-recognition of a particular group."[128] This sets the bar quite high, but we may hope for it to be lowered as courts develop more familiarity with interpreting this form of violation of dignity.

So far, this theme has remained relatively underdeveloped in Canadian jurisprudence. It has the potential to increase the scope of the equality rights in the *Charter*. Unfortunately, that potential was not fulfilled in *Gosselin v. Quebec (Attorney General)*.[129] The case involved a challenge to the social assistance regime in place in Quebec between 1984 and 1989. That regime declared that welfare recipients under the age of thirty were entitled only to one-third of the benefits provided to those over thirty. Regular benefits were not exactly generous, being set at what the government regarded as subsistence level. Thus, someone under thirty received a fraction of a subsistence level income. The scheme then provided that younger recipients could qualify to have their benefits raised by participating in remedial education programs or job training programs. Participation in the former would bring one's benefits up to about 75 percent of the regular benefit, while participation in the latter would put one on a par with those over thirty.[130] In a five-to-four decision, the Supreme Court held that the scheme was not discriminatory — in particular, it did not violate the dignity of those under thirty, but was aimed at supporting their dignity by providing an incentive to young people to participate in programs that would improve their chances of integrating into the workforce. In the context of the high rate of youth unemployment in the early 1980s, this was held to be important to their long term well-being.

The case demonstrates that it is not only indirect discrimination cases of the *Eldridge* sort that can exemplify a culpable indifference to the needs of a particular group serious enough to constitute a violation of dignity. *Gosselin* involved the explicit use of age as a criterion determining the level of social assistance benefits. In most cases in which an enumerated characteristic is explicitly used, the analysis revolves around whether its use is grounded in prejudice or stereotype. The presence of either of these features is sufficient to decide the case in the complainant's favour (absent section 1 justification). The consensus on the Court seemed to be that those under thirty are not likely victims of prejudice or stereotyping;[131] hence, if violation of dignity was to be found it had to be because the benefit denied to those under thirty could be regarded as important enough to be dignity-constituting.

The majority, in a judgment written by McLachlin C.J., relies very heavily on the findings of the trial judge that no "adverse effects" on the claimant or the class she represented[132] had been proven. This conclusion seriously misunderstands the nature of the benefit at stake here that might be classified as dignity-constituting. The majority conclusion is in part based on the fact that the Court did not have detailed evidence about precisely how many eligible welfare recipients under thirty might have been denied access to one of the programs that would have qualified them for a top-up of benefits, nor on the exact economic consequences of this.[133] This argument systematically blurs the question of whether a violation of section 15 had been shown and that of the appropriate remedy for any such violation. Given that the claimant was asking for monetary damages on behalf of the entire class, one might argue that the quantification of such damages is impossible without more information about numbers and precise effects. But that remedial difficulty should not have been allowed to determine the question of whether there was a violation of equality rights to begin with. This confusion seems to have prevented the majority from really grappling with the issue of whether there was a denial of a dignity-constituting benefit here.

In fact, the scheme was designed in a way that certainly placed those under thirty *at risk* of deprivation of an important benefit — the means of basic subsistence. This conclusion is supported by three features of the scheme. First, there were significantly fewer places in education and job training programs than there were eligible welfare recipients under thirty.[134] Second, there were restrictions on eligibility for these programs and on their length, making it impossible for someone under thirty to access the programs seamlessly and maintain the higher benefit level. Finally, the government offered no evidence for its hypothesis that the level of financial need was lower for those under thirty because many of them had the option of living with their parents. While not everyone under thirty would suffer under this scheme, that group was at greater risk of being plunged into abject poverty than those over thirty; nor was the risk merely hypothetical, as Ms. Gosselin's own circumstances showed.[135] The majority's premature worry about the appropriate remedy seems to have distracted it from noticing that there was a real risk here and that for those for whom it materialized the consequences would be devastating. The real question, then, was whether creating a serious risk for those under thirty that they might end up with no more to live on than $170 per month in an economic context of high unemployment show sufficient lack of regard for their welfare to qualify as a violation of dignity. It is hard to imagine how anyone could live a life with dignity under such circumstances.[136] In addition, as Bastarache J. notes in dissent, the constant fear of being reduced to such dire straits was itself likely to impair the dignity of its victims.[137]

I would go further still and argue that there is another layer of indignity inflicted by this legislative scheme. In order to find a violation of dignity, Bastarache J. focuses mainly on the economic hardship imposed on those who are unable to rely on their family for support.[138] Insofar as he attends to the assumption lying behind the legislation that many young people would be able to live with their parents, it is in order to point out that the government provided no proof of its accuracy and did not make reduction of benefits contingent on whether parental support was available to an applicant.[139] This is designed to set up his analysis of what he sees as the indignity of the scheme — subjecting young people to severe poverty.[140] I would argue that the assumption that anyone under thirty should live with his or her parents if unable to find work constitutes a violation of dignity even to those who are fortunate enough to have parents willing and able to provide living accommodations. It suggests that nothing of any significance is lost in remaining under parental authority until one reaches the age of thirty. This surely requires closer examination. In the worst case scenario, the scheme may have put some young people to the choice of life in an abusive family situation or abject poverty. Even if we postulate reasonably healthy relations between young welfare recipients and their parents, the prospect of living with one's parents means foregoing any aspiration to an independent life. It means postponing until age thirty (or a dramatic turn-around in the economy) many of the experiences that we regard as formative of young adulthood; it means retaining a child-like status until age thirty. This, in itself, constitutes some harm to dignity. This is a kind of harm that is not acknowledged at all in the majority judgment, making it easier for it to treat as fatal to the claim whatever imperfections there may have been in the factual record about the degree and extent of the purely economic deprivation inflicted by the scheme.

Although the dissenting judgment of Bastarache J. comes much closer to seeing the real issue in this case, he sticks very closely to the conventional post-*Law* format for equality analysis, and this inhibits a clear expression of the idea that the third form of indignity that counts as a violation of section 15 is the denial of benefits so important as to be integral to dignity. He proceeds systematically through a discussion of each of the four contextual factors laid down in *Law*, even though the crux of his argument falls under the fourth factor — the nature of the interest affected. Some of the reasons that support the conclusion that the interest affected is crucial to dignity are sprinkled throughout the analysis of the other factors, particularly the first and second, obscuring their significance. Recognizing that there are three forms of indignity and that some of the *Law* contextual factors are more relevant to some than to others would make it easier for courts to zero in on the essential features of a particular case.

F. CONCLUSION

This analysis of equality claims places an enormous responsibility on the courts, because they are the ultimate arbiters of the social meaning of the distinctions used to define entitlement to various benefits. They must decide, and try to justify to the rest of us, when use of a distinction attributes lesser worth and when it does not. The Supreme Court has begun to define some of the contextual features that can help us interpret the meaning of a given legislative distinction. These are usefully grouped, as suggested by L'Heureux-Dubé J.'s suggested framework for analysis, according to whether they direct our focus to the nature of the excluded group itself or to the nature of the benefit denied them. The former typically lead us to reasons to suspect that prejudice or stereotype may have been operating in the drafting of the legislation. The latter should lead to a debate over whether the benefit denied is crucial to a life with dignity.

The key factor coming out of an examination of the group itself is whether it has been historically marginalized from the mainstream. The more we are aware of a lengthy past practice of exclusion, the more wary we should be that any modern exclusion, even a seemingly minor one, may reinforce old attitudes and values. Similarly, the more widespread and systematic past practices of exclusion have been, the more careful we should be to ferret out any whiff of continuing attribution of lesser worth. The systemic imposition of disadvantage can create social dynamics that reinforce exclusion without being directly tied to the initial contexts of discrimination. Courts should be alert to ensure that new distinctions do not contribute to such dynamics because they are as capable of creating an aura of inferiority around a group as direct imputations to that effect. Noticing that a group is in a chronic minority status in society operates in a similar fashion, since its lesser political power makes it members vulnerable to victimization. On the other side of the ledger, the more important a particular benefit is to one's ability to participate fully in society, or the more it is a marker of true belonging in society, the more one should worry that exclusion from it will carry the connotation that members of the excluded group deserve less respect.

None of this produces a bright-line test for discrimination nor simply a strategy for encouraging better judging. None is possible, or even desirable. Rigid formulas cannot capture the interpretive exercise that is at the heart of a determination as to whether equality rights have been violated. Rather, we more urgently need to begin a social conversation about dignity and its meaning in our political culture. Its meaning will vary from one set of social circumstances to another, making context crucial to the discussion in any given case. Legal argument should focus on connecting the meaning of legislative distinctions in the lives of the people they affect to one of the three forms of indignity and fleshing out the implication of inferiority they contain. The discrete factors identified by the case law so far can be used as shorthand when appropriate, but they should not substitute for an analysis of how the distinction can be tied back to dignity. It is out of the close study of the political, historical, and social contexts within which distinctions between groups arise that we will develop an increasingly rich concept of dignity, one which will over time provide increasingly greater guidance to future courts.

ENDNOTES

1 © 2003, Louisiana Law Review. First published (2004) 63 Louisiana L.R. 645. The development of this article has benefitted from many forms of support and many kinds of help. The opportunity to visit the College of Law at the University of Saskatchewan as the Law Foundation Chair gave me the luxury to carry out the research necessary, as well as a warm and collegial environment in which to do so. I have also benefited from the chance to present earlier versions of this work both at the University of Saskatchewan and the University of Victoria, as well as at the conference at the Louisiana State University Law School which gave rise to this symposium issue. In addition, I am grateful for individual feedback from Donna Greschner, Ken Norman, and Hester Lessard and encouragement from Colleen Sheppard. Lastly, thanks must also go out to Zoe Oxäal for her meticulous research assistance.

2 *Canadian Charter of Rights and Freedoms*, Part 1 of the *Constitution Act, 1982*, being Schedule B of the *Canada Act*, 1982 (U.K.), 1982, c. 11 [the *Charter*].

3 Section 15(1) of the *Charter* provides that "[e]very individual is equal before and under the law and has the right to the equal protection and equal benefit of the law without discrimination and, in particular, without discrimination based on race, national or ethnic origin, colour, religion, sex, age or mental or physical disability." All rights in the *Charter* are subject to s. 1, which provides: "The Canadian Charter of Rights and Freedoms guarantees the rights and freedoms set out in it subject only to such reasonable limits prescribed by law as can be demonstrably justified in a free and democratic society."

4 See, for example, Peter W. Hogg, *Constitutional Law of Canada*, 4th ed., looseleaf (Toronto: Carswell, 1997–) at 52:26–52:27; Sheilah Martin, "Balancing Individual Rights to Equality and Social Goods" (2001) 80 Can. Bar Rev. 299 at 328–30; June Ross, "A Flawed Synthesis of the Law" (2000) 11 Const. Forum 74 at 83; Roger Gibbins, "How in the World Can You Contest Equal Human Dignity" (2000–2001) 12 N.J.C.L. 25.

5 See, for example, *Gosselin v. Quebec (Attorney General)*, [2002] 4 S.C.R. 429 [*Gosselin*].

6 Donna Greschner, "Does Law Advance the Cause of Equality?" (2001) 27 Queen's L. J. 299 at 306.

7 In analyzing the case law, I will take a somewhat broad-brush approach — in particular, I will not do justice to the debate about the proper division of labour between s. 15 and s. 1 of the *Charter*. For purposes of this argument, I accept the trend in the case law toward doing at least some of the work of determining the limits of the right to equality within s. 15 rather than leaving it all to be done under the rubric of determining what are the limits on rights demonstrably justifiable in a free and democratic society, the criteria provided by s. 1.

8 The *Canadian Bill of Rights*, S.C. 1960, c. 44, reprinted in R.S.C. 1985, App. III, was an ordinary statute adopted by the federal government in 1960. Although the courts occasionally treated it as having quasi-constitutional status, the fact that it was not entrenched, combined with the conservatism of the bench, meant that it was

often interpreted in a way that was extremely deferential toward Parliament. This
was especially so with the equality provision, which guaranteed "equality before the
law without discrimination on the basis of" various designated characteristics. The
high-water mark of this judicial conservatism was reached in the sex equality case
A.G. Canada v. Lavell, [1974] S.C.R. 1349, in which the Supreme Court of Canada
held that a provision of the *Indian Act* which deprived only Indian women of their
status under the Act upon marriage to a non-Indian did not violate the *Bill of Rights*
because the law applied equally to all those, Indian women, at whom it was directed.
Five years later, the Court decided in *Bliss v. A.G. Canada*, [1979] 1 S.C.R. 183 that
a provision of the *Unemployment Insurance Act* making regular sick leave benefits
unavailable for work absences caused by pregnancy and confining pregnant women
to more restrictive benefits did not deny equality before the law because it treated all
"pregnant persons" alike. For a brief history of this case law, see Walter S. Tarnopolsky, "The Equality Rights (ss. 15, 27 and 28)" in Walter S. Tarnopolsky & Gérald
A. Beaudoin eds., *The Canadian Charter of Rights and Freedoms: Commentary*
(Toronto: Carswell, 1982) at 395; Beverley Baines, "Women, Human Rights and the
Constitution" in A. Doerr & M. Carrier, eds., *Women and the Constitution* (Ottawa:
Canadian Advisory on the Status of Women, 1981) at 31–63.

9   Gwen Brodsky & Shelagh Day, *Canadian Charter Equality Rights for Women: One
Step Forward or Two Steps Back?* (Ottawa: Canadian Advisory on the Status of
Women, 1989) at 185ff.

10   For the sake of brevity, henceforth I will use "benefit" to refer to both benefits and
burdens, since relief from a burden can be conceived of as a benefit.

11   Isaiah Berlin, "Equality as an Ideal" in Frederick A. Olafson, ed., *Justice and Social
Policy* (Englewood Cliffs: Prentice-Hall, 1961) at 134–35 describes such a claim as
pointing out the "unfairness" of the existing distribution, an argument grounded in
the value of equality, as opposed to criticizing it for violating some other value, such as
the promotion of virtue or happiness, not necessarily tending toward greater equality.

12   *Ibid.* at 132.

13   *Andrews v. Law Society of British Columbia*, [1989] 1 S.C.R. 143 [*Andrews*].

14   For example, Kathleen A. Lahey succinctly states the approach as follows: "the
evaluation of sex equality challenges would require judges to ask whether the rule or
practice that is being challenged contributes to the actual inequality of women, and
whether changing the rule or practice will actually produce an improvement in the
specific material conditions of the specific woman or women before them." Kathleen
A. Lahey, "Feminist Theories of (In)Equality" in Sheilah L. Martin & Kathleen
Mahoney, eds., *Equality and Judicial Neutrality* (Toronto: Carswell, 1987) at 83.

15   Note that the list of benefits covered by such universal principles must be limited for
the theory to be coherent. Since some forms of equal distribution will deny equality
along some other dimension, there is no way to distribute every benefit and burden
equally. For example, the equal satisfaction of need may conflict with equality of
resources. A theory of substantive equality must specify the benefits over which it
ranges, mindful of the fact that the wider its swath, the more likely conflict will arise
between competing aspirations toward equality.

16 For an example of this kind of approach, see David M. Beatty, "The Canadian Conception of Equality" (1996) 46 U.T.L.J. 349. Although Beatty appears to adopt the rather radical view that *all* goods should be divided equally making every legislative distinction a violation of s. 15, in the final analysis, by incorporating the s. 1 analysis of whether the legislative means are calibrated to its ends, he effectively ends up with an account of equality that holds that "gratuitous" distinctions should not be made between people in distributing benefits. Such approaches can vary from weak to strong depending on how tight the connection they insist on between legislative means and end. At the weaker end of the spectrum, advocates require only that there be some rational connection, that the means used bear some relationship to the objectives sought, and the objectives be permissible. Versions with more teeth require that the means be necessary, or virtually so, to the achievement of an important objective.

17 For just a taste of the complexities, see Ronald M. Dworkin, *Sovereign Virtue: The Theory and Practice of Equality* (Cambridge: Harvard University Press, 2000).

18 *Andrews*, above note 13.

19 *Ibid.* at 168.

20 N. Colleen Sheppard, "Recognition of the Disadvantaging of Women: The Promise of *Andrews v. Law Society of British Columbia*" (1989) 39 McGill L.J. 207 at 211–18; Brodsky & Day, *Canadian Charter Equality Rights for Women*, above note 9 at 205–7.

21 Thus, for example, Peter Hogg's analysis of the analogous ground jurisprudence fastens onto the element of immutability as the conceptual common link between all the enumerated grounds in s. 15. Hogg, *Constitutional Law of Canada*, above note 4 at 52:29–52:35 .

22 [1990] 3 S.C.R. 229 [*McKinney*]. *McKinney* dealt with whether a statutory permission to private sector employers to impose mandatory retirement at age sixty-five constituted a violation of s. 15. A majority held that since the legislation made a clear distinction on the basis of age, an enumerated characteristic, and mandatory retirement could be experienced as a disadvantage, the s. 15 test was met. However, the Court upheld the legislation under s. 1.

23 See, for example, Hogg, above note 4 at 52:16.1–52:19.

24 See, for example, *R. v. Hess*, [1990] 2 S.C.R. 906 [*Hess*], and *Weatherall v. Canada*, [1993] 2 S.C.R. 872 [*Weatherall*], in both of which it was held that a distinction on the basis of sex was not discriminatory — the former involving a *Criminal Code* provision specifying that only men can be guilty of the offence of statutory rape, and the latter deciding that a prohibition on male prison guards performing frisk searches of female prisoners while female prison guards were not restricted from performing such searches on male prisoners is not discriminatory. Note, though, that in *Weatherall*, the Court hedged its bets, finding merely that is it "doubtful" that the rules about cross-gender frisking were discriminatory (at 877), and holding that they would be justified under s. 1 in any event. In *Hess*, while the dissent followed the "grounds approach" strictly, finding that the statutory rape provision was a violation of s. 15 simply because it distinguished in a disadvantaging way on the basis

of an enumerated ground, the majority held that there was no infringement of s. 15 despite the use of sex in defining the criteria for criminal liability for this offence (the dissent nevertheless held that the violation of s. 15 was justified under s. 1, beginning what has come to be a constant pattern of confusion about which considerations belong under the s. 15 analysis and which under s. 1). Another case illustrating that a finding of discrimination is more complicated than determining that a distinction was based on an enumerated characteristic is *R. v. Swain*, [1991] 1 S.C.R. 933. Here the Court found no violation of equality in a rule allowing the Crown to decline to prosecute an insane accused in favour of pursuing a trial simply on the issue of insanity with the result that a finding of insanity would leave the accused open to detention indefinitely in a psychiatric facility rather than subject to a fixed sentence as would result from an ordinary conviction. The rule clearly distinguished on the basis of an enumerated characteristic — mental disability — but the Court found that indefinite detention under these circumstances did not constitute a disadvantage. Furthermore, reading s. 15(1) as a prohibition of the use of certain characteristics would have required s. 15(2) to be read as an equally categorical *exception* to that rule. Section 15(2) provides "[S]ubsection (1) does not preclude any law, program or activity that has as its object the amelioration of conditions of disadvantaged individuals or groups including those that are disadvantaged because of race, national or ethnic origin, colour, religion, sex, age or mental or physical disability."

25 Daniel Proulx, "Les droits a l'égalité revus et corrigés par la Cour suprême du Canada dans l'arrêt Law: un pas en avant ou un pas en arrière" (2001) 61 R. du B. 185 at 234–35; Ross, above note 4; Hogg, above note 4.

26 For an alternative explanation of the trajectory of the early case law, see Daniel Proulx, "Le concept de dignité et son usage en context de discrimination: deux Chartes, deux modèles" (2003) 63 R. du B. 485 at 502–13. Proulx treats the emergence of a substantive condition that a legislative distinction must violate dignity in order to be in violation of s. 15 as designed to stave off challenges to social welfare programs for being under-inclusive and as required to explain the denial of discrimination in *Hess* and *Weatherall* (both above note 24). This sort of explanation seems to be consistent with mine, but operates on a different plane.

27 *Corbière v. Canada*, [1999] 2 S.C.R. 203 at para. 11 [*Corbière*].

28 In *Andrews*, McIntyre J. quotes with approval Hugessen J.A. in *Smith, Kline & French Labs v. AG Canada (Attorney General)*, [1987] 2 F.C. 359 at 367–69 as follows: "[t]he inquiry, in effect, concentrates upon the personal characteristics of those who claim to have been unequally treated. Questions of stereotyping, of historical disadvantagement, in a word, of prejudice, are the focus and there may even be a recognition that for some people equality has a different meaning than for others."

29 Brodsky & Day, *Charter Equality Rights for Women*, above note 9 at 207.

30 The explanation may lie in the fact that McIntyre J., despite his conclusion that the legislation violated s. 15, would have upheld the legislation under s. 1 as a reasonable limit demonstrably justified in a free and democratic society. Had he developed an account of how the use of citizenship as a criterion is based on stereotype and prejudice, he might have found it harder to find it nevertheless justified. Indeed, the s. 1

argument wholeheartedly accepts the government's argument that an insistence on citizenship is a reasonable way to ensure commitment to the country and adequate acquaintance with the Canadian system of government, as well as a reasonable condition on access to the privileges of a life in the law. The implication in the s. 15 analysis that the legislation was grounded in prejudice and stereotype seems completely negated by the justification offered under s. 1 — at least if one accepts that justification. That is, the harm done by the provisions, conceived of as having something to do with the wrong of prejudice, is not only outweighed by the beneficial purpose, but entirely washed away. In fact, MacIntyre J.'s s. 15 analysis makes more sense if we locate the violation of inequality simply in the concrete disadvantage of being denied access to a profession based on a characteristic closely analogous to specifically prohibited ones like nationality; that is, just in the making of a distinction on prohibited grounds. This leaves all the important questions about equality begged — what kind of disadvantage counts and what kind of basis for distinction is impermissible — but it salvages some intelligibility for McIntyre J.'s division of labour between s. 15 and s. 1. This is the first hint that there must be something wrong with the way the division of labour between s. 15 and s. 1 has been developed. If one did think the legislation exhibited prejudice, one would be hard-pressed to uphold it, and if one found it completely reasonable under s. 1, how could it be discriminatory to begin with?

31 *Andrews*, above note 13 at 154.

32 This point adopts the language of the Supreme Court of the United States in *United States v. Carolene Products Co.*, 304 U.S. 144, 152–53 n.4, 58 S. Ct. 778, 783–84 n.4 (1938).

33 *Andrews*, above note 13 at 194.

34 *Ibid.* at 195.

35 *Ibid.* at 197, quoting *Kask v. Shimizu*, [1986] 4 W.W.R. 154 at 161, McDonald J.

36 La Forest J. sums up his analysis with the comment that those subjected to such a law would rightly feel that "Canadian society is not free or democratic as far as they are concerned," *Andrews, ibid.*, quoting *Kask v. Shimizu, ibid.* at 161, McDonald J.

37 See, for example, *R. v. Hess*, above note 24. By contrast, in *McKinney*, above note 22, the adoption by all members of the Court of a fairly simplistic conclusion that the simple fact of the use of an enumerated ground to impose a burden constituted discrimination pushed all the substantive disagreement between the majority and the dissent into the s. 1 analysis. The ultimate conclusion that illicit distinctions must not only use an enumerated or analogous ground, but must also be discriminatory, has brought these arguments into the discussion of what counts as a violation of s. 15 to begin with.

38 With *Thibaudeau v. Canada*, [1995] 2 S.C.R. 627, decided at the same time, these cases constitute a trilogy in which the pervasive disagreements on the Court about equality became apparent.

39 [1995] 2 S.C.R. 418 [*Miron*].

40 [1995] 2 S.C.R. 513 [*Egan*].

41 In *Miron*, the same majority denied the s. 1 argument and the provision was held to be unconstitutional; in *Egan*, one member of the majority on the s. 15 issue, Sopinka J., defected on the s. 1 question, so the denial of pension benefits to same-sex couples was found to be discriminatory, but upheld. Since my discussion of these cases is confined to the s. 15 analysis, I will use "majority judgment(s)" to refer to the five judges who accepted the argument that there was a s. 15 violation, and "minority judgement(s)" to refer to the four judges who denied the s. 15 violation.

42 The other four members of the majority were McLachlin, Cory, Iacobucci, and Sopinka JJ. McLachlin J. wrote the judgment for this group in *Miron*, while Cory J. wrote the s. 15 judgment for the same group in *Egan*.

43 The other three justices were Major, La Forest, and Lamer JJ.

44 Although in *McKinney*, above note 22, there is considerable discussion of dignity and whether it is infringed by mandatory retirement, this discussion tended to come up in the context of the s. 1 argument rather than in the s. 15 analysis, because all members of the Court were content to hold that there was a violation of s. 15 simply by virtue of the legislature's explicit use of age to impose a disadvantage. In retrospect, one can see some of the later s. 15 disagreements foreshadowed in the s. 1 dispute in *McKinney*.

45 *Miron*, above note 39 at para. 23.

46 *Ibid.* at para. 15.

47 Greschner, above note 6 at 307.

48 *Miron*, above note 39 at 438–39, 441; *Egan*, above note 40 at 535–36, 538–39.

49 By contrast, the majority characterized the legislation in both cases as designed to provide for the needs of economically interdependent family units, and judged by this standard, holding a marriage license or being of the opposite sex is simply irrelevant to the question of need. For the majority, this is part of the s. 1 analysis, not part of the determination of whether the use of the distinction is discriminatory.

50 That the legislative purpose must not itself be discriminatory has been reiterated in *Benner v. Canada (Secretary of State)*, [1997] 1 S.C.R. 358 at para. 64. The cases in which the acceptability of the objective is the central issue have an all-or-nothing quality. If the judges "see" the discriminatory nature of the entire scheme, the rest of the legal analysis follows easily; if they do not, the reasoning upholding the legislation is circular.

51 This point was made forcefully in *Canada (Attorney-General) v. Mossop*, [1993] 1 S.C.R. 554 at 634, L'Heureux-Dubé J.

52 The use of relevance in Gonthier J.'s judgment to assess constitutionality provoked a strong reaction from both McLachlin J. in *Miron* and L'Heureux-Dubé J. in *Egan*, leading them both to reject it altogether as part of the s. 15 test. This, however, throws the baby out with the bath water. The way relevance is used by Gonthier J. and La Forest J. is deeply problematic, but used properly, some form of assessment of the relevance of the statutory criteria to the objectives sought is an important part of the s. 15 analysis. Indeed, both McLachlin J. and L'Heureux-Dubé J. rely equally heavily on the idea of relevance; it is just that they start from a different view of the objective of the legislation. They tend to talk about whether legislative criteria are

"appropriate" rather than "relevant" to what they think are the legislative ends, but the same means/ends assessment is in issue.

53   *Miron*, above note 39 at para. 131.

54   "Logic suggests that in determining whether a particular group characteristic is an analogous ground, the fundamental consideration is whether the characteristic may serve as an irrelevant basis of exclusion and a denial of essential human dignity in the human rights tradition. In other words, *may it serve as a basis for unequal treatment based on stereotypical attributes ascribed to the group, rather than on the true worth and ability or circumstances of the individual*? An affirmative answer to this question indicates that the characteristic may be used in a manner which is violative of human dignity and freedom." *Miron*, above note 39 at at para. 147, McLachlin J. (emphasis added).

55   *Ibid.* at para. 149.

56   *Ibid.* at para. 148.

57   *Ibid.* at para. 156.

58   In *Corbière*, above note 27, McLachlin J., writing with Bastarache J. for the majority, seems to identify the characteristics that indicate stereotypes with features of the person that are actually or constructively immutable. It is not clear what is thought to justify this apparent retreat from an open-ended, multi-faceted account of the indicators of stereotype in favour of reliance on a single factor. I am grateful to Hester Lessard for pointing out the potential significance of this development.

59   The only mention of inaccurate, preconceived notions about common law couples mentioned in McLachlin J.'s judgment comes not in her s. 15 discussion, but in her analysis of whether the exclusion can be saved under s. 1. At this stage, she notes, having decided that the objective of the legislation is to provide for financially needy families, the exclusion of common law couples seems to be based on the assumption that such couples are not stable, financially dependent units. This she finds to be inaccurate.

60   Instead, the same form of words, declaring it wrong to impose "limitations, disadvantages or burdens through the stereotypical application of presumed group characteristics rather than on the basis of individual merit, capacity, or circumstance" is simply repeated at several crucial junctures in the argument. *Miron*, above note 39 at para. 131. A very similar form of words is used at paras. 134, 140, 146, 147, 149, & 156.

61   In *Eaton v. Brant County Board of Education*, [1997] 1 S.C.R. 241 [*Eaton*] at paras. 66–67, and *Vriend v. Alberta*, [1998] 1 S.C.R. 493 [*Vriend*] at paras. 70–72, the Court has since stated that the use of stereotype is not the only means of discriminating. Below, in articulating a concept of dignity capable of guiding equality jurisprudence I take a stab at mapping out the various types of discrimination as different ways of violating dignity in order to try to make sense of the case law so far.

62   The fullest description of her approach is in *Egan*, above note 40 at para. 51.

63   She notes in *Egan*, *ibid.* at para. 51, that since not every distinction based on an enumerated or analogous ground constitutes discrimination, "[a]n additional dimension of analysis is needed."

64 *Egan, ibid.* at para. 48.

65 *Ibid.* at para. 37; see also *ibid.* at para. 56: "A distinction is discriminatory ... where it is capable of either promoting or perpetuating the view that the individual adversely affected by this distinction is less capable, or less worthy of recognition or value as a human being or as a member of Canadian society, equally deserving of concern, respect, and consideration."

66 *Ibid.* at para. 36.

67 *Ibid.*

68 *Ibid.* at para. 39; see also her judgment in *Miron,* above note 39 at para. 107.

69 In *Miron, ibid.* at para. 94, L'Heureux-Dubé J. introduces what may be an additional factor indicating that the basis for a legislative distinction is one that has the effect of discrimination — "whether the impugned distinction is based upon a fundamental attribute of 'personness' or 'humanness.'" This factor is designed to counter the argument that since whether to marry or not is a matter of choice, it cannot be an immutable aspect of a person's situation, and distinctions based on marital status cannot be discriminatory. Marital status may be able to be chosen (yet is not always so), according to L'Heureux-Dubé J., but the choice is fundamental to one's personality and so deserving of protection against being made the basis for legislated disadvantages.

70 *Egan,* above note 40 at para. 90.

71 *Ibid.* at paras. 160–61.

72 *Ibid.* at para. 161.

73 *Ibid.* at para. 171: "The fundamental consideration underlying the analogous grounds analysis is whether the basis of distinction may serve to deny the essential human dignity of the *Charter* claimant." It is interesting that Cory J. places so much weight on the issue of whether the legislation could be said to be based on an analogous ground, since according to La Forest J., the Attorney-General of Canada conceded that sexual orientation is an analogous ground.

74 Much has been made of the apparent methodological disagreement between L'Heureux-Dubé J. and her colleagues, even those with whom she often agrees in result. The disagreement appeared to deepen still further in *Vriend,* above note 61, in which L'Heureux-Dubé J. declared "I do not agree with the centrality of enumerated or analogous grounds in Cory J.'s approach to s. 15(1). Although the presence of enumerated or analogous grounds may be indicia of discrimination, or may even raise a presumption of discrimination, it is in the appreciation of the nature of the individual or group who is being negatively affected that they should be examined. Of greatest significance to a finding of discrimination is the effect of the legislative distinction on that individual or group." *Vriend* at para. 185. Although I prefer L'Heureux-Dubé J.'s analytical framework because it more carefully ties all the reasoning to the search for violations of dignity, I think the differences between her approach and those of McLachlin J. and Cory J. are exaggerated. Making the case for this view is, however, beyond the scope of the present article.

75 *Egan,* above note 40 at para. 180.

76 [1999] 1 S.C.R. 497 [*Law*]. For a sampling of the academic commentary on *Law*, see Martin, "Balancing Individual Rights to Equality and Social Goods," above note 4; Ross, "A Flawed Synthesis of the Law," above note 4; Donna Greschner, "Does Law Advance the Cause of Equality?" (2001) 27 Queen's L.J. 299; Proulx, "Les droits a l'égalité revus et corrigés," above note 25; Beverley Baines, "*Law v. Canada*: Formatting Equality" (2000) 11 Const. Forum 65.

77 Other cases, such as *Vriend*, above note 61, also invoke dignity as the ground of the analysis, but it is in *Law* that the Court made an effort to develop a consensus on how it operates.

78 *Law*, above note 76 at para. 51.

79 *Ibid.* at para. 53.

80 In the course of this analysis, Iacobucci J. also tries to move away from a rigid, two- or three-step test for s. 15. "It is inappropriate to attempt to confine analysis under s. 15(1) of the *Charter* to a fixed and limited formula." *Ibid.* at paras. 82, 88. He acknowledges that there will be some circumstances in which the analysis that establishes a violation of dignity will take place in the first step of the traditional analysis, usually described as that of determining whether the law imposes differential treatment on the claimant by comparison to others, and sometimes in the determination of whether the differential treatment constitutes discrimination in a substantive sense, which is itself a matter of deciding whether the basis for the difference is an enumerated or analogous ground and whether it "has the effect of perpetuating or promoting the view that the individual is less capable or worthy of recognition or value as a human being or as a member of Canadian society, equally deserving of concern, respect, and consideration." *Ibid.* at para. 88. Thus, it is the overarching purpose of s. 15(1) of protecting dignity that should guide the analysis and not any specific set of analytical steps. This seems to bring him closer to L'Heureux-Dubé J.'s approach which recommends abandoning a rigid focus on searching for enumerated or analogous grounds in favour of asking more loosely whether the legislative distinction violates dignity. Nevertheless, when Iacobucci J. restates the three "broad inquiries" that a court should make to determine a s. 15(1) claim, he reverts to describing the first two — whether there is a formal distinction or a differential impact, and whether it is based on an enumerated or analogous ground — in rather mechanical terms, apparently leaving the consideration of whether dignity is violated to the third inquiry.

81 *Ibid.* at para. 88.

82 *Ibid.* at para. 63.

83 *Ibid.*

84 *Ibid.* at para. 64.

85 *Ibid.* at para. 69.

86 Although used to reaffirm the need to take difference into account in the design of rules, this factor is at risk of collapsing into or at least re-incorporating the discredited "relevance" argument offered by La Forest J. and Gonthier J. in *Egan* and *Miron*. See Baines, "*Law v. Canada*: Formatting Equality," above note 76 at 71.

87 *Law*, above note 76 at para. 72. In *Lovelace v. Ontario*, [2000] 1 S.C.R. 950 [*Lovelace*], this was apparently watered down so that the fact that legislation is designed to benefit *a* disadvantaged group is treated as a counter-indicator of dignity violation even if those excluded from the benefit are just as bad off.

88 *Law, ibid.* at para. 75.

89 *Ibid.* at para. 74.

90 Proulx, "Les droits a l'égalité revus et corrigés," above note 25 at 240–55, usefully notices that these contextual factors divide into two categories: "*facteurs aggravants,*" or ones indicative of violation of dignity, and "*facteurs disculpants,*" ones that are counter-indicative of violation of dignity.

91 *Law*, above note 76 at para. 104.

92 Because the class of persons into which the claimant falls is not a historically disadvantaged group, Iacobucci J. is not concerned to impose an extremely high standard of accuracy in his factual assumptions on the government. However, he acknowledges that other situations may require a stricter standard.

93 There might be a plausible public policy argument that the short-term economic loss of losing a spouse should be better dealt with by government assistance programs, but this would have to be formulated not as an argument that it is discriminatory to refuse a long-term pension to those under thirty-five, but rather that it is discriminatory to provide for long-term need in these circumstances and not short-term need. On this argument age becomes a proxy for short-term need and the real question is whether it is demeaning or derogatory to fail to respond to those in short-term economic need as a result of the death of a spouse.

94 The post-*Law* cases include *M. v. H.*, [1999] 2 S.C.R. 3; *Corbière*, above note 27; *Winko v. B.C.*, [1999] 2 S.C.R. 625; *Lovelace*, above note 87; *Granovsky v. Canada (Minister of Employment and Immigration)*, [2000] 1 S.C.R. 703; *Lavoie v. Canada*, [2002] 1 S.C.R. 769 [*Lavoie*]; *Nova Scotia (Attorney-General) v. Walsh*, [2002] 4 S.C.R. 325; and *Gosselin*, above note 5. In all of the last six of these, the claim was denied on the basis that the legislative distinction did not violate human dignity.

95 *Law*, above note 76 at para. 62; *Gosselin, ibid.* at para. 29, McLachlin, C.J.

96 La Forest J. in *Andrews*, above note 13 at 197.

97 Herbert Spielberg, "Human Dignity: A Challenge to Contemporary Philosophy" (1971) 9 Philosophy Forum 39.

98 Charles Taylor, "The Politics of Recognition" in Amy Gutman, ed., *Multiculturalism and the Politics of Recognition* (Princeton: Princeton University Press, 1992) at 26–27; Spielberg, *ibid.*

99 Aurel Kolnai, "Dignity" in Robin S. Dillon, ed., *Dignity, Character, and Self-Respect* (New York: Routledge, 1995).

100 *Ibid.* at 57–59.

101 I borrow the language of belonging from Donna Greschner, "The Purpose of Canadian Equality Rights" (2002) 6 Rev. Const. Stud. 291, but use it as a component of the concept of dignity rather than as a separate purpose informing equality rights.

102 Immanuel Kant, *Groundwork of the Metaphysics of Morals*, trans. by H.L. Paton (New York: Harper and Row, 1964) at 96. For an extended account of Kant's view,

see c. 2 of Thomas E. Hill Jr., "Dignity and Practical Reason" in *Kant's Moral Theory* (Ithaca: Cornell University Press, 1992) at 38–57.

103 Kolnai, above note 99 at 56. See also Thomas E. Hill, Jr., "Social Snobbery and Human Dignity" in *Autonomy and Self-Respect* (Cambridge: Cambridge University Press, 1991) at 161.

104 Hill, Jr., "Dignity and Practical Reason," above note 102 at 50–51.

105 For just two of the many political theorists who have noted this connection, see John Rawls, *A Theory of Justice* (Oxford: Clarendon Press, 1972) at 62; Taylor, "The Politics of Recognition," above note 98 at 25–26.

106 Indeed, there is an even more basic form of respect for dignity than the one I explicate here, one which governs treatment of those who may, temporarily or permanently, be deprived of the capacity for full-fledged autonomy that figures prominently in the following analysis. This more basic form requires respect for the integrity and essential needs of the human person whatever his or her capacities, and is the backbone of any concept of dignity. It may at some point be necessary to bring this to the surface and subject it to more careful scrutiny and elaboration, but this has not been necessary in the equality contexts examined in this article.

107 See, for example, Taylor's association of Kantian conceptions of dignity as grounded in the universal capacity for rational agency with a conception of rights that insists on uniformity — each individual to enjoy an identical bundle of rights and entitlements. In "The Politics of Recognition," above note 98 at 37–44, Taylor correctly notes that this kind of approach is hostile to any kind of special rights or any deviation from universality in the interpretation of a given right. I take issue, however, with his labeling of such approaches as a "politics of dignity," since it gives the impression that the concept of dignity is integrally tied to this model of rights. My articulation of an alternative is meant to show that dignity can take account of the importance of recognizing the capacity for rational agency without adopting this homogenizing approach. In other words, I seek to unite the two streams that Taylor labels the "politics of dignity" and the "politics of recognition" and which he treats as seriously at odds with one another.

108 This is meant to signal disagreement with Taylor's assumption, in "The Politics of Recognition," *ibid.* at 56–58, that an autonomy-focused conception of dignity must be individualistic in the sense of valuing individual rights above any collective goals. Obviously, this requires much fuller argument than I can provide here, but since it seems to me that it is often the perceived individualism of classic conceptions of dignity that motivate suspicion about the concept, it is important to at least stake out a conception that is not rigidly individualistic.

109 David Feldman, "Human Dignity as a Legal Value (Part 1)" (1999) P.L. 682. For a similar exercise in the context of a Canadian-German comparison, see Dierk Ullrich, "Concurring Visions: Human Dignity in the *Canadian Charter of Rights and Freedoms* and the Basic Law of the Federal Republic of Germany" (2003) 3 Global Jurist Frontiers.

110 It has sometimes been said that the fact that dignity ultimately underpins *all* human rights makes it an insufficiently specific value to guide thinking about equality. See,

for example, Greschner, "Does Law Advance the Cause of Equality," above note 6 at 312; Greschner, "The Purpose of Canadian Equality Rights," above note 101 at 316–17. I am unpersuaded that the fact that dignity may have something to tell us about the foundation of the right to security of the person and freedom of expression etc., means it cannot inform equality as well. A fully fleshed-out concept of dignity should help explain a range of, if not all of, the human rights typically entrenched in constitutions, just as the value of liberty does. Different rights will reflect different aspects or dimensions of the concept. However, this concern is a useful reminder that we need to be looking for the dimensions of dignity that help with the work of s. 15 in particular.

111 Greschner, "The Purpose of Canadian Equality Rights," *ibid.* at 298. It should be remembered, of course, that individuals can identify with more than one such group.

112 *Ibid.* at 304–5.

113 In many everyday contexts, we understand the socially constructed nature of indignity more readily than is often the case in the constitutional context. For example, in some societies showing another person the palm of one's hand is an insult. This is the case even if the actor does not intend to show disrespect. On a first occasion, he might be forgiven the insult — even though the fact of the insult remains — but if he continues to act this way, no one would accept the excuse that he does not mean to insult. The meaning of the action is a question of how it is socially understood, not a matter of the actor's intention. Such social meanings are open to change — new forms of insult develop and old ones fade in significance. So, for example, I would argue that the apparently innocent question, "where are you from" asked of a non-white immigrant to Canada has become an insult because it has come to stand for an assumption that immigrants do not really belong, especially if they are non-white. It is the experience of many racialized people in having to answer the question too frequently, including people who were born in Canada but are taken to be immigrants, that has turned the question into an insult. However innocently someone asks it now, it is insulting. Contrarily, it is no longer taken as insulting to the Irish to refer to a police wagon as a "paddywagon."

114 As Richard Wollheim remarks, "Good intentions in a ruler are of little interest except in so far as they augur good results." Wollheim, "Equality and Equal Rights," in Olafson, ed., *Justice and Social Policy*, above note 11 at 116.

115 *Egan*, above note 40 at para. 41, L'Heureux-Dubé J. This way of formulating the appropriate perspective was adopted by the Court as a whole in *Law*.

116 See, for example, *ibid.* at para. 40, L'Heureux-Dubé J.; *Gosselin*, above note 5 at para. 245, Bastarache J.

117 From this perspective, the majority opinion in *Gosselin* gives reason for worry. Not only was the question of whether prejudice or stereotyping might have been operating not very sensitively handled (see the analysis at note 131, below), but also the majority's deployment of the subjective/objective standard comes perilously close to collapsing into an assessment of the legislature's *bona fides*.

118 In *Lavoie*, above note 94, the Court had another opportunity to consider a citizenship-based restriction on employment — this time with respect to federal civil

service jobs. A majority of the Court (seven Justices) held the restriction to be a violation of dignity. However, the restriction was upheld because four members of the s. 15 majority found the distinction to be justified under s. 1, these votes combining in result with the two judges denying a s. 15 violation. The interplay of s. 15 and s. 1 arguments in this case complicates the dignity issue in ways that go beyond the scope of this article to untangle.

119 For a more extended analysis of this phenomenon in the context of gender-biased rules, see Denise G. Réaume, "What's Distinctive about a Feminist Analysis of Law? A Conceptual Analysis of Women's Exclusion from Law" (1996) 2 Legal Theory 265.

120 It follows from this argument that I must disagree with L'Heureux-Dubé J.'s claim in *Gosselin*, above note 5 at para. 120, that "[a] neutral distinction, or one that 'unwittingly' yields negative effects, is by definition not premised on a negative stereotype." An unwittingly negative distinction shows no intention to discriminate, but it does not necessarily show no stereotyping.

121 [1997] 2 S.C.R. 624 [*Eldridge*].

122 *Ibid.* at para. 62.

123 *Ibid.*

124 *Eaton*, above note 61 at para. 67.

125 *Eldridge*, above note 121 at para. 65. For a comprehensive analysis of this phenomenon in the context of the exclusion of those with disabilities, see M.D. Lepofsky, "Report Card on the *Charter*'s Guarantee of Equality to Persons with Disabilities After 10 Years: What Progress? What Prospects?" (1997) 7 N. J. C. L. 263; M.D. Lepofsky, "The *Charter*'s Guarantee of Equality to People with Disabilities — How Well is it Working?" (1998) 16 Windsor Y.B. Access Just. 155.

126 *Eldridge, ibid.* at para. 71.

127 Although La Forest J. briefly mentions the duty of physicians to disclose the risks and benefits of medical treatment, he concentrates more on the fact that the absence of interpreters may put doctors in the position of being unable to treat deaf patients without breaching their professional responsibilities than on the denial to patients of the opportunity to consent or refuse consent. *Ibid.* at para. 70.

128 *Law*, above note 76 at para. 74.

129 *Gosselin*, above note 5.

130 See the overview of the scheme provided by Bastarache J. in his dissenting judgment. *Ibid.* at paras. 155–71.

131 This issue was not as carefully attended to as one might like, but I will leave that aside for purposes of the present discussion. Briefly, the conclusion of the majority that there was no prejudice or stereotyping here was premised on a refusal to take into account that the group affected by the legislation was not simply those under thirty, but welfare recipients under thirty. If one asks whether welfare recipients constitute a group which has historically been subjected to prejudice and stereotype, and whether this might have led the government to impose a special hardship on the subset of welfare recipients under thirty, the answer might well be different. Bastarache J. mentions in passing that the legislation seemed to be premised on the assumption that those under thirty were in greater need of incentives to improve their

job prospects than those over thirty (*Gosselin, ibid.* at para. 250), but he makes little, in his reasoning, of the insult embedded in that assumption — that young people are less motivated to pursue self-sufficiency. Nevertheless, I accept for the sake of argument that if there is prejudicial thinking lying behind the legislation, it is merely a tinge. The firmer ground for finding a violation of dignity is in the importance of the benefit at issue.

132 *Gosselin, ibid.* at paras. 46–47. The case was brought as a class action on behalf of 75,000 persons under thirty eligible for welfare during the relevant period. The only evidence presented as to concrete effects on individuals was that regarding the personal circumstances of Louise Gosselin, the named plaintiff.

133 *Ibid.*

134 The gap was very large — 30,000 placements originally established when there were 85,000 eligible welfare recipients under thirty. *Ibid.* at para. 283, Bastarache J.

135 *Ibid.* at paras. 164–70, Bastarache J.

136 For a description of the sorts of conditions disproportionately affecting young female welfare recipients in particular, see Gwen Brodsky & Shelagh Day, "Beyond the Social and Economic Rights Debate: Substantive Equality Speaks to Poverty" (2002) 14 C.J.W.L. 185 at 217–20.

137 *Gosselin*, above note 5 at para. 256.

138 Bastarache J. wrote the main dissenting judgment on the equality issue, Arbour J. and LeBel J. agreeing with his analysis. L'Heureux-Dubé J. wrote separate reasons concurring with Bastarache J. in the result, focusing equally strongly on the nature of the benefit — freedom from poverty — denied by the legislation. Bastarache J. treats the stipulation that those under thirty should get a reduced benefit as the violation of s. 15, and the creation of remedial programs permitting one to increase one's benefit to the regular level as the government's attempt to mitigate the rights violation. He therefore examines the satisfactoriness of this effort under the rubric of his analysis of whether the impairment of s. 15 had been minimal so that it can be justified, concluding that the gaps in access to the remedial programs showed that the impairment was not minimal. This allows him to treat the rights violation more categorically — not as the mere imposition of a risk of poverty, but as a certainty of poverty. My characterization of the s. 15 violation has been more modest, considering the entire scheme as a whole, but nevertheless arguing that the imposition of a real risk of severe poverty on one class of citizens should be sufficient to conclude that a dignity-constituting benefit has been denied.

139 *Gosselin*, above note 5 at paras. 246–47.

140 Most of this analysis takes place under Bastarache J.'s consideration of the fourth contextual factor — the nature of the interest affected — confirming my hypothesis that this fourth factor is likely to be the vehicle for arguments that the denial of some benefits can themselves constitute a violation of dignity. *Ibid.* at paras. 251–59.

five

Law v. Meiorin:
EXPLORING THE GOVERNMENTAL RESPONSIBILITY TO
PROMOTE EQUALITY UNDER SECTION 15 OF THE *CHARTER*

Melina Buckley

A. INTRODUCTION

Canadian equality jurisprudence recognizes that section 15 of the *Charter* and human rights legislation encompass both a duty to refrain from discrimination and an obligation to promote equality. The Supreme Court of Canada has consistently held that section 15(1) requires governments to both refrain from discrimination and to ameliorate the position of groups within Canadian society who have suffered disadvantage by taking into account their needs in formulating law and policy.[1] In my view, the latter positive obligation to promote equality is underdeveloped and requires further exploration at both the theoretical and practical levels. In particular, further theoretical development is necessary because the framework set out in *Law v. Canada*[2] does not adequately address how governments have failed to take into account women's substantive inequality in legislative and policy-making processes.[3] By contrast, the Supreme Court of Canada's decision in Tawney Meiorin's case[4] — an equality analysis developed under a provincial human rights code — is an important breakthrough in providing a framework of analysis concerning an employer's obligation to create equality in the workplace pursuant to human rights legislation. In my view, *Meiorin* provides an important foundation for the needed theoretical development and can advance an alternative approach to section 15 analysis that is better suited to judicial review of the governmental responsibility to promote equality.

This paper underscores the transformative nature of the project of achieving substantive equality for women. Calling this project transformative highlights the degree, breadth, and number of changes that are required to achieve women's substantive equality. It is not enough to accept existing formal and social institutions as they are and only work toward ensuring that opportunities within society are equally available to all. The institutions themselves have to be transformed. Substantive equality entails changes at all levels of society: individual behaviour, perceptions, and attitudes; ideas and ideology; community and culture; institutions and institutional practices; and, deeper structures of social and economic power. Thinking about social transformation helps us to understand that discrimination is not merely about isolated incidents but also about the patterns of violations of the right to equality. The focus on transformation is inextricably tied to an inquiry into positive government obligations since the levels of change required clearly necessitate state action as an important component of achieving women's equality.

In setting up the distinction between the duty of non-discrimination and the responsibility to promote equality, I do not mean to incorporate the "negative" versus "positive" rights dichotomy. The literature on human rights, particularly at the international level, is quite clear that there is no persuasive difference between a negative constraint on government to not interfere with human rights and a positive requirement on government to act to ensure human rights. They are merely two sides of the same coin of rights protection. However, there may be important differences in the way that rights infringements are analysed and remedied depending upon whether the cause of action is rooted in a claim of state action or inaction. Similarly, even though discrimination is discrimination, conceptualizing an equality rights infringement as direct, adverse effects, or systemic discrimination may be helpful in litigating and analysing the case to the extent that it helps illuminate the dynamics by which discrimination is imposed. It is the issues related to equality analysis, and remedies in cases involving the positive obligation to promote equality, that are explored here.

The first section of this paper provides a brief overview of the limited *Charter* jurisprudence that recognizes the government's responsibility to promote equality. Given the underdevelopment of this aspect of section 15 to date and consequent doctrinal uncertainty, the paper provides an initial inquiry into a principled basis for determining the content of this positive obligation. Toward this end, the second section assesses what lessons can be drawn from the *Meiorin* decision. The last section explores approaches to extending the positive duty to promote equality through test-case litigation.

B. RECOGNITION OF POSITIVE OBLIGATION TO DATE

The Supreme Court of Canada has recognized the governmental obligation to promote equality in several cases. The general framework for analysing equality rights claims as laid out in *Andrews* and restated in *Law*, is premised on a broad purposive understanding of the objects of section 15 as promoting substantive equality both through refraining from discrimination and taking into account the situation of those who have historically been treated unequally.[5] This was made clear in *Eldridge* where the Court stressed that section 15(1) serves two distinct but related purposes: "First, it expresses a commitment deeply engrained in our social, political and legal culture — to the equal worth and human dignity of all persons" and "Secondly, it instantiates a desire to rectify and prevent discrimination against particular groups suffering social, political and legal disadvantage in our society."[6]

Section 15 is not a general guarantee of equality as it is only concerned with the application or operation of the law.[7] However, section 15(1) read as a whole "constitutes a compendious expression of a positive right to equality in both the substance and the administration of the law."[8] Furthermore, the Supreme Court has recognized that "the accommodation of differences" is the essence of "true equality."[9] The concept of accommodation goes beyond the duty to refrain from discrimination within an existing situation and extends to a responsibility to change the situation itself in order to ameliorate the position of the disadvantaged. One of the strongest statements of this positive obligation to accommodate under section 15 was made by Sopinka J. in *Eaton*:

> This emphasizes that the purpose of s. 15(1) of the *Charter* is not only to prevent discrimination by the attribution of stereotypical characteristics to individuals, but also to ameliorate the position of groups within Canadian society who have suffered disadvantage by exclusion from mainstream society as has been the case with disabled persons.
>
> The principal object of certain of the prohibited grounds is the elimination of discrimination by the attribution of untrue characteristics based on stereotypical attitudes relating to immutable conditions such as race or sex. In the case of disability, this is one of the objectives. The other equally

important objective seeks to take into account the true characteristics of this group which act as headwinds to the enjoyment of society's benefits and to accommodate them. Exclusion from the mainstream of society results from the construction of a society based solely on "mainstream" attributes to which disabled persons will never be able to gain access.[10]

Three lines of cases shape the parameters of an exploration of the governmental responsibility to promote equality. The first and most extensively developed line deals with inclusiveness of legal provisions and benefits. In some cases, the extension of a legal regime to excluded groups is simply a question of refraining from direct discrimination. The courts have repeatedly held that if the government is going to provide a benefit it must do so in a non-discriminatory manner.[11] In other cases, though, the extension involves recognizing a positive obligation to take into accounts the needs of a particular group by providing a service not originally contemplated by the scheme, but related directly to it. For example, in *Eldridge*, the Court held that discrimination could arise from a governmental failure to take positive steps to ensure that deaf persons could access medical care through the assistance of sign language interpreters. The British Columbia courts took this one step further in *Auton* in holding that the government breached section 15 by failing to provide effective health treatment to children with autism, though this was later overturned.[12]

However, the fixing of exclusions does not fully satisfy the positive *Charter* requirements; much more is required to fulfil the promise of substantive equality. The limitations of focusing on the under-inclusiveness of government actions is heightened in situations where the adverse effects of exclusion are more subtle allowing the courts to defer to legislatures on where to draw the line between those who are in and out. The courts have stated that the *Charter* does not require "perfect correspondence" between a benefit program and the actual needs and circumstances of the claimant group.[13] But substantive equality requires more than correspondence; in situations of structural inequality it requires a fundamental rethinking of a law or program and the norms that underlie it. For example, in *Brooks* the extension of a health insurance scheme to cover pregnancy-related benefits amounted to much more than including a previously excluded group.[14] It involved an examination and rejection of the normative basis upon which the health accident and sickness insurance plan was based, given its lack of congruence with women's needs in the context of the role of childbearing, and the way that this perpetuated sex inequality.

A second important line of cases deals with the obligation of public officials to administer legislation and policy consistent with *Charter* rights, including the right to equality.[15] In *Baker*, the Supreme Court of Canada concluded that even discretionary decisions must be exercised in accordance with the boundaries imposed by the statute, the principles of the rule of law, the principles of administrative law, the fundamental values of Canadian society, and the principles of the *Charter*.[16] In particular, equality values have a pervasive role in interpreting and applying all Canadian laws, even those situations not directly involving governmental action.[17] The *Charter* does in fact require all legislators, policy-makers, and administrators to carry out their duties in a manner that is proactive and fully consistent with the guarantee of substantive equality. This statement is at once self-evident to the point of triteness and also a powerful recognition of the transformative potential of constitutional human rights. The Supreme Court has reaffirmed this fundamental norm in confirming that the "question of constitutional validity inheres in every legislative enactment"[18] as it does in every executive decision.[19] Perhaps the most passionate statement of this principle was made by McLachlin J. (as she then was) in her dissent in *Cooper*: "The *Charter* is not some holy grail which only judicial initiates of the superior courts may touch. The *Charter* belongs to the people. All law and law-makers that touch the people must conform to it."[20]

Finding effective means to ensure that *Charter* values are incorporated into administrative decision-making is a central task in efforts to realize substantive equality. This incorporation of values has the potential to transform the operation of many state activities by putting the obligation to protect and promote equality rights at the forefront of state decision-making. For example, the decision in *Jane Doe* that the police failure to warn women of a serial rapist in their neighbourhood, and their handling of the serial rape investigation infringed women's rights to equal benefit and equal protection of the law, created some momentum toward systemic change in policing.[21] Similarly, the finding in *Little Sisters* that the operation of the customs system to prohibit gay and lesbian publications from entering the country infringed the freedom of expression and equality rights of gays and lesbians heralded a similar opportunity for substantive change.[22] It is important to highlight that these cases contain transformative *potential*, but to date neither case appears to have resulted in the necessary degree of systemic change to achieve equality in practice. As Iacobucci J. noted in his partial dissent in *Little Sisters,* it will often be necessary to develop more forceful remedies that are consistent with and able to enforce the positive obligation that where "a government delegates powers it does so in a way that ensures — or at the very least attempts to ensure — that *Charter* rights will be respected."[23]

The third line of cases relevant to this discussion are ones decided under the rubric of other *Charter* rights but which relate in fundamental ways to the positive obligation to promote equality. The Supreme Court of Canada has used the strongest language in the context of section 2 fundamental freedoms and sections 16–23 official language minority rights. For example, decisions with respect to freedom of expression and freedom of religion have held that the absence of government intervention may in effect substantially impede the enjoyment of fundamental freedoms and therefore regulation may be required to ensure that these guarantees are meaningful in practice.[24] The minority language rights guarantees are expressed as affirmative entitlements that clearly impose positive duties requiring state action and the courts have been expansive in their interpretation of these provisions as guaranteeing substantive equality for official language minorities.[25]

In two recent cases, members of the Supreme Court of Canada have begun to develop a more general theory of positive state obligations under the *Charter*. In *Dunmore*, a majority of the Court held that the Ontario government had infringed the right to freedom of association protected by section 2(d) of the *Charter* by failing to provide a statutory labour relations regime to protect agricultural workers.[26] In the circumstances of the case, the government had a positive obligation to provide a labour relations and collective bargaining regime for this specific group of workers because without such government action they were unable to exercise one of their fundamental freedoms, the freedom of association.[27] This case stands for the proposition that a positive duty to assist excluded groups generally arises when the claimants are in practice unable to exercise a *Charter* right without state action. The Court held that:

> ... exclusion from a protected regime may in some contexts amount to an affirmative interference with the effective exercise of a protected freedom. In such a case, it is not so much the differential treatment that is at issue, but the fact that the government is creating conditions which in effect substantially interfere with the exercise of a constitutional right.[28]

The majority clarified that this does not mean that there is a constitutional right to protective legislation *per se*, it means legislation that is under-inclusive may, in unique contexts, substantially impact the exercise of a constitutional freedoms.[29]

Dunmore sets out the criteria for founding a positive constitutional obligation. First, a constitutional right must be at stake, not merely access to a statutory right.[30] Secondly, the state must be truly held accountable for any inability to exercise a fundamental freedom. There must be strong evidence that the right cannot be enjoyed without government action. However, the contribution of private actors to a violation does not immunize the state from *Charter* review or from a finding of a duty to act. The claimant is not required to prove a causal nexus tying the state to the claimant's inability to exercise his or her constitutional right. In claims asserting the infringement of a positive right, the focus is on whether the state is under an obligation of performance to alleviate the claimants' condition, and not on whether it can be held causally responsible for that condition in the first place.[31]

The important step taken in *Dunmore* was expanded upon by Arbour J. in her dissent in *Gosselin* in which she, among other things, explores the idea of positive state obligations under the *Charter* in a sophisticated and lengthy analysis.[32] Arbour J. finds that section 7 of the *Charter* does impose positive obligations on governments to offer basic protection for the life, liberty, and security of its citizens. She found that excluding the applicants from the full benefits of the Quebec social assistance scheme, which effectively excluded them from any real possibility of having their basic needs met, violated their section 7 right to security of the person and perhaps even their right to life. While her analysis did not win favour with her colleagues on the facts of *Gosselin,* the potential of section 7 to impose positive obligations was left open by eight of the nine judges.[33]

Arbour J. reviews the differences in conducting an analysis in claims to positive obligations as opposed to claims to non-interference by the state. She concludes that when a claim is that the state must take action to ensure that a right is fulfilled it is extremely difficult (if not impossible) for claimants to point to some positive state act that constitutes an interference with their rights, and it is inappropriate to expect this of them. Instead, the claim will essentially be grounded in a lack of effective state action.[34] In conceiving of state accountability in terms of the breach of a positive duty of performance, it becomes possible to recognize how under-inclusive legislation can violate a fundamental right by "effectively turning a blind eye to, or *sustaining*, independently existing threats to that right."[35] In effect, the exclusion is substantially reinforced by lack of effective state action.

Whether or not the *Charter* obliges the state to take positive actions such as providing services to ameliorate the symptoms of systemic inequality is a question that has consistently been left open by the Supreme Court of Canada. For example, in *Haig*, a majority of the Court wrote that "a government may be required to take positive steps to ensure the equality of people or groups who come within the scope of section 15."[36] In her *obiter* comments in *McKinney*, Wilson J. stated: "It is not self-evident to me that government could not be found to be in breach of the *Charter* for failing to act." In *Vriend* the Court went further in discussing the scope of government obligations under section 32 of the *Charter*:

> The relevant subsection, s. 32(1)(*b*), states that the *Charter* applies to "the legislature and government of each province in respect of all matters within the authority of the legislature of each province." There is nothing in that wording to suggest that a *positive act* encroaching on rights is required; rather the subsection speaks only of *matters within the authority of the legislature*. Dianne Pothier has correctly observed that s. 32 is "worded broadly enough to cover positive obligations on a legislature such that the *Charter* will be engaged even if the legislature refuses to exercise its authority" ("The Sounds of Silence: *Charter* Application when the Legislature Declines to Speak" (1996), 7 *Constitutional Forum* 113, at p. 115). The application of the *Charter* is not restricted to situations where the government actively encroaches on rights.

On the other hand, the courts have been less than open in recognizing a positive duty to ameliorate pre-existing conditions of disadvantage where they cannot be linked specifically to state action. In *Ferrell*, the Ontario Court of Appeal held that there was no constitutional obligation to enact employment equity legislation and therefore under the *Charter* the legislature was not precluded from repealing it.[37] Given the discussion in *Dunmore*, it is important to note the Court found that the human rights commission could deal with claims of employment discrimination. As a result, the case could be characterized as an issue of choice of legislative means rather than total exclusion. Nevertheless, *Ferrell* and a number of other cases contain problematic assertions that appear to limit the nature of governmental obligations under section 15. Much emphasis is placed on the language of section 15: "the wording indicates that the purpose of section 15 is to require that when laws are enacted they do not incorporate distinctions that discriminate on *Charter* grounds. With this in mind, it is difficult to see section

15 as imposing a general obligation to advance equality values."[38] Similarly, in *Lovelace*, the Ontario Court of Appeal held that "governments have no constitutional obligation to remedy all conditions of disadvantage in our society."[39] Even L'Heureux-Dubé J., a more consistent supporter of substantive equality analyses, has made similar statements in her dissents in *Egan*[40] and *Thibaudeau*: "Although section 15 of the *Charter* does not impose upon governments the obligation to take positive actions to remedy the symptoms of systemic inequality, it does require that the government not be the source of further inequality."[41] The underlying concern is that courts are not in a position to answer questions concerning the nature and scope of a positive obligation. Questions of institutional competence are clearly key to progress on these issues.[42] However, the development of a rigorous framework for assessing claims to positive obligations under section 15 will play a leading role in overcoming these institutional concerns.

A principled framework for analysing the nature and scope of the government's positive obligation under section 15 is required to overcome these judicial concerns and to build upon the foundation established by the other lines of cases discussed above. The majority decision in *Dunmore* and Arbour J.'s exploration in *Gosselin* are particularly important in this respect. However, the unanimous Supreme Court of Canada decision in *Meiorin* is the most promising step in this direction.

C. LESSONS FROM *MEIORIN*

The *Meiorin* decision originated in a labour arbitration where the employer, the Government of British Columbia, had imposed a new aerobic fitness standard on firefighters. The grievor, Ms. Meiorin, who had worked as a firefighter for a number of years without problem, was fired when she could not meet that new standard. In its unanimous decision, the Supreme Court of Canada concluded that the running test was not justifiable and in its reasoning revolutionized the analysis and standards for accommodation and justification under human rights legislation. The Court did so with a clear recognition that the jurisprudential changes it made were needed in order to ensure that human rights law fulfills "the promise of substantive equality."[43]

The Court noted the many problems that had developed in the case law with respect to the different approaches available to employers to show that an employment standard, while discriminatory on its face, was nevertheless justifiable in that specific work environment. There were different tests depending on whether the standard was characterized as direct discrimination or adverse effects discrimination. Given the overwhelming critique that had built up over the years, the Court took the opportunity in *Meiorin* to develop a new framework of analysis. In particular, it was noted that under the pre-existing or "conventional" analysis, if a standard was classified as being "neutral" at the initial stage of the inquiry, its legitimacy was never questioned. The focus shifted immediately to whether the individual claimant could be accommodated, and the formal standard itself always remained intact. The conventional analysis thus shifted attention away from the substantive norms underlying the standard, to how "different" individuals can fit into the "mainstream," represented by the standard. The Court declared that while this approach might satisfy the requirements of formal equality, it was inconsistent with substantive equality central to Canadian equality rights law.[44]

The Court elaborated a three-step test for determining whether a standard that had been shown to discriminate is nevertheless justifiable because it is a *bona fide* occupational requirement. An employer has to justify the impugned standard by establishing on the balance of probabilities:

i) that the employer adopted the standard for a purpose rationally connected to the performance of the job;

ii) that the employer adopted the particular standard in an honest and good faith belief that it was necessary to the fulfilment of that legitimate work-related purpose; and

iii) that the standard is reasonably necessary to the accomplishment of that legitimate work-related purpose. To show that the standard is reasonably necessary, it must be demonstrated that it is impossible to accommodate individual employees sharing the characteristics of the claimant without imposing undue hardship upon the employer.

In stating that in order to justify a discriminatory standard an employer must actively demonstrate that it is "impossible" to make changes without imposing undue hardship, the Court sent a clear signal of the heavy onus on employers to take active steps to avoid discrimination wherever and however possible.

In *Meiorin,* the Supreme Court of Canada went further than simply reformulating this legal test and clarifying that it applied both to direct and adverse effects discrimination. It also provided general guidance on the nature of the employer's positive obligation under human rights law to build equality into the workplace. It used these strong words:

Employees designing workplace standards owe an obligation to be aware of both the differences between individuals and the differences that characterize groups of individuals. They must build conceptions of equality into workplace standards.[45]

The decision greatly expands the nature and extent of the employer's duty to accommodate. This obligation has both *procedural* and *substantive* dimensions. Employers must demonstrate that they have undertaken an active, pro-active, and good-faith process in considering how workplace rules or policies have an adverse impact on a group of employees and how these discriminatory effects could be reduced or eliminated. Employers should be "innovative, yet practical" in fulfilling this obligation. This process should be an inclusive one as employers, employees, and unions have a shared role in meeting this obligation. Courts will also review whether or not the employer has successfully discharged the substantive content of this obligation; that is, whether or not they have been successful in redesigning rules and policies to accord with substantive equality principles.

The Court went on to illustrate the nature of the duty to accommodate by listing some of the important questions that a tribunal or court may ask in the course of reviewing whether or not a workplace standard is justified:

(a) Has the employer investigated alternative approaches that do not have a discriminatory effect, such as individual testing against a more individually sensitive standard?

(b) If alternative standards were investigated and found to be capable of fulfilling the employer's purpose, why were they not implemented?

(c) Is it necessary to have *all* employees meet the single standard for the employer to accomplish its legitimate purpose or could standards reflective of group or individual differences and capabilities be established?

(d) Is there a way to do the job that is less discriminatory while still accomplishing the employer's legitimate purpose?

(e) Is the standard properly designed to ensure that the desired qualification is met without placing an undue burden on those to whom the standard applies?

(f) Have other parties who are obliged to assist in the search for possible accommodation fulfilled their roles? (For example, the empoyee herself and/or a union).[46]

Although this list of factors is written from the perspective of a human rights review of what the employer has done, in effect it provides explicit instructions as to what steps must be taken in order to avoid discrimination.

Meiorin introduced profound changes in the legal conception of accommodation and what has been called a "comprehensive accommodation analysis."[47] Before this decision, employers had only to consider accommodation of an individual by assisting those who didn't fit the existing standard, without changing the discrimination standard. Now, the duty is two-fold. First, an employer must consider whether the standard itself can be changed so as to be more inclusive and promote substantive equality in the workplace. Second, if this is not possible, or if the standard is fully justifiable under the new higher legal threshold, then substantial efforts toward individual accommodation are still required. The comprehensive accommodation analysis provides a principled framework for a consideration of whether or not an employer has carried out its positive duty to create equality in the workplace. It delineates a deliberative and participatory process that encourages the parties involved to scrutinize underlying norms in a reflective manner. It integrates a consideration of the individual and systemic manifestations of discrimination. Further, it builds in consideration of equality norms into the reconstruction of workplace policies and practices. It articulates a "transformative ideal for equality law"[48] that is fully consistent with the norm of substantive equality.

A few months later, in *Grismer*, the Supreme Court of Canada confirmed that this new approach to justification and accommodation applied in all cases of discrimination — not just in the workplace — and more specifically, that it applies to governments.[49] Everyone governed by human rights legislation is required:

> to accommodate the characteristics of affected groups within their standards, rather than maintaining discriminatory standards supplemented by accommodation for those who cannot meet them. Incorporating accommodation into the standard itself ensures that each person is assessed according to her or his own personal abilities, instead of being judged against presumed group characteristics.[50]

In order to prove that its standard is "reasonably necessary," the defendant always bears the burden of demonstrating that the standard incorporates every possible accommodation to the point of undue hardship, whether that hardship takes the form of impossibility, serious risk, or excessive cost.

Meiorin has had an immediate and profound effect in the workplace both through informal voluntary application in the employment context,[51] in workplace grievances processes,[52] and in the review of these efforts by human rights tribunals and the courts.[53] There is general agreement that the threshold for accommodation is high. With only a few exceptions, tribunals and courts have been unwilling to defer to employers or others and require evidence of the steps taken to accommodate employees, both at the systemic level in terms of changing the standard itself and at the individual level where it is impossible to change the standard. Where no steps have been taken to accommodate, the discriminatory standard cannot be justified. Similarly, where the Tribunal has not undertaken a substantive and comprehensive accommodation analysis, this has been overturned upon judicial review. Some tribunals and courts have rejected the *Meiorin* test as being inapplicable in a given case. For example, in *Robb,* a case dealing with whether or not a school had discriminated against a child with a learning disability, the BC Human Rights Tribunal decided that because the complainants alleged a series of discriminatory actions rather than a discriminatory policy or standard, the three-part analysis is difficult to apply.[54] Here, the Tribunal effectively applied the relevant principles from *Meiorin* without strictly following the three-step analysis. *Robb* is a positive development because it focuses on the application of the substance of *Meiorin* in a flexible way rather than being unduly concerned with framing the analysis in the formal steps outlined by the Supreme Court of Canada's decision.

Meiorin did not provide guidance on the issue of what constitutes undue hardship. The post-*Meiorin* cases make it very clear that the respondent must have taken some steps to ascertain whether accommodation was possible, both on a systemic and an individual basis. A defence of undue hardship requires more than impressionistic evidence. Where the issue is the cost of accommodation, tribunals have been willing to weigh this as a factor relative to the respondent's ability to pay and the evidence of actual harm. However, in the majority of cases the cost argument has not won out.[55] An important factor has been evidence of what types of accommodation have been undertaken by other comparable organizations. A tribunal's willingness to look at what types of alternatives have worked elsewhere is a positive development since it makes it harder for governments to argue that no alternatives are available. In essence, the novel practices developed in other contexts provide new minimum standards of equality-promoting practices. However, it is important that these new practices not become reified as the only possible. The search for more fully inclusive workplaces, laws, and policies is an ongoing one.

The *Meiorin* approach also fosters a greater emphasis on the prospective impact of remedies beyond the specific case and can lead to the generation of solutions that address individual and systemic inequalities. Remedies must operate at various levels of change in order to enhance transformative possibilities. Litigation strategies should encompass remedial approaches that facilitate the integration of human rights norms at the individual, doctrinal, institutional, and structural levels. The strength of *Meiorin* lies in the fact that the Court provided guidance at the individual level in terms of the duty on employers, at the institutional level with respect to procedures to be followed, and at the analytic level in terms of substance of the duty to accommodate. In the *Beaulac* case, the Supreme Court recognized that governments are obliged to do all that is "practically possible" to ensure minority language rights, a comment that helps to shape government attitudes in addition to setting out the specific approach to remedy in the case.[56] In effect, *Meiorin* tells employers to do all that is "practically possible" with respect to ensuring equality rights in the workplace. The time has come for the Court to tell governments that they are obliged to do all that is "practically possible" to promote substantive equality in Canada.

D. EXTENDING THE GOVERNMENT'S POSITIVE DUTY

One goal for future equality litigation could be to develop and promote a principled basis for determining the content of this positive governmental obligation to do all that is "practically possible" to promote equality through test-case intervention. This appears to be of particular importance in the pursuit of women's substantive equality given the difficulties the courts have had in recognizing adverse effects discrimination against women.[57] There have been clear victories in many sex equality cases, including in interpreting and applying section 15.[58] However, a full-out section 15 win for women on the basis of sex discrimination has eluded us at the Supreme Court of Canada level. The first section 15 "victory" on the basis of sex discrimination came in July 2003, when a *man* won a challenge to the provisions in the birth registration process which had provided the mother with a privileged role in deciding whether or not to acknowledge the father and in naming her child.[59] This inequality was the very "definition of discrimination" in the view of a unanimous Court. The irony of this outcome — in the ready recognition of sex discrimination which overturned a statutory provision which had been directed at protecting vulnerable women — should be a galvanizing point for a new approach to constitutional equality analysis. Framing future cases as governmental failure to take into account women's already disadvantaged position in Canadian society may help to overcome the court's difficulties in appreciating the nexus between legislation or governmental action and the adverse effect on women. The following section is an initial inquiry into some of the elements that could comprise such a strategy.

1) Limitations of *Law*

There is a much greater emphasis on substantive equality in *Meiorin* by comparison with the Court's approach in *Law*. The limitations of *Law* have been widely discussed and include: the overemphasis on stereotype; the narrow focus on an infringement of "human dignity" as an indicator of substantive discrimination; a tendency toward focusing the contextual analysis on the legislative scheme rather than on the claimant's situation; and an enhanced inclination to consider justifications of differential treatment within the finding of a *prima facie* case of discrimination under section 15 rather than as a reasonable limit under section 1. The problems associated with the *Law* framework suggest the need to develop an alternative approach to section 15 analysis concerning the nature and scope of the state's positive obligation. The Supreme Court has recognized that the correct approach to section 15 is a flexible and nuanced analysis, not a rigid test. It has also recognized the need for evolution and adaptation of equality analysis over time in order to accommodate new or different understandings of equality as well as new issues raised by varying fact situations.[60]

In many post-*Law* cases, both the comparative analysis and the dignity inquiry have been used to shield differential treatment. The courts appear to be getting it backwards. Rather than conducting a contextual analysis from the perspective of the claimant and then measuring whether impact falls below the standard of substantive equality, the courts increasingly assign a contextual primacy to a purported legislative purpose and conduct an equality analysis solely with reference to its relationship to achieve the purpose which is not critically analysed. The effect is to conduct an analysis within the four corners of the challenged legislation — an approach expressly rejected by the Supreme Court of Canada in *Andrews*. The purpose of the section 15 analysis is to act as a shield for positive differential treatment that in fact assists members of disadvantaged groups, not to protect distinctions that have an adverse impact on the claimant.

It may be possible to argue that the *Law* framework is inapplicable to claims based on the positive obligation under section 15. For example, one should ask: What is the role of comparative analysis in the context of claims that a government has failed to take into account women's substantive inequality? The fundamental purpose of the comparative analysis is to reveal the differential treatment. Where a section 15 claim is based on a failure to accommodate, comparing the treatment between two groups tends to obscure rather than clarify the discriminatory treatment and the required remedy. Several appellate courts stressed that a more flexible comparator analysis is required in these cases. For example, in *Falkiner*, the Ontario Court of Appeal shifted between three separate comparators (based on sex, marital status, and receipt of social assistance) and discussed how these grounds interacted.[61]

A section 15 analysis should assist the courts in moving away from abstract notions of equality and toward critical reflection; that is, the rethinking of basic premises and norms. The latter is key because: "Fundamentally an equality analysis ought to be about questioning basic premises to test whether they are consistent with constitutional norms."[62] This is what the Court did in *Meiorin*. It carried out a close examination of the beliefs, assumptions, and norms that shaped the employment standard within the whole factual context. It was a true substantive equality analyses because it extended to how the differences between men and women were recognized, given meaning, and valued (or not). Rather than being preoccupied with a comparative analysis, the approach took into account the systems and structures that reproduce these inequalities (the way the test was designed as being based on the norms of those who had traditionally occupied the position) and examined the whole equality picture surrounding Ms. Meiorin and her claim.

Similarly, the dignity inquiry fulfils only one part of the purpose of section 15. Other types of harm, ones that are less individualistic and more relational and systemic than dignity, may be more helpful in dealing with the second, positive aspect of the right to equality. A focus on human dignity does not require the courts to examine the nature of structural inequality and its impact on individuals. It encompasses a limited conception of equality that is based foremost on an understanding of discrimination as operating through stereotypes and assumptions. It cannot adequately capture the differential effects that discrimination imposes through the operation of relations of power, patterns, practices, and norms.[63]

In essence, the *Law* framework has not demonstrated its ability to overcome the fixation on formal equality. It may be that only limited gains can be made from trying to work within its narrow confines or focusing on incremental change to the more problematic aspects of analysis under it. While these are worthwhile projects, greater potential lies in relegating *Law* to anti-discrimination cases and proposing an alternative approach to cases that bring into question the governments' positive obligations under section 15. *Meiorin* is founded on a profound substantive equality analysis and is inconsistent with a formal equality approach. Further work is required on how to translate this inquiry into the *Charter* context. It would involve the courts affirming that governments have an obligation to "be aware of both the differences between individuals and the differences that characterize groups of individuals" and that they must "build conceptions of equality" into legislative and policymaking procedures and resulting standards and provisions.[64]

2) Location of Accommodation Analysis: Section 15 or Section 1

A second important issue is where to locate the comprehensive accommodation analysis. Should it be seen as part of the section 15 or section 1 analysis? Whereas before *Meiorin* reasonable accommodation was equivalent to a reasonable limit under section 1, now it is something much more. This suggests to me that in the *Charter* context the accommodation analysis should have two aspects: as part of the evidence of discriminatory effects and as part of the justification under section 1.

The level of proof required to make out a *prima facie* case of discrimination is generally lower under human rights legislation than under section 15. The *Andrews* and *Law* approach has been to integrate some justificatory analysis within the three-stage section 15 inquiry. While initially motivated by a desire to protect distinctions designed to ameliorate conditions of disadvantage, this approach has placed additional hurdles on claimants to prove that differential treatment amounts to discrimination. It has also led to a blurring of the section 15 and section 1 considerations, to the detriment of claimants. It is important to keep these two as distinct stages of inquiry because of the relative burden of proof on the claimant and the government in each of the stages.

The comprehensive accommodation analysis established in *Meiorin* requires that the responsible party take active steps to take into account the needs and/or characteristics of the claimant/group. In order to avoid a finding of discrimination, the government would have to show that it has taken steps to avoid discrimination and that the impugned law or policy is as inclusive as possible. This is the procedural component of the *Meiorin* accommodation analysis and could be incorporated into the inquiry under section 15. Where there is no evidence of attempts to accommodate, the section 1 defence would not be available to the government. It is also important to note that section 1 only applies to legislation since a reasonable limit must be "prescribed by law." Thus, a comprehensive accommodation analysis could be of particular importance in respect of the administration of a law or policy by government.

The *Meiorin* approach also assists in refining the existing section 1 test that would now be analogous to the "undue hardship" analysis. To begin, it would assist in giving meaning to the phrase "demonstrably justified" as an element of the section 1 test because it would encompass an inquiry into what the government had actually done to ameliorate the experience of disadvantage — simple claims that a state action has an overall ameliorative purpose would be insufficient. In addition, the analysis of the government objectives would be more critical and transformative under the *Meiorin* approach by comparison with the deference conventionally bestowed in *Charter* litigation. Finally, the *substantive* dimensions of the duty to accommodate are more extensive than the current considerations of rational connection and minimal impairment. The substantive dimension speaks of investigating "how the discriminatory effects could be reduced or eliminated"; it is phrased as a positive duty to promote equality rather than a negative one to minimize harm. At the section 1 stage the courts will also review whether the government has successfully discharged the substantive content of this obligation; that is, whether or not they have been successful in redesigning laws and policies to accord with substantive equality principles.

There are a number of outstanding issues that also should be taken into consideration here. It is important to question whether the *Meiorin* approach to accommodation goes far enough. What other elements might we want to build into the comprehensive accommodation analysis if it is to be imported into the section 15 framework? Secondly, there is the problem of the conventional limited approach to accommodation that may hamper its transformative potential, just as traditional formal equality notions continue to plague section 15 analyses. The LEAF National Legal Committee's Sub-Committee that worked on the *Meiorin* factum talked about the advantages of finding new terminology to distinguish between the two types of accommodation at the systemic and individual levels. In the end, we opted to stay with the term "accommodation" because we felt the court would be more comfortable with it. However, there may be different considerations in the *Charter* context.

3) Invigorating Section 15 with Substantive Content

Andrews recognized that section 15 read as a whole "constitutes a compendious expression of a positive right to equality in both the substance and the administration of the law." However, very little doctrine has been developed on the content of the four basic rights protected by this *Charter* provision: (1) the right to equality before the law; (2) the right to equality under the law; (3) the right to equal protection of the law; and (4) the right to equal benefit of the law. The focus of analysis is almost solely on the second part of this section; that is, on the modifier of "without discrimination" on the enumerated or analogous grounds. Yet these four rights could provide a set of boundaries to the amorphous concept of equality, boundaries that could provide the courts with the limits that they are continually searching for in their section 15 analysis. Invigorating these phrases as substantive guarantees would also assist in responding to some of the questions over institutional competence of the courts when dealing with positive state obligations.

A related goal is to develop a refined theory of sex inequality stated as a legal principle. This is an integral part of this focus on giving content to the concept of substantive equality, thereby enhancing the courts' ability to recognize sex discrimination issues. The Court has made important strides in its ability to succinctly state the nature of discrimination on the basis of disability.[65] While their discussion is far from perfect, it underscores the fact that Canadian courts do not have such a clear or coherent understanding of the rationale underlying the prohibition of discrimination on the basis of sex. In a trilogy of cases decided more than fifteen years ago, the Supreme Court made important headway on this task by recognizing some of the dimensions of sex inequality, including those related to women's role as childbearers,[66] sexual harassment,[67] and systemic discrimination in the workplace.[68] However, little progress has been made since then toward a broad judicial understanding of the complex facets affecting women's inequality, both in terms of the general structures affecting all women and the diverse and intersecting experience of identifiable groups of women. Judicial recognition of a general theory of women's substantive inequality would provide a framework against which the specific facts of a case could be further elucidated.[69] In many cases, this type of reference point would provide the required comparative analysis, rendering visible the needs of women, by comparison with men, that governments are obliged to take into account in legislative and policy-making processes.

4) Integration of Equality Analysis and Remedy

One of the continuing issues in achieving substantive equality is how to craft legal remedies that substantively contribute to the eradication of inequality and the creation of equality. Criticisms that the courts are being too "activist" often focus on the remedy ordered by the court. In the context of *Charter* litigation, the courts have favoured granting declaratory relief in very broad terms that provide governments with a large degree of latitude to formulate a specific response. This "remedial consensus" is generally seen to be an appropriate and balanced approach, with the court elaborating the constitutional standard and leaving the government with the responsibility of making the necessary changes.[70] However, a simple declaration that a provision or act violates the *Charter* may not go far enough toward creating substantive equality. Legal strategies need to incorporate careful thought about remedies that will serve this ultimate objective. Winning the case on legal principles is not usually enough.

The *Meiorin* approach lends itself to greater integration between analysis of *Charter* breach and remedy by comparison with the *Law* framework. *Meiorin* requires that the parties and the court take one further step in the contextual inquiry by deconstructing and reconstructing an impugned standard or provision so that it is consistent with substantive equality principles. This approach would go further than current section 15 equality analysis because rather than simply considering wider social conditions that cause laws to have unequal effects, reconstruction requires the court to consider how unequal social conditions can be changed.

Other promising developments on the remedial front should be borne in mind in elaborating the governmental responsibility to promote equality.

In *Auton*, the Court found that the lack of treatment for autistic children infringed their right to equality, ordered the government to begin providing a specific type of treatment to them, and awarded symbolic damages to the claimants. In making the order, the Court noted "the apparent and regrettable intransigence on the issue of this therapy by those administering the province's program for children justifies an order beyond the usual *Charter* remedy of mere declaration." The approach taken was seen to serve the twin remedial purposes of "governmental behaviour modification and compensation for an applicant whose *Charter* rights have been breached." The BC Court of Appeal upheld this order and left open the possibility of an order in the nature of mandamus if the government did not respond adequately. In *Auton* the Supreme Court of Canada ultimately overturned the finding of a *Charter* breach and so did not address the question of remedy.[71] However, in other cases the Supreme Court has expressly recognized that novel and creative approaches are often necessary to ensure an effective and meaningful remedy "because tradition and history cannot be barriers to what reasoned and compelling notions of appropriate and just remedies demand."[72] This decision invites claimants to propose remedies that are responsive to the facts of their case, keeping in mind the overarching goal of substantive equality.

The human rights context provides an alternative, more proactive approach to remedies by comparison with section 15 jurisprudence to date. Human rights tribunals have large remedial powers to order that the discrimination cease and that steps be taken to ensure that the same or similar contravention is not repeated, and to order parties to take other steps to ameliorate the effects of the discriminatory practice. The only jurisprudential limitation placed on the remedial powers of human rights tribunals comes from a series of cases that assert human rights remedies are compensatory, rather than punitive, and are aimed at ameliorating discrimination. In the leading case of *Action Travail*, the order extended to the implementation of specific pro-active and systemic ameliorative programs or measures, with obvious cost implications, in order to resolve patterns of discrimination. These programs can require continuing consultation between the respondent and a human rights commission, or the issuing of "Ministry-wide systemic directives" in order to achieve compliance with human rights legislation. Tribunals have held that the government's rights to allocate resources cannot override human rights legislation although tribunals will not tell the government how to pay for costs involved in meeting their orders. Recent cases of note include: *Sparkes*,[73] where the government was ordered to abolish wait-lists for early intervention treatment for autistic children; *Gwinner*, where the government was ordered to extend widow's pensions to women who were divorced or separated at the time of their former spouse's death;[74] and *McKinnon*, where the government was ordered to undertake an extensive range of systemic remedies to eradicate racial discrimination in the provincial corrections system.[75]

One of the procedural aspects of the duty to accommodate elaborated in *Meiorin* is the requirement that all the parties have a voice in the development of a standard that is consistent with equality rights norms. While this process is easier to imagine in a contained workplace, the approach could be incorporated into the *Charter* context. First, courts could require governments to consult both with the claimant and other affected parties during the process of formulating a response when the Court declares that a given law is invalid because it infringes a *Charter* right. In some cases, governments have engaged in a public dialogue as part of the policy-making process to formulate a response to the declaratory order. For example, the federal government undertook consultations following the Supreme Court's declaration in *Corbière* that the exclusion of off-reserve Indians from band elections violated the equality rights of this group.[76] However, claimants and groups have not always been happy with the consultation process or the outcome.[77]

Beyond participation, *Charter* decisions should set out the substantive principles flowing from equality norms that should structure the remedial dialogue between the parties. This is the substantive side of the duty to accommodate in *Meiorin*. This approach does not involve judges dictating the details of compliance. However, courts and human rights commissions can help to foster remedial discourse by maintaining jurisdiction until the remedy is fully implemented. The courts have a long history of retaining jurisdiction for this purpose in a number of *Charter* language rights cases,[78] and, as discussed above, in at least one section 15 case.[79] The Supreme Court of Canada affirmed the court's ability to retain jurisdiction in *Charter* cases in *Doucet-Boudreau v. Nova Scotia*.[80] The retention of jurisdiction allows the court to do more than simply enforce remedies — it provides a forum for the court to resolve disputes about the meaning and implications of a general declaration. In the words of the dissenting Court of Appeal judge in *Doucet-Boudreau*, court supervision provides "a means of mediation" to achieve the result in a case.[81]

E. CONCLUSION

The limited development of the jurisprudence on the government's positive obligation to promote equality results in both impatience and hope. The creative tension between the two can be harnessed to infuse the transformative potential of equality rights litigation with renewed energy. In 1999, the Supreme Court of Canada provided us with two radically different approaches to equality rights analysis. In this paper, I have argued that there is no doubt as to the outcome of the *"Law v. Meiorin"* case. Despite its incorporation of the language and some of the concepts of substantive equality, the *Law* framework has clearly shown itself to be a vehicle for mechanical application, allowing the resurgence of formal equality thinking. By contrast, *Meiorin's* comprehensive accommodation analysis, with its emphasis on critical review of how underlying norms privilege some and disadvantage others, is fully consistent with substantive equality analysis. Our goal is to work toward a case in which the courts tell governments that they are obliged to do all that is "practically possible" to promote substantive equality in Canada. It is clear that *Law* will not get us there. This paper is a first step into an inquiry on how the approach adopted in *Meiorin* could assist us in furthering the positive obligation on governments under section 15 of the *Charter*.

ENDNOTES

1   *Andrews v. Law Society of British Columbia*, [1989] 1 S.C.R. 143 [*Andrews*]; *Eaton Brant County Board of Education*, [1997] 1 S.C.R. 241 [*Eaton*]; *Eldridge v. British Columbia (Attorney General)*, [1997] 3 S.C.R. 624 [*Eldridge*]; *Law v. Canada (Minister of Employment and Immigration)*, [1999] 1 S.C.R. 497 [*Law*].

2   *Law, ibid.*

3   This paper does not provide an overview and critique of the problems experienced with the *Law* framework of analysis. However, several of the papers in this volume undertake this important task.

4   *British Columbia (Public Service Employee Relations Commission) v. BCGSEU*, [1999] 3 S.C.R. 3. This case is often referred to as the *Meiorin* case after the claimant firefighter, Tawney Meiorin [*Meiorin*].

5   See for example, *Law*, above note 1 at paras. 41 & 88.

6   *Eldridge*, above note 1 at para. 54.

7   *Andrews*, above note 1 at 163–64, McIntyre J.

8   *Ibid.* at 171.

9   *Ibid.* at 169.

10   *Eaton*, above note 1 at paras. 66–68.

11   See for example *Shachter v. Canada*, [1992] 2 S.C.R. 679; *Vriend v. Alberta*, [1998] 1 S.C.R. 493.

12   *Auton (Guardian ad litem of) v. British Columbia* (2000), 80 C.R.R.(3D.) 333 (B.C.S.C.); (2002), 220 D.L.R. (4th) 41 (BCCA) [*Auton*]. The Supreme Court of Canada reversed this decision in finding that there was no discrimination on the facts of this case, [2004] 3 S.C.R. 657.

13   See for example *Law*, above note 1 at para.105.

14   *Brooks v. Canada Safeway Ltd.* [1989] 1 S.C.R. 1291 [*Brooks*].

15   See *Slaight Communications Inc. v. Davidson*, [1989] 1 S.C.R. 1038 where the Court held that an adjudicator, who exercises delegated powers, does not have the power to make an order that would result in an infringement of the *Charter*.

16   *Baker v. Canada*, [1999] 2 S.C.R. 817 at para. 56.

17   See for example *Hill v. Church of Scientology of Toronto*, [1995] 2 S.C.R. 1130. For a discussion see Peter Hogg, "Equality as a *Charter* Value in Constitutional Interpretation" (2003), 20 S.C.L.R. (2d) 113.

18   *Nova Scotia v. Martin*, [2003] 2 S.C.R. 504 at para. 28 [*Martin*].

19   See for example *Operation Dismantle v. The Queen*, [1985] 1 S.C.R. 441.

20   *Cooper v. Canada (Human Rights Commission)*, [1996] 3 S.C.R. 854 at para. 70. Quoted with approval by the majority in *Martin*, above note 18 at para. 28.

21   *Jane Doe v. Metro Toronto Police et al.* (1998), 160 D.L.R. (4th) 697 (Ont. Gen. Div.). The decision led to an audit of policing practices resulting in recommendations for sweeping changes to the state response to sexual assault cases.

22   *Little Sisters Book and Art Emporium v. Canada (Minister of Justice)*, [2000] 2 S.C.R. 1120.

23   *Ibid.* at para. 256.

24 *Haig v. Canada (Chief Electoral Officer)*, [1993] 2 S.C.R. 995 [*Haig*]; *Native Women's Association of Canada v. Canada*, [1994] 3 S.C.R. 267; *R. v. Big M Drug Mart Ltd.*, [1985] 1 S.C.R. 295.

25 Two clear examples are *R. v. Beaulac*, [1999] 1 S.C.R. 768 at para. 24 [*Beaulac*] and *Moncton (City) v. Charlesbois*, [2001] N.B.J. No. 480, 2001 NBCA 117.

26 *Dunmore v. Ontario (Attorney General)*, [2001] 3 S.C.R. 1016 [*Dunmore*].

27 This case is also instructive regarding the importance of a complementary s. 15 argument. Because the majority decided solely on the basis of the s. 2(d) freedom to associate and did not deal with the equality argument put forward by the claimants, the Court did not provide them with the full relief they sought. As result, the equality argument will have to be re-litigated. *Dunmore* underscores the importance of fully integrating equality with arguments based on other constitutional provisions or principles. See Dianne Pothier, "Twenty Years of Labour Law and the *Charter*" (2002) 40 Osgoode Hall L.J. 369 at 386.

28 *Ibid.* at para. 22.

29 *Ibid.*

30 Where the claim deals with access to a statutory right, it should be brought under s.15.

31 *Dunmore*, above note 26 at para. 26, Bastarache J.

32 *Gosselin v. Quebec*, [2002] 4 S.C.R. 429 [*Gosselin*]. Arbour J.'s dissenting reasons are at paras. 305–98.

33 Only Justice Bastarache foreclosed this line of argument, and his reasons in *Gosselin* appear to be at odds with his reasoning in *Dunmore* (there is a lively and illuminating difference of opinion whether or not the *Dunmore* criteria are satisfied on the facts of *Gosselin*).

34 *Gosselin*, above note 32, Arbour J. dissenting at para. 362.

35 *Ibid.* at para. 379.

36 *Haig*, above note 24 at 1041. See also *Eldridge*, above note 1 at para. 73.

37 *Ferrell v. Ontario (A.G.)* (1998), 42 O.R. (3d) 97 (C.A.).

38 *Ibid.* at para. 46.

39 *Lovelace v. Ontario* (1977), 33 O.R. (3d) 735 (C.A.) at para. 64.

40 *Egan v. Canada*, [1995] 2 S.C.R. 513 at 541–44.

41 *Thibaudeau v. Canada*, [1995] 2 S.C.R. 627 at 655.

42 This aspect of the issue is discussed in detail in Jamie Cameron, "Positive Obligations under Sections 15 and 7 of the *Charter*: A Comment on *Gosselin v. Quebec*" (2003) 20 S.C.L.R. 65.

43 *Meiorin*, above note 4 at para. 41.

44 *Ibid.* In making this finding the Court relied on Shelagh Day & Gwen Brodsky. "The Duty to Accommodate: Who Will Benefit?" (1996) 75 Can. Bar Rev. 433.

45 *Meiorin*, above note 4 at para. 68.

46 *Ibid.* at para. 65.

47 This is the term adopted by Greckol J. in *Gwinner v. Alberta* (2002), 44 C.H.R.R. D/52, 2002 ABQB 685 [*Gwinner*].

48　Colleen Sheppard, "Of Forest Fires and Systemic Discrimination: A Review of *British Columbia (Public Service Employee Relations Commission) v. B.C.G.S.E.U*" (2001) 46 McGill L.J. 533 at 550.

49　*British Columbia (Superintendent of Motor Vehicles) v. British Columbia (Council of Human Rights)*, [1999] 3 S.C.R. 868.

50　*Ibid.* at para. 19.

51　At a conference organized by Women in Trades and Technologies in March 2001, many participants provided examples of how the decision had been utilized to address discriminatory practices in the workplace. For example, a representative from BC Hydro discussed how she had brought the decision to the attention of senior management and how it had led to major changes within that workplace.

52　This is the consensus of labour arbitrators whom I have interviewed.

53　I reviewed how *Meiorin* was being applied by tribunals and courts across Canada using the Canadian Human Rights Reporter database in September 2003 and draw the conclusions discussed here based on my reading of all these cases (approximately sixty).

54　*Robb v. St.Margaret's School* (2003), 45 C.H.R.R. D/276, 2003 BCHRT 4.

55　This is equally true in several recent tribunal decisions dealing with legislation and government policy. See the discussion below in the section on remedies.

56　*Beaulac*, above note 25 at para. 24.

57　These difficulties have been well documented: see for example Shelagh Day & Gwen Brodsky, *Women and the Equality Deficit: The Impact of Restructuring Canada's Social Program* (Status of Women Canada, March 1998) and Dianne Pothier "M'Aider, Mayday: Section 15 of the *Charter* in Distress" (1996) 6 N.J.C.L. 295.

58　Interestingly many of the legal victories at the Supreme Court of Canada with the greatest impact on ameliorating women's inequality in the non-criminal/penal context have been in non-constitutional cases where equality analysis has permeated common law and statutory interpretations (i.e., *Norberg v. Wynrib*, [1992] 2 S.C.R. 226 and *Moge v. Moge*, [1992] 3 S.C.R. 813) and in the human rights context (i.e., *Action Travail*, below note 68; *Brooks*, above note 14; and *Janzen*, below note 67).

59　*Trociuk v. BC (Attorney General)*, [2003] 1 S.C.R. 835.

60　*Law*, above note 1 at para. 3.

61　*Falkiner v. Ontario (Minister of Community and Social Services)* (2002), 59 O.R. (3d) 481 (C.A.). Note that the Ontario government withdrew its appeal to the Supreme Court of Canada in September 2004.

62　Pothier, above note 57 at 310.

63　However, the court does state that it will "always be helpful for the claimant to identify a pattern of discrimination against a class of persons with traits similar to the claimant." *Law*, above note 1 at para. 66.

64　*Meiorin*, above note 4 at para. 68.

65　Including most recently in *Martin*, above note 18.

66　*Brooks*, above note 14.

67　*Janzen v. Platy Enterprises Ltd.*, [1989] 1 S.C.R. 1252 [*Janzen*].

68   *Canadian National Railway Co. v. Canada (Canadian Human Rights Commission)*,
     [1987] 1 S.C.R. 1114 (often referred to as *Action Travail* after the original complain-
     ants Action Travail des femmes).
69   For examples of this type of encapsulated statement that could inform my proposal,
     see Day & Brodsky, *Women and the Equality Deficit*, above note 57 at 7; and Susan
     Okin, *Justice, Gender and the Family* (New York: Basic Books, 1989) and discussion
     on the latter in Iris Young, *Inclusion and Democracy* (Oxford: Oxford University
     Press, 2000) at 94.
70   Kent Roach, "Remedial Consensus and Challenge in Equality Rights and Minority
     Language Rights Cases" (Winnipeg: Court Challenges Program of Canada, 2001).
71   *Auton*, above note 12.
72   *Doucet-Boudreau v. Nova Scotia (Minister of Education)*, [2003] 3 S.C.R. 3 at para.
     59.
73   *Newfoundland and Labrador (Ministry of Health and Community Services) v.
     Sparkes* (2002), 45 C.H.R.R. D/225 (Nfld. Bd. Inq.), upheld on appeal *Newfound-
     land and Labrador (Ministry of Health and Community Services) v. Sparkes* (2004),
     48 C.H.R.R. D/457, 2004 NLSCTD 16.
74   *Gwinner*, above note 47. Affirmed by the Alberta Court of Appeal: *Gwinner v. Al-
     berta (Minister of Human Resources and Employment)* (2004), CHRR Doc. 04-151,
     2004 ABCA 210.
75   *McKinnon v. Ontario (Ministry of Correctional Services) (No. 1)* (1996), C.H.R.R.
     Doc. NP/96-131 (Ont. Bd. Inq.); *(No. 2)* (1997), C.H.R.R. NP/97-77 (Ont. Bd.
     Inq.); *(No. 3)* (1998), 32 C.H.R.R. D/1 (Ont. Bd. Inq.); *(No. 4)* (1999), 35 C.H.R.R.
     D/191 (Ont. Bd. Inq.); *(sub nom. Ontario (Ministry of Correctional Services) v.
     Ontario (Human Rights Comm.))* (2001), 39 C.H.R.R. D/308 (Ont. Sup. Ct.); *(No.
     5)* (2001), CHRR Doc. 01-202 (Ont. Bd. Inq.); *(No. 6)* (2001), 41 C.H.R.R. D/234
     (Ont. Bd. Inq.). The Ontario courts have supportive of the Human Rights Commis-
     sion's attempts to supervise the enforcement of this order. See most recently, *Ontario
     (Ministry of Correctional Services) v. Ontario (Human Rights Comm.)* (2004),
     CHRR Doc. 04-419 (Ont. C.A.).
76   *Corbière v. Canada*, [1999] 2 S.C.R. 203. The first stage of the government's response
     included funding for four Aboriginal groups to participate in this process as well as
     training sessions for bands to facilitate their participation.
77   For example, in applying the decision in *M. v. H.*, [1999] 2 S.C.R. 3 (a declaration
     that exclusion of same sex couples from support provisions of family law legislation
     was unconstitutional because it infringed the claimant's s.15 right to equality), the
     successful *Charter* applicant, as well as some organizations representing gays and
     lesbians were strongly opposed to the manner the Ontario government took in
     extending benefits and obligations in light of the court's ruling because it amounted
     to further discrimination. Jason Murphy, "Dialogic Responses to *M. v. H.*: From
     Compliance to Defiance" (2001) 59 U.T. Fac. L. Rev. 299. The successful applicant
     asked the Supreme Court to re-visit the matter but her request was denied without
     reasons from the court. Many Aboriginal groups have also expressed their dissat-
     isfaction with the federal government's approach to implementing the decision in

Corbière, especially in terms of the amount of time taken to develop a plan of action. Roach, "Remedial Consensus," above note 70 at 30–31.

78 Numerous examples exist in litigation concerning official minority language rights claims under ss. 16–23 of the *Charter*. Two examples will suffice. First, in the *Manitoba Language Reference*, the Supreme Court of Canada retained jurisdiction over the matter by suspending the declaration of invalidity for the minimum period of time necessary to translate the unilingual laws. This issue returned to court a number of times as information emerged on what the minimum time was for the translation process. See, for example, *Reference re Manitoba Language Rights supplementary reasons*, [1985] 2 S.C.R. 347, [1990] 3 S.C.R. 1417, [1992] 1 S.C.R. 212. A second example can be found in *Marchand v. Simcoe County Board of Education (No.2)* (1987), 44 D.L.R. (4th) 171 (Ont. S.C.), where court ordered injunctive relief against a school board and retained jurisdiction to the extent that it was willing to consider whether the school board's proposed plan satisfied the requirements of the *Charter*.

79 In *Auton*, at the B.C. Supreme Court, Allan J. issued a general declaration but maintained a "limited supervisory role" so that the applicants could renew their premature application for mandatory relief if the government did not implement an effective program in a timely manner. *Auton*, above note 12, at para. 47 (B.C.S.C). This approach was upheld by the BC Court of Appeal but was not addressed by the Supreme Court of Canada.

80 2000 N.S.J. No. 191 (T.D.), rev'd with respect to remedies 2001 N.S.J. No. 240 (C.A.). In this case, the trial judge issued a declaration of entitlement to homogeneous facilities and programs for French language education without unreasonable delay and the that the defendants were to make their best efforts to provide such programs and facilities.

81 *Ibid.* at para. 12, Freeman J.A.

Part Two

EQUALITY CLAIMS IN CONTEXT

six

Women Are Themselves to Blame:
CHOICE AS A JUSTIFICATION FOR UNEQUAL TREATMENT[1]

Diana Majury[2]

> Speech that seeks power to transform the world, as well as the human subject, must embrace a political language that moves the subject *into* the world without locking her into the *terms* of ongoing social arrangements. It is here that the language of liberal feminism falls short.[3]

A. INTRODUCTION

In this paper, I explore how the language of choice falls short in the context of the feminist equality project, even though "choice" has been a central plank of feminist movements since their inception. I argue that "choice" does exactly what Jean Bethke Elshtain warns against in the epigraph above; that is, choice locks us into existing social arrangements and into a liberal perspective rather than offering movement through and beyond the status quo of inequality.

I have, for some time, been troubled by the concept of choice and the ways in which it has been deployed by feminists and within feminist debates. These debates have for me raised questions about the meaning and significance of choice and about our[4] strong inclination to defer to choice. More recently, I have been alarmed by the Supreme Court of Canada's invocation of choice as a shield against equality claims. As my title suggests, I see the Court as blaming women for having "chosen" to put themselves in a situation that they later claim to be unequal. The Court seems to see these women as crying inequality simply because things didn't work out.

Unsympathetic to women perceived as wanting to have their cake and eat it too, the Court uses respect for individual choice as the justification for allowing that inequality to persist, unexamined. Once the situation can be ascribed to the claimant's "choice," it seems that the Court feels that there is no need to investigate the inequality claimed, to examine impact or effect. This is a decontextualized invocation of choice that looks at a specific choice in a vacuum and fails to examine the limits on available alternatives, constraints on the chooser, conflicting motivations, interrelated potential impacts, and other factors that might affect the decision. Choice signals the termination of the discussion rather than the beginning of the inquiry. I am not sure what is operating here — perhaps a presumption that if one chose it, it can't be unequal or that one has to live with the consequences of one's choice, however unequal. Either way, such presumptions beget an extremely punitive approach to both choice and equality. This decontextualized approach to choice applied in recent Supreme Court of Canada decisions is clearly problematic, from a feminist standpoint. However, recognizing the problems with the approach to choice employed by the Court has helped me to crystallize my discomfort with much of the feminist reliance on choice which I think is similarly haunted by a decontextualized approach. So in what follows, I offer some preliminary thoughts on the problems with feminist reliance on choice and on how similar problems surface in egregious ways in the Supreme Court's reliance on choice.

In *Attorney General of Nova Scotia v. Walsh and Bona*,[5] the use of choice as a shield against equality by the majority of the Court is glaring. This case thus provides an excellent vehicle for exploring what the concept of choice represents to the Court and how choice is used to foreclose an equality analysis. The decision in *Walsh* is the focus of this paper. But there are more subtle invocations of choice underlying such decisions as the majority in *Gosselin v. Attorney General of Quebec*[6] and the section 15 analysis by the dissent in *Sauvé v. Canada (Chief Electoral Officer)*.[7] In the interest of examining some quite different invocations of choice, I look briefly at these two decisions solely in terms of their use of choice to justify the rejection of an equality claim. While I have restricted myself to looking at these cases for the purposes of this paper, choice is seen as an underlying issue/assumption/good to be preferred over equality in many section 15 claims. The analysis that I offer here could be applied and refined in relation to a number of equality decisions.

On the other hand, there are cases, such as *Rodriguez v. British Columbia (Attorney General)*,[8] in which the claimant's choice is rejected, not deferred to. In *Rodriguez* it was the failure to respect the claimant's choice to decide the timing and circumstances of her own death that gave rise to, even constituted, the *Charter* breach that was claimed but not recognized by the Court. Perhaps the lesson from cases like *Rodriguez* is, to borrow from a legalism, that choice is not generally effective as a sword on behalf of equality claimants, but is frequently employed as a shield against equality claimants. Those cases in which choice does operate as a sword, and the claimant successfully asserts choice as a *Charter* right, may be cases in which choice becomes a basis for furthering privilege. In those situations, choice is not an equality-promoting strategy, but is asserted as a right in and of itself.[9] I am not able to deal with these aspects of choice in this paper, but ultimately they are necessary parts of the discussion. We need to understand all aspects of choice and its usages in order to be able to challenge how this concept is used and to decide whether to try to de-centre or transform it.

The other context in which choice is invoked in law is in relation to parliamentary supremacy and the choices made by legislatures with respect to the legislation they pass or the policies they promote. In *Charter* terms, this is the issue of deference to Parliament. My Quicklaw word search using "choice" and "*Charter*" sent me mostly to discussions by courts of the issue of whether or not to defer to the choice made by the legislature; that is, to allow the challenged legislation to stand on the basis that the government was acting within their authority and made a legitimate and reasonable choice. Courts' most frequent discussion of choice is really the court's "choice" to avoid dealing with the merits of a claim, described neither as choice nor avoidance but as deference. In this context, the courts' reliance on legislative choice is often the justification for supporting a *Charter* breach. It would be interesting to explore in what circumstances the Court's deference tends to be to legislative choice generally, that is deferring to the right of government to make poor choices, rather than to the choice of the specific legislation being challenged.

All of these aspects of choice are, I think, interconnected and warrant exploration, critique and strategizing in terms of their relationship with and impact on section 15 equality.[10] In what follows, I offer some preliminary thoughts on some aspects of the critique of choice, starting with how choice has been invoked in controversies among feminists.

B. FEMINIST INVOCATIONS OF CHOICE

I offer the following in order to situate myself in relation to the feminist debates in which "choice" has played an important role. I have a long history of working on issues of male violence against women. In this, I include pornography and prostitution as forms of male violence against women and thus I resist the characterization of prostitution and pornography as freely chosen forms of women's work.[11] I have an almost equally long history of activism in women's health, focusing initially on abortion and then shifting to include reproductive technologies and reproductive issues more generally. I participated in a call for a moratorium on the development and availability of reproductive technologies in Canada. I have worked on family law issues and was initially very drawn to mediation as a potential means of resolving disputes but I have become increasingly sceptical of mediation's ability to deal with the systemic gendered power imbalances in heterosexual relationships. On related grounds, I am critical of domestic contracts and the right to contract out of family law legislation. I resist the claims of transgendered women to a right of access to women-only space, or rather I support the right of feminist organizations to define their membership based in part on a shared experience of growing up female in a male-dominated society. I base my position on this issue on a systemic, as opposed to an individualistic, understanding of gender. I am disturbed by the uncritical endorsement of, and focus of activity on, lesbian and gay marriage that ignore, or even reject, the feminist critiques of the institution of marriage.

I find that choice seems frequently to be raised as a shield to protect practices of which I am critical.[12] With respect to each of these issues, choice has been a significant argument put forward in support of the practice.[13] For example, women are said to choose to participate in pornography and prostitution, to choose to go to mediation or to choose a domestic contract. And because women choose these things, feminism requires us to respect and support these choices. Some unacknowledged slippage then seems to take place whereby it is not just the individual choice that should be accepted and supported but the practice itself. From this perspective, critical examination of these practices is seen as critique of the women who engage in the practices.[14] Critical positions on these issues inevitably spark charges of paternalism, judgmentalism, essentialism, and ideological determinism;[15] serious criticisms that warrant serious attention. In making such critiques, I have been told that I am arguing for the limitation of women's choice as if that is *per se* and necessarily a bad thing, as if the limiting of women's choice is the limiting of women. But I see myself as arguing for a more complex understanding of choice, a recognition of the gendered and systemic constraints on choice and of the contradictions and reservations that haunt many of our choices. It is not clear to me that the liberal concept of choice, as unencumbered and free, is not also paternalistic nor why it is necessarily a preferable route. Not infrequently choice seems to be seen as a sufficient answer such that there is no need for further discussion on the meaning and impact of that choice in a larger social context. However, while I find the facile assertion of choice to be seriously lacking in substance, I nonetheless seem to have trouble responding to it or getting behind it or inside it or around it. It does seem problematic to be arguing against choice.

These differing feminist views on the relative importance of choice to some extent flow from our different feminist responses to the state and our understandings of the role of the state, positions that in the past have been simplistically ascribed to differences between liberal feminists, socialist feminists, and radical feminists. From these bailiwicks, feminists who champion choice would tend to favour less government intervention and to be more sceptical of government attempts to encroach on important freedoms. From such a perspective, choice would be seen as itself a fundamental freedom to be jealously protected against state interference.[16] Socialist feminists tend to view the state as oppressive and repressive and not to be trusted. Liberal feminists would view the state as more benign, but would nonetheless tend to argue against state intrusion into the private affairs of its citizens. On the other hand, those of us who are more cautious about choice as an inherent good are less distressed by the prospect of government intervention, often seeing it as the lesser and more controllable among many potential evils. The state is still seen as oppressive, but as no more so than other institutions. The state is seen as capable of providing some limited protection against more powerful individuals and organizations.

These positions are hold-overs from our feminist history; feminist analysis has long since moved beyond the basic equation of the state with government, to recognize that the state operates at many levels and through many institutions and structures. Also, there are many modes of regulation other than through government. These alternative modes may be more pernicious because more subtle and more opaque. Our more complex and sophisticated understanding of the state and of governance should translate into more complex and sophisticated understandings of choice and of the meaning and significance of state limits on choice. And it should, and has, led us to move beyond a simplistic dichotomy between individual liberty to choose and government interference with that liberty. We are now raising questions about the potential, and/or obligation, for the state and other governing apparatuses to facilitate meaningful choice.[17] However, because choice seems simple and because it feels empowering[18] and positive, the attraction to choice as an unencumbered concept and as a slogan persists, serving to insulate choice from critical scrutiny.

A related artifact that promotes unreflective deference to choice is the characterization of some strands of feminism as promoting a view of women as victims,[19] as opposed to women as agents. This characterization represents a false dichotomy, in which, as feminists, we frequently find ourselves trapped — as if it were a question of one or the other (choice or no choice), as if we have to choose to which oversimplified vision of women we subscribe (whether we see women as victims or agents) as if these are mutually exclusive visions.[20] From within this dichotomy, feminists who argue for a more critical approach to choice are accused of portraying women as victims and, in this polarized picture, victim is associated with passivity and helplessness, rather than seen as one who is wronged or harmed. Choice is an underlying theme in this dichotomy, with one side portraying victims as having no choices and as therefore not being responsible for their actions; and the opposite side portraying agents as having choices and therefore being responsible for the choices they make. Choice is thus seen as the defining distinction between victimhood and agency so that, if we want to see ourselves as autonomous, responsible agents, rather than as passive helpless victims, we need to support an uncritical approach to choice.

As is so often the case, the problem with this critique of "victim feminism" is that it distorts the object of the critique. Those who argue, for example, that women are victims of pornography and prostitution are not making the argument that women are victims pure and simple or that women have no choices or that women should not be held accountable. Women are simultaneously both victims and agents; which means they are both and neither and that it is a disservice to see them in exclusive terms, at either end of the control spectrum. When made fully and appropriately, the "victim" argument presents a gender-based, systemic analysis that recognizes the social, economic, and institutional factors that constrain or direct women's choices and seeks to have these factors considered when it comes to taking account and holding women accountable.

Choice itself is similarly premised on a dualism, an either/or model that tends to oversimplify the items between which one is supposed to be choosing. The false dichotomy that inheres in the abstract notion of choice is then replicated in the particularities of the so-called choice being made. While I do not think that we should abandon choice altogether,[21] I think we need to take a more sceptical, problematized approach to choice. We would do better, wherever possible, to talk about choices rather than choice and to recognize the complexity and multiplicity of choices, as well as the factors that circumscribe those choices.[22]

It may be a contradiction to argue that we should simultaneously be critiquing and redefining concepts such as choice, but it is a contradiction that I embrace. It is a contradiction and a challenge captured in the above epigraph from Jean Bethke Elshtain which invites us to engage with the prevailing tenets of liberal individualism, without accepting its terms. An individualized approach to choice depoliticizes the choices that are made and the context within which they are made, as well as the more abstract discussion of choice itself. Once choice is thus depoliticized, discussion about a specific choice is necessarily circumscribed. In such a context, it becomes difficult, even non-sensical, to talk about the socially imposed restrictions and the social structures that limit or direct choices or to argue that the impact of those limits needs to be taken into consideration as we seek to hold the person accountable for their choice. In an attempt to avoid the much-maligned victim label, we abandon women to their deficient, circumscribed, inequality-perpetuating choices. Instead, we need to abandon the focus on the individual. The more we ensure that we are talking about the liberation of all women, the more we are forced to recognize the limits of liberalism and of individualism and to look critically at the fundamental values, like choice, on which they rest.[23]

Part of my acceptance of the contradiction lies in the acknowledgement that we can't totally opt out of these concepts in any concrete practical sense, even if we want to. Choice, equality, dignity, rights, privacy are words with long histories that have firmly embedded them in liberal democracy. They are concepts that currently have a strong presence in public discourse and a strong resonance with the general public, in part due to feminists' efforts to raise their profile. Given their present currency, these concepts will definitely be used against us, so it would be short-sighted to take the high road and simply abandon them. And it is not as if these are the wrong concepts *per se* and it is simply a matter of finding the right words with which to communicate our arguments; it is our radical equality arguments themselves that are challenging and difficult to "sell."

Situations and circumstances change over time, as do our understandings. One of the things we need to guard against is a tendency to see concepts as static rather than fluid and the related tendency toward universalizing concepts rather than contextualizing them. If we succumb to these tendencies, we can become wedded to our limited applications of abstract concepts and vulnerable to becoming trapped by our own slogans. They are just words (not that words are not incredibly powerful and important — that is the point — they are); but we are part of creating and living their meaning and we need to engage in that process of re-creating and re-assessing meaning on an ongoing basis. We need to grow with, through, and beyond our own watchwords, strategies, and goals; to be flexible and open to change, to self-reflection, to criticism, and to re-evaluation.

What is missing from the assertion that choice is *per se* a good thing are the issues of power and inequality that underlie and circumscribe any particular choice. The availability of any choice must be examined in its context which would include factors pertaining to race, class, gender, (dis)ability, age, or sexual orientation that may limit or coerce "choice" or render a choice in effect unchoosable. Another aspect of the context of a particular choice is the other choices that are precluded or enhanced by the availability of this choice, in conjunction with the question to whom are these choices made more or less available. And the impact of the choice must be examined, not just the impact on the individual or the disadvantaged group(s) to which she belongs but on other disadvantaged groups as well. A contextualized approach to choice raises questions such as, choice to do what? What is being chosen between? And at what costs to whom? Who gets to decide what choices are made available? And on what basis are those decisions made? Who has choice? Who doesn't? Why is this a choice to be protected?

Recently,[24] judicial deference to choice has been a key factor in some of the Supreme Court of Canada's rejection of section 15 equality claims. The concerns and frustrations that I have with feminist deference to choice surface in more heinous and pernicious ways in these cases and make the need for feminist re-examination of choice more urgent and clear. I fear, to some extent, that as feminists we are being hoist by our own petard.

Before I get into the section 15 cases, I look at an infamous U.S. case in which the sex discrimination of relegating women to poorly-paid sales positions was explained away as women's choice of that type of work and thus found to be non-discriminatory. It is the U.S. Supreme Court's explicit reliance on and distortion of feminist work that makes this case so disturbing and so instructive.

C. A SEARING EXAMPLE OF CHOICE AS A DEFENCE TO INEQUALITY

The dangers of a simplistic reliance on choice and the ways in which it can be used against women were dramatically illustrated in the 1988 *Sears* case in the U.S.[25] In this case, Sears successfully defended itself against a systemic sex discrimination claim relating to their failure to hire women into the better paid commission sales jobs. Sears argued that women had different values, interests, and goals than men and that these natural "differences" led them to not "choose" the highly competitive aggressive world of commission sales. According to Sears, women did not want these jobs and thus the fact that women were not awarded commission sales jobs could not be characterized as discrimination. To support this argument and to garner credibility for their position, Sears enlisted the aid of feminist historian, Rosalind Rosenberg, whose historical work explores women's "difference," based on women's domestic roles and related family values. Her testimony on behalf of Sears effectively held women responsible for the sexual division of labour, portrayed as a result of women's freely-made choices.[26] The choice to which Rosenberg's evidence attested assumed conditions of full equality within a completely open labour market. Such a concept of women choosing lower paid work is compatible with a reading of feminist history relating to women's "difference" (from men),[27] but through such a reading the structural, economic, political, and social "differences" in and of which women partake are decontextualized into choice. In portraying the choice as unqualified and unrestricted, Rosenberg glossed over gendered socialization, the gendered nature of the structure and organization of the paid workplace, the underlying assumptions that lead to the gendered division of labour, and the coercive power of gender stereotypes, all of which function so as to limit and direct women's choices and to pre-determine the impact of those choices. Women's responses to gendered family expectations and commitments are seen unproblematically as women's choices, simply as a function of women's different values and goals which are assumed to apply to all women.

Alice Kessler-Harris, the feminist historian brought in by the Equal Employment Opportunity Commission (EEOC) to counteract Rosenberg, explained the problem of acknowledging "difference" in a context of unacknowledged inequality:

> [O]ne of the tensions in women's history that arguably described much of the dynamic of change in women's lives over time was the tension between women's own conception of "difference" and the objective condition of inequality. We had all observed that women, to live, had participated in, even colluded in, their own oppression. But that was not the sum total of their perceptions and understandings of the world around them. Nor did that truth wipe out the ways in which women had continually exerted themselves (in ways consonant with their access to money, resources and education) in a centuries-long struggle for emancipation.[28]

Choice limited by a context of inequality; coercion labelled as choice; choice restricted by access to money, resources, and education; qualified choice as part of a struggle for emancipation — these are women's choices. There is no unqualified choice and the extent to which such choice is assumed is the extent to which equality is similarly assumed and inequality thereby rendered invisible and unchallengeable.

An uncritical, decontextualized endorsement of choice could lead to the invocation of feminist analysis in support of the argument that "any situation that results from choice or preferences vitiates the charge of oppression or discrimination"[29] — that is, women choose their oppression and therefore it cannot be characterized as oppression. A more nuanced, in-depth examination of choice will lead to the conclusion that in some circumstances, discrimination lies in the limited choices or in the limits on choices and that sometimes every available choice is a choice of oppression and sometimes oppression is the only choice.

As Joan Scott describes the decision in the *Sears* case, "[d]iscrimination was redefined as simply the recognition of 'natural difference' (however culturally or historically produced).... Difference was substituted for inequality, the appropriate antithesis of equality, becoming inequality's explanation and legitimation."[30] In *Sears*, choice was the vehicle used to transform inequality into difference, thus rendering inequality benign. A similar process is at work in Supreme Court of Canada decisions in which choice is substituted for inequality and then used to legitimate the inequality, obviating the need for further exploration or explanation.

D. THE INSULATING LABEL OF CHOICE IN THE SUPREME COURT OF CANADA

> Insulating a rights restriction from scrutiny by labelling it a matter of so-cial philosophy ... removes the infringement from our radar screen, in-stead of enabling us to zero in on it to decide whether it is demonstrably justified as required by the *Charter*.[31]

These are the words of Justice McLachlin in her majority judgement in *Sauvé*. I see the label "choice" being used by the Court in a similar way so as to protect the challenged inequality from scrutiny, effectively taking it off the radar screen so as to circumvent examination of the equality is-sues at stake. Such insulation from scrutiny is even more insidious when it is invoked at the section 15 determination of discrimination stage, than when it is resorted to at the section 1 justification stage (as referred to in the above quote by Justice McLachlin in relation to social policy as an insulat-ing label). The choice insulation is used under section 15 as the basis for the determination that there has been no discrimination, thus precluding exploration of the context and impact of the choice, including any systemic inequalities that may have affected or circumscribed the alleged choice that was made. Equality scrutiny under the equality section is obviated by the ascription of the choice label. I am not sure that it would be any less un-palatable for the Court to find that a discriminatory breach of section 15 is justified under section 1 by using the label "choice" to insulate the breach from section 1 scrutiny. However, the sleight of hand of using choice to override equality when used at the section 15 stage might at least be exposed when performed as a section 1 justification.

The Supreme Court's invocation of choice as a shield against equality claims largely takes place in relation to the contextual factors set out as part of the third element in the guidelines for assessing a section 15 equal-ity claim established by the Supreme Court of Canada in *Law v. Canada* (the *Law* test).[32] There is a disturbing irony in the Court applying what, as the analysis provided below indicates, is a decontextualized or acontextual notion of choice in relation to the application of so-called contextual fac-tors. This incongruity calls into question the Court's understanding and application of the notion of context.[33]

Choice, as the Court has interpreted and applied it, is inextricably linked with the concept of dignity, a key factor in the *Law* test, such that if the situation can be ascribed to choice it is likely to be left unexamined in the name of dignity; that is, dignity requires automatic deference to the claimant's choice. Choice is similarly linked with notions of autonomy, agency, and self-determination and, like all of these, is highly individualistic. Choice as a dichotomizing concept fits more comfortably with a formal equality approach than a substantive equality approach. In relation to a section 15 analysis, choice raises issues with respect to comparator groups, similarly situatedness, intersectionality, context, group-based as opposed to individual rights, immutability, and analogous grounds. Choice is thus embroiled in many of the issues and concerns that feminists have articulated with respect to the interpretation and application of section 15.

E. OVER-READING THE "CHOICE" NOT TO MARRY: *WALSH AND BONA*

Choice and the language of choice play a central role in the decision in *Walsh and Bona*.[34] In the words of Justice Bastarache writing for the majority,[35] "choice must be paramount;"[36] paramount over equality as it turns out. In this case, Ms. Walsh unsuccessfully challenged the exclusion of unmarried heterosexual cohabitants (hereinafter cohabitants)[37] from the statutory marital property regime. She argued that the failure to accord unmarried cohabitants the same property rights and protections provided to married cohabitants constituted discrimination on the basis of marital status. The majority of the Court held that Ms. Walsh's "choice" not to marry precluded her from the equality-promoting presumption of an equal division of matrimonial property as provided to heterosexual married couples upon marriage breakdown under the *Nova Scotia Matrimonial Property Act (MPA)*.[38] According to the majority, Ms. Walsh could have chosen to marry the man with whom she cohabited. Her choice not to marry was her choice not to be covered by the *MPA*. She cannot after the fact claim that she was discriminated against because she did not like the consequences of the choice that she made. The majority's exclusive focus on a narrow understanding of choice allowed them to avoid exploring systemic inequalities that may have affected the choice that Ms. Walsh made, as well as the equality impacts of such a choice. Neither did the Court see it as necessary, given the claimant's choice, to examine the equality implications of the changing relationship between married and unmarried cohabitants, the ways in which cohabiting couples actually structure their relationships and of the expectations and interdependencies that may arise as a result.

There are two related but distinct concerns with the Court's deference to "choice" in this case.[39] One concern relates to the systemic gendered equality issues that render the so-called choice on which this decision rests highly questionable; the second concern relates to the equality impact of that choice. The first concern is that the "choice" on which this decision is premised constitutes a gross oversimplification; it is "highly abstract and idealized";[40] it is an illusion. Except at its most simplistic and basic level (that is, the level of the decision not to marry; a decision that may or may not have been the claimant's choice), there is no indication in this case of any choice having been made at the time of cohabitation with respect to opting in or out of the marital property regime which is the issue in the case. In their references to Ms. Walsh's choice to opt out of the *MPA*, the majority rely upon ungrounded assumptions and speculation. The second concern is basically: so what if she did choose not to be governed by the marital property regime. Why defer to choice? Even if none of the factors that would render the notion of choice an illusion were actually present for Ms. Walsh, why would the fact that she "chose" to put herself in a situation of inequality necessarily preclude a *Charter* remedy? The *Walsh* decision illustrates the vacuousness of choice as a sole rationale.

The illusory nature of the choice relied upon in this decision has a number of interrelated components. The first illusion is that married couples have chosen to be bound by the laws governing the dissolution of marriage — the laws relating to support, property, custody, etc. — and that conversely unmarried cohabitants have chosen not to be bound by those laws. As Justice L'Heureux-Dubé points out, most people are not aware of what the law requires and many have serious misconceptions about the legal obligations of marriage, as well as of cohabiation.[41] Additionally, in my experience, most people who are getting married are not interested in knowing or thinking about what happens if/when they split up.[42] It is hard to say that people have chosen something when they either do not know what that something is, or they think they know what it is but they are wrong, or they are deliberately avoiding knowing what it is. I would describe this as the illusion of informed choice.

The second illusion, the illusion of intentional choice, is that the marital regime property imposed by the law is a major factor, or the primary factor, in the choice to marry. People choose to marry or not to marry for a wide range of complex reasons; to ascribe a single intention to that "choice" is a gross generalization. The Court collapses the choice with the consequences of that choice, but those consequences may well not have been chosen, perhaps not even contemplated. Some people make the (non)marriage choice despite, rather than because of, the property consequences of that choice. Feminists have fallen into this same intentional choice trap in their attempt to protect non-marriage from state intervention. The feminist argument that unmarried cohabitants have consciously and deliberately chosen not to have the state dictate the terms of their relationship is similarly troubling. This feminist invocation of choice is relied upon by the majority in their decision, in the form of endorsing the words of feminist sociologist, Margrit Eichler:

> Treating all common-law relationships like legal marriages in terms of support obligations and property division ignores the very different circumstances under which people may enter a common-law union. If they choose to marry, they make a positive choice to live under one type of regime. If they have chosen not to marry, is it the state's task to impose a marriage-like regime on them retroactively?[43]

Whether articulated by feminists or judges, the assumption that the decision to marry or not to marry reflects a specific intent with respect to property and support is a problematic over-generalization, made more problematic when used as the basis for a judicial decision and as a counter to equality.[44]

Conversely, in relation to the question of intent, some unmarried cohabitants will choose to conduct their financial relationship in a way that coincides with the presumption of a mutual intention to enter into an economic partnership that informs the *MPA*. In fact, as Justice Bastarache notes, this is what the parties in this case did.[45] The particular circumstances of this couple's economic relationship would seem to be highly relevant with respect to the second contextual factor under the *Law* test in which the Court is to consider the legislation in relation to the actual needs, capacity and circumstances of the claimant. But this circumstance of the claimant is dismissed by the majority because the parties' intent to share an economic partnership would not necessarily carry through to agreement with respect to the disposition of property upon relationship breakdown.[46] Of course, such an intent, if it was there in the first place, often does not carry through in marriages either. Ironically, this is exactly why legislation like the *MPA* is necessary. It is often the case that a mutual intent on the part of the couple to have an economic partnership, agreed to in the early years of their relationship, falls apart when the relationship breaks down. At that point, the partner with the greater economic assets often wants to renege on the shared intention. In the interests of equality, the *MPA* precludes such reneging.

The third illusion is that choice is unconstrained, that it is freely and individually made and reflects what each person truly wants. This assumption ignores the many constraints and barriers that may affect the decision to marry or not to marry. For example, for those whose religion condemns unmarried cohabitation, marriage is the only option. Some couples marry for immigration purposes. Conversely, there are religious, legal, and cultural impediments to marriage. The decision to marry or not is a relational decision that requires negotiation and often compromise and not infrequently coercion. It is not necessarily about individual choice. If one party refuses to marry, the other's "choices" are limited to cohabitation or nothing. As Justice L'Heureux-Dubé points out in her dissent, unilateral refusal to marry in order to avoid the legal consequences of marriage can "create a situation of exploitation."[47] It is this situation of exploitation/inequality that the claimant is alleging and that the majority of the Court refuses even to consider.

The fact that the *MPA* has created "a significant alteration to the status quo of an individual's proprietary rights and obligations,"[48] as is clearly of major concern to the majority,[49] is arguably an indication of the significance of the potential inequality of the status quo. This status quo was the situation of exploitation/inequality that married women were in twenty-five years ago and that shared marital property regimes were introduced to correct. This is the situation of exploitation/inequality to which Ms. Walsh is now abandoned in the name of choice and in order to protect her dignity. The alternative modes of addressing spousal property division through unjust enrichment and constructive trust were found inadequate to protect married women's interests twenty-five years ago. They are no more adequate to protect the property interests of unmarried cohabitants in the present.[50]

The final illusion of choice that underlies the majority decision is that the marital property regime is a matter of choice at all. Married couples did not choose the marital property regime, that is they did not choose the presumption of equal division of property upon marriage break up. The state, in response in large part to feminist advocacy, imposed this regime in an attempt to redress marital gender inequalities. The judges in *Walsh* refer to the marital property regime as a "benefit," but this is surely a misnomer. To the extent that the statutorily imposed regime can be described as a benefit, it is only so for the spouse who is in the less strong economic position. But the benefit label is more egregiously a misnomer because the *MPA* was not about conferring a benefit; it was about redressing an imbalance, about remedying inequality. This marital property regime is imposed, as an equality-promoting measure, on couples who choose to marry. It seems disingenuous to suggest that couples who marry are choosing the marital property regime.

The second concern, what I referred to above as the "so what" concern, relates to this point of the inequality-redressing nature and purpose of the scheme to which Ms. Walsh sought access. In setting out and discussing the history and purpose of the legislation, the Court clearly recognizes that equality is the key principle underlying the *MPA* and that the Act was "designed to alleviate the [gendered] inequities of the past."[51] While all of the judges in *Walsh* clearly know and seem to understand this history, its significance in the context of a section 15 *Charter* claim seems to escape them. The equality purpose of the *MPA* should constitute strong support for a section 15 equality-focused analysis of the situation of unmarried cohabitants. But instead of focusing on equality and inequality, or on the actual circumstances and needs of unmarried cohabitants, the majority focus on consent and choice because they are seen as the features that distinguish marital cohabitation from non-marital cohabitation. In this shift from equality to choice, the Court is doing what Dorothy Roberts describes as "separating private choices from social power ... [and preferring] private remedies for individuals' problems to collective responsibility for social conditions."[52] But it is not clear why choice would be considered an answer to an equality claim. Section 15 is/should be about systemic issues, not confined to the circumstances or decisions of the individual claimant. Equality is not about what the individual necessarily wants or chooses; its presence in section 15 of the *Charter* reflects its status as a fundamental Canadian value that, when the circumstances warrant, we are willing to impose upon those who are reluctant to conform to equality's dictates. That is what the *MPA* is about; that is what section 15 is about.

When and how and why did choice become a *Charter* value that has paramountcy over equality? There is a dangerous sleight of hand going on here. Why does choice have this caché; what does choice stand for? Choice becomes the stand-in for individualism, liberty, and autonomy; these are what are in conflict with and trumping equality.[53] But these things are only meaningful in a context of equality. You can't have a meaningful exercise of individualism, liberty, or autonomy — that is, you can't have meaningful choice — in a situation of inequality. Equality has to provide the foundation and the context. The marital property regime was imposed in order to address existing gender inequalities. If a claimant finds herself in the same situation of inequality that married women were in twenty-five years ago, why would the *Charter* not apply to remedy it? What is it about choice that would foreclose such an inquiry?

These questions raise the further question as to whether Ms. Walsh's claim would have been better made on the basis of sex equality, alone or in addition to marital status. While the "chosen" distinction is marital status, the inequality to be addressed relates to gender. Marital status is the vehicle through which the sex discrimination is being perpetrated. Sex discrimination would be a disparate impact argument rather than a direct discrimination case and, in relation to disparate impact, the choice argument would be more difficult to sustain.[54] A sex discrimination claim would have provided the opportunity to introduce evidence of the gendered impact of exclusion from the *MPA*, as well as given greater weight to the history and purpose of the *MPA*. Additionally, a sex claim would pose more complicated comparator group questions and might potentially expose the limits of comparator group analysis.[55] And finally, a sex discrimination claim would have undermined the distinction made by the majority in relation to the *Miron* case, where the Court held that "an unmarried spouse was entitled to insurance benefits because she lived in a relationship analogous to marriage."[56] According to Justice Bastarache, "the discriminatory distinction at issue in *Miron* concerned the relationship of the couple as a unit, to third parties"[57] whereas *Walsh* was about the rights and responsibilities of the couple in relation to each other. If discriminatory distinction within the couple is the focus, the discriminatory distinction is sex, not marital status.

As is clear from *Walsh*, choice is strongly linked to dignity. According to the majority, to not respect someone's choice is to infringe their dignity, to treat them as less than a fully autonomous, responsible person.[58] Given the central role currently played by dignity in section 15 analysis,[59] the conflation of choice and dignity makes choice a virtually impenetrable shield against an equality claim.[60] Once the discrimination is accepted as a matter of the claimant's choice, dignity easily falls into line to protect that choice, even against the chooser herself. The flourishing of dignity as a section 15 principle has allowed its offshoot, choice, to surface as a serious hurdle for equality claimants. It creates an hermetic layer of abstraction and assumptions. Most, if not all, of the concerns that have been raised with respect to dignity in the section 15 context apply similarly to choice.

While the majority sees denying the applicant's equality claim as a dignity-enhancing measure, Justice L'Heureux-Dubé, in her dissent in *Walsh*, accepts the equality claim and finds that the *MPA* "demeans the dignity of heterosexual unmarried cohabitants."[61] She attaches the dignity problem to the lack of acknowledgement of the relationship; that is, to the failure to recognize common-law relationships as legitimate family forms.[62] However, her characterization of the absence of state recognition as a harm to dignity seems a bit of a stretch. I am not sure how the application of the marital property regime to unmarried cohabitants confers legitimacy on their relationship and I do not think acknowledgement of legitimacy is what Ms. Walsh was concerned about. This is one of the central critiques of dignity, that is that it diverts the analysis to focus on the claimant's feelings and sense of self-worth rather than on her material and social circumstances.[63] To assume that unmarried cohabitants are seeking acknowledgement and legitimation of their relationship echoes the "women want to be men" approach to sex equality, rather than the "women want the benefits men enjoy" version of sex equality. To me the indignity in this case lies in the inequality and inequity experienced by the unmarried cohabitant who has suffered economically as a result of the relationship (usually the woman in a heterosexual couple). I recognize that to define dignity violations in terms of inequality creates a circular argument when the point of turning to dignity is to assist in the determination of whether there is inequality. But this is precisely why I do not find dignity a helpful tool in the section 15 analysis. As a primary focus, dignity clouds the analysis rather than clarifies it, adding an additional layer of obscurity to be defined and dissected, much the same as equality needs to be. To me, dignity is a partial and watered-down proxy for equality and choice an even weaker, more watered-down proxy. Equality is a concept that needs strengthening and animation, not dilution.

F. WELFARE RECIPIENTS AND PRISONERS — THE CHOICELESS IN *GOSSELIN* AND *SAUVÉ*

The use of choice to justify inequality through the conflation of choice and dignity that is at the heart of the decision in *Walsh* is also present in other recent Supreme Court of Canada decisions. The *Walsh* case initially sparked my outrage at the Court's deference to choice, but given its use there, I wanted to see if and how choice was being used in other contemporaneous decisions. In search of possible parallel invocations of choice or echoes of the *Walsh* choice analysis, I turned to *Gosselin v. The Attorney General of Quebec*,[64] a decision released at the same time as *Walsh* and to *Sauvé v. Canada (Chief Electoral Officer)*,[65] which was released two months earlier. I found choice operating as an underlying rationale in the majority decision in *Gosselin* and as the basis for denying analogous ground status to prisoners in the dissenting decision in *Sauvé*.

Gosselin was a class action challenge to regulations under Quebec's social assistance legislation that reduced the benefits of single "employable" people under the age of thirty to one third of the base amount payable to welfare recipients over thirty, unless the person under thirty participated in an education or work experience program.[66] As a result, those who were subject to these regulations received the unlivable-on sum of $170 per month in social assistance. The section 15 portion of Ms. Gosselin's claim was based on age.[67]

After reading *Walsh*, I (re)turned to *Gosselin*, based on my recollection/assumption that the Court had dismissed the claim in part based on a choice argument. I had understood the majority of the Court to be saying that welfare recipients are free to choose not to attend the programs but they do so with full knowledge of the consequences of that choice and they must be held responsible for that choice and its consequences, that it would be an affront to their dignity to treat their choice otherwise. On rereading the case, I was surprised to find that this choice argument is not actually articulated anywhere in the case. There is no discussion of choice and choice is not explicitly a basis for denying the claim. Given the absence of any explicit reference to choice, I may be overreaching in trying to make the argument that choice was an underlying rationale for this decision. But if a choice analysis is the underpinning, then the invocation of choice in *Gosselin* is in many ways even more pernicious than in *Walsh*. This kind of implicit reliance on choice will be more difficult to get at, to dissect, and to refute.

The claimant, Louise Gosselin, is described by Justice McLachlin, writing for the majority,[68] as having "led a difficult life, complicated by a struggle with psychological problems and drug and alcohol addictions."[69] With respect to Ms. Gosselin's participation in the required programs, Justice McLachlin states:

> She ended up dropping out of virtually every program she started, apparently because of her own personal problems and personality traits. The testimony from one social worker, particularly as his clinic was attached to a psychiatric hospital and therefore received a disproportionate number of welfare recipients who also had serious psychological problems, does not give us a better or more accurate picture of the situation of other class members, or of the relationship between Ms. Gosselin's personal difficulties and the structure of the welfare program.[70]

Further on in the judgment, Justice McLachlin again refers to Ms. Gosselin dropping out of the programs, with the implication that she could have persevered if she had wanted to:

> In fact, contrary to her allegation, Ms. Gosselin's own experience clearly establishes that participation was a real possibility.... On those occasions when Ms. Gosselin dropped out of programs, the record indicates that this was due to personal problems, which included psychological and substance abuse components, rather than to flaws in the programs themselves. Ms. Gosselin's experience suggests that even individuals with serious problems were capable of supplementing their income under the impugned regime.[71]

These statements, as is much of the decision, are full of demeaning and dismissive language. It is the language of disbelief — "dropping out," "apparently," "better or more accurate," "contrary to her allegation." It is the language of individualized responsibility/blame, accompanied by diminution — "dropping out," "personal problems," "personality traits," "personal difficulties," "supplementing their income." There is an unmistakable tone of blame and censure. While there is no explicit reference to choice here, there is a clear sense that Ms. Gosselin could have participated in the programs if she had just pulled up her socks and got on with it; that, instead of choosing to try harder to avail herself of the benefits offered, she chose to wallow in her personal problems and to allow herself to fall into "the habit of relying on social assistance,"[72] consigning herself to a life of dependence on welfare. The later reference to the "programs [as] designed specifically to integrate her into the work force and to promote her long-term self-sufficiency"[73] carries the same message of disbelief and blame. This is the extreme of the punitive approach to choice — she made her bed and now she has to lie in it.

The Court discredits Ms. Gosselin's testimony and treats it as woefully inadequate for the class action claim that she is making. Ms. Gosselin and her particular circumstances may garner some sympathy,[74] but she — or perhaps it is the sympathy — is dismissed as not representative of the group of over 75,000 unnamed class members on whose behalf she is making the claim. The implication is that even if Ms. Gosselin's circumstances were so debilitating that she could not take advantage of these programs, others who suffered under these regulations were simply choosing not to participate. Welfare stereotypes and, as in *Walsh,* unfounded assumptions seem to underlie much of the majority reasoning. Similarly Ms. Walsh was not seen as representative of unmarried cohabitants. Both are treated as anomalies within their group and dismissed as such.[75] The Court in *Gosselin* is clearly overwhelmed by the prospect of "tens of thousands of unidentified people" being owed "hundreds of millions of taxpayer dollars"[76] and dismisses the claim based on the absence of evidence that these tens of thousands have been adversely affected by their social assistance being reduced by two thirds. But the huge number of non-participants in the programs (about two thirds of the eligible welfare recipients[77]) alone is surely damming evidence that the programs are seriously not working. Who would choose to live on one third of an already less than poverty level income unless they clearly had no "choice"?

The Court held that the "incentive" programs not only did not constitute an affront to human dignity but actually promoted human dignity:[78]

> The participation incentive worked towards the realization of goals that go to the heart of the equality guarantee: self-determination, personal autonomy, self-respect, feelings of self-worth and empowerment. These are the stuff and substance of essential human dignity. [79]

Equality has been totally eviscerated, reduced to individual feelgoodisms, or perhaps in this case feelbetterisms. Choice and the right to choose are implicit in all of these attributes now seen as the essence of dignity, the diluted proxy for equality. You have to make the "right" choice or you suffer the consequences. These feelgoodisms premised on choice are celebrated in this case despite the Court's recognition that these "incentive" programs were introduced by the Quebec Government as a way to circumvent the federal prohibition against mandatory programs — "Because federal rules in effect at the time prohibited making participation in the programs mandatory, the province's only real leverage in promoting these programs lay in making participation a prerequisite for increases in welfare."[80] This is unabashed coercion, not incentive, not choice, not autonomy, not self-determination, not empowerment — not equality.

The distortion of choice is more overt, and arguably even more perverse, in the dissenting decision of Justice Gonthier in *Sauvé*, the case in which the denial of the right to vote to federally sentenced prisoners was found to be unconstitutional. The majority decision in the case does not address the section 15 argument because they find the contravention of section 3 of the *Charter* (the right of all citizens to vote) not justifiable under section 1. However, having found the infringement of section 3 justifiable under section 1, Justice Gonthier, writing on behalf of the four dissenting judges, is required to deal with the argument that the denial of the right to vote is an infringement of federally incarcerated prisoners' section 15 right to equality, based on the analogous ground of prisoner status. The discussion is brief and dismissive but it reflects the same decontextualized, punitive attitude to choice that I argue underlies *Gosselin*. In *Sauvé*, the choice argument is explicit and, as in *Walsh*, respecting choice, regardless of the consequences of that choice, is described as a dignity-enhancing measure.

Early on in his judgment, in his preliminary remarks on the challenged legislation, Justice Gonthier rejects the majority view that temporary disenfranchisement undermines the dignity of serious criminal offenders. He goes so far as to take the opposite position, that punishment shows respect for dignity by respecting choice: "In fact, it could be said that the notion of punishment is predicated on the dignity of the individual: it recognizes serious criminals as rational, autonomous individuals who have made choices."[81] This is a perverse understanding of dignity and a paternalistic and decontextualized notion of choice. Justice Gonthier applies this same logic to the analogous ground question, arguing that the status of being a prisoner was brought on by the individual him or herself, not by "the stereotypical application of a presumed characteristic."[82] Incarceration is "the result of their criminal activity, the commission of which was in their control."[83] According to Justice Gonthier, this choice to engage in criminal behaviour is in contrast to the immutable (or close to immutable) characteristics reflected in the section 15 grounds, characteristics that "do not reflect a voluntary choice by anyone, but rather an involuntary inheritance."[84] "Choice" is thus implicated in the determination of grounds, providing the basis, at this very early stage, for denying access to the equality guarantee, of shielding the alleged inequality from any scrutiny whatsoever. Here again, choice is a unidimensional, decontextualized concept through which those who make the wrong choices are denied their basic rights.

G. CONCLUSION

In each of these three cases, choice is used explicitly, or in *Gosselin* implicitly, as the basis for the determination that there was no breach of the section 15 equality guarantee. Other recent section 1 decisions contain similar invocations of choice.[85] I expect that we will see choice playing an increasingly prominent role as a justification for inequality. The reliance on choice is in part, I think, due to the increased focus on dignity since the *Law* decision. Abstract concept after abstract concept is being deployed in the attempt to define equality and as a result we are moving further and further away from examining the concrete inequalities at issue. We (feminists, as well as members of the Supreme Court) are mired in the language of liberalism and that language locks us into the "terms of ongoing social arrangements";[86] the status quo prevails.

Once the situation has been determined to have been a matter of the claimant's "choice," the Court defers to that choice in the name of not infringing dignity. They refuse to look behind or beyond the choice *simpliciter* at the inequalities that the claimant argues have resulted. Equality has been conflated with dignity and dignity has been conflated with choice, so that it is assumed that if we have freedom of choice, we have equality. But this is backwards; equality is the prerequisite for choice, not the corollary of choice; only if you have equality can you have meaningful choice.

In response to the Court's automatic deference to choice, we need, at the very least, to be arguing for a conceptualized understanding of choice. However, this might not provide much assistance. In light of the application of *Law*'s contextual factors, context itself has become suspect. What does a conceptualized understanding of choice mean? Look like? Is context just another empty, self-serving concept? Do we simply choose the pieces of the context that suit our purpose/goal? I am not sure that providing context is enough. Perhaps we should be going a step further to argue that choice can never be a rejoinder to a discrimination/inequality claim because choice assumes equality and freedom and a section 15 claim is, by definition, challenging that assumption. From this perspective, only the claimant could rely upon choice as an equality-promoting measure. Choice could never be used as a shield against an equality claim; choice could not be used to justify inequality, only to support equality.

ENDNOTES

1   The first half of this title came from Alice Kessler-Harris, "*Equal Employment Opportunity Commission v. Sears, Roebuck and Company*: A Personal Account" in D. Kelly Weisberg, ed., *Applications of Feminist Legal Theory to Women's Lives: Sex, Violence, Work and Reproduction* (Philadelphia: Temple University Press, 1996) 594 at 595; the second half of this title came from Ann Cudd, "Oppression by Choice" (1994) 25 Journal of Social Philosophy 22 at 22.

2   I would like to thank LEAF for providing the impetus for writing this paper and the opportunity to present it at such an interesting and supportive forum. And I would like to express my deep appreciation to the National Legal Committee of LEAF for the many, many hours of stimulating and challenging discussion that have strongly shaped my thinking for this paper and on equality more generally. In particular, I thank Margaret Denike and Fay Faraday for their painstaking and thoughtful editorial comments — I could not do justice to all (or I fear any) of their more substantive suggestions but they all were extremely helpful and thought-provoking. And my thanks to Megan Reid for the research that she did so quickly, effectively, and enthusiastically, and to Constance Backhouse for her generous support.

3   Jean Bethke Elshtain, "Feminist Discourse and its Discontents: Language, Power and Meaning" in Nannerl Keohane, Michelle Rosaldo, & Barbara Gelpi, eds., *Feminist Theory: A Critique of Ideology* (Chicago: University of Chicago Press, 1982) at 127. I would not attribute this problem exclusively to liberal feminism. In relation to the subject of this paper, I think many feminists, from diverse strands of feminism, have adopted the language of choice and in doing so have bought into, or been unable to extricate themselves from, a quintessentially liberal concept, thus locking themselves into "the terms of ongoing social arrangements."

4   In this context, my use of "our" refers not just to feminists but also to liberal, left-leaning, progressive people.

5   *Attorney General of Nova Scotia v. Walsh and Bona*, [2002] 4 S.C.R. 325 [*Walsh*].

6   *Gosselin v. Attorney General of Quebec*, [2002] 4 S.C.R. 429 [*Gosselin*].

7   *Sauvé v. Canada (Chief Electoral Officer)*, [2002] 3 S.C.R. 519 [*Sauvé*].

8   *Rodriguez v. British Columbia (Attorney General)*, [1993] 3 S.C.R. 103.

9   For an example of this, see Daphne Gilbert & Diana Majury, "Infertility and the Parameters of Discrimination Discourse" in Dianne Pothier & Richard Devlin, eds., in *Critical Disability Theory: Essays in Philosophy, Politics, Policy and Law* (Vancouver: University of British Columbia Press, 2005). In this paper we discuss the Nova Scotia Court of Appeal decision in *Cameron v. Nova Scotia (Attorney General)* (1999), 177 D.L.R. (4th) 611. The case involves a claim that failure to fund specialized IVF treatments constitutes discrimination on the basis of disability (infertility). The majority decision concluded that infertility is a disability and that the funding disparity was discriminatory but that the breach of equality rights was justifiable under s. 1 of the *Charter*. Choice has been at the centre of many of the debates about IVF and other reproductive technologies, such that limits placed on the availability of reproductive technologies are characterized as paternalistic incursions into a woman's right to

choose to do what she can to bear her own child. While there is very little explicit mention of choice in the *Cameron* decision, choice is clearly a critical factor. But, unlike the cases that I review in this paper in which choice is used against the claimants, the choice to bear a child and access to the technologies required to do so, are in *Cameron* transformed into a right, without discussion, or perhaps even without any recognition of the shift from choice to right occurring.

Dorothy Roberts' critique of state protection and state privileging of the choices of white people would be extremely helpful in pursuing this analysis of choice as a right that operates counter to equality ("The Priority Paradigm: Private Choices and the Limits of Equality" (1996) 57 U. Pitt. L. Rev. 363). In the introduction to her article, Roberts explains (at 367),

> Herbert Wechsler's resolution of conflicting human claims reflects a central tenet of prevailing equality jurisprudence: human freedom requires that protection of private interests from government intrusion must supersede government promotion of equality. The prioritizing of individual liberty over equality (what I call the "priority paradigm") serves to maintain white supremacy because it means that white people's private choices outweigh concern for black people's equal status.

10 In her reviewer's comments on this paper, Fay Faraday made the following interesting connection between choice and consent:

> [I]n reading your paper I thought about the contrast/similarity between concepts of "consent" and "choice." While there has been intense judicial scrutiny and feminist critique around the notion of "consent," the same is not true with respect to "choice" ... [and] the uncritical assumption that a vulnerable person has "consented" to the consequences of her so-called "choice."

The examples Fay gave me related to "informed consent" to standard form contracts and medical treatment. In addition to those areas, extensive critical feminist analysis and law reform work has been done on the issue of consent in the context of sexual assault charges. I am intrigued by these connections and the deepening-the-thinking possibilities they present. But I could not do justice to any of these in this paper, so I leave it to a later paper and/or to others to pursue the possibilities.

11 The inclusion of pornography and prostitution under the umbrella of violence against women positions me clearly on one side of the "debate." The categorization of these practices as forms of violence against women is a controversial position in and of itself, especially with respect to prostitution.

12 Abortion is the only "practice" that I listed that I am not critical of *per se*. However, like many feminists, I have become critical of our/feminist reliance on choice as the defining rationale for support of abortion rights. Choice has been the key slogan of the abortion rights movement in North America. We define ourselves as pro-choice rather than pro-abortion in recognition that the decision to have an abortion is, for most women, a difficult and painful one and that it is possible to be in favour of the right to abortion even though one would never choose an abortion for oneself. It has

been a critical component of this pro-choice position that we not question individual women's reasons for having an abortion, that we not try to go behind that decision to challenge its legitimacy or appropriateness. However, feminists have come to recognize that this exclusive and unproblematized deference to choice glosses over a number of troubling issues. Ableism and negative assumptions about the quality of life for a person with a disability are often the basis for the decision to abort a disabled fetus. Some women feel forced to abort a fetus with a disability because of the absence of services and support for raising a child with a disability. Some women are coerced by male partners to have an abortion. For some staunch pro-choice feminists, the spectre of abortions for the purpose of sex selection (that is — almost always — the choice to abort a fetus because it is female) has shaken the commitment to unexamined choice and has led to questions about choice *simpliciter* being promoted as the key value to be protected. As well, the adoption of unqualified support for choice has been critiqued in the larger reproductive context as a gross oversimplification. Poor and racialized women, in particular, are sometimes forced to have abortions they don't want or are required to undergo sterilization as the price of their choice to abort. Like any other choice, the choice to have an abortion is not just about the right to choose; it is complicated and circumscribed and has significant impacts. As described by Rosalind Petchesky in "Reproductive Freedom: Beyond a Woman's Right to Choose" (1980) 5 Signs: The Journal of Women in Culture 661 at 673, abortion is "irreducibly social and individual at the same time." Accordingly, both the social and the individual aspects need to be attended to, at the same time. Have we done women a disservice in championing abortion solely as an issue of individual choice? On the other hand, when the right to abortion is precarious, as it perhaps always has been and certainly is now (see Sanda Rogers, "Abortion Denied: Bearing the Limits of Law" in Colleen Flood, ed., *Frontiers of Fairness* (Toronto: University of Toronto Press, forthcoming), is it irresponsible to open the door to questions about why and how women exercise that choice?

13   With respect to some of these issues, both sides of the debate frame their arguments in terms of choice. For example, one of the ways that the issue of access to women-only space by transgendered women has been framed is as a contest between the rights of an individual and the rights of a collective of women, seen simply as conflicting choices.

14   Despite best efforts to focus critique on the object of the choice, not the woman doing the choosing, the two often, or perhaps inevitably, collapse at some level. It is impossible, and counter to the analysis, totally to abstract the people from the practice.

15   For a full discussion of these critiques, see Kathryn Abrams, "Ideology and Women's Choices" (1990) 24 Georgia L. Rev. 761.

16   Such an oppositional position fails to consider the state authority that inevitably operates behind the scenes to make "choices" available and to control to whom and on what terms choices are available. As Dorothy Roberts puts it, "when courts protect white preferences as private choices, they often ignore how those choices are shaped, supported and even mandated by state authority." Above note 9 at 391.

17 The Supreme Court of Canada's decision in *Dunmore v. Attorney General for Ontario*, [2001] 3 S.C.R. 1016 in which the Court struck down the exclusion of agricultural workers from Ontario's labour relations regime may open up possibilities for arguments that, in some circumstances, the state has a positive obligation to facilitate choice.

18 The language of empowerment is often linked with choice and dignity (see, for example, *Walsh*, above note 5 at para. 81 and *Gosselin*, above note 6 at para. 65) and shares many of choice's problems. Feminists seem to have been drawn to the notion of empowerment, even though it denotes an outside source that bestows or facilitates the power transfer and even though the power so transferred always seems rather impalpable. To me empowerment seems more a feel betterism than a meaningful concept.

19 This has often been a characterization of radical feminism, particularly radical feminist work on violence against women.

20 See Frances Olsen, "The Sex of Law" in David Kairys, ed., *The Politics of Law: A Progressive Critique*, 3d ed. (New York: Basic Books, 1998) at 691–707 for a discussion of how law is premised on dichotomies and is therefore not very receptive to the more complex and nuanced arguments of feminism.

21 I do think the question of whether to reject or redefine a concept is important because exploration of the question helps to crystallize and clarify the issues. At the same time, it can be a problematic question because it too sets up a false dichotomy that promotes an either/or proposition rather than a more cogent continuum, both-at-the-same-time, kind of approach.

22 Abrams, above note 15 at 795–801, reaches a similar conclusion in which she suggests that we need to shift the choice discourse to explore multi-causal explanations for women's choices and to integrate more complex narrative accounts of women's choices.

23 Confronting the limits of liberalism is, I think, what Zillah Eisenstein was talking about in her book *The Radical Future of Liberal Feminism* (Boston: Northeastern University Press, 1981), a title that itself reflects a promising contradiction. As this, and many other of my references, reveal, when I was thinking about this paper and where I might find critical feminist analyses of choice, I was repeatedly drawn back to feminist critiques of liberalism written twenty years ago. I am intrigued by my return to what I would have thought of as dated feminist literature. But it occurs to me that, in the *Charter* equality context, we may well have run head on into the limits of liberalism, which would make this literature a potentially fruitful starting point for us in terms of analyzing what is currently going on in our courts with respect to s.15.

24 I assume that this is a recent, post-*Law* occurrence, not that I have only become aware of it recently, but I would need to review earlier *Charter* cases to confirm that the language of choice did not play a significant role before the *Law* decision and the resulting shift to dignity as the defining feature of equality.

25 *EEOC v. Sears*, 628 F. Supp. 1264 (N.D. Ill. 1986), aff'd 839 F.2d 302 (7th Cir. 1988) [*Sears*].

26 Kessler Harris, above note 1 at 600. Lest we think that this kind of simplistic reliance on gender difference as choice is an historical artefact, we need only turn to the factum of the Attorney General of Alberta (paras. 25–29) in the NAPE appeal before the Supreme Court of Canada. This case involved a s. 15 claim brought against the Government of Newfoundland for reneging on their pay equity agreement to compensate women working in the health care sector for longstanding pay inequities. Among a number of arguments that echo those made by Sears twenty years ago in defence of their discriminatory wages is the following statement from the Attorney General of Alberta:

> An inquiry into whether s.9 is [*sic*] discriminates in substance must also consider the significance of the fact that no person is affected by the impugned legislation but for the decisions they have made in their working lives. (para. 25)

For the (devastating) decision in this case, see *Newfoundland (Treasury Board) v. N.A.P.E.*, [2004] 3 S.C.R. 381.

27 Such a reading of women's history would now probably be characterized as essentialist and be dismissed. However, essentialism can be another dichotomizing, discussion-stopping label that tends to oversimplify and belie issues that warrant further examination. It is not necessary to argue that differences are innate or "real" in order to argue that gender differences might exist and might need to be taken into account. The tricky question is how they are taken into account and to what short term and long-term effect. See Martha Minow, "Sources of Difference" in Martha Minow, ed., *Making All the Difference: Inclusion, Exclusion and American Law* (Ithaca: Cornell University Press, 1990) at 49–78.

28 *Ibid.* at 603.

29 Ann Cudd, above note 1 at 22.

30 Joan Scott, "Deconstructing Equality-versus-Difference: Or, the Uses of Poststructuralist Theory for Feminism" in D. Kelly Weisberg, ed., *Applications of Feminist Legal Theory to Women's Lives: Sex, Violence, Work and Reproduction* (Philadelphia: Temple University Press, 1996) 611 at 617.

31 *Sauvé*, above note 7 at para. 10.

32 These guidelines were set out and unanimously endorsed by the Court in *Law*, above note 1. As described by the Court in *Law* at para. 51, the purpose of s. 15 is "to prevent the violation of essential human dignity and freedom through the imposition of disadvantage, stereotyping, or political or social prejudice, and to promote a society in which all persons enjoy equal recognition at law as human beings or as members of Canadian society, equally capable and equally deserving of concern, respect and consideration." In furthering this purpose, the s. 15 test sets out the following three central elements for analysis:

1) whether the law imposes differential treatment between the claimant and others, on its face or through impact;

2) whether one or more of the enumerated or analogous grounds is the basis for the differential treatment;

3) whether the differential treatment discriminates in a substantive sense in light of the purpose of s. 15 [paras. 23 & 39].

The Court in *Law* sets out the following non-exclusive list of four contextual factors as potentially relevant to the consideration of the third element, the question of whether there was discrimination:

i) pre-existing disadvantage, stereotyping or vulnerability of the claimant;

ii) the correspondence between the claim and the actual need or circumstances of the claimant;

iii) the ameliorative purpose or effects of the impugned law on other groups in society; and

iv) the nature and scope of the interest affected [as listed in *Walsh*, above note 5 at para. 33].

It is the discussion of this third element and these contextual factors that choice supersedes. For example in *Walsh,* the appellant conceded the first two elements of the *Law* test and Justice Bastarache dispensed with them in a single paragraph (para. 32) before moving on to consider the four contextual factors relating to the determination of whether or not there had been discrimination. And in that consideration, Ms. Walsh's choice not to marry becomes "a significant aspect of the context in which the respondent's claim of discrimination arises" (para. 35).

33 Like choice and dignity, context is a concept that warrants serious critical attention with respect to its interpretation and application under s. 15. Context has long been a cornerstone of feminist theory and methodology. Since the inception of s. 15, feminists have been calling for a conceptualized approach to equality. For feminists, context refers to social context in which gender and other systemic power dynamics are central to the analysis. The Court, however, views context much more broadly (see *ibid.*) and as a result, the significance of social factors is seriously diluted and a power analysis is circumvented.

34 *Walsh*, above note 5.

35 Justice Bastarache wrote the decision on behalf of the seven-member majority; Justice Gonthier wrote concurring reasons to add "his own distinct, and now familiar, take on the 'fundamental institution' of marriage" (Rollie Thompson, "Annotation" (2002) 32 R.F.L. (5th) 87 at 88) to the reasons of the majority with which he agreed; and Justice L'Heureux-Dubé was on her own in dissent.

36 His full sentence is "Where legislation has the effect of dramatically altering the legal obligations of partners, as between themselves, choice must be paramount." The rationale for deferring to choice in this case appears to be because marriage is "intensely personal and engages a complex interplay of social, political, religious and financial considerations by the individual" (*Walsh*, above note 5 at para. 43). However, this argument could as easily apply the other direction. The fact the state felt it necessary to intervene in this most personal and individual of decisions in order to dramatically alter the legal obligations of married couples would seem to be a strong argument that a similar legal intervention might be necessary to protect the interests of those who, for whatever reasons, have "chosen" not to marry, but have otherwise

undertaken a similar commitment and obligation. From this perspective, the issue would then be whether some married cohabitants could (or should) be assumed to have undertaken similar spousal commitments and obligations, rather than assuming they had chosen not to.

37 Justice Bastarache makes a point of noting the introduction of the *Law Reform (2000) Act*, S.N.S. 2000, c. 29 (*LRA*) enacted in response to the Court of Appeal decision in this case (above note 5 at paras. 5 & 6). The *LRA* provides for heterosexual and lesbian/gay registered partnerships to be eligible for the benefits of the *MPA*. It is perhaps a sign of (slight) progress that the Court in *Walsh* at least feels that it has to acknowledge that the constitutional question in this case is limited to *heterosexual* unmarried cohabitants. Not too long ago the unstated, subconscious assumption would have been that all coupled cohabitants were heterosexual. However, the repeated reference to unmarried heterosexual cohabitants is a constant reminder of the discriminatory exclusion of gays and lesbians from marriage. For those lesbians and gays for whom the right to marry is an important and meaningful right that has been denied them, this type of language is painful salt in the wound. Ironically of course the majority's reliance in this case on choice as the meaningful distinction between married and unmarried cohabitants that renders the challenged exclusion nondiscriminatory opens the door to the argument that the *MPA* exclusion discriminates against lesbian and gay cohabitants who are denied the choice to marry. Significantly, the majority in *Walsh* do not attempt to distinguish the decision in *M. v. H.*, [1999] 2 S.C.R. 2 [*M. v. H.*], in which spousal support obligations were extended to lesbian and gay couples, a case in which the choice rationale for exclusion is eliminated by discriminatory definitions of who can marry. This ironic implication of the Court's reliance on "choice" reinforces my perception that the *Walsh* decision is not really about respecting "choice" but is more about protecting the sanctity of marriage as somehow a meaningful and distinct legal institution, despite the almost complete erosion of any legal distinctiveness. Justice Gonthier's concurring decision in *Walsh* is a desperate, and tautological (in that he uses the *MPA*, the legislation under challenge, as a distinguishing characteristic) attempt to identify the "characteristics that distinguish marriage from other forms of cohabitation" so as to preserve the "unique character of marriage" (para. 191). Unlike the majority, Justice Gonthier does attempt to distinguish *M. v. H.* His assertion that spousal support fulfills a social objective relating to need and dependency, whereas the *MPA* is contractual and relates to the division of matrimonial assets without regard to need (paras. 203–4) is a similarly suspect and circular attempt to shore up the distinctiveness of marriage. The *Walsh* case would have been so much more interesting and had so much more depth if it had involved more than a single claimant; if for example a lesbian or gay couple had joined the claim. *Charter* litigation and jurisprudence more generally are severely limited by the fact that they are largely based on individual claims and individual fact situations that restrict the evidence, the understanding of the issue, and the analysis of impact; and no doubt of remedy as well.

38 R.S.N.S. 1989, c. 275.

39   Most of these issues are canvassed by Justice L'Heureux-Dubé in her dissent. She
goes into the choice issue in depth and provides a strong critique of the reliance on
choice as the salient feature in this case. In so doing, she explores the complexity and
contradictions that inhere in cohabitants' relationships, whether married or not.

40   I borrow this terminology from Carol Rogerson, "Developments in Family Law: The
2002–2003 Term" (2003) 22 Sup. Ct. L. Rev. 273 at 301, which she uses to describe
the Court's view of family relationships.

41   *Walsh*, above note 5 at para. 143.

42   As is often the case with law students and new lawyers, I used to insist on burdening
friends who were getting married with the details of my newfound knowledge as
to their legal rights and obligations, particularly with respect to marriage breakdown. Not one of them was the least bit interested; most of them found my patter
extremely annoying and depressing and all assured me that they were going to stay
together so this information was irrelevant to them.

43   *Walsh*, above note 5 at para. 43, quoting Margrit Eichler, *Family Shifts: Families,
Policies and Gender Equality* (Toronto: Oxford University Press, 1997) at 96. While
this is nowhere near as extreme as the *Sears* case's (mis)use of feminist historical work
on women's difference, it does echo that case in its (mis)use of feminist work to support the rejection of a women's equality argument.

44   If the decision not to marry is a decision to keep the state out of one's relationship,
this case ironically confirms the impossibility of fully achieving that goal. The Court
seeks to support "the individual's freedom to choose alternative family forms and
to *have that choice respected and legitimated by the state*," *Walsh, ibid.* at para. 44
(emphasis added).

45   "It may very well be true that some, if not many, unmarried cohabitants have agreed as
between themselves to live as economic partners for the duration of their relationship.
Indeed, the factual circumstances of the parties' relationship bear this out," *Walsh,
ibid.* at para. 54. These factors would seem to counter the majority's assumption that in
choosing not to marry, Ms. Walsh was choosing to opt out of the marital property regime imposed by the *MPA*. If anything, the economic relationship between the parties
indicated an intention to adopt the regime. But the specifics of the claimant's situation
are ignored in favour of an unfounded generalized assumption.

46   *Ibid.*

47   *Ibid.* at para. 171.

48   *Ibid.* at para. 48.

49   Because the change brought about by the *MPA* is so significant, the majority is
unwilling to impose the legislation on couples who have not explicitly chosen to be
bound by it. Justice L'Heureux-Dubé points out the hypocrisy of such an argument
given that the *MPA* applied retroactively to couples who were already married when
the legislation came into effect, *ibid.* at para. 147.

50   Justice L'Heureux-Dubé, in her dissent, is the only one to examine the alternative
remedies available to unmarried cohabitants. For the majority, the shield of choice
renders such an examination unnecessary. According to the majority, the fact that
Ms. Walsh chose not to marry means that she chose to be governed by these alterna-

tive remedies. Thus, however inadequate the remedies may be, that was her choice and it must be "respected." And, according to Justice L'Heureux-Dubé, *ibid.* at para. 168, the alternatives are seriously inadequate:

> The situation facing heterosexual unmarried cohabitants today is no different than the one facing married couples in the late 1970s. The same inadequate, costly remedies that led to reform for married couples are now the only remedies available to non-marital-cohabitants.

See also Thompson, above note 35; Daniel Melamed & Stefanie Brull, "Constructive/Resulting Trust: A Review of Where We Were and Where We Are Going" (2003) 18 Money and Family Law 57, and Rogerson, above note 40 at 285–86 and 302. All of these authors, in different words, describe the current state of the law of unjust enrichment and constructive trust as "suffer[ing] from a high degree of conceptual confusion" (Rogerson at 302). Thompson goes so far as to ask "Will *Walsh v. Bona* be another *Murdoch*?" (at 87). *Murdoch v Murdoch* (1973), 13 R.F.L. 185 (S.C.C.) was the case that exposed the shortcomings of unjust enrichment and constructive trust doctrines in relation to married women, giving rise to major public outcry and resulting in the kinds of legislative changes embodied in the *MPA*.

51 *Walsh*, above note 5 at para. 47.

52 Roberts, above note 9 at 396. And in the context of this case, the private remedies that are preferred by the courts are totally inadequate (see above note 50).

53 In concluding his decision, Justice Bastarache explicitly invokes liberty, a right protected by s. 7 of the *Charter*, as the "essential value" that correlates with freedom of choice (*Walsh*, above note 5 at para. 63).

54 I recognize that after the decision in *British Columbia (Public Service Employee Relations Commission) v. BCGSEU*, [1999] 3 S.C.R. 3, these categories no longer exist for litigation purposes. My point here is that it would be more difficult to argue that a person has consciously chosen hidden (indirect) effects than to argue that the (direct) discriminatory effects were readily apparent as part of the choice that was made.

55 This case is a clear example of comparator groups constituting a proxy for the similarly-situated analysis that was supposedly renounced in *Andrews v. Law Society of British Columbia*, [1989] 1 S.C.R. 143. For Justices Bastarache and L'Heureux-Dubé, married couples are clearly the appropriate comparator group for unmarried heterosexual couples. For each of them, the s. 15 exercise then becomes assessing the extent and significance of the similarities and differences between the two groups. According to Justice Bastarache, the couple themselves, in choosing to get married or choosing not to get married, creates the definitive difference that renders the two groups not similarly situated with respect to the *MPA*. Justice L'Heureux-Dubé employed the prevailing functional approach to family law by assessing the two groups as "functionally equivalent," with few distinctions and the same needs when the relationship comes to an end. Clearly for both judges the question is one of sameness or difference — one has to be able to assert one's strong similarity to another better-off group in order to proceed with an equality claim. In this, we are still stuck in at least

half of the Aristotelean model of formal equality that substantive equality was supposed to have moved us beyond. We may have grasped the notion that equality does
not mean that we have to treat everyone the same, but we do not seem to have fully
grasped that equality does not require that groups be substantially similar in order
for inequality to exist. We have repudiated the "alike" but not the "likes" half of the
definition of equality as being about "treating likes alike," and thus are still focused
on finding "like" groups for comparison. Yet it is usually those who are perceived as
most unalike who experience the greatest inequalities and are most in need of s. 15
protection.

On the other hand, Justice Gonthier, in his concurring decision, rejects married
couples as the appropriate comparator group in this case, based on what he sees as a
fundamental difference between married couples and common law couples (*Walsh*,
above note 5 at para. 205). The fundamental difference, according to Justice Gonthier, is the absence of a permanent and reciprocal life commitment, which according
to the statistics he quotes earlier, means that 90 percent of marriages last at least ten
years, a sort of appliance-lifetime notion of permanence. He makes no mention of
the fact that, having cohabited for ten years, Ms. Walsh and Mr. Bona fit into this 90
percent cohort. Justice Gonthier offers no alternative comparator group, leaving one
with the impression that unmarried heterosexual couples are a group unto themselves, without an appropriate comparator. Given the Court's insistence that every
s. 15 claim requires a comparator group, this would leave unmarried heterosexual
couples without access to s. 15. For a fuller discussion of the problems with comparator groups, see Leslie Reaume, this volume.

Confirming the slippage of comparator groups into a "similarly situated" analysis, Justice McLachlin in *Gosselin*, above note 6 at para. 61, explicitly employs the language of "similarly situated" (albeit in quotation marks) in her discussion of welfare
recipients over thirty years of age and welfare recipients under thirty as comparator
groups.

56 *Miron v. Trudel*, [1995] 2 S.C.R. 418 (referred to in *Walsh, ibid.* at para. 10). Justice
Gonthier, writing on behalf of four judges, dissented in *Miron*, relying upon a choice
argument to find that the distinction between married and unmarried cohabitants in relation to eligibility for insurance benefits was not discriminatory. Some of
Justice Gonthier's thinking in his dissent in *Miron* finds its way into the majority
decision in *Walsh*.

57 *Walsh, ibid.* at para. 53.

58 *Ibid.* at paras. 43, 62–63.

59 In the post-*Law* application of the *Law* test, harm to dignity has become the defining feature of the discrimination determination. In *Law*, dignity was given primary
place in the stated purpose of s. 15 (see above note 32) and it has retained that centrality since the *Law* decision, despite extensive critiques that dignity is not up to the
equality task. For critiques of the focus on dignity, see, for example, Sheilah Martin,
"Balancing Individual Rights to Equality and Social Goods" (2001) 80 Can. Bar Rev.
299; and June Ross, "A Flawed Synthesis of Law" (2000) 11 Const. Forum 74. In this
volume see Beverley Baines, "Equality, Comparison, Discrimination, Status" and

Sheila McIntyre, "Answering the Siren Call of Abstract Formalism with the Subjects and Verbs of Domination." For a thoughtful attempt to flesh out the concept of dignity as a substantive value underpinning s. 15, see Denise Réaume, "Discrimination and Dignity" (2003) 63 La. L. Rev. 645, reprinted in this volume.

60   As described so aptly by Sonia Lawrence: "In both *Gosselin* and *Walsh*, the Court suggests: choice = liberty = human dignity = equality." ("Harsh, Perhaps Even Misguided: Developments in Law, 2002" (2003) 20 S.C.L.R. (2d) 93 at 96.) Roberts, above note 9 at 396, makes the opposite point about seeing these values as in conflict: "The priority paradigm's assumption that liberty may be pitted against equality, as if they were two isolated values, ignores the relationship between individual choice and social power." Either way, through conflation or through conflict, equality gets trounced. Instead, these values need to be reconceived; to be seen, understood, and applied as complementary; as separate but mutually supportive.

61   *Walsh*, above note 5 at para. 157. Justice L'Heureux-Dubé's discussion of the impact on dignity (at paras. 141–57) is all about choice. She too falls into the trap of equating dignity and choice and premises her finding that the *MPA* demeans the claimant's dignity on the *MPA's* "failure to appreciate the absence of choice many cohabitants face with its concomitant exploitative features" (at para. 157). As I argue above, an equality analysis should focus on the "concomitant exploitative features" of which the absence of choice may be one, rather than on choice *per se*.

62   *Ibid.* at paras. 170–71.

63   This is not to say that feelings and sense of self-worth are not important. But they are only a component of an equality analysis, not the primary issue. I am not arguing that dignity should not be a factor in a s. 15 analysis, just that it should not be the determining factor; it should not be used to stand in for equality.

64   *Gosselin*, above note 6.

65   *Sauvé*, above note 7.

66   The regulation at issue in *Gosselin*, above note 6, was replaced in 1989.

67   Ms. Gosselin also brought claims under s. 7 of the Canadian *Charter* and under s. 45 of the *Quebec Charter*. Although there were differing judgements on each of these claims, none of the claims were supported by a majority of the Court. As in *Walsh*, it would have been interesting if Ms. Gosselin's s. 15 claim had been based on multiple grounds (in her case possibly gender, mental disability, and poverty/receipt of welfare) and if the case had included other individual claimants raising other combinations of grounds. The majority looks at age in isolation from any other factors and is thereby able to assert that "young adults as a class simply do not seem especially vulnerable or undervalued" (*ibid.* at para. 33) (even though this too is a questionable assertion) and to dismiss the proposed sub-category of welfare recipients between eighteen and thirty (*ibid.* at para. 35). Whatever one thinks about the accuracy of the description as it pertains to "young adults," the claim in this case is about young welfare recipients who are unquestionably vulnerable and undervalued.

68   Justice McLachlin wrote the majority reasons for the decision that the impugned provision did not infringe s. 15 of the *Charter*, on behalf of five judges. For the purposes of this paper, I am only looking at the majority decision on the s. 15 claim

and only with respect to the narrow issue of the implicit treatment of Ms. Gosselin's situation as flowing from her "choice." There are a number of excellent, comprehensive critiques of the decision in *Gosselin*. In this volume, see Andrée Côté and Gwen Brodsky,

69 *Gosselin*, above note 6 at para. 1.

70 *Ibid.* at para. 8.

71 *Ibid.* at para. 48.

72 *Ibid.* at para. 7.

73 *Ibid.* at para. 19.

74 "The situation of those who, for whatever reason, may have been incapable of participating in the programs attracts sympathy. Yet the inability of a given social program to meet the needs of each and every individual does not permit us to conclude that the program failed to correspond to the actual needs and circumstances of the affected group," *ibid.* at para. 55.

75 Justice McLachlin repeatedly refers to the fact that some people may fall through a program's cracks, as if this explains or somehow justifies Ms. Gosselin's dire situation.

76 *Gosselin*, above note 6 at para. 47.

77 *Ibid.* at para. 51.

78 This echoes the majority decision in *Walsh* that respecting Ms. Walsh's decision not to marry was not only not an infringement of her dignity but was actually dignity-enhancing.

79 *Gosselin,* above note 6 at para. 65.

80 *Ibid.* at para. 44.

81 *Ibid.* at para. 73.

82 *Ibid.* at para. 195.

83 *Ibid.* at para. 197.

84 *Ibid.* There is no mention here of non-immutable characteristics that have been held to constitute grounds, such as the non-immutable characteristic of marital status which was accepted in *Walsh* as an analogous ground in a decision that turns on marital status as a voluntary choice.

85 See for example *Hodge v. Canada (Minister of Human Resources Development)*, [2004] 3 S.C.R. 357, in which Ms. Hodge challenged the denial to her of a survivor's pension under the Canada Pension Plan. She was held ineligible for the pension because she had separated from her abusive common law spouse five months prior to his death. While the logic of this decision very much echoes that of *Walsh,* choice is an implicit rather than explicit basis for denying her claim, as it was in *Gosselin.* The choice implication is, however, very clear in the Court's rejection of her choice of separated married spouses as the appropriate comparator group and the insertion of former married spouses as the basis for comparison.

86 See above note 3.

seven

The *Law* Test for Discrimination and Gendered Disability Inequality

Fiona Sampson

A. INTRODUCTION

Contextualized equality rights arguments, specific to the experience of gendered disability, constitute a potentially viable mechanism to advance the equality rights of disabled women. However, the successful advancement of such analyses has become more difficult in the post-*Law* (*Law v. Canada (Minister of Employment and Immigration)*[1] equality rights era, with the introduction of a new, more onerous, and complicated test for discrimination. The *Law* test for discrimination has compounded pre-existing problems with section 15 *Charter*-based[2] equality rights analyses, and introduced new challenges for equality claimants seeking to advance claims pursuant to section 15. The introduction of these new challenges comes at a time in Canadian history when those who are most disadvantaged in our society, such as disabled women, are experiencing increased disadvantage as a result of the neo-liberal political-economic agenda.[3] This reality makes the need to overcome the challenges associated with the *Law* test, and the need to fulfill the potential of section 15 to protect and promote equality, more important than ever.

This chapter will provide a critique of the components of the *Law* test that are of particular concern from a gendered disability perspective: the comparator group analysis and the injury to dignity analysis. It will also include a critique of the one post-*Law* decision to date in which gendered disability discrimination has been argued, *Auton v. British Columbia*.[4] The analysis of this case will be used as a prism through which the problems with the *Law* test will be exposed and assessed. The paper will conclude with an analysis of why the weaknesses with the *Law* test for discrimination need to be challenged, and why section 15 equality analyses have to be more honest and direct in their approach to provide for meaningful substantive equality, and more than just symbolic rhetoric.

B. THE TEST FOR DISCRIMINATION

The Court's early interpretation of section 15 of the *Charter* in *Andrews v. Law Society of British Columbia*[5] and *R. v. Turpin*[6] established equality rights tests that were quite helpful indicators of whether a person's equality rights had been violated. Several years after the release of *Andrews* and *Turpin* the Court became divided about how to interpret and apply section 15, and some members of the Court adopted more restrictive interpretations of equality than had been stated in *Andrews* and *Turpin*.[7] In 1999 the Court, in an apparent effort to clarify and harmonize its equality rights analyses, released its unanimous decision in *Law v. Canada* — a decision that has seriously narrowed the judicial scope of *Charter*-based equality rights, and made it more difficult to advance successful equality rights claims.

In the first decisions involving the application of section 15, it was decided that the purpose of the *Charter*'s equality rights guarantees was "to remedy historical disadvantage."[8] The major goal for equality rights advocates was to ensure that the *Charter* equality guarantees provided for substantive equality, which takes into account systemic disadvantage and provides for an equality of results, rather than just formal equality. Formal equality, which provides that likes be treated alike, provides little or no protection against discrimination for most disadvantaged persons. Formal equality invokes the similarly situated test[9] that holds that an equality violation exists where there is different treatment of similarly situated individuals. Formal equality does not take into account the ways in which different groups in society have experienced systemic disadvantages. Under a formal model of equality, the disadvantaged only get equality in the areas of life in which they are most like the dominant norm; Catharine McKinnon has described the limitations with formal equality as "if men don't need it, women don't get it."[10] The fundamental difficulty with formal equality theory is that it makes disadvantage invisible through a consideration of equality in terms of sameness and difference, rather than in terms of dominance and subordination.[11] The theory asserts a neutral standard that fails to take into consideration the power imbalances that have resulted from years of oppression.

In *Andrews* and *Turpin*, the Court reached the important conclusion that the section 15 equality guarantees provide for substantive equality rather than just formal equality. The Court adopted a two-step test for establishing discrimination: first, did the legislation create a distinction; second, was this distinction discriminatory?[12] The second part of the test required the claimant to prove that the legislation imposed a burden, or that a benefit was denied based upon an enumerated or analogous ground under section 15.[13] Adopting much of the rationale of substantive equality that had informed radical feminist theoretical analyses of equality,[14] the Court decided "equality may well require differentiation in treatment."[15] The Court found that in determining whether there is discrimination it is important to look at:

> The larger social, political and legal context. ... Accordingly, it is only by examining the larger context that a court can determine whether differential treatment results in inequality or whether, contrariwise, it would be identical treatment which would in the particular context result in inequality or foster disadvantage.[16]

The endorsement of contextualized analyses represented a significant advancement for equality rights law. Through a contextualized approach, equality claimants can educate the judiciary about their actual experiences, contributing to the broadening of the theoretical base of the legal concept of equality, and providing for improved legal reasoning based on more informed understandings of experiences of discrimination. Part of the attraction of the contextualized approach to equality is that it diminishes the focus on the sameness/difference dichotomy.[17] The goal of a contextualized equality rights analysis is to identify the source of the claimant's subordination in order to eradicate it.

A contextualized approach to equality is attractive to equality claimants such as disabled women, because they need not necessarily argue that they are the same as either non-disabled women and/or disabled men and so deserve the same treatment, nor that they are different from non-disabled women and/or disabled men so that they deserve different treatment. Through a contextualized analysis, disabled women can argue that their subordination has been socially constructed and legally enforced. The focus is thereby switched from the individual to systemic discrimination, allowing for a more comprehensive understanding of the subordination experienced by women with disabilities. Unfortunately, the *Law* test for discrimination has moved discrimination analyses away from examinations of substantive (in)equality grounded in contextualized thinking, and has thereby created a significant disadvantage for equality claimants, including disabled women.

In *Law* the Supreme Court set out a three-step test for discrimination: i) is there differential treatment; ii) is the differential treatment based on an enumerated ground; iii) is the differential treatment discriminatory. According to Iacobucci J., writing for a unanimous Court in *Law*, the purpose of section 15(1) is "... to prevent the violation of essential human dignity and freedom through the imposition of disadvantage, stereotyping, or political or social prejudice, and to promote a society in which all persons enjoy equal recognition at law as human beings or as members of Canadian society, equally capable and deserving of concern, respect, and consideration."[18] Central to Iacobucci J.'s redevelopment of the section 15 equality rights analysis in *Law* is the injury to dignity test that is understood to constitute the third step of the *Law* test. The injury to dignity test has now assumed a pivotal role in the analysis of discrimination claims advanced under section 15 of the *Charter*.[19] In *Law*, Iacobucci J. found that the purpose of section 15(1) is "... to prevent the violation of essential human dignity and freedom through the imposition of disadvantage, stereotyping, or political or social prejudice, and to promote a society in which all persons enjoy equal recognition at law as human beings or as members of Canadian society, equally capable and equally deserving of concern, respect and consideration."[20] In *Law* Iacobucci J. suggested four "contextual" factors that may be referred to by a claimant to demonstrate legislative injury to a person's dignity so as to establish differential treatment that is discriminatory and in violation of section 15. The four factors identified by Iacobucci J. are:

i) Is pre-existing disadvantage, stereotyping, prejudice, or vulnerability experienced by the individual or group at issue?

ii) Is there correspondence, or lack of it, between the ground on which a claim is based and the actual need, capacity, or circumstances of the claimant or others?

iii) Does the legislation have an ameliorative purpose or effect for a group which has been historically disadvantaged in the context of the legislation?

iv) What is the nature of the interest affected by the legislation?[21]

Iacobucci J. cautioned in *Law* that the list of factors in the dignity test is not closed and that there is no specific formula to be applied in the consideration of a violation of human dignity. The Court stated that the factors identified in *Law* should not be applied "too mechanically."[22] While the *Law* test for discrimination may have been developed in an effort to improve the quality and predictability of equality analyses, it has failed to address pre-existing problems that arose through the section 15 jurisprudence (for example, problems with comparator analyses, as discussed below), and has unfairly created additional hurdles for section 15 equality claimants, hurdles that are especially difficult for disabled women to clear. What follows is a critique of those hurdles conducted from a gendered disability perspective.

C. THE COMPARATOR GROUP ANALYSIS

There are significant problems with the *Law* test for discrimination, many of which are analyzed by other authors who have contributed to this collection of papers. Two problems with the test are of particular concern from the perspective of gendered disability, because they have an especially onerous impact on disabled women advancing equality claims. These problems are the comparator group analysis and the injury to dignity analysis, which are discussed below.

The inclusion of a comparator analysis in section 15 jurisprudence is not a novel idea. The idea that equality is a comparative concept was endorsed early on by the Supreme Court in its decision in *Andrews v. British Columbia*. The Court in *Andrews* wrote that equality "is a comparative concept, the condition of which may only be attained or discerned by comparison with the condition of others in the social and political setting in which the question arises."[23] The Supreme Court in *Andrews* also stated that "It must be recognized at once, however, that every difference in treatment between individuals under the law will not necessarily result in inequality and, as well, that identical treatment may frequently produce serious inequality."[24] The importance of comparator analyses has been reaffirmed under the *Law* test. Unfortunately pre-exiting problems with this concept have been compounded, while the focus on the critical guiding principles has been diminished. The emphasis on comparative analyses, and the way in which the concept of difference has been (mis)applied has made it increasingly difficult for equality claimants to successfully advance section 15 claims post-*Law*.[25]

For the Supreme Court post-*Law*, a "crucial" element of the section 15 discrimination test is the identification of the comparator group — the group in relation to which the equality claimant can properly claim "unequal treatment,"[26] as per the first branch of the *Law* test.[27] According to the principles established in *Law*, the Court is not bound by the claimant's characterization of the appropriate comparator group and has the authority to redefine it where warranted.[28] In *Granovsky v. Canada (Minister of Employment and Immigration)*,[29] Binnie J., writing for a unanimous Court, decided that Mr. Granovsky inaccurately identified the proper comparator group for purposes of the first step of the section 15(1) test; namely, differential treatment. Binnie J. noted that pursuant to the Court's decision in *Law*, a section 15 claimant is given considerable scope to identify the appropriate group for comparison.[30] However, he went on to find that:

> Such identification has to bear an appropriate relationship between the group selected for comparison and the benefit that constitutes the subject matter of the complaint. As was pointed out in *Law*, at para. 57: "Both the purpose and the effect of the legislation must be considered in determining the appropriate comparison group or groups." [31]

The role of the "comparator group" in section 15 analyses was further elaborated upon by Iacobucci J. in *Lovelace v. Ontario*[32] as follows:

> ... there are three basic stages to establishing a breach of s. 15. Briefly, the Court must find (i) differential treatment, (ii) on the basis of an enumerated or analogous ground, (iii) which conflicts with the purpose of s. 15(1) and, thus, amounts to substantive discrimination. *Each of these inquiries proceeds on the basis of a comparison with another relevant group or groups*, and locating the relevant comparison groups requires an examination of the *subject-matter of the law, program or activity and its effects, as well as a full appreciation of the context.* [Emphasis added.]

In *Hodge v. Canada*[33] Binnie J. writing for a unanimous Court, repeated that the selection of the comparator group is not a threshold issue that, once decided, can be put aside. He found that, on the contrary, each step in the section 15(1) analysis proceeds "on the basis of a comparison."[34] Indeed in many of the decided cases, the characteristics of the "comparator group" are only developed as the analysis proceeds, especially when consid-

seven • THE LAW TEST FOR DISCRIMINATION

ering the "contextual" factors relevant at the third stage; that is, whether discrimination, as opposed to just a "distinction," has been established. Binnie J. went on to find that the criteria for identifying the appropriate comparator group is as follows:

> The appropriate comparator group is the one which *mirrors* the characteristics of the claimant (or claimant group) relevant to the benefit or advantage sought except that the statutory definition includes a personal characteristic that is offensive to the *Charter* or omits a personal characteristic in a way that is offensive to the *Charter*.[35] [Emphasis added.]

Herein lies the heart of the critical problems with the comparator group analysis.

The problems relating to the comparator analysis are that it is overly formalistic and artificial. However, the primary problem is that it reinforces the dominant norm that is usually the source of the subject oppression. It is an analysis that is very much removed from what should be at the core of a discrimination analysis; namely, whether the claimant, a member of a protected or analogous group, has experienced treatment that exacerbates or perpetuates a pre-existing disadvantage. The comparator group analysis operates to reinforce the dominant norm, invites analyses of formal discrimination, and is especially problematic for claimants who are more than one step removed from the dominant norm,[36] such as disabled women, for whom it is especially difficult to identify an appropriate comparator group.

The problem may be rooted in the fact that discrimination analyses traditionally focus on equality, which assumes analyses of difference, rather than on inequality; namely, the effect of the impugned treatment. Analyses of inequality do not demand the same referential or comparative examination as analyses of equality because the manifestations of inequality, for example marginalization, oppression, disempowerment, etc., are readily apparent. Therefore a shift to a focus on inequality may offer some liberation from the Byzantine convolutions of the comparator group exercise. At the very least, the ways in which the comparator group exercise is vulnerable to actually perpetuating disadvantage need to be made front and centre in discrimination analyses.

Analyses of difference within equality claims need to be informed by theoretical understandings of difference. Differential treatment is not an "impartial" or "neutral" legal principle;[37] differential treatment is a value-packed concept that operates to the disadvantage of those outside of the dominant norm by reinforcing and privileging the dominant norm. For example, the analysis in *Hodge v. Canada*[38] was entirely focused on the similarity or dissimilarity between the claimant, a former common-law spouse, and the potential different comparator groups in the case, separated vs. divorced formerly married persons. The focus was on the dominant norm of marriage, and it formed the main reference for the analysis. This focus on the dominant norm distracted from what should be the focus of the analysis; namely, the discriminatory effect of the denial of the benefit on the claimant, a member of a protected group.

The Court in *Hodge* decided that there was no discrimination in that case. It rejected the claimant's choice of comparator group, separated married spouses who are entitled to receive the subject benefits, and decided instead that the appropriate comparator group was divorced spouses. The Court concluded that divorced spouses were the appropriate comparator group because they were like non-co-habiting former common law spouses as they had no continuing legal relationship with each other (this finding is confusing in that non-co-habiting, former common-law spouses may be entitled to receive spousal support and therefore may maintain a legal relationship). The Court's focus on finding a group that "mirrored" the claimant's group and was the same as or similar to the claimant's group not only forced a focus on the dominant norm, it also forced a formal equality analysis focused on sameness and difference. What should have been the focus of the analysis, the disadvantageous effect of the impugned legislation on the claimant, was not factored into the discrimination analysis. The Court did acknowledge the arguments made by the claimant relating to the disadvantageous effect of the impugned legislation on her.[39] However, the Court only made a passing reference to those arguments. It then came to the somewhat confusing conclusion that because the definition of "co-habitation" had not been challenged, only the requirement that a non-married spouse be cohabiting with the contributor at the time of the contributor's death to be eligible for a survivor's benefit at issue[40] (which amounts to a distinction without a difference in this case), it could not provide any relief.[41] The artificial effort of attempting to make the comparator group analysis work seems to invite this kind of specious thinking — thinking that does not assist in the identification and verification of discriminatory (in)actions.

An alternative to the current comparator group analysis would be to re-think the "differential" treatment examination. Consider that the concept of "differential" treatment invites the inquiry of, "difference with respect to whom?" The attribution of difference, and the affirmation of the dominant norm as inherent and natural, hide the power of the dominant groups,[42] thus disadvantaging oppressed groups such as disabled persons, and espe-cially disabled women who are often quite "different" from the dominant norm. Attributions of difference can work against equality claimants as they can distance them from the norm, and work to reinforce the power of the norm. The effect that the difference of gendered disability makes in the context of equality claims is complicated, however, by the fact that some consideration of difference is sometimes a legitimate consideration, and therefore some differences may deserve recognition. The problem in judicial decision-making occurs when the difference that constitutes dis-ability or gendered disability becomes a focus for the wrong reasons; that is, consciously or unconsciously, to justify unequal treatment (as happened in *Granovsky*).[43]

The key to understanding the various implications of difference, and thus to engage in equality analyses in which difference is used to under-stand disadvantage and expose its origins, is to distinguish the various ways in which difference operates. Martha Minow has argued, "the stigma of difference may be recreated both by ignoring *and* by focusing on it" (em-phasis added).[44] This is particularly true with respect to disabled persons and especially disabled women. For disabled persons, the stigma of differ-ence can be created by ignoring a disability that needs accommodation; it can also be created by focusing on a physical or mental distinction that is irrelevant. Relational difference imposed by the dominant group on the subordinate group, is an instrument of stigmatization and power. Differ-ence may also be a distinction that requires recognition and accommoda-tion, but difference as a distinction should not result in stigmatization. The primary problem occurs when relational difference operates to impose an unstated norm, so that those outside of the norm are labeled as abnormal and stigmatized through difference.

The value of the differential treatment exercise as it relates to the com-parator group analysis is threatened by these intrinsic problems with the concept of difference. The impossibility of ever identifying a single, full-proof comparator group for the purposes of establishing differential treat-ment, especially with respect to claimants more than one step removed from the dominant norm, demonstrates that the exercise is seriously flawed. For example, are disabled women to compare themselves to non-disabled women, non-disabled men, disabled men, or some combination of these different groups? What is the appropriate comparator group for a disabled, racialized, Muslim lesbian?

Rather than asking whether the equality claimant has experienced differential treatment, a more appropriate question to ask is, has the claimant been subject to oppression, disadvantage, devaluation, marginalization, violence, colonization, etc., based on an enumerated or analogous ground? This would focus the analysis on the effects of the impugned treatment on the claimant and on the inequality experienced, rather than on the experience of the comparator group, presumably the (relatively) privileged dominant norm. While analyses focused on the experience of marginalization, oppression, colonization, etc., could involve reference to the dominant norm as a source of the discriminatory treatment, that reference would be about identifying the source of a power imbalance, rather than privileging the dominant norm, which would provide for a more satisfactory substantive equality analysis.

By asking the question of whether the claimant is the same as or different than the dominant norm, the dominant norm gets normalized and reinforced, and it encourages analyses of formal equality. The focus needs to be on the effect of the treatment on the claimant, and whether a power imbalance has resulted in oppression, devaluation, marginalization, etc. The claimant should need to prove membership within a protected group and that she has experienced disadvantageous treatment, and the focus on the comparison with the dominant norm should be eliminated. Such an analysis would contribute to the advancement of improved understandings of the oppression and subordination responsible for inequality — the relational source of inequality — thereby providing the opportunity to expose the origin of the inequality and to provide meaningful redress.

D. INJURY TO DIGNITY

Pursuant to the *Law* test for discrimination, the injury to dignity analysis has now assumed a critical role in discrimination analyses. The placement of a priority focus on the concept of human dignity sounds positive and relevant to the experience of equality. However the concept of human dignity is both qualitatively and quantitatively difficult to measure, and the

injury to dignity test developed in *Law* has led to increased confusion surrounding section 15 analyses — confusion that has disadvantaged equality
rights claimants, including disabled women. Since the release of its decision in *Law,* the Court has attempted to provide some clarification of the
dignity test. In *Gosselin v. Quebec*[45] it stated that "a distinction made on an
enumerated or analogous ground violates essential human dignity to the
extent that it reflects or promotes the view that the individuals affected are
less deserving of concern, respect, and consideration than others."[46] Despite this effort to explain the relevance of human dignity to the equality
rights analysis, problems remain in its application.

The injury to dignity test introduces a concept that primarily relates to
an experience of personal injury as a threshold requirement for a section 15
violation. One of the general problems with the test is that the concept of
human dignity is abstract and nebulous, which makes it a difficult fit with
an analysis of human rights violations that demands concrete assessments
of context and disadvantage. Dianne Pothier has argued that the Court's
concept of human dignity is too easily manipulated:[47]

> Thus, in light of recent jurisprudence, the limitation on the scope of the s. 15
> protection is coming not from the requirement of enumerated or analogous
> grounds, but from the conceptualization of discrimination around "human
> dignity." Human dignity is a malleable enough concept to mean whatever
> the judges want it to mean. It thus enables a brake on judicial intervention
> if the Court thinks that it would be usurping a legislative role.[48]

It is difficult for equality claimants to anticipate how the concept of dignity might be used to act as judicial brake, and this unpredictability makes
the dignity test especially problematic. Part of the problem may be that
while Iacobucci J. did provide a helpful definition of what constitutes "dignity" in *Law,*[49] the judicial focus on the specific technical elements of the
"contextual" factors associated with the dignity test (discussed below), has
shifted the discrimination analysis away from a connection to the concept
of dignity itself. The link between the four different "contextual" factors
identified by Iacobucci J. and the concept of dignity has not been well-de-
veloped in the jurisprudence. This lack of development has facilitated the
cursory dismissal of equality claims on the basis that there is no injury to
dignity, without any reference to or analysis of any of the four contextual
factors, or any other factors that might be examined to determine injury to
dignity.[50] Without a strong link between the contextual factors that may be

referenced to demonstrate an injury to dignity and the concept of dignity itself, the concern is that there is a tendency to come to arbitrary conclusions that an equality claimant has not experienced the necessary hurt, humiliation, disempowerment, etc., to demonstrate an injury to dignity.

The problem with the injury to dignity test is therefore two-fold. The test is problematic because the abstract concept of dignity is now a threshold requirement for a section 15 violation, and in the absence of concrete links between dignity and the "contextual" factors referenced in *Law*, the concept is left vulnerable to manipulation and superficial analyses.[51] The second problem with the dignity test lies with the application of the specifics of the test as articulated within the four contextual factors, a problem that is manifested when the test is applied in a mechanical fashion (as discussed below). Unfortunately, equality claimants may be damned if the dignity analysis is applied too loosely, or if it is applied too mechanically.

One of the primary problems with the contextual factors involved in the dignity analysis is that they introduce a focus on the purpose of the law/legislation within the section 15 analysis, as opposed to within the section 1 analysis where the government has the onus of justifying an established breach.[52] The introduction of analyses relating to legislative purpose usually happen through the second step of the injury to dignity analysis, the "correspondence" step, and sometimes through the fourth step relating to the nature of the interest affected by the legislation. While the idea of human dignity infers a focus on personal feelings (for better or worse), the introduction of analyses relating to the purpose of the law detract from the personal. The focus on the purpose of the law means that provisions/actions under review may not be deemed discriminatory if they have a beneficial effect on others. The dignity analysis has come to include analyses of the broad, societal purpose of the legislation, not analyses focused on the effect of the legislation on the individual claimant as a member of a disadvantaged group.[53] Iacobucci J. in *Law* did make reference to the need to consider the "purpose and effect" of the impugned legislation.[54] However this reference to the effect of the law seems to be generally either overlooked or interpreted to apply to the larger societal context.[55] The result is a departure from an effects-based analysis of a discrimination claim. The new dignity-based approach to the determination of equality rights violations represents a serious divergence from established human rights law wherein it was clearly established that intention (that is, the purpose of the law), is irrelevant to a section 15 discrimination analysis.[56]

A related problem with the dignity analysis is the apparent confusion within the Court about what exactly constitutes a contextual analysis under the new dignity test. McLachlin C.J. in *Gosselin* stated that a contextual analysis involves a determination of whether "'the legislation which imposes differential treatment has the effect of demeaning [his or her] dignity' having regard to the individual's or group's traits, history, and circumstances."[37] This approach sounds appropriate, as a contextual analysis should include a comprehensive examination of the effect of the legislation in consideration of historical socio-political disadvantage experienced by the claimant as a member of a disadvantaged group. However, the focus on the legislation's effect on the claimant is sacrificed with the introduction of the competing analysis relating to the purpose of the legislation. McLachlin C.J. concluded in *Gosselin* that "the context of a given legislative scheme also includes its purpose,"[38] and therefore intent, while perhaps not technically determinative, is significantly relevant. McLachlin C.J. did concede that a beneficial purpose will not shield a discriminatory distinction,[59] but the fact remains that the focus of the effect of the impugned law/practice on the claimant is diluted as the context is broadened to consider the legislature's perspective in the section 15 analysis. Conducting contextualized analyses that incorporate analyses of the purpose of the legislation — which will almost always have some beneficial purpose attached to it — shifts the focus away from the effect of the distinction on the claimant as a member of a disadvantaged group. This kind of confusion about the meaning and nature of a section 15 contextual analysis is problematic and clearly works to the disadvantage of equality rights claimants.

The subjective-objective standard of assessment used in the injury to dignity test is also problematic.[60] Both elements of this test may be problematic for equality rights claimants, and particularly for disabled women. The subjective element of the test may not be passed if the claimant fails to persuade the Court that she has suffered an injury to her dignity. In order to make this argument the claimant must portray herself as a victim, a portrait that many who experience discrimination find offensive and reject. The need to establish an injury to dignity forces an equality rights claimant to describe in detail the hurt, disempowerment, humiliation, and/or degradation that may be associated with an experience of discrimination (or, at least, these are the kinds of harm generally associated with an injury to dignity; the Court in *Law* did provide reference to injury to dignity involving these kinds of harm,[61] but, as discussed earlier, the analysis itself does not necessarily get at these elements of the concept). The need for a claimant to paint a picture of herself as damaged and pitiful is problematic. The concept is also problematic; as the possibility exists that a victim of discrimination may be thick-skinned and may not actually experience any injury to dignity resulting from the discriminatory experience. The need to demonstrate an injury to dignity could disadvantage thick-skinned claimants who survive the discriminatory experience with their self-respect and self-worth intact. The Court appears to have assumed that if your dignity is intact, or if it should be intact, you cannot have experienced discrimination or inequality.

Problems also exist with the objective element of the test. The primary problem with the objective element of the test is the way in which the reasonable person test is used to the disadvantage of those outside of the dominant norm, such as women with disabilities. The concept of reasonableness is a product of non-disabled male perspectives and experiences imposed on the law as an allegedly "neutral" standard.[62] It is through the imposition of this standard that the dominant norm maintains power and control over the exercise of the law to the disadvantage of those outside of the norm. For example, feminist legal theorists Karen Busby, and Lise Gotell,[63] have analyzed how the standard of the "reasonable" person has worked to the disadvantage of women who are primary witnesses in sexual assault trials, as rape mythologies remain deeply engrained in the thinking of many judges about what constitutes "reasonable" doubt. The reasonableness standard decontextualizes the inquiry, as its goal is to achieve a neutral and universal perspective on the matter. It distances the decision maker from the context of the inquiry. It invokes principles of universality that favour the non-disabled, white male. The determination of whether or not the claimant's personal feelings of hurt are reasonable or not is open to the imposition of biased norms that can work to the disadvantage of those who appear "unreasonable" from the perspective of the decision maker. Dianne Pothier has legitimately argued that judicial assessments of human dignity need to be scrutinized for discriminatory tendencies.[64] This is because the objective approach to the dignity question provides no guarantee of impartial decision-making.

The injury to dignity test constitutes a serious challenge for disabled women advancing *Charter*-based equality rights claims. Additional challenges now face all claimants advancing equality rights claims, challenges associated with the importation of section 1 considerations into section 15, and challenges associated with the need to provide evidential records relating to a concept that is ambiguous and difficult to address in concrete terms. However, women with disabilities may be especially disadvantaged by the new approach to equality rights analyses, including the application of the subjective/objective assessment of an injury to dignity. For example, some women with mental disabilities may not be able to communicate effectively so as to articulate a case in satisfaction of the subjective element of the test. The test requires the claimant to provide evidence of personal harm that includes psychological and political damage. Some disabled women may not experience this kind of harm as a result of a discriminatory experience, either because of a mental incapacity or because of a resilient personality — the result being that it may prove difficult to provide the necessary evidence of humiliation, disempowerment, marginalization, devaluation, etc. The fact that the lived experience of many women with disabilities is so different than that of the norm, may make it especially difficult for them to persuade the judiciary of the legitimacy of their claim in consideration of the subjective element of the dignity test. The difficulties posed by the dignity test for women with disabilities raises what Denise Réaume has identified as the "dilemma" of framing legal claims around a dignity standard.[65] Réaume's argument that the harm to dignity of marginalized groups "is precisely the harm that the courts are least likely to see,"[66] seems especially apt with respect to disabled women.

The objective element of the test may also prove particularly challenging to meet for women with disabilities. The test involves an inquiry to determine whether a challenged distinction, viewed from the perspective of a reasonable person in the claimant's circumstances, violates that person's dignity and fails to respect her as a full and equal member of society. What constitutes a "reasonable" personal response for a woman with a disability, someone so far removed from the dominant norm usually represented on the judiciary, may be difficult to assess. The "reasonable person" analysis inevitably incorporates elements of the decision maker's perspective and value system — the analysis becomes, "how would I respond in that situation?" It may be very difficult for someone who has not experienced gendered disability to assess what constitutes a reasonable or unreasonable reaction for that person. Because the experience of gendered disability is often so far removed from the dominant norm, the circumstances of a woman with a disability as an equality claimant may be impossible to assess from the perspective of a "reasonable" person. For example, how would the reasonable woman with the mental equivalency of a four-year-old respond to being forced to testify at the sexual assault trial of her rapist?[67] These problems with the injury to dignity test, and the *Law* test more generally, make it difficult to apply as a fair and just indicator of discrimination, as was demonstrated by the Supreme Court's decision in *Auton v. British Columbia*, discussed below.

1) *Auton v. British Columbia*

In the face of the challenges associated with *Law* test, the potential of equality rights claims to work as an effective mechanism to advance the equality rights of women with disabilities seems dubious. Few claims involving gendered disability discrimination were successfully litigated pre-*Law*.[68] In the post-*Law* era, the challenges associated with successfully litigating such claims have increased. The following is an analysis of the Supreme Court's decision in *Auton v. British Columbia*, the Court's only post-*Law* opportunity to date to consider a claim involving gendered disability discrimination. The Court's decision in *Auton* provides a useful example of the detrimental effect that the *Law* test has had on the analysis of equality claims, and specifically claims of disability and gendered disability discrimination. The problems with the *Law* analysis which are apparent in the Court's decision in *Auton* include problems with the comparator group analysis, problems with the imposition of the dominant norm in general, and problems with analyses of intersectional discrimination.

At issue in *Auton* was whether the BC Government's refusal to fund health services to ameliorate the effects of autism violated the equality rights of autistic children. The Court found that the failure to provide autism-related health services did not constitute a breach of the *Charter*'s section 15 equality guarantees. It found that there was no discrimination because the services were not provided. The Court also found that there was no evidence suggesting that the government's approach to the requested therapy was different than its approach to other comparable, "novel" therapies for non-disabled persons or persons with a different type of disability. In making this finding, the Court unilaterally re-defined the comparator group to such a narrow spectrum of the population that it shut down the claim before the examination even reached the discrimination stage of the *Law* analysis.

There are several concerns with the Court's approach to the equality rights analysis in *Auton*. The comparator group analysis and the circular reasoning that informed the analysis in general stand out as concerns with the Court's decision. However, another serious flaw with the Court's analysis is apparent early in its decision. At paragraph 2, McLachlin C.J., writing for a unanimous Court, states that "One sympathizes with the petitioners"[69] — autistic children and their parents. This approach to the discrimination analysis constitutes a serious problem because it is difficult to recognize and respect disabled persons as equals, and thus to recognize their rights to equal treatment, when the starting place for the analysis is one of sympathy. The emotion of sympathy provides a convenient cover for what's really happening relationally between the non-disabled and the disabled; that is, between the dominant norm and the oppressed group. To declare sympathy for the disabled allows the person making the declaration to portray her/his self as a benevolent humanitarian. Cast in this light, the non-disabled can justify their actions, or decision making, as virtuous and proper, and they can continue to assert a relationship of domination over the disabled, as happened in *Auton*.

The Court in *Auton* did not conduct an injury to dignity analysis because it shut down the discrimination inquiry at the first stage of the test. However, knowing that the Court's perspective on the claim was grounded in sympathy provides some indication of how an injury to dignity analysis might have gone astray in this case. As discussed above, the objective element of the injury to dignity analysis is problematic, especially so for disabled women, because it is based on the reasonable person inquiry that invokes principles of universality favouring the non-disabled, white male. The reasonable person analysis inevitably incorporates elements of the decision maker's perspective and value system. When the decision maker's emotional perspective is one of sympathy, the possibility of conducting analyses that are truly objective and divorced from the dominant norm is questionable. The concern is that emotions of sympathy in the disability context may be informed by feelings of superiority and pity for the disabled, because they do not conform to the dominant norm of the non-disabled. In this way, sympathy can be indicative of dominance, a dominance that may make it difficult for a decision maker to determine as part of the injury to dignity analysis, what is a "reasonable" response for a disabled woman so far removed from the dominant norm. This kind of weakness with the dignity analysis jeopardizes its utility as an impartial and truly neutral indicator of discrimination.

Because the Court found that there was no section 15 breach in *Auton*, it did not have to consider section 1 in its decision. The section 1 cost factor was the dominant focus of the BC Attorney General in this case, and the eight other governments that intervened in support of the BC Attorney General also made it their focus. The Court never officially dealt with the cost issue in *Auton*, as noted. However, given the Court's declared sympathy for the petitioners, it leads one to speculate that it was easier for the Court to dismiss the equality claim at the section 15 stage, than to deny the sympathetic claimants their rights for cost-related reasons — reasons that would seem callous and difficult to justify when applied in the context of "sympathetic" disabled children.

The Court in *Auton* found that "there is no magic in a particular statement of the elements that must be established to prove a claim under section 15(1). It is the words of the provision that must guide. ... The important thing is to ensure that all the requirements of section 15(1), as they apply to the case at hand, are met."[70] The Court's commitment to this kind of flexible, more holistic analysis of section 15 claims is encouraging, and represents perhaps a willingness to rethink the *Law* test. Unfortunately the Court failed to apply this kind of analysis to its decision making in *Auton*. The Court started (and effectively concluded) its discrimination analysis in *Auton* by asking the question:

> Is the claim for a benefit *provided by law*? If not, what relevant benefit is provided by law?[71]

The fact that the benefit at issue was not provided by law was at the heart of this claim; the discrimination lay in the under-inclusive nature of the health care system. Turning the analysis to other "relevant" benefits provided by law once under-inclusiveness is established invites a formal equality analysis, and lead the Court to the question of whether the legislative scheme in fact provides anyone with all medically-required treatment[72] — this was not the question before the Court in this case (although the Attorneys General tried hard to create the impression that it was the question). The concept of equality that the Court articulated in *Auton* relates only to formal equality — everyone has the equal right to sleep under the bridges. There is no recognition of, or provision for, substantive equality. The Court found that there was no section 15 breach in this case because the services were not provided, but that was the very basis for the claim. The discrimination lay in the failure to provide the services. This kind of restrictive and circular reasoning is a betrayal of the Court's early promise to apply the equality guarantees in a broad and purposive manner.

A holistic substantive equality approach would have required the Court to take proper account of the specific needs of children with autism, and would have provided for them accordingly.

The Court further justified its decision that there was no discrimination in *Auton* through its application of the comparator group analysis. As it has done in other recent equality rights cases, the Court unilaterally changed the comparator group that was the reference for the discrimination analysis in *Auton*. The petitioners had argued that the appropriate comparator was non-disabled children and their parents, as well as adult persons with mental illness.[73] The LEAF/DAWN Canada Coalition intervened before the Court in *Auton* and argued that the differential treatment between the claimants and others was based on disability and gendered disability.[74] The Coalition argued the differential treatment in this case was grounded in the statutory framework giving primacy to hospitals and doctors, and reinforced by the administrative refusal to exercise the available statutory discretion to deviate from that primacy, and to provide autism services. It was argued that the delivery of health services primarily from doctors and hospitals is designed, for the most part, to meet the usual health concerns of the non-disabled population, typically neglecting the isolating and marginalizing effects of disability.[75] The Coalition argued that the refusal to respond to the needs of autistic children failed to take into account the claimants' already disadvantaged position, including the particular oppression of females with autism, within Canadian society, resulting in substantively differential treatment between the claimants and others on the basis of disability and gendered disability.[76]

The Court did not agree with the comparator analyses adopted by the claimants and the Coalition.[77] It decided that the appropriate comparator was a non-disabled person or a person suffering a disability other than a mental disability (here autism) seeking or receiving funding for a non-core therapy important for his or her present and future health, which is emergent and only recently becoming recognized as medically required.[78] The identification of such a narrow and obscure comparator group is almost impossible to predict, and seriously reduces the chances of success for equality claimants. The Court's choice of comparator group in *Auton* meant that the petitioners were essentially guaranteed to lose. The Court's identification of such an obscure and unpredictable comparator group is demonstrative of how easily the comparator group analysis can be manipulated — a critical problem with the analysis.

Another problem with the Court's decision in *Auton* concerns the lack of analysis relating to the intersectional discrimination involved in the case. Arguments that the BC government's refusal to fund autism services constituted gendered disability discrimination were advanced before the Supreme Court in *Auton* by the LEAF/DAWN Canada Coalition[79] — unfortunately these arguments were not addressed by the Court. The Coalition argued that although autism is more common amongst boys than girls, girls with autism, particularly as they grow older, may experience compounded and extreme discrimination because of their gendered disability. The Coalition argued that not addressing the effects of autism will likely lead to lives of isolation and institutionalization for both male and female children. However, the negative effects will be compounded for girls with autism. For example, women with autism who are institutionalized are liable to experience one of the most serious forms of gendered disability discrimination — the physical and sexual abuse that is prevalent in institutions. Because of their gendered disability, women with certain disabilities are in some circumstances vulnerable in ways that neither non-disabled women nor disabled men would be vulnerable.[80] The Court did not address the Coalition's arguments relating to gendered disability discrimination, and the Court provided no reasons why these arguments about intersectional discrimination were not addressed.

In *Law*, the Court attempted to address the rigidity of equality law relating to intersecting claims of discrimination, such as those involved in claims of gendered disability discrimination, by recognizing the need for a more holistic approach:

> [I]t is open to a claimant to articulate a discrimination claim under more than one of the enumerated and analogous grounds. ... If the court determines that recognition of a ground or confluence of grounds as analogous would serve to advance the fundamental purpose of s. 15(1), the ground or grounds will then be so recognized.
>
> There is no reason in principle, therefore, why a discrimination claim positing an intersection of grounds cannot be understood as analogous to, or as a synthesis of, the grounds listed in s. 15(1).[81]

In *Corbiere v. Canada (Minister of Indian and Northern Affairs)*[82] the Court had an opportunity to apply its thinking about intersectional discrimination as articulated in *Law*. *Corbiere* dealt with a claim that voter eligibility requirements under the *Indian Act*, specifically legislation that provided that only band members "ordinarily resident on reserve" were entitled to vote in band elections, violated section 15 of the *Charter*. Writing for the majority of the Court, McLachlin C.J. and Bastarche J. recognized "Aboriginality-residence"[83] as an analogous ground, conforming to the "central concept of immutable or constructively immutable personal characteristics, which too often have served as illegitimate and demeaning proxies for merit-based decision making."[84] L'Heureux-Dubé J., writing for four of nine judges in *Corbiere*, stated that the characteristics that may comprise analogous grounds should be considered in a fluid and contextual manner so that intersecting discrimination can be addressed:

> I should also note that if indicia of an analogous ground are not present in general, or among a certain group in Canadian society, they may nevertheless be present in another social or legislative context, within a different group in Canadian society, or in a given geographic area, to give only a few examples. ... The second stage must therefore be flexible enough to adapt to stereotyping, prejudice, or denials of human dignity and worth that might occur in specific ways for specific groups of people, to recognize that personal characteristics may overlap or intersect (such as race, band membership, and place of residence in this case), and to reflect changing social phenomena or new or different forms of stereotyping or prejudice.[85]

L'Heureux-Dubé J.'s approach to intersectional analyses provides a clear articulation of the analytical flexibility necessary to accommodate claims of intersectional discrimination in equality law.

Unfortunately the promise of the Court's rhetoric about intersectional analyses was not realized in *Auton*. It is difficult to say why arguments related to the gendered disability analysis were ignored by the Court, but the premature closure on the discrimination analysis in the case meant that there was no opportunity for the Court to engage in the complex and somewhat complicated arguments relating to gendered disability. This is an ominous sign for disabled women whose equality claims will likely always be complex and complicated because the social construction and legal enforcement of their experiences of discrimination are unique and usually unfamiliar to the non-disabled, demanding fully developed and non-mechanical equality rights analyses. Only the application of a holistic and non-aggregated equality rights analysis that leaves room for the deconstruction of the complex experiences of intersectional discrimination, such as gendered disability discrimination, will provide for justice in the context of such equality claims.

LEAF has argued in support of holistic substantive equality rights analyses that expose unequal power relationships as an alternative to the disaggregated and overly formalistic analyses associated with the *Law* test.[86] Holistic substantive equality analyses promote equality by paying close attention to the unequal effects that are revealed when examining the interrelationships amongst differential treatment, grounds, and discrimination. The Court in *Auton* did endorse a flexible approach to section 15 analyses — an approach that is preferable to the overly mechanical analyses associated with section 15 analyses since the introduction of the *Law* test. However, the Court's analysis in *Auton*, while it can be understood to constitute a departure from the mechanical application of the *Law* test, is disappointing as it did not provide for clarification of how more flexible, effective equality analyses might operate. The idea of applying flexible analyses is promising as it seems to offer some liberation from the strictures of the *Law* test, but unfortunately the Court in *Auton* was unable to disentangle the mess of problems that has come to be associated with the *Law* test for discrimination.

E. CONCLUSION

As equality rights jurisprudence has evolved, there has been progress and reversals of progress relating to the development of the Supreme Court's understanding of (in)equality in general.[87] While equality rights law may be an imperfect instrument through which to advance the cause of social justice, it is a critical site of struggle, and one that cannot be ignored.[88] The *Law* test for discrimination has made the advancement of successful equality rights complaints more difficult, and it is clear that there is lots of work to be done to fulfill the potential that the *Charter* first offered equality rights advocates twenty years ago. However, there are ways in which to constructively critique the *Law* test, and ways in which the analysis can be improved.

Based on the equality rights jurisprudence that has evolved to date, it is apparent that the power relations at the source of discriminatory behaviour need to be closely examined, and the impugned law or (in)action need to be linked more clearly to the relations of domination that perpetuate and rationalize the systemic inequality of oppressed groups, including disabled women. Unfortunately, due to the challenges associated with the *Law* test, including the comparator group analysis and the increased focus on human dignity, the law has not yet developed sufficiently in this direction, and the risk of undermining substantive equality is very real. What is required is an analysis of inequality that challenges the norm and fulfils the goal of section 15 to promote substantive equality.

To date, section 15 of the *Charter* has not fulfilled all of its potential; and more recently, post-*Law*, the Supreme Court's section 15 analyses have become more regressive and confusing in relation to goals of substantive equality and the legal elimination of disadvantage. As a result, the tentative advances made during the early days of *Charter* litigation have been threatened. It is still possible to achieve results that are supportive of equality rights, as demonstrated by the Court's decision in *Martin v. Nova Scotia (Workers' Compensation Board)*;[89] however, the Court's application of equality rights analyses has become unnecessarily complicated and unpredictable, so that its value as an equality rights mechanism has been jeopardized. This development constitutes a step backwards for all equality seekers; however, it is particularly bad news for disabled women whose difference from the dominant norms has made it especially challenging for them to advance successful equality rights challenges. There is a critical need to expose the weaknesses with the *Law* test for discrimination, and to advance alternative analyses that will operate to protect and promote equality. In the absence of this work, the equality rights of the disadvantaged will remain in legal jeopardy, and those at particular risk of being subsumed by the dominant legal paradigm, such as disabled women, will be denied their rights to equality, and the unique potential of section 15 will remain unfulfilled.

ENDNOTES

1 [1999] 1 S.C.R. 497 [*Law*].

2 Section 15 of the *Canadian Charter of Rights and Freedoms, Constitution Act*, 1982, as enacted by the *Canada Act* 1981 (UK), 1982, c.11.

3 See Fiona Sampson, "Globalization and the Inequality of Women with Disabilities" (2003) 2 J.L. & Equality 2; Janice Gross Stein, *The Cult of Efficiency* (Toronto: Anansi, 2001) at 9.

4 [2004] 3 S.C.R. 657 [*Auton*].

5 [1989] 1 S.C.R. 143 [*Andrews*].

6 [1989] 1 S.C.R. 1296 [*Turpin*].

7 See *Egan v. Canada*, [1995] 2 S.C.R. 513 [*Egan*] (*Egan* challenged the *Old Age Security Act* as discriminatory on the basis of sexual orientation); *Miron v. Trudel*, [1995] 2 S.C.R. 418 [*Miron*] (*Miron* challenged the exclusion of common law couples from the definition of "spouse" in the *Insurance Act*, R.S.O. 1980, c. 218, ss. 231, 233, Sch. C); *Thibaudeau v. Canada*, [1995] 2 S.C.R. 627 [*Thibaudeau*] (*Thibaudeau* challenged the constitutionality of the *Income Tax Act*, S.C. 1970–71–72, c. 65, s. 56(1)(b) which permitted a non-custodial parent to deduct his/her child support payments from his or her personal income tax calculations, and required a custodial parent to include these payments in her or his income). The decisions in these cases revealed three different approaches to s. 15. Four judges, La Forest, Gonthier, Major JJ., & Lamer C.J.C., used the "relevance" approach (the relevance criterion referred to here is whether a challenged distinction is relevant to the functional values of the legislation. *Miron*, above at paras. 15 and 31–38). Four other judges, McLachlin, Cory, Iacobucci, & Sopinka JJ., continued to use the *Andrews* approach and rejected the relevance approach as too narrow; while L'Heureux-Dubé J. adopted her own distinctive approach and argued that the s. 15 analysis should turn on the nature of the group adversely affected by a distinction and the nature of the interest adversely affected.

8 *Andrews*, above note 5; *Turpin*, above note 6.

9 Robert Sharpe & Kent Roach, *The Charter of Rights and Freedoms*, 3d ed. (Toronto: Irwin Law, 2005) c. 15, "Equality."

10 Catharine McKinnon, "Reflections on Sex Equality Under the Law" (1991) 100 Yale L.J. 1281.

11 Shelagh Day, "The Process of Achieving Equality" in Ryszard Cholewinski, ed., *Human Rights in Canada: Into the 1990s and Beyond* (Ottawa: M.O.M. Printing, 1990) at 18.

12 *Andrews*, above note 5 at 168.

13 *Ibid.*

14 Catharine MacKinnon's work, including *Feminism Unmodified: Discourses on Life and Law* (Cambridge, Mass.: Harvard University Press, 1987), is recognized as the quintessential theorization of radical feminism and the law, and she is credited with advancing feminist legal theory beyond the limits of liberal feminism [Carol Smart, *Feminism and the Power of Law* (New York: Routledge, 1989) at 76]. MacKinnon

and other radical feminists advocate for socio-political, legal, and economic transformation or major structural change as a means to achieve equality for women.

15 *Andrews*, above note 5 at 165.

16 *Turpin*, above note 6 at para. 45.

17 Radha Jhappan, "The Equality Pit or the Rehabilitation of Justice" (1998) 10 C.J.W.L. 60 at 72–74.

18 *Law*, above note 1 at para. 51.

19 Recently the injury to dignity test has been imported into discrimination analyses advanced relating to federal and provincial human rights legislation. See, for example, *Wignall v. Department of National Revenue*, [2004] 1 F.C.R. 679 and *Vancouver Rape Relief Society v. Nixon*, [2003] B.C.J. No. 2899.

20 *Law*, above note 1 at para. 51.

21 *Ibid.* at paras. 62–75.

22 *Law*, above note 1 at para. 88; see also McLachlin C.J.'s decision in *Auton*, above note 4 at para. 23, in which she states "There is no magic in a particular statement of the elements that must be established to prove a claim under s. 15(1). It is the words of the provision that must guide."

23 *Andrews*, above note 5 at para. 26.

24 *Ibid.*

25 For further discussion of the problems with the comparator group analysis see Beverly Baines, "*Law and Canada:* Formatting Equality," (2000) 11(3) Const. Forum 65 at 89; and Jennifer Koshan, "Alberta (Dis)Advantage: *The Protection of Children Involved in Prostitution Act* and the Equality Rights of Young Women" Fall 2003, J.L. & Equality, 211 at 238–39.

26 *Granovsky*, below note 29 at para. 45.

27 *Law,* above note 1 at para. 24.

28 *Ibid.* at para. 58.

29 [2000] 1 S.C.R. 703 [*Granovsky*]. At issue was the constitutionality of s. 44(2)(b) of the *Canada Pension Plan Act*, R.S.C., 1985, c. C-8, as it relates to persons with disabilities. The Plan was designed to be a comprehensive social insurance scheme for Canadians who experience a loss of earnings owing to retirement, disability, or the death of a wage-earning spouse or parent. The disability pension, an integral element of the Plan since that scheme came into force in 1966, is an income replacement measure for those persons determined to be "disabled" within the meaning of the Plan. See Allan Puttee, "Reforming the Disability Insurance System: A Collaborative Approach," in Allan Puttee, ed., *Federalism, Democracy and Disability Policy in Canada* (Montreal: McGill-Queen's University Press, 2002). The constitutional questions in this case dealt with the drop-out provisions of the Plan, and whether these provisions discriminate against persons with a physical or mental disability claiming a disability pension under the Act, contrary to s. 15 of the *Charter*.

30 *Granovsky, ibid.* at para. 46.

31 *Ibid.* at paras. 47–49.

32 [2000] 1 S.C.R. 950 at para. 62.

33 [2004] 3 S.C.R. 357 [*Hodge*].

34 *Ibid.* at para. 17.

35 *Ibid.* at para. 23.

36 Feminist critical race theorist Nitya Duclos (now Iyer) has explored the relevance of the imposition of the dominant perspective onto equality rights claims in an effort to explain the disappearance of racial minority women from anti-discrimination cases. Iyer has concluded that anti-discrimination law is not well designed to assist persons more than one step removed from the dominant norm, that norm being the white, able-bodied, heterosexual man: Nitya Duclos, "Disappearing Women: Racial Minority Women in Human Rights Cases" (1993) 6:1 C.J.W.L. 25; Nitya Iyer, "Categorical Denials: Equality Rights and the Shaping of Social Identity" (1994) 19 Queen's L.J. 179.

37 For an analysis of how "the official version of the law," including the legal principles of impartiality and neutrality work against those outside of the dominant norm, see Ngaire Naffine, *The Law and the Sexes: Explorations in Feminist Jurisprudence* (Sydney: Allen and Unwin, 1990) at 24.

38 The *Hodge* case, above note 33, dealt with a challenge to the constitutionality of s. 2(1)(a)(ii) of the *Canada Pension Plan* based on discrimination because of marital status. The claimant, Betty Hodge, a former common-law spouse, argued that the requirement that a common law spouse, but not a married spouse, have cohabited with the CPP contributor at the date of death and for one year prior to that date in order to be eligible for a survivor's pension violated her equality rights under s. 15 of the *Charter*.

39 *Ibid.* at para. 44.

40 *Ibid.*

41 *Ibid.*

42 Martha Minow, *Making All the Difference: Inclusion, Exclusion, and American Law* (Ithaca: Cornell University Press, 1990) at 111.

43 See Fiona Sampson "The Supreme Court of Canada's Decision in *Granovsky*: Adding Insult to Injury?" C.J.W.L. (forthcoming).

44 Minow, above note 42.

45 [2002] 4 S.C.R. 429 [*Gosselin*]. The *Gosselin* case was based on a claim that the social assistance regulations in Quebec during the 1980s were discriminatory: single mothers under the age of thirty, who were considered employable, received only one third of the assistance granted to their older counterparts. This was the first case in which the Supreme Court dealt directly with the constitutionality of social and economic rights.

46 *Gosselin, ibid.* at para. 18, citing *Law*, above note 1 at para. 42 and *Andrews*, above note 5 at 171.

47 Dianne Pothier, "Connecting Grounds of Discrimination to Real People's Real Experiences" (2001) 13 C.J.W.L. 37.

48 *Ibid.* at 24–25.

49 Iacobucci J. found that: "... Human dignity means that an individual or group feels self-respect and self-worth. It is concerned with physical and psychological integrity and empowerment. Human dignity is harmed by unfair treatment premised upon

personal traits or circumstances which do not relate to individual needs, capacities, or merits. It is enhanced by laws which are sensitive to the needs, capacities, and merits of different individuals, taking into account the context underlying their differences. Human dignity is harmed when individuals and groups are marginalized, ignored, or devalued, and is enhanced when laws recognize the full place of all individuals and groups within Canadian society. Human dignity within the meaning of the equality guarantee does not relate to the status or position of an individual in society per se, but rather concerns the manner in which a person legitimately feels when confronted with a particular law." (*Law*, above note 1 at para. 53.)

50　For an example of this phenomenon, see the trial decision in *Health Services and Support-Facilities Subsector Bargaining Assn. v. British Columbia*, [2004] B.C.J. No. 1354 in which, with respect to the third part of the *Law* test, the trial judge's entire injury to dignity analysis is as follows (at para. 189):

> While the plaintiffs are clearly aggrieved by the legislation for various justifiable reasons, the impact upon them is not of the quality or characteristic that impacts their dignity in the sense that engages s. 15.

There is no substantive analysis to support this finding, just an assertion on the judge's part, seemingly based upon her own subjective appraisal of the situation.

51　An alternative yet substantive application of the dignity concept to equality analyses is developed by Denise Réaume, in her chapter, "Discrimination and Dignity" which appears in this collection. This analysis relates to the recognition of dignity-constituting benefits.

52　Binnie J. in *Canadian Foundation for Children, Youth and the Law v. Canada (Attorney General)*, [2004] 1 S.C.R. 76 at para. 72, did acknowledge the risk that the "correspondence" factor under the dignity analysis could inappropriately "... become a sort of Trojan horse to bring into s. 15(1) matters that are more properly regarded as 'reasonable limits ... demonstrably justified in a free and democratic society' (s. 1)."

53　See, for example, *Gosselin*, above note 45 at para. 65.

54　*Law*, above note 1 at paras. 80 & 88(5).

55　*Gosselin*, above note 45.

56　*O'Malley v. Simpsons-Sears*, [1985] 2 S.C.R. 536.

57　*Gosselin*, above note 45 at para. 25.

58　*Ibid.* at para. 26.

59　*Ibid.* at para. 27.

60　"The appropriate perspective is subjective-objective. Equality analysis under the *Charter* is concerned with the perspective of a person in circumstances similar to those of the claimant, who is informed of and rationally takes into account the various contextual factors which determine whether an impugned law infringes human dignity, as that concept is understood for the purpose of s. 15(1)." *Law*, above note 1 at para. 61.

61　*Law, ibid.* at para. 53.

62　Iacobucci J. does acknowledge the potential of the reasonable person standard to "... act as a vehicle for the imposition of community prejudices," which is why he concludes that the appropriate standard of assessment is the subjective-objective standard. (*Law, ibid.* at para. 61).

63 Karen Busby, "Discriminatory Uses of Records In Sexual Violence Cases" (1997) 9 C.J.W.L. 148; Lise Gotell, "Colonization through Disclosure: Confidential Records, Sexual Assault Complainants and Canadian Law" (2001) 10 Social and Legal Studies 315.

64 Dianne Pothier, "But It's for Your Own Good," submitted for publication as a chapter in Margot Young, Gwen Brodsky, Shelagh Day, & Susan Boyd, eds., *Poverty Rights, Social Citizenship and Governance* (forthcoming from UBC Press).

65 Denise Réaume, "Indignities: Making a Place for Dignity in Modern Legal Thought" (2002) 28 Queen's L.J. 61 at para. 44.

66 *Ibid.*

67 See Fiona Sampson, "Beyond Compassion and Sympathy to Respect and Equality: Gendered Disability and Equality Rights Law" in Dianne Pothier & Richard Devlin, eds., *Disability Law, Theory and Policy* (forthcoming from UBC Press).

68 Examples of successful pre-*Law* cases that involved claims of gendered disability discrimination include *Eldridge v. British Columbia (A-G)*, [1997] 3 S.C.R. 624, and *Norberg v. Wynrib*, [1992] 2 S.C.R. 226. The Supreme Court did not explicitly acknowledge the gendered disability discrimination at issue in its decisions in these cases. However, LEAF did advance arguments analyzing the gendered disability discrimination at issue in its interventions before the Court in these cases, and the Court did decide these cases in the claimants' favour. (See the LEAF facta in *Norberg* in *Equality and the Charter: Ten Years of Feminist Advocacy Before the Supreme Court of Canada*, Women's Legal Education and Action Fund (Toronto: Emond Montgomery Publications Limited, 1996) at 226; the LEAF/DAWN Canada factum in *Eldridge* is available online: www.leaf.ca/facta/eldridge.pdf).

69 *Auton*, above note 4 at para. 2.

70 *Ibid.* at para. 23.

71 *Ibid.* at para. 26.

72 *Ibid.* at para. 31.

73 *Ibid.* at para. 49.

74 LEAF/DAWN Supreme Court of Canada factum in *Auton, ibid.* at para. 36; reproduced in this book and also available online: www.leaf.ca.

75 *Ibid.* at para. 8.

76 *Ibid.* at para. 36.

77 The Court found that the claimants' comparators were deficient because they focused on the non-existent medical benefit of medically required care; thus the Court's circular reasoning about the nature of the benefit fed into the comparator analysis and confused it as well, *ibid.* at para. 56.

78 *Ibid.* at para. 55.

79 See the LEAF/DAWN Supreme Court of Canada factum in *Auton, ibid.*

80 *Ibid.* at para. 15.

81 *Law,* above note 1 at paras. 93–94.

82 [1999] 2 S.C.R. 203.

83   *Ibid.* at para. 6.

84   *Ibid.* at para. 13.

85   *Ibid.* at para. 61.

86   See the LEAF Supreme Court of Canada factum in *NAPE v. Newfoundland* and the LEAF/DAWN Supreme Court of Canada factum in *Auton v. British Columbia*, both reproduced in this book and available online: www.leaf.ca.

87   See Diana Majury, "The *Charter*, Equality Rights, and Women's Equivocation and Celebration" (2002) 40 Osgoode Hall L.J. 297.

88   See Susan B. Boyd & Amy Bartholomew, "Toward a Political Economy of Law" in Wallace Clement & Glen Williams, eds., *The New Canadian Political Economy* (Kingston: McGill-Queen's University Press, 1989); Stephen Brickey & Elizabeth Comack, "The Role of Law in Social Transformation: Is a Jurisprudence of Insurgency Possible?" (1990) 5 C.J.L.S. 47; Patricia Williams, *The Alchemy of Race and Rights* (Cambridge: Harvard University Press, 1991) at 149; Carol Smart, *Feminism and the Power of Law*, above note 14 at 164; Radha Jhappan, "Introduction: Feminist Adventures in Law" in *Women's Legal Strategies in Canada* (Toronto: University of Toronto Press, 2002) at 22–23.

89   [2003] 2 S.C.R. 504. The *Martin* case involved a successful s. 15 challenge to the constitutionality of the Nova Scotia Worker's Compensation Plan that excluded chronic pain sufferers from coverage under the Plan.

eight

Equality Rights and the *Charter*:

RECONCEPTUALIZING STATE ACCOUNTABILITY

FOR ENDING DOMESTIC VIOLENCE

Melanie Randall[1]

The entry of feminists into law has turned law into a site of struggle rather than being taken only as a tool of struggle.[2]

A. INTRODUCTION

The state's major response to the problem of violence against women in intimate relationships — what is most commonly described as "domestic violence" — has been a legal one. While government initiatives have taken place on other fronts as well, through for example, the funding of shelters for assaulted women, the commissioning of reports[3] and the provision of other victim services, the main and most comprehensive site of state intervention and response has been through law. This legal response largely began with directives mandating that police arrest those suspected of perpetrating "domestic violence," and that Crowns prosecute these cases,[4] and progressed to legal reforms in the criminal justice system including the more recent establishment of specialized courts exclusively focusing on domestic violence throughout many Canadian jurisdictions.[5]

In addition to law reform as a response to violence against women, some branches of the state have acknowledged — even if in an incomplete and rudimentary manner — that domestic violence is a gender issue, and to this extent, have recognized its implication in the larger problem of gender inequality.[6] While this linking of domestic violence and gender remains contested[7] it is significant that it has been officially adopted in various state pronouncements[8] and this insight is certainly central to feminist activist[9] and scholarly work in this area.

How is it, then, given law as the major terrain of state reform and of much feminist advocacy in relation to domestic violence, that this prominent and concrete expression of gender inequality has been largely untouched by a direct *Charter*[10] equality rights challenge?[11] Why has section 15 been virtually dormant in relation to the specific legal reforms undertaken to respond to domestic violence and in relation to the broader political and legal challenges around this issue? An equality rights analysis has infused much significant legal reform work in the area of sexual violence, most especially regarding sexual assault law, yet in terms of the violence perpetrated against women in their intimate adult relationships ("domestic violence") there has not to date been a direct constitutional challenge based on the section 15 equality provision of the *Charter*.[12]

There has, in fact, been extensive legal reform in relation to criminal law governing sexual assault and the direct impact of a feminist-inspired gender analysis and section 15 *Charter* equality rights in this area. Advocates, academics, and policy-makers have been both successful and influential in having courts (and the legislature) address equality concerns in sexual assault law, including in challenging the traditional reliance on corroboration, the use of past sexual history, and the use of third party records.[13] While the successes are in no way complete, and while the treatment of sexual assault survivors in the criminal justice system remains highly problematic, this does not negate the fact that some significant and positive legal developments have taken place in relation to equality concerns in sexual assault law.

Given, then, that much effort to redress women's subordination has taken place in the area of equality rights in law, and given that a core feature of this gender subordination is intimate violence against women, it seems a paradox that the legal guarantee of equality enshrined in the *Charter* has barely been expressly activated in this struggle, at least not in any direct and explicit way. But in thinking about what such a legal challenge would look like, the difficulties become ever more evident. This is largely because the direction of equality rights interpretation taken by the Canadian Supreme Court suggests an ever narrowing of the possibilities for capturing the nature and complexities of discrimination and inequality, particularly within the restrictive confines of the *Law* test and the restrictive judicial lens through which many judges at the Supreme Court approach equality claims.

Thinking about how to engage an equality rights analysis under the *Charter* in relation to the complicated and seemingly intractable social, legal, and political problems of violence against women in intimate relationships, then, poses a series of questions and challenges. Of greatest conceptual difficulty is thinking about how to frame the problem in terms of the ways in which equality claims have been understood and analyzed in *Charter* jurisprudence. It appears, in fact, that there is an increasing disconnect between the actual contexts and conditions of lived gender inequality and the arid application of legal tests for and approaches to recognizing it. That the gendered problem of domestic violence and the legal terrain of equality rights under the *Charter* have yet to make much direct or meaningful contact, then, is perhaps less surprising than it would initially appear.

This argument is not intended to disparage the *Charter* or to be aligned with those *Charter* critics (including those on the right and left), whom Sheila McIntyre has so effectively excoriated in an analysis of "Feminist Movement in Law."[14] I am not arguing that we should abandon the language of rights or the struggle to push the limits of the *Charter* at every possible opportunity. But it does appear, as I elaborate more fully below, that the nature of the specific problem of intimate gendered violence and abuse in women's lives, its complexity and its vastness (implicating so many institutions and social relations at the macro and micro levels), exceeds the restrictive — even anemic? — scope of *Charter* rights as they are currently interpreted.

In this paper I outline the nature of the gendered problem of domestic violence within an equality framework. I then outline in broad terms the kinds of initiatives that need to be undertaken in order to move towards eradicating violence against women in intimate relationships. I juxtapose the kinds of redress and remedies needed against the inadequate conceptual framework offered by the current legal approach to equality articulated by the Supreme Court. Finally, I offer some initial and broad suggestions about what some possible legal strategies might look like which engage equality and other *Charter* rights to address and end the problem of domestic violence in women's lives. Specifically, I suggest that even though the opportunity of posing a direct section 15 challenge in relation to domestic violence has yet to materialize or be seized, the failure of state action in this area — the absence of adequate legal protections for assaulted women — poses a violation of a number of *Charter* rights that should be actionable.

These suggestions for legal claims are necessarily ambitious and difficult, given the current state of the law, and given the Supreme Court's tendency to treat some social problems as not justiciable.[15] But in spite of how formidable the challenges might be, I offer these considerations as part of a dialogue on how to advance towards the realization of substantive equality for women in Canada and how law might play a significant, if partial, role in that advance.

B. THE GENDERED HARMS OF DOMESTIC VIOLENCE: THE LINKS TO SEXUAL INEQUALITY AND THEIR LEGAL RECOGNITION

Violence against women and children is a constitutive feature of women's inequality as it is produced and reproduced throughout society at large in both the macro (institutional) and micro (interpersonal) levels. This has long been a central component of feminist analyses of the conditions of women's subordination. The issues relating to sexual violence in women's lives have been at the forefront of feminist activism, scholarship, and advocacy.[16]

The violence and abuse so many women experience can also be understood as a "gendered harm."[17] This concept involves making explicit and cognizable in law, an element of women's experience, which is at once a cause and effect of gender inequality. It is a way of "recognizing that injury has a social as well as an individual dimension: people suffer harm not just because they are individuals but also because they are part of a particular class, group, race, or gender."[18]

That violence against women is inextricably an expression of gender subordination, and that it is a violation of women's rights, including fundamental human rights, has been recognized repeatedly and by organizations such as the United Nations. The U.N. observes that:

> Violence against women is an obstacle to the achievement of the objectives of equality, development and peace. Violence against women both violates and impairs or nullifies the enjoyment by women of their human rights and fundamental freedoms .... [19]

The link between violence against women and gender inequality has also been acknowledged by the Supreme Court of Canada in numerous judgments engaging issues of sexualized and intimate violence. While it is Justice L'Heureux-Dube who has most forcefully made these connections starkly explicit over a series of her judgments, other Justices, including some male Justices, have recognized, for example, that sexual assault is a gendered problem, an assault on women's dignity, and a violation of women's equality rights.[20] While this recognition has been most explicit in the greater number of sexual assault cases which have reached the Supreme Court, the gendered dimensions of intimate violence in intimate relationships (that is, "domestic violence") has also been recognized. Speaking specifically of domestic violence in *R. v. Lavallee*,[21] for example, Wilson J. observes that:

> The gravity, indeed, the tragedy of domestic violence can hardly be overstated. Greater media attention to this phenomenon in recent years has revealed both its prevalence and its horrific impact on women from all walks of life. Far from protecting women from it the law historically sanctioned the abuse of women within marriage as an aspect of the husband's ownership of his wife and his "right" to chastise her. One need only recall the centuries old law that a man is entitled to beat his wife with a stick "no thicker than his thumb."

She continues to explain that

> Laws do not spring out of a social vacuum. The notion that a man has a right to "discipline" his wife is deeply rooted in the history of our society. The woman's duty was to serve her husband and to stay in the marriage at all costs "till death do us part" and to accept as her due any "punishment" that was meted out for failing to please her husband. One consequence of this attitude was that "wife battering" was rarely spoken of, rarely reported, rarely prosecuted, and even more rarely punished. Long after society abandoned its formal approval of spousal abuse tolerance of it continued and continues in some circles to this day.[22]

Despite this encouraging judicial recognition in some of the caselaw of the context of gender inequality, an opposing and worrying trend coexists, which is especially evident in the expanding body of equality rights decisions. That is, the ways in which the concrete and harsh realities of what inequality actually looks like in women's lives, tends to be neutralized or even disappeared in the language used to describe it in the equality rights jurisprudence. For example, the somewhat anesthetized language of "disadvantage" and "stereotyping" sanitizes what feminists would more aptly describe as inequality, subordination, domination, or oppression, and identify as the harms and injuries flowing from that inequality. The idea of deeply-structured relations of power tends to disappear within the Supreme Court's favoured terminology, as does the notion of any agency, complicity, and responsibility on the part of those who are afforded and enjoy greater power and privilege in social, economic, and political terms.[23] Of course, the Supreme Court's legal discourse surrounding *Charter* equality rights easily accomplishes this erasure partly because of its highly abstracted focus on appropriate state and legal responses to inequality, rather than on the nature of inequality itself.

The power of naming has long been identified as a staple of feminist analysis. The language chosen to describe a problem is highly significant to the way in which it is understood and identified, as well as to the kinds of solutions sought. This is particularly evident in relation to men's violence against women and children.[24] Yet even this descriptor is considered controversial in a political climate of increasing backlash and hostility to women's equality claims,[25] for it names both the perpetrators and the victims. Many would prefer the use of bland and gender neutral terms, such as interpersonal violence, family violence, or even domestic violence — terms which don't focus on or even identify gender patterns regarding who perpetrators and victims overwhelmingly are, but which expressly avoid doing so.

The increasingly impatient reaction to discussions of gender discrimination and "women's issues" appears to be a society-wide phenomenon. But it is also traceable in Canadian case law, in the Supreme Court's tepid reception to discrimination analyses in general, and in the diminishing rates of success of *Charter* equality claims, evidenced in the court's failure to apprehend adequately the equality issues advanced in *Symes*,[26] *NWAC*,[27] *Thibadeau*,[28] *Vancouver Society of Immigrant and Visible Minority Women*,[29] *Law*, *Lovelace*,[30] *Walsh*,[31] *Gosselin*,[32] *N.A.P.E.*,[33] and *Auton*.[34]

Without suggesting that there is a hierarchy of issues in relation to gender inequality and its imbrications with the other equally profound and interconnected forms of inequality structured around race, class, sexuality, ability/disability, I do argue that the problem of men's violence against women and children reveals a particularly *gendered* aspect of inequality in one of its more stark and brutal forms. In describing this violence I think it is critical that we struggle to retain language which does justice, so to speak, to what exactly it is we are talking about.[35] This is especially critical given the trend towards degendering these issues, particularly in government programs, policy and pronouncements, but also in many of the academic disciplines which address these issues.[36]

The politics of terminology aside, and in spite of the heated controversies about its causes, solutions, and pervasiveness, almost everyone can be made to agree that violence in intimate relationships is a serious problem. The research in this area is now vast and ever expanding, documenting the damaging and devastating effects of this violence in women's lives.[37]

One more extreme manifestation of this violence is found in the phenomenon of intimate femicide. Every year in Canada (and around the world) too many women die at the hands of their male intimates — often estranged ones, demonstrating that assaulted women simply "leaving" is not necessarily a strategy that ensures their safety.[38] In addition to being a leading cause of physical injury, domestic violence is also associated with long-term significant mental health consequences, including trauma.[39] And while the feminist insight that all women are vulnerable to violence is and remains a critically important one to make people aware of its pervasiveness and its social control function, it is also true that some women are more vulnerable than others, and there is a research literature documenting this. In particular, Aboriginal women, women living with disabilities, racialized women, and women with fewer economic means experience violence in their intimate relationships with men at disproportionate rates. Moreover, violence against women in intimate relationships is very often linked with poverty and homelessness.[40] Clearly, then, while domestic violence is a gender issue, it is also inextricably, necessarily, and simultaneously also an issue implicating class, race, and other relations of socially constructed inequalities.

The Supreme Court has, in recent judgments, signaled an increasing cognizance of and concern about the so-called "costs" of equality.[41] While this was abundantly clear in, for example, *Granovsky v. Canada (Minister of Employment and Immigration)*,[42] and *Gosselin*, the trend has become even more starkly apparent with the release of the judgments in *Newfoundland Treasury Board v. Newfoundland and Labrador Association of Public and Private Employees (N.A.P.E)*[43] and *Auton (Guardian ad litem of) v. British Columbia (Attorney General)*.[44] In each of these section 15 claims, the former addressing women's right to equal pay, the latter addressing autistic children's rights to state-funded specialized therapy, the Court denied the claims in part based on an explicit concern to protect state resources and a concomitant denial of the existence of discrimination in *Auton*.

This concern is tied to a reluctance to recognize some equality claims and corresponding refusal to impose on the state what is perceived to be an unfair burden in relation to remedying inequality. But to counter this ascending approach, a powerful argument can and needs to be ever more forcefully made about the *costs of inequality*, and the costs associated with *failing* to remedy structured, socially-produced inequalities in people's lives.

We must remain cautious (ambivalent even) about deploying these kinds of arguments because they typify the crass cost/benefit approach to human welfare which so neatly fits into the right-wing economic market approach, commodifying all aspects of social life. Nevertheless, to the extent that they can move us further towards challenging dominant misperceptions, we should not hesitate to utilize these approaches strategically, if they can assist us with our larger goals.

There is, in fact, an emerging and increasingly sophisticated literature documenting the economic costs of violence against women,[45] and assessing these costs in terms of the operation of the criminal justice system, related health and mental health care costs, and lost productivity in the workforce, to name just a few.[46] These calculations can also be used to construct arguments about the costs associated with inequality, and the social and economic costs which attach to doing nothing about this inequality. This kind of perspective can reframe and challenge the fiscally conservative approach which sees establishing more services for victims, expanding the welfare net, and undertaking education and prevention initiatives, as "too expensive" and as negotiable frills. The claim that the costs to the state of achieving equality are too prohibitive must be vociferously met with a documentation of the ongoing costs of *in*equality, and of who bears these costs.

To develop some of these themes further, I briefly sketch, in the broadest and most general of terms, what seriously and contextually addressing the problem of men's violence against women in intimate relationships would necessarily involve, if the provision of effective responses to victims and eradication of the problem through its ultimate prevention are the goals. These kinds of issues are then juxtaposed against the current legal framework required for an equality rights claim in order to cast light on the uneasy fit, at best, and disjuncture, at worst, existing between them.

C. ENDING VIOLENCE AGAINST WOMEN: WHAT WOULD THE "SUBSTANCE" OF "SUBSTANTIVE EQUALITY" REQUIRE?

… it has turned out to be easier to avoid pure formal equality than to articulate the substance of substantive equality.[47]

If law is to play a central role in the struggle to remedy inequality, how would this be situated in an overarching agenda for the eradication — even more modestly, the amelioration — of violence against women in intimate relationships? In other words, what significant things need to be done if we are serious about eliminating the social problem of violence against women and children?

In the words of one group of writers, to end violence against women an agenda for change must include "empowering women and girls; raising the costs to abusers; providing for the needs of victims; co-ordinating institutional and individual responses; involving youth; reaching out to men; and changing community norms."[48] In the broadest of strokes, then, because it is intimately connected to sexual domination and gender inequality, an adequate agenda to end men's violence against women and children necessarily involves tackling the relations of gender inequality itself, as these are embedded structurally (in public institutions, the state, the labour market, etc.) and in social relationships both writ large and as these are lived at the micro level.

In terms of the narrower goal of meeting the needs of victims and providing effective legal remedies, what is needed is a transformed criminal justice system response at all levels, which doesn't revictimize women, pathologize their coping, or penalize their reluctance and ambivalence about prosecutions.[49] This would include a prioritizing of women's safety concerns as a paramount interest guiding criminal justice system responses.

Moreover, an integration of criminal justice system and family law matters where domestic violence is involved would assist with the multitude of problems associated with conflicting legal responses which fracture assaulted women's already complicated lives. Some specialized domestic violence courts are experimenting with this kind of integration. Additionally, access to justice for assaulted women and their children must be made real rather than chimerical, in terms of providing adequate legal representation and legal aid to women who cannot afford it themselves — in criminal and civil matters, and most especially in the area of family law.

An improved legal system response to domestic violence also requires the imposition of adequate criminal sanctions and sentences for convicted offenders to demonstrate public intolerance for this privatized violence,[50] while simultaneously, expanded and sufficient mandated treatment interventions for batterers are needed. These programs must address and interrupt the attitudes and issues legitimating men's use of violence and coercion in their intimate relationships with women, integrating an understanding of their backgrounds and individual psychological issues without positioning them as victims *vis-à-vis* their own use of violence. In other words, effective interventions — both legal and extra-legal — must retain a simultaneous focus on perpetrators' responsibility and agency, situated within a critical framework which challenges traditional masculine entitlement and assists perpetrators of violence in developing the psychological, emotional, and other resources needed to change.[51]

Beyond the myriad reforms needed to the legal system's response to domestic violence, a range of social supports and resources must also be in place if our society really takes seriously the eradication of violence against women in intimate relationships. This includes the provision of adequate emergency shelters, as well as second-stage housing to ensure that women escaping violent men have safe accommodation. More broadly still, it requires the provision of adequate child care (a need not unique to women assaulted by their male intimates), and the provision of adequate social assistance to allow women and their children a decent standard of living. Finally, the provision of an adequate mental health and counseling network of services, as well as advocacy and other support programs is needed for navigating the criminal justice and other systems assaulted women face.

These recommendations are related to but don't directly touch the larger set of social beliefs, attitudes and practices, and relationships in which the undervaluing and denigration of women and the valorization of masculine superiority and entitlement are inscribed and reinforced. To begin to address this level of the problem, broad-based education and community violence prevention programs which *centrally address ending inequality* — based on gender, as well as race, class, and other relations of subordination — must be undertaken. This means delivering prevention programs which are built around and concretize the idea that "healthy relationships" are "*equal* relationships," which are categorically not built on fixed or hierarchical gender roles. Too often, public education campaigns to raise awareness on the issue don't challenge the "societal failure to understand the gendered nature of violence,"[52] or make the links between violence against women and gender inequality. As a result, they remain decontextualized and individualized in focus, and fail to foster social responsibility for a social (and not an individual) problem. Finally, there must be a continued and intensified emphasis on state and community accountability for violence against women and children, and for ending the structured inequalities in which this violence is situated and which it expresses.

It may reasonably be pointed out that this kind of agenda and the level and kinds of structural changes I have sketched out above, are not the kinds of things that lend themselves to something a court could simply "order," or that lend themselves to a legal remedy imposed under the *Charter*. While I would agree with this assessment, it does not follow that it is impossible to pursue *Charter* and other legal claims to pursue discrete components of the overarching kinds of changes needed to end violence against women and children. These more discrete goals might include, to cite only a very few specific examples, forcing the state to enforce restraining and protective orders, to provide adequate publicly funded legal representation (legal aid) to assaulted women in family law proceedings,[53] and to ensure that there is an adequate procedure for retrieving the weapons and gun licenses of violent men.[54] While we cannot naively expect to use the law to oblige the state to undertake a sweeping social revolution towards establishing equality, we can certainly use whatever creative legal arguments and openings might be afforded through law's power to make specific, incremental improvements and to remedy particular instances of discrimination, as part of a broader political strategy to effect social change and achieve substantive equality.

D. THE ROLE AND LIMITS OF LAW IN ESTABLISHING EQUALITY: THE LEGAL TEST FOR AN EQUALITY CLAIM AND ITS APPLICATIONS

Many of us working within the legal profession tend to overestimate law's power and significance *vis-à-vis* social problems such as gender inequality, to take just one example, and underestimate its complicity in them. As Sheila Martin points out, "[t]o the extent that law either is, or is about, politics and power, there can be no doubt that law has played a significant and complex role in reinforcing gender based and other power imbalances."[55] Law is, therefore, both deeply implicated in social inequalities, yet also a potentially transformative force in relation to remedying these inequalities.

Law's contradictory pulls are especially evident in Canadian equality rights jurisprudence. The guarantee of equality, entrenched in the *Charter* and articulated in the case law since its inception, is one which is at once critically important in terms of feminist social justice goals, and yet simultaneously severely restricted. In thinking more specifically about the ways in which the social problem of violence against women in intimate relationships is constructed and requires deconstruction, and the ways in which the appeal to *Charter* rights might play a role in this project, this paradox became even more sharply clear.

The now authoritative test for a breach of the section 15 equality rights guarantee of the *Charter* is articulated in a unanimous judgment of the Supreme Court in *Law v. Canada (Minister of Employment and Immigration)*.[56] The test comprises three major questions:

1. Does the impugned law (a) draw a formal distinction between the claimant and others on the basis of one or more personal characteristics, or (b) fail to take into account the claimant's already disadvantaged position within Canadian society resulting in substantively differential treatment between the claimant and others on the basis of one or more personal characteristics?
2. Is the claimant subject to differential treatment based on one or more enumerated and analogous grounds?
3. Does the differential treatment discriminate, by imposing a burden upon or withholding a benefit from the claimant in a manner which reflects the stereotypical application of presumed group or personal characteristics, or which otherwise has the effect of perpetuating or promoting the view that the individual is less capable or worthy of recognition or value as a human being or as a member of Canadian society, equally deserving of concern, respect, and consideration.

The third component of the *Law* test requires that four contextual factors be taken into consideration. These include (i) pre-existing disadvantage, (ii) correspondence between ground and actual circumstances and need of group, (iii) the purpose or effects of the impugned law upon a more disadvantaged person or group in society, and (iv) the nature and scope of the affected interests.[57]

Many commentators have effectively identified and exposed the profound deficiencies in much of the body of *Charter* equality rights jurisprudence since the test established in *Law v. Canada*. These deficiencies include the return to formalism,[58] the problematic and vague complication of equality with the equally unclear idea of "dignity,"[59] the problems of comparator groups,[60] the decontextualized and individualized focus of much equality rights analysis,[61] the preoccupation with "stereotyping" as the paradigmatic example or essential core of discrimination,[62] and the minimalist approach to section 1 which relieves the state of articulating a defence and justification of its policies and violations of rights,[63] among others.

Among the more astonishing and disappointing equality cases recently decided by the Supreme Court is *N.A.P.E.*, a case in which the Court had no difficulty recognizing the glaring equality rights violation yet nevertheless blithely defended the violation as an economically defensible excercise of government priorities. In *N.A.P.E.*, Binnie J. writing for the Court, found that the provincial government of Newfoundland and Labrador violated women hospital workers' section 15(1) equality rights by passing legislation (the *Public Sector Restraint Act*) which deferred payment of the hard-won and promised pay equity agreements from 1988 to 1991. Worse still than deferring the payment of money owed, the legislation arbitrarily simply extinguished arrears owed to the women workers for a three-year period (1988–1991). Although he could not resist commenting on a perceived lack of "nuance" in N.A.P.E.'s counsel's assessment of the implications of this legislation (perhaps the perplexing call for "nuance" expressed the Court's uneasiness with the forceful and incontrovertible nature of the analysis?), Binnie J. nevertheless accepted the veracity of the argument she advanced:

> [The *Public Service Restraint Act*] repudiates recognition by the state of the undervaluation of work done by women, it identifies pay inequity for women as acceptable and it repudiates state responsibility [as employer] for redressing systemic discrimination for women.[64]

The fact that pay equity settlements constituted a state obligation undertaken to remedy sex discrimination in remuneration was unambiguous, as was the fact that their retraction and delay of the settlements represented a breach of section 15(1) of the *Charter*.[65] The Court grasped the gender discrimination which inhered in the violation of the women's equality rights. In Binnie J.'s words:

> Postponement of pay equity and extinguishment of the 1988–91 arrears could reasonably be taken by the women, already underpaid, as confirmation that their work was valued less highly than the work of those in male-dominated jobs. The *Public Sector Restraint Act* reinforced an inferior status by taking away the remedial benefits their unions had negotiated on their behalf. This perpetuated and reinforced the idea that women could be paid less for no reason other than the fact they are women....[66]

What the Court appeared to have trouble with, however, was the idea that women's equality rights are not for sale or cannot be trumped by other pressing economic issues. Despite acknowledging the "casually introduced section 1 record"[67] and the government's failure to call witnesses to describe alternative cost reduction strategies,[68] Binnie J.'s section 1 analysis, departing from the principles previously articulated by the Court, affords the provincial government a "large margin of appreciation" within which to make its policy and budgetary choices.[69] He finds that each stage of the section 1 analysis is satisfied, therefore justifying the acknowledged violation of the equality rights guaranteed by section 15(1).

Ironically, the Court recognizes the enormousness of the debt owed to the women workers for the unequal wages they had been (under)paid, and observes that "in one sense, the size of the debt illustrates the scale of discrimination experienced by women hospital workers" (though it is not made clear in what "other" sense it can possibly represent anything else with regard to the relevant equality analysis). To add insult to injury the Court then advances the perverse argument that the very piece of legislation (the *Public Sector Restrain Act*) which obliterates some and defers the rest of the pay equality settlement actually represents an "affirmation"[70] of the principle of pay equity, as if this is some sort of consolation prize after the trampling of the very rights the pay equity settlements were to remedy. The Court finds that the deferral of some and the wholesale elimination of other portions of the pay equity settlements owed to the women workers who had been discriminated against, represents a "minimal impairment" to the equality rights of the women, "serious and deeply regrettable" though such adverse affects were.[71]

The equality rights judgment in *N.A.P.E.*, therefore, suggests that even in the face of glaringly obvious, systemic, and profound violations of women's equality rights (such as the right to equal and fair remuneration, not assessed against a discriminatory standard or an assumption that women's "dignity" is of lesser monetary worth) equality can be subordinated to other pressing governmental concerns such as a temporary budget crisis. Although the equality rights guarantee in the *Charter* has been described by the Court as one of the most fundamental and searching rights, cutting across and implicating all of the others, the deleterious effect on women's rights to equality in *N.A.P.E.* was of less concern to the Supreme Court than was the Newfoundland government's concern not to create "even greater grief and social disruption"[72] by actually honouring the payments in full. The "legal strongbox" Binnie identifies as protecting *Charter* rights[73] appears to be not so strong, after all.

While *N.A.P.E.* is the most recent case to target equality claims based on gender a range of other section 15 claims have reached the Supreme

Court and all have lost. In *Auton*, for example, the claim advanced by autistic children and their parents was that the refusal to fund ABA/IBI therapy (a specialized treatment) for these children represented an infringement of their equality rights and discriminated on the grounds of disability. The Chief Justice, writing for the unanimous Court, found that no discrimination existed. In the Court's view, a benefit provided must not be provided in a discriminatory manner, but the refusal to fund the medically required ABA/IBI treatment — reframed as a "benefit" rather than a necessity — was deemed to be legitimate because it was not a "medically necessary" service, and the state is "under no obligation to create a particular benefit."[74] In this judgment not only is the excessively high level of deference shown to the government again on full display, but so is the Court's reluctance to examine the effects and impact of the government's refusal to fund a medical service to a vulnerable group of children facing lifelong adverse consequences and limitations without this early intervention. Here we see a particularly formalistic and decontextualized approach to an equality problem, in which the focus is on the reasonableness of the state's delivery of health care and not on the plight and circumstances of a group of children (and their parents) struggling to cope with a profound disability.

Auton represents a paradigmatic example of a simultaneous failure to grasp the nature of the discrimination at issue and over-sensitivity to the burden on governments which equality claims might pose. *N.A.P.E.* represents a specific kind of low point among cases where equality rights violations are actually recognized and the blatant nature of the discrimination is judicially recognized, but it is nevertheless subordinated to the greater recognition of the heavy cost imposed on the state in order to achieve equality and remedy inequality. While these are only two recent examples, too many of the other recent section 15 decisions by the Supreme Court represent a failure to grasp the substantive implications of the equality rights analysis advanced by the plaintiffs (and the supporting interveners) and an increasing narrowing of the equality rights lens.

This does not bode well for those seeking an expanded equality rights approach and hoping that legal remedies framed around section 15 challenges might contribute to the realization of substantive equality. But the impoverished analyses of equality recently on view in the Supreme Court of Canada jurisprudence must not limit our insistence on and continued efforts towards realization of the early promise of the *Charter* and the expectations of rights holders. Although they exist in a sea of opposing currents, there are enough glimmers of possibility in the case law to sustain hope in law's transformative potential in the struggle for equality, and it is on these that we must anchor and expand our legal challenges.

E. DOMESTIC VIOLENCE, STATE ACCOUNTABILITY, AND *CHARTER* RIGHTS

Stepping back somewhat and widening the lens still further away from the *Law* test for a section 15 breach, the conceptual straitjacket which the *Charter* rights legal framework seems to impose become even more clear.[75] Because it guarantees equality only in terms of equal benefit and protection of law, section 15 of the *Charter* necessarily engages only those instances of inequality which can be demonstrated in relation to state-provided and legal entitlements, benefits, and programs. Given that the *Charter* applies to state action and doesn't, therefore, govern "private relationships" — which is precisely where intimate violence is lived and takes place — constructing a *Charter* challenge to work towards eradicating domestic violence becomes an extremely difficult task.

The obvious "state action" in relation to domestic violence is the criminal justice system response, including the role of the judiciary, the legal profession, the police, probation, and parole. The criminalization of violence in intimate relationships has, in fact, been the state's largest response to the problem; despite important reforms, many defects continue to exist in terms of that response. But the issues which confront women using the criminal justice system because of their experiences of domestic violence do not directly or easily lend themselves to a traditional equality analysis framed in terms of section 15 claim.

It is in terms of enforcing state accountability for men's violence against women and children that further legal interventions using *Charter* rights might be most fruitfully launched. This accountability necessarily has a dual quality. That is, state accountability lies in the duty to protect women from violence (through, for example, adequate legal responses such as an effective criminal justice system),[76] and also lies in *a duty to take proactive measures to prevent violence*. In the same way that negative and positive aspects inhere in the concept of "rights," the idea of state accountability for violence necessarily engages negative and positive dimensions of responsibility. This duality is, in fact, entrenched in the language of the equality guarantee of the *Charter*, a duality which has been expressly recognized by the Supreme Court. But its negative aspects — the focus on the bundle of negative liberties and on remedying denials of rights and benefits — have been overwhelmingly emphasized in the jurisprudence, while the positive aspects — attention to the imposition of affirmative duties — have only barely been acknowledged.

The state's demonstrated failure to protect in too many cases — in other words, the state's failure to deliver equal benefit of and protection of the law to assaulted women — is an avenue warranting legal innovation and effort, not only for its symbolic, public, and educative value, but also in order to marshal state resources and power towards meaningful social solutions to the problem of men's violence against women.

Pointing out failures in state response is not to suggest, of course, that the state always fails in this regard. Fortunately, there are many examples where the criminal justice system has afforded assaulted women some measure of meaningful protection and assistance, often because of the extraordinary efforts of committed people working within this system (in the police services, Crown offices, judiciary, and victim support services). But there is both a historical and contemporary reality of inadequate understanding, resources, and responses of state agencies to the situations of danger and risk faced by assaulted women, and these remain real instances of rights violations.

In addition to the state's well-documented failure to protect women from criminal harm, another and inter-related area in which creative *Charter* challenges might usefully — if also not without difficulty — be mounted, revolves around the state's obligation to promote social conditions conducive to equality. This latter theme represents a move beyond the remedying of discriminatory *denials* of rights and/or benefits, towards the imposition of positive duties on the state towards actualizing equality and creating the material conditions necessary for its actualization.

Because, in a context of an escalating antipathy to equality claims and an increasingly negative and minimalist liberal state, feminists and other equality seekers are so often in a defensive and reactive position, it is refreshing to have the opportunity to think more proactively and creatively about ways to engage law more fully to push at and challenge the interpretive limits which have been imposed on its relationship to equality. We should not allow the fact that the legal developments around equality rights in Canada to date have been uneven, limited, and often disappointing, to result in the imposition of restrictions on our imaginations or on our efforts to push at these boundaries in order to expand the scope of what is or what might be justifiable. I turn first to a consideration of the legal possibilities surrounding *Charter* challenges to the state's failure to protect, then to the even more difficult question of using the *Charter* to promote positive obligations to end violence and concretize equality.

F. THE DENIAL OF EQUAL PROTECTION: PUBLIC RESPONSIBILITY FOR PRIVATE VIOLENCE

> Treating women as dis-embodied objects constructs women's relationship to the physical self and to the state.[77]

Challenging the state for its inaction in the face of men's violence against women and children in the private sphere is consistent with the struggle to deprivatize this issue and frame it as one of social and community responsibility. One of the more significant issues in relation to the criminal justice system's response to domestic violence is its failure, once it has been engaged, to protect women from known violent and dangerous men. In fact, containing violent men — men who have already been abusive towards their female intimates and who have threatened further violence or murder — is one of the greatest social and legal challenges facing those working to end violence against women in intimate relationships.[78] Not only does this effort directly personalize and concretize the issue of violence against women by focusing on the perpetrators of this violence, but it also focuses on the state's responsibility to ensure women's safety.

The claim that the state fails to protect women from intimate violence necessarily confronts the public/private split which ideologically limits how state action is understood. Because in a traditional liberal political and legal framework the minimally interventionist state's role is to protect negative rights and liberties, what counts as state action is significantly circumscribed. Attached to this is the view that the state, through the power of law, has little if any legitimate role in interfering in those relationships characterized as fundamentally "private." This conception is built into the way that the scope and applicability of *Charter* rights are typically understood;[79] that is, as actionable only in relation to state action (law) and not directly extending to the realm of the private.[80] This, of course, has significant implications for interpretations of the state's role in relation to violence in the so-called "private" sphere, and in particular in relation to the state's absence of intervention in this problem. In other words, if the state isn't seen as responsible for directly creating the harm, then it is under no constitutionally imposed and affirmative duty to protect those injured or to take action to prevent the harm in the first place.

Analyzing the legal scope and interpretations of the Equal Protection Clause of the Fourteenth Amendment in the US, Robin West argues that because its textual language is clearly directed at states and law *and not at private actors* it has been erroneously assumed (by Owen Fiss and others) that it is directed only at state action, rather than state inaction. The logical error West identifies is the assumption that if state inaction in the face of egregious private conduct attracts constitutional sanction then what is really being targeted is private conduct and that, by definition, can't be the case according to the very terms of the clause.[81] According to West, it doesn't follow that because the constitutional provision is aimed at state action (via law) rather than private parties it is only state action, rather than inaction, which is the exclusive target.

This analysis is equally applicable, I think, to section 15 of the *Charter* as well as the rights engaged by sections 7 and 28. And this reasoning — what West describes as an unnecessary conflation — has resulted in a complete "shielding" of the "moral and political problem of egregious state inaction, or neglect, from constitutional scrutiny."[82] This is precisely what I am problematizing in the Canadian context with regard to state failure in the lives of assaulted women and the violations of a constitutional right to protection from known and specific sources of violence, such as violent male intimates.

West illustrates this argument with precisely the kind of issue which might be legally actionable as a *Charter* challenge. As West explains it:

> A state's failure to criminalize private violence perpetrated by one group of citizens against another group of citizens (such as violence visited upon freed blacks, for example, in the wake of the civil war, or violence inflicted in patriarchal families upon spouses, or children) might well be an example, even a paradigmatic example, of a state's denial of equal protection.[83]

This kind of analysis doesn't render the private conduct as the focus of the US equal protection clause. Similarly, nor would the private conduct be the focus, in the Canadian context, of section 15 *Charter* claim in cases of state accountability for violence against women. Instead it is the state *inaction* in the face of the private conduct which triggers the constitutional issues regarding the failure to provide equal protection and benefit of the law. And this is exactly what a *Charter* challenge should make actionable.

G. FAILING TO PROTECT: PRIVATE LAW ACTIONS WITH CONSTITUTIONAL DIMENSIONS

Additionally, private law actions, framed in relation to and informed by *Charter* values, might also yield some further options for advancing the legal possibilities for equality rights and a discrimination analysis to impose state accountability for violence against women.[84] An important case in this regard has reached the Supreme Court in the United States. In *Castle Rock v. Gonzales et al.*[85] Gonzales' claim is that her procedural due process rights were violated when police officers in Colorado failed to enforce a restraining order against her estranged and violent husband after he abducted their three daughters, in violation of a court order. While Gonzales repeatedly and frantically sought police enforcement of the order, contacting police six times over an eight hour period, the husband proceeded to murder each of the children. In an astonishing and disturbing decision issued 27 June 2005, the majority of the Court (in a judgment written by arch-Conservative Supreme Court Justice Antonin Scalia) ruled that the police are not required to enforce restraining orders, even in the face of state law explicitly mandating that they do so.[86]

Despite the state's statute which unambiguously compelled police to enforce restraining orders using "every reasonable means," the majority of the U.S. Supreme Court managed to (mis)construe the state's legislative intent as enabling officer "discretion" in the matter of enforcement. In a powerful dissent, Justice Stevens, joined by Justice Ruth Bader Ginsburg, to the contrary, observed that, "the crucial point is that, under the statute, the police were required to provide enforcement; *they lacked the discretion to do nothing*" (emphasis in original). Clearly, the promise of the Appeals Court (the Tenth Circuit) ruling which created an entitlement for Ms. Gonzales to receive police protection based on the mandatory language of the Colorado statute was crushed by the Supreme Court's refusal to impose state accountability for the abject failure of police protection directly resulting in the death of three children.

In a recent Canadian case, which the Supreme Court disappointingly refused to hear, the BC Court of Appeal denied a woman's claim against the police, in negligence, for their failure to investigate a complaint of domestic violence. The offender, R.K., who was B.M.'s estranged common law husband, had a lengthy history of criminal violence, including a conviction for assault against B.M. Following his conviction (and brief incarceration) and after their separation B.M. reported a threatening incident with R.K. to the police, but they declined to take any action. R.K. subsequently arrived at B.M.'s property, smashed open her door, entered the house, shot and killed B.M.'s friend Hazel White, and shot B.M.'s twelve-year-old daughter in the shoulder.

The tort action failed at the BC Court of Appeal on the issue of causation,[87] with two of the judges supporting the trial judge's finding that the temporal remove between the time of the RCMP's failure to investigate and R.K.'s shooting spree negated the finding of any factual causal connection, and, more fundamentally, that the RCMP Constable's failure to investigate B.M.'s complaint against R.K. was unrelated to his "murderous rage."[88]

The disappointing analysis in this case can be critiqued on numerous levels, too many to advance here. But for the purposes of this analysis the case is significant because the trial and Court of Appeal decisions all found a private law duty of care owed by the police to the plaintiff. Moreover, Donald J.A., writing in dissent at the Court of Appeal advanced a powerful argument about the state's duty to protect victims of domestic violence. In his words, in analyzing the cause of action,

> Reference must be made to the policies laid down by the Ministry of the Attorney General and adopted by the RCMP in relation to domestic violence. They relate not only to the special proximity between police and complainants but they also give content to the duty of care and set the standard of care. The general duty of the police is to protect, but in the area of domestic violence the degree of protection is heightened by government policy. *The discretion whether to act on a complaint is very limited.*[89]

Justice Donald argues that the action should not be defeated because of an overly restrictive analysis of factual causation, explaining that:

> In the present matter, the general duty of care on the police to provide protection was heightened by government policy addressing the serious problem of domestic violence. The duty owed to potential victims of spousal abuse would be virtually unenforceable if claimants had to do more than show a material contribution of the risk because of the difficulty of proof to which I have referred. To insist upon strict proof would leave a right without a remedy.

Although the outcome of *B.M. v. British Columbia (Attorney General)* is disappointing, there is no reason to suggest that future actions along these lines might not succeed. Given that the duty analysis seems uncontentious, the greatest hurdles appear to lie in mounting a successful causation analysis, something which will no doubt be easier to do on different facts, which might, for example, involve a more specific breach of police duty, such as failure to enforce a restraining or other court-ordered protective measure. And, surprisingly, B.M.'s cause of action appears to have been pled strictly in private law terms, around a claim of negligence, while the facts seem to call out for a legal analysis which centrally foregrounds the constitutional issues also at stake. These include not only the discrimination analysis of a section 15 claim, but also the breach of section 7 rights to security of the person, all of which are implicated in state actors' failure to act effectively — *in the face of an explicit set of policies mandating them to do so* — to protect assaulted women.

Jane Doe v. Metropolitan Toronto (Municipality) Commissioners of Police[90] is an obvious example of the integration of a private law action — a negligence claim against the state — fused with constitutional claims about section 15 and section 7 rights. In this case, in which a woman successfully sued the police for their failure to warn her that she was at specific risk of attack by a serial rapist, a sex discrimination argument was central to the legal analysis and actually underpinned both the negligence analysis and the constitutional claims.[91]

Other possibilities for suing the state are waiting to be found. Given the dramatic expansion of negligence doctrine, this might be an approach worth pursuing in terms of making legally actionable the state failure to protect and the state failure to provide protection adequately and equally.

H. *CHARTER* RIGHTS AND WOMEN'S SAFETY: MAPPING THE LEGAL CONTOURS OF STATE ACCOUNTABILITY FOR FAILURE TO PROTECT

When the state fails to take affirmative steps to protect battered women from intra-familial violence, it is complicit in creating the harm.[92]

Charter challenges grounded in inadequacies in the criminal justice system response which jeopardize assaulted women's safety are one potential source of legal activism integrating an equality rights perspective in the context of domestic violence. Failure to remove weapons from violent men; to enforce restraining and other protective orders; to adequately investigate, charge, and arrest in domestic violence situations; and to undertake adequate risk assessments in legal proceedings, especially including bail, sentencing, and parole, are all potential sources of *Charter* challenges. To take one specific example, rights to a protective order from the state are meaningless if these orders are not state-enforced, and if there is no remedy for state failure to enforce.

The media regularly reports on cases of women being killed by male intimates who have already had plenty of contact with the criminal justice system but whose violence is unrestrained. The problem of spousal homicide is one extreme end of the larger issue of domestic violence. For example, the findings and recommendations from the Ontario coroners' inquests into the deaths of Arlene May and Gillian Hadley,[93] both of whom were killed at the hands of their male partners, starkly demonstrate the failure of state protection and concretize the kinds of system failures which should be legally actionable. The juries in both inquests received submissions from a broad range of parties, including some which where explicitly informed by an equality rights perspective.[94]

In both cases, women who had been subjected to ongoing and escalating abuse perpetrated by their male intimates repeatedly sought the intervention and protection of the police and the criminal justice system — for example, by reporting the assaults against them to the police, and seeking protective orders. Despite this, each woman ended up dead. Their stories are, unfortunately, more typical than not in cases of spousal homicide.

When Randy Iles killed his estranged spouse, Arlene May, he had a lengthy criminal history including convictions for indecent exposure, harassing phone calls, probation breaches, possession of stolen property, and a weapons offence. At the time of the murder (and his suicide) there was one warrant for his arrest in a neighbouring jurisdiction, and another warrant for breaching his recognizance by contacting Arlene May in defiance of a court order not to do so. A condition of his bail terms was the surrender of his Firearms Acquisition Certificate, yet he was not actually compelled to relinquish it by anyone associated with the criminal justice system. As a result, while out on bail Iles was able to purchase the gun with which he killed his spouse.

When Gillian Hadley was killed by her estranged husband in her own house, just moments before her death she had handed her baby to a neighbour, who had desperately tried to intervene in the stand-off. This was a particularly dramatic aspect of the story which received much media attention. Less attention was paid, however, to the fact that her killer was, at the time he perpetrated this murder, facing charges for criminal harassment and was also under court order to keep away from her.

While their experiences may seem extreme, what the tragic stories of Arlene May and Gillian Hadley illustrate is the more typical pattern of on-going abuse and failed state interventions which characterize so many cases of intimate femicide. Moreover, in direct contradiction to dominant myths about assaulted women's passivity, helplessness, and/or complicity in the face of domestic violence, both of these deceased women's stories are filled with examples of their *repeated and persistent attempts to engage the criminal justice system* and use all legal remedies available to them to secure their own safety. The extensive and sweeping set of recommendations issued from each of these inquests (many of which were originally issued in the first report and then repeated in the second) languish largely unimplemented.

The even more recently released report of the Ontario Death Review Committee provides further documentation[95] that many intimate femicides are preventable with co-ordinated and skilled intervention. Based on a review of actual case files of women murdered by their intimates, the report identified common risk factors which were often present and which could have led properly trained domestic violence professionals to predict and intervene to prevent a domestic homicide, if an effective system wide response had been in place.

The specific sets of circumstances surrounding the deaths of Arlene May and Gillian Hadley, and their well-documented and multiple points of intervention with the criminal justice system, provide clear examples of the kinds of tragedies which give rise to justiciable claims. I am certainly not suggesting that only spousal homicide situations call out for a legal remedy, but am using these well-publicized examples to illustrate the ways in which too many women encounter massive gaps in criminal justice system responses — gaps, omissions, and failure to protect which render them vulnerable to further harm, and deny them equal protection of and under the law.

Given the gendered and discriminatory nature of men's violence against women and given the profound threat this violence poses to women's security of the person and liberty interests, legal challenges about state failure to protect might involve claims framed around section 15, section 7, and even section 28. In *Gosselin v. Quebec (Attorney General)*, L'Heureux-Dubé J. argues that section 15 rights must be interpreted in relation to section 7 rights.[96] If that is correct, then the obverse must also be true — that security of the person rights can be articulated in terms of an equality claim. In fact, the minority judgment in *New Brunswick (Minister of Health and Community Services) v. G. (J.)*[97] expressly recognized that some fact situations simultaneously implicate section 7 and section 15 rights, stating that: "[t]he rights in section 7 must be interpreted through the lens of ss. 15 and 28, to recognize the importance of ensuring that our interpretation of the Constitution responds to the realities and needs of all members of society."[98] The paradigmatic example of the intertwining of these security of the person and equality rights is found in women's experiences of intimate violence.

I. POSITIVE STATE DUTIES: AFFIRMATIVE OBLIGATIONS TO PROMOTE EQUALITY UNDER THE *CHARTER*

> [T]he section 7 rights to "life, liberty and security of the person" include a positive dimension. Few would dispute that an advanced modern welfare state like Canada has a positive moral obligation to protect the life, liberty and security of its citizens.[99]

Rights necessarily involve negative and positive dimensions. Justice Arbour explains how this is the case with regard to some of the *Charter* rights guaranteed in Canada and the positive duties this imposes on the state to ensure their realization. In her words:

> The rights to vote (s. 3), to trial within a reasonable time (s. 11(b)), to be presumed innocent (s. 11(d)), to trial by jury in certain cases (s. 11(f)), to an interpreter in penal proceedings (s. 14), and minority language education rights (s. 23) to name but some, all impose positive obligations of performance on the state and are therefore best viewed as positive rights (at least in part). By finding that the state has a positive obligation in certain cases to ensure that its labour legislation is properly inclusive, this Court has also found there to be a positive dimension to the section 2(d) right to associate (*Dunmore v. Ontario (Attorney General)*, [2001] 3 S.C.R. 1016, 2001 SCC 94). Finally, decisions like *Schachter v. Canada*, [1992] 2 S.C.R. 679, and *Vriend, supra*, confirm that "[i]n some contexts it will be proper to characterize section 15 as providing positive rights" (*Schachter, supra*, at p. 721). This list is illustrative rather than exhaustive.[100]

The dual negative and positive aspects of the equality rights protected in the *Charter* were recognized in the first section 15 decision of the Supreme Court of Canada. In the still foundational *Andrews* decision, Justice Wilson stipulated that section 15 is designed to "protect those groups who suffer social, political, and legal disadvantage in our society."[101] In this way, section 15 has always had twin goals, articulated in *Andrews* and echoed (if at a diminished volume) throughout the case law since. These dual purposes of section 15 include both *the prevention* of legal denials of equality and *the promotion* of equality.

As others have begun to argue, this latter and expressly identified *constitutional obligation to promote equality* has yet to be developed in any meaningful way. Yet it is potentially a rich source of legal action and intervention, particularly when constitutional guarantees of equality are read in conjunction with section 7 guarantees of life, liberty, and security of the person. This has particular currency in relation to the issue of violence against women. Intimate violence in women's lives simultaneously represents an expression of gender inequality (and concomitant denial of equality), and a violation and invasion of autonomy, liberty, and security of the person. Writing about law in relation to sexual assault, for example, Sheilah Martin posits that that the *Charter* can be read to suggest that the state is under an obligation to "actively create and rigorously enforce policies and procedures designed to promote the equality, liberty and security of women's persons."[102]

Jurisprudential support for the view that the state is positively obligated to provide the conditions required to actualize equality as guaranteed by section 15, and to ensure that section 7 rights to security of the person have a material base (such as the right to housing, welfare, and other necessities of life) might be characterized as thin, at best, in Canadian case law. Nevertheless, there are enough glimpses of the possibility of Supreme Court judgments opening the door in this direction, to warrant pursuing and pushing for this possibility to be more fully realized in practice.

Melina Buckley has effectively woven together examples from the equality rights and section 7 jurisprudence under the *Charter* to demonstrate doctrinal support for the possibility of legally establishing a positive equality obligation.[103] Though this argument clearly goes against the direction of the legal tide, support can nevertheless be gleaned from judicial pronouncements in *Eaton*, *Eldridge*, and from the untapped potential of section 7 acknowledged by a majority of the judges in *Gosselin*, particularly in the luminous and path-breaking judgment written by Justice Arbour.[104]

In *Gosselin* it is significant that McLachlin C. J., writing for the majority, expressly accepts that section 7 of the *Charter* might ground a positive duty on the state to uphold the rights the provision engages. Although she did not find a section 7 violation on the facts of the case, she nevertheless imagines the possibility in future jurisprudence. In her words,

> I leave open the possibility that a positive obligation to sustain life, liberty, or security of the person may be made out in special circumstances.[105]

LeBel J. agreed that section 7 might require positive state action, as did Justices L'Heureux-Dubé and Arbour.[106] This judicial recognition of section 7's potential builds on that proffered by the Supreme Court in *Dunmore v. Ontario (Attorney General)*,[107] in which Bastarache J., writing for the majority, found that the *Charter* can require that the state take positive steps to protect groups from having their *Charter*-guaranteed rights breached.

In *Gosselin*, Justice Arbour stakes out the largest legal space for a set of rights in section 7 of the *Charter* imposing positive duties on the state. In fact, Arbour goes further than restricting her analysis to section 7 rights, and claims that: "As a theory of the Charter as a whole, any claim that only negative rights are constitutionally recognized is of course patently defective."[108] In arguing that section 7 can and does impose positive duties on the state, Arbour J. explains that "Section 7 must be interpreted as protecting something more than merely negative rights."[109] Justice Arbour then expands this analysis, pointing out that:

> Clearly, positive rights are not at odds with the purpose of the *Charter*. Indeed, the *Charter* compels the state to act positively to ensure the protection of a significant number of rights .... Positive rights are not an exception to the usual application of the *Charter*, but an inherent part of its structure. The *Charter* as a whole can be said to have a positive purpose in that at least some of its constituent parts do.[110]

Though not definitive, then, the support found in *Gosselin* for a reading of section 7 which includes the imposition of positive duties on the state has significant implications for feminist legal challenges in the area of violence against women.

A number of areas more directly linked to the problem of domestic violence have been identified as ripe for creative legal intervention, and fall easily under the rubric of positive state obligation. For example, an area crying out for reform is the grossly inadequate access to legal representation for assaulted women in family law proceedings, especially dealing with custody and access issues. If the state is to make the promise of equal benefit of the law have any substance, access to legal services is essential. The women in most dire need are obviously most often marginalized and racialized women, those with the fewest resources. This reveals the compounding and intersecting nature of multiple grounds of oppression. Given that the vast majority of the (admittedly limited) legal aid funding goes to criminal defence work, which largely involves providing legal representation to defend men charged criminally, it seems that the gender dimensions of this distribution of state resources might be receptive to a legal challenge.[111] The gendered dimensions of the distribution of legal aid, in the context of the utter inadequacy of legal aid more generally, are areas some activist lawyers and academics are already working on.

Tying this larger issue in to the specific vulnerability of women abused in intimate relationships might productively advance the struggle on a number of fronts. Again, and even if only from a part of the Court, support for a recognition of the gender discrimination elements of the state's denial of legal aid to women seeking legal representation (in this case in custody proceedings) is found in *New Brunswick (Minister of Health and Community Services) v. G. (J.)*.[112] In that case, the entire Court found that the provincial government's failure to provide legal aid to a woman engaged in custody proceedings was a violation of her section 7 security of the person rights, and therefore found that, in some circumstances, the state is positively and constitutionally obligated to provide state-funded counsel to litigants in these legal proceedings. In a separate decision, L'Heureux-Dubé, Gonthier, and McLachlin JJ. also explicitly identified the inextricably interconnected gender dimensions of this denial of legal representation and found that the section 15 and section 28 guarantees of equality in the *Charter* can significantly influence the scope of the rights protected by section 7 of the *Charter*.

In *Auton*, McLachlin C.J. writes that:

Whatever framework is used, an overly technical approach to section 15(1) is to be avoided. In *Andrews, supra*, at pp. 168–69, McIntyre J. warned against adopting a narrow, formalistic analytical approach, and stressed the need to look at equality issues substantively and contextually. *The Court must look at the reality of the situation and assess whether there has been discriminatory treatment having regard to the purpose of section 15(1), which is to prevent the perpetuation of pre-existing disadvantage through unequal treatment.*[113]

While it seems obvious that the actual interpretation of the facts and the legal analysis of equality deeply fails to deliver on this promise in the *Auton* decision, the Court's fulsome rhetoric about equality (there and elsewhere) and about the purpose of the *Charter*'s section 15 guarantees of it — contradicted as they are in much of the case law — must be pushed towards concrete realization. And, the imbrications of section 15 equality rights with section 7 security of the person rights (as well as section 28's promise that all *Charter* rights are guaranteed equally to men and women) can fruitfully be pursued in legal analyses and legal actions which continue to push the boundaries of the liberal negative state towards a state committed to substantive equality and positively bound to provide the conditions for it.

J. INTERNATIONAL AUTHORITY FOR STATE OBLIGATIONS TO PROTECT WOMEN FROM PRIVATE VIOLENCE

Support for greater state accountability not only to protect women from intimate violence but also to undertake positive steps to prevent this violence, is found in international law and covenants, case law interpreting these covenants, and the legal framework which has been established around legal obligations to protect human rights. For example, the *Convention on the Elimination of all Forms of Discrimination Against Women* (*CEDAW*), the *Beijing Platform for Action*, and the *Vienna Declaration and Programme of Action*[114] all expressly link gender inequality and domestic violence, and suggest that systemic state failure to deal with the problem of violence against women is discriminatory.

CEDAW came into force in 1981 and was signed and ratified by the Canadian government in 1982, making the convention binding in Canada.[115] *CEDAW* imposes broad positive and remedial obligations on the states to ensure discrimination against women is eliminated. Article 2 sets forth the declarations of positive obligations imposed on states:

> Article 2: States Parties condemn discrimination against women in all its forms, agree to pursue by all appropriate means and without delay a policy of eliminating discrimination against women and, to this end, undertake:
>
> (c) To establish legal protection of the rights of women on an equal basis with men and to ensure through competent national tribunals and other public institutions the effective protection of women against any act of discrimination; ...

(e) To take all appropriate measures to eliminate discrimination against women by any person, organization or enterprise;

(f) To take all appropriate measures, including legislation, to modify or abolish existing laws, regulations, customs and practices which constitute discrimination against women.

In 1992, the General Recommendations of the Committee specifically addressed violence against women. While the General Recommendations are not binding on the states, they are considered to provide guidance on the implementation of *CEDAW* at the national level. Gender-based violence is described as discrimination within the meaning of article 1 of the Convention.

The Committee emphasized that,

> ... discrimination under the Convention is not restricted to action by or on behalf of Governments (articles 2(e), 2(f) and 5).... Under general international law and specific human rights covenants, States may also be responsible for private acts *if they fail to act with due diligence to prevent violations of rights* or to investigate and punish acts of violence, and for providing compensation. [Emphasis added.]

And, in its 1992 report the Committee reiterated that states are *positively obligated* to ensure the elimination of discrimination against women.

The Committee advised all state parties to take all appropriate and effective measures to overcome all forms of gender-based violence, whether caused by public *or private* actions. States are obliged to ensure that laws addressing domestic violence, sexual assault, and other gender-based violence provide adequate protection to all women, and to provide adequate support services and protective services to victims. Training in gender-sensitivity for judges, law enforcement officers, and public officials is necessary to effectively implement the Convention. Effective legal measures including penal sanctions, civil remedies, and compensatory provisions are also identified as necessary to protect women from violence.

The Committee recommends that overcoming domestic violence requires measure such as:

- criminal penalties where necessary, as well as civil remedies, for domestic violence
- legislation removing the defence of honour for assaulting or murdering a female family member

- services ensuring the safety of victims of family violence
- rehabilitation for perpetrators of domestic violence
- support services for families affected by sexual abuse

Canada has recently also ratified the *Optional Protocol* that allows individual complaints to be advanced to the Committee for allegations of breaches to *CEDAW*. Complaints can be advanced by individuals or groups who allege their rights in *CEDAW* have been infringed. This is another route for women to pursue claims of discrimination after all the domestic remedies have been exhausted. As of yet, no claims have been advanced against Canada under this mechanism, although this Protocol was only ratified by Canada in 2003.

In 1994 a United Nations General Assembly Resolution was issued addressing the elimination of violence against women. Under article 4, states have positive obligations to take all appropriate measures towards eliminating violence against women. States should *prevent*, investigate, and punish acts of violence against women committed by both public and private individuals, and should develop sanctions to punish and redress the harm caused. Laws and enforcement mechanisms should be gender-sensitive to ensure that re-victimization does not occur.

Article 4 stipulates that:

States should condemn violence against women and should not invoke any custom, tradition or religious consideration to avoid their obligations with respect to its elimination. States should pursue by all appropriate means and without delay a policy of eliminating violence against women and, to this end, should:

(c) Exercise due diligence to prevent, investigate and, in accordance with national legislation, punish acts of violence against women, whether those acts are perpetrated by the State or by private persons;

(d) Develop penal, civil, labour and administrative sanctions in domestic legislation to punish and redress the wrongs caused to women who are subjected to violence; women who are subjected to violence should be provided with access to the mechanisms of justice and, as provided for by national legislation, to just and effective remedies for the harm that they have suffered; States should also inform women of their rights in seeking redress through such mechanisms;

(e) Consider the possibility of developing national plans of action to promote the protection of women against any form of violence, or to include provisions for that purpose in plans already existing, taking into account, as appropriate, such cooperation as can be provided by non-governmental organizations, particularly those concerned with the issue of violence against women;

(f) Develop, in a comprehensive way, preventive approaches and all those measures of a legal, political, administrative and cultural nature that promote the protection of women against any form of violence, and ensure that the re-victimization of women does not occur because of laws insensitive to gender considerations, enforcement practices or other interventions.

Finally, the *International Covenant on Civil and Political Rights (IC-CPR)*[116] was ratified by Canada on 19 May 1976. It does not expressly name a right to state protection from gender violence but since the early 1990s the monitoring body, the Human Rights Committee, has identified that this protection is implicit in numerous of the Covenant's Articles.[117]

Kristian Miccio has effectively developed the themes of state accountability for "private" violence against women in a pair of articles which draw on international and US domestic law to bolster the claim for holding the state accountable for its complicity in this aspect of gender inequality.[118] As she argues,

> Because international standards and customary law articulate positive obligations as well as specific human rights, constitutional protection of fundamental rights should expand beyond the rigid and tautly drawn boundaries implicit in the negativist concept of the state.[119]

An emerging and clear international consensus has been established, therefore, that frames women's (and children's) rights to be protected from sexual and intimate violence as a fundamental human right; that obliges states to be proactive and effective in delivering this protection; and that, as part of this right, obliges states to provide legal remedies to victims of violence in the face of failures of this protection.[120] This body of international law, principles, and treaties provide further legal authority for efforts undertaken within Canada to use domestic law to enforce women's constitutional right to state protection from private violence, a fundamental right underpinned by *Charter* rights to equality and to security of the person.

K. EQUALITY, *CHARTER* RIGHTS, AND *LAW*

> The *Charter* gives state actors the opportunity and mandate to make laws
> more responsive to the various realities of women's lives.[121]

The equality rights guarantees under the *Charter* are of real as well as symbolic importance, and there have been some important legal victories (of which we need to remind ourselves when the picture looks bleak). But the ways in which the conditions of inequality surrounding domestic violence are actually experienced in women's lives continue to be resisted by the legal categories and approaches which have been constructed ostensibly to remedy these very conditions of inequality. These legal tests and approaches require revision and reformulation.

As an instrument for advancing the struggle for equality in Canada, the *Charter* appears to be inherently limited by its narrowed focus on legal equality, and by its corresponding interpretation as applicable only to denials of equality which can be demonstrated in relation to what gets recognized as state action. And what typically counts as state action is seen through the lens of the liberal, negative state. Even within this frame, many commentators have pointed to the constricted and individualistic approach the Supreme Court has taken to equality rights analyses as a result of the legal test and approach to equality rights articulated in *Law* and in the equality rights case law since.

In thinking about how the law's power can be utilized as a vehicle for moving towards social relations characterized by equality, we find that the *Charter's* focus on law makes the inquiry profoundly self-referential. Stepping back and widening the lens, then, we can see that the field on which the equality game is currently played *vis-à-vis* the *Charter*, is a very pared-down one.

This raises the question, then, of the efficacy and utility of pursuing a strategy of engaging law in the quest for substantive equality. If, in other words, *Charter* equality rights jurisprudence has been so impoverished and inadequate from a substantive equality point of view, then why bother expending more effort on this front? The answer lies, in part, in the fact that legal strategies and struggles are necessarily simultaneously political strategies and struggles. While the difficulties encountering feminist engagements with law are daunting, the prospects of abandoning law as a site of struggle are even more so. Furthermore, we must not lose sight of the transformative potential of legal intervention, on levels extending beyond what we consider a "successful" legal outcome to be. What is required, in part, is a political and legal exercise of refusing the traditional categories and boundaries as an act of resistance in the struggle to achieve substantive equality.

Subjecting state failures, inaction, and neglect to constitutional scrutiny and pursuing test case litigation to establish positive duties flowing from the constitutional guarantee of equality and other rights, is a way of posing a direct legal challenge to the dominant construction of the liberal, minimalist, and non-interventionist capitalist state. Again, as West argues,

> it is often the unduly minimal state, not the unduly irrational state, that is the cause of the unaddressed wrongful group disadvantage caused by social circumstances, and it is thus the unduly minimal state, rather than the unduly irrational state, that might best be viewed as the target of the equal protection clause.

She continues to explain that:

> The failure of the state to take actions that alleviate the disadvantage caused to poor women and their children by virtue of the nonexistence of publicly funded child care, or the failure of states to enact appropriately progressive taxation schemes, or to enforce laws against criminal violence, or to enact laws against hate crimes, or to address the consequences of private sphere racial discrimination, all appear as logical and straightforward targets of Equal Protection challenges, rather than as simply the inevitable consequence of private actions and a passive state, if we view state inaction rather than state action (or individual action) as the nub of the phrase.[122]

Although the struggle to disrupt and transgress the boundaries of the playing field of equality rights necessarily encounters formidable obstacles, these should not deter us. As Mari Matsuda reminded us some years ago, feminists engage the law as a "tool of necessity."[123]

ENDNOTES

1 An earlier version of this paper was originally prepared for LEAF Community and Legal Consultations, Toronto, 26–27 February 2004. Thanks to Sonia Lawrence, Osgoode Hall, and to Fay Faraday and M. Kate Stephenson for helpful comments on this paper.

2 Carol Smart, "The Woman of Legal Discourse" (1992) 1 Social and Legal Studies 29 at 30.

3 See, for example, *Changing the Landscape/Achieving Equality: Final Report of the Canadian Panel on Violence Against Women* (Ottawa: Minister of Supply and Services, 1993) for an articulation of the links between gender, inequality, and violence.

4 For a critical examination of these policies, see FREDA Centre for Research on Violence Against Women and Children, *"Arresting" Violence in Relationships: An Analysis of the Attorney General's Mandatory Arrest Policy* (Vancouver: FREDA, 1997).

5 A number of Canadian jurisdictions have also introduced other approaches, including specialized domestic violence police units; diversion and treatment programs for batterers who plead guilty; more intensive training of those within the criminal justice system, including judges; and provincial domestic violence legislation.

6 See, for example, the work of the Ontario Women's Directorate, online: www.gov.on.ca/citizenship/owd/. See also *Changing the Landscape,* above note 3, for an articulation of the links between gender, inequality, and violence.

7 The gendered nature of domestic violence is, in fact, vigorously contested by some, including so-called "father's rights" groups which are explicitly anti-feminist in agenda, but also by other segments of society resistant to recognizing gender and/or gender inequality.

8 See, for example, *Changing the Landscape*, above note 3.

9 See, for example, Lee Lakeman for Canadian Association of Sexual Assault Centres (CASAC), *Canada's Promises to Keep: The Charter and Violence Against Women* (Vancouver: CASAC, 2003).

10 *Canadian Charter of Rights and Freedoms*, Part 1 of the *Constitution Act, 1982* being Schedule B to the *Canada Act* 1982 (UK), 1982, c. 11, s. 15 [*Charter*].

11 One example of a private law claim, framed in tort, is found in *Bonnie Mooney v. Solicitor General of Canada, the Attorney General & RCMP*. For information on the case, see online: www.rapereliefshelter.bc.ca/issues/bonnie_mooney_Tyee_03042004.html. Leave to appeal to S.C.C. denied, see *Mooney v. Canada (Attorney General)*, [2004] S.C.C.A. No. 428.

12 This is not to imply, of course, that sexual assault and sexual violence is not a dimension or component of "domestic violence." But to the extent that the issues of sexual assault and domestic violence have been treated somewhat distinctly in terms of feminist advocacy, service provision, and legal strategy, I am posing the question in this way, to explore why the former issue but not the latter has received so much *Charter* analysis.

13 See, for example, *R. v. Shearing*, [2002] 3 S.C.R. 33.

14 Sheila McIntyre, "Feminist Movement in Law: Beyond Privilege and Privileging Theory" in Radha Jhappan, ed., *Women's Legal Strategies in Canada* (Toronto: University of Toronto Press, 2002) at 42.

15 This point was raised by Fay Faraday, "Opening Comments" (Paper presented to LEAF Community Consultation, Toronto, February 2004) [unpublished] and furthered by LEAF initiatives such as the 2003–2004 colloquia on equality rights.

16 See, for example, Catharine MacKinnon, for a compelling analysis of the interconnection between violence against women and gender inequality. See also *Changing the Landscape*, above note 3, for an articulation of the links between gender, inequality, and violence.

17 The idea of a "gendered harm" has been advanced by various feminist scholars to capture the specific and gendered nature of the injuries associated with women's inequality. For an elaborated discussion of this concept see, for example, Robin West, "Jurisprudence and Gender" 55 U. Chi. L. Rev. 1 (1988); see also Adrian Howe, "The Problem of Privatized Injuries: Feminist Strategies for Litigation" in M. Fineman & N. Thadsen, eds., *At the Boundaries of Law: Feminism and Legal Theory* (New York: Routledge, 1991).

18 J. Conaghan, "Gendered Harms and the Law of Tort: Remedying (Sexual) Harassment" (1996) 16 Oxford J. Legal Stud. 407 at 408.

19 United Nations Fourth World Conference on Women, "United Nations' Beijing Declaration and Platform for Action — FWCW Platform for Action: Violence Against Women," online: www.un.org/womenwatch/daw/beijing/platform/violence.htm. This Platform for Action was adopted at the Fourth United Nations World Conference on Women, 1995.

20 See, for example, *R v. Osolin*, [1993] 4 S.C.R. 595 at paras. 165–66, Cory J.; *R v. McCraw*, [1991] 3 S.C.R. 72 at para. 29, Cory J.; *Janzen v. Platy Enterprises*, [1989] 1 S.C.R. 252 at para. 57, Dickson C.J. In *R. v. Mills*, [1999] 3 S.C.R. 668, the Supreme Court expressly foregrounded equality concerns, and a recognition of gender inequality in relation to sexual assault myths, in the battle over access to third party records (typically used to impugn victim credibility) in sexual assault trials.

21 *R. v. Lavallee*, [1990] 1 S.C.R. 842.

22 *Ibid.*

23 Sheila McIntyre has potently raised this same issue in her writing on the subject. See "Answering the Siren Call of Abstract Formalism with the Subjects and Verbs of Domination" in this volume. In McIntyre's words,

> There are stronger umbrella terms than "disadvantaged" for the situations of the groups in question. Dispossessed, disempowered, demonized, dehumanized, degraded, debased, demeaned, discredited. If a single generic is required, I propose, "oppressed." These more starkly violative verbs evoke an active subject and invite critical judgment, not pious abstractions about concern, respect and dignity, far less condescending pity about "the disadvantaged." They imply wrongdoing against the targets of discrimination; and leave little room for disagreement over whether the target should "feel" injured. The focus shifts from debates about

appropriate comparators to analysis of relations between excluders and excluded; stigmatizers and stigmatized; expropriator and dispossessed.

24 Most feminist researchers and writers, for example, resort to inserting a footnote which references the statistics demonstrating that men are overwhelmingly the perpetrators and women overwhelmingly the victims of this violence, in order to legitimate the use of gender-specific language to describe the problem. This appears to be necessary to defeat the increasing tendency to obscure this issue in gender-neutral language, a tendency which is related to the concomitant anti-feminist assertion that interpersonal violence simply "affects everybody" and should not be seen as a "women's issue."

25 For critical assessments of the Supreme Court's record with regard to s. 15 cases see Diana Majury, "The *Charter*, Equality Rights and Women: Equivocation and Celebration" (2002) 40 Osgoode Hall L.J. 297; and Sheilah Martin, "Balancing Individual Rights to Equality and Social Goals" (2001) 80 Can. Bar Rev. 299.

26 *Symes v. Canada*, [1993] 4 S.C.R. 695 [*Symes*].

27 *Native Women's Association of Canada v. Canada*, [1994] 3 S.C.R. 627 [*NWAC*].

28 *Thibaudeau v. Canada*, [1995] 2 S.C.R. 627 [*Thibaudeau*].

29 *Vancouver Society of Immigrant and Visible Minority Women v. M.N.R.*, [1999] 1 S.C.R. 10 [*Vancouver Society of Immigrant And Visible Minority Women*].

30 *Lovelace v. Ontario*, [2000] 1 S.C.R. 250 [*Lovelace*].

31 *Nova Scotia [Attorney-General] v. Walsh*, [2002] 4 S.C.R. 325 [*Walsh*].

32 *Gosselin v. Quebec (Attorney-General)*, [2002] 4 S.C.R. 429 [*Gosselin*].

33 *Newfoundland Treasury Board v. Newfoundland and Labrador Association of Public and Private Employees (N.A.P.E.)*, [2004] 3 S.C.R. 381 [*N.A.P.E.*].

34 *Auton (Guardian ad litem of) v. British Columbia (Attorney General)*, [2004] 3 S.C.R. 657 [*Auton*].

35 Many of the most favoured and frequently used terms in much of the literature are gender neutral. These include descriptors such as family violence, family abuse, domestic violence, intimate partner violence, violence and abuse and relationships, etc. Though I am critical of its limitations, I nevertheless continue at times to use the term domestic violence, because it has extensive currency. But more generally I aim to frame and identify the issue more specifically as one of men's violence against women and children. This does not, obviously, imply that it is a problem, which implicates all men, or all women for that matter, but it does describe the gender-specific reality of the vast majority of the problem.

36 These disciplines include, but are certainly not limited to, the field of psychology. For example, the burgeoning literature and industry being developed around victimization and trauma, especially in relation to sexual abuse in childhood, by and large expressly excludes a gender analysis and analyses the phenomenon and its effects as if they are unmediated by gender socialization, gender relations, and inequalities. See Lori Haskell, *First Stage Trauma Treatment: A Guide for Mental Health Professionals* (Toronto: CAMH, 2003), for some correction of this tendency by discussing trauma as it specifically affects women, and as it is connected to gendered violence.

37 In addition to an increasing number of published books on the subject, there is, for example, a proliferation of scholarly journals devoted exclusively to violence and abuse issues, including *Violence Against Women: An International and Interdisciplinary Journal* (Sage), *Journal of Interpersonal Violence* (Sage), *Trauma and Abuse*, *Violence and Victims* (Springer), and *International Journal of Victimology*, to name a few.

38 There is a direct and empirically-documented link between domestic violence and intimate femicide. In most cases of the killing of women by their male intimates, a previous history of physical abuse exists. For example, in 59 percent of all spousal homicide cases between 1991 and 2001, police were aware of a history of domestic violence between the accused and victim — and this refers only to those cases of domestic violence reported to the police (in fact, the majority are not). See Canadian Centre for Justice Statistics, *Family Violence in Canada: A Statistical Profile 2003* (Ottawa: Statistics Canada, 2003).

39 See, for example, "Post-traumatic Stress Disorder and the Perpetration of Domestic Violence," online: www.ncptsd.va.gov/publications/cq/v7/n2/riggs.html/. See also, Gillian Mezey, Loraine Bacchus, Susan Bewley, & Sarah White, "Domestic Violence, Lifetime Trauma and Psychological Health of Childbearing Women" BJOG: An International Journal of Obstetrics & Gynaecology, February 2005 at 197, abstract online: www.blackwell-synergy.com/links/doi/10.1111/j.1471-0528.2004.00307.x/abs.

40 In fact, an expanding recognition of this fact has been mirrored by an expanding literature on this interconnection. See, for example, Janet Mosher *et al.*, *Walking on Eggshells: Abused Women's Experiences of Ontario's Welfare System: Final Report of Research Findings from the Woman and Abuse Welfare Research Project* (April, 2004) online: DAWN Ontario http://dawn.thot.net/walking-on-eggshells.htm.

41 This concern was pointed out by Fay Faraday, above note 15.

42 *Granovsky v. Canada (Minister of Employment and Immigration)*, [2000] 1 S.C.R. 703.

43 *N.A.P.E.*, above note 33.

44 *Auton*, above note 34.

45 Most recently and comprehensively, the World Health Organization has released a report entitled *The Economic Dimensions of Interpersonal Violence*, which examines the problem of violence against women from a public health economics vantage point. Specifically, the report documents the ways in which the social problem of violence against women is also fundamentally an economic problem, insofar as it imposes major economic costs on nations the world over. The report documents that "some nations spend more than four percent of their Gross Domestic Product (GDP) on violence-related injuries, and low-income nations may be hardest hit. [For example] Colombia and El Salvador spend 4.3 percent of their GDP on violence-related expenditures — the highest of any nations. The United States spends 3.3 percent of GDP on violence-related matters." See H. Waters, Y. Rajkotia, S. Basu, J.A. Rehwinkel, & A. Butchart, *The Economic Dimensions of Interpersonal Violence* (Geneva: Department of Injuries and Violence Prevention, World Health Organization, 2004)

online: World Health Organization, www.who.int/violence_injury_prevention/
publications/violence/en/economic_dimensions.pdf.

46 There is also a rich US literature relating to violence against women, the state, and
the passage of the federal *Violence Against Women Act*, with particular reference to
the federal government's argument that it was entitled to legislate against this Act
because it affected interstate commerce. For the case striking down the civil rights
remedy afforded by *VAWA*, see *United States v. Morrison* (99-5) 169 F.3d 820, aff'd,
online: supct.law.cornell.edu/supct/html/99-5.ZS.html.

47 Denise Reaume, "Discrimination and Dignity," in this volume, reprinted from
(2003) 63 Louisiana L. Rev. 645.

48 L. Heise, M. Ellsberg, & M. Gottemoeller, "Ending Violence Against Women"
Population Reports, Series L, No. 11, December 1999, online: Baltimore, Johns Hop-
kins University School of Public Health, Population Information Program, www.
infoforhealth.org/pr/l11edsum.shtml.

49 And especially a criminal justice system which refrains from criminalizing women
who are reluctant witnesses by charging them with public mischief or obstruction
of justice, as some frustrated Crown Attorneys have done in relation to assaulted
women who have elected not to testify in the prosecution of domestic violence cases.

50 While I obviously reject the alignment of feminist goals with a right-wing "law and
order" agenda in this area, the punitive arm of the state does have critical role to
play in demonstrating social approbation of the conduct and in imposing individual
accountability. As one legal researcher has pointed out, in the majority of cases (and
those are only the relatively few which reach the criminal justice system), offenders
escape any significant sanctions. In her words, "[f]ew batterers ever see the inside of a
jail cell, even when convicted of a serious offense." See Cheryl Hanna, "The Paradox
of Hope: The Crime and Punishment of Domestic Violence" (1998) 39 Wm. & Mary
L. Rev. 1505 at 1523.

51 For examples of leading work in this area see R. E. Dobash *et al.*, *Changing Violent
Men* (Thousand Oaks: Sage Publications, 2000), and Edward Gondolf, *Batterer
Intervention Systems: Issues, Outcomes and Recommendations* (Thousand Oaks: Sage,
2002).

52 Martha McMahon & Ellen Pence, "Making Social Change: Reflections on Individual and Institutional Advocacy With Women Arrested For Domestic Violence"
(2003) 9 Violence Against Women 47.

53 The provision of adequate legal aid is, of course, a larger issue, but my point here is
simply to highlight the discriminatory and compounding effects of state failures in
relation to the experiences and needs of assaulted women.

54 See the story of Randy Isles' murder of his spouse, Gillian Hadley, discussed below.

55 Sheilah Martin, "Some Constitutional Considerations of Sexual Violence Against
Women" (1994) 32 Alberta L. Rev. 535 at 539 ["Constitutional Considerations"].

56 *Law v. Canada (Minister of Employment and Immigration)*, [1999] 1 S.C.C. 497 at
para. 88 [*Law*].

57 *Ibid.* at para. 88.

58   See Sheila McIntyre, "Answering the Siren Call of Abstract Formalism with the Subjects and Verbs of Domination," in this volume.

59   See, for example, Diane Pothier, "Connecting Grounds of Discrimination to Real Peoples' Real Experiences" (2001) 13 C.J.W.L. 37; Donna Greschner, "Does *Law* Advance the Cause of Equality?" (2001) 27 Queen's L J. 299.

60   See, for example, June Ross, "A Flawed Synthesis of the Law" (2000) 11 Const. Forum 74.

61   See Majury, above note 25.

62   See Gwen Brodsky, "Gosselin v. Quebec (Attorney General): Autonomy with a Vengeance" (2003) 15 C.J.W.L. 194 ["Autonomy"].

63   See, for example, Ross, above note 60.

64   *N.A.P.E.*, above note 33 at para. 38.

65   *Ibid.* at para. 51.

66   *Ibid.* at para. 46.

67   *Ibid.* at para. 56.

68   *Ibid.* at para. 58.

69   *Ibid.* at para. 84.

70   *Ibid.* at para. 88.

71   *Ibid.* at para. 88.

72   *Ibid.* at para. 88.

73   *Ibid.* at para. 95.

74   *Auton*, above note 34 at para. 41.

75   The exercise of trying to fit the brief but multi-layered fact pattern attached to the legal aid problem discussed at the LEAF community consultation into the test articulated in the *Law* decision, sharply illustrated the constrictions at the very first stage (that of defining the nature of the distinction/differentiation).

76   An interesting example of a successful legal action in private law enforcing a woman's right to police protection, specifically through the duty owed to warn her of the risk of a serial rapist, is found in *Doe v. Metropolitan Toronto (Municipality) Commissioners of Police* (1989), 58 D.L.R. (4th) 396 at 430 (Ont. H.C.J.), aff'd (1990), 74 O.R. (2d) 225 (Div. Ct.). For an analysis of this case see: Melanie Randall, "Sex Discrimination, Accountability of Public Authorities, and the Public/Private Divide in Tort Law: An Analysis of *Doe v. Metropolitan Toronto (Municipality) Commissioners of Police*" (2001) 26 Queen's L.J. 451.

77   G. Kristian Miccio, "Notes from the Underground: Battered Women, the State Conceptions of Accountability" (2000) 23 Harv. Women's L.J. 133 at 163 ["Notes From the Underground"].

78   This was pointed out in a feminist report submitted to the Ontario Women's Directorate focusing on risk assessment in cases of spousal homicide. See Lori Haskell, Maria Crawford, & Joanne Bacon, "Proposed Model/Framework for an Enhanced Response to Intimate Femicide: Final Report of Intimate Femicide Working Group" (Toronto: Ontario Women's Directorate, 2000) (unpublished, on file with author).

79   For an analysis of the *Charter* as a fundamentally liberal legal document see Andrew Petter & Allan Hutchinson, "Private Rights/Public Wrongs: The Liberal Lie of the

Charter" (1988) 38 U.T.L.J. 278, and Joel Bakan, *Just Words: Constitutional Rights and Social Wrongs* (Toronto: University of Toronto Press, 1997).

80 See *RWDSU v. Dolphin Delivery Ltd.*, [1986] 2 S.C.R. 573.

81 Robin West, "Groups, Equal Protection and Law" in Issues in Legal Scholarship: The Origins and Fate of AntiSubordination Theory: A Symposium on Owen Fiss' "Groups and the Equal Protection Clause" (2002) Article 8 at 2 ["Groups, Equal Protection and Law"].

82 *Ibid.* at 2.

83 *Ibid.*

84 See *Seneca College of Applied Arts and Technology v. Bhadauria*, [1981] 2 S.C.R. 281 [*Bhadauria*]. While *Bhaduaria* appears to foreclose the possibility of a common law action for discrimination there is evidence that some lower courts are open to a reconsideration, especially in relation to common law claims engaging issues of sexual harassment. In the US there has been judicial recognition of domestic violence as a distinct tort; when infused with a gender and discrimination analysis, this opens up another possibility for legal exploration and intervention to be pursued in the Canadian context.

85 *Castle Rock v. Gonzales et al.*, 366 F.3d 1093 (10th Cir. 2004).

86 See *Castle Rock v. Gonzales*, 545 U. S. (2005), decision available online at: www. supremecourtus.gov/opinions/04pdf/04-278.pdf. See also *"Castle Rock v. Gonzales* Brief of Amici Curiae National Coalition Against Domestic Violence, *et al.*," online: www.aclu.org/WomensRights/WomensRights.cfm?ID=17666&c=173.

87 *B.M. v. British Columbia (Attorney General)*, [2004] B.C.J. No. 1506 at para. 141 [*B.M.*].

88 *Ibid.* at 143.

89 *Ibid.* at para. 50.

90 *Doe v. Metropolitan Toronto (Municipality) Commissioners of Police* (1998), 39 O.R. (3d) 487 (Gen. Div.).

91 See Randall, "Sex Discrimination," above note 76 at 451–95 for an analysis of the case and its significance.

92 G. Kristian Miccio, "With All Due Deliberate Care: Using International Law and the *Federal Violence Against Women Act* to Locate the Contours of State Responsibility for Violence Against Mothers in the Age of *DeShaney*" (1998) 29 Colum. H.R.L. Rev. 641 at 645 ["Deliberate Care"].

93 See "Arlene May — Coroner's Inquest: Jury's Verdict and Recommendations" online: Ontario Women's Justice Network, www.owijn.org/archive/arlene3.htm; and "Hadley Inquest Jury Recommendations," online: Ontario Women's Justice Network, www.owijn.org/issues/w-abuse/hadley2.htm.

94 See, for example, the Recommendations by METRAC (Metro Action Committee on Violence Against Women and Children) and OAITH (Ontario Association of Interval Transition Houses), online: www.owijn.org/archive/arlene2.htm.

95 Ontario Death Review Committee, *Annual Report to the Chief Coroner, Case Review of Domestic Violence Deaths, 2002* (March 31, 2004), online: Government of Ontario,

www.mpss.jus.gov.on.ca/english/publications/comm_safety/DVDRC_Report_ 2003.pdf.

96 Brodsky, "Autonomy," above note 62.

97 *New Brunswick (Minister of Health and Community Services) v. G.(J.)*, [1999] 3 S.C.R. 46 [*G.(J.)*].

98 *Ibid.* at para 115.

99 *Gosselin*, Arbour J. (in dissent), above note 32 at para. 306.

100 *Gosselin, ibid*, Arbour J. (in dissent) at para. 318.

101 *Andrews v. Law Society of British Columbia*, [1989] 1 SCR 143 [*Andrews*].

102 Martin, "Constitutional Considerations," above note 55 at 537.

103 See Melina Buckley, "*Law v. Meiorin*: Exploring the Governmental Responsibility to Promote Equality under Section 15 of the *Charter*," in this volume.

104 Even the dismal example provided by *Gosselin* should not deter us from pursuing the strategy of pushing for an expanded conception of equality which imposes positive legal duties, because it has a profound political and educative function even if legal success on this front remains elusive for some time.

105 *Gosselin*, above note 32 at para. 83.

106 Only Bastarache J. declined to comment on this particular aspect in his much narrower s. 7 analysis.

107 *Dunmore v. Ontario (Attorney General)*, [2001] 3 S.C.R. 1016 [*Dunmore*].

108 *Gosselin*, above note 32 at para. 318.

109 *Ibid.* at para. 346.

110 *Ibid.* at para. 348.

111 Patricia Hughes, "A Constitutional Right to Legal Aid" (paper presented to LEAF conference, Toronto, May 2002) [unpublished]; and "The Gendered Nature of Legal Aid" in Frederick H. Zemans, Patrick J. Monahan, & Aneurin Thomas, eds., *A New Legal Aid Plan for Ontario: Background Papers* (Toronto: Osgoode Hall Law School, York University Centre for Public Law and Public Policy, 1997) at 29.

112 *G.(J.)*, above note 97.

113 *Auton*, above note 34 at para. 25 [emphasis added].

114 *The Convention on the Elimination of All Forms of Discrimination against Women* (*CEDAW*) adopted in 1979 by the UN General Assembly, online: www.un.org/ womenwatch/daw/cedaw/; *Beijing Declaration* and *Platform for Action*, Fourth World Conference on Women, 15 September 1995, A/CONF.177/20 (1995) and A/CONF.177/20/Add.1 (1995), online: www1.umn.edu/humanrts/instree/e5dplw. htm; *Vienna Declaration* and *Programme of Action* adopted by the World Conference on Human Rights on 25 June 1993, online: www.unhchr.ch/huridocda/huri-doca.nsf/(Symbol)/A.CONF.157.23.En?OpenDocument.

115 The supervisory body of the Convention is the Committee on the Elimination of Discrimination Against Women. This Committee is mandated with overseeing the implementation of *CEDAW* at the national level. It has the capacity to issue general comments and provide commentary in response to state reports on the implementation process.

116 Adopted by General Assembly Resolution 2200 A (XXI) of 16 December 1966, entry into force on 23 March 1976, in accordance with Article 49.

117 Including articles 6, 7, 12, 18, & 24 (protecting rights to life, from torture, from cruel or inhuman or degrading treatment or punishment, etc.).

118 See Miccio, "Notes from the Underground," above note 77; and Miccio, "Deliberate Care," above note 92.

119 Miccio, "Deliberate Care," *ibid.* at 683.

120 An excellent overview of some of these International legal authorities on state obligation to protect victims of domestic violence, written in support of a US law suit recently decided by the US Supreme Court, is the "Brief of International Law Scholars and Women's Civil Rights and Human Rights Organizations as Amici Curiae in Support of Respondents," *Town of Castle Rock, Colorado v. Jessica Gonzales*, Docket Number: 04-278, argued before the US Supreme Court, March 21, 2005. Decision available online: www.justia.us/us/545/04-278/case.html.

In this case the plaintiff sought and was denied a federal civil rights remedy for the police's failure to enforce a mandatory restraining order against her violent estranged husband, who then murdered their three girls.

The decision is a deeply disappointing and flawed one. Sara Buel, an expert on domestic violence law in the US, writes in the *Los Angeles Times* that, "What's stunning about the Supreme Court's decision is its reliance on Orwellian doublespeak. Even though Colorado specifically mandates that a police officer 'shall use every reasonable means to enforce' a restraining order, the court concluded that Colorado law was actually to permit officer discretion." Sara Buel, "Battered Women Betrayed" *Los Angeles Times,* 4 July 2005, online : www.ncdsv.org/publications_castlerock.html.

121 Martin, "Constitutional Considerations," above note 55 at 556.

122 West, "Groups, Equal Protection and Law," above note 81.

123 Mari Matsuda, "When the First Quail Calls: Multiple Consciousness as Jurisprudential Method" (1989) 11 Women's Rights Law Reporter 7 at 8.

nine

Women's Poverty is an Equality Violation

Gwen Brodsky & Shelagh Day

A. INTRODUCTION

Poverty is an urgent equality issue for women all over the world. Since the Depression of the 1930s, Canada has had a history of good social programmes, and those programmes have been a central egalitarian force in women's lives. Public health care, childcare, affordable public education, unemployment insurance, and social assistance have all provided ways of ameliorating women's inequality, shifting some of the burden of unpaid caregiving to the state, and making available more opportunities for women to engage in paid work, education, and community life. Income security programs like employment insurance and social assistance have also softened women's dependence on men, ensuring that women have independent income at crucial times in their lives.

But this has changed in Canada. For some time now we have been experiencing restructuring "Canadian-style," including a race to the bottom among provincial governments to eliminate the entitlement to social assistance, narrow eligibility rules, and reduce welfare benefits. In recent years, successive governments have hacked away at the social safety net. Cuts to social programmes have hurt women.

The picture of women's poverty and overall economic inequality is shocking in a country as wealthy as Canada. Women have moved into the paid labour force in ever-increasing numbers over the last two decades,[1] but they do not enjoy equality there: not in earnings, in access to nontraditional jobs and managerial positions,[2] or in benefits.[3] The gap between men's and women's full-time, full-year wages is due in part to occupational segregation in the workforce, which remains entrenched, and to the lower pay accorded to traditionally female jobs. Although the wage gap has decreased in recent years, with women who are employed on a full-time, full-year basis now earning about 71 percent of comparable men, part of the narrowing of this gap is due to a decline in men's earnings, rather than to an increase in women's.[4]

Women's annual average income from all sources is about 62 percent of men's.[5] This significant difference in income is partly attributable to the wage gap, but also partly attributable to the fact that women work fewer hours than men in the paid labour force because they cannot obtain full-time work[6] and because they carry more responsibility for unpaid caregiving duties.[7] In 1999, 41 percent of women, compared to 29 percent of men, held non-standard jobs[8] — that is, they were self-employed, had multiple jobs, or jobs that were temporary or part-time. These jobs are unlikely to be unionized and unlikely to provide pensions or benefits.[9]

Some groups of women in Canada are more marginalized than others in the labour force. Aboriginal women are heavily concentrated in low-paying sales, service, and clerical jobs. They also have higher unemployment rates and lower earnings levels than other women.[10] Women of colour have higher education levels than other women, but not better jobs and better earnings. Instead, they too have higher unemployment rates and lower earnings than other women and than their male counterparts.[11] Immigrant women also generally earn less than other women and initially accept employment for which they are overqualified. They are more likely than other women to be employed in manufacturing work.[12] Women with disabilities earn less than their male counterparts and less than other women in most age groups.[13]

Even though women's earnings are substantially lower than men's, women play a significant role in keeping their families out of poverty through their earnings. Without women's earnings, poverty rates would rise dramatically and the number of poor families would more than triple.[14] In addition to diminished rewards for their labour, women do not enjoy an equal share of wealth, including property, savings, and other resources.[15]

The extreme manifestation of women's economic inequality is women's disproportionate poverty. More women than men are poor. Between 1984 and 2003, the poverty rate for women fluctuated between 22.1 percent and 15.9 percent, always higher than the rate of poverty for men.[16]

Even the lower rate is still extremely high. It means that, in one of the wealthiest countries in the world, one in six women is living below the poverty line. Further, the overall poverty rates mask the high rates of poverty of particular groups of women.

Single mothers and other "unattached women" are most likely to be poor. In 2003, 49.4 percent of all unattached women and 58.8 percent of single mothers were living below the poverty line. Unattached men have significantly lower poverty rates.[17]

The shockingly high rate of poverty among single mothers is even higher when the figures are disaggregated by race and by the mothers' ages. In 1996, 73 percent of Aboriginal single mothers were living below the poverty line.[18] In 1998, 85.4 percent of single mothers under twenty-five were living in poverty.[19]

Also, Aboriginal women, immigrant women, women of colour, and women with disabilities are significantly more vulnerable to poverty than other women in Canada. In 2000, 42 percent of Aboriginal women, 29 percent of women of colour, and 35 percent of women who are recent immigrants (those who arrived between 1991 and 2000) were living below the poverty line.[20] Aboriginal women and women of colour also have higher rates of poverty and substantially lower incomes than their male counterparts.[21] Women with disabilities had a poverty rate of 26 percent in 2000.[22]

The fact that women are economically unequal to men, and more likely to be poor, is not mere coincidence. It is the result of women's work not being properly valued; of women being penalized because they are the principal caregivers for children, old people, men, and those who are ill or disabled; and of systemic discrimination in the workforce which devalues the work of women, and marginalizes women workers who are Aboriginal, of colour, immigrants, or disabled. Income and poverty data not only reveal a general picture of material inequality in relation to the distribution of the society's wealth. They show the lower value that is assigned to women, and women's work, and particularly to single mothers, racialized women, and women with disabilities.

In an article published by the *Canadian Journal of Women and the Law* in 2002,[23] we advanced the argument that a substantive approach to equality under the *Canadian Charter of Rights and Freedoms*[24] requires recognition of positive constitutional rights compelling governments to ensure that everyone has adequate food, clothing, and housing. To be clear, this is an interpretive argument. This is not a call to amend the *Canadian Charter* to add explicit references to social and economic entitlements, such as those that appear in the South African *Constitution*,[25] but rather an argument that equality rights guarantees are capable of doing this work. We argued more particularly that the idea of a hierarchy between civil and political rights and economic, social, and cultural rights comes from an outmoded constitutional paradigm — one which clings to a negative rights model of constitutional rights, envisioning them only as restraints on harmful state action.

We suggested that a formal conception of equality rights fits well within such an outmoded negative rights paradigm, but that a substantive conception of equality rights does not. Rather, substantive equality, by definition, requires governments to take positive steps towards remedying group disadvantage, including the poverty of women. We put forward an analysis of women's poverty as a sex equality issue on the basis that it is a manifestation of discrimination against women, that affects women, and particular groups of women disproportionately, by exacerbating every form of social and sexual subordination that women experience. We concluded that women's right to substantive equality must be understood to encompass a basic right to income security because without that security, profound deprivations of personal autonomy, and of physical and psychological integrity — which are incompatible with women's equality — result. A shorthand way of summarizing our position might be: social and economic rights are civil and political rights.

A primary focus of our 2002 article was the case of *Gosselin* v. *Quebec (Attorney General)*,[26] which at the time was pending in the Supreme Court of Canada. Louise Gosselin's was the first *Charter* case concerning social assistance to reach the Supreme Court of Canada.

Since the publication of our earlier article, judgment in the *Gosselin* decision was rendered. Louise Gosselin's claim was unsuccessful. However, the decision was divided, and the majority decision purported to turn on the sufficiency of the evidence rather than legal principle. Because of this, its importance as a precedent may be negligible. Nonetheless, certain theoretical issues emerged that will be of enduring importance, as the struggle to address the injustices caused by cutbacks to social programmes continues. One crucial issue, which arose in the context of the section 15 reasoning, is whether discrimination is only about stereotyping. The central goal of this paper is to comment on how the Court dealt with the issue of stereotyping, in light of the analysis advanced in our earlier article. For the future of constitutional jurisprudence and women's equality it is critically important that there was a consensus on the Court — albeit incompletely developed or applied — that equality is not confined to protecting individuals from group stereotypes. The paper also touches upon the Court's decision concerning the section 7 rights to life, liberty, and security of the person, which confirms that the door is open for the Court to recognize that the *Charter* encompasses a positive obligation to ensure that everyone has a subsistence income.

B. *GOSSELIN v. ATTORNEY GENERAL (QUEBEC)*: OVERVIEW OF THE DECISION

In 1984, the Quebec government altered its social assistance scheme in an effort to coerce young people into the labour force, through denial of the means of subsistence. Section 29(a) of the *Regulation Respecting Social Aid*[27] set the rate of welfare for adults between the ages of eighteen and thirty at roughly one-third of the regular rate paid to those thirty years of age and over. In dollar terms, the difference was $170 per month compared to $466 per month — $466 per month being the amount the Quebec Legislature had defined as "the bare minimum for the sustainment of life."[28] The monthly cost of proper nourishment alone was $152 per month.[29]

The under-thirties could increase their rate by participating in three different "employability programs." But the government's employability programs were structurally incapable of allowing all the under-thirty recipients to reach the regular rate of welfare, defined as necessary to meet basic needs. This was so because: not all of the programs provided participants with a full top-up to the basic level; there were temporal gaps in the availability of the various programmes to willing participants; welfare recipients who were illiterate or severely under-educated, or "over-educated," could not participate in certain programs; and only 30,000 program places were available for 75,000 under-thirty welfare recipients.

Although some people in the under-thirty age group were able to access employability programs through which they could get themselves back to the regular rate, for the vast majority, the regular rate was out of reach.[30]

Living on the reduced rate had severe physical and psychological effects. The reduced rate did not provide enough income to allow the men and women in the under-thirty group to meet basic needs for food, clothing, and shelter. They resorted to degrading and criminalized survival strategies, such as begging and petty theft. They were often homeless and malnourished. They experienced psychological stress, anxiety, and despair.

The reduced rate put women at risk in specific ways. For example, as a survival strategy, some young women on the reduced rate became pregnant and had children in order to become eligible for benefits at the regular rate of social assistance. A number of young women on the reduced rate engaged in prostitution, or accepted unwanted sexual advances to try to keep their apartments, to pay monthly expenses, such as heat and electricity, or to buy food.

The appellant Louise Gosselin brought a class action on behalf of herself and approximately 75,000 other young people who were affected by the regulation between 1985 and 1989. The constitutional issue before the Supreme Court of Canada was whether the challenged regulation violated section 7 or 15 of the *Charter*. Louise Gosselin's claim was rejected on all grounds.

As we have said, the decision was deeply divided. The section 15 decision was particularly close, a 5–4 split. In its section 15 decision, the majority ruled that cutting the social assistance rate of adults under thirty to a below-subsistence rate was not a violation of section 15. The five-judge majority identified the disagreement with respect to section 15 as not being about the "fundamental approach" to section 15 but rather about whether the claimant had discharged her burden of proof. Similarly, regarding the section 7 rights to life, liberty, and security of the person, the decision was split (7–2). That decision features a particularly strong dissenting opinion by Arbour J. concurred in by L'Heureux-Dubé J. As with section 15, the explanation of the majority for refusing the section 7 claim was that the evidence was insufficient, not that there is no constitutional right to social assistance.

C. DISCRIMINATION IS NOT ONLY ABOUT STEREOTYPES

1) Stereotyping

One of the traditional understandings of anti-discrimination and equality guarantees is that their purpose is to protect individuals from the evil of stereotyping. The insight that discrimination may result from reliance on stereotype is important. Women have often benefited from the norm against stereotyping, particularly in the employment context, by demonstrating their individual competence and thereby exposing the inaccuracy of generalized assumptions (stereotypes) about what women can and cannot do.

Similarly, in rental housing situations women have also benefited from the legally established principle that landlords are not permitted to refuse housing to single mothers based on a blanket assumption that single mothers do not pay their rent. Human rights jurisprudence says that the ability of prospective renters must be individually assessed, based on financial criteria, not negative group stereotype. Although this does nothing for the woman who cannot afford to pay for housing, it does afford some measure of protection for those who can afford to pay, but face stereotypes about their reliability.

As we argue elsewhere,[31] the challenged legislative scheme in the *Gosselin* case was discriminatory in the very way that discrimination has most traditionally been defined. It rested on a negative stereotype of people who are reliant on social assistance, and of young people reliant on social assistance in particular. Young people are particularly subject to the generalized assumption that laziness is at the root of their reliance on welfare. They are perceived to be the "sturdy beggars" who first appeared in the Elizabethan poor laws.[32] "Sturdy beggars" were the ones whom the parish was to punish if they did not work, while other indigents were to be fed and housed. In the *Gosselin* decision, various judges including LeBel J. addressed the problem of stereotyping. LeBel J. explained that withdrawing social assistance from young people was not related to the needs or abilities of welfare recipients under thirty years of age, but rather flowed from and reinforced a stereotype of social assistance recipients as "parasites." LeBel J. pointed out that young people are the first to feel the impact of an economic crisis in the labour market, and that the problem in Quebec in the economic crisis in the 1980s was not that young people latched on to social assistance because of laziness but rather that there were no jobs available.[33] The stereotype was disproved by numerous experts. One example identified by LeBel J. was the report of Professor Gilles Guérin in which he wrote, *inter alia* (at page 65):

> [TRANSLATION] An estimated proportion of 91% of young people (counting only those capable of working) perceive their situation on social aid as temporary and have a fierce desire to work, to have a "real" job, to collect a "real" wage, and to acquire socio-economic autonomy. An IQOP study shows that young people value being productive workers, that it is

preferable in their eyes to hold a job, even one that does not interest them, than to be unemployed. *The myth of the young social assistance recipient who is capable of working and is happy with social assistance is therefore completely false; work is what is most highly valued by the people around them, their friends and family and their neighbours, and by the young people themselves.*[34] [Emphasis added.]

Four of the five judges in *Gosselin* had no difficulty in perceiving the stereotype that was embedded in the regulation, of a young person as, by definition, lazy and unwilling to work. Louise Gosselin's story of having repeatedly tried and sometimes succeeded but other times failed at employment and job training, demonstrated the inaccuracy of the generalization. However, apparently the majority did not see this.

In the majority's view, the evidence established that the government's purpose was to help young adults achieve long-term autonomy,[35] by creating an incentive to compel young adults to participate in training programs that would increase their employability.[36] According to the majority, this purpose was not based on stereotype because it "corresponded to the actual needs and circumstances of individuals under 30,"[37] and was "an affirmation of their potential."[38] Although some under-thirty individuals may have fallen "through the cracks of the system and suffered poverty,"[39] this fact was not, in the majority's view, sufficient to establish discrimination.[40] The majority found that the negative financial incentive imposed on the under thirty group "was not imposed as a result of negative stereotypes."[41]

This conclusion is disturbing. The majority is guilty not only of refusing to closely scrutinize generalized and overly broad assumptions about young people's needs and capacities, and of failing to distinguish theoretical employability from a *de facto* crisis in the employment market, but also of embracing and perpetuating contempt for a vulnerable and historically marginalized group. However, the main point of this paper is not to argue that the majority should have recognized and rejected both the stereotype (of young welfare recipients as parasites) and the challenged regulation because it was poisoned by that stereotype. Rather, our main point is to reconsider the sufficiency of stereotyping as an understanding of what counts as discrimination, and to suggest that discrimination has other dimensions that should be more fully considered and developed.

There are various reasons why we should not treat stereotyping as the *sine qua non* of discrimination. One important reason is that insistence on proof of stereotyping can too easily slide into a requirement for proof of malicious intent, contrary to the well-established principle that proving discrimination does not necessitate proving bad motive. Even before the *Charter*, anti-discrimination law in Canada held that it was not necessary to prove that discrimination was intentional and ill-motivated, and acknowledged that discrimination could result from the adverse effects of a facially neutral rule. It is also settled law that discrimination may result from the adverse effects of a seemingly neutral system of rules and practices, or from a combination of seemingly neutral rules and blatant prejudice. And yet, a decision such as *Gosselin* shows that judges may have difficulty in perceiving a negative stereotype embedded in a rule that the respondent believes has been imposed for the claimant's "own good."

Further, stereotyping consists of an unfounded or mistaken generalization about a group that is applied to individual members of the group, denying their individual capacity or needs. However, some differences between groups, such as those relating to pregnancy, certain disabilities, and historic disadvantages experienced by some groups, are real and not mistaken. Nonetheless, we do not or at least should not accept those differences, which are real, and not the product of mistaken generalizations, as a legitimate basis for practices that have the effect of reinforcing and perpetuating marginalization, material inequality, and subordination.

There is an additional problem; namely, the insufficiency of the responses to stereotyping. The antidotes to stereotyping are usually thought to be facial neutrality, and where necessary, individual assessment. However, when the problem is that social programmes that are vital to women's equality are being eroded, and poverty-reducing benefits that were formerly taken for granted are being cut, facial neutrality and individual assessment are not effective responses. Neither a facially neutral welfare scheme nor individual assessment can provide any comfort to a woman, if the scheme has been eliminated or rates have been reduced for all recipients.

We are aided in our endeavour to de-centre stereotyping by the fact that in *Gosselin* the Court agreed that the identification of an underlying stereotype is not an essential element of discrimination. On behalf of the majority McLachlin C.J. said that the absence of stereotypical thinking is only one factor to be considered, and that stereotypical thinking need not always be present for discrimination to be established. Implicit in this comment is the recognition that there are other factors that can give rise to a finding of discrimination. Although McLachlin C.J. did not develop this point further, a door has been left open for developmental work to be done.

Claire L'Heureux-Dubé J., in her judgement, addressed the point, and there was no disagreement expressed by any member of the Court with her comment.

As we have noted, Supreme Court of Canada human rights jurisprudence[42] has never insisted on proof of stereotyping, intentional or otherwise. Sexual harassment is one example of a practice that has been found to be discriminatory, not because it is premised on a stereotype of women workers, but rather because it is an exercise of power, and a form of abuse, that reinforces women's inequality in their workplaces. Similarly, in *Meiorin*,[43] also known as the women firefighter's case, the Court held that a fitness standard which excluded many women from firefighting work and which had not been shown by the employer to be necessary to job performance, was discriminatory. If one digs deeply enough and examines the assumptions underlying the fitness standard that had been adopted, a sexist stereotype of who is a competent firefighter can be found, but this was not necessary to the Court's analysis.

In *Gosselin*, L'Heureux-Dubé J. points out that support for a fuller understanding of discrimination can be found in the Court's jurisprudence. As one example, she points to the Court's unanimous decision in *Law*[44] and notes that discrimination may result from differential treatment that reflects stereotyping "or otherwise has the effect of perpetuating or promoting the view that the individual is less capable, or less worthy of recognition or value as a human being or as a member of Canadian society."[45]

L'Heureux-Dubé J. states that the Court's concern for human dignity means that the equality guarantee "is concerned with physical and psychological integrity and empowerment,"[46] and the severe impairment of an extremely important interest — such as physical and psychological integrity — may itself be sufficient to ground a claim of discrimination. Applying the analysis to the facts of the *Gosselin* case, L'Heureux-Dubé J. concludes that section 29(a) was discriminatory because of the harm to physical and psychological integrity resulting from the fact of poverty and the constant fear caused by poverty. She concludes that Louise Gosselin was treated as less deserving of respect. In keeping with the point that human dignity is not only about stereotyping, but also about physical and psychological integrity, L'Heureux-Dubé J. also knits together the section 15 right to equality and the section 7 right to security of the person, opining that where, as in *Gosselin,* harm is severe enough to give rise to a breach of the right to security of the person, there will be *prima facie* grounds for a claim of discrimination.

By drawing out the section 15 purpose of preventing the violation of human dignity L'Heureux-Dubé J. helps us to understand why the denial of subsistence should be considered discrimination. Judging people based on group stereotype rather than individuality is only one possible manifestation of discrimination. A consideration of other ways in which essential human dignity may be violated, and other purposes of section 15, provides a leaping-off point from which to identify additional bases for recognizing that a denial of the means of subsistence should be understood to constitute discrimination.

In *Law*, the Court said:

> [the] purpose of section 15(1) is to prevent the violation of essential human dignity and freedom through the imposition of disadvantage, stereotyping, or political or social prejudice, and to promote a society in which all persons enjoy equal recognition at law as human beings or as members of Canadian society, equally capable and equally deserving of concern, respect and consideration."[47]

Taking a purposive approach, here then are some additional reasons for recognizing that denying social assistance to women — and men — in need is discriminatory.

2) Equality-Constituting Benefits[48]

Equality guarantees are concerned with ameliorating the inequality of major groups in society, including women. This can be understood either as another dimension of what it means to prevent the violation of essential human dignity through the imposition of disadvantage, or as another section 15 purpose; namely, the pursuit of substantive equality. The Supreme Court of Canada has used the terms "dignity" and "substantive equality" interchangeably.[49] Regardless, substantive equality's associations, more so than the term "human dignity," lie with group disadvantage, marginalization, and subordination. The concept of substantive equality recognizes that certain groups in society suffer from entrenched inequality, and that members of those groups are systematically denied basic rights, freedoms, and influence in the political process that others take for granted.

Government denial of the means of subsistence engages the section 15 goal of ameliorating group disadvantage. Poverty affects disadvantaged groups disproportionately. In Canada, the group "poor people" is disproportionately composed of Aboriginal peoples, women, people with disabilities, recent immigrants, people of colour, and single mothers. These groups have higher rates of poverty than average, some shockingly high. The economic inequality, as well as the social and political inequality, of members of these groups is part of the "fall-out" from complex and deeply rooted forms of discrimination. For this reason, it is necessary to deal with poverty as an aspect of sex, race, and disability discrimination. A central cause of poverty is entrenched patterns of systemic discrimination.

But poverty also exacerbates and deepens the inequality of members of already disadvantaged groups. Poor women get sex inequality writ large. As the facts in *Gosselin* showed, poverty forces women to accept sexual commodification and subordination to men in order to survive. They engage in prostitution or "survival sex" to get by. They lose autonomy to choose freely with whom and when they will have sex, and even whether and when they will have children. They are more vulnerable to rape, assault, and sexual harassment because they live in unsafe places, and they are not free to walk away from workplaces that are poisoned. They are not free to leave abusive relationships when destitution is the alternative. Poverty perpetuates women's under-representation in governments and in decision-making and their lack of political influence.

Laws or policies that perpetuate or hold in place the disproportionate poverty of women, Aboriginal peoples, people of colour, or people with disabilities necessarily engage section 15 because they maintain or reinforce the disadvantage of already disadvantaged groups. Effective protection of the groups who suffer social, political, and legal disadvantage in Canada requires governments to address structural or systemic forms of discrimination and their effects.

Viewed from a women's equality perspective, the section 15 guarantee of sex equality, on its own, imposes an obligation on governments to ensure that women are not denied income security adequate to meet basic needs.

We are supported in our analysis of social assistance as an equality-consituting benefit by the comments of the South African Constitutional Court in *Grootboom*.[50] The South African Constitutional Court held in *Grootboom* that it was a violation of the Constitution for the government to approve a development plan which entailed the displacement of homeless people, without making reasonable provision for people with no access to land, no roof over their heads, and who were living in intolerable situations or in crisis situations. The Court explained in *Grootboom* that, "The realization of rights to housing are "a key to the advancement of race and gender equality and the evolution of a society in which men and women are able to achieve their full potential."[31] The logic of the South African Constitutional Court's decision in *Grootboom*, particularly as it relates to the interdependency of social and economic rights and sex and race equality is also applicable in the Canadian context.

Although the South African Constitution contains explicit guarantees to social and economic rights, including access to housing, the absence of identical provisions in the *Canadian Charter* is not a persuasive reason for reading such entitlements out of the *Charter*. On the contrary, our argument is that in the name of realizing women's rights to equality, governments in Canada must provide social programmes, and that the obligation to do so is necessarily incidental to women's rights to equality, and to life, liberty, and security of the person.

A corollary is that an equality analysis is always relevant to poverty, even though there may be other rights that also apply. Seeing the group dimensions of poverty, and the layers of rights infringements it both causes and reflects, strengthens the claim that there is a societal obligation to address it. When we look at poverty through a group-based equality lens we open up new opportunities to see that poverty is more than an individual problem, because the patterns of who is poor are entrenched and reflect long-standing discrimination in the society. The analytical risk of failing to take account of the particular effects on disadvantaged groups is that the nature and extent of the harm of poverty-producing measures and their potential to reinforce pre-existing disadvantage and compromise fundamental interests may not be fully appreciated. Purely individualistic and gender-, race-, and disability-neutral explanations of poverty are just too simplistic. Commentary about group-based effects tells more of the truth of what is happening; it can show that there are qualitatively different impacts on certain groups; it may implicate a range of different constitutional rights and treaty provisions; and it can help to call into question the validity of the thesis that poverty is all about individual irresponsibility.

3) Equal Concern, Respect, and Consideration

Notwithstanding poverty's group dimensions, we do not suggest that the denial of the means of subsistence is an issue of discrimination only because the group, poor people, is disproportionately composed of members of historically disadvantaged groups, such as women.

Embracing the normative value of equality means that each person is understood to be inherently equal in dignity, equally worthy of respect, and equally entitled to share in the decision-making, responsibilities, opportunities, resources, and benefits of their society. Conditions that have the effect of obstructing equal participation by groups and individuals in the political, economic, and social life of their society, and equal enjoyment of widely agreed-to rights, including the rights to life, liberty, and security of the person, contravene the equality principle.

Poverty is one of the conditions that impedes equal participation in society, and puts people at greater risk with respect to the maintenance of life, health, and physical and psychological integrity.

In Canada, social assistance has been the established means of ensuring that even the poorest people are not deprived of the means of subsistence and totally banished from society. Social assistance is a fundamental social institution.

In a country as wealthy as Canada, for a government to refuse adequate social assistance to meet basic needs to a person in need is a blatant signal that that person is not regarded as equal in worth and dignity.

D. THE RIGHTS TO LIFE, LIBERTY, AND SECURITY OF THE PERSON

Section 7 of the *Canadian Charter* reads:

> Every person has the right to life, liberty and security of the person, and the right not to be deprived thereof, except in accordance with the principles of fundamental justice.

The Court's handling of section 7 of the *Charter* was also significant in *Gosselin*. The majority chose not to apply section 7 in this case, not because section 7 does not include positive obligations, but rather because, in the majority's view, the evidence was insufficient to warrant the application of section 7. The majority left the door open for future section 7 challenges based on government inaction, saying that "it would be a mistake to regard section 7 as frozen, or its content as having been exhaustively defined in previous cases," and stated that "[o]ne day section 7 may be interpreted to include positive obligations." [52] McLachlin C.J. said, "I leave open the possibility that a positive obligation to sustain life, liberty, or security of the person may be made out in special circumstances."[53]

Arbour J., with the concurrence of L'Heureux-Dubé, went much further. Even though her decision regarding the application of section 7 is a dissent and even though it is about section 7 rather than section 15, it is relevant to our topic, and it is a resource for future litigation because it "deconstructs the various firewalls"[54] that are said to preclude the courts from finding that there is a legal obligation on the state to provide basic protection for life, liberty, and security of the person. Much of the analysis is just as applicable to section 15 as it is to section 7 of the *Charter* because Arbour J. addresses centrally the question of negative versus positive rights and the requirement of state action. Here lies a terrain of dispute that is vital not only to section 7 jurisprudence but also to section 15 and to the *Charter* as a whole. Thus, Arbour J.'s comments have helpful implications for the interpretation of section 15.

Arbour J. acknowledges that it is commonly said that section 7 contains only negative rights of non-interference and therefore cannot be implicated, absent any overt state action. However, she examines this common view, framing the question this way:

> One should first ask, however, whether there is in fact any requirement, in order to ground a section 7 claim, that there be some affirmative state action interfering with life, liberty or security of the person, or whether section 7 can impose on the state a duty to act where it has not done so. (I use the terms "affirmative," "definitive" or "positive" to mean an identifiable action in contrast to mere inaction.) No doubt if section 7 contemplates the existence only of negative rights, which are best described as rights of "non-interference," then active state interference with one's life, liberty or security of the person by way of some definitive act will be necessary in order to engage the protection of that section. But if, instead, section 7 rights include a positive dimension, such that they are not merely rights of non-interference but also what might be described as rights of "performance," then they may be violable by mere inaction or failure by the state to actively provide the conditions necessary for their fulfillment. We must not sidestep a determination of this issue by assuming from the start that

section 7 includes a requirement of affirmative state action. That would be to beg the very question that needs answering.[55]

Arbour J. points out that it is often not clear whether the theory of negative rights underlying section 7 is intended to be one of general application, extending to the *Charter* as a whole, or one that applies strictly to section 7. She concludes that as a theory of the *Charter* as a whole, any claim that only negative rights are constitutionally protected is "patently defective."[56] She points to other *Charter* provisions that all impose positive obligations of performance on the state, including but not limited to: rights to vote (section 3), to trial within a reasonable time (section 11(b)), to be presumed innocent (section 11(d)), to trial by jury in certain cases (section 11(f)), to an interpreter in penal proceedings (section 14), and minority language education rights (section 23). She also points to leading sections 2 and 15 jurisprudence, noting that the Court has found there to be a positive dimension to the section 2(d) right to associate,[57] and that decisions like *Schachter v. Canada*[58] and *Vriend*[59] confirmed that "[i]n some contexts it will be proper to characterize section 15 as providing positive rights."[60]

Arbour J. also notes that in *G.(J.)*[61] the Court held that section 7 provided a positive right to state-funded counsel in the context of a child custody hearing. Arbour J. points out that Lamer C.J. put the proposition quite baldly saying: "'The omission of a positive right to state-funded counsel in s. 10 … does not preclude an interpretation of section 7 that imposes a positive constitutional obligation on governments to provide counsel in those cases when it is necessary to ensure a fair hearing.'"[62] Arbour says, "It is in the very nature of such obligations that they can be violated by mere inaction, or failure to perform the actions that one is duty-bound to perform."[63] Arbour J. emphasizes that it is important not to dilute the obvious significance of *G.(J.)* by attempting to locate the threat to security of the person in state action. She notes that Lamer C.J. said that it was not the *action* of the state in initiating the proceedings *per se* that gave rise to the potential section 7 violation, but rather the *failure* of the government to provide the appellant with state-funded counsel after initiating child protection proceedings.

Arbour then turns to *Dunmore*,[64] and points out that in that case, the Court held that "exclusion from a protective regime may in some contexts amount to an affirmative interference with the effective exercise of a protected freedom." Arbour J. finds that *Dunmore* confirms that state inaction — the mere failure of the state to exercise its legislative choice in connection with the protected interests of some societal group, while exercising it in connection with those of others — may at times constitute "affirmative interference" with one's *Charter* rights. Thus in certain contexts, Arbour J. reasons, the state is under a positive duty to extend legislative protections where it fails to do so inclusively.

Arbour J. says further that,

> ... it may well be that in order for such positive obligations to arise the state must first do *something* that will bring it under a duty to perform. But even if this is so, it is important to recognize that the kind of state action required will not be action that is causally determinative of a right violation, but merely action that "triggers," or gives rise to, a positive obligation on the part of the state. Depending on the context, we might even expect to see altogether different kinds of state action giving rise to a positive obligation under section 7. In the judicial context, it will be natural to find such a state action in the initiation by the state of judicial proceedings. In the legislative context, however, it may be more appropriate, following cases like *Vriend* and *Dunmore*, to search for it in the state's decision to exercise its legislative choice in a non-inclusive manner that significantly affects a person's enjoyment of a *Charter* right. In other words, in certain contexts the state's choice to legislate over some matter may constitute state action giving rise to a positive obligation under section 7.[65]

Arbour J. acknowledges that justiciability issues regarding the allocation of scarce resources may arise in some cases, but finds that this does not preclude consideration of the claim in this case; namely, that the state is under a positive obligation to provide basic means of subsistence to those who cannot provide for themselves. On the facts of this case, finds Arbour J., the Court does not need to determine what would satisfy a basic level of welfare because that determination had already been made by the legislature.[66]

Arbour J. concludes that "any acceptable approach to *Charter* interpretation — be it textual, contextual, or purposive — quickly makes apparent that interpreting rights contained in section 7 as including a positive component is not only possible, but necessary."[67]

Regarding the application of section 7 to the facts of the case, Arbour J. says,

> [A] minimum level of welfare is so closely connected to issues relating to one's basic health (or security of the person), and potentially even to one's

survival (or life interest), that it appears inevitable that a positive right to life, liberty and security of the person must provide for it.[68]

Arbour then explains that what is at stake in *Gosselin* is not exclusion from the *particular* statutory regime but, more basically, the claimants' fundamental rights to security of the person and life itself.[69] She finds that there was ample evidence that the "lack of government intervention 'substantially impeded' the enjoyment of their section 7 rights."[70] Government intervention was necessary to render their section 7 rights meaningful.

Arbour J. concludes that the state does have an obligation to address basic needs relating to the personal security and survival of indigent members of society.

Arbour J.'s opinion is a well-reasoned argument grounded in the Court's own jurisprudence, holding that there is a positive obligation on the state to provide a minimum level of assistance to persons in need. The state action requirement was satisfied by the existence of the *Social Aid Act* which was directed at addressing basic needs, but Arbour J. did not make the existence of the *Social Aid Act* a precondition for her decision. Rather, she said, "It is almost a cliché that the modern welfare state has developed in response to the obvious failure of the free market economy to provide these basic needs for everyone."[71]

There is a significant cross-over in logic between L'Heureux-Dubé J.'s section 15 opinion and Arbour J.'s section 7 opinion in *Gosselin*. Both judges are concerned to ensure that *Charter* rights are understood to have positive content so that the rights are capable of giving effect to the values that underlie the rights.

Arbour J.'s insights about the potential for section 7 rights to be violated by state inaction are more than a potential source of enrichment for section 7 of the *Charter*. They also provide a trajectory for equality jurisprudence, to move beyond stereotyping, to contend with women's inequality of conditions that cannot be properly addressed unless governments are understood to have positive obligations to act, and equality rights are understood to have positive content.

E. CONCLUSION

The decision in *Gosselin* provides clear openings for equality jurisprudence to move beyond the limitations of a conception of discrimination as consisting only of stereotyping, and of constitutional rights generally as consisting only of negative restraints on governments. The Court was unanimous in its agreement that discrimination may exist without the presence of a stereotype. In addition, the majority agreed that the door should be left open for a claim that governments have a positive obligation to sustain life, liberty, or security of the person. In the opinions of L'Heureux-Dubé and Arbour JJ. lie some particularly useful resources for the consolidation of an understanding of equality rights as imposing a positive obligation on governments to take measures to ensure that everyone has access to a subsistence income.

However, the story of *Gosselin* is not only a story of these agreements. It has also been felt as a direct insult to poor people, and few of those who are familiar with the record accept the majority's view that it was insufficient to support a finding of discrimination. The decision has caused great concern in Canada that the Court has decided to turn its back on the stark realities of the poorest residents, preferring to back away when equality guarantees raise distributive issues. Concerns about the divisions on the Court that *Gosselin* reveals, the underlying conceptual tensions, and the unsettled jurisprudence are also intensified by the fact that the composition of the Court has changed very significantly since *Gosselin*. Four of the judges who sat on *Gosselin*, including L'Heureux-Dubé and Arbour JJ., who wrote most imaginatively, are no longer on the Court. L'Heureux-Dube J. has retired and Arbour J. is now the High Commissioner for Human Rights at the United Nations.

The newly-composed Court is positioned at a crucial crossroads. Will it revert to a narrow, negative, formalistic conception of equality that is indifferent to material conditions of inequality and deprivation, or move forward with a substantive conception of equality? That choice will determine whether Canadian women's constitutional rights can speak to poverty. Should our Court choose the narrow, formalistic course, it will betray the inherent logic, and promise, of those rights.

This paper is primarily about equality theory rather than institutional relationships between courts and governments. However, in closing, a word about institutional responsibilities may be in order. The purpose of having constitutional equality guarantees is not only to establish a mechanism for judicial review. The point is to set a standard that governments agree to live up to, whether or not they are taken to court. In Canada this is declared by section 32 of the Constitution, which states that the *Charter* applies to the Parliament and the government of Canada, and to the legislature and governments of the provinces and the territories, in all matters within their authority.

The result of adopting a constitutional guarantee of equality, in any country in the world, should be that governments monitor and assess their own legislative programmes and decisions about resource allocation, to ensure that they do not make women worse off, but rather improve their situation.[72] Unfortunately, women in Canada have not been able to count on governments to engage in voluntary compliance.[73] On the contrary, governments in Canada have persistently refused to reverse the train of neo-liberal economics and social programme cutbacks, even though they are well aware of the implications of their conduct for women's equality, and even though they have been criticized for the harms caused by these policies by United Nations treaty bodies.[74] In such a circumstance of blatant government refusal to live up to their rights obligations, women should without doubt be able to turn to the domestic constitutional human rights framework for a principled determination of their rights and remedies, and for assistance in recalling governments to the equality-promoting tasks that governments agreed to when they made the commitment to women's equality.

As Canada implements neo-liberal economic formulas, distributional fairness is out of fashion. At such a time, courts, which should have a longer view, have a heightened obligation not to turn their backs on the human rights of the most vulnerable groups. However, recently, Louise Arbour, speaking in Canada in her new role as United Nations High Commissioner for Human Rights, expressed her concern about the "timidity" of the Canadian judiciary in tackling the claims emerging from the right to be free from want.[75] We share her concern.

ENDNOTES

1   Statistics Canada, *Women in Canada 2005: A Gender-Based Statistical Report* (Ottawa: Statistics Canada, 2005) at 103 [*Women in Canada 2005*].

2   *Ibid.* at 113. *Women in Canada 2005* notes that "[t]he majority of employed women continue to work in occupations in which women have traditionally been concentrated. In 2004, 67 percent of all employed women were working in teaching, nursing and related health occupations, clerical or other administrative positions and sales and service occupations." The report also notes that "women continue to account for large shares of total employment in each of these occupational groups. In 2004, women made up 87 percent of nurses and health-related therapists, 75 percent of clerks and other administrators, 65 percent of teachers, 57 percent of those working in sales and service." The report also notes that "women tend to be better represented in lower-level positions as opposed to those at more senior levels. In 2004 women made up only 22 percent of senior managers, whereas in 1996, the figure had been 27 percent" (at 113).

3   *Ibid.* at 279. *Women in Canada 2005* states that in 2003 private employment-related retirement pensions provide 26 percent of the income of senior women, as opposed to 41 percent of the income of senior men. While payments from public pension plans provide about the same percentage of the income of senior women and men, since benefit amounts are tied to earnings senior women receive less per year than senior men. Monica Townson also notes in *Independent Means: A Woman's Guide to Pensions and a Secure Financial Future* (Toronto: Macmillan, 1997) at 98–100 that pension rules in the 1970s and 1980s that discriminated against women by requiring them to work longer to be eligible for a pension or to retire earlier than men, still have a lingering effect both on the amount of women's pension benefits and on access to a pension because when the rules were changed those changes were not retroactive.

4   *Women in Canada 2005, ibid.* at 139. See also Isabella Bakker, "Introduction: The Gendered Foundations of Restructuring in Canada" in Isabella Bakker, ed., *Rethinking Restructuring: Gender and Change in Canada* (Toronto: University of Toronto Press, 1996) at 13–14; Pat Armstrong, "The Feminization of the Labour Force: Harmonizing Down in a Global Economy" in Bakker, *Rethinking Restructuring* at 29–54. See also Katherine Scott & Clarence Lochhead, *Are Women Catching Up in the Earnings Race?* (Ottawa: Canadian Council on Social Development, 1997) at 2. Scott & Lochhead state that "[p]reliminary analysis shows that the women who made wage gains over the last decade were the beneficiaries of a pool of good jobs in the health, education and social service sectors. However, as the structure of the economy continues to change, with the continuing polarization of job opportunities, there is a real danger that women's economic advances will be halted. And such a situation would herald greater economic insecurity for all Canadians."

5   *Women in Canada 2005, ibid.* at 133.

6   In 2004, 26 percent of part-time women workers indicated that they wanted full-time work but could not find it. See *ibid.* at 109.

7 Women's care of children affects their participation in employment and, consequently, their incomes. Women with pre-school-aged children are less likely than those with school-aged children to be employed. In 2004, 67 percent of women with children under age six were employed, compared to 77 percent of women with children aged six to fifteen. *Ibid.* at 105. Single mothers are less likely than women in two-parent families to be employed. In 2004, 68 percent of single mothers with children under sixteen were employed, compared to 73 percent of women in two-parent families with children the same age. *Ibid.* at 106.

8 *Ibid.* at 110–11.

9 Monica Townson, "Non-Standard Work: The Implications for Pension Policy and Retirement Readiness," report from the Women's Bureau, Human Resources Development Canada, 1996 at 1 & 3 [unpublished].

10 *Women in Canada 2005*, above note 1 at 198–99.

11 *Ibid.* at 223–28.

12 *Ibid.* at 224–25.

13 *Ibid.* at 296.

14 *Ibid.* at 142.

15 Bakker, "Introduction: The Gendered Foundations of Restructuring in Canada," above note 4 at 18–19; Lisa Philipps, "Tax Policy and the Gendered Distribution of Wealth," in Bakker, *Rethinking Restructuring*, above note 4 at 141–62.

16 Statistics Canada, Persons in low income before tax, by prevalence in percent. Source CANSIM table 202-0802 and Catalogue no. 75-202-XIE, online: www40.statcan.ca/l01/cst01/famil41a.htm (accessed: 15 December 2005).

17 *Ibid.*

18 *Women in Canada 2000: A Gender-Based Statistical Report* (Ottawa: Statistics Canada, 2000) at 259.

19 National Council of Welfare, *Poverty Profile 1998* (Ottawa: National Council of Welfare, 2000) at 32.

20 *Women in Canada 2005*, above note 1 at 201, 252, & 226.

21 *Ibid.* at 200, 199, 253, & 252. In 1996, 43 percent of Aboriginal women were living in poverty, compared to 35 percent of Aboriginal men and 20 percent of non-Aboriginal women. Wherever their place of residence, the incomes of Aboriginal women were less than those of Aboriginal men. In 2000, 29 percent of visible minority women were living in poverty, compared to 28 percent of visible minority men, and 16 percent of other women. In 2000, the average incomes of visible minority women were 90 percent of their male counterparts.

22 *Ibid.* at 297. See also G. Fawcett, *Living with Disability in Canada* (Ottawa: Human Resources Canada, 1996) at 131. Similar documentation of this pattern of women's poverty can be found in Shelagh Day & Gwen Brodsky, "Beyond the Social and Economic Rights Debate: Equality Speaks to Poverty" (2002) 14:1 Canadian Journal of Women and the Law/Revue Femmes et Droit 185 at 190–93 ["Beyond the Social and Economic Rights Debate"] and in the 2004 report of the Canadian Feminist Alliance for International Action entitled *A Decade of Going Backwards: Canada in the Post-Beijing Era*, online: www.fafia-afai.org/docs/B10_shadow_10CCE.6.doc (date

accessed: 30 September 2005). That report was authored by Shelagh Day & Natalie McMullen.

23   "Beyond the Social and Economic Rights Debate," *ibid*.

24   *Canadian Charter of Rights and Freedoms*, Part I of the *Constitution Act, 1982*, being Schedule B to the *Canada Act 1982* (U.K.), 1982, c. 11.

25   *Constitution of the Republic of South Africa, 1996*.

26   *Gosselin v. Quebec (Attorney General)*, [2002] 4 S.C.R. 429 [*Gosselin*].

27   *Regulation Respecting Social Aid*, R.R.Q., c. A-16, r. 1, s. 29(a).

28   *Gosselin*, above note 26 at paras. 251 and 285, Bastarache J. Similarly, at para. 334, Arbour J. put it this way: "This is the amount that was deemed by the legislature itself to be sufficient to meet the 'ordinary needs' of a single adult." At para. 372, Arbour J. stated:

> On $170/month, paying rent is impossible. Indeed, in 1987, the rent for a bachelor apartment in the Montreal Metropolitan Area was approximately $237 to $412/month, depending on the location. Two-bedroom apartments went for about $368 to $463/month. As a result, while some welfare recipients were able to live with parents, many became homeless. During the period at issue, it is estimated that over 5,000 young adults lived on the streets of the Montreal Metropolitan Area. Arthur Sandborn, a social worker, testified that young welfare recipients would often combine their funds and share a small apartment. After paying rent however, very little money was left to pay for the other basic necessities of life, including hot water, electricity and food. No telephone meant further marginalization and made job hunting very difficult, as did the inability to afford suitable clothes and transportation.

29   *Ibid*. at para. 130, L'Heureux-Dubé J.

30   *Ibid*. at para. 130, L'Heureux-Dubé J. Similarly, at para. 371, Arbour J. stated that

> [t]he various remedial programs put in place in 1984 simply did not work: a startling 88.8 percent of the young adults who were eligible to participate in the programs were unable to increase their benefits to the level payable to adults 30 and over. In these conditions, the physical and psychological security of young adults was severely compromised during the period at issue." At para. 254, Bastarache J. stated that "any reading of the evidence indicates that it was highly improbable that a person under 30, with the best intentions, could at all times until he or she was 30 years old be registered in a program and therefore receive the full subsistence amount."

31   Gwen Brodsky, "*Gosselin v. Quebec (Attorney General)*: Autonomy With a Vengeance" (2003) 15 Canadian Journal of Women and the Law 194. See also Shelagh Day, "Majority Embraces Stereotype of Poor" in Jurisfemme (Newsletter of the National Association of Women and the Law) vol. 22, Winter 2003, online: www.povertyandhumanrights.org/html/centrepubs/gosselinopfinal.pdf (accessed: 15 December 2005).

32   The *Poor Law* of 1601 placed every English parish under an obligation to relieve the aged and ill and to provide work for the able-bodied poor. See *An Act for the Relief of*

the Poor, 1601, 43 Eliz., ch. 2 (Eng.) reprinted in 7 Stat. At Large (Eng. 37-37) (Danby Pickering ed., 1762). A 1697 amendment to the English poor laws aimed to distinguish the "genuinely deserving" recipients from "the idle, sturdy, and disorderly beggars." See *An Act for Supplying Some Defects in the Law for the Relief of the Poor of This Kingdom, 1696–97*, 8 and 9 Will. 3, ch. 30, § 2 (Eng.), reprinted in 10 Stat. At Large (Eng) 106 (Danby Pickering ed., 1762) amending *Poor Relief Act, 1662*, 14 Car. 2, ch. 12 (Eng., reprinted in 8 Stat. At Large (Eng.) 94–95 (Danby Pickering ed., 1762). A provision of the Act required all people who received poor relief to wear the letter "P" in red or blue cloth on the right shoulder of their clothing. Refusal to wear the badge resulted in a reduction or elimination of relief, or imprisonment with hard labour for up to twenty days. This amendment introduced the notion, that still has currency today, that it is legitimate to subject beneficiaries of public relief to stigmatizing and humiliating treatment, both as a means of deterring the poor from relying on public relief, and in order to ensure that the non-deserving poor do not receive it.

33 *Gosselin*, above note 26 at para. 407, Lebel J.

34 *Ibid.* at para. 405.

35 *Ibid.* at paras. 27, 43–44, and 65.

36 *Ibid.* at paras. 41–42

37 *Ibid.* at para. 38.

38 *Ibid.* at para. 19.

39 *Ibid.* at para. 54.

40 *Ibid.* at paras. 55–56.

41 *Ibid.* at para. 52, McLachlin C.J.

42 By "human rights jurisprudence" we mean case law arising under both statutory human rights instruments and the equality provisions of the *Charter*.

43 *British Columbia (Public Service Employee Relations Commission) v. BCGSEU*, [1999] 3 S.C.R. 3.

44 *Law v. Canada (Minister of Employment and Immigration)*, [1999] 1 S.C.R. 497 [*Law*].

45 *Gosselin*, above note 26 at para. 116, L'Heureux-Dubé J.

46 *Ibid.* at para. 121.

47 *Law*, above note 44 at para. 88.

48 In "Dignity, Equality and Second Generation Rights" in *Poverty: Rights, Social Citizenship*, and *Governance*, eds. Boyd, Brodsky, Day, & Young, forthcoming from UBC Press, 2006, Denise Réaume argues that social assistance is a "dignity-constituting benefit." She asserts that the underlying s. 15 value of human dignity grounds an entitlement to social assistance because poverty is so profoundly threatening to identity and autonomy. Dignity can be dishonoured in different ways. But, importantly, the dignity of a person is dependent on material conditions that permit her to participate in social, political, and economic life in her society as an equal member; and to make choices about her life, including sexual and reproductive choices, as an autonomous creature. About social assistance, Réaume writes:

> Social assistance recognizes that those unable to find adequate employment nevertheless need a roof over their heads and food on the table. The alternative

is life on the streets, having to beg or pilfer, exclusion from most social activities, subjection to the constant risk of violence and disease, the waste of one's talents, and the likelihood of premature death. Someone confined to a hand-to-mouth existence can form no meaningful life plan; she is driven by necessity. The impairment of autonomy is comprehensive and extreme. The additional psychological toll of living such a life, including constantly dealing with the misunderstanding and prejudice of others, is staggering. The need created by poverty is ... urgent; its alleviation is ... integral to human dignity.

Our thinking about "equality-constituting benefits," and our adoption of this term, is influenced by Réaume's work.

49   See, for example, *Nova Scotia (Workers' Compensation Board) v. Martin; Nova Scotia (Workers' Compensation Board) v. Laseur*, [2003] 2 S.C.R. 504 at para. 85.

50   *RSA and others v. Grootboom* (2001) (1) South African Law Reports 46 (Const. Ct.).

51   *Ibid.* at para. 23.

52   *Gosselin*, above note 26 at para. 82.

53   *Ibid.* at para. 83.

54   *Ibid.* at para. 309.

55   *Ibid.* at para. 319.

56   *Ibid.* at para. 320.

57   *Dunmore v. Ontario (Attorney General)*, [2001] 3 S.C.R. 1016 [*Dunmore*].

58   *Schachter v. Canada*, [1992] 2 S.C.R. 679 [*Schachter*].

59   *Vriend v. Alberta*, [1998] 1 S.C.R. 493.

60   *Schachter*, above note 58 at 721.

61   *New Brunswick (Minister of Health and Community Services) v. G.(J.)*, [1999] 3 S.C.R. 46.

62   *Gosselin*, above note 26 at para. 324.

63   *Ibid.*

64   *Dunmore*, above note 57.

65   *Gosselin*, above note 26 at para. 329.

66   *Ibid.* at para. 334.

67   *Ibid.* at para. 335.

68   *Ibid.* at para. 358.

69   *Ibid.* at para. 368.

70   *Ibid.* at para. 370.

71   *Ibid.* at para. 383.

72   Ken Norman, "The Charter as a Barrier Against Welfare Roll Backs: A Meditation on the 'Difference Principle' as a 'Bedrock Value' of the Canadian Democratic Project" in *Poverty: Rights, Social Citizenship and Governance*, above note 48.

73   This is a point that Mary Eberts has made in various meetings of equality-seeking groups and lawyers in Canada, including at the 2003 annual meeting of the Court Challenges Programme in Winnipeg, Manitoba.

74   See *Concluding Observations of the Committee on Economic, Social and Cultural Rights: Canada*, UN CESCR, 1998, UN Doc. E/C.12/1/Add.31 at paras. 23, 28,

and 54; *Concluding Observations of the Human Rights Committee: Canada,* UN Doc. CCPR/C/79/Add.105 (1999) at para. 20; *Committee on the Elimination of Discrimination Against Women, Concluding Observations of the Committee: Canada* (A/58/38), 2003, at paras. 357–58.

75   Louise Arbour, United Nations High Commissioner for Human Rights, LaFontaine-Baldwin Symposium 2005 Lecture, online: www.lafontaine-baldwin.com/lafontaine-baldwin/e/2005_speech_1.html (accessed: 15 December 2005).

ten

The Supreme Court, the *Law* Decision, and Social Programs:

THE SUBSTANTIVE EQUALITY DEFICIT

Judith Keene[1]

A. INTRODUCTION

Recently, there has been a growing concern among many advocates[2] about the frequency with which the Supreme Court has used the language of equality to deny the claims of equality-seekers, producing a body of decisions that narrows the scope of section 15, imports into it issues that should arise only under section 1, and seems to limit its application to situations in which formal inequality can be demonstrated. In large part, this result has been associated with the effect of the *Law*[3] decision on the development of section 15 of the *Charter*.[4]

Prior to the *Law* decision, the Supreme Court's section 15 decisions had been proceeding cautiously in the direction indicated by substantive equality, with the high point being the decision in *Eldridge v. British Columbia (Attorney General)*.[5] In *Eldridge*, the Court found that the denial of interpreter services by a provincial health care system breached the equality rights of deaf users of the system and was not saved by section 1. The Court rejected an argument that government inaction was not constitutionally reviewable.

While the *Eldridge* decision was unanimous, a number of the Court's other section 15 decisions clearly demonstrated that a minority of the Court was alarmed by the implications in the Canadian context of the right to equality "without discrimination."[6] The *Law* decision was an attempt to create an approach to section 15 that all members of the Supreme Court could live with. Unfortunately, that anxiety about section 15's implications is obviously still felt, at present by a majority of the Court. Because the utility of the *Law* analysis as a vehicle to promote substantive equality depends entirely on the individual judge's understanding of the concept and commitment to it, *Law* can and has been used by all members of the Court as a rationale for decisions that are philosophically poles apart.

The most challenging test of judicial reasoning and commitment to substantive equality arises in the context of the redistributive implications of section 15. The Court's discomfort and divisions are nowhere more evident than in cases brought by the most disadvantaged equality claimants; those who have been excluded, despite personal characteristics and circumstances that should qualify them for assistance, from government programs designed to ameliorate poverty and disability. The decisions of the Court, in these areas in particular, feature few statements of principle. Principles that are expressed are not applied, or are claimed as the basis of both majority and dissenting opinions, so that we are left to guess what unstated principles might be at play. The Court is obviously struggling with section 15, and at this point, it has given us only a list of things to consider when trying to predict what will be considered discriminatory. At present, the only certainty is that a section 15 claim is not likely to be successful, particularly one in respect of government benefit programs.

Using a broad definition of "government benefit programs" the important cases to date in addition to *Law* itself are *Granovsky v. Canada (Minister of Employment and Immigration)*,[7] *Gosselin v. Quebec (Attorney General)*,[8] *Hodge v. Canada (Minister of Human Resources Development)*,[9] *Auton (Guardian ad litem of) v. British Columbia (Attorney General)*,[10] and *Newfoundland (Treasury Board) v. N.A.P.E.*[11] Because it displays most of the current problems, I have chosen the *Gosselin* decision for detailed examination.

This paper will

- discuss the decision in *Gosselin v. Quebec (Attorney General)*,
- briefly outline the more generous and liberal approach used by the Supreme Court in dealing with the concept of discrimination in human rights legislation, and illustrate the effect of that approach in *Hutchinson* and *Gwinner*, cases involving complaints of discrimination in respect of government benefits, and
- summarize some of the current difficulties, making some suggestions as to arguments that may be made in section 15 government benefit cases in the future.

B. *GOSSELIN v. QUEBEC (ATTORNEY GENERAL)*

In a decision handed down on 19 December 2002, the Supreme Court of Canada dismissed the appeal in *Gosselin v. Quebec (Attorney General).*[12] Ms. Gosselin challenged a Quebec *Social Aid Act* regulation under sections 7 and 15 of the *Canadian Charter of Rights and Freedoms*, and section 45 of the *Quebec Charter of Human Rights and Freedoms*.

Section 29(a) of the Quebec *Regulation respecting social aid*[13] made the amount of benefits for single "employables" under age thirty conditional on participation in "employability" programs. Section 29(a) of the regulation set the base amount of welfare payable to persons under the age of thirty at one-third of the base amount payable to those thirty and over. This reduced welfare for those between eighteen and thirty to $170 a month. Participation in one of three education or work experience programs allowed people under thirty to increase their welfare payments to either the same as, or within $100 of, the base amount payable to those thirty and over.

Gwen Brodsky and Shelagh Day summarize some of the effects of the regulation:[14]

... the effects on young adults of the section 29(a) cuts were devastating, from malnutrition, to being forced into demeaning survival strategies, to depression, despondency, and acute psychological stress.

For the young women in the group there were also gender specific effects. As a survival strategy, some young women on the reduced rate bore children in order to become eligible for benefits at the regular rate. Women who were pregnant while on the reduced rate were particularly likely to have low birth-weight babies, who are known to have a high incidence of health and learning problems. According to accounts of the Montreal Dietary Dispensary, the nutritional status of some of these pregnant women was comparable to that of pregnant women in Holland during the Great Famines of the World War II period.

A number of young women on the reduced rate engaged in prostitution, or accepted unwanted sexual advances to try to keep their apartments, to pay monthly expenses, such as heat and electricity, or to buy food. The appellant, Louise Gosselin, was no exception. She had to resort to what the trial judge described as "degrading ways of surviving." She exchanged her sexual availability for shelter and food; she engaged in prostitution to get money to buy clothes so that she could look for a job; she survived an attempted rape by a man from whom she was obtaining food; she was sexually harassed by male boarders when renting a room in a mixed Boarding House.

Louise Gosselin sued on behalf of a class of persons under thirty who were affected by the regulation between 1985 and 1989 (the year the impugned scheme was replaced by legislation that no longer made this age-based distinction). She sought a declaration of invalidity and an order that Quebec pay the members of the class the difference between what they receive and what they would have received in social assistance had the regulation not created the differentiation.

A five-judge majority of the Supreme Court of Canada found that the regulation did not infringe section 15 of the *Charter*. L'Heureux-Dubé, Bastarache, Arbour, and LeBel JJ., in dissent, found that section 15 was breached, and that the breach was not saved by section 1. A seven-judge majority found that the facts did not establish a breach of section 7, although six of these found that section 7 could encompass "a positive obligation to sustain life, liberty, or security of person," given the right facts. Justices L'Heureux-Dubé and Arbour, in dissent, found that the regulation violated section 7 by depriving those to whom it applied of their right to security of the person, contrary to the principles of fundamental justice. Only Justice Bastarache found that section 7 was inapplicable in situations that do not involve the judicial system or its administration.

Chief Justice McLachlin, for Justices Gonthier, Iacobucci, Major, and Binnie, made it clear that her failure to recognize a breach of sections 15 and 7 was purely fact-based.[15] Justice LeBel also clearly rejected the section 7 claim on facts alone. The recognition by the majority that both section 15 and section 7 could be implicated in regard to the adequacy of welfare is encouraging in respect of the possibility of success in future cases. However, there are certainly indications that establishing future claims will be an uphill struggle, since the basis on which evidence was rejected is arguably no clearer to most readers than it was to the dissenting Justices, and the problem has not been addressed by the majority in subsequent cases.[16]

The section 15 decision was a close one: a five-to-four split.

1) The Majority Decision

Chief Justice McLachlin delivered the majority judgment, for Justices Gonthier, Iacobucci, Major, and Binnie. The lengthy majority decision illustrates how the *Law* analysis may be used to define substantive inequality out of existence. Briefly, McLachlin C.J. found that Ms. Gosselin and the group she represented

- did not qualify for section 15 protection. This exclusion was effected by confining the inquiry to age discrimination, while ignoring the factual context and other personal characteristics of the group. Refusing to recognize intersecting grounds of discrimination is a problem that predates *Law*, but *Law* is the source of this kind of narrow focus applied to enumerated grounds.
- suffered no adversity, despite the acknowledgement that even those able and willing to participate in the impugned scheme could be reduced to attempting to survive on $170 a month. This finding was reached by rejecting the evidence that was rejected by the trial judge (but not by the dissenting Supreme Court Justices) and allowing a focus on the alleged motives of the government to displace consideration of the impact on the affected group. The last-noted problem is a clear product of the *Law* analysis.

Finding that the claimant had met the first two parts of the *Law* test, McLachlin C.J. went straight to the four "factors" identified in *Law* as relevant to ascertaining whether a distinction is discriminatory:

i)   pre-existing disadvantage;
ii) relationship between grounds and the claimant's characteristics or circumstances;
iii) ameliorative purposes or effects; and
iv) the nature of the interest affected.

McLachlin C.J. found that there was nothing to suggest that people in the eighteen to thirty age group in Quebec had been treated historically as less worthy than older people, and that there was "no reason to believe" that they "are or were particularly susceptible to negative preconceptions.... If anything, people under thirty appear to be advantaged over older people in finding employment."[17]

McLachlin C.J. arrived at this assessment by declining to consider the evidence of the stereotyping and vulnerability of welfare recipients, because "[t]he ground of discrimination upon which she founds her claim is age.... Re-defining the group as welfare recipients aged 18 to thirty does not help us answer that question, in particular because the thirty-and-over group that Ms. Gosselin asks us to use as a basis of comparison also consists entirely of welfare recipients."[18] Thus, McLachlin C.J. seems to have dismissed or over-looked the possibility that, among a population subject to negative stereotyping (that is, welfare recipients), those under thirty might more frequently be subject to negative stereotyping, or be subject to more negative stereotyping, than older welfare recipients. She also appeared to disregard the undisputed fact that persons under thirty had for many years prior to the impugned scheme had a lower social assistance allowance than older persons.

Before considering the second contextual factor, McLachlin C.J. noted that "a law that imposes restrictions or denies benefits on account of pre-sumed or unjustly attributed characteristics is likely to deny essential hu-man worth and to be discriminatory."[19] However, she failed to see any evidence of "presumed or unjustly attributed characteristics" in the Que-bec government's obvious belief that younger welfare recipients were too ir-responsible to take advantage of remedial programs without coercion. She avoided having to address the implications of trying to survive on $170 a month by focusing on the government's stated rationale for its scheme:

> The government's longer-term purpose was to provide young welfare re-cipients with precisely the kind of remedial education and skills training they lacked and needed in order eventually to integrate into the work force and become self-sufficient.... This was not a denial of young people's dignity; it was an affirmation of their potential.[20]

Despite the above statement, the Chief Justice did not appear to be troubled by the implications for young people's "potential" of the fact that those who opted for education (to complete a high school diploma) rather than training or community service would be penalized by some $100 a month. She saw no implications for "essential human dignity" in welfare recipients under thirty being discouraged from completing high school.[21]

By contrast, Bastararche and LeBel JJ. did recognize the logic on which the impugned provisions were based. Bastararche J., in rejecting arguments by the government based on the "assumption that there would be less in-centive to enter the workforce or to participate in the programs if the full benefit was provided unconditionally" referred to those arguments as "sup-porting the contention that the provisions reflect a discriminatory and ste-reotypical view of irresponsible youth."[22] LeBel J. noted that

> By trying to combat the pull of social assistance, for the "good" of the young people themselves who depended on it, the distinction perpetuated

the stereotypical view that a majority of young social assistance recipients choose to freeload off society permanently and have no desire to get out of that comfortable situation. There is no basis for that vision of young social assistance recipients as "parasites."[23]

Astonishingly, McLachlin C.J. found that Ms. Gosselin had failed to establish adverse effect. Relying on the opinion of the trial judge, who had rejected Ms. Gosselin's statistical and expert evidence, she held that there was no evidence that any welfare recipient under thirty wanting to participate in one of the programs had been refused enrollment or that the programs were designed in such a way as to systematically exclude persons under thirty from participating.[24] Among her remarks that could be seen to pertain to adversity is a statement of belief, presumably but not clearly arising from evidence, that people whose allowance was only $170 must have been getting some other money from somewhere.[25] In fact, it might be possible to infer from her judgment that she believed that, despite the fact that the impugned scheme could reduce a person to trying to survive on $170 a month, there was no evidence that anyone had had that experience, but for the fact that she appeared to accept that at least Ms. Gosselin had, for twelve months, been so reduced, becoming homeless in the process.

McLachlin C.J. acknowledged that Ms. Gosselin had failed to stay with the programs she tried, but held that this did not mean that the program had failed to correspond to the needs of the under-thirty age group. She concluded:

> The fact that some people may fall through a program's cracks does not show that the law fails to consider the overall needs and circumstances of the group of individuals affected, or that distinctions contained in the law amount to discrimination in the substantive sense intended by s. 15(1).[26]

This remark raises the possibility that McLachlin C.J. was ready to entertain the notion that no adversity is proven unless an (unstated) number of people or proportion of a class suffer the consequence that a law makes possible.

Even where she accepted the evidence, the Chief Justice downplayed its implications. She refused to "infer from the apparent lack of widespread participation in programs that some recipients under thirty must at some time have been reduced to utter poverty," or to "infer that at least some of these people's human dignity and ability to participate as fully equal members of society were compromised."[27]

McLachlin C.J. commented that disparity between the purpose and effect of a legislative scheme could not be inferred from the government's failure to prove that its assumptions were correct, holding that legislators were "entitled to proceed on informed general assumptions without running afoul of s. 15."[28] She also rejected the argument that the choice of thirty as an age cut-off was arbitrary and therefore failed to correspond to the actual circumstances of young adults, noting that all age-based distinctions had an element of arbitrariness and that the age chosen need only be "reasonably related to the legislative goal."[29]

In this decision, as in a number of previous decisions including *Law*, McLachlin C.J. took judicial notice[30] of a "fact" that served to weaken the case for the equality claimant. As in the *Law* decision, she concluded without evidence that older people (no age is specified, but the inference is that the Court was referring to people over 35 in *Law* and over thirty in *Gosselin*), have more difficulty in getting employment than younger people. The programs at issue in both *Law* and *Gosselin* were intended to provide a safety net when employment income was reduced or eliminated, and a cut-off age was the impugned provision in each case. Getting to the truth about the relative ease of finding employment was fundamental to doing justice in each of these cases. The failure to require evidence to back up the government's assumptions is disturbing.

By contrast, the Chief Justice held the claimant rigidly to the requirement that adversity be proven; there was no judicial notice that trying to survive on $170 a month might cause adversity.

A final disturbing feature of the majority judgment is McLachlin C.J.'s indication that the legislature's actions are to be reviewed in the light of their foundation in "reality," "everyday experience," and "common sense."[31] She does not acknowledge that, in a discrimination context, the invocation of "common sense," which is rooted in common practice based on common beliefs of the majority, is particularly suspect.[32] In this way, the majority decision in *Gosselin* is reminiscent of *Bliss v. Canada (Attorney General).*[33]

2) The Section 15 Dissents

a) Differences Concerning Facts

The most striking feature of the *Gosselin* decision was the remarkable differences between the majority and the minority in regard to what facts were accepted as proven. Unlike the Chief Justice, few of the dissenting Justices appear to have declined to consider evidence, and all were able and willing to draw inferences from the evidence that demonstrate an appreciation of the relevant context.

The facts relied upon by the minority were set out by L'Heureux-Dubé and Bastarache J.J. L'Heureux-Dubé J. summed up as follows:

> As a result of s. 29(a), adults under 30 were uniquely exposed by the legislative scheme to the threat of living beneath what the government itself considered to be a subsistence level of income. Of those eligible to participate in the programs, 88.8 percent were unable to increase their benefits to the level payable to those over 30 and over. Ms. Gosselin was exposed to the risk of severe poverty as a sole consequence of being under 30 years of age. Ms. Gosselin's psychological and physical integrity were breached. There is little question that living with the constant threat of poverty is psychologically harmful. There is no dispute that Ms. Gosselin lived at times below the government's own standard of bare subsistence. In 1987, the monthly cost of proper nourishment was $152. The guaranteed monthly payment to young adults was $170. I cannot imagine how it can be maintained that Ms. Gosselin's physical integrity was not breached.[34]

A review of the facts was a feature of Justice Bastarache's section 1 analysis. He cited the following problems:

- Only 11 percent of social assistance recipients under the age of thirty were in fact enrolled in the employment programs that allowed them to receive the base amount allocated to beneficiaries thirty years of age and over: "This in and of itself is not determinative of the fact that the legislation was not minimally impairing, but it does bring to our attention the real possibility that the programs were not designed in a manner that would infringe upon the appellant's rights as little as is reasonably possible."[35]
- One major branch of the scheme, the Remedial Education Program, did not provide for full benefits for those who participated, leaving them $100 short of the base benefit.[36]
- The design of the programs was not tailored in such a way as to ensure that there would always be programs available to those who wanted to participate.[37]
- Illiterate or severely undereducated persons were unable to participate in the Remedial Education Program. While ineligible for the

Remedial Education Program, such persons would also face difficulty entering On-the-job Training, and would thus be left with the Community Work Program, which was limited to one year.[38]

- The administrative hurdles were such that, in the course of his or her time on social assistance, a young person desiring to receive the full benefit of the programs would most likely spend at least a month or two on the reduced benefit.[39]

- Even though 85,000 single people under thirty years of age were on social assistance, the government at first only made 30,000 program places available. "The government did not have to prove that it had 85,000 empty chairs waiting in classrooms and elsewhere. However, the very fact that it was expecting such low levels of participation brings into question the degree to which the distinction in section 29(a) was geared towards improving the situation of those under 30, as opposed to simply saving money."[40]

b) Differences in Application of the *Law* Analysis

Justice L'Heureux-Dubé began by pointing out that presumptively excluding younger people from the protection of section 15 constitutes a failure to respect the express wording of the *Charter*, as well as being out of step with much of the relevant Supreme Court jurisprudence. She then reviewed the four factors outlined in the *Law* decision, and pointed out that, as noted in *Law*, the presence of a problem related to just one of these factors is sufficient to ground a finding of discrimination. She opined that "the severe impairment of an extremely important interest may be sufficient to ground a claim of discrimination:

> [E]ven if we accept for the moment that youth are generally an advantaged group, if a distinction were to severely harm the fundamental interests of youth and only youth, that distinction would be found to be discriminatory.[41]

Justice L'Heureux-Dubé went on to find that the fourth factor in the *Law* analysis — the nature of the interest affected — was clearly engaged in this case. The legislative distinction in this case had severe negative effects on Ms. Gosselin; solely because she was under thirty.

In conformity with the *Law* test, L'Heureux-Dubé J. assessed the threat to dignity from the viewpoint of a reasonable person in the claimant's position, apprised of all the circumstances. She noted that the reasonable person would have been informed that the Quebec government's intention was to help young people enter the marketplace, and to affirm their dignity: "She would have been informed that those thirty and over have more difficulty changing careers, and that those under thirty run serious social and personal risks if they do not enter the job market in a timely manner."

L'Heureux-Dubé J. then compared this information with the context, the circumstances of this "reasonable person":

> ... [T]he reasonable claimant would also likely have been a member of the 88.8 percent who were eligible for the programs and whose income did not rise to the levels available to all adults 30 years of age and over. Even if she wished to participate in training programs, she would have found that there were intervals between the completion of one program and the starting of another, during which the amount of her social assistance benefit would have plunged. The reasonable claimant would have made daily life choices in the face of an imminent and severe threat of poverty. The reasonable claimant would likely have suffered malnourishment. She might have turned to prostitution and crime to make ends meet. The reasonable claimant would have perceived that as a result of her deep poverty, she had been excluded from full participation in Canadian society. She would have perceived that her right to dignity was infringed as a sole consequence of being under 30 years of age, a factor over which, at any given moment, she had no control. While individuals may be able to strive to overcome the detriment imposed by merit-based distinctions, Ms. Gosselin was powerless to alter the single personal characteristic that the government's scheme made determinative for her level of benefits.[42]

L'Heureux-Dubé J. concluded Ms. Gosselin would reasonably have felt that she was being less valued as a member of society than people thirty and over and that she was being treated as less deserving of respect.[43]

Touching briefly on the remaining factors in the *Law* analysis, Justice L'Heureux-Dubé noted that, in respect of the relationship between grounds and the claimant's characteristics, "there should be a strong presumption that a legislative scheme which causes individuals to suffer severe threats to their physical and psychological integrity as a result of their possessing a characteristic which cannot be changed does not adequately take into account the needs, capacity or circumstances of the individual or group in question."[44]

In respect of the third factor, ameliorative purposes or effects, Justice L'Heureux-Dubé took note of the factual context of young adults in Quebec, rather than considering young adults in a vacuum:

... if 23 percent of young adults were unemployed by comparison with 14 percent of the general active population, and if an unprecedented number of young people were entering the job market at a time when federal social assistance programs were faltering, I fail to see how young adults did not suffer from a pre-existing disadvantage."[45]

In regard to section 1, Justice L'Heureux-Dubé concurred "entirely" with Justice Bastarache's section 1 analysis in respect of section 15, and substantially concurred with Justice Arbour's section 1 analysis in respect of section 7.

Justice Bastarache had no difficulty in concluding that the regulatory regime was discriminatory on its face. In considering the "four contextual factors" relevant to section 15, he made the following findings:

- The group at issue was subject to pre-existing disadvantage and stereotyping: unlike McLachlin C.J., Justice Bastarache took into account that the group was not just made up of young adults, but young adult welfare recipients. He also noted that "the stereotypical view upon which the distinction was based, that the young social welfare recipients suffer no special economic disadvantages, was not grounded in fact; it was based on old assumptions regarding the employability of young people." He added that the creation of the social assistance programs themselves demonstrated the government's awareness of the disadvantage facing youth.[46]

- In respect of the second *Law* factor, correspondence between grounds and the claimant's circumstances, "the assumption that long-term benefits of training are greater for younger persons has nothing to do with the present need of all persons for a minimum amount of support and their likely response to the availability of training programs through penalties or incentives."[47]

- Importantly, he stressed that, given the existence of section 1, "it is not appropriate to accept at face value the legislature's characterization of the purpose of the legislation and then use that to negate the otherwise discriminatory effects" at the section 15 stage. He set out some pointed criticism of the Chief Justice's approach in this respect.[48]

- Ameliorative purpose may be relevant to dignity if the impugned provision's purpose or effect is to help a more disadvantaged person or group in society, but "[g]roups that are the subject of an inferior differential treatment based on an enumerated or analogous ground are not treated with dignity just because the government claims that the detrimental provisions are "for their own good."[49]

• "[A]s this Court's jurisprudence makes clear, the fourth contextual inquiry focuses on the particular interest denied or limited in respect of the claimant, not the societal interests engaged by the legislature's broader program or another particular benefit purportedly being provided to the claimant. In my view, the interests that the Chief Justice discusses under the fourth inquiry of the *Law* test at para. 65 belong properly under the section 1 justification. The interest denied the appellant in this case was not 'faith in the usefulness of education,' but rather welfare payments at the government's own recognized subsistence level. Consideration of any 'positive impact of the legislation' belongs in the proportionality analysis at s. 1."[50]

Justice Bastarache went on to find that the impugned provision was not saved by section 1 of the *Charter*. He considered that the provision passed the "pressing and substantial" and "rational connection" part of the test. However, he concluded "upon examination of the manner in which the legislation in question was implemented," that "the government's initiative was not designed in a sufficiently careful manner to pass the minimally impairing test."[51]

Bastarache J. held that, while "the government was not required to demonstrate that the programs had any actual significant salutary effect on the well-being of young people; it nevertheless had to demonstrate that the reduction in benefits would reasonably be expected to facilitate the integration of the younger social assistance beneficiaries in the workplace."[52] However, he held that the onus had not been met.

Justice Arbour, in dissent, focused her decision almost entirely on an extremely thorough analysis section 7, which will not be discussed here. She agreed with Justice Bastarache in regard to section 15. Pointing out that a limitation on *Charter* rights under section 1 will only be justified where it furthers the values at which the rights are themselves directed, Arbour J. found no section 1 justification.[53]

Justice LeBel concurred with Justice Bastarache in regard to section 15, making some particularly pointed observations about the stereotypical thinking that underlay the coercive nature of the program,[54] and concurred with his section 1 analysis.

To sum up, the majority decision in *Gosselin* contains most of the elements that have been used against equality claimants in previous and subsequent cases. Perhaps the primary problem is the majority's practice of disaggregating the elements of the test set out in *Law* and giving each meticulous but separate consideration, with the result that there is never a focus on the larger, substantive picture: the effect of the impugned government action on the claimant.

C. CONSTRUCTION OF "DISCRIMINATION" FOR THE PURPOSES OF HUMAN RIGHTS LEGISLATION — A MORE EQUALITY-POSITIVE APPROACH

In contrast to our experience with section 15 so far, the Supreme Court since the 1980s and 90s has laid down clear principles for the generous and liberal construction of human rights legislation, and, with rare exceptions, demonstrated a willingness to recognize the experience of people whose voices are not routinely heard and valued, and to redress entrenched inequities.

Human rights legislation has been described by the Supreme Court as "quasi-constitutional."[55] It is applicable to government actions and government programs within its specified areas of application. Where other legislation and human rights legislation conflict, the Supreme Court has ruled that human rights legislation prevails, even where the human rights legislation has no specific paramountcy clause.[56] However, despite all these similarities to section 15 of the *Charter*, the Supreme Court has rarely demonstrated any reluctance to take a purposive and liberal approach to the scope of human rights legislation. As with the *Charter*, the Supreme Court has stressed that the purpose of human rights legislation is to achieve substantive, not just formal equality. However, unlike the situation with the *Charter* to date, the Court has quite consistently demonstrated its commitment to that goal.[57] The clear result of this is that courts and tribunals interpreting federal and provincial human rights legislation often show a more sophisticated understanding of the context of claimants' situations than has been evident in the Supreme Court's most recent section 15 decisions.

To date, the Supreme Court has not applied *Law* in dealing with appeals based on federal or provincial human rights legislation.[58] The practice of lower courts and tribunals has varied in this respect.[59] While there have been some decisions in which the application of *Law* has had the predictable chilling effect,[60] to date *Law* has not had nearly so negative an effect as it has in the *Charter* jurisprudence.

A recent example can be seen in *Hutchinson v. B.C. (Ministry of Health)*,[61] in which a British Columbia Human Rights Tribunal essentially applied the *Law* test despite ruling that it need not do so.

In *Hutchinson*, a disabled woman successfully challenged a Ministry of Health policy that prohibited the hiring of family members by adults with disabilities who qualified for and received Ministry funding to cover the cost of long-term, in-home care services.

Cheryl Hutchinson, who has cerebral palsy, was denied program funds to pay her father, who had provided care to her all her life. She complained of discrimination under British Columbia's *Human Rights Code*, on the basis of family status and disability. Her father also filed a complaint of discrimination on the basis of family status. Both were successful.

In a lengthy decision, the Tribunal concluded that the blanket prohibition against the hiring of family members as caretakers had breached the BC *Code*, as the respondent Ministry had not established that it would suffer undue hardship if it amended its policy to allow for exceptions for cases like that of Ms. Hutchinson.

In coming to its decision, the tribunal clearly accepted evidence concerning the intimate nature of the care involved in respect of claimants with Ms. Hutchinson's type of disability.[62] The Tribunal goes on to quote the *Law* decision concerning the nature of human dignity, to note the claimant's pre-existing disadvantage as a person with a severe disability, and to base its decision on a "reasonable" claimant in her circumstances:

> ... the reasonable person in circumstances similar to those of Ms. Hutchinson, who is informed of, and rationally takes into account, the various contextual factors, including that one of the purposes of CSIL is to facilitate greater autonomy and choice for its clients while adhering to the Ministry's philosophy that family members have the primary responsibility to care for one another, and cognizant of the Ministry's concern with costs, would experience a violation of her dignity when the blanket prohibition against the hiring of family members is applied to her without consideration of her particular circumstances.[63]

Gwinner v. Alberta (Minister of Human Resources and Employment)[64] involved a challenge, under Alberta's *Human Rights, Citizenship and Multiculturalism Act*[65] (HRCMA), to the *Widows' Pension Act*[66] (WPA), which made pensions available to persons who were married at the date of their spouse's death but not to persons who were divorced or separated at the date of their former spouse's death. The Alberta Court of Appeal upheld the decision of the Chambers Judge below, without comment on the issue of the application of the *Law* test. An application by the Crown for leave to appeal to the Supreme Court of Canada was dismissed.[67]

The judge below, Greckol J., had held that the *WPA* discriminated on the ground of marital status. In coming to this conclusion, she applied the *Law* test, although she held that it is not appropriate in "many, if not most, cases" to apply *Law*.[68]

The claimants in *Gwinner* had challenged the exclusion on the basis of section 3(a) and (b) of the *HRCMA*,[69] which prohibited the denial of "services customarily available to the public," or discrimination in respect of those services, on the basis, *inter alia*, of marital status." The specific defence provided under the *HRCMA* was set out in section 11.1,[70] which provides that

> A contravention of this Act shall be deemed not to have occurred if the person who is alleged to have contravened the Act shows that the alleged contravention was reasonable and justifiable in the circumstances.

The Human Rights Panel appointed under the *HRCMA* ruled that the government's exclusion was reasonable and justifiable pursuant to section 11.1.

In applying the *Law* test on appeal, Greckol J. displayed an understanding, lacking in the decision of the majority in *Gosselin*, of the pre-existing disadvantage, the stigma of being poor, and the further stigma attaching to receipt of social assistance:

> ... The WPA has the effect of perpetuating the disadvantage and stereotyping of the poor who are divorced, separated and single in two ways. First, by denying access, the WPA suggests that people in these groups are less worthy. Second, the denial of access means that the Claimants must rely on social assistance or "welfare," the term used by the Deputy Minister in his response to the complaint. Social assistance provides lower benefits, is more difficult to qualify for, requires an in-depth monthly review and, by the Crown's own evidence, is laden with social stigma.
>
> ... Those who seek to qualify for Widows' Pension and benefits, but who are denied access on the basis of their marital status and therefore must turn to welfare, will reasonably perceive that they are marginalized,

ignored and devalued when compared to the widowed in the community in identically impoverished or better circumstances. They will feel unfairly treated by the government, which is to say, their community. They will feel this is a perpetuation of their disadvantage. They will correctly perceive that their human dignity has been violated. In my view, this is not "one of those rare cases" described by Iacobucci J. in *Law* at para. 110 where differential treatment based on an enumerated ground is not discriminatory.[71]

D. SUMMARY OF SOME CURRENT DIFFICULTIES; SUGGESTIONS FOR ARGUMENTS IN SECTION 15 CASES IN THE FUTURE

In *Twenty Years of Equality Rights: Reclaiming Expectations*,[72] Bruce Porter ably reviews the history of the drafting process with reference to section 15, and sets out the expectations of equality-seeking groups. He also points out the grim statistics:

> Since the Supreme Court issued its first decisions under section 15 in *Andrews*, half a million more households have fallen into poverty. The number of single mothers living in poverty has increased by more than 50% and their poverty has in many cases deepened to the point of extreme destitution. Foodbanks, a rare phenomenon in the early 1980s, are now a critical means of survival for three quarters of a million people every month, including over 300,000 children, but still fail to come close to meeting the needs of an estimated 2.4 million hungry adults and children. A national child-care program, first promised by the Mulroney Government in 1984 and then by the Liberal Government in 1993, remains the "longest-running broken political promise in Canada." Women and children have been the most dramatically affected by the epidemic of homelessness, with the number of homeless women and children living in shelters in Toronto more than doubling since 1989. The poverty rate for visible minority women is now as high as 37%. One third of households in which one parent is an immigrant now live in poverty, which includes 231,000 children. The average income of Aboriginal women is $13,300.[73]

Porter notes that treaty-monitoring bodies of the United Nations have identified "critical areas in which governments in Canada have failed to meet their human rights obligations, and provided sensible and reasoned recommendations for remedying them."[74]

At the same time, in *Gosselin* and in subsequent decisions such as *Hodge*,[75] and *Auton*,[76] the majority of the Supreme Court has used various aspects of the *Law* approach to put a stop to an emerging tendency by the courts to take seriously the guarantee of equality provided by section 15 in respect of government programs. Why is this, and what can be done about it?

It is possible that the position of the current majority of the Court is reflective of no more than the personal beliefs of the individuals concerned. No one who has studied discrimination could dismiss the possibility that judges themselves, consciously or unconsciously, hold discriminatory opinions and views that are endemic within society and are reflected in the law or government action under challenge. This would explain some of the recent results of the Supreme Court's application of the "dignity" test that is featured in *Law*.

As Dianne Pothier observes, "[h]uman dignity is a malleable enough concept to mean whatever the judges want it to mean."[77] Even if a judge wants to invest the term with a breadth and depth that is congruent with the appropriate interpretation of section 15, his or her own background may limit that judge's understanding of what dignity means to a person whose background is very different. The Supreme Court in *Law* noted that in some cases it would not be necessary for the claimant to adduce evidence because an impairment of dignity can be "evident on the basis of judicial notice and logical reasoning."[78] This is useful as far as it goes, but the problem with this part of the section 15 analysis is that any individual's concept of dignity is heavily class- and culture-bound, in ways of which she or he may be quite unconscious. The average judge, who is still a white, affluent, able-bodied man, may be unable to appreciate what factors negatively affect the dignity of someone of whose life he can have little real understanding.[79] Further, a judge may, consciously or unconsciously, maintain a double standard that conceives of some types of indignity as simply part of life for other people. This is particularly true in cases of constructive or adverse-effect discrimination,[80] which by definition involve norms that are unquestioned by the majority, and in cases involving access to government-provided benefits, of which the majority has no need.

It is also possible that, despite its repeated defences of its role under the *Charter*, and its avowal that the *Charter* must be interpreted liberally and broadly, the Court has simply been ground down by critics who call down the wrath of heaven on "judicial activism." By definition, any decision that accords rights to those to whom "common sense" accords none is breaking new ground, and attracts criticism from the advantaged majority who define the popular notion of "common sense." In such circumstances, the easiest way to deflect criticism is to exclude from protection the most vulnerable claimants, who are the most vulnerable precisely because the same segments of society that criticize judicial activism despise "dependent" people, remain deliberately ignorant of their circumstances, and have no interest in ameliorating their disadvantages.

To date, the Supreme Court has not imposed a similar chill on the interpretation of human rights legislation. It is clear that most decisions of courts and tribunals construing human rights legislation display a deeper understanding of the dynamics of substantive discrimination and of the disadvantaged position of persons protected by that legislation than do those of courts and tribunals construing section 15 of the *Charter*. This may suggest some ideas for how to persuade the courts to take a closer look at the concept of equality under section 15.

The Court is on relatively safer ground with human rights legislation. By definition, human rights legislation has made it past democratically elected legislatures and Parliament. Further, it is legislation rather than a constitution, and as such is subject to the familiar rules of statutory interpretation, foremost among them being the rule that legislation is to be interpreted in a "fair, large and liberal" manner. This means that a Court that interprets human rights legislation broadly has relatively little fear of allegations of judicial activism. However, it can also be pointed out to the Court that the existence of long-established human rights legislation, which is applicable to government as well as to the private sector, is evidence of the will of the Canadian people, through their democratically elected governments, to accept the consequences of substantive equality.

The Court in *Law* acknowledged that "[t]here can be different conceptions of what human dignity means,"[81] and that "controversy ... exists regarding the biases implicit in some applications of the "reasonable person" standard."[82] When dealing with social benefits cases, counsel will need to focus on the Supreme Court's general description, in *Law*, of the purpose of section 15:

> In general terms, the purpose of s. 15(1) is to prevent the violation of essential human dignity and freedom through the imposition of disadvantage, stereotyping, or political or social prejudice, and to promote a society in which all persons enjoy equal recognition at law as human beings or as

members of Canadian society, equally capable and equally deserving of concern, respect and consideration [paragraph 88].

In social benefits cases, the focus should be on the second part of the paragraph, which states the purpose of section 15 in a positive way. In respect of government benefit programs, the phrase "equally deserving of concern ... and consideration" is particularly important. In these cases, it is arguable that where legislation and government practice has a comparatively adverse impact on people whose subordination is related to personal characteristics enumerated in section 15, or analogous personal characteristics, they are being denied equal concern and consideration.

The second step is to squarely address, through evidence and argument, how being excluded from a benefit program in itself "perpetuates the view" that persons excluded "are less capable or less worthy of recognition or value as human beings or as members of Canadian society." As noted above, the Justices of the Supreme Court have, so far, implicitly failed to recognize exclusion from a benefit program itself as having this effect, but have made no explicit judgments saying so. More importantly, they have never repudiated jurisprudence such as *Eldridge v. British Columbia*,[83] which recognises the effect of exclusion from an important government service. In fact, they continue to cite and to rely on *Eldridge*.

Advocates for the most disadvantaged section 15 claimants are faced with reluctant, frightened, and sometimes hostile courts. Those with long memories will remember that, in the early years of human rights legislation, they were faced with reluctant, frightened, and sometimes hostile legislatures. It might be useful to consider and apply the same approaches that were used then.

Chief among these is doggedly and repeatedly explaining to the advantaged the circumstances of the disadvantaged, in an attempt to remind them that our clients are human and deserving of dignity. This is horribly difficult to do within the artificial constraints imposed by litigation. Frequently, we will fail as we did in *Masse v. Ontario (Ministry of Community and Social Services)*,[84] *Gosselin*, and *Hodge*. Occasionally we will succeed, as we did in *Dartmouth/Halifax County Regional Housing Authority v. Sparks*[85] and in *Falkiner v. Ontario (Ministry of Community and Social Services)*.[86] Repeatedly, we will be obliged to remind the courts of some forty years of human rights jurisprudence that the Supreme Court has repeatedly indicated is instructive.[87] In this way, we may see more decisions such as *Eldridge*,[88] in which the Court took an approach to section 15 that accorded with its approach to provincial and federal equality-rights legislation and promoted substantive equality for subordinated groups.

Like other *Charter* rights, section 15 is an expression of the values by which we aspire to govern our state actions. To borrow a phrase from Justice La Forest in *Eldridge*,[89] we can do better than a "thin and impoverished vision of s. 15."

ENDNOTES

1   Judith Keene is a lawyer with the Clinic Resource Office of Legal Aid Ontario. Opin-
    ions expressed herein are those of the author and not those of Legal Aid Ontario.

2   Recent commentary includes Bruce Ryder, Cidalia Faria, & Emily Lawrence,
    "What's *Law* Good For? An Empirical Overview of *Charter* Equality Rights
    Decisions" (2004) 24 Sup. Ct. L. Rev. (2d) 103; Mary C. O'Donoghue, "Section 15
    Charter Update: Developments since *Law*," Conference Materials, Third Annual
    Charter Conference (15 October, 2004) Ontario Bar Association; Ena Chadha &
    Laura Shatz, "Human Dignity and Economic Integrity for Persons with Disabilities"
    (2004) 16 N.J.C.L. 27; Dianne Pothier, "Connecting Grounds of Discrimination
    to Real People's Real Experiences" (2001) 13 C.J.W.L. 1; Gwen Brodsky & Shelagh
    Day, "Beyond the Social and Economic Rights Debate: Substantive Equality Speaks
    to Poverty" (2002) 14 C.J.W.L./R.F.D. 184; Gwen Brodsky, "Autonomy with a Ven-
    geance" (2003) 15 C.J.W.L./R.F.D. 194; Sheila McIntyre, "Answering the Siren Call
    of Abstract Formalism with the Subjects and Verbs of Domination," in this volume;
    Sheilah Martin, "Court Challenges: *Law*" (Winnipeg: Court Challenges Program,
    2002) and "Balancing Individual Rights to Equality and Social Goals" (2001) 80
    Can. Bar Rev. 299; June Ross, "A Flawed Synthesis of the Law" (2000) 11:3 Const.
    Forum 74; Christopher D. Bredt & Adam M. Dodek, "Breaking the Law's Grip on
    Equality: A New Paradigm" (2003) 20 Sup. Ct. L. Rev. (2d) 33.

3   *Law v. Canada (Minister of Employment and Immigration)*, [1999] 1 S.C.R. 497.

4   *Canadian Charter of Rights and Freedoms,* Part I of the Constitution Act, 1982,
    Schedule B to the Canada Act 1982 (U.K.), 1982, c. 11 [*Charter*].

5   [1997] 3 S.C.R. 624, [1997] S.C.J. No. 86, 218 N.R. 161 [*Eldridge*].

6   Professor Hogg provides an insightful brief history of competing views as to how
    discrimination was to be defined, put forward before the *Andrews* case was decided,
    as well as a summary of how Supreme Court decisions have developed since then, in
    Peter W. Hogg, *Constitutional Law of Canada*, vol. 2, 3d ed. (supplemented) (Scar-
    borough: Carswell, 1992) loose-leaf at 52:17–52:29.

7   [2000] 1 S.C.R. 703 [*Granovsky*].

8   [2002] 4 S.C.R. 429 [*Gosselin*].

9   [2004] 3 S.C.R. 357 [*Hodge*].

10 [2004] 3 S.C.R. 657 [*Auton*].

11 [2004] 3 S.C.R. 381 [*N.A.P.E.*].

12 *Gosselin*, above note 8.

13 R.R.Q., c. A-16, r. 1.

14 Gwen Brodsky & Shelagh Day, "Poverty is a Human Rights Violation" (December
    2001) consultation paper, The Poverty and Human Rights Project. This paper is
    published on the website of the Poverty and Human Rights Centre, at the University
    of British Columbia, online: www.povertyandhumanrights.org.

15 *Gosselin*, above note 8 at paras. 19, 75, & 83.

16 See *Chaoulli v. Quebec (Attorney General)*, [2005] 1 S.C.R. 791.

17 *Gosselin*, above note 8 at paras. 33–34.

18 *Ibid.* at para. 35.

19 *Ibid.* at para. 37.

20 *Ibid.* at para. 42.

21 *Ibid.* at para. 49.

22 *Ibid.* at paras. 250 & 272.

23 *Ibid.* at para. 407.

24 *Ibid.* at para. 47.

25 *Ibid.* at paras. 51 & 71.

26 *Ibid.* at para. 55.

27 *Ibid.* at para. 71.

28 *Ibid.* at para. 56.

29 *Ibid.* at para. 57.

30 *Ibid.* at paras. 34 & 61.

31 *Ibid.* at paras. 44 & 56.

32 As John Stuart Mill observed, our legal system and those who operate within it tend to assume that existing relationships of domination and subordination are "natural." Mill argued that the law, in adopting the status quo, then plays an even more insidious role, from an equality perspective: that of converting into a legal right a relationship of inequality which was previously a mere physical fact. Mill points out that a position of advantage always appears "natural" to those who possess it. In the same way, the unquestioning acceptance of "common sense" can simply perpetuate the self-serving beliefs of those in a dominant position.

33 [1979] 1 S.C.R. 183, 23 N.R. 527 [*Bliss*]. (In *Bliss*, a *Canadian Bill of Rights* case, the Supreme Court ruled that denying benefits to pregnant women under the *Unemployment Insurance Act* was not discriminatory, on the reasoning that the distinction drawn under the Act was based on relevant biological differences. Ten years later, in *Brooks v. Canada Safeway Ltd.*, [1989] 1 S.C.R. 1219, the Supreme Court acknowledged that the superficial relevance of the biological difference between women and men had led it astray in *Bliss*.)

34 *Gosselin*, above note 8 at para. 130.

35 *Ibid.* at para. 276.

36 *Ibid.* at para. 277.

37 *Ibid.* at para. 279.

38 *Ibid.* at para. 280.

39 *Ibid.* at para. 281.

40 *Ibid.* at para. 283.

41 *Ibid.* at para. 128.

42 *Ibid.* at paras 132.

43 *Ibid.* at paras 130–33.

44 *Ibid.* at para. 135.

45 *Ibid.* at para. 137.

46 *Ibid.* at para. 235.

47 *Ibid.* at para. 243.

48 *Ibid.* at paras. 244–47 & 250.

49 *Ibid.* at para. 250.

50 *Ibid.* at para. 257.

51 *Ibid.* at para. 275.

52 *Ibid.* at para. 288.

53 *Ibid.* at paras. 391–93.

54 *Ibid.* at paras. 407–10.

55 *Dickason v. University of Alberta* (1992), 95 D.L.R. (4th) 439 (S.C.C.) at 454; *Insurance Corporation of British Columbia v. Heerspink*, [1982] 2 S.C.R. 145. See also *O'Malley v. Simpson-Sears*, [1985] 2 S.C.R. 536, 64 N.R. 161, 23 D.L.R. (4th) 321 at D.L.R. 329, where the Supreme Court describes human rights legislation as "not quite constitutional but certainly more than the ordinary."

56 *Insurance Corporation of British Columbia v. Heerspink, ibid.; O'Malley v. Simpson-Sears, ibid.; Singh v. MEI*, [1985] 1 S.C.R. 177; *Winnipeg School Division No. 1 v. Craton*, [1985] 2 S.C.R. 150, 6 CHRR D/3014.

57 *Canadian National Railway Co. v. Canada (Human Rights Commission)*, [1987] 1 S.C.R. 1114; *O'Malley v. Simpson-Sears*, above note 55; *Central Alberta Dairy Pool v. Human Rights Commission (Alta)*, [1990] 2 S.C.R. 489, 113 N.R. 161; *Renaud v. Board of Education of Central Okanagan No. 23 and C.U.P.E. Local 523* [1992] 2 S.C.R. 970, 141 N.R. 185.

58 See, for example, the decision in *British Columbia (Public Service Employee Relations Commission) v. B.C.G.S.E.U*, [1999] 3 S.C.R. 3, which was decided after *Law*.

59 See J. Keene, "A Graft from the Constitutional Tree: The *Law* test and Human Rights Legislation" (2005) L.S.U.C. Human Rights Update 2005. Note that, after the LSUC Update and this chapter were written, the Ontario Divisional Court applied the *Law* analysis to the definition of discrimination in the Ontario *Human Rights Code* in reviewing the operation of a government program in *Ontario Secondary School Teachers' Federation v. Upper Canada District School Board*, [2005] O.J. No. 4057 (Div. Ct.). Leave to appeal has been recently refused.

60 See for example *Vancouver Rape Relief Society v. Nixon*, 2003 BCSC 1936, 48 C.H.R.R. D/123. In *Nixon*, the BC Supreme Court overturned a decision of the BC Human Rights Tribunal, which ruled that Vancouver Rape Relief and Women's Shelter discriminated against Kimberly Nixon, a male-to-female transsexual, by refusing to accept her as a volunteer peer counsellor for victims of male violence. The Tribunal had found that Rape Relief was not entitled to rely on the exemption in s. 41 of BC's *Code* that permits a non-profit organization, which has as a primary purpose the promotion of the interests or welfare of an identifiable group, to grant a preference to members of that group.

On appeal, the BC Supreme Court overturned the Tribunal decision for two reasons. The first was that Rape Relief is protected by s. 41, which may be, depending on the facts, the correct reason. However, the second was because, under the test in *Law*, the refusal did not constitute discrimination. The Court found that Rape Relief's decision to exclude Kimberly Nixon did not violate dignity because "exclusion by a small, relatively obscure, self-defining private organization cannot have the same impact on human dignity as legislated exclusion from a statutory benefit program.

This is because any stereotyping or prejudice arising from legislated exclusion bears the imprimatur of state approval and therefore some wide public acceptance" (at para. 145). Despite the fact that provincial human rights legislation governs actions by individuals, and by small as well as large corporations, the court's astonishingly stringent test apparently could not be met unless the claimant could reasonably feel that he or she could "no longer participate fully in the economic, social and cultural life of the province" (para. 151). The decision rather unconvincingly distinguishes the refusal at issue from "Ms. Nixon being excluded from a restaurant because of her transsexual characteristics" (para. 158).

61 2004 BCHRT 58.

62 *Ibid.* at para. 110.

63 *Ibid.* at para. 141.

64 (2002), 44 C.H.R.R. D/52, 2002 ABQB 685, appeal to Alta. C.A. dismissed; *Gwinner v. Alberta (Minister of Human Resources and Employment)* (2004), CHRR Doc. 04-151, 2004 ABCA 210, leave application to S.C.C. dismissed; *The Crown in Right of Alberta as represented by the Minister responsible for Alberta Human Resources and Employment v. Director of the Human Rights and Citizenship Commission* (Alta. C.A., May 10, 2004) (30449) [*Gwinner*].

65 R.S.A. 1980, c. H-11.7 (now R.S.A. 2000, c. H-14).

66 S.A. 1983, c. W-7.5 (now R.S.A. 2000, c. W.-7).

67 *Gwinner*, above note 64.

68 *Ibid.* at paras. 94–96. Greckol J. based the application of *Law* in this case on "the interplay between human rights legislation and the *Charter*," citing cases in which the Supreme Court had relied on human rights jurisprudence in interpreting the *Charter*.

69 Now s. 4(a) & (b).

70 Now s. 11.

71 *Gwinner*, above note 64 at paras. 158 & 163.

72 Paper prepared for the Equality Advisory Committee of the Court Challenges Program, presented at the Equality Rights Review Consultation on October 1–2, 2004, at the Four Points Sheraton Hotel, Hull, Quebec. I am indebted to Mr. Porter for the opportunity to see this article before it was published.

73 *Ibid.* at 45, footnotes deleted. For more detailed comment on the feminization of poverty in Canada, see Gwen Brodsky & Shelagh Day, "Beyond the Social and Economic Rights Debate," above note 2.

74 *Ibid.* at 44. Also see Bruce Porter, "Judging Poverty: Using International Human Rights Law to Refine the Scope of Charter Rights" (2000) 15 J. Law & Soc. Pol'y 117; and Craig Scott, "Canada's International Human Rights Obligations and Disadvantaged Members of Society: Finally Into the Spotlight" (1999) 10 Const. Forum.

75 *Hodge*, above note 9.

76 *Auton*, above note 10.

77 Dianne Pothier, "Connecting Grounds of Discrimination to Real People's Real Experiences," above note 2 at 56.

78 *Law*, above note 3 at para. 88.

79 In addition to the *Gosselin* decision, an example can be seen in *Granovsky*, above note 7, another case in which the Supreme Court failed to address the issue that exclusion from a benefit scheme could reduce a person's dignity. In *Granovsky*, Justice Binnie mentioned but clearly failed to appreciate the nuances of the applicant's assertion (quoted at para. 69) of the harm that resulted from his exclusion: "He says he will be thrown onto the welfare rolls." It is part of the social context of the poorest Canadians that a person "on disability benefits" is considered morally superior to a person "on welfare." More fortunate classes fail to appreciate this type of fine gradation. It is possible that the Court simply did not understand the dignity interest of Mr. Granovsky in having a public acknowledgement that the reason he could not work was disability.

80 Constructive discrimination (a term borrowed from Ontario's *Human Rights Code*, R.S.O. 1990, c. H.19 [*Code*], arises where a requirement, qualification, consideration, or practice that does not itself expressly distinguish on impermissible grounds results in a disadvantage, that is not felt or is less felt by others, for persons with a personal characteristic identified for protection under human rights legislation or the *Charter*, or imposes a disadvantage on a group, and the group that suffers the disadvantage is disproportionately composed of persons with a personal characteristic identified for protection under human rights legislation or the *Charter*.

81 *Law*, above note 3 at para. 53.

82 *Ibid.* at para. 61.

83 *Eldridge*, above note 5.

84 (1996), 134 D.L.R. (4th) 20 (Ont. Div. Ct.), leave to appeal to Ont. C.A. refused [1996] O.J. No. 1526, leave to appeal to S.C.C. refused [1996] S.C.C.A. No. 373.

85 (1993), 101 D.L.R. (4th) 224 (N.S.C.A.), rev'g (1992), 112 N.S.R. (2d) 389, 307 A.P.R. 389 (Co. Ct.).

86 (2002), 59 O.R. (3d) 481 (C.A.), aff'g (2000), 188 D.L.R. (4th) 52 (Ont. Div. Ct.), leave to appeal to S.C.C. granted (20 March 2003). The Crown withdrew its appeal to the Supreme Court in *Falkiner*.

87 See remarks of the Court in, for example, *Andrews v. Law Society of British Columbia*, [1989] 1 S.C.R. 143, 56 D.L.R. (4th) 1 at D.L.R. 18; *Eldridge*, above note 5 at N.R. para 63; *Symes v. Minister of National Revenue*, [1993] 4 S.C.R. 695.

88 *Eldridge, ibid.*

89 *Ibid.* at para. 73.

Part Three

SHIFTING AND BLENDING PARADIGMS:

eleven

Postcards from *O'Malley*:

REINVIGORATING STATUTORY HUMAN RIGHTS
JURISPRUDENCE IN THE AGE OF THE *CHARTER*

Leslie A. Reaume[1]

A. INTRODUCTION

The *O'Malley*[2] decision, released by the Supreme Court of Canada in 1985, is one of the cornerstones of statutory human rights interpretation in Canada.[3] Twenty years after its release, it remains the definitive statement on the shifting evidentiary burdens borne by parties in the adjudication of a statutory human rights claim, including the vital concept of the *prima facie* case.[4] The decision in *O'Malley* also resulted in the progression of other important substantive equality principles: emphasizing the broad public policy reflected in the purpose of the enabling statute; shifting the focus from the purpose of an impugned rule to its effect: affirming prior findings that motive or intent to discriminate was not an evidentiary requirement in construing statutory human rights violations. While the Supreme Court of Canada has yet to supplant this important decision, human rights tribunals and courts have effectively taken on this task. Together they have contributed to a patchwork of decisions across a new jurisprudential landscape where *O'Malley* has retreated to the background while the *Charter*[5] and its attendant analytical concepts have slid into the foreground.[6]

This paper explores one of the important developments in statutory human rights jurisprudence which has consequences for the development of substantive equality theory and practice: the import, into statutory adjudications, of the *Charter* decision in *Law v. Canada (Minister of Employment and Immigration)*.[7] The range of potential consequences depends on what is imported from *Law* and how those concepts are applied in statutory human rights adjudications. As is discussed in greater detail below, *Law* appears in the statutory human rights context on a continuum. On the one end is the recognition of the interplay between the *Charter* and provincial and federal human rights instruments which does not result in the principles from *Law* dominating the statutory analysis. On the other end is the wholesale application of the three-stage analysis from *Law,* including the inquiry into the effect of the impugned rule or conduct on the claimant's dignity. The closer a statutory adjudicator moves to the latter end of the spectrum, the more dominant the *Charter* analysis becomes and the greater the potential for adverse consequences. Among the most important of those consequences is the potential for an elevated burden on a human rights claimant which effectively supplants the more appropriate evidentiary principles articulated in *O'Malley*. This is of particular concern when only a small fraction of the complaints filed with human rights commissions result in a public hearing, limiting the possibilities for evolving the jurisprudence in this important emerging area of law.[8]

Allowing interpretive elements associated with *Law* to dominate a statutory human rights analysis changes how statutory human rights adjudications unfold. It diverts the attention of decision-makers from the language of the enabling statute, the principles which have evolved through statutory human rights adjudications, the regulatory context in which statutory human rights allegations arise, the intent of the framers of the legislation, and the quasi-constitutional nature of human rights.[9] Although some statutory cases certainly cross over into the realm of constitutionally-protected rights in the sense that they could be adjudicated under either instrument, statutory human rights are not constitutionally entrenched and they require the appropriate contextual interpretation to give life to the values which underlie them. Provincial and federal politicians framed human rights legislation in a manner which provides broad public access to remedies for both private and public sector forms of discrimination which are not contemplated by the *Charter* in the service, accommodation, facilities, and employment arenas.[10] It is not suggested here that statutory human rights claims are inferior, but they are contextually different from *Charter* claims.[11]

Principles developed in the *Charter* context can be given consideration in the adjudication of human rights complaints. Indeed there is a relationship between these two equality rights instruments which can enrich the development of jurisprudence in both contexts.[12]

The interplay between the *Charter* and statutory human rights instruments, which began with the analysis of discrimination in *Andrews*,[13] is examined in more detail later in this paper, as is the question of the appropriate limits on borrowing concepts from one context to another. Simply put, borrowing from the *Charter* context to the statutory context is appropriate so long as the exercise enriches the substantive equality analysis, is consistent with the limits of statutory interpretation and advances the purpose and quasi-constitutional status of the enabling statute. The objection raised in this paper is not to the interplay but to the manner in which *Charter* principles, specifically those articulated in the decision in *Law*, are imported and then allowed to dominate an analysis which should be driven first by the principles of statutory interpretation, and second by the jurisprudence which has developed specifically in the regulatory context.[14]

Statutory human rights jurisprudence has its roots in both the principles of statutory interpretation and the broader public policy principles associated with human rights which are often expressly articulated in the enabling legislation. Purposes and preambles are replete with language drafted in the broadest imaginable public policy terms, such as the purpose of the *Canadian Human Rights Act* which references "equality of opportunity" for individuals to "make for themselves the lives that they are able and wish to have";[15] the preamble to the *Human Rights, Citizenship and Multiculturalism Act*,[16] which provides "that all Albertans should share in an awareness and appreciation of the diverse racial and cultural composition of society and that the richness of life in Alberta is enhanced by sharing that diversity"; the British Columbia *Human Rights Code*[17] (*BCHRC*) which articulates as one of its purposes "to foster a society in British Columbia in which there are no impediments to full and free participation in the economic, social, political and cultural life of British Columbia." Contrast these public policy statements with the policy statement implicit in the limited entitlements under section 15(1) of the *Charter* to "equality before and under the law" and the right to "equal protection and equal benefit of the law;" highlighting, again, the importance of context to deliberations which take place under these two important equality instruments.

Apart from the shift in the complainant's evidentiary burden, reliance on *Law* creates a number of other problems in the statutory human rights context, all of which are addressed in greater detail later in the paper. It introduces, for example, an improper method for "screening" complaints in circumstances where a human rights commission employs the test to determine whether a case merits public inquiry by a human rights tribunal.[18]

The concept of human dignity becomes an element of the burden of proof rather than a value which underlies the entire statutory scheme.[19] Reliance on *Law* also supplants statutory definitions of "discrimination" and interferes with the analytical relationship between the *prima facie* case and the defence.[20] Importing *Law* creates defences against a finding of discrimination which are inconsistent with statutory language and the development of statutory human rights principles.[21] Not all adjudicators in the statutory human rights context who engage with the decision in *Law* rely on the three stages which have come to be known as the "*Law* test." When they do, however, the adoption of a formal, mechanistic approach to determining discrimination puts adjudicators directly at odds with their enabling legislation and the open, contextual language of *O'Malley*.

All of these important considerations might give way if the analysis developed in *Law* presented opportunities for a positive and appropriate evolution of substantive equality theory in the statutory human rights context. In writing for the Court, Iacobucci J. sought to synthesize the divergent views which had arisen since the decision in *Andrews* on the appropriate framework for determining section 15(1) claims. That effort resulted in a series of guidelines which have subsequently become entrenched as a formal, mechanistic "three-part test" involving an inquiry into whether there is a) a distinction (or failure to take disadvantage into account); b) based on an enumerated or analogous ground; c) which is discriminatory in the sense that it imposes a burden on the claimant based on a view (stereotypic) of the claimant as less capable or less worthy of recognition.[22] On its face, the analysis looks much like the analysis developed in *Andrews*.

However, the last stage of the analysis has come to involve an inquiry into the extent to which the impugned rule violates the human dignity of the claimant. While the guidelines have been formally articulated as a three-part test, it is this "dignity inquiry" which distinguishes *Law* from *Andrews* — not on a conceptual level, since human dignity clearly animates the analysis developed in *Andrews*, but from a practical evidentiary perspective. From the claimant's perspective what has been articulated as a three-part test actually imposes four separate evidentiary requirements: a distinction, based on a ground, which imposes the burden described above *and* which undermines the claimant's dignity. This dignity inquiry, which is carried out not from the subjective view of the claimant but from a "subjective/objective" perspective has been described as "onerous, vague, and beset by significant judicial subjectivism."[23]

The guidelines have also been described by Daphne Gilbert as a "compromise" which is now "badly fractured" following the decisions in *Lavoie* and *Gosselin*, which contained four and five separate opinions respectively.[24] Gilbert argues that the many decisions "were more than just interpretive differences; instead, each represented significant problems with the *Law* framework."[25] Importing this fractured case law into a context where cases are decided by publicly-appointed citizens who are not necessarily required to have legal training, is impractical. There would be no end to the judicial review applications and appeals against the decisions of these adjudicators, who would be assessed on a standard of correctness for applying the wrong interpretation of *Law* and its many incarnations since the original decision.[26] More importantly, to the extent that *Law* has entrenched the mechanistic application of a formal test, which places a burden on the claimant to prove impairment to dignity assessed against something other than the claimant's subjective view of their own experience, the "test" is at odds with the burdens already established by provincial and federal statutes.

The paper begins with a review of the legal principles applicable to the statutory human rights context including the similarities, differences, and interplay between the statutory and *Charter* contexts. This is followed by a brief review of the jurisprudence from the Supreme Court of Canada since the decision in *Law* in which statutory human rights instruments were engaged — in none of those cases did the Supreme Court of Canada move to supplant the *prima facie* case as it was originally defined in *O'Malley*. The final section of the paper deals with the myriad ways in which *Law* has manifested in the statutory context and the dangers those cases pose to the development of substantive equality theory and practice.

B. LEGAL PRINCIPLES APPLICABLE TO THE STATUTORY HUMAN RIGHTS CONTEXT

This section addresses two broad issues. The first is the application of the principles of statutory interpretation and the requirement to interpret human rights statutes in a broad, liberal, purposive manner. That requirement is rooted in the quasi-constitutional nature of statutory human rights legislation which has specific implications for how one interprets the scope of both the statutory entitlement and the defence. The second issue is that despite the quasi-constitutional status accorded human rights legislation, it creates specifically defined statutory rights rather than general entitlements which affects how parties must prove their case. Statutes are not "living trees," a concept which is central to constitutional interpretation. Human rights statutes specifically limit entitlement to particular public and private contexts and prohibit discrimination on the basis of fixed grounds which are not open to expansion through the analogous grounds approach taken under the *Charter.*

Statutory human rights legislation is remedial in nature and requires a broad, liberal, purposive interpretation to the adjudication of claims.[27] However, the Supreme Court has noted that in conducting a purposive analysis, an adjudicator cannot ignore the words and definitions contained in the statute itself. As Iacobucci J. stated in *Gould v. Yukon Order of Pioneers,* "a true purposive approach looks at the wording of the statute itself, with a view to discerning and advancing the legislature's intent. Our task is to breath life, and generously so, into the particular statutory provisions that are before us."[28] The interpretation is conducted, therefore, in accordance with the rules of statutory interpretation, within the context of the purpose of the statute in question and in a manner which recognizes the quasi-constitutional status of human rights legislation.[29] This status provides the rationale for a more organic and flexible interpretation of general terms and concepts and allows for key provisions of the legislation to be adapted not only to changing social conditions but also to evolving conceptions of human rights. This approach was taken, for example, in *O'Malley* in the context of the application of the principles of adverse impact discrimination, which were not expressly provided for in the statute in question. McLachlin J. (as she was then), writing for the majority of the Supreme Court in *Meiorin,* was similarly engaged in this more organic, flexible approach when she dismantled the distinctions between direct and adverse impact discrimination in the statutory context.[30]

The opposite is true for statutory defences and exemptions which must be construed narrowly. The goal of statutory human rights legislation is to remedy discrimination, not to punish. Defences must be construed in a manner which is consistent with the overarching goal to reveal and remedy discrimination. According to Sopinka J., writing for the majority in *Zurich Insurance Co. v. Ontario (Human Rights Commission),* defences are interpreted narrowly because human rights legislation is "the last protection of the most vulnerable members of society."[31]

The onus on the parties in a statutory human rights case lies in the language of the enabling statute and statutory human rights jurisprudence.

The standard is the ordinary civil standard or the "balance of probabilities" and the burden is a shifting one: the complaint must prove a *prima facie* case of discrimination; the burden then shifts to the respondent to establish an explanation or defence; the burden shifts back to the complainant to prove that the explanation is a pretext.[32] The Supreme Court of Canada established the test for finding a *prima facie* case which is articulated in the decision in *O'Malley* at page 558:

> A *prima facie* case is one which covers the allegations made, and which, if believed, is complete and sufficient to justify a verdict in the complainant's favour in the absence of an answer from the respondent.

It is not necessary for the complainant to prove that the prohibited ground was the only operative factor or the most important factor in the effect of the impugned policy or conduct. It is sufficient to prove that the prohibited ground was "a" factor in the treatment experienced by the claimant.[33] The *prima facie* case may also be proven by circumstantial evidence creating what was described in *Basi* as the "subtle scent of discrimination."[34]

The *O'Malley* definition of *prima facie* case does not establish exactly what evidence is required in each case to satisfy the "complete and sufficient" element of the test. The evidentiary burden associated with the *prima facie* case is discerned in each case by reference first to the wording of the enabling statute. In employment cases, for example, most statutes contain prohibitions against the denial of employment ("denial cases") as well as the alternative prohibition against discrimination in the course of employment ("discrimination cases"). In denial cases, the claimant meets the test of *prima facie* case simply by proving that she or he was denied employment and that a prohibited ground was a factor in the denial. In these cases, the framers of the legislation have already determined that such a denial constitutes a violation of the legislation and there is no requirement for further evidence on whether the denial constitutes discrimination. In *Charter* cases, by contrast, the claimant is required to prove that the denial constitutes discrimination. This is one of the critical differences between the statutory and the *Charter* contexts: some statutory human rights provisions contain the key to the evidentiary burden associated with the *prima facie* case in the wording of the statute itself.

In other employment-related cases, a claimant may allege "discrimination in the course of employment." In those cases, the statute may or may not define the word "discrimination." Under the *CHRA,* for example, the Act prohibits "discriminatory practices" and defines those practices as "adverse differentiation on a prohibited ground."[35] The burden on the claimant under the *CHRA* is to lead sufficient evidence to establish that they were treated adversely and that the prohibited ground was a factor in their experience.[36] In other cases, the statute is silent on the meaning of discrimination. In those cases, the adjudicator has been required to define discrimination so as to establish the claimant's evidentiary burden.

Section 15(1) of the *Charter* also refers to, but does not define the word "discrimination." The *Andrews* decision established the definition of discrimination for *Charter* adjudications, drawing on the history of statutory human rights jurisprudence which preceded the *Charter*. This is an important aspect of the interplay between these two equality arenas which is explored in detail later in the paper. Since the decision in *Andrews*, human rights adjudicators have drawn on that definition in circumstances where they have been required to define discrimination in the context of the statutory complaint before them. *Andrews* defines the evidentiary burden in essentially the same terms as the wording of the *CHRA*.[37] In other words, most claimants in statutory human rights adjudications have been required to prove a distinction, which has adverse consequences and which is connected to a prohibited ground. Since the decision in *Law*, it is in cases where the adjudicator defines the case as one of "discrimination" rather than plain denial, in circumstances where discrimination is undefined in the statute, where the import of *Law* occurs most frequently.[38]

The pursuit of evidence which connects adverse differential treatment to a prohibited ground is conducted largely through the subjective experience of the claimant. Claims in the statutory context are often articulated in highly individual terms and as a result, the analysis undertaken by an adjudicator is largely fact-driven. The claimant's storytelling has real evidentiary weight in human rights adjudications and they are not required to take anything more than a subjective perspective on their own experience. The test for *prima facie* case specifically precludes reference to the explanation of the respondent. This can be contrasted with *Charter* adjudications conducted within the parameters of the *Law* test, which requires the adjudicator to take a subjective/objective approach to the claimant's experience and who is permitted to consider the "context" of the claim by reference to the purpose of the impugned rule.

The relatively low evidentiary threshold associated with the *prima facie* case takes into consideration the difficulties associated with proving discrimination in the variety of contexts which are regulated by statutory human rights instruments. The lower threshold is also partly attributable to the fact that the *prima facie* case is rebuttable, since it is decided in the absence of any explanation or justification offered by the respondent. It is only after the *prima facie* case of discrimination has been established that the evidentiary burden shifts to the respondent to establish an exemption or defence to the *prima facie* case. The final verdict on whether the conduct constitutes discrimination is delivered at the conclusion of the evidence lead by both parties. Contrast this with the burden on a *Charter* claimant, which is to definitively prove discrimination and therefore a violation of section 15(1). The *Charter* claimant under the *Law* test bears not just the burden of articulating their own experience, but the additional burden of disproving the justificatory claims of the state which are to some extent permitted in the analysis of the context of the claim.[39]

Once the statutory claimant proves a *prima facie* case, the respondent's burden is to establish a defence or an exemption. The defences and exemptions are at times articulated in the statute[40] or are derived from the Supreme Court of Canada's jurisprudence in *Meiorin*[41] in which the Court undertook a historic re-examination of the concepts of direct and adverse impact discrimination, accommodation, undue hardship, *bona fide* occupational requirement, and *bona fide* justification.[42] Where the employer or service provider disputes the allegation that a prohibited ground was a factor in the decision or practice, the respondent must provide an explanation that proves their assertion on the balance of probabilities that:

a) it adopted the standard for a purpose or goal that is rationally connected to the function being performed;

b) it adopted the standard in good faith, in the belief that it is necessary for the fulfillment of the purpose or goal; and

c) the standard is reasonably necessary to accomplish its purpose or goal in the sense that the respondent cannot accommodate persons with the characteristics of the complainant without incurring undue hardship.

Where the respondent has discharged this evidentiary burden, the burden shifts back to the complainant to establish that the explanation is a pretext designed to mask the fact that considerations related to the prohibited ground were factors in the respondent's decision making or conduct.

C. SIMILARITIES, DIFFERENCES, AND BORROWING BETWEEN THE *CHARTER* AND THE STATUTORY HUMAN RIGHTS CONTEXT

This section deals with some of the similarities between the two arenas, which has lead to a history of each borrowing concepts from the other. This section also canvasses the differences, both conceptual and practical, between constitutional and statutory human rights, including the interpretive distinctions which arise as a result of the differences in the relationships regulated by these regimes. The relationships governed by statutory instruments, namely those between citizens themselves and between citizens and their government employers and service providers, is distinct from the relationship between the citizen and the state in its role in enacting and enforcing law.

Both the *Charter* and human rights statutes share the goal of achieving substantive equality, and are driven by similar underlying principles, such as the promotion of human dignity, the recognition of the benefits of diversity, and the pursuit of activities related to full citizenship: all of these principles ground a broad, liberal, purposive interpretation by adjudicators and courts. In both arenas, discrimination means something more than mere distinction. Both schemes are also anti-majoritarian instruments, and adjudicators and judges frequently attract criticism for "activism" in interpreting them in favour of claimants. They are also beset by the same challenges in attempting to advance substantive equality within the limits of "prohibited grounds." L'Heureux-Dubé J. articulated this problem in her dissent in *Egan v. Canada* that the prohibited grounds approach did not focus sufficient attention on the purpose of section 15 and specifically on those individuals who belong to groups that have suffered historic disadvantage.[43] Denise Réaume makes the related point that prohibited grounds or "pigeonholes" "encourage adjudicators to analyze fact situations through the lens of one alleged ground of discrimination at a time," limiting the possibilities for an intersectional analysis in those cases which engage more than one prohibited ground.[44]

The similarities between these instruments have created a jurisprudential interplay which began with the decision in *Andrews*. In fashioning an analytical framework for determining the scope of discrimination under section 15(1), the Court borrowed elements from the statutory human rights jurisprudence which preceded the *Charter*. Since the decision in

Andrews, statutory adjudicators working without the benefit of a statutory definition of discrimination have borrowed back McIntyre J.'s description of the burden on the claimant to prove more than mere distinction on the basis of a prohibited ground. In *Meiorin*, McLachlin J. borrowed from the *Charter* context to dismantle the distinctions between direct and adverse effect discrimination which were incorporated into statutory human rights law in the 1985 decision in *O'Malley*. In *Maksteel*, the Supreme Court borrowed from the *Charter* decision in *R. v. Big M Drug Mart Ltd.*, [1985] 1 S.C.R. 295 at 344 in emphasizing the importance of not "overshooting the actual purpose of the right or freedom in question," and construing the purpose of the legislation in the appropriate context. In *Baylis-Flannery v. DeWilde (No. 2)*,[45] a decision of the Human Rights Tribunal of Ontario, the adjudicator borrowed from *Law* in describing the role of dignity in the assessment of damages after a finding of discrimination.

What distinguishes this practice of borrowing from the act of importing *Law* into statutory human rights adjudications is that each of these examples enhances or is illustrative of the underlying analytical framework and the interpretive requirements of the statute in question. In other words, borrowing does not result in supplanting the proper interpretive framework. An example of the danger associated with extending beyond the proper limits of borrowing is in the circularity of the decisions in *Reaney, Schafer,* and *McLeod*.[46] The complaint in *Reaney* involved distinctions in benefits between biological and adoptive parents. It started as a labour case to which the provincial human rights legislation applied. In *Reaney*, the British Columbia Court of Appeal decided as a matter of judicial comity to follow the reasoning in *Schafer,* a similar-fact case with a critical distinction — *Schafer* was a *Charter* case not a statutory case, and the *Law* test governed the analysis. Since *Reaney* was decided by the Court of Appeal, the British Columbia Human Rights Tribunal adjudicator in *McLeod,* deciding a similar-fact statutory case, followed the result in *Reaney*. *Reaney* and *McLeod* have their origins in the wrong equality analysis and, as a result, this entire line of cases which could be decided in either the *Charter* or the statutory context is now trapped in this circular analysis in which the *Charter* dominates no matter what statutory instrument is engaged.

The *Charter* and statutory human rights instruments arise in different social and legal contexts which is a significant factor in the interpretation of those instruments, including the development of definitions of discrimination. Madame Falardeau-Ramsay, former Chief Commissioner of the Canadian Human Rights Commission, distinguished statutory human rights instruments and the *Charter* in this way:

> Equality rights are the primary focus of Canadian human rights legislation. Particularly, these include rights to equal and non-discriminatory treatment in employment and in the provision of goods, services and accommodation. This legislation governs relationships between private actors, although, effectively, the state may wear a "private actor" hat as an employer, landlord, or provider of goods and services. In comparison, when a state is wearing its "state" hat, the civil rights which define the relationship between the individual and the state which restrain or compel the state to act (for example, rights of freedom of expression and association, and legal process rights) are addressed by the *Canadian Charter of Rights and Freedoms.*[47]

Human rights legislation is regulatory in nature. It establishes and regulates a limited set of entitlements and expectations between individuals in the context of their private relationships and in the interaction of individuals with government service providers and employers. Most statutes are confined to conduct and policies arising in relation to employment, services, goods, facilities, and accommodation. Cases in the statutory context relate at times to broad public policy issues, but they also focus considerable attention on the individual circumstances of each complainant. The statutes are not drafted in such a way as to empower commissions and tribunals to focus their resources on cases involving complainants who identify with groups that have suffered historic disadvantage. While they are not constitutional in nature, these statutes play an important role in establishing the boundaries and contours of acceptable conduct in the important public and private contexts of employment and service provision.

The *Charter,* by contrast, prohibits discrimination which arises by the application or operation of law and is invoked only against a government actor. The *Charter* has much greater potential for advancing the equality rights of historically disadvantaged groups, through a focus on the experiences of dominance and subordination that arise through the operation of law and government policy. As was suggested earlier, unlike statutory human rights legislation, the *Charter* is interpreted in a manner which allows for the expansion of the prohibited grounds of discrimination.[48]

The section 15(1) test has evolved not in the regulatory context of statutory human rights disputes, but in the context of challenges to legislation or government policy or programs. As Cynthia Petersen points out in her arguments on behalf of the intervener EGALE in *Nixon*,[49] the application of the *Charter* analysis to the regulatory human rights context, could have significant negative consequences:

> The "contextual factors" which comprise the s. 15 test consist, inter alia, of considering the "constitutional and social significance of the interests affected," whether the claimant has been denied access to a "fundamental social institution," and whether their exclusion from an under-inclusive law or program "affects a basic aspect of full membership in Canadian society." These questions are frequently answered affirmatively in the context of under-inclusive legislative schemes because of the significant impact of state-sanctioned exclusion from a public program. These same questions would, however, hardly ever be answered affirmatively in the context of assessing the effect of private sector policies, practices or programs. Consequently, importing these *Charter* factors into the human rights context, where complaints are usually against private sector entities, sets a virtually unreachable threshold for establishing *prima facie* discrimination.[50]

In reviewing the decision of the tribunal in *Nixon*, Edwards J. applied the *Law* test, but made note of the difficulties associated with its application at paragraphs 127 through 129:

> Application of the *Law* analytical framework presents difficulties in this case because it was articulated in *Law* as the appropriate analysis for *Charter* scrutiny of exclusion from financial benefit entitlement legislation, not for scrutiny of exclusion from a service or employment provided by a non-governmental entity such as Rape Relief, alleged to be discrimination under the *Code*.

These observations highlight the importance of context in choosing an analytical framework for the adjudication of statutory human rights claims. The differences between the context in which statutory instruments and the *Charter* have evolved, combined with the nature of the claims and relationships at stake in those arenas, is what makes the application of different interpretive frameworks appropriate. There is no "one size fits all" analysis which would capture the complexities of these important but distinctive equality rights instruments.

D. SUPREME COURT OF CANADA DECISIONS SINCE *LAW*

Since *Law*, the Supreme Court has considered five notable cases which engage with the discrimination analysis required under statutory human rights legislation.[51] In none of those cases did the Supreme Court supplant *O'Malley* with *Law*. To take an even broader view, the decisions of the Supreme Court since *O'Malley*, including the seminal *Charter* decision in *Andrews*, have consistently reinforced the distinct legal analysis associated with statutory human rights instruments. In *Andrews*, while the Supreme Court borrowed definitions of discrimination from human rights law, the Court rejected the convergence of the *Charter* with the statutory human rights instruments which preceded it and articulated a distinct framework for discerning discrimination under section 15(1).[52]

The *Meiorin* decision, which was released just months after the decision in *Law*, arose in the context of an arbitration in which the issue of discrimination and therefore the provisions of the *BCHRC* were engaged. The Court undertook an historic re-examination of the concepts of direct and adverse impact discrimination as they related to the complex web of defences to which this distinction had given rise. The approach taken by the Court unified what had previously been distinct evidentiary burdens on respondents in defending allegations of discrimination, depending on whether those allegations could be described in "direct" or "adverse impact" terms. The distinctions, to the extent that they remain on a conceptual level, no longer have any bearing on the respondent's evidentiary burden.

In the decision in *Meiorin*, the Court made reference to the "dissonance" between *Charter* and human rights analysis. The "dissonance" argument is the last and least significant of the seven arguments in favour of the new approach. The narrow scope of the dissonance identified by the Court between statutory instruments and the *Charter* was articulated in paragraph 48:

> Where it is possible to make a *Charter* claim in the course of an employment relationship, the employer cannot dictate the nature of what it must prove in justification simply by altering the *method* of discrimination. I see little reason for adopting a different approach when the claim is brought under human rights legislation which, while it may have a different legal orientation, is aimed at the same general wrong as s. 15(1) of the *Charter*.

This statement does not, in any way, suggest support for the adoption of the test in *Law* into statutory human rights cases. In fact, in paragraph 43, the Court affirmed that human rights statutes are "legislative pronouncements" which must be interpreted according to their terms and in light of their purposes. It is clear that the purpose of the analysis in *Meiorin* was not to harmonize statutory human rights legislation with the *Charter,* but to evolve statutory human rights law in a manner which was more consistent with the purpose of contemporary human rights legislation. At paragraph 25, McLachlin J. (as she was then) writes:

> The conventional analysis was helpful in the interpretation of the early human rights statutes, and indeed represented a significant step forward in that it recognized for the first time the harm of adverse effect discrimination. The distinction it drew between the available remedies may also have reflected the apparent differences between direct and adverse effect discrimination. However well this approach may have served us in the past, many commentators have suggested that it ill-serves the purpose of contemporary human rights legislation. I agree. In my view, the complexity and unnecessary artificiality of aspects of the conventional analysis attest to the desirability of now simplifying the guidelines that structure the interpretation of human rights legislation in Canada.

While the focus of *Meiorin* is on the development of the principles of accommodation, undue hardship, *bona fide* occupational requirement (BFOR), and *bona fide* justification (BFJ), what is sometimes overlooked by adjudicators and courts is that McLachlin J. began her analysis by confirming the finding of *prima facie* case made by the original arbitrator. In *Meiorin* the *prima facie* case was established in a manner consistent with *O'Malley*, through evidence identifying adverse treatment on the basis of a prohibited ground. And yet, respondents have urged adjudicators and courts to adopt a "unified" approach to defining discrimination on the basis of the "dissonance" argument, which they articulate in broader terms than is actually reflected in the *Meiorin* decision. In the British Columbia Human Rights Tribunal decision in *Dame,*[53] for example, the argument was raised but ultimately rejected by the adjudicator. However, in the Albert Court of Queen's Bench decision in *Gwinner,*[54] the Court accepted this argument as support for the import and application of the decision in *Law* in the adjudication of a statutory human rights claim.

The decision of the Supreme Court of Canada in *Grismer* was released at the same time as *Meiorin* and confirmed that the *Meiorin* analysis applied in both the labour and statutory human rights contexts. Like *Meiorin*, the Court in *Grismer* confirmed the finding that the claimant had established a *prima facie* case by proving that he had been denied a driver's license because of his disability (visual impairment). In both *Meiorin* and *Grismer*, the Court in fact affirmed that the claimants had discharged their burden to prove a *prima facie* case by proving adverse treatment on the basis of a prohibited ground. There was no inquiry, in either case, into the manner in which the impugned standards engaged with the dignity of the claimants.

Similarly, in the *City of Montreal* case, L'Heureux-Dubé J. did not follow the *Law* decision in determining the elements of the complainant's burden under the provincial human rights charter in Quebec.[55] Instead, she focused her analysis on the statute itself, confirming the importance of context and the specific wording of the act in question. In "*B*,"[56] which involved the question of the scope of the prohibited ground of family status, Iacobucci J. did not supplant *O'Malley* with his own reasoning in *Law*. He focused his analysis on the statutory context of the appeal, the wording of the statute, and the quasi-constitutional nature of human rights legislation. Similarly, in *Maksteel*, decided in 2003, the most recent of the statutory human rights cases cited here, the Supreme Court of Canada expressly considered the elements of the *prima facie* case without reference to the decision in *Law* affirming that the burden of proof associated with the *prima facie* will depend on the wording of the provision in question.[57]

E. ILLUSTRATIONS OF *LAW* IN THE STATUTORY HUMAN RIGHTS CONTEXT

What follows is an analysis of some of the notable cases which are illustrative of the arguments raised earlier in the paper and which demonstrate the dangers associated with merging statutory adjudications with the analytical concepts drawn from *Law*. The analysis begins with two cases, *Barrett* and *Nixon*,[58] in which the import of *Law* was specifically addressed and originally rejected creating a framework for understanding the interplay between *Law* and *O'Malley*. Those cases are followed by a discussion of the challenges associated with "cross-over" cases or cases which could be adjudicated in either the statutory or constitutional context. The section concludes with more thematic observations derived from a variety of other cases which demonstrate the myriad ways in which *Law* has manifested in the statutory context.

1) *Barrett* and *Nixon*: Rejecting *Law*

In the Federal context and in various provincial jurisdictions such as Ontario and Alberta, the import of principles from the *Law* decision began without much analysis of the propriety of that approach.[59] By contrast, in British Columbia, the issue appears to have arisen first in the context of the very thoughtful analysis conducted in *Barrett* in December 2001. In that case, the British Columbia Human Rights Tribunal rejected a claim by Elizabeth Barrett that two groups of employees of Cominco Ltd. were discriminated against on the basis of age with respect to pension and severance packages that were made available to employees in anticipation of the closure of Cominco's operations in Kimberley, BC The union was added as a respondent because the issue involved provisions in a collective agreement. The employer and the union claimed that they were attempting to balance the needs of various groups of employees by creating a tiered system of severance pay which reflected their understanding that older workers would have a harder time finding alternate employment.

The tribunal found that in the case of workers under the age of forty-six, the claimant was able to make out a *prima facie* case on the basis of an adverse distinction on the prohibited ground of age. As has been suggested above, this is the classic formulation of the *prima facie* analysis in statutory human rights adjudications. The tribunal ultimately dismissed the case on the basis of the exemption for *bona fide* pension plan schemes in section 13(3) of the *BCHRC*. Barrett's second complaint, relating to employees fifty-five and over, was dismissed on the basis that there was no disadvantage flowing from the differential treatment of this group, which also represents the classic requirement to prove more than mere distinction.

In deciding the case, the tribunal conducted a discussion of the application of the decision in *Law* to the concept of *prima facie* discrimination. The analysis began, appropriately, with a restatement of the test in *O'Malley*. It was the respondent in this case who urged the *Law* decision upon the tribunal and suggested that *Law* required the claimant to prove injury to dignity as an element of the burden of proving a *prima facie* case. After a review of the *Law* decision itself, the tribunal made the following findings, which are located at paragraphs 75 through 102 of the decision:

1. In *Charter* cases, the *Law* decision does not necessarily require evidence of dignity — it may be apparent on the record.

2. While the *Code* requires a substantive discrimination analysis, the decision in *Law* has not imported a requirement that a complainant establish a violation of human dignity as an element of the *prima facie* case.

3. Nowhere in *Law* does the Court suggest that the *Charter* analysis applies to statutory human rights adjudications.

4. In cases decided by the Supreme Court since *Law*, the Court has not imported a requirement to adduce evidence of impairment to dignity before the *prima facie* case is established and the burden shifts to the respondent to establish a BFOR.

5. The differences between the *Charter* and the *Code* suggest different evidentiary burdens.

6. The development of the concept of discrimination is flexible and is informed by developments in both arenas.

7. In many cases, the analysis under the *Charter* and the *Code* will be the same — if a distinction is based on an enumerated ground and results in a disadvantage to the complainant, it will likely be self-evident that the distinction is discriminatory.

8. The assessment of whether there is disadvantage resulting in discrimination requires consideration of the context of the claim and a purposive analysis; however, none of this is new to human rights adjudications.

The *Barrett* decision was not appealed and it was followed within approximately one month by a similar decision from the tribunal in *Nixon*. As of this writing, the *Nixon* tribunal decision had been overturned by the British Columbia Supreme Court and was awaiting argument before the British Columbia Court of Appeal.

Kimberley Nixon alleged that she was denied a volunteer counseling position with Rape Relief in Vancouver on the basis that she was a post-operative male to female transexual. Rape Relief is a non-profit, feminist organization whose mandate is to provide services to women who have experienced male violence and to work toward the eradication of male violence toward women. This equality-seeking mandate distinguishes Rape Relief from almost all other respondents in human rights claims and represents one of the most important complexities of this case.[60]

There are a number of similarities between the tribunal decisions in *Barrett* and *Nixon*. Both affirmed the application of the *prima facie* analysis from the *O'Malley* decision. In both cases the *respondents* urged the tribunal to adopt the analysis in *Law* and require evidence of impairment to dignity as an element of proving a *prima facie* case. In both decisions, the tribunals pointed out that it had been long settled in the statutory human rights context that mere distinctions do not constitute substantive discrimination and that the analysis must be conducted purposively. In both cases, the tribunals conducted the purposive analysis appropriately by reference to the purpose of the *BCHRC* of which human dignity is but one aspect.

> The concept of human dignity is one aspect of the vision of equality that the Code aims to achieve. Following *Law*, it may be appropriate to affirm the principle that the conduct prohibited by the Code is discriminatory conduct within the meaning of the legislation. I do not accept the respondent's argument, however, that a violation of human dignity is an independent and necessary element of a *prima facie* case.[61]

Both adjudicators agreed that there was nothing in the decision itself or the Supreme Court of Canada's subsequent jurisprudence to suggest that the Court intended a change in the elements of the *prima facie* case. In *Nixon*, the adjudicator evolved this argument by pointing out that in neither *Meiorin* nor *Grismer* did the Court embark on an analysis of whether the distinction made by the respondents affected the claimant's dignity.

In both cases the respondents relied on the exemptions available under the *BCHRC*, which is one of the factors distinguishing the *Charter* from statutory human rights legislation.[62] In *Barrett*, the respondents successfully pleaded the exemption available for "*bona fide* pension plans." In *Nixon*, three exemptions were pleaded, all of which were rejected: first, that the *Code* does not govern relationships between non-profit organizations and their volunteers because those relationships cannot be defined as "employment" within the meaning of the *Code*; second, that the ability to volunteer does not constitute a service; and third, that section 41 of the *Code*, which purports to balance freedom of association with freedom from discrimination, protects Rape Relief in its ability to define membership in its organization according to sex, and in this case, sex as a broader construct than the binary male and female. In the appeal of the tribunal's decision by the British Columbia Supreme Court, which is reviewed in more detail below, Rape Relief was successful in invoking this last exemption.

The existence of statutory exemptions and defences is critically important to the question of importing *Law*. These exemptions and defences represent explicit legislative mechanisms which, if successfully invoked by a respondent, result in a finding of no discrimination. However, a finding of no discrimination in the statutory human rights context is limited to either the failure of the claimant to prove a *prima facie* case, or the success of the respondent in invoking a statutory exemption or defence. If the adjudicator in *Nixon* had accepted the argument of the respondent that *Law* requires proof of impairment to dignity on the "subjective/objective" evidentiary standard, there would be a resulting elevation in the burden on the claimant. This elevation in the burden would be tantamount to creating a defence which is not articulated in either the statute or the *Meiorin* framework. As discussed earlier in the paper, the Supreme Court of Canada has repeatedly reinforced the quasi-constitutional nature of human rights legislation, including the requirement to construe defences and exemptions as narrowly as possible.

In *Nixon*, as in *Barrett*, the adjudicator relied on a variety of distinctions between the *Charter* and human rights legislation, all of which have been canvassed in detail above. In both cases, the tribunals reinforced that in most human rights cases a discriminatory effect will be apparent where there is differential adverse treatment on the basis of a prohibited ground.

However, there is at least one troubling departure from the classic statutory human rights analysis by the adjudicator in *Nixon* which appears at the conclusion of the analysis on the application of *Law*. The adjudicator is clear that proof of injury to dignity is not a requirement of the *prima facie* case. She goes on to say that once the *prima facie* case is proven and the onus has shifted to the respondent to provide an explanation, the tribunal will then assess both the differential treatment and the respondent's explanation for it. It is in this context, "and where it is not evident that the differential treatment is discriminatory," that the tribunal may consider the impact on the complainant's dignity and the contextual factors that were set out in *Law*.[63]

This assertion seems out of place, coming as it does at the conclusion of a lengthy critical analysis of the application of *Law* to statutory human rights cases. It is also inconsistent with statutory human rights law and an example of an adjudicator exceeding the appropriate limits of borrowing from the *Charter*. If a claimant is successful in proving the *prima facie* element of the case, their complaint will be successful unless the employer proves a defence or exemption. The adjudicator's analysis in this case, however, suggests that a claimant could be successful in proving a *prima facie* case and then find the case dismissed, not because the respondent asserted a successful defence, but on some other analysis which engages with the contextual factors that were set out in *Law*. The myriad questions about how this analysis might unfold are not answered in this case, where the adjudicator goes on to find that the discrimination was "self-evident."

Ultimately the tribunal found that "it is self-evident that this type of exclusion is *prima facie* discriminatory with the meaning of the Code," given the admissions by Rape Relief that Ms. Nixon was excluded solely because she was transexual.[64] The tribunal also concluded that even if the subjective/objective perspective were applied to Ms. Nixon's evidence, her dignity was clearly impaired.

The onus having shifted to the respondent, the tribunal engaged in the undue hardship analysis established in *Meiorin*. While the *prima facie* case is self-evident, Rape Relief's argument that socialization as a female is a *bona fide* occupational requirement remains one of the most challenging arguments ever raised under the *Meiorin* framework. This case is one which could have significantly advanced the jurisprudence on the defence of undue hardship. Like most human rights cases, it poses the greatest challenge to the third stage of the *Meiorin* analysis which requires a respondent to demonstrate that the standard they have adopted (in this case, socialization as a female) incorporates every possible accommodation to the point of undue hardship. In the appeal of the tribunal's decision the British Columbia Supreme Court focused first on the exemption available to Rape Relief and second on confirming the import of the *Law* decision into the *prima facie* analysis. The Court did not deal with the *Meiorin* stage of the analysis and therefore never clarified whether the tribunal conducted the appropriate undue hardship analysis. The focus on *Law* in this case impaired the development of this important aspect of human rights jurisprudence.[65]

In December 2003, the British Columbia Supreme Court released its decision in the appeal of the *Nixon* tribunal decision. The Court decided the case in favour of Rape Relief on the statutory exemption, overturning the tribunal's decision in that respect. Despite this finding, which was dispositive of the appeal, the Court went further; it overturned the tribunal's decision on the application of the *Law* test, concluding that it was bound by the decision of the British Columbia Court of Appeal in *Reaney*. The Court found that Ms. Nixon was required, but had failed, to establish impairment to dignity on the appropriate subjective/objective perspective.

This is a direct example of a Court adopting an inappropriate evidentiary standard, the outcome of which is to directly interfere with the wording of the statute, which itself contains the key to the evidentiary burden. Like many statutory human rights instruments, it is a *prima facie* violation of the *BCHRC* to deny a public service or to deny employment on the basis of a prohibited ground. Inherent in this kind of statutory provision is the conclusion by the drafters of the legislation that denying employment or public services on a prohibited ground constitutes *prima facie* discrimination. Once the denial is connected to a prohibited ground, the respondent is required to provide a justification. In "denial" cases it is a mistake to apply either the elaborate *Law* analysis or the definition of discrimination from *Andrews*. The drafters of the legislation have already established the evidentiary equation: denial + prohibited ground = *prima facie* case.

In circumstances where a prospective employer is not so forthcoming, the evidentiary burden on the complainant is more difficult to discharge, but still limited to proof that the prohibited ground was a factor in the decision not to hire. In Nixon's case, there was no dispute that the prohibited ground was connected to the denial. Once it was established that Kimberley Nixon was denied the opportunity to volunteer with Rape Relief on the basis of the prohibited ground of sex, the *prima facie* analysis was complete. The tribunal made the same mistake, although the consequences were obviously less significant. As was suggested above, had the tribunal and the Courts proceeded in a manner which was consistent with the statutory language, this case would have had the potential to advance the jurisprudence through a much more significant focus on the undue hardship analysis and the exemptions.

2) *Gwinner*: The Challenge of "Cross-Over" Cases Involving Government Respondents

Cases which could be adjudicated in either the statutory or constitutional forum, referred to here as "cross-over" cases, present significant challenges to maintaining clear analytical boundaries between statutory and *Charter* interpretation. These cases usually arise in the context of a challenge to a government benefit program and raise questions about the propriety of attaching two discrete definitions of discrimination to the same government program. The decision in *Gwinner*[66] is an example of a cross-over case where this question was resolved in favour of allowing *Law* to dominate.

An alternative to this approach would be to consider the extent to which *borrowing* concepts from the *Charter* might enhance the statutory analysis in cases where government policy is impugned.

Despite the fact that the Alberta human rights legislation under which *Gwinner* was adjudicated does not contain explicit statutory provisions entrenching a different analytical framework for private respondents as opposed to public sector respondents, that is precisely the approach taken in this case. The Alberta Court of Queens Bench accepted the propriety of relying on the decision in *Law* in circumstances where the issue was one which could be raised either under the *Charter* or under the provincial human rights statute. This is not an approach which takes into consideration the possibility of borrowing *Charter* concepts to enhance the adjudication of statutory claims that have significant public interest components. This approach simply supplants the statutory framework with the *Law* test.

In *Gwinner*, the respondent was the Alberta government in its capacity as service provider and the benefits at issue were provided under the provincial *Widow's Pension Act*.[67] The *Act* provided pension benefits to widows and widowers between the ages of fifty-five and sixty-four. The intention of the Act, according to the province, was to provide a pension to married women who stayed at home to raise children and therefore relied on their husband's income, who found themselves without support on the death of their spouse.[68] The claimants alleged that the deprivation of the benefit was discriminatory since divorced women and women who have never married but have taken care of an aged parent who dies can find themselves in very similar financial circumstances as widows and widowers. In the original tribunal decision, the claimants were able to establish a *prima facie* case; however, the respondents were ultimately successful in invoking the "reasonable and justifiable" defence provided for in the statute, and the complaints were dismissed.

The tribunal decision was appealed to and overturned by the Alberta Queen's Bench. The Court adopted the *Law* analysis, interpreting the "dignity inquiry" as an elaboration of the third step of the traditional equality analysis, made necessary because it was not readily apparent that the impugned legislation violated Nancy Law's dignity. The Court then affirmed that in many, if not most, cases under human rights legislation, the elaborate third step scrutiny to determine if the dignity interest of the claimant was truly engaged, would not be necessary. Yet the Court applied the test to this case without first establishing its necessity, except to say that the claimants were challenging a government program and the respondent raised the question about the impact of the exclusion from the program on the claimant's dignity.

The Court engaged in the elaborate *Law* analysis despite the fact that the legislation clearly precluded the denial of any service on a prohibited ground — like *Nixon*, this case should have been decided simply on that basis. It matters not that the outcome in this case is ultimately favourable to the claimants. What matters is that the claimants were all living in a state of extreme financial hardship which was no doubt exacerbated by the kind of protracted proceedings which ensued when the Court engaged in a more complex analysis than was required to resolve the issue. There is a serious concern that the more complex and protracted the proceedings, the more potential there is for a tribunal or court to deviate from the proper interpretation of the statute to the detriment of an otherwise deserving complainant.

It remains a challenge to determine how best to resolve these cross-over cases, many of which, because of their engagement with issues of broad public policy, present opportunities for achieving real substantive-equality ends through statutory human rights legislation. Is there a principled approach to the development of a hybrid analysis of statutory human rights principles and *Charter* principles in cross-over claims? Is there room, for example, in the defence of undue hardship, for an analysis which accords some deference to government respondents with respect to their legislative choices? Does tailoring the analysis to the nature of the claim undermine the intent of the framers of statutory human rights legislation? Must discrimination be construed in monolithic terms? Is it more or less consistent with the principles of substantive equality to accept that some conduct may be discriminatory on a quasi-constitutional standard but not on a constitutional one? Is the potential for different outcomes related to the claims that *Law* imposes a higher evidentiary burden on claimants, and if so, does that place an even greater limit on the potential for borrowing? The Court in *Gwinner* did not engage in this analysis, opting instead for the dominance of *Law*.

3) The *Law* Continuum

As was suggested above, the *Law* decision appears in the statutory human rights context on a continuum. On the one end are cases which recognize the interplay, but not the dominance, of the *Charter* analysis. On the other end are cases where *Law* is imported along with the requirement to prove impairment to dignity.[69]

In *Brock* and *Turnbull*, two Ontario cases dealing with the exclusion of persons in wheelchairs from movie theatres, the adjudicator applied *Law*, but in a way which simply recognizes dignity as a value underlying both the *Charter* and the Ontario legislation. In both of these cases impairment to dignity was obvious to the adjudicator, who only referenced the concept of dignity from *Law* as being "at the heart of discrimination."[70] Similarly, in the *Friday* case, decided under the Saskatchewan legislation, the adjudicator referenced *Law* in finding that a disabled aboriginal man had been profoundly humiliated when the security guard in a grocery store treated him as if he was drunk.[71] In that case, the adjudicator relied on the decision in *Andrews* as having been confirmed conceptually by *Law*.

In *Waters*, the tribunal concluded that the *Law* test did not apply to the discrimination analysis but that it was useful in considerations associated with remedy.[72] Similarly in *Baylis-Flannery*, the adjudicator rejected the application of *Law* in the *prima facie* analysis but undertook a very thoughtful application of *Law* on the issue of remedy in this complex intersectional case.[73] The case involved serious allegations of sexual and racial harassment in the context of employment, culminating in sexual assault for which the respondent was criminally prosecuted. Since the issue of impairment to dignity is central to the question of quantum of damages, the language in *Law* may be of assistance to tribunals in developing the evidentiary framework for these awards. The issue of general damages, which is highly discretionary, is one of the least predictable elements of trying a case before a tribunal.

In some cases, the formal three-part test from *Law* has not been applied directly, but the requirement to prove impairment to dignity has opened the door to requiring complainants to prove that their claims violate the purpose of the legislation in question. In other words, apart from the evidentiary burdens to prove a *prima facie* case on the basis of a denial or differential treatment, the claimant now has the additional hurdle of proving that an infringement of the purpose of the legislation on the basis that the dignity of the claimant is impaired.

A number of provincial statutes reference the preservation of human dignity as one of the goals of the legislation. This general purpose section, in which dignity underpins the entire legislative scheme, should be understood as a recognition that the preservation of human dignity is achieved by remedying discrimination. The enhancement of human dignity is an outcome of a properly-administered human rights dispute resolution process. However, post-*Law*, this purpose has, in some cases, been transformed into an evidentiary burden.

In *Bigsby*, for example, the Alberta Commission dismissed a complaint rather than refer it to a public inquiry.[74] Commission staff found that there was no impairment to human dignity and therefore, the complaint was not a "human rights issue." This analysis was developed by reference both to *Law* and to the underlying purpose of the Alberta human rights legislation. *Bigsby* is also an example of the implications of importing *Law* into statutory human rights adjudications — there is a risk that it will become the new standard by which commissions carry out their "gatekeeping" function and determine which cases merit public inquiry.

In several of the cases described above, the *Law* analysis was directly imported and allowed to dominate the statutory analysis for various reasons: judicial comity in cases involving similar fact patterns; as a natural part of the evolution of the concept of discrimination; and where the conduct of a government rather than a private respondent is impugned. In *Wignall*, for example, the *prima facie* case should have been easily proven on the basis that the complainant was deaf, and that because he was deaf he received an education grant which, because of Revenue Canada's policy, attracted adverse tax consequences. *Wignall* was a classic example of a seemingly neutral rule with unintended adverse consequences. The loss in that case is directly attributable to the adjudicator's misapprehension that a "convergence in the approach taken to define discrimination" had occurred between the *Charter* and the statutory analysis.[75] Similarly, in *Pringle*, the statutory analysis was completely eradicated through the application of the *Law* test. The adjudicator dismissed the claim of Ms. Pringle, who was adopted as a child and later sought access to her birth registration, finding that there was no objective evidence of impairment to dignity as a result of the denial.[76]

The *Brown* decision is yet another case involving of a government respondent (although in this case, government as employer) where *Law* was imported creating significant consequences for the discrimination analysis.[77] *Brown* involved differential treatment in the provision of employment benefits to persons disabled by alcoholism. The application of the *Law* test in this case was an invitation to the government to engage in defending the purpose and operation of the impugned rule at the very commencement of the discrimination analysis.[78] In this case, the government asserted that there was no distinction between alcoholics and other disabled employees because ultimately, the same benefits were available to both groups. Compare that analysis to the *prima facie* case analysis which is determined without reference to the evidence of the respondent and on the basis of the claimant's subjective experience of adverse differential treatment on a prohibited ground. The government's argument was ultimately rejected in this case. However, the use of the *Law* framework to introduce justificatory evidence at the commencement of the discrimination analysis creates opportunities for defending the impugned rule which are inconsistent with the decision of the Supreme Court of Canada in *O'Malley* and the statutory defences.

There are cases where the *Law* analysis has been applied and the outcome has been consistent with statutory instruments. In *A.A. v. New Brunswick (Department of Family and Community Services)*[79] a New Brunswick adjudicator found in favour of a lesbian couple who had been refused the parental rights of registration and adoption of the daughter they had conceived through alternative fertilization. The adjudicator found that the denial was an affront to the dignity of both parents, particularly the non-biological parent. At paragraph 54, the adjudicator stated that "... the discriminatory action concerning the efforts to adopt C.C. by A.A. and B.B. reflects a difference in treatment based on marital status implying that same-sex couples are less worthy of consideration as adoptive parents than heterosexual couples with the resulting injury to their self-esteem." As was suggested earlier in the paper, the dignity inquiry is fraught with potential for judicial subjectivism, and the outcome in this case would not necessarily be universal. Only a short while ago, the government of Canada was taking the legal position in the same-sex marriage cases that the "heterosexual" definition of marriage, when viewed by gays and lesbians from the appropriate subjective/objective perspective, would not been seen as undermining their dignity.[80] In cases where anti-discrimination law is most underdeveloped, and conduct least recognized as "self-evidently" discriminatory, this subjectivism could seriously impair the progression of substantive equality theory and practice in the statutory human rights context.

F. CONCLUSION

The *Charter* and statutory human rights legislation are distinct instruments designed to advance substantive equality in important but different forums. The *Charter* cannot be invoked to remedy discrimination in the vast majority of relationships regulated by statutory instruments, nor would it be desirable to characterize every statutory claim as constitutional in nature. Because of those distinctions, the evidentiary burdens borne by parties must correspond to the circumstances in which their claims arise. The historic analysis applied to the resolution of statutory human rights claims, drawn largely from the decision in *O'Malley*, represents the appropriate evidentiary standard in a context where statutory interpretation governs the analysis, where the *prima facie* case is rebuttable, and where the respondent is able to draw on a range of statutory and jurisprudential exceptions and defences.

The application of the *Law* test in the statutory context can result in an elevation in the burden on the claimant directly contributing to dismissals in cases which would have succeeded under the traditional analytical framework. The focus on the application of the complex principles from *Law* can shift the focus from the development of other important principles such as the defence of undue hardship. The *Law* analysis is also complex and its application poses serious challenges to adjudicators, many of whom are appointed with limited experience in human rights adjudications. The current jurisprudence contains several examples of the improper application of *Law*. One of the best examples was cited earlier in the paper where the burden of proof was raised to "compelling objective evidence" rather than the subjective/objective perspective required by *Law*.

There is considerable promise in maintaining distinct analytical frameworks between the *Charter* and the statutory human rights arenas. The challenge will be to find ways to develop analytical concepts which give life to the purposes which underlie these important instruments, appreciating that they are linked by the grander purpose of eradicating discrimination. The goal should be an interactive framework which provides opportunities for enriching equality rights jurisprudence and advancing substantive equality without supplanting the principles developed specifically for the issues which arise in these two distinct contexts.

ENDNOTES

1   Leslie A. Reaume is counsel to the Canadian Human Rights Commission. The author's views do not necessarily reflect the views of the Commission.

I wish to thank the participants of "In Pursuit of Substantive Equality: A Two-Part Colloquium to Reinvigorate and Advance Equality Rights Under the *Charter*: September 2003 and February 2004" and particularly Fay Faraday, whose contributions enriched the final version of this paper. Andrea Wright has written a paper which also appears in this collection and addresses another important concern: that comparative methodologies, which are fundamental to *Charter* applications, have been increasingly relied upon as a necessary element in proving statutory human rights violations.

2   *Ontario Human Rights Commission and O'Malley v. Simpson Sears Limited*, [1985] 2 S.C.R. 536 [*O'Malley*].

3   In this paper the phrases "statutory human rights," "regulatory context," or "statutory context" are used to distinguish provincial and federal human rights statutes from the *Charter*.

4   The status of the *O'Malley* decision was recently affirmed by the Federal Court of Appeal in *Lincoln v. Bay Ferries*, [2004] SCCA (leave to appeal to S.C.C. denied), [2004] FCA 204 [*Lincoln*].

5   Part I of the *Constitution Act, 1982*, being Schedule B to the *Canada Act 1982* (U.K.), c. 11 [*Charter*].

6   We may now be perched on the edge of losing the important distinctions between these two equality rights arenas, which is why this paper might have been more aptly entitled "Postcards from the Edge," but for the fact that a thoughtful American writer came up with it first. Carrie Fisher, *Postcards from the Edge* (New York: Simon and Shuster, 1987). See, for example, W.S. Tarnopolsky in *Discrimination and the Law*, looseleaf (Toronto: R. De Boo, 1985) at 4.7B who says that jurisprudence pertaining to *Charter* interpretation, particularly s. 15(1), may be relied upon in interpreting human rights code guarantees, citing *Ontario (Human Rights Commission) v. Ontario (Ministry of Health)* (1994), 21 C.H.R.R. D/259 (Ont. C.A.). The discussion continues at 4.8 where the author states that: "... principles of constitutional paramountcy and *in pari materia* operate jointly to homogenize the interpretation of anti-discrimination language in human rights codes with that of s. 15(1). If not a 'mirror,' *Charter* jurisprudence might fairly be described as a 'template' for decision-making under other anti-discrimination statutes." See also Walter S. Tarnopolsky & William F. Pentney, *Discrimination and the Law: Including Equality Rights Under the Charter*, looseleaf (Scarborough: Carswell, 2001) at 4-102,11-12: "*Charter* jurisprudence is a source of authority for cases involving the anti-discrimination provisions of human rights codes. Indeed it would be remarkable if this were not the case, in view of the paramount authority of the *Charter* and the almost precise identity between the grounds enumerated under s. 15 and those identified in human rights enactments ...."

7   *Law v. Canada (Minister of Employment and Immigration)*, [1999] 1 S.C.R. 497
     [*Law*].

8   At the Federal level and in most provinces, human rights commissions play a screen-
     ing function and resolve through settlement, dismissal, or deferral to other forums
     the vast majority of complaints filed. Of those cases that are referred for public
     inquiry, many settle before a public hearing. In 2004, for example, the Canadian
     Human Rights Tribunal released public decisions in approximately eighteen cases
     (online: www.chrt-tcdp.gc.ca). The Human Rights Tribunal of Ontario also released
     approximately eighteen decisions in 2004 (online: www.hrto.on.ca). The rate of final
     public decisions from the British Columbia Human Rights Tribunal, however, is
     expected to rise significantly in comparison to other tribunals because of the imple-
     mentation of "direct access." This is not to suggest that direct access will create more
     opportunities to evolve the jurisprudence since the screening function simply moves
     from the Commission to the Tribunal. The evolution of the jurisprudence depends
     on the existence of public institutions, like human rights commissions and private
     advocates, with well-developed strategic litigation plans which allow them to screen
     cases and deploy litigation resources for maximum human rights impact.

9   There are a considerable number of cases in which courts and tribunals have pro-
     nounced on the quasi-constitutional nature of human rights legislation. See, for
     example, the often-cited decision *Insurance Corporation of B.C. v. Heerspink*, [1982] 2
     S.C.R. 145.

10 The statutory human rights context is replete with examples of claims which would
     not be described as "constitutional" in nature but which are consistent with the
     importance provincial and federal legislators have placed on eradicating discrimina-
     tion in the regulatory context. See, for example, *Daily v. Sears Canada Inc.* (2003), 49
     C.H.R.R. D/506 (Sask. H.R.T.) in which the complainant successfully retained her
     retail discount card after retirement; or any number of complaints based on transient
     disabilities like temporary back injuries which an employer has failed to accommo-
     date.

11 Indeed, there are many examples of cases in the statutory context, particularly in
     the context of harassment claims, for which the emotional and financial costs are
     devastating. Some of these cases include allegations of criminal assault. In 1996 a
     Coroner's Inquest was conducted into the death of Theresa Vince who was murdered
     by her supervisor at the Sears store in Chatham, Ontario where she worked. The
     Coroner heard evidence that Mrs. Vince had complained to the company of sexual
     harassment by the same supervisor prior to her death.

12 This is precisely the approach taken by the Supreme Court in cases such as *B v.
     Ontario (Human Rights Commission)*, [2002] 3 S.C.R. 403 [*B*] and *British Columbia
     (P.S.E.R.C.) v. BCGSEU*, [1999] 3 S.C.R. 3 [*Meiorin*].

13 *Andrews v. Law Society of British Columbia*, [1989] 1 S.C.R. 143 [*Andrews*].

14 There is, of course, one arena in which it is appropriate for the *Charter* to dominate
     statutory human rights legislation: in cases in which it is alleged that the legislation
     itself fails to comply with the *Charter*. In *Vriend v. Alberta*, [1998] 1 S.C.R. 493, for
     example, the *Charter* was used to remedy the absence of sexual orientation discrimi-

nation protection in employment under the provincial human rights legislation. The Supreme Court read in sexual orientation as a prohibited ground of discrimination. This kind of interaction between the *Charter* and the statutory human rights instruments is vital to ensuring that provincial and federal statutes comply with the *Charter* and the policy goals of the statute in question.

15 *Canadian Human Rights Act*, R.S. 1985, c. H-6 [*CHRA*].

16 *Alberta Human Rights, Citizenship and Multiculturalism Act*, c. H-14 [*HRCMA*].

17 *Human Rights Code*, R.S.B.C. 1996, c. 210 [*BCHRC*].

18 *Bigsby v. Alberta (Human Rights and Citizenship Comm.)* (2002), 45 C.H.R.R. D/178, 2002 ABQB 574 [*Bigsby*].

19 *Ibid.*

20 For example, under the *CHRA*, "discriminatory practice" is defined as either the denial of employment, goods, services, facilities, or accommodation on a prohibited ground of discrimination, or "adverse differentiation" in relation to any individual on a prohibited ground of discrimination. Under the principles of statutory interpretation, an adjudicator is not empowered by the statute to ascribe any other definition to discrimination and particularly not one which would change the evidentiary burden inherent in the wording of the statute. See, for example, *Canada (Human Rights Commission) v. M.N.R.*, [2004] 1 F.C.R. 679, *Canada (Human Rights Comm.) v. M.N.R.* (2001), 40 C.H.R.R. D/117 (C.H.R.T.) [*Wignall*] which upheld in the final result by the Federal Court of Canada (Trial Division) but overturned on the improper application of the *Law* test.

21 Federal and provincial human rights statutes contain specific, limited, statutory defences against a finding of discrimination. The statutes do not include as a defence the claimant's failure to meet the three stages of the *Law* test or to prove impairment to dignity. Increasing the claimant's evidentiary burden is tantamount to introducing a new avenue for defending against the allegations.

22 *Law*, above note 7 at para. 88.

23 Daphne Gilbert, "Rethinking Section 15 of the Charter" (2003) 48 McGill L.J. 627. See also Peter Hogg, *Constitutional Law of Canada* (Toronto: Thomson Canada, 2002) at 52.7(b). It is not the concept of human dignity which is objected to here, but the conversion of the concept into a distinct evidentiary burden. For a discussion of the role of dignity and its connection to constitutional equality protections see Denise G. Réaume, "Indignities: Making a Place for Dignity in Modern Legal Thought" (2002) 28 Queen's L.J. 61.

24 Gilbert, *ibid.* at 633; *Lavoie v. Canada*, [2002] 1 S.C.R. 769 [*Lavoie*]; *Gosselin v. Quebec (A.G.)*, [2002] 4 S.C.R. 429 [*Gosselin*]. Gilbert also references the decision in *Trociuk v. British Columbia (A.G.)*, [2003] 1 S.C.R. 835 [*Trociuk*] as an "ironic and disheartening" example of a recent equality decision which actually garnered unanimity from the Court. In that case the Court upheld a male claimant's challenge on the ground of sex discrimination without any analysis of the historic "advantage" of the group to which the claimant belonged.

25 Gilbert, *ibid.* at 629.

26　See, for example, *Pringle v. Alberta (Municipal Affairs)* (2003), 48 C.H.R.R. D/111 (Alta. H.R.P.) [*Pringle*] where the adjudicator applied *Law* and required the complainant to produce "compelling objective evidence" of impairment to dignity.

27　See, for example, *Québec (Commission des droits de la personne et des droits de la jeunesse) v. Montréal (City)*, [2000] 1 S.C.R. 665 at para. 34 [*City of Montreal*].

28　[1996] 1 S.C.R. 571 at para. 7.

29　*City of Montreal*, above note 27.

30　*Meiorin*, above note 12.

31　[1992] 2 S.C.R. 321 at 18.

32　It is also important to point out that this "test" is not quite as linear as it appears. Human rights tribunals tend to hear the entire case before conducting the analysis. The decision in *O'Malley* prevents the adjudicator from taking into consideration the explanation of the respondent in determining whether the complainant has met the *prima facie* burden. He or she is precluded, for example, from finding against a complainant on this element of the analysis because of the respondent's evidence of the purpose behind the impugned rule or conduct. However, the adjudicator is not prevented from taking into consideration admissions and other evidence from the witnesses for the respondent which are relevant to the question whether the complainant was denied or adversely treated on the basis of a prohibited ground.

33　*Holden v. Canadian National Railway Co.* (1990), 14 C.H.R.R. D/12 (F.C.A.).

34　*Basi v. Canadian National Railway Co.* (No. 1) (1988), 9 C.H.R.R. D/5029 (C.H.R.T.) [*Basi*].

35　*CHRA*, above note 15 at s. 7.

36　This analysis was recently confirmed by the Federal Court of Appeal in *Lincoln*, above note 4.

37　*Andrews*, above note 13 at 145.

38　Included in this reference are those cases which should have been defined as "denial" cases but were mischaracterized as "discrimination" cases. In the three jurisdictions where "discrimination" is defined by the legislation (Manitoba, Quebec, and the *CHRA*), there is no evidence of the import of the *Law* decision into statutory human rights adjudications. The only exception to this is the anomalous decision in *Wignall*, above note 20, where the adjudicator imported and applied *Law* in the context of a complaint under the *CHRA*. This case was overturned by the Federal Court; not in the result, but in the application of the *Law* test, and there has since been no recurrence of the analysis in decisions from the Canadian Human Rights Tribunal.

39　If *Charter* claimants are required to take a subjective/objective view of their own experiences, as required by *Law,* they will be required to call evidence which disproves the evidence associated with the objective element of that standard, such as the purpose of the legislation and its impact on other groups.

40　See, for example, the *CHRA*, above note 15, s. 65 (due diligence) & s. 15 (undue hardship exceptions).

41　*Meiorin*, above note 12; this case involved the application of certain aerobic standards in the testing of firefighters in British Columbia which created adverse consequences for women. In *British Columbia (Superintendent of Motor Vehicles) v. British Columbia (Council of Human Rights)*, [1999] 3 S.C.R. 868 [*Grismer*] the claimant case was denied a driver's license because of his visual impairment. The Supreme Court confirmed in this case that the *Meiorin* analysis applies in the context of statutory human rights complaints.

42 The Supreme Court of Canada undertook an analysis of the duty to accommodate narrowing the test of undue hardship to considerations of health, safety, and cost.

43 [1995] 2 S.C.R. 513 [*Egan*].

44 Denise G. Réaume, "Of Pigeonholes and Principles: A Reconsideration of Discrimination Law" (2002) 40 Osgoode Hall L.J. 113 at para. 33. See also Gilbert, above note 23 at 638, for a discussion of the absence of an intersectional analysis in the *Lavoie* case where the court did not engage with the issue of gender.

45 (2003), 48 C.H.R.R. D/197 [*Baylis-Flannery*].

46 *BC Government & Service Employees Union v. H.M.T.*, 2002 B.C.C.A. 476 [*Reaney*]; *Schafer v. Attorney General of Canada* (1997), 149 D.L.R. (4th) 705 [*Schafer*]; *McLeod v. British Columbia Medical Assn.* (2004), C.H.R.R. Doc. 04-375, 2004 B.C.H.R.T. 240 [*McLeod*].

47 Michelle Falardeau-Ramsay, Q.C. "Human Rights Legislation: The Path Ahead" (1998) 47 U.N.B.L.J 165 at 166. As is discussed later in the paper, claims which could be adjudicated in either the statutory or constitutional forum, pose a significant challenge to this relatively compartmentalized description.

48 Perhaps the best illustration of this principle is *Canada (Attorney General) v. Mossup*, [1994] 1 S.C.R. 554, which pre-dated the inclusion of sexual orientation protection under the *CHRA*. The complainant was denied bereavement leave to attend the funeral of the father of his same-sex partner. The case was heard on the prohibited ground of family status. The Court accepted that Parliament's failure to include sexual orientation protection in the *Act* precluded a claim related to sexual orientation under any other ground, including family status. The decision implies that the use of family status was a "colourable" attempt to get around the fact that gays and lesbians were not meant to be protected in the context of benefits such as family leave. Thankfully, the decision was short-lived and the remarkable dissent of L'Heureux-Dubé J. in that case has since prevailed.

49 The decision of the British Columbia Supreme Court in *Vancouver Rape Relief Society v. Nixon* 2003 BCSC 1936 [*Nixon*]. At the time of writing, the case was before the British Columbia Court of Appeal. Although he applied the *Law* test in reviewing the tribunal's decision in *Nixon*, Edwards J. noted the difficulties associated with the application of that test in the context of a private respondent.

50 Factum of the Intervener EGALE (cited with permission of the author, Cynthia Petersen). This issue is addressed more fully below, in the discussion of the *Nixon* case. The issue also arises in jurisdictions where adjudicators and courts have determined that the *Charter* analysis is a "good fit" in those human rights cases where the impugned policy or conduct could be adjudicated under either the *Charter* or a statutory human rights instrument (referred to later in the paper as cross-over cases).

51 *Meiorin*, above note 12; *Grismer*, above note 41; *B*, above note 12; *City of Montreal*,
    above note 27; and *Quebec (Commission des droits de la personne et des droits de la
    jeunesse) v. Maksteel Québec Inc.*, [2003] 3 S.C.R. 228 [*Maksteel*].

52 *Andrews*, above note 13 at para. 39.

53 *Dame v. South Fraser Health Region* (2002), 43 C.H.R.R. D/251, 2002 B.C.H.R.T. 22.

54 *Gwinner v. Alberta (Minister of Human Resources and Employment)* (2002), 44
    C.H.R.R. D/52, 2002 ABQB 685 [*Gwinner*]. See also the decision from the Nova
    Scotia Tribunal in *Redden v. Saberi* 1999 N.S.H.R.B.I.D. No. 3, where the adjudica-
    tor stated: "... the Supreme Court has labelled as problematic the traditional disson-
    ance between the analysis of discrimination under the Charter and under 'human
    rights legislation which, while it may have a different legal orientation, is aimed
    at the same general wrong as s. 15(1) of the Charter' (at para. 47 of unpublished
    judgment). McLachlin J. for the Court disapproved of '[i]nterpreting human rights
    legislation primarily in terms of formal equality, [which] undermines its promise of
    substantive equality' (at para. 41)." This statement is clearly much broader than what
    is actually articulated in *Meiorin*.

55 *City of Montreal*, above note 27 at para. 84.

56 *B*, above note 12.

57 *Maksteel*, above note 51 at para. 47 where Deschamps J. said: "In discrimination
    cases, it is settled law that the onus is on the complainant to establish *prima facie*
    proof that a protected right has been infringed": *Meiorin*, above note 12, and *Gris-
    mer*, above note 41. The content of that evidence will depend on the wording of the
    provision in question. See also paras. 48 & 49.

58 *Barrett v. Cominco Ltd.* (2001), 41 C.H.R.R. D/367, 2001 B.C.H.R.T. 46 [*Barrett*];
    Vancouver Rape Relief Society v. Nixon (No. 2) (2002), 42 C.H.R.R. D/20, 2002
    B.C.H.R.T. 1 [*Nixon Tribunal*].

59 See for example at the Federal level *Wignall*, above note 20; *Brock v. Tarrant Film
    Factory Ltd.* (2000), 37 C.H.R.R. D/305 (Ont. Bd. Inq.) [*Brock*] in Ontario, and
    Gwinner v. Alberta (Minister of Human Resources and Employment) (2001), 40
    C.H.R.R. D/202 (Alta. H.R.P.) in Alberta.

60 This case has incited a debate among equality rights advocates which is captured in
    part in the articles published recently by barbara findlay, "Real Women: *Kimberly
    Nixon v. Vancouver Rape Relief*" (2003) 36 U.B.C.L. Rev. 57, and Christine Boyle,
    "The Anti-Discrimination Norm in Human Rights and *Charter* Law: *Nixon v. Van-
    couver Rape Relief*" (2004) 37 U.B.C.L.Rev. 31. The findlay article is consistent with
    the history of statutory human rights interpretation.

61 *Nixon Tribunal*, above note 58 at para. 114.

62 With the exception of s. 15(2) of the *Charter* which is rarely invoked and limited by
    comparison to the statutory exemptions available in the *BCHRC* and other human
    rights statutes.

63 *Nixon Tribunal*, above note 58 at para. 124.

64 *Ibid.* at para. 133. Ultimately, this is the proper finding — it is self-evident that the
    denial was connected to a prohibited ground which is the extent of the *prima facie*
    analysis in this case.

65 In the intervening period between the decision of the tribunal in *Nixon* and the decision of the British Columbia Supreme Court, the British Columbia Court of Appeal released its decision in *Reaney*, above note 46. The Court adopted the *Law* analysis as a requirement for the adjudication of claims which engage with statutory human rights legislation. The decision is deeply flawed, not only because of the lack of analysis associated with the import of the *Law* decision but also because of its tautological reasoning. The Court concluded that the denial of benefits to adoptive mothers was not discriminatory because the purpose of the benefit was to support the particular circumstances of biological mothers, re-introducing the long discarded defence of "intent" in statutory cases. Under a conventional statutory human rights analysis there was ample evidence to establish a *prima facie* case of discrimination, and it is unlikely that the defendant would have been able to establish undue hardship. *Reaney* appears to have been treated largely as anomalous by both tribunals and courts. The British Columbia Human Rights Tribunal, for example, has since released the decision in *British Columbia v. Hutchinson* (2004), C.H.R.R. Doc. 04-369, 2004 BCSC 1536 [*Hutchinson*] in which the tribunal interpreted *Reaney* in light of the Supreme Court jurisprudence since *Law* and refused to import *Law*. There have also been at least two human rights-related decisions from the British Columbia Court of Appeal which do not reference *Reaney* and which do not import *Law: Oak Bay Marina Limited v. British Columbia (Human Rights Commission)*, [2002] B.C.J. 2029 and *Health Sciences Association of British Columbia v. Campbell River and North Island Transition Society*, [2004] B.C.J. 922.

66 *Gwinner*, above note 54. See also the decision in *Mis v. Alberta (Human Rights and Citizenship Comm.)* (No. 2) (2002), 48 C.H.R.R. D/360, 2002 ABQB 570.

67 S.A. 1990, c. W-7.5.

68 This Act was both over-inclusive, in that it provided benefits to those who did not necessarily meet the core requirements (it was available to women, for example, who did not stay home to raise children), and under-inclusive in that it excluded others whose dependency on a supporting person was disrupted by their death.

69 There are also cases where an adjudicator has "hedged their bet" by engaging in both the classic *prima facie* analysis and the *Law* analysis. See, for example, the original tribunal decision in *Nixon*, above note 58, or *Moser v. Sechelt (Dist.)* (2004), 50 C.H.R.R. D/202, 2004 B.C.H.R.T. 72.

70 *Brock*, above note 59; *Turnbull v. Famous Players Inc.* (No. 1) (2001), 40 C.H.R.R. D/333 (Ont. Bd. Inq.) at para. 191.

71 *Friday v. Westfair Foods Ltd.* (2002), 45 C.H.R.R. D/218 (Sask. H.R.T.) [*Friday*].

72 *Waters v. British Columbia (Ministry of Health Services)* (2003), 46 C.H.R.R. D/139, 2003 B.C.H.R.T. 13.

73 *Baylis-Flannery*, above note 45.

74 *Bigsby*, above note 18.

75 *Wignall* Tribunal decision, above note 20 at para. 30. In addition to the losses that are directly attributable to the import of *Law* there are also examples of cases where the ambiguity about *Law* creates opportunities for escalating the costs of human rights proceedings through procedural motions. In *Gibbons v. Vancouver (City)*

    Board of Parks and Recreation (2004), C.H.R.R. Doc. 04-272, 2004 B.C.H.R.T. 145, the respondent brought a preliminary motion before the tribunal to dismiss the claim on the basis that the complainant could not succeed as there was no evidence of impairment to dignity as required by *Law*.

76 *Pringle*, above note 26.

77 *Saskatchewan (Dept. of Finance) v. Saskatchewan (Human Rights Comm.)* (2004), C.H.R.R. Doc. 04-300, 2004 SKCA 134.

78 See also the decision in *Canada Safeway Ltd. v. Alberta (Human Rights and Citizenship Comm.)*, (2003), 47 C.H.R.R. D/220, 2003 ABCA 246. *Law* was applied in this case, not as test, but as a direction to consider the entire context of the impugned rule in a statutory claim. The analysis shifts the focus from the *prima facie* analysis to the purpose and effect of the rule, turning a classic disability case into something much more complex. A further example of the problems associated with this approach, which actually resurrects the concept of intent, can be found in the decision in *Hwe v. Saskatchewan (Dept. Of Social Services)* (2003), 47 C.H.R.R. D/337 (Sask. H.R.T.)

79 [2004] N.B.H.R.B.I.D. No. 4.

80 *Halpern v. Canada (Attorney General)* (2003), 65 O.R. (3d) 161 (C.A.).

twelve

Formulaic Comparisons:
STOPPING THE *CHARTER* AT THE STATUTORY HUMAN
RIGHTS GATE

Andrea Wright[1]

A. INTRODUCTION

This paper examines the emergence of another[2] troubling trend in statutory human rights jurisprudence: the increasing reliance on and misuse of rigid comparative formulas. Statutory human rights tribunals and reviewing courts are frequently neglecting or displacing the broad and adaptable *O'Malley* test — the flagship test for a *prima facie* case of discrimination — in favour of restrictive comparator-group analyses, and reductive tests that require comparative evidence in order to meet the *prima facie* burden. A principal source of this trend is the ascendancy of comparative formulas in *Charter* jurisprudence. These formulas cause claimants to thread their discrimination experiences through templates that are ill-fitting and rigid, and that often operate like formal-equality analyses. The result is often the de-contextualization of the complaint, and the denial of substantive equality. The *O'Malley* test does not require such formulaic rigidity, and its application in statutory human rights jurisprudence should be revitalized. Indeed, the *O'Malley* test, like many other governing principles of statutory human rights jurisprudence, reflects a conceptualization of equality that focuses on the flourishing of every individual in all her or his particularity, not on formalistic comparisons of societal groups. Its reinvigoration is therefore all the more imperative.

Specifically, this paper first reviews two methodologies increasingly being applied by statutory human rights tribunals: comparator-group analyses, and the *Shakes/Israeli* test. It examines their effects, particularly in contrast to the analysis that the neglected *O'Malley* test affords. It posits that the comparator-group test requires artificial and precarious comparisons with "others," which look and operate like formal-equality analyses, lead to poor choices of "comparator groups," and often neglect the essential question of the discrimination complaint — what position the claimant would have been in were it not for the gravamen of the complaint. The paper next examines the perils of the *Shakes/Israeli* test, which, while easing a claimant's burden in some ways, requires the claimant to adduce evidence of the treatment or qualifications of others. This is evidence which is usually not within the complainant's control, is often imbued with the same hidden discriminatory norms that are impugned in the first place, and most importantly, takes on conclusory status to the exclusion of the vast scope of potential evidence that might otherwise establish a discrimination claim. Fact patterns of discrimination are infinitely diverse, and there should be as many avenues to establishing a *prima facie* case of discrimination as there are manifestations of discrimination.

This paper posits that the roomy *O'Malley* test allows for such plenteous consideration of discrimination complaints, in all their variety; while the formulaic use of rigid comparative tests reduces a discrimination fact pattern to a thread of itself, a thread which must be woven through narrow comparative-formula templates if a complaint is to succeed. The result is often formalist analysis, the effacement of the gravamen of the complaint, the de-contextualizing of a claimant's experience, and the denial of substantive equality. The continued application of these comparative formulas threatens the gainful equality framework that the *O'Malley* test affords.

This paper therefore urges steadfast application of the *O'Malley* test in statutory human rights cases, whatever the formulaic, comparative trends in the *Charter* context. It questions the *Charter* proposition that equality is necessarily comparative, and highlights further flaws of such a conceptualization, including the abstractionist, essentialist, and contradictory premise that a historically-disadvantaged group can be tidily compared to an identifiable and historically-advantaged "other" group. It posits that while comparisons with the conditions of others may be the long-established convention of equality discourse, they should at most be *probative* of an ideal condition, not *conclusory*. It urges a conceptualization of equality as the attainment of *particularized* ideals, not comparative ones; and discusses numerous statutory human rights principles and cases that apply individualized, unipolar considerations of a claimant's circumstance, such as *Meiorin* and *Brooks*. It concludes that as long as *Charter* jurisprudence rigidly conceptualizes equality as comparative, and as long as statutory human rights jurisprudence plenteously conceptualizes equality as the attainment of societal conditions that allow the flourishing of every individual in all her or his particularity, it is the latter framework that offers the greater potential for the achievement of substantive equality in Canada. The *O'Malley* test, and other statutory human rights constructs, must therefore be reinvigorated, and the *Charter*'s increasing comparative formulism should be stopped at the statutory human rights gate.

B. COMPARATIVE METHODOLOGIES IN STATUTORY HUMAN RIGHTS JURISPRUDENCE: A SURVEY OF SOME PROMINENT AND/OR RECENT EXAMPLES OF THEIR ERRONEOUS APPLICATION

Statutory human rights cases in the employment context can roughly be categorized into three types of complaints: (1) complaints that allege that a rule, standard, or practice in the employment context was discriminatory,[3] or that the denial of a benefit or service was discriminatory; (2) complaints that a hiring, promotion, or dismissal decision was discriminatory; and (3) complaints of harassment or other discriminatory conduct. The governing test for whether a complaint of discrimination has been made out — the *O'Malley* test — is broad and adaptable enough to be applied in all three categories of cases. It states:

The complainant must first establish a *prima facie* case of discrimination; that is, one that covers the allegations made and which, if they are believed, is complete and sufficient to justify a verdict in the complainant's favour in the absence of an answer from the respondent. The burden then shifts to the respondent to provide a reasonable explanation for the otherwise discriminatory rule/practice/conduct. If the respondent provides such an explanation, the complainant has the evidentiary burden of demonstrating that the explanation provided was merely a pretext and that the true motivation behind the employer's actions was in fact discriminatory.[4]

In its generality, the *O'Malley* test appropriately offers to complainants, who would otherwise have a "herculean"[5] task, the chance to prove a *prima facie* case of discrimination in a vitally large number of ways: through indirect evidence, through "subtle scent(s),"[6] through aggregated pieces of evidence, through clumsy sums of evidence, through consideration of their particularized circumstances and the opportunities they should properly have to flourish, and so forth. However, despite the polyvalence of the *O'Malley* test, or perhaps because of its non-specificity, tribunals and courts have often chosen to apply more formulaic tests. This has typically occurred in those cases in which comparisons appear to be the self-evident approach; that is, cases in which there are identifiable others who are subject to the same rule, or who got the job instead of the complainant, and so forth. These cases fall into categories 1 and 2 above.

In this section, a number of cases falling into categories 1 and 2 are surveyed in which tribunals and courts have applied comparative formulas instead of the *O'Malley* test and have thereby dismissed discrimination allegations.[7] In the first category, the methodological culprit is the "comparator group" approach; and in the second category, it is the *Shakes/Israeli* test. I examine a selection of these cases in detail, with a view to other historical and case law currents, in order to identify and elucidate the sources of this ascendant trend.

1) Use of Comparator Groups

There are several cases in the statutory human rights context that are well-known to equality advocates for their misconceived comparator-group analyses.

a) *Dumont-Ferlatte*

The first is *Canada (Human Rights Commission) v. Canada (Human Rights Tribunal) (re Canada (Employment and Immigration Commission))*.[8] In *Re Dumont-Ferlatte*, as the case is better known, the complainants alleged that a collective agreement provision discriminated against women. Specifically, the collective agreement provided that women who were on maternity leave were not part of the "paid" work force, and were therefore disentitled from accumulating the minimum ten "work days" per calendar month that were needed for vacation leave, sick leave, and bilingualism bonus calculations. In other words, in being denied the accumulation of these benefits while on maternity leave, women were subject to disadvantage in the workplace because they were women — society's only childbearers.

Even though this was a statutory human rights case, the Federal Court did not begin its analysis with a statement of the *O'Malley* test. It began by citing the test which governed *Charter* jurisprudence at the time — *Andrews*:

... discrimination may be described as a distinction, whether intentional or not, but based on grounds relating to personal characteristics of the individual or group, which has the effect of imposing burdens, obligations or disadvantages on such individual or group *not imposed upon others*, or which withholds or limits access to opportunities, benefits, and advantages *available to other members of society.*[9]

The Court stated that this amounted to a definition of discrimination in three elements: (1) a distinction, (2) based on a personal characteristic that corresponds to a prohibited ground of discrimination, and that (3) imposes a burden on some individuals *and not on others.*[10]

The Court *then* cited the *O'Malley* test, and wondered, "(j)ust what is a *prima facie* case of discrimination?" Without any instructive ratio, the Court concluded that a *prima facie* case of discrimination is one in which "the three (*Andrews*) elements of the definition of discrimination are present."[11] The Court therefore used *Andrews* as a (more rigid) formula for the application of the *O'Malley* test.[12] It stated: "(d)iscrimination is (therefore) established by doing a comparative analysis."[13]

The next task, in the Court's view, was to choose a "comparator group." The Court stated that since the "very essence of the contract of employment" is that "pay is conditional on work being performed," the claimant group had to establish that it was treated no more adversely than other employees who were doing "no work."[14] The claimant group, the Court held, could not be compared "with other groups that are not affected by the rule."[15] In other words, in Tremblay-Lamer J.'s view, the claimant group (women) could not be compared with society's non-childbearers (men), even though childbearing is the (tautologically) distinguishing reason that women take maternity leave and men need not. Instead, women, or rather that "sub-group of employees" who take maternity leave, were compared to the other "sub-groups" of employees who took leave, either for gender-neutral reasons (such as leave without pay for education and training; and leave without pay to participate in the activities of an international organization), or for reasons that also deserved human rights protection (such as paternity leave and adoption leave).

This is a misconceptualized, formalistic approach to a discrimination claim. It is far removed from the *O'Malley* test and especially from substantive equality goals. By comparing women to a random assortment of other employees who were off on unpaid leave, the Court wholly ignored the unique feature of women that had left them historically disadvantaged: their childbearing capacity. The Court de-contextualized the claim. It dislodged it from its human rights bearings, and converted it into a battle for superior benefits between ordinary "sub-groups" of employees. It did so by applying a rigid formula that it had derived from the *Andrews* definition of discrimination, rather than by applying the more expansive *O'Malley* test. The latter would have prevented such a de-contextualization, at least insomuch as it allows for myriad considerations to enter into the *prima facie* test. The *O'Malley* test also contains no express requirement that a comparison be made, nor a requirement that a comparative methodology be the sole avenue for proof of discrimination. Application of the *O'Malley* test in *Dumont-Ferlatte* would have allowed, not precluded, the true central question: in what position would the claimants have been in, had they not been women; that is, society's only childbearers?

b) *Re Cramm*

The Federal Court arrived at a similar result in *Canada (Human Rights Commission) v. Canadian National Railway,*[16] better known as *Re Cramm.* CN Railway had shut down, and any employees who had accumulated eight years of "working service" were entitled to employment security benefits. To be eligible, however, employees needed to have worked at least one day in each calendar year. Disability leave (and other forms of leave) were included in the calculation, but were not to exceed one hundred days in a calendar year. If a disability leave exceeded one hundred days in a calendar year, that year could not be included in the calculation of an employee's "working service." In this case, the claimant Cramm had taken numerous short-term disability leaves over his years of employment, all due to a work-related injury. A number of these leaves exceeded one hundred days in a calendar year, causing those calendar years to be excluded from the calculation of Cramm's years of "working service." The net result was that Cramm did not meet the eight-year "working service" minimum, and was ineligible for the security benefits. He filed a discrimination complaint with the Canadian Human Rights Commission on the ground of disability.

The Federal Court did not cite the *O'Malley* test.[17] Instead, it cited *Dumont-Ferlatte,* as well as the Supreme Court decision in *Gibbs,*[18] both of which applied the *Andrews* definition of discrimination as a formula or replacement for the *O'Malley* test. The *Cramm* Court used these two cases to substantiate its "comparator group" methodology. "[T]he appropriate comparator group," the Court ruled, was "the others to whom (the impugned clause) applied"; that is, other employees absent from work "for whatever reason."[19] The claimant group was therefore compared to employees who were absent from work for reasons such as "authorized maternity leave ... attendance at committee meetings, and so on." The Court therefore found that Mr. Cramm had not been discriminated against, because "his disability did not result in any different treatment than was applicable to those who were not working for the (other) designated reasons...."[20]

Like the Court in *Dumont-Ferlatte* then, the Court in *Cramm* entirely failed to focus on the gravamen of the complaint — the claimant's disability — in order to determine whether the claimant was disadvantaged as a result of that disability. The Court failed to ask what position the claimant would have been in if he had not been disabled. Instead, it asked the misplaced question of whether Mr. Cramm was treated the same as other subgroups of employees who were subject to the same rule. The Court should have compared Mr. Cramm with those who had not been disabled over the years and who had therefore been on the job. Ironically, in the Court's concluding paragraph, it recognized this very distinction, but effectively found it a matter of "sympathy" only, not discrimination:

> It is impossible not to have sympathy for Mr. Cramm. He worked for the railway for a long time and had considerable seniority. *Had he not been injured at work, he would have been eligible for the full benefits of the (plan)....*[21]

The fact that the Court did not find room for this vital observation in the actual analysis of Mr. Cramm's discrimination complaint, but rather relegated it to an after-thought of condolence,[22] is a grim illustration of the hazards of the narrow comparator-group approach.

c) *Wignall*

A similar analysis has been applied more recently as well. In *Canada (Human Rights Commission) v. M.N.R.*,[23] the Federal Court reviewed a case in which the Canadian Human Rights Tribunal had determined that the complainant, Scott Wignall, had not been discriminated against when the federal government caused him to pay tax on the bursary he had received as a deaf university student. The bursary helped pay for interpretation services. Showing shades of the *Cramm* Court's reasoning that the adverse consequence to the complainant was a matter of "sympathy" but not discrimination, the Tribunal had recognized that "the ultimate effect of the ... tax treatment of the grant ... was a financial penalty," but had concluded that this did not amount to discrimination.[24] The Federal Court affirmed this finding. In its reasoning, it compared Mr. Wignall to all others who had received bursaries, for whatever reason, and even all "other taxpayers."[25] In so doing, the Court only ensured that Mr. Wignall was treated the same as other "subgroups" — various categories of taxpayers — insomuch as he was taxed. This is again a formalist approach that effaces the gravamen of the complaint.[26] The Tribunal needed to ask the question that the *O'Malley* test would have afforded: what position Mr. Wignall would have been in had he not been disabled; that is, would Mr. Wignall have had the impugned tax burden if he had not been disabled? In precluding this question, the narrow comparator-group approach once again denied the complainant the possibility of substantive equality. It prevented an assessment of whether Mr. Wignall had truly achieved equality when he incurred tax liability for the government's assistance in removing a barrier to his self-fulfillment.

d) *Ontario Nurses' Association*

Unfortunately, it is not only the Federal Court that has erred in comparator-group reasoning in statutory human rights jurisprudence. For example, the Ontario Court of Appeal reached a similar result in *Ontario Nurses' Association v. Orillia Memorial Hospital et al.*[27] It relied on the Supreme Court's comparative methodology in *Gibbs*, which, as mentioned, derived from an application of *Andrews* instead of an application of the *O'Malley* test, to find that the denial of certain benefits to disabled employees was not discriminatory. Specifically, in reasoning that echoed *Dumont-Ferlatte*, the Court stated that since the purpose of two of the benefit schemes in issue[28] was to provide compensation "in exchange for work," disabled employees had to be compared to "other employees not providing work." Carrying out this comparison, not only did the Court find that disabled employees were treated no worse than this comparator group, but it stated that "the benefits provided to handicapped employees not providing work" were actually "*more generous*" than those afforded to other employees not providing work."[29] The Court therefore found that the employer had not discriminated against the claimant group.

This reasoning makes the same errors as *Dumont-Ferlatte*, *Cramm*, and *Wignall*. It asks a misplaced question that effaces the gravamen of the complaint — the claimants' disability. It fails to pose the proper equality-advancing question, which the *O'Malley* test would have allowed, of what position the claimants would have been in had they not been disabled.

Notably, the Ontario Court of Appeal came to a superior conclusion in its consideration of a third benefits scheme in issue in the case: the accrual of seniority. For reasons which are unclear, the Court used a far more plenteous definition of the purpose of seniority benefits than its casting of the other benefit schemes as mere "compensation for work." The Court called seniority benefits an instrument that allows employees "to access, remain in, and thrive in the workplace ... a right that is therefore at the core of human rights legislation."[30] It thereby compared disabled employees to "all other employees" and reached the conclusion that the claimant group had suffered discrimination.

The Court in *Ontario Nurses* therefore reached opposite conclusions about the denial of benefit schemes to the same claimant group of disabled employees. It did so by choosing different comparator groups, based on puzzlingly divergent definitions of the "purpose" of the benefit schemes.[31] This is yet another illustration of the inherent risks of a dominant comparator-group methodology: arbitrary and discordant results. The comparator-group approach is an artificial, formalist search for a comparable "other," which leads to unpredictable results, in part because there are myriad ways to reasonably articulate a basis of comparison,[32] and in part because the approach often neglects the gravamen of the complaint and the objective of substantive equality. Put simply, it is easy to get the choice of comparator group wrong, it is easy to reasonably justify several different comparator-group choices, and it is easy to lose sight of the objective of substantive equality when searching for comparisons based on formalistic assessments of sameness and difference.

e) Similar Analyses in *Charter* Jurisprudence

Notably, courts in *Charter* jurisprudence have frequently applied erroneous comparator-group reasoning to reach conclusions that deny section 15 claims and/or contort the discrimination analysis so significantly as to neglect or efface the necessary discourse of historical and contextual disadvantage.[33] They have done so largely based on a conceptualization of discrimination that was articulated in the *Law*[34] case, which in turn drew from a slightly-evolved version of the *Andrews* conceptualization of discrimination.

The sheer volume of these cases is compelling evidence that they have influenced statutory human rights adjudicators, but as mentioned above, in many circumstances their reasoning has been expressly imported into the statutory human rights context. This trend is perhaps nowhere more express than in *Canada (Attorney General) v. Brown*.[35] In that case, the Federal Court of Appeal was called upon once again to determine whether the adverse consequences of maternity leave constituted gender discrimination under the *Canadian Human Rights Act*. Specifically, the claimant alleged that the *Employment Insurance Act*[36] was discriminatory because it diminished a woman's entitlement to employment insurance benefits by the number of weeks of maternity leave that she had already taken in that year. The same provision of the *Employment Insurance Act* had in fact been impugned several years earlier in a *Charter* allegation of discrimination. In that case, *Sollbach*, the Federal Court of Appeal had compared women to others subject to the same statutory cap, and had concluded that there was no discrimination.[37] The Court in *Brown* ruled that since it had already adjudicated the claim in the *Charter* context in *Sollbach*, "it would be unjustifiable to hold that the same provision is discriminatory for the purpose of the *Canadian Human Rights Act*."

Not only were the comparative formula of a *Charter* case and its flawed application therefore expressly imported into a statutory human rights case, but the court did so with the summary objective of harmonizing the two equality landscapes. This is disturbing reasoning, as long as the statutory human rights context affords the plenteous and gainful equality framework of *O'Malley*, and the *Charter* context continues its predominant formulaic trajectory. As discussed above, the rigid comparator-group test requires formalistic and precarious comparisons, and too often precludes a substantive-equality analysis. As long as the comparator-group test is a prescribed and conclusory formula in the *Charter* context, harmonization of the two contexts should be avoided, at least insomuch as it risks suppression of the *O'Malley* test.

2) Reliance on Comparative Evidence

There is another prominent comparative formula in statutory human rights jurisprudence: the *Shakes/Israeli* test. This test requires that a complainant prove a *prima facie* case by slotting her or his evidence into a three-part framework that compares his or her treatment to that of others. While in many cases this formula lessens the burden on complainants to adduce direct evidence of *prima facie* discrimination, it can also act to preclude the consideration by tribunals of a host of relevant evidence. In other words, this formula can narrow the potential of the broader *O'Malley* test, because it causes complainants to fit their infinitely-varied discrimination experience into a rigid three-slot test.

As I illustrate below, although the *Shakes/Israeli* test is a home-grown vehicle, it is inevitably influenced by the focus in *Charter* jurisprudence on rigid comparisons, in particular as this focus has drifted into statutory human rights jurisprudence.

a) The *Shakes/Israeli* Test

In 1982, Florence Shakes applied for a job at a food-packaging plant. She was one of a handful of candidates for the job, she was black, and the woman who received the job instead of her was white. Ms. Shakes filed a complaint with the Ontario Human Rights Commission alleging discrimination on the basis of race. In *Shakes v. Rex Pak Limited,*[38] the Ontario Board of Inquiry formulated a test to analyze her claim. It stated that in employment-hiring cases, a *prima facie* case is "usually"[39] established by proving:

a   that the complainant was qualified for the particular employment;

b.   that the complainant was not hired; and

c.   that someone no better qualified but lacking the distinguishing feature which is the gravamen of the human rights complaint (i.e., race, colour, etc.) subsequently obtained the position.[40]

A year later, the Canadian Human Rights Tribunal developed a slightly altered test in *Israeli v. Canadian Human Rights Commission*[41] to suit a fact pattern in which the complainant had not been promoted, and the employer continued to look for other candidates. Stating that the test was "relatively fixed in the case law," the Tribunal held that in order to prove a *prima facie* complaint of discrimination, a complainant must show that:

a.   the complainant applied and was qualified for a job the employer wished to fill;

b.   the complainant was rejected; and

c.   thereafter the employer continued to seek applicants with the complainant's qualifications.[42]

The *Shakes/Israeli* test has been routinely applied in statutory human rights cases ever since. It is in many ways a helpful test for complainants, because it lessens their evidentiary burden. Not only can complainants avoid the "herculean" task of adducing direct evidence of discrimination,[43] but they can surmount their initial hurdle simply by showing that someone no more qualified, but lacking the gravamen of the complaint, received the job or promotion in question. The burden then shifts to the respondent employer to explain how this sequence of events did *not* constitute discrimination. The test can be especially helpful where, as in most cases, there is no intention to discriminate, or there is no overtly discriminatory behaviour. For example, the discrimination may be hidden in an employer's unconscious norms, subjective assessments, and discretionary decision-making, as it was in *McAvinn v. Strait Crossing Bridge Ltd.*[44] However, for the very same reason — the fact that discrimination can be hidden in an employer's norms and discretionary decision-making — the *McAvinn* case also illustrates the risks of the *Shakes/Israeli* test for a complainant. This case is discussed below.

Phyllis McAvinn held all the qualifications for a bridge patroller job, but she was not hired. Only men were hired, and some were less qualified than Ms. McAvinn. Ms. McAvinn therefore met the three-part *Shakes/Israeli* test, and the burden shifted to the employer to provide a reasonable explanation for its failure to hire her. The employer could not, and the Tribunal awarded Ms. McAvinn a set of remedies pursuant to the *Canadian Human Rights Act*. Inasmuch as Ms. McAvinn needed only to satisfy the template requirements of the *Shakes/Israeli* test, and did not require evidence of overtly discriminatory statements or actions, the test was of considerable assistance to her.

But the case also provides an illustration of one of the significant risks of the *Shakes/Israeli* test: that the complainant will not meet her *prima facie* burden because the discrimination is hidden in the assessment of whether she is indeed qualified for the position. That is, as equality advocates well know, a determination of whether a candidate is qualified for a position often includes subjective assessments of vague concepts such as communication skills, judgment, suitability, or potential[45] — assessments which very often disguise the discriminatory norms and attitudes that are unconsciously applied by the employer. Unless these assessments are properly deconstructed by a tribunal or court, there is a considerable risk that a complainant will not even succeed in establishing that she or he was at least as qualified as the other candidates. And there is nothing on the face of the *Shakes/Israeli* test that calls on tribunals and courts to engage in such a deconstruction. In other words, the *Shakes/Israeli* formula allows a tribunal or court to accept at face value the employer's method for assessment of the candidates, such that any comparison between the complainant and the successful candidates will in no way be probative of whether discrimination was a factor in the decision-making. Put simply, when the tribunal uses the same evaluative method as the employer to compare the complainant to the other candidates, the comparison will be probative of nothing at all.

Fortunately this did not happen in *McAvinn*, because the Tribunal approached the employer's assessment method with scepticism.[46] The employer had argued that Ms. McAvinn did not perform as well as the successful candidates in the "important" interview stage of the hiring process, in which qualifications such as "communications skills," "general attitude," and ability to "handle situations" were assessed.[47] But the Tribunal declined to accept the employer's evaluations at face value, and refused to limit its analysis to a simple comparison of candidates using these evaluations. It considered other evidence, such as the "maleness" of the job profile as reflected by some of the interview questions, and concluded that "gender was a factor, albeit not the only one, in the selection process."[48] It therefore effectively deconstructed the employer's own comparative method, rather than simply reproduce it for the *prima facie* inquiry.

Given that the *Shakes/Israeli* test does not call for such a skeptical examination of the criteria used by an employer to evaluate candidates' "qualifications," one could argue that Ms. McAvinn's *prima facie* case had been won exceptionally, in spite of the test. The case provided a typical example of the masked manifestations of discriminatory norms, which the *Shakes/Israeli* test in its simple requirement for a comparison of "qualifications," does not challenge. Nor does the *Shakes/Israeli* template call for a critical consideration of an employer's evaluative methods or a search for the myriad, but hidden, ways in which discriminatory attitudes can enter an evaluative process. In other words, had it not been for the critical and ultimately highly probative analysis that the Tribunal undertook *in addition* to the template requirements of the *Shakes* test, Ms. McAvinn might not have won her case.

In other words, although the *McAvinn* case provides an illustration of the potential advantage of the *Shakes/Israeli* test, insomuch as it diminishes a complainant's evidentiary burden, it also demonstrates its risks. The *Shakes/Israeli* formula narrows the *O'Malley* test to the point that a human rights complaint is easily de-contextualized and stripped of a truly probative inquiry into the subtle manifestations of discrimination; and it causes evidence to be slotted into a formula of comparison that reproduces the employer's own flawed methodology. In this respect, the trend highly resembles the courts' and tribunals' increasing reliance on comparator group methodologies, instead of the *O'Malley* test. Given the import of comparator-group analyses from the *Charter* context — as well as the growing trend toward import of the governing *Law* test from *Charter* jurisprudence, as asserted in another paper in this text[49] — the conclusion arguably follows that this trend is one of several that exhibit the growing influence, indeed ascendancy, of the *Charter*'s conceptualization of discrimination.

There are numerous examples of cases in which the *Shakes/Israeli* test has narrowed the discrimination inquiry,[50] either to the detriment[51] or the narrow benefit[52] of the complainant's *prima facie* case. But one recent case provides perhaps a particularly stark example of the adverse consequences of a mechanical reliance on the comparative *Shakes/Israeli* formula. In *Canada (Attorney General) v. Canada (Human Rights Commission)* (*Morris* (FCTD)),[53] the Federal Court held that "[c]omparison [e]vidence [is] *required* to establish a *prima facie* case of discrimination."[54] In so doing, it quashed a decision by the Canadian Human Rights Tribunal[55] that had applied the *O'Malley* test instead of the "rigid" Shakes/Israeli test. While the Federal Court's decision has since been set aside on appeal,[56] the reasoning remains a disturbing example of the impact of a reasoning process that effaces the flexible *O'Malley* test and that fails to recognize that discrimination can be established in many ways.

b) *Morris* (CHRT) and *Morris* (FCTD)

George Morris filed a complaint with the Canadian Human Rights Commission alleging that the Canadian Armed Forces had discriminated against him on the basis of age. He had worked for the Forces from the age of nineteen to fifty-five and had been regularly promoted until the age of forty-six. But he was not promoted between the age of forty-six and his mandatory retirement age of fifty-five. The Forces promoted members according to a number of criteria, including objective prerequisites such as the attainment of certain courses, but also including a complicated process of subjective evaluations by a large number of senior Forces members. Morris alleged that although he met all of the Forces' objective criteria, as well as many of its subjective criteria, he did not receive any further promotions because the senior decision-makers took his age into account when making certain of the more critical subjective assessments, such as their evaluation of his "potential."

The Canadian Human Rights Tribunal conducted a hearing into Mr. Morris' complaint. A large amount of documentary and testimonial evidence was adduced by both the Commission and the Forces. Importantly, very little evidence had been disclosed by the Forces about the age and qualifications of the candidates who had successfully been promoted in the years when Mr. Morris was refused a promotion; and therefore very little of this evidence was adduced by either side. The Tribunal thus saw very little "comparative evidence" of the type that would normally be slotted into a *Shakes/Israeli*-like inquiry.

Nonetheless, there was a significant amount of evidence before the Tribunal, which it rigorously reviewed. It applied the *O'Malley* test, and made detailed rulings as to whether the various pieces of evidence assisted Mr. Morris in meeting his *prima facie* case, or assisted the Forces in meeting its reasonable-explanation defence. Evidence that helped Mr. Morris meet his *prima facie* burden included testimony by senior members of the Forces about Mr. Morris' career, the decision-making surrounding his promotion, and the Forces' practices in general; testimony by Mr. Morris that was corroborated by other evidence; and documentary evidence from Forces' manuals and various performance reports and promotion records. The Tribunal also scrutinized the Forces' subjective evaluations of Mr. Morris in a manner akin to its approach in *McAvinn*.[57]

Ultimately the Tribunal held that the Canadian Human Rights Commission had met the *prima facie* burden of proving that Mr. Morris had been discriminated against, and that the Forces had not met its reasonable-explanation burden. The Tribunal therefore concluded that Mr. Morris had been discriminated against by the Forces. In discussing the applicable legal principles, the Tribunal noted the existence of the *Shakes* and *Israeli* tests, but properly held, citing prior jurisprudence, that these tests serve as "useful guides" at most, and that the broader *O'Malley* test was clearly the governing test:

> Neither (the *Shakes* nor *Israeli*) test should ... be automatically applied in
> a rigid or arbitrary fashion in every hiring or promotion case: rather the

circumstances of each case should be considered to determine if the application of either of the tests, in whole or in part, is appropriate. Ultimately, the question will be whether the complainant has satisfied the *O'Malley* test, that is: if accepted, is the evidence before the Tribunal complete and sufficient to justify a verdict in the complainant's favour in the absence of an answer from the respondent?

The present case does not fall squarely within the fact patterns of either *Shakes* or *Israeli....*

It is not necessary to know whether (the successful candidates for promotion) were in fact qualified or were perhaps of the same age as Mr. Morris, in order for a *prima facie* case to be made out.... If the evidence establishes that discrimination was a factor in denying the Complainant an employment opportunity, irrespective of the qualifications and characteristics of the other candidate, the *prima facie* case will have been made out and the burden will have shifted to the Respondent to provide an explanation.

The Tribunal's application of the more adaptable *O'Malley* test, rather than the formulaic *Shakes* and *Israeli* tests, was particularly important in the *Morris* case, because the Forces had not disclosed the vast majority of information about the ages and qualifications of the successful promotion candidates. If the Tribunal had insisted on applying the *Israeli* test, it would effectively have imposed an obligation on Mr. Morris to adduce evidence that was not within his possession or control. This result would have been doubly disadvantaging: not only would Mr. Morris have been obliged to satisfy the narrow requirements of an overly simplistic test, but he would have been obliged to do so using evidence that was not within his possession or control. As I discuss below, I think this latter burden a particularly unreasonable one to place on complainants in the human rights context.

Despite these arguments against the necessary application of the *Shakes* and *Israeli* tests, the Federal Court quashed the Tribunal's decision and ruled that comparative evidence was indeed a prerequisite to a finding of discrimination. In so doing, the Court omitted any mention or consideration of the *O'Malley* test; and it stated that it was not persuaded of the correctness of other Canadian Human Rights Tribunal decisions that had applied the *O'Malley* test instead of the *Shakes/Israeli* templates: *Singh v. Canada (Statistics Canada)*[58] and *Chander v. Department of National Health and Welfare.*[59] Yet both of these decisions had been affirmed by the

Federal Court,[60] and both, evidently, had applied the governing Supreme Court test in *O'Malley*. And in so doing, the Federal Court overlooked myriad evidence upon which the Tribunal had relied to found its conclusion of discrimination.[61]

c) *Morris* FCA

Encouragingly, the Federal Court of Appeal recently set aside the Federal Court's decision. Relying in part on another recent Federal Court of Appeal decision,[62] it affirmed the proposition that *O'Malley* is the governing test and that the *Shakes/Israeli* test is but one way to meet the *prima facie* burden.[63] It went further:

> [a] flexible legal test of a *prima facie* case is better able than more precise tests to advance the broad purpose underlying the *Canadian Human Rights Act*, namely, the elimination in the federal legislative sphere of discrimination from employment, and from the provision of goods, services, facilities, and accommodation. Discrimination takes new and subtle forms. Moreover, as counsel for the Commission pointed out, it is now recognized that comparative evidence of discrimination comes in many more forms than the particular one identified in *Shakes*.[64]

This is a promising recognition by the Federal Court of Appeal of the plenteous and necessary potential of the *O'Malley* discrimination framework for adjudication of statutory human rights complaints.[65] Together with the Court's decision in *Lincoln*,[66] it appears to smooth the way for complainants to prove their discrimination allegations in the variety with which they have been experienced, and to impliedly depart from the increasing formalistic and formulaic trends of *Charter* jurisprudence.

In the meantime, the Federal Court ratio, which this decision set aside, remains a disturbing illustration of the risks that a culture of formulaic comparison can pose for anti-discrimination law. It shows the propensity of courts to summarily or mechanically rely on rudimentary, analytical frameworks of limited suitability. It shows their propensity to revert to "no assembly required" formulas, rather than broader Supreme Court statements of the applicable law. It shows the onerous burden for a complainant to adduce evidence that is not within his or her control, in the face of a vast quantity of other evidence. It even hints at the possibility that complaints may be rejected at human rights commissions' intake and investigation stages because a "requisite" type of evidence is missing. It insidiously calls for the absolute use of the same comparisons that the employer used to make the impugned hiring decision, without any automatic scrutiny of this methodology.

Perhaps most significant of all, the Federal Court decision hints at the vast scope of evidence that can be ignored by a court if a part of the comparative formula is missing. That is, a Court may shut down its discrimination inquiry because a certain limited kind of evidence is missing, when fact patterns of alleged discriminatory conduct are infinitely diverse. They range from expressly discriminatory statements, to systemically discriminatory norms, to unconscious discriminatory attitudes, to hostile but facially-neutral treatment, to "subtle scent(s),"[67] to intersectional experiences of discrimination, and so forth. Given this range of complexities, it is, at minimum, only logical that tests as simplistic as *Shakes* and *Israeli* would fail to adequately address a large number of fact patterns. Discrimination can occur, and therefore should be susceptible to being proven, in a variety of ways. Formulas that preclude access to these alternative avenues, as the *Shakes* and *Israeli* tests do, can therefore produce inimical results.

C. COMPARATIVE FORMULAS: A DISCUSSION OF THEIR SOURCES AND FLAWS

Why the emphasis on comparative formulas? Did it begin with the *Charter*, where comparator-group analyses have become so common, or is the *Charter* simply the dominant vehicle and influence for such formulas in the modern Canadian jurisprudential era?

Comparative methodologies appear to be long entrenched in equality discourse, whether the discourse is situated in philosophy,[68] in history,[69] in seminal jurisprudence,[70] even in logic.[71] For example, in the case of patent legal distinction between blacks and whites,[72] or between men and women,[73] it made intuitive sense and compelling argument to *compare* the rights that whites enjoyed, or that men enjoyed, in order to demonstrate the prejudice that the claimants were experiencing. The pursuit of equality was the pursuit by the oppressed of those positive rights that dominant groups enjoyed. It was the pursuit of the equal application of the law, the equal treatment of the law.[74] It was the pursuit of the elimination of "hierarchies of status (and associated rights and privileges)," based on foundational notions that all individuals are "'equally human,' 'equally worthy,' and 'equally deserving.'"[75] It was the pursuit of the concrete (and reductive) "goods" of distributive justice.[76]

Academic scholarship emerged, as did jurisprudence, replete with positive and negative comparative terminology such as "differential," "distinction," and "disproportionate," all necessarily evoking comparisons with the conditions experienced by others; that is, the dominant group. Indeed, in two of Canada's seminal equality law decisions, the Supreme Court discussed at length the proposition that equality is a *comparative* concept.[77] For example, in *Andrews*, citing "Western thought"[78] McIntyre J. stated that equality "... is a comparative concept, the condition of which may only be attained or discerned by comparison with the condition of others in the social and political setting in which the question arises."[79] A decade later, in *Law*, the Court affirmed that "the equality guarantee is a comparative concept" and that "... locat(ion) of the appropriate comparator is necessary in identifying differential treatment...."[80] Indeed, it used the discourse of comparison, differential treatment and distinction in each part of the landmark three-part test that it formulated.[81] In the Supreme Court's first post-*Law* equality case in which the ground of disability was invoked, Binnie J., writing for the Court, stated: "[t]he identification of the group in relation to which the appellant can properly claim 'unequal treatment' is crucial."[82]

Is this so? Is equality *necessarily* a comparative concept? Even if it is, should comparative formulas have conclusory status? Should they be the exclusive avenue for establishing discrimination?

Notably, statutory human rights jurisprudence contains a significantly lesser amount of strictly comparative discourse and methodology. Apart from its increasing reliance on the comparator-group approach and on the comparative-evidence requirements of the *Shakes/Israeli* test — a trend which I argue has its sources in the ascendancy of *Charter* principles — statutory human rights jurisprudence is actually replete with concepts that allow for broad, flexible inquiries and that call for *particularization*, and for *individualized* consideration, rather than *comparison*. The *O'Malley* test, already discussed at length, is a primary example: a complainant can establish a *prima facie* case by adducing enough evidence to justify a finding of discrimination in the absence of a reasonable explanation by the respondent. Implicit in this non-specific *prima facie* test is the recognition that discrimination in the post-express-discrimination era is almost always a subtle or veiled or systemic or unconscious act. The test therefore allows a complainant to adduce any manner of evidence that she or he may be able to find — indirect, circumstantial, "subtle scent(s)," systemic, past practice, personal impact and experience, comparative, contextual, etc. As one court put it, such flexibility "gives teeth to" and is "faithful to" the underlying purpose of human rights legislation: "assuring that persons are judged or dealt with on individual merit."[83]

The *Meiorin*[84] test is another example of the broad and individualized analyses that statutory human rights jurisprudence offers. In order to prove that a rule or standard is a *bona fide* occupational requirement, and therefore not discriminatory, a respondent employer must establish, *inter alia*, that it is impossible to accommodate a claimant without undue hardship. That is, the employer must take an individual's particular characteristics into account, and show that a "more individually sensitive (job) standard" would not be workable. It must afford a claimant an opportunity to perform her or his job in a different way, a way which accommodates her or his individual differences.[85] The possibilities for such accommodation will be case-specific, and effectively infinite. Most importantly, it certainly does not suffice for a respondent to establish that the claimant is simply subject to the same rule as other employees are, as the comparator-group test allows.[86]

The *Canadian Human Rights Act*, in particular the French version, also proffers an example of a conceptualization of equality that is particularized, rather than formulaically comparative. Section 2 states that the objective of the *Act* is to:

> ... extend the laws in Canada to give effect, within the purview of matters coming within the legislative authority of Parliament, to the principle that *all individuals should have an opportunity equal with other individuals to make for themselves the lives that they are able and wish to have and to have their needs accommodated, consistent with their duties and obligations as members of society, without being hindered in or prevented from doing so by discriminatory practices* based on race, national or ethnic origin, colour, religion, age, sex, sexual orientation, marital status, family status, disability or conviction for an offence for which a pardon has been granted. [Emphasis added.]

> ... compléter la législation canadienne en donnant effet, dans le champ de compétence du Parlement du Canada, au principe suivant: *le droit de tous les individus, dans la mesure compatible avec leurs devoirs et obligations au sein de la société, à l'égalité des chances d'épanouissement et à la prise de mesures visant à la satisfaction de leurs besoins, indépendamment des considérations fondées sur la race*, l'origine nationale ou ethnique, la couleur, le religion, l'âge, le sexe, l'orientation sexuelle, l'état matrimonial, la si-

tuation de famille, la déficience ou l'état de personne graciée. [Emphasis added.]

According to these statements, in particular the French version's use of the lustrous word "épanouissement,"[87] the purpose of equality law is the flourishing of every individual. It is the pursuit of particularized ideals, not comparative ones.

This conceptualization of equality is echoed elsewhere in statutory human rights cases. For example, in landmark cases on sexual harassment,[88] systemic discrimination,[89] and the discriminatory impact on women of certain benefit-plan exclusions,[90] the Supreme Court endorsed the following definition of discrimination:

> Equality in employment means that no one is denied opportunities for reasons that have nothing to do with inherent ability. It means equal access free from arbitrary obstructions. *Discrimination means that an arbitrary barrier stands between a person's ability and his or her opportunity to demonstrate it.* If the access is genuinely available in a way that *permits everyone who so wishes the opportunity to fully develop his or her potential, we have achieved a kind of equality. It is equality defined as equal freedom from discrimination.*[91]

Notably, the Court in *Janzen* went on to expressly reject the proposition that a finding of discrimination requires that all members of a protected group be "mistreated identically," as comparative formulas appear to presume:

> ... discrimination does not require uniform treatment of all members of a particular group.... If a finding of discrimination required that every individual in the affected group be treated identically, legislative protection against discrimination would be of little or no value. It is rare that a discriminatory action is so bluntly expressed as to treat all members of the relevant group identically. In nearly every instance of discrimination the discriminatory action is composed of various ingredients with the result that some members of the pertinent group are not adversely affected, at least in a direct sense, by the discriminatory action. To deny a finding of discrimination (in such a circumstance) is to deny the existence of discrimination in any situation where discriminatory practices are less than perfectly inclusive. It is to argue, for example, that an employer who will only hire a woman if she had twice the qualifications required of a man is

not guilty of sex discrimination if, despite this policy, the employer never-theless manages to hire some women.[92]

In so holding, the Supreme Court was effectively highlighting a serious pitfall of a formulaically comparative approach to discrimination: the possibility that discrimination will be overlooked by a court because the claimant cannot prove that others were similarly mistreated. Conversely, discrimination may be overlooked because a claimant cannot prove *different* treatment of certain others; namely, others who lack the gravamen of the complaint.

A formulaic comparative approach is even more fundamentally flawed. For example, it presumes that there *exists* an identifiable "other" with whom a claimant or claimant group can be adequately compared in her or his or its search for an idealized condition, despite the fact that "other" groups do not even share the characteristics nor especially the societal experience of disadvantage of the claimant group.[93] This amounts to a presumption that ideal societal and organizational conditions can necessarily be universally defined and universally applicable, despite inherent differences among in-dividuals and groups.[94] This is simply a lofty formulation of base formal-ism. The strictly comparative approach is also abstractionist,[95] and grossly essentialist.[96] At least one commentator has called it assimilationist,[97] and "fundamentally contradictory insomuch as it seeks the attainment of the privileged position of "others" in society, when such privilege is "contin-gent upon" the historical and continued oppression of the claimant and other groups.[98] Put another way, the conventional comparative approach "does not challenge mainstream norms and structures."[99]

D. CONCLUDING THOUGHTS: COMPARISON AS ONE POSSIBLE METHODOLOGY, NEITHER CONCLUSIVE NOR NECESSARY

In summary then, formulaic comparative methodologies appear to be the understandable result of an historic emphasis on the condition of the "other," despite the artificiality or inappropriateness of such reflexive com-parisons in a substantive-equality era. They have become particularly pre-dominant in the section 15 context, by virtue of the rigid application of definitions of equality that were formulated by the Supreme Court, first in *Andrews*, and later in *Law*. And they are gaining increasing prominence in the statutory human rights context, in part due to the drift of *Char-*

ter concepts and methods into statutory human rights cases. This drift is occurring *despite* the fact that the statutory human rights context has its own governing tests that are more flexible, and more favourable to the achievement of substantive equality, because they allow for individualized approaches.

Indeed there is a seminal equality case in the statutory human rights context that illustrates the full substantive-equality and individualized-consideration potential of statutory human rights concepts, in particular when unimpeded by a formulaic comparative approach. In *Brooks*,[100] the Supreme Court held that it was discriminatory to exclude women on maternity leave from employment benefit plans. In so doing, the Court not only overruled the formal-equality approach it had applied to deny a similar claim in *Bliss*[101] ten years earlier, but it reached its conclusion *without resort* to the formulaic comparator-group test that has since become the conclusory methodology of such cases.[102] That is, the Court did not engage in a contextual analysis of which other "sub-groups" of employees were also excluded, to ensure that all sub-groups were equally adversely affected, as courts have often since done. Rather, the Court looked at the "unique"[103] situation of women as society's only childbearers, and determined that they should not be subject to any employment disadvantage — they should not be "défavorisées"[104] — because of this unique and necessary role. The Court's ratio is substantivist and enlightened, and far removed from the effacing methodologies of subsequent comparative formulas:

> Combining paid work with motherhood and accommodating the child-bearing needs of working women are ever-increasing imperatives. That those who bear children and benefit society as a whole thereby should not be economically or socially disadvantaged seems to bespeak the obvious. It is only women who bear children; no man can become pregnant. As I argued earlier, it is unfair to impose all of the costs of pregnancy upon one half of the population.... The capacity to become pregnant is unique to the female gender....[105]

Citing a number of its prior decisions in statutory human rights claims, including *O'Malley*, as well as the guiding principle set out in section 2 of the *Canadian Human Rights Act*, the Court stated that this analysis was consistent with the proper approach to interpreting human rights legislation.[106]

The Supreme Court's decision in *Brooks* illustrates the potential of the *O'Malley* test and statutory human rights legislation in general. Their promise is illustrated by the broadly-stated and flexible emphasis on the achievement of self-fulfillment, not on the rigid achievement of only that which certain proximate others may be accorded by employers or by government.

Statutory human rights principles therefore offer a rich and deeply necessary possibility for unipolar analyses of the particular condition of the claimant or claimant group. Comparative evidence may have more or less probative value in any given case, depending on the circumstances, but such methodologies should never ascend to rigid formula, as has happened so starkly in the *Charter* context and as appears to be happening in the statutory context. The circumstances of equality claimants and equality claims are too diverse, too particularized, for rigid comparative formulas to take on conclusory status. Discrimination can manifest itself in infinitely subtle ways, and the threads of a claimant's discrimination fact pattern should not be forced through the eyes of narrow comparative-formula templates.

Equality principles must be broad enough and adaptable enough to allow for identification of discrimination, whatever substantive form it may take; and rigid comparative methodologies are antithetical to this objective. Statutory human rights tools, such as the *O'Malley* test, offer the flexibility and emphasis on individual self-fulfillment that equality claims require and pursue. These tools must therefore be reinforced, and reinvigorated, not replaced or undermined by rigid comparative formulas. In other words, ascendant or predominant *Charter* methodologies should not be allowed to supercede the plenteous potential of well-established statutory human rights methods. They should be stopped at the statutory human rights gate.

ENDNOTES

1 Andrea Wright was Legal Counsel with the Canadian Human Rights Commission at the time that this paper was originally presented. The views expressed herein are her own, and should not be taken to represent those of the Commission.

2 Leslie Reaume, who also presented at the conference, and whose paper appears in this text, discusses another trend in statutory human rights jurisprudence: its increasing reliance on the *Law* test.

3 This category would include the distinct subset of "pay equity" complaints. See discussion at below note 7.

4 *Ontario (Human Rights Commission) v. Simpsons Sears Ltd.*, [1985] 2 S.C.R. 536 at para. 28 [*O'Malley*].

5 *Basi v. Canadian National Railway Co. (No. 1)* (1988), 9 C.H.R.R. D/5209 (C.H.R.T.) at para. 34841 [*Basi*].

6 *Ibid.* at para. 38493.

7 A distinct and substantial subset of the first category is the pay equity complaint. In the federal statutory human rights context, pay equity complaints are filed and adjudicated pursuant to s. 11 of the *Canadian Human Rights Act*, R.S.C. 1985, c. H-6. This paper does not posit that comparative methodology is an ascendant jurisprudential trend in the pay equity domain, because formulaic comparison is expressly prescribed by the legislation. That is, in contrast with the assertion for other types of complaints that discrimination can be proved through other methods and evidence, pay inequity can only be proven, pursuant to statute, by virtue of a formula of comparison.

8 [1997] F.C.J. No. 1734 (T.D.) [*Dumont-Ferlatte*].

9 *Andrews v. Law Society of British Columbia*, [1989] 1 S.C.R. 143 at para. 37 [*Andrews*]. Emphasis added.

10 *Dumont-Ferlatte*, above note 8 at para. 37. Emphasis added.

11 *Ibid.* at paras. 28–32.

12 This was not quite unprecedented at the time. A year earlier, in *Battlefords and District Co-operative Ltd. v. Gibbs*, [1996] 3 S.C.R. 566 [*Gibbs*], the Supreme Court used the same *Andrews* passage to substantiate its use of a comparison of the claimant group (the mentally disabled) with "others" (in this case, the physically disabled). Surprisingly, the Court did not even cite the *O'Malley* test, even though this was a statutory human rights case, and the *O'Malley* test was the Court's own product.

13 *Dumont-Ferlatte*, above note 8 at para. 33.

14 *Ibid.* at para. 47.

15 *Ibid.* at para. 34.

16 [2000] F.C.J. No. 881 (T.D.) [*Cramm*].

17 The Court did cite the *O'Malley* case, but for a different proposition. See *O'Malley*, above note 4 at para. 16.

18 *Gibbs*, above note 12.

19 *Cramm*, above note 16 at paras. 16–24.

20 *Ibid.* at para. 24.

21 *Ibid.* at para. 30. Emphasis added.

22 The Court's statement of "sympathy" has shades of the "pity, patronization and paternalism" that disability advocates have long decried. See D. Lepofsky, "Discussion: The *Charter*'s Guarantee of Equality to People with Disabilities — How Well is it Working?" (1998) 16 Windsor Y.B. Access Just. 155 at 4.

23 [2004] 1 F.C.R. 679 (T.D.) [*Wignall* FCTD], aff'd in its application of comparator-group analysis and finding of no discrimination [2001] C.H.R.D. No. 9 (C.H.R.T.) [*Wignall* CHRT].

24 *Wignall* FCTD, *ibid.* at para. 26, describing C.H.R.T.'s reasoning.

25 *Ibid.* at para. 25.

26 Indeed the reasoning of the C.H.R.T. and the F.C.T.D. is *Bliss*-like in its conclusion that Mr. Wignall "was not taxed because he was disabled," but rather, because he required exceptional services to pursue his education (*Wignall* CHRT, above note 23 at para. 48). The fact that such exceptional services were required because he was disabled is not a part of the reasoning, just like the fact that only women can become pregnant was ignored by the Supreme Court in its conclusion that Ms. Bliss was not discriminated against. *Bliss v. Canada (A.G.)*, [1979] 1 S.C.R. 183 [*Bliss*].

27 (1999), 42 O.R. (3d) 692 (C.A.), leave to appeal dismissed [1999] S.C.C.A. No. 118 [*Ontario Nurses*].

28 There was a third benefit scheme in issue, on which the Court came to a different conclusion. See discussion below.

29 Shades of a similar conclusion can be found in the Tribunal's and the Federal Court's decisions in *Wignall* FCTD, above note 23. For example, the Tribunal stated at para. 47: "[t]he creation of the Special Opportunity Grant in the first place was obviously a recognition by the Government of Canada that students with disabilities were in need of special financial assistance...."

30 *Ontario Nurses*, above note 27 at 21.

31 Assessment of the "purpose" of a benefits scheme has become a common element of the comparator-group methodology. It first appeared in *Gibbs*, above note 12, in which Sopinka J., writing for the majority, ruled that the purpose of a benefits scheme must be identified in order to identify an appropriate comparator group and thereby assess the discrimination allegation. The parameters of this paper do not allow for a critique of the "purpose" test, but McLachlin J. (as she then was) ably predicted its pitfalls, in a separate concurring judgment in *Gibbs* (see paras. 45–54). McLachlin J.'s principal critique was that the "purpose" of any given scheme could be articulated in numerous ways, including narrow ones that would effectively exclude a claimant group by definition, or by a facially-neutral, yet discriminatory, statement of purpose. The test therefore created a risk of *Bliss*-like reasoning, because the inquiry could fail to focus on the gravamen of the complaint. This failure to focus on the gravamen of the complaint — a de-contextualization of the discrimination claim — is precisely what happened in *Dumont-Ferlatte*, as discussed above. The Court defined the purpose of the scheme as the provision of benefits to employees who were "at work," and thereby determined that the claimant group was treated no

differently than others who were not at work. In other words, a facially-neutral statement of purpose became the vehicle for effacement of the gravamen of the complaint.

32 See *Gibbs*, above note 12 at paras. 45–54, discussed *ibid*.

33 See, for example, *Sollbach v. Canada*, [1999] F.C.J. No. 1912 (C.A.) [*Sollbach*], in which the Court compared women on maternity leave to other employees on leave who were subject to the same provision, and therefore found no violation of s. 15; *Nishri v. Canada*, [2001] F.C.J. No. 563 (C.A.), in which identical comparator group reasoning was used to similarly deny a s. 15 claim of gender discrimination; *Miller v. Canada*, [2002] F.C.J. No. 1375 (C.A.), leave to appeal dismissed [2002] S.C.C.A. No. 505, in which the Court declined to overrule the comparator-group reasoning of *Sollbach*; and *Power v. Canada (Attorney General)*, [2003] N.J. No. 104 (C.A.), leave to appeal dismissed [2003] S.C.C.A. No. 353, in which the Newfoundland and Labrador Court of Appeal applied reasoning similar to the Federal Court's in *Cramm*.

See also *Granovsky v. Canada (Minister of Employment and Immigration)*, [2000] 1 S.C.R. 703 [*Granovsky*], in which the Court compared the "temporarily" disabled to the "permanently" disabled to dismiss an allegation of s. 15 discrimination and engage in a discourse of disability hierarchy (see, for example, paras. 27, 60, 67, and especially 81) (for similar comparisons of the variously-disabled, see also *Gibbs*, above note 12, a statutory human rights case; and *Nova Scotia (Workers' Compensation Board) v. Martin*, [2003] 2 S.C.R. 504); *Lovelace v. Ontario*, [2000] 1 S.C.R. 950, in which the Court compared non-band aboriginal communities to band aboriginal communities to dismiss an allegation of s. 15 discrimination, even though it noted at length the "overlapping and largely shared histories of discrimination, poverty, and systemic disadvantage (of the two groups) that cry out for improvement" (see, for example, paras. 6, 7, & 66); and *Bear v. Canada (Attorney General)*, [2003] 3 F.C. 456 (C.A.), leave to appeal dismissed [2003] S.C.C.A. No. 115, in which the Court compared the improbably de-contextualized sub-groups of "individuals who earn their income on an Indian reserve" to "Canadians who do not earn their income on an Indian reserve," as if the fact that the claimant was an aboriginal person had nothing to do with the s. 15 claim.

Perhaps the most recent example of the contortions of a comparator-group analysis is the Supreme Court's decision in *Auton (Guardian ad litem of) v. British Columbia (Attorney General)*, [2004] S.C.J. No. 71, in which the Supreme Court held, in overturning a finding of discrimination by the British Columbia Court of Appeal, that the appropriate comparator group was "a member of a non-disabled group or a person suffering a disability other than a mental disability that requests or receives funding for non-core therapy important to present and future health, but which is emergent and only recently becoming recognized as medically required" (at para. 58). One might posit that the ponderous, chain-linked description of the comparator group alone suggests that equality jurisprudence has gone horribly awry; that surely there must be a less encumbered, less formulaic, purer way to assess an equality claim.

34 *Law v. Canada (Minister of Employment and Immigration)*, [1999] 1 S.C.R. 497 [*Law*].

35 [2001] F.C.J. No. 1882 (C.A.).

36 S.C. 1996, c. 23.

37 *Sollbach*, above note 33.

38 (1981), 3 C.H.R.R. D/001 (Ont. Bd. Inq.) [*Shakes*].

39 *Ibid.* at para. 8918.

40 *Ibid.* at para. 8918.

41 (1983), 4 C.H.R.R. D/1616 (C.H.R.T.) [*Israeli*], aff'd (1984), C.H.R.R. D/2147 (C.H.R.R.T.). All further references herein are to C.H.R.T. decision.

42 *Ibid.* at para. 13865.

43 *Basi*, above note 5 at para. 38481.

44 [2001] C.H.R.D. No. 36 (C.H.R.T.) [*McAvinn*].

45 See for example *Offierski v. Peterborough Board of Education*, [1980] C.H.R.R. D/33 (Ont. Bd. Inq.) [*Offierski*]; *Folch v. Canadian Airlines International*, [1992] C.H.R.D. No. 5 (C.H.R.T.) [*Folch*]; *Oxley v. British Columbia Institute of Technology*, [2002] B.C.H.R.T.D. No. 33 [*Oxley*]; *Ayangama v. French Language School Board of Prince Edward Island*, [2003] P.E.I.H.R.P.D. No. 2 [*Ayangama Tribunal decision*], aff'd [2004] P.E.I.J. No. 41 (Sup. Ct. T.D.) [*Ayangama judicial review decision*]; *Morris v. Canadian Armed Forces*, [2001] C.H.R.R. no. 41 (C.H.R.T.) [*Morris (CHRT)*], quashed [2003] F.C.J. 1746 (T.D.) [*Morris (FCTD)*], restored [2005] F.C.J. 731 [*Morris (FCA)*].

46 *McAvinn*, above note 44; see, for example, para. 137*ff.*

47 *Ibid.* at paras. 116–17.

48 *Ibid.* at para. 169. Ms. McAvinn herself perhaps provided the best description of the many ways in which the employer's process evidenced discrimination. The Tribunal cited this excerpt from her testimony in full, but did not engage in an express or plenteous consideration of how these elements fit into the *prima facie* case. See para. 109.

49 See Leslie Reaume, "Postcards from *O'Malley*: Reinvigorating Statutory Human Rights Jurisprudence in the Age of the *Charter*," in this volume.

50 See, for example, *Offierski*, above note 45; *Folch*, above note 45; *Oxley*, above note 45; *Lincoln v. Bay Ferries Ltd.*, [2002] C.H.R.D. No. 5 (C.H.R.T.) [*Lincoln CHRT*], aff'd [2003] F.C.J. No. 1462 (T.D.) [*Lincoln FCTD*], rev'd [2004] F.C.J. 941 (C.A.) [*Lincoln FCA*], leave to appeal dismissed [2004] S.C.C.A. No. 367; *Garand v. K.E. Gostlin Enterprises Ltd. (c.o.b. Canadian Tire Corp.)*, [2002] B.C.H.R.T.D. No. 8 [*Garand*]; *Martin v. Saulteaux Band*, [2002] C.H.R.D. No. 10 (C.H.R.T.) [*Martin*]; *Montreuil v. National Bank of Canada*, [2004] C.H.R.D. NO. 4 (C.H.R.T.) [*Montreuil*]; *Milano v. Triple K. Transport Ltd.*, [2003] C.H.R.D. No. 23 (C.H.R.T.) [*Milano*]; *Mbaruk v. Surrey School District No. 36*, [1996] B.C.C.H.R.D. No. 50 [*Mbaruk*]; *Corrigan v. Pacific Western Airlines Ltd.*, [1988] C.H.R.D. No. 6 (C.H.R.T.) [*Corrigan*]. For an example of cases in which tribunals have rejected "rigid application" of the *Shakes/Israeli* test in favour of the more adaptable *O'Malley* test, see *Singh v. Canada (Statistics Canada)*, [1998] C.H.R.D. No. 7 (C.H.R.T.), aff'd [2000] F.C.J. No. 417 (T.D.) [*Singh*]; *Chander v. Canada (Department of National Health and Welfare)*, [1995] C.H.R.D. No. 16 (C.H.R.T.), aff'd [1997] F.C.J. No. 692 (T.D.) [*Chander*]; *Crouse v. Canadian Steamship Lines Inc.*, [2001]

C.H.R.D. No. 12 (C.H.R.T.); *Premakumar v. Air Canada*, [2002] C.H.R.D. No. 3 (C.H.R.T.); *Oster v. International Longshore & Warehouse Union (Marine Section)*, [2000] C.H.R.D. No. 2 (C.H.R.T.), aff'd [2002] 2 F.C. 430 (T.D.); *Abouchar v. Metropolitan Toronto School Board*, [1998] O.H.R.B.I.D. No. 6.

51 See, for example, *Shakes*, above note 38; *Israeli*, above note 41; *Offierski*, *ibid.*; *Folch*, *ibid.*; *Lincoln CHRT*, *ibid.*; and *Oxley*, *ibid.* In *Oxley*, the Tribunal cited the *O'Malley* test as the governing test, and professed that the *Shakes/Israeli* test need not be applied rigidly, but proceeded to apply the latter nonetheless (at para. 78*ff*). Perhaps most unfortunate is that the Tribunal expressly rejected the possibility that a "flawed" selection process could impugn the applicability of the *Shakes* test or otherwise change the Tribunal's conclusion on the *prima facie* case. In so doing, it effectively even required that an intention to discriminate be shown. It stated:

> Even if I were to accept the Complainant's allegation that the selection process was flawed, this would not be sufficient to justify a complaint of discrimination on the basis of race, colour or ancestry. Even if the selection criteria were skewed to favour a particular candidate ... unless a link can be made to a discriminatory reason for such a decision, a case of discrimination is not made out.

52 See, for example, *Garand*, above note 50; *Martin*, above note 50; *Montreuil*, above note 50; *Milano*, above note 50; *Mbaruk*, above note 50; *Corrigan*, above note 50.

53 *Morris* (FCTD), above note 45. The author of this paper represented the Commission in the Federal Court Trial Division. As stated at the beginning of this paper, the views expressed herein are personal, and should not be taken to necessarily represent those of the Canadian Human Rights Commission.

54 *Ibid.* at para. 25. Emphasis added.

55 *Morris* (CHRT), above note 45.

56 *Morris* (FCA), above note 45.

57 *Morris* (CHRT), above note 45: see, for example, para. 124*ff*.

58 *Singh*, above note 50.

59 *Chander*, above note 50.

60 *Ibid.*

61 See the Tribunal's detailed consideration of evidence at para. 77*ff*, and its summary of the evidence upon which it relied, at para. 134*ff*.

62 *Lincoln FCA*, above note 50.

63 *Morris* (FCA), above note 45 at para. 26.

64 *Ibid.* at para. 28.

65 This said, one can be concerned that the Federal Court of Appeal stated only that "comparative evidence of discrimination comes in many more forms than the particular one identified in *Shakes*," rather than stating that evidence of discrimination, generally, comes in many more forms than the particular one identified in *Shakes*.

66 *Lincoln FCA*, above note 50.

67 *Basi*, above note 5 at para. 38493.

68 Aristotle is often cited as one of the first to posit that "like cases should be treated alike"; see, for example, D. Lepofsky, above note 22 at 7. This proposition appears

to have been the foundation for the "similarly situated" test in modern Canadian equality doctrine and law. For a discussion, see, for example, *Andrews*, above note 9 at para. 25*ff*; D. Lepofsky, *ibid.* at 7*ff*; *Brooks*, below note 90 at para. 42*ff*.

69 The highest-profile equality struggles in the modern era defined the measure of disadvantage by reference to the rights and privileges that the dominant majority enjoyed; for example, the right to vote, the right to attend the same schools, the right to drink from the same water fountain, the right to the status of "person," the right to access to the same jobs, the right to marriage, etc.

70 See discussion below this paragraph.

71 Laws, rules, regulations, policies, and standards all inherently make distinctions between persons and conditions in society. It becomes only logical then, in the challenge of a rule or practice that distinguishes between groups, that the relative effects of such distinction be compared.

72 For example, *Plessy v. Ferguson*, 163 U.S. 537 (1896); *Brown v. Board of Education*, 345 U.S. 972 (1953); *Loving v. Virginia*, 388 U.S. 1 (1967).

73 For example, *Edwards v. Canada (A.G.)*, [1930] A.C. 124 (P.C.) (the "Persons" case).

74 See, for example, Ronald Dworkin, *Taking Rights Seriously* (Cambridge: Harvard University Press, 1977) at 272*ff*. The concept of "juridical equality" has also been used: see Alan Brudner, "What are Reasonable Limits to Equality Rights?" (1986) 64 Can. Bar. Rev. 469, cited in Diana Majury, "Equality and Discrimination According to the Supreme Court of Canada" (1991) 4 C.J.W.L. 407 at 413.

75 Radha Jhappan, "The Equality Pit or the Rehabilitation of Justice" 10 C.J.W.L. 60 at 66.

76 See, for example, Iris Marion Young, "Equality of Whom? Social Groups and Judgments of Injustice" (2001) 9 J. Pol. Phil. 1.

77 *Andrews*, above note 9; *Law*, above note 34.

78 *Andrews*, *ibid.* at 164.

79 *Ibid.* See also *Gibbs*, above note 12 at paras. 28–29, in which the Supreme Court cited this dictum from McIntyre J. in reaffirming the "comparative" nature of equality.

80 *Law*, above note 34 at para. 56*ff*.

81 *Ibid.* In 2001, while still a Supreme Court justice, L'Heureux-Dubé J. also confirmed in academic writing that "equality continues to be a comparative concept." See "A Conversation About Equality" in Joseph E. Magnet, ed., *Constitutional Law of Canada*, 8th ed. (Edmonton: Juriliber, 2001).

82 *Granovsky*, above note 33 at para. 45, citing *Andrews*, above note 9 at 164, and *Law*, *ibid.* at para. 24.

83 *Power v. Wabush Mines*, [1997] N.J. No. 255 (C.A.) at para. 29.

84 *B.C.(Public Service Employee Relations Commission) v. BCGSEU*, [1999] 3 S.C.R. 3 [*Meiorin*]. The Supreme Court formulated a similar test for the non-employment context in *British Columbia (Superintendent of Motor Vehicles) v. British Columbia (Council of Human Rights)*, [1999] 3 S.C.R. 868 [*Grismer*].

85 *Meiorin*, *ibid.* at paras. 54–68. See also *Grismer*, *ibid.* at paras. 20–22 and 30–45; and *Air Canada v. Carson*, [1985] 1 F.C. 209 (C.A.) in which the court stated at 217:

Thus, in asking what is reasonably necessary to ensure the safe performance by pilots of their duties as they age, it seems entirely reasonable to enquire if it is not possible or practical to deal with those pilots on an individual basis rather than preventing their initial employment by a blanket refusal to hire (candidates over the age of 27).

86 See discussion above at section B.I. See also *Saskatchewan (Human Rights Commission) v. Saskatoon (City)*, [1989] 2 S.C.R. 1297 at para. 20, in which the Court stated that the "general philosophy of human rights legislation" is that "persons are not to be judged or dealt with on the basis of external characteristics such as race, age, sex, etc. but on individual merit.... The dichotomy between an individualized approach and an approach based on average characteristics is of the very essence of a defence (to discrimination)."

87 Indeed, the French version goes on to define "*actes discriminatoires*" as practices which "*défavorisent*" a claimant. This choice of language appears to reflect a conceptualization of equality that is, and has the potential to be, vastly different from the conventional comparative conceptualization of equality discussed above. That is, to determine whether someone is "défavorisé" by a particular rule or standard or practice, one engages in a much more individualized, unipolar analysis of the conditions of the claimant, rather than a comparative analysis of how the person's experience stacks up *vis à vis* that of others.

88 *Janzen v. Platy*, [1989] 1 S.C.R. 1252 [*Janzen*].

89 *Canadian National Railway Co. v. Canada (Human Rights Commission)*, [1987] 1 S.C.R. 1114 [*Action Travail*].

90 *Brooks v. Canada Safeway Ltd.*, [1989] 1 S.C.R. 1219 [*Brooks*].

91 *Janzen*, above note 88 at para. 48, citing *Action Travail*, above note 89 at 1138–39; *Brooks*, *ibid.* at 1234, all citing *Equality in Employment: Royal Commission Report*, 1984 (*Abella Report*) at 2. Emphasis added.

This reasoning is echoed by D. Lepofsky, above note 22 at 13, in his discussion of the goals of equality guarantees for people with disabilities:

The aim is to have people fairly and accurately judged on their individual ability, based on what they can do in a barrier-free context, and not on what they cannot do or on what others think they cannot do. The goal is to achieve a barrier-free society for persons with disabilities which accommodates a wide spectrum of individual abilities, and not a society which simply expects all to conform to one hypothetical, typically fictional "normalcy" standard before they "fit in."

92 *Janzen*, *ibid.* at para. 62.

93 Patricia Hughes has commented: "The mainstream or dominant view is not necessarily the only view and the goals which the mainstream or dominant group seek are not necessarily those sought by non-dominant members of society," in "Recognizing Substantive Equality as a Foundational Constitutional Principle" (1999) 22 Dalhousie L.J. 5 at 17. Hughes cites, *inter alia*, Leon E. Trakman who commented that "... the ends of privileged groups are not coincident with those whom privileged groups supposedly empower" in "Substantive Equality in Constitutional Jurisprudence:

Meaning within Meaning" (1994) 7 Can. J. L. & Jur. 27 at 31. See also Mary Ellen Turpel-Lafond, "Patriarchy and Paternalism: The Legacy of the Canadian State for First Nations Women" (1993) 6 C.J.W.L. 174.

94 bell hooks has said "(m)ost people in the United States think of feminism ... as a movement that aims to make women the social equals of men.... Since men are not equals in white supremacist, capitalist, patriarchal class structure, which men do women want to be equal to?" See bell hooks, "Feminism: A Movement to End Sexist Oppression" in Anne Phillips *et al.*, *Feminism and Equality* (Oxford: Basil Blackwell, 1987) at 62, cited in Jhappan, above note 75 at 79.

The inappropriateness of a comparative conceptualization of equality — for example, that men and women should be equal — is especially salient for Aboriginal people. See for example Mary Ellen Turpel, "Patriarchy and Paternalism: The Legacy of the Canadian State for First Nations Women" (1993) 6 C.J.W.L. 174 at 179–80, and Sharon McIvor, "Aboriginal Women's Legal Strategies" in Radha Jhappan, ed., *Women's Legal Strategies in Canada: A Friendly Assessment* (Toronto: University of Toronto Press, forthcoming), both cited in Jhappan, *ibid.* at 79–80.

A similar criticism exists in examinations of disability equality theory. Jonathan Penney has written: "... substantive equality demands that differences between people be taken into consideration. This does not mean that people are defined as different from a norm, however. Rather, people are to be seen as different from each other." J. Penney, "A Constitution for the Disabled or a Disabled Constitution? Toward a New Approach to Disability for the Purposes of Section 15(1)" (2002) 1 J.L. & Equality 83 at para. 55, citing P. Hughes, "Recognizing Substantive Equality as a Foundational Constitutional Principle," *ibid.* at 35.

95 See, for example, Donna Greschner, "Equality and Critical Legal Studies" in Sheilah Martin & Kathleen Mahoney, eds., *Equality and Judicial Neutrality* (Toronto: Carswell, 1987).

96 Numerous commentators have pointed out the "forced essentialism" (Jhappan, above note 75 at 63) of the present equality jurisprudential framework. See, for example, K. Crenshaw, "Demarginalizing the Intersection of Race and Sex: A Black Feminist Critique of Antidiscrimination Doctrine, Feminist Theory and Antiracist Politics" (1989) U. Chicago Legal Forum 139; A. Harris, "Race and Essentialism in Feminist Legal Theory" (1990) Stan. L. Rev. 581; M. Eaton, "Patently Confused: Complex Inequality and *Canada v. Mossop*" (1994) 1 Rev. of Con. Stud. 203; M. Eaton, "Homosexual Unmodified: Speculations on Law's Discourse, Race and the Construction of Sexual Identity" in D. Herman & C. Stychin, eds. *Legal Inversions: Lesbians, Gay Men, and the Politics of Law* (Philadelphia: Temple University Press, 1995) cited in Carl F. Stychin, "Essential Rights and Contested Identities: Sexual Orientation and Equality Rights Jurisprudence in Canada" (1995) 8 Can. J.L. & Juris. 49; Jhappan, *ibid.* at 68–79; Penney, above note 94.

97 Jhappan, *ibid.*

98 *Ibid.* at 81.

99 Penney, above note 94 at para. 29.

100 *Brooks*, above note 90.

101 *Bliss*, above note 26.

102 Examples in the statutory context have already been canvassed in this paper: *Dumont-Ferlatte*, above note 8; *Cramm*, above note 16; *Ontario Nurses*, above note 27; *Wignall*, above note 23. Examples in the s. 15 *Charter* context have also been noted above note 33.

103 *Brooks*, above note 90 at para. 38.

104 *Canadian Human Rights Act*, R.S.C. 1985, c. H-6, s. 2 of French version.

105 *Brooks*, above note 90 at para. 40.

106 *Ibid.* at para. 42*ff.*

thirteen

International Law as a Strategic Tool for Equality Rights Litigation:
A CAUTIONARY TALE

Jennifer Koshan[1]

A. INTRODUCTION

Since the early days of equality rights jurisprudence under the *Canadian Charter of Rights and Freedoms*,[2] the concept of human dignity has played an important role in defining the goal of constitutional equality protections.[3] The role of dignity has become even more central since the Supreme Court of Canada's 1999 decision in *Law v. Canada*, where the Court described the purpose of section 15(1) of the *Charter* as follows:[4]

> to prevent the violation of *essential human dignity* and freedom through the imposition of disadvantage, stereotyping, or political or social prejudice, and to promote a society in which all persons enjoy equal recognition at law as human beings or as members of Canadian society, equally capable and equally deserving of concern, respect and consideration.

Similarly, dignity has a prominent place in international human rights documents. The *Universal Declaration of Human Rights (UDHR)* notes in its preamble "that recognition of the *inherent dignity* and of the equal and inalienable rights of all members of the human family is the foundation of freedom, justice and peace in the world."[5] The *International Covenant on Civil and Political Rights (the ICCPR)*[6] and the *International Covenant on Economic, Social and Cultural Rights (the ICESCR)*[7] also refer in their preambles to "the *inherent dignity* of the human person" as the source of human rights. More specifically, the *Convention on the Elimination of All*

Forms of Discrimination Against Women (*the CEDAW*) states "discrimination against women violates the principles of equality of rights and respect for *human dignity*."[8]

Given their intersection at the point of dignity, one might expect that Canadian courts would find international human rights instruments to be a fruitful source for interpreting the scope of section 15(1) of the *Charter*. This is not to accede to the argument that "dignity" should be maintained as the centerpiece of equality rights.[9] However, as long as dignity remains at the core of section 15(1) of the *Charter*, international human rights norms have a potential role to play in the interpretation of section 15(1).

Even if dignity were displaced this would be the case, given the similarity of equality norms at the domestic and international levels. International human rights instruments, like the *Charter*, protect against discrimination generally,[10] and in more specific contexts.[11] Regional human rights documents also include equality guarantees.[12] Some international human rights conventions have mechanisms for complaints,[13] or reports by international bodies,[14] offering further opportunities for pronouncements on equality and discrimination at the international level. International human rights sources thus provide fertile ground for Canadian courts in their interpretation of section 15(1) of the *Charter*.

My analysis will show that despite the richness of international human rights material, the Supreme Court of Canada has been reticent in using international law in relation to section 15 of the *Charter*. The Court's silence is particularly pronounced with respect to social and economic rights, and women's equality guarantees. When the Court does refer to international law in its equality rights decisions, it often fails to provide reasons for why it is doing so, making it difficult to assess the basis upon which the Court finds international human rights law to be a compelling source in the domestic context. In the absence of a clear explanation from the Court, I will explore possible reasons for its reluctance to apply international law in the equality context.

Another trend that I will expose is the Supreme Court's use of international law to narrow the scope of section 15 of the *Charter*. International human rights norms have been put forward by conservative interveners, and used by members of the Court to defeat equality rights claims under the *Charter* as often as they have been used to support a substantive equality approach. In other cases, international law seems to make little difference to the Court's reasons for decision.

I will argue that these trends have implications for parties and interveners in assessing the utility of employing international human rights law to support substantive equality claims before the courts. While international law can be used to further a more substantive approach to equality, this remains a risky strategy until a theory of substantive equality and international law is put forward. Relying upon the work of Gibran van Ert, I sketch out some of the parameters of such a theory in my conclusion.

B. SOURCES OF INTERNATIONAL LAW

Before turning to an analysis of international law in *Charter* equality cases, the scope of "international law" and of the rules surrounding the interplay between international law and domestic law will be briefly reviewed. According to van Ert,[15]

> The sources of international law are not to be sought in any authoritative constitution or text. Rather, they are established by the practice of states. As state practice changes, new sources may arise and old sources fade.

Although international law is in a constant state of flux, van Ert also notes that article 38 of the *Statute of the International Court of Justice* is "an important statement of the sources of international law."[16] Article 38 includes the following as established sources of international law: international conventions (treaties); international custom (general practices accepted as law); general principles of law recognized by civilized nations; and judicial decisions and the teachings of the most highly qualified publicists (both subsidiary sources).[17]

In addition to these sources of "hard" law, there are also "soft law" sources, those that describe developing norms of international law. Soft law sources include draft treaties, as well as declarations, reports, guides, and recommendations of international bodies.[18] While "soft law" is not actually "law" in the true sense, it may express "international values," and is thus important in the domestic context, as I will discuss below.

Turning to the second preliminary issue, what is the relationship between international law and domestic law? A distinction is often made between sources of international law which are binding in the domestic context, and those which are not. Customary international law applies domestically without any explicit act of incorporation into Canadian law, unless it conflicts with existing legislation or common law rules.[19] In contrast, international treaties must be incorporated in order to apply at the domestic level. This typically requires implementation of international treaty obligations through legislation.[20]

It is not settled whether international human rights treaties to which Canada is a party[21] have been incorporated into domestic law.[22] In one sense, this is an important debate — if such treaties have been incorporated, then one would expect Canadian courts to refer to them as a matter of obligation in interpreting the *Charter*. Until this debate is settled, there is continuing scope for a lack of coherence in the courts' use of international human rights treaties in the domestic context.

However, even if this issue is not settled, international human rights treaties can be useful in a second sense. Courts are bound by a presumption that the *Charter* should be interpreted in a way that is consistent with international law.[23] This presumption is reflected in statements from the Supreme Court of Canada on the interplay between international human rights law and the *Charter*. In *Reference Re Public Service Employee Relations Act (Alta.)*, Dickson C.J., writing in dissent, noted that "the *Charter* should generally be presumed to provide protection at least as great as that afforded by similar provisions in international human rights documents which Canada has ratified."[24] In *Slaight Communications Inc. v. Davidson*, a majority of the Court held that "Canada's international human rights obligations should inform ... the interpretation of the content of the rights guaranteed by the *Charter*...."[25]

However, in *R. v. Keegstra*, McLachlin J., in dissent, noted that international conventions may not be useful where their guarantees are less fulsome than those of the *Charter*:[26]

> Canada's international obligations, and the accords negotiated between international governments may well be helpful in placing *Charter* interpretation in a larger context. Principles agreed upon by free and democratic societies may inform the reading given to certain of its guarantees. It would be wrong, however, to consider these obligations as determinative of or limiting the scope of those guarantees. The provisions of the *Charter*, though drawing on a political and social philosophy shared with other democratic societies, are uniquely Canadian. As a result, considerations may point, as they do in this case, to a conclusion regarding a rights violation which is not necessarily in accord with those international covenants.

Recent decisions of the Supreme Court of Canada highlight the interpretive role of a broader range of international human rights instruments. In *Baker v. Canada (Minister of Citizenship and Immigration)*, a majority of the Supreme Court held that "the values reflected in international human rights law may help inform the contextual approach to statutory interpretation and judicial review.... It is also a critical influence on the interpretation of the scope of the rights included in the *Charter*."[27] As sources of international values, the majority relied on the *Convention on the Rights of the Child*, a treaty not yet implemented by Canada, as well as the *Universal Declaration of Human Rights* and the *United Nations Declaration of the Rights of the Child* (1959), "soft law" sources.

Subsequently, in *Suresh v. Canada (Minister of Citizenship and Immigration)*, the Court was unanimous in finding that the scope of the principles of fundamental justice under section 7 of the *Charter* should be informed by "Canada's international obligations and values as expressed in '[t]he various sources of international human rights law — declarations, covenants, conventions, judicial and quasi-judicial decisions of international tribunals, [and] customary norms'."[28] Even more forcefully, the Court stated that the provisions of the *Charter* "cannot be considered in isolation from the international norms which they reflect. A complete understanding of the Act and the *Charter* requires consideration of the international perspective."[29] The Court went on to refer to a number of international treaties, declarations, and decisions of United Nations bodies in its interpretation of section 7 of the *Charter*.

The Court's pronouncements in *Baker* and *Suresh* can be compared to the Court's use of "*Charter* values" to inform the interpretation of the common law. Although the common law cannot be directly challenged as contrary to the *Charter*,[30] the Supreme Court has noted that *Charter* values should be used to ensure that the common law develops in a way that is consistent with the *Charter*.[31] I will return to this analogy in my conclusion, as it bears relevance for the development of a theory of international law and substantive equality.

The *Baker* and *Suresh* decisions thus confirm the possibility of making *Charter* equality arguments that rely upon a broad range of international materials, including treaties which have not been incorporated, and "soft law" sources. In fact, while the Court's willingness to entertain arguments based upon international law may appear to have increased following *Baker* and *Suresh*, my survey of cases will show that the Supreme Court did not restrict itself to considering binding sources of international law even before these cases.

Therefore, I have used a broad definition of "international law" in this survey — conventions, whether or not Canada is a party; customary international law; declarations; resolutions; and reports and decisions of international bodies. In the next part of my paper, I will draw out the trends in the Supreme Court's use of international law, broadly defined, under section 15 of the *Charter*. My analysis will show that, even using a broad definition, the Court's references to international law in its section 15 cases are sparse, and are not always in furtherance of a substantive approach to equality.

C. SECTION 15 AND INTERNATIONAL LAW, 1989–2004: TRENDS IN THE CASE LAW

In this section, I analyze the Supreme Court of Canada's use of international law in its *Charter* equality rights cases from 1989 to 2004. I have reviewed only those equality rights cases involving a challenge to a law or government practice under section 15(1) of the *Charter*, and not those cases where section 15(1) was cited in relation to the interpretation of a law, or to support a law being upheld as constitutional where it was challenged under another section.[32] In my view, the "pure" equality rights cases canvassed here are most relevant to a discussion of the possibilities of using international law to support section 15(1) claims.[33] My sample is also limited to those cases where the Supreme Court actually dealt with the section 15 submissions raised by the parties, although I include cases where only a minority of judges considered section 15, as these are still germane for analyzing trends and predicting how the courts will respond to international law arguments in future equality rights cases.[34]

The Supreme Court of Canada decided a total of sixty section 15(1) cases from 1989 to 2004.[35] Out of these sixty cases, the Court cited international law in only sixteen. When these sixteen cases are examined, the sample can be further narrowed to eight cases where the Court actually referred to international law in its section 15 reasons,[36] rather than in relation to one of the other rights or freedoms at issue, or in relation to section 1 of the *Charter*.[37] The eight decisions where international law was cited in relation to section 15(1) of the *Charter* are set out in Table 1.

Table 1 — International Law in *Charter* Section 15 Cases, 1989–2004

Case	Source(s) of International Law	Cited By
McKinney v. University of Guelph, [1990] 3 S.C.R. 229	U.N. General Assembly Resolution 3137	La Forest J. (plurality) (at 296)
Miron v. Trudel, [1995] 2 S.C.R. 418	*European Convention*, Article 12; *Universal Declaration*, Article 16	Gonthier J. (dissent)(at 450)
Egan v. Canada, [1995] 2 S.C.R. 213	*Resolution on Equal Rights for Homosexuals and Lesbians in the European Community* (A3-0028/94)	Cory J. (plurality) (at 602)
Granovsky v. Canada, [2000] 1 S.C.R. 703	World Health Organization, *International Classification of Impairments*; United Nations, *World Programme Of Action concerning Disabled Persons*	Binnie J. (unanimous) (at para. 34)
Lovelace v. Ontario, [2000] 1 S.C.R. 950	*Concluding Observations of the Committee on Economic, Social and Cultural Rights* (Canada, 1998)	Iacobucci J. (unanimous) (at para. 69)
Lavoie v. Canada, [2002] 1 S.C.R. 769	*International Covenant on Civil and Political Rights*, Art. 25(c); *Universal Declaration*, Art. 21(2)	Bastarache J. (plurality) (at paras. 46–48); Arbour J. (concurring) (at para. 101)
Nova Scotia v. Walsh, [2002] 4 S.C.R. 325	*Universal Declaration*, Art. 16	Gonthier J. (concurring) (at para. 193)
Canadian Foundation for Children, Youth and the Law v. Canada, [2004] 1 S.C.R. 76	*Convention on the Rights of the Child*; *International Covenant on Civil and Political Rights*, Art. 24	Deschamps J. (dissent) (at paras. 225-26)

The first observation to make in relation to this data is that the Court seems reluctant to cite international law in its equality rights decisions. In only eight out of sixty, or 13.33 percent of the cases did the Court refer to international law in relation to section 15(1) of the *Charter*. Put another way, the Court was silent on international law in 86.67 percent of the cases. Although this number is somewhat inflated, as some of the cases were decided in groups, it is nevertheless true that the vast majority of the Supreme Court's section 15(1) reasons did not refer to international law.

The Court's reticence with respect to international law cannot be explained simply by a lack of argumentation. In many section 15(1) cases, the parties and/or interveners cited international law in their *facta*, but the

Court did not refer to these arguments in its reasons for decision.[38] For example, the Charter Committee on Poverty Issues routinely relies upon international law in its section 15 interventions, primarily the *ICESCR*, but the Court has failed to advert to these arguments in most of these cases.[39] In *Vriend*, the Alberta Civil Liberties Association and the Canadian Association of Statutory Human Rights Agencies cited international law in their *facta* to support the position that Alberta was obliged to protect against discrimination on the basis of sexual orientation, but again, the Court did not refer to international law in its judgment.[40]

Importantly, parties and interveners seeking to restrict the scope of equality rights have also relied upon international law to support their arguments. In *Vriend*, for example, the Christian Legal Fellowship argued that the omission of sexual orientation from Alberta's human rights legislation was consistent with the *ICCPR*, the *Universal Declaration of Human Rights*, and decisions of the European Court of Human Rights.[41] Similarly, in *M. v. H.*, a church coalition relied on the *ICCPR* and the *Universal Declaration of Human Rights* to restrict the rights of gays and lesbians.[42] International law was not referred to by the Court in either case.

The fact that international law has been used by parties and interveners both for and against substantive equality interpretations of section 15 is telling. It may be that, faced with such conflicting arguments, the Court simply chooses not to wade into the debate about the implications of international law for the case at hand. If international human rights law is broad enough to support conflicting positions in an equality rights case, progressive parties and interveners will need to rely upon an approach to international law that is supportive of substantive equality in order to persuade the Court that their interpretation of international norms is the more compelling one.

A second observation from this survey of cases is that some sources of international human rights law are notably absent from the Court's reasons for decision. Customary international law has never been cited by the Court in relation to section 15(1) of the *Charter*, despite the fact that customary norms of international law relating to non-discrimination have been recognized.[43] This omission is not surprising, as Anne Bayesfky notes that courts tend to refer to customary international law infrequently where they can rely on conventional international law, given the problems of proof inherent in international custom.[44]

More surprising is the fact that the Court has yet to cite the *ICESCR* in relation to section 15(1) of the *Charter*.[45] The *ICESCR* was cited in *Gosselin*, but this was with respect to section 45 of the *Quebec Charter* rather than section 15(1) of the *Canadian Charter of Rights and Freedoms*.[46] Again, this is not for lack of argument on the point, as a number of interveners and parties cited the *ICESCR* in support of their section 15 *Charter* arguments in *Gosselin* and other cases.[47]

Similarly, the Court has never cited the *CEDAW* in relation to section 15(1) of the *Charter*. This Convention was referred to by the Court in *Canadian Foundation for Children, Youth and the Law*, but this was in the majority's section 7 reasons. In part, this may be because parties and interveners seldom rely upon the *CEDAW*.[48] Still, this cannot be the only explanation, given the Court's approach to the *ICESCR*.

The *ICESCR* is an important instrument to the project of advancing substantive equality, with its guarantees of the right to work, the right to social security, and the right to an adequate standard of living.[49] Similarly, the *CEDAW* has the potential to support a substantive equality approach, with its specific guarantees of women's equality, and its imposition upon state parties of the obligation to take "all appropriate measures ... to ensure the full development and advancement of women."[50]

The Court's refusal to cite these human rights instruments under section 15 of the *Charter* coincides with its dismissal of substantive equality arguments in some of its recent cases involving social and economic rights, and women's equality.[51] Again, the Court's utter lack of attention to these international instruments signals the need for an approach to international law that is supportive of substantive equality.

The Court's disregard for the *ICESCR* and the *CEDAW* is consistent with a third observation — when the Court does turn to international law, it is often to narrow the scope of section 15(1) of the *Charter* rather than to support a substantive equality approach. This is apparent in three cases from my survey.

First, in *Miron v. Trudel*, the Court addressed the question of whether the definition of "spouse" under Ontario's insurance legislation violated the equality rights of persons living in common law relationships. A majority of the Court answered this question in the affirmative, but did not refer to international law in doing so.[52] In his dissenting judgment, Gonthier J. referred to the *European Convention for the Protection of Human Rights and Fundamental Freedoms* (article 12) and the *Universal Declaration of Human Rights* (article 16) as support for his finding that "marriage is both a basic social institution and a fundamental right which states can legitimately legislate to foster."[33] Both of these Articles guarantee the right to marry and found a family. Ultimately, Justice Gonthier found that there was no violation of section 15(1) in the circumstances of this case.

Similarly, in *Nova Scotia (Attorney General) v. Walsh*, the issue was whether the exclusion of common law couples from matrimonial property legislation in Nova Scotia violated their equality rights. The majority judgment, written by Bastarache J., held that this exclusion did not infringe section 15(1) of the *Charter*, and was silent on international law. Gonthier J., in a concurring judgment, again referred to article 16 of the *Universal Declaration of Human Rights*, in support of the link between marriage and family and "their central importance to our society."[34] As in *Miron*, international law was thus used to support a finding that narrowed the scope of section 15, and was more in keeping with a formal rather than substantive approach to equality.

A third example is found in *Lavoie v. Canada*, where the Court considered whether the citizenship requirement for employment with the federal public service violated the equality rights of non-citizens. In a concurring judgement, Arbour J. found that there was no breach of section 15(1) of the *Charter*, and relied upon "the international context" to support the finding that there was no violation of the "essential human dignity" of non-citizens.[35]

It is unlikely that international law was the decisive factor in any of these decisions. They may simply reflect the Court's discomfort with its role in enforcing substantive equality, regardless of international law.[36] However, given that *Charter* interpretation requires analysis of relevant international norms, there is still a role to play for progressive parties and interveners in this area. To avoid the possibility that the Court will rely upon international norms to restrict the scope of equality rights, their arguments should include analysis of the proper use of international law.

There are also a number of cases in this sample where international law was cited by judges who went on to find that there was no violation of section 15(1) in any event, or in spite of international law.

In *Granovsky v. Canada*, the Court reviewed the unavailability of disability pensions under the Canada Pension Plan to persons with temporary disabilities. Writing for a unanimous Court, Binnie J. referred to two international reports to support the differentiation between physical and mental impairments, and socially constructed limitations: the World Health Organization's *International Classification of Impairments, Disabilities, and Handicaps: A Manual of Classification Relating to the Consequences of*

Disease (1980), and the United Nations *Decade of Disabled Persons, 1983-1992: World Programme of Action concerning Disabled Persons.*[57] The Court noted that these reports "[help] to bring into sharper focus the disability ground within the larger s. 15(1) framework set out in *Law*, supra."[58] The Court ultimately went on to find that the impugned CPP provision did not violate section 15(1), as the denial of benefits did not "demean the dignity" of those with temporary disabilities.[59]

In *Lovelace v. Ontario*, the issue was whether the exclusion of non-status First Nations and Métis communities from a casino project agreement between the Ontario government and status First Nations contravened section 15(1) of the *Charter*. Iacobucci J., writing for a unanimous Court, cited the *Concluding Observations of the Committee on Economic, Social and Cultural Rights* (Canada, 1998) as evidence of the fact that "Aboriginal peoples experience high rates of unemployment and poverty, and face serious disadvantages in the areas of education, health, and housing."[60] This was noted under the first contextual factor from the *Law v. Canada* test, which considers whether the claimant group has experienced pre-existing vulnerability, stereotyping, prejudice, or disadvantage. Despite this finding, the Court unanimously held that there was no violation of section 15(1) in light of the other contextual factors from *Law*.

One way to view *Granovsky* and *Lovelace* is that international law ultimately had no positive bearing on the outcome, as the section 15 claims were denied in both cases. For interveners facing limited space for written arguments, these cases may suggest that international law is not worth the bother. On the other hand, it could be argued that international law was germane to a substantive equality interpretation of disability in *Granovsky*, even if his claim failed. Similarly, in *Lovelace*, international law was supportive of a finding of pre-existing disadvantage amongst Aboriginal peoples, even though the other contextual factors from *Law* weighed more heavily in the end. Thus, although international law was not used to support the finding of a section 15(1) violation in these cases, it may nevertheless have lent a substantive equality approach to the interpretation of section 15(1) of the *Charter*.

There are three other cases in this survey where international law was cited in support of a substantive equality approach to section 15.

In *McKinney v. University of Guelph*, the Court considered whether a mandatory retirement policy violated the equality rights of university professors. A majority of the Court found that the *Charter* did not apply, as the university was found to be a non-government actor. In *obiter*, La Forest J., for the plurality, referred to United Nations General Assembly Resolution 3137 (1973), in which the General Assembly called upon member states to "discourage, whenever and wherever the overall situation allows, discriminatory attitudes, policies and measures in employment practices based exclusively on age." This was cited as evidence in support of an "evolving right against discrimination on the ground of age," such that if the *Charter* had applied, the university's mandatory retirement policy would have violated section 15(1).[61] Thus, in *McKinney*, international law seems to have had some impact on the plurality's position that there would be a violation under section 15 if the *Charter* had applied.

In *Egan v. Canada*, the Court reviewed the exclusion of same-sex couples from benefits under the *Old Age Security Act* under section 15(1) of the *Charter*. A four-person plurality of the Court referred to the European Parliament's *Resolution on Equal Rights for Homosexuals and Lesbians in the European Community* in finding in favour of the argument that sexual orientation should be recognized as a protected ground under section 15 of the *Charter*.[62] This Resolution prohibits discrimination based on sexual orientation for both individuals and couples, and was taken by the plurality as evidence that gays and lesbians, "whether as individuals or couples, form an identifiable minority who have suffered and continue to suffer serious social, political and economic disadvantage."[63] The Resolution had been cited by EGALE in its factum in *Egan*.[64] While the intervener Inter-faith Coalition on Marriage and the Family cited international law in support of its argument that sexual orientation should not be recognized,[65] the minority of the Court that adopted this position did not rely on international law.[66] Thus international law did have a positive impact on the interpretation of section 15(1) of the *Charter* for at least some of the judges in *Egan*.

In the third case, *Canadian Foundation for Children, Youth and the Law v. Canada*, the Court reviewed the constitutionality of section 43 of the *Criminal Code*, which provides a defence to assault for schoolteachers, parents, and persons in the place of parents who use reasonable force to discipline their children. Only Deschamps J. referred to international law in her section 15(1) reasons, citing the *Convention on the Rights of the Child* and article 24 of the *ICCPR* as evidence that children have "the right to have their security and safety protected by their parents, families and society at large."[67] Section 43 was found to be at odds with this right, and children were recognized as a group facing pre-existing disadvantage under the first contextual factor from the *Law* case. Justice Deschamps went on to find that section 43 was an unjustifiable limitation on children's equality rights, and was in dissent on this point.[68] The majority, which upheld section 43, did not cite international law in its section 15 reasons.[69] Thus *Canadian Foundation for Children, Youth and the Law* is another case where international law had a positive impact on the finding that there was a violation of equality rights.

The plurality decision in *Lavoie v. Canada* establishes a different relationship between *Charter* equality and international law. Bastarache J., writing for four judges, noted that international treaties (unnamed) support the proposition that distinctions based on citizenship do not necessarily "[perpetuate] the view that non-citizens are less capable or less worthy of recognition or value as human beings or as members of Canadian society" for the purposes of the *Law* test.[70] Regardless, the plurality found that the citizenship requirement was a violation of section 15(1) of the *Charter*, noting that laws are not "non-discriminatory" simply because they "[reflect] an international consensus as to the appropriate limits on equality rights." These were said to be "highly relevant considerations at the section 1 stage," however.[71] In relation to its section 15(1) reasons, though, the Court found a violation in spite of international law rather than because of it.

The *Lavoie* case is the only section 15 decision where the Court actually engaged with the question of why, and in what circumstances, international law was useful to the interpretation of section 15. However, it is a case where the Court was divided. As noted, the plurality was of the view that international covenants and practice relating to citizenship requirements for the public service were not relevant as an internal limitation under section 15(1) of the *Charter*.[72] In contrast, Arbour J., in concurring reasons, found that international law was germane as a limit to the scope of section 15 of the *Charter*.

While this debate about the use of international law was not ultimately significant to the outcome of the case, it nevertheless sheds light on an important point. The Supreme Court is not agreed on the extent to which international law should be permitted to narrow the scope of equality rights under the *Charter*. As my analysis has shown, international law has been used in this way in several cases, but never by a majority of the Supreme Court.[73] This issue is an important one to address in a theory of substantive equality and international law, as I will discuss below in my conclusion.

More broadly, there is no majority statement on the utility of international law under section 15 of the *Charter* from the Supreme Court. In the eight cases in this survey, international law was cited in majority reasons in only two cases: *Granovsky* and *Lovelace*. In neither of these cases was international law discussed in any detail in terms of its relationship to the interpretation of section 15(1) of the *Charter*. The preponderance of citations of international law in the section 15 context are in dissenting or concurring judgments, or in *obiter*. [74]

A related observation is that where it is cited, international law is often treated as an add-on to other, typically domestic sources of law. There tends to be little or no engagement with the text of the international provisions in question, and no reasons provided for why international law is being mentioned — as an interpretive tool, as a binding source of law, or otherwise. An exception is found in *Canadian Foundation for Children, Youth and the Law*, where the majority referred to international law as creating "obligations" (although this was in its section 7 reasons).[75] The same observation has been made with respect to the Court's treatment of international law outside the equality rights context, leading some commentators to argue that the Court's approach to international law is "unprincipled," "instrumental," "erratic," and "haphazard."[76] While others have argued that principles can be discerned from the Court's judgments,[77] the paucity of reasons makes it difficult to assess the Court's basis for citing or ignoring international law in a given case.

Even without a clear statement from the Court, it is possible to speculate as to why it has relied on international law so infrequently in the equality rights context. One possible explanation is offered by van Ert, who posits that international anti-discrimination provisions protect grounds no broader than those enumerated under section 15 of the *Charter*.[78] While this may be true, it only relates to one aspect of section 15 interpretation — grounds — and cannot explain the more general reluctance to cite international law in support of section 15 claims.

Another possible reason for the Court's reticence can be drawn from the work of feminist international law scholars, who argue that international anti-discrimination norms are modelled on a formal equality paradigm.[79] If this argument is accepted, it would render these provisions of limited utility in supporting substantive equality rights. Indeed, the Supreme Court has often been noted as an international leader in a substantive approach to equality. To the extent that international human rights law constitutes a formal equality approach, it may be inconsistent with the Supreme Court's stated approach to section 15 of the *Charter*. [80]

On the other hand, recent reports by United Nations committees support the view that international law should be given an interpretation that is in keeping with substantive equality principles. For example, in its *General Comment on Non-discrimination*, the United Nations Human Rights Committee stated "the principle of equality sometimes requires States parties to take affirmative action in order to diminish or eliminate conditions which cause or help to perpetuate discrimination prohibited by the Covenant."[81] Similarly, the Committee on the Elimination of Discrimination Against Women recommended that parties to the *CEDAW* "make more use of temporary special measures such as positive action, preferential treatment or quota systems to advance women's integration into education, the economy, politics and employment."[82]

Other international instruments also have the potential to support a substantive equality analysis under section 15 of the *Charter*. As noted above, the *ICESCR* and the *CEDAW* are two such sources, but the Court has yet to cite these treaties in relation to section 15(1) of the *Charter*.[83]

Interestingly, the *ICESCR* and the *CEDAW* are international treaties ratified by Canada, yet under section 15(1) of the *Charter*, the Court has referred more often to sources of international law to which Canada is not a party, such as the European Convention on Human Rights,[84] or to "soft" sources of international law, such as reports of United Nations Committees and the World Health Organization.[85]

It is important to note that the Court has cited international law more frequently since the *Baker* case: five out of the eight cases in this study where the Court referred to international law were decided after *Baker*.[86] This may suggest that the Court is now more open to entertaining arguments based on international law than it has been in the past.[87] Members of the Supreme Court have also been writing about international law, indicating an interest in this area.[88]

Although there may be an increased readiness on the part of the Court to entertain arguments based upon international law, this is not to say that international norms will necessarily be utilized to further a substantive approach to equality, as my analysis has shown. The frequency with which conservative interveners cite international law indicates that there are some provisions of international treaties that may hinder a substantive equality approach, or that international norms are broad and malleable, and open to a formal equality interpretation. This is similar to aspects of the critique that has been made with respect to the Court's recent section 15 *Charter* jurisprudence, particularly the *Law* test.[89] Just as a new approach to substantive equality is required under section 15 of the *Charter*, a new approach to international law and substantive equality is required.[90]

D. CONCLUSION: A COHERENT APPROACH TO INTERNATIONAL LAW AND SUBSTANTIVE EQUALITY

As a means of providing coherence to the courts' use of international law more broadly, Gibran van Ert has put forward a theory he calls the "universal presumption of international legality."[91] While van Ert does not look specifically at the application of this theory to the equality rights context, he provides a useful set of general principles that I believe would further the substantive equality project.

The theory is grounded upon the accepted presumption that Parliament does not intend to act contrary to its international obligations. Van Ert extends the presumption to apply to non-binding sources of international norms as well, based upon the fact that these sources are an important part of the international human rights picture, and have been supported by Canada internationally and at home. The presumption would require the courts to consider international human rights instruments when interpreting the *Charter*, rather than permitting a pick and choose approach.[92]

The presumption thus entails a comprehensive use of international human rights sources, and would make it difficult for the courts to ignore particular documents such as the *ICESCR*, and the *CEDAW*. Reliance upon more specific human rights guarantees, such as those regarding race and disability, would also be required, and may assist the courts with an intersectional analysis of equality. This is a critical component of any theory of international law that will further substantive equality.

Support for this theory can be found in the Supreme Court's general approach to *Charter* interpretation. According to the *Big M Drug Mart* case, the *Charter* should be applied in a way that is contextual, and "generous rather than ... legalistic ..., aimed at fulfilling the purpose of the guarantee and securing for individuals the full benefit of the *Charter*'s protection."[93] The Court's use of *Charter* values to interpret the common law is further support for an approach that takes a broad view of international human rights sources falling within the presumption.

It is also significant that the presumption is rebuttable — international law that is inconsistent with the *Charter* should not be followed.[94] This is another critical component of the theory from the substantive equality perspective. It means that in order to be applied by the courts, international human rights norms must be consistent with substantive equality as it is understood under Canadian law. Applications of international law that impede a substantive equality analysis — such as Justice Gonthier's judgments in *Miron* and *Walsh* — would thus be improper.[95] Conversely, uses of international norms as exemplified in *McKinney*, *Egan*, and *Canadian Foundation for Children, Youth and the Law* would be correct.

Van Ert's theory also has the advantage of extending to the interpretation of statutory human rights provisions in addition to the *Charter*. It thus has the potential to create coherence between the courts' approach to rights under statutory and constitutional human rights regimes.[96]

In my view, this theory must be built upon and applied by progressive parties and interveners if international law is to promote substantive equality in the domestic context. While it is certainly open to the Court to clarify this area of its own accord, international law is an area where the Court has specifically called for the assistance of interveners.[97] This will remain a difficult decision strategically, as interveners have limited time and space to develop such arguments. However, it is a worthwhile effort, as the Court is floundering in the area of substantive equality. Until this work is undertaken, international law will continue to be a double-edged sword in the equality rights context, and should be approached with caution.

APPENDIX I

1. *Andrews v. Law Society of British Columbia*, [1989] 1 S.C.R. 143**
2. *Reference re Workers Compensation Act*, [1989] 1 S.C.R. 922
3. *R. v. Turpin*, [1989] 1 S.C.R. 1296
4. *Rudolph Wolff v. Canada*, [1990] 1 S.C.R. 695
5. *Dywidag Systems Int'l Canada Ltd. v. Zutphen Brothers Construction Ltd.*, [1990] 1 S.C.R. 705
6. *R. v. S.(S.)*, [1990] 2 S.C.R. 254
7. *R. v. Hess and Nguyen*, [1990] 2 S.C.R. 906
8. *McKinney v. University of Guelph*, [1990] 3 S.C.R. 229*
9. *Harrison v. University of British Columbia*, [1990] 3 S.C.R. 451
10. *Stoffman v. Vancouver General Hospital*, [1990] 3 S.C.R. 483
11. *Douglas/Kwantlen Faculty Assn. v. Douglas College*, [1990] 3 S.C.R. 570
12. *R. v. Swain*, [1991] 1 S.C.R. 933
13. *Tétreault-Gadoury v. Canada*, [1991] 2 S.C.R. 22
14. *R. v. Généreux*, [1992] 1 S.C.R. 259
15. *Canada (Minister of Employment and Immigration) v. Chiarelli*, [1992] 1 S.C.R. 711
16. *Schacter v. Canada*, [1992] 2 S.C.R. 679
17. *Weatherall v. Canada (Attorney General)*, [1993] 2 S.C.R. 872
18. *Haig v. Canada*, [1993] 2 S.C.R. 995
19. *Rodriguez v. British Columbia (Attorney General)*, [1993] 3 S.C.R. 519**
20. *Symes v. Canada*, [1993] 4 S.C.R. 695
21. *R. v. Finta*, [1994] 1 S.C.R. 701
22. *Native Women's Association of Canada v. Canada*, [1994] 3 S.C.R. 627
23. *Miron v. Trudel*, [1995] 2 S.C.R. 418*
24. *Egan v. Canada*, [1995] 2 S.C.R. 513*
25. *Thibaudeau v. Canada*, [1995] 2 S.C.R. 627
26. *Ontario Home Builders' Association v. York Region Board of Education*, [1996] 2 S.C.R. 929
27. *Adler v. Ontario*, [1996] 3 S.C.R. 609
28. *Eaton v. Brant County Board of Education*, [1997] 1 S.C.R. 241
29. *Benner v. Canada (Secretary of State)*, [1997] 1 S.C.R 358
30. *Eldridge v. British Columbia (Attorney General)*, [1997] 3 S.C.R. 624
31. *Vriend v. Alberta*, [1998] 1 S.C.R. 493
32. *Vancouver Society of Immigrant and Visible Minority Women v. Canada*, [1999] 1 S.C.R. 10
33. *Law v. Canada*, [1999] 1 S.C.R. 497
34. *M. v. H.*, [1999] 2 S.C.R. 3
35. *Corbière v. Canada*, [1999] 2 S.C.R. 203

36. *Winko v. B.C.*, [1999] 2 S.C.R. 625
37. *Bese v. B.C.*, [1999] 2 S.C.R. 722
38. *Orlowski v. B.C.*, [1999] 2 S.C.R. 733
39. *R. v. LePage*, [1999] 2 S.C.R. 744
40. *Delisle v. Canada (Deputy Attorney General)*, [1999] 2 S.CR. 989**
41. *New Brunswick (Minister of Health and Community Services) v. G. (J.)*, [1999] 3 S.C.R. 46
42. *Granovsky v. Canada*, [2000] 1 S.C.R. 703*
43. *Lovelace v. Ontario*, [2000] 1 S.C.R. 950*
44. *Little Sisters Book and Art Emporium v. Canada (Minister of Justice)*, [2000] 2 S.C.R. 1120
45. *Trinity Western University v. British Columbia College of Teachers*, [2001] 1 S.C.R. 772
46. *Re Therrien*, [2001] 2 S.C.R. 3
47. *Dunmore v. Ontario (Attorney General)*, [2001] 3 S.C.R. 1016**
48. *Lavoie v. Canada*, [2002] 1 S.C.R. 769*
49. *Sauvé v. Canada (Chief Electoral Officer)*, [2002] 3 S.C.R. 519**
50. *Gosselin v. Quebec*, [2002] 4 S.C.R. 429**
51. *Nova Scotia (Attorney General) v. Walsh*, [2002] 4 S.C.R. 325*
52. *Siemens v. Manitoba (Attorney General)*, [2003] 1 S.C.R. 6
53. *Trociuk v. British Columbia*, [2003] 1 S.C.R. 835
54. *Nova Scotia (Workers' Compensation Board) v. Martin; Nova Scotia (Workers' Compensation Board) v. Laseur*, [2003] 2 S.C.R. 504
55. *R. v. Malmo-Levine, R. v. Caine*, [2003] 3 S.C.R. 571**
56. *Canadian Foundation for Children, Youth and the Law v. Canada*, [2004] 1 S.C.R. 76*
57. *Hodge v. Canada (Minister of Human Resources Development)*, [2004] 3 S.C.R. 357
58. *Newfoundland (Treasury Board) v. N.A.P.E.*, [2004] 3 S.C.R. 381
59. *Auton (Guardian ad litem of) v. British Columbia (Attorney General)*, [2004] 3 S.C.R. 657
60. *Reference re Same-Sex Marriage*, [2004] 3 S.C.R. 698

* Cases where the Court cited international law in relation to section 15(1) of the *Charter*.

** Cases where the Court cited international law in relation to another right or freedom, or under section 1.

ENDNOTES

1 This paper was originally prepared for LEAF's Colloquium "In Pursuit of Substantive Equality," held in Toronto from 19–21 September 2003. Versions of the paper were also presented at the Canadian Association of Law Teachers conference in Winnipeg, June 2004, and at a seminar at the University of Calgary Faculty of Law in November 2004. The author wishes to thank Amy Nixon for her research assistance, and colloquium, conference, and seminar participants for their feedback. A special thank you goes out to the editors of this collection for their very helpful comments on an earlier draft of this paper.

2 *Canadian Charter of Rights and Freedoms*, Part I, *Constitution Act 1982*, Schedule B to *Canada Act, 1982*, U.K. 1982, c.11 [*Charter*].

3 See *McKinney v. University of Guelph*, [1990] 3 S.C.R. 229 at 391, Wilson J. in dissent [*McKinney*]; *Miron v. Trudel*, [1995] 2 S.C.R. 418 at para. 131, McLachlin J. [*Miron*]; *Egan v. Canada*, [1995] 2 S.C.R. 513 at para. 128, Cory J. [*Egan*]; *Vriend v. Alberta*, [1998] 1 S.C.R. 493 at para. 67, Cory & Iacobucci JJ.).

4 [1999] 1 S.C.R. 497 at para. 51, Iacobucci J. (emphasis added).

5 G.A. Res. 217A (III), U.N. Doc A/810 at 71 (1948) [*UDHR*] (emphasis added). See also article 1: "All human beings are born free and equal in *dignity* and rights. They are endowed with reason and conscience and should act towards one another in a spirit of brotherhood." (Emphasis added.)

6 G.A. Res. 2200A (XXI), 21 U.N. GAOR Supp. (No. 16) at 52, U.N. Doc. A/6316 (1966), 999 U.N.T.S. 171, entered into force for Canada August 19, 1976 [*ICCPR*].

7 G.A. Res. 2200A (XXI), 21 U.N.GAOR Supp. (No. 16) at 49, U.N. Doc. A/6316 (1966), 993 U.N.T.S. 3, entered into force for Canada August 19, 1976 [*ICESCR*]. Emphasis added in quote.

8 G.A. Res. 34/180, 34 U.N. GAOR Supp. (No. 46) at 193, U.N. Doc. A/34/46, entered into force for Canada January 9, 1982 [*CEDAW*] (emphasis added). See also the United Nations *Declaration on the Elimination of All Forms of Racial Discrimination*, (General Assembly Resolution 1904 (XVIII)) (1963), which notes that racial discrimination is an issue of respect for human dignity.

9 For pieces in this collection that grapple with the issue of dignity, see Sophia Moreau, "The Wrongs of Unequal Treatment"; Beverley Baines, "Equality, Comparison, Discrimination, Status"; Sheila McIntyre, "Answering the Siren Call of Abstract Formalism with the Subjects and Verbs of Domination"; Denise G. Réaume, "Discrimination and Dignity"; Melina Buckley, "*Law v. Meiorin*: Exploring the Governmental Responsibility to Promote Equality under Section 15 of the *Charter*"; Fiona Sampson, "The *Law* Test for Discrimination and Gendered Disability Inequality," in this volume.

10 *UDHR*, above note 5, articles 1, 2, & 7; *ICCPR*, above note 6, articles 2, 3, & 26; *ICESCR*, above note 7, articles 2 & 3.

11 See, for example, the *CEDAW*, above note 8. Section 28 of the *Charter* similarly guarantees equal rights for male and female persons. Other specific guarantees against discrimination at the international level include the *International Con-*

vention on the Elimination of All Forms of Racial Discrimination, G.A. Res. 2106 (XX), Annex, 20 U.N. GAOR Supp. (No. 14) at 47, U.N. Doc. A/6014 (1966), 660 U.N.T.S. 195, entered into force for Canada November 13, 1970; *Discrimination (Employment and Occupation) Convention* (ILO No. 111), 362 U.N.T.S. 31, entered into force for Canada June 15, 1960; *Declaration on the Rights of Disabled Persons,* G.A. Res. 3447 (XXX), 30 U.N. GAOR Supp. (No. 34) at 88, U.N. Doc. A/10034 (1975).

12 See *American Convention on Human Rights,* O.A.S.Treaty Series No. 36, 1144 U.N.T.S. 123, reprinted in *Basic Documents Pertaining to Human Rights in the Inter-American System,* OEA/Ser.L.V/II.82 doc.6 rev.1 at 25 (1992). Canada is not a signatory to this Convention. See also *African [Banjul] Charter on Human and Peoples' Rights,* adopted June 27, 1981, OAU Doc. CAB/LEG/67/3 rev. 5, 21 I.L.M. 58 (1982), entered into force October 21, 1986; *[European] Convention for the Protection of Human Rights and Fundamental Freedoms,* 213 U.N.T.S. 222, entered into force September 3, 1953, as amended.

13 See *Optional Protocol to the International Covenant on Civil and Political Rights,* G.A. Res. 2200A (XXI), 21 U.N. GAOR Supp. (No. 16) at 59, U.N. Doc. A/6316 (1966), 999 U.N.T.S. 302, entered into force for Canada August 19, 1976; *Optional Protocol to the Convention on the Elimination of Discrimination Against Women,* G.A. Res. 54/4, annex, 54 U.N. GAOR Supp. (No. 49) at 5, U.N. Doc. A/54/49 (Vol. I) (2000), entered into force for Canada January 18, 2003; *European Convention for the Protection of Human Rights and Fundamental Freedoms, ibid.,* article 19.

14 See, for example, *ICESCR,* above note 7, article 16; *CEDAW,* above note 8, article 17; *International Convention on the Elimination of All Forms of Racial Discrimination,* above note 11, article 9.

15 Gibran van Ert, *Using International Law in Canadian Courts* (The Hague: Kluwer Law International, 2002) at 15.

16 *Ibid.* at 16.

17 *Statute of the International Court of Justice,* [1945] Can. T.S. no. 7, article 38(1).

18 van Ert, above note 15 at 29–30.

19 Anne Bayefsky, *International Human Rights Law: Use in Canadian Charter of Rights and Freedoms Litigation* (Toronto: Butterworths, 1992) at 5. Bayefsky notes that while there is "no clear statement to this effect from the Supreme Court," the case law suggests that this approach applies. This approach is variously called "adoption," "incorporation," or "monism." For a discussion of these terms, see van Ert, above note 15 at 50. See also William A. Schabas, *International Human Rights Law and the Canadian Charter,* 2d ed. (Toronto: Thomson Canada, 1996).

20 Bayefsky, *ibid.* at 25–26, citing *Arrow River & Tributaries Slide & Boom Co. v. Pigeon Timber Ltd.,* [1932] S.C.R. 495. The approach is called "the transformation theory," "implementation," or "dualism." See van Ert, above note 15 at 51; Schabas, *ibid.* at 21. See also *Baker v. Canada (Minister of Citizenship and Immigration),* [1999] 2 S.C.R. 817 at para. 69 [*Baker*]; *Suresh,* below note 28 at para. 60.

21 International human rights treaties to which Canada is a party include the *ICCPR;* the *ICESCR;* the *CEDAW;* and the *International Convention on the Elimination of*

All Forms of Racial Discrimination. See Canada Treaty Information, online: www. treaty-accord.gc.ca.

22 Bayesfsky notes that case law is inconsistent on this point, above note 19 at 63–66. See also Schabas, above note 19 at 26–27; van Ert, above note 15 at 239.

23 See Bayefsky, *ibid.* at 20–21; Ruth Sullivan, *Driedger on the Construction of Statutes*, 3d ed., (Toronto: Butterworths, 1994) at 330. van Ert notes that this presumption "is vigorously applied" by the courts. See van Ert, above note 15 at 101.

24 [1987] 1 S.C.R. 313 at 349.

25 [1989] 1 S.C.R. 1038 at 1056–57.

26 [1990] 3 S.C.R. 697 at 838 [*Keegstra*].

27 *Baker*, above note 20 at para. 70, L'Heureux-Dubé J., Iacobucci & Cory JJ. disagreed with this approach, and held that only treaties which were ratified by Canada and incorporated into domestic law through implementing legislation should be used to interpret domestic law (at paras. 79–80).

28 [2002] 1 S.C.R. 3 at para. 46 [*Suresh*], quoting from *United States v. Burns*, [2001] 1 S.C.R. 283, and citing *Re B.C. Motor Vehicle Act*, [1985] 2 S.C.R. 486 at 512; *Baker*, *ibid.*; *Reference re Public Service Employee Relations Act (Alta.)*, above note 24; *Slaight Communications Inc. v. Davidson*, above note 25; *R. v. Keegstra*, above note 26. *Suresh* concerned the compliance of a deportation hearing with the principles of fundamental justice. The Court referred to international law as establishing a norm against deportation to torture.

29 *Suresh*, *ibid.* at para. 59.

30 *RWDSU v. Dolphin Delivery*, [1986] 2 S.C.R. 573.

31 See *Dolphin Delivery*, *ibid.*; *Hill v. Church of Scientology*, [1995] 2 S.C.R. 1130.

32 I have also included reference cases involving s. 15(1) of the *Charter*.

33 International law may also be relevant to the interpretation of s. 15(2) of the *Charter*, the affirmative action provision. To date, the Supreme Court has not considered s. 15(2) apart from s. 15(1) of the *Charter*. See *Lovelace v. Ontario*, [2000] 1 S.C.R. 950 [*Lovelace*].

34 Given the parameters for my selection of cases, my sample size is somewhat different from those in other recent studies of s. 15(1).

35 See Appendix I.

36 *McKinney*, above note 3; *Miron*, above note 3; *Egan*, above note 3; *Granovsky v. Canada*, [2000] 1 S.C.R. 703 [*Granovsky*]; *Lovelace*, above note 33; *Lavoie v. Canada*, [2002] 1 S.C.R. 769 [*Lavoie*]; *Nova Scotia (Attorney General) v. Walsh*, [2002] 4 S.C.R. 325 [*Walsh*]; *Canadian Foundation for Children, Youth and the Law v. Canada*, [2004] 1 S.C.R. 76 [*Canadian Foundation*].

37 van Ert also notes this trend, above note 15 at 249–50. In *Andrews*, above Appendix I at 177, the *European Convention on Human Rights* was cited by McIntyre J., but this was in his reasons under s. 1 of the *Charter*; in *Rodriguez*, above Appendix I at 602–3, Sopinka J., for the majority, referred to several decisions of the European Commission of Human Rights under s. 7 of the *Charter*; in *Finta*, above Appendix I at 787, 875–76, several international documents were referred to in the Court's judgments, but none were cited in the context of the s. 15 issues; in *Delisle*, above

Appendix I at paras. 71, 141, Cory and Iacobucci JJ., in dissent, referred to a range of international documents protecting freedom of association under s. 2(d) of the *Charter*; in *Dunmore*, above Appendix I at paras. 27, 41, Bastarache J., for a majority of the Court, cited international labour conventions in relation to s. 2(d) of the *Charter*, while L'Heureux-Dubé and Major JJ., the only justices considering s. 15, did not cite international law in their reasons; in *Sauvé*, above Appendix I at paras. 108, 133, the four dissenting justices (per Gonthier J.) relied on the *European Convention on Human Rights*, the *ICCPR*, and a General Comment on the Covenant by the United Nations Human Rights Committee under s. 1 of the *Charter*; in *Gosselin*, above Appendix I at paras. 93, 147, and 419–20, McLachlin C.J. (for the majority), L'Heureux-Dubé J. (in dissent), and LeBel J. (concurring on this point) all cited the *ICESCR* in relation to s. 45 of the *Quebec Charter*; and in *Malmo-Levine*, above Appendix I at paras. 270–71, Arbour J., in dissent, referred to international narcotics conventions under s. 1 of the *Charter*.

38 This aspect of my research is anecdotal rather than being based on a systematic review of parties and interveners' arguments in all sixty cases.

39 See Factum of the Intervener Charter Committee on Poverty Issues in *Symes* (at para. 53–54, citing the *ICESCR*); Factum of the Interveners Charter Committee on Poverty Issues, Federated Anti-Poverty Groups of BC, National Action Committee on the Status of Women, and LEAF in *Thibaudeau* (at para. 16, citing the *ICESCR*); Factum of the Intervener Charter Committee on Poverty Issues in *Eldridge* (at paras. 16–20, 31–33, & 39, citing the *ICESCR* and the *UDHR*); Factum of the Intervener Charter Committee on Poverty Issues in *New Brunswick v. G.(J.)* (at paras. 17–22, citing the *UDHR*, the *ICESCR*, the *ICCPR*, the *Convention on the Rights of the Child*, and the *European Convention on Human Rights*). The Charter Committee on Poverty Issues also cited international law in its facta in *Lovelace* and *Gosselin*. For a discussion of the use of international law by the Charter Committee on Poverty Issues and other interveners, see Jennifer Koshan, "Dialogue or Conversation? The Impact of Public Interest Interveners on Judicial Decision Making," in Patricia Hughes & Partick Molinari, eds., *Participatory Justice in a Global Economy: The New Rule of Law?* (Montreal: Les Editions Themis, 2004).

40 Factum of the Intervener the Alberta Civil Liberties Association in *Vriend v. Alberta* (at para. 6), citing the *ICCPR*, the *European Convention on Human Rights*, and case law under the *European Convention* (at para. 7); Factum of the Intervener Canadian Association of Statutory Human Rights Agencies [CASHRA] in *Vriend* (at para. 11, citing the *UDHR*, the *ICCPR*, and the *ICESCR*). See also Factum of the Intervener Canadian AIDS Society in *Vriend* (at para. 42, citing World Health Association Resolution 41.24).

41 Factum of the Intervener Christian Legal Fellowship in *Vriend* (at paras. 11–13). See also Factum of the Intervener Inter-faith Coalition on Marriage and the Family in *Egan*.

42 Factum of the Interveners Evangelical Fellowship of Canada, Ontario Council of Sikhs, Islamic Society of North America, and Focus on the Family in *M. v. H.* (at para. 36).

43   For example, freedom from racial discrimination has been recognized as a customary norm of international law. See Bayefsky, above note 19 at 13; Schabas, above note 19 at 17, citing *Barcelona Traction, Light & Power Co. (Belgium v. Spain)*, I.C.J. Reports 1970 at 3. Freedom from gender discrimination might also be a customary norm of international law, although this is not settled. See Bayefsky at 15, citing the *Restatement of the Foreign Relations Law of the United States*, vol. 2, Comment 1 at 166, where it is stated that "freedom from gender discrimination as state policy ... may already be a principle of customary international law."

44   See Bayefsky, *ibid.* at 23–25. Proof that state practice has achieved the level of customary international law requires "evidence of a sufficient degree of state practice" and "a determination that states conceive themselves as acting under a legal obligation" (Bayefsky at 10).

45   The Court did cite a Report of the Committee on Economic, Social and Cultural Rights in *Lovelace*, above note 33.

46   See discussion of *Gosselin*, above. Section 45 of the *Quebec Charter* guarantees that every person in need has a right to "measures of financial assistance and to social measures provided for by law, susceptible of ensuring such person an acceptable standard of living."

47   See Factum of the Appellant Louise Gosselin in *Gosselin v. Quebec*, citing the *UDHR*, the *ICCPR*, the *ICESCR*, and the *Convention on the Rights of the Child*; Factum of the Intervener Charter Committee on Poverty Issues in *Gosselin*, citing the *UDHR*, the *ICESCR*, the *ICCPR*, the *CEDAW*, the *Convention on the Rights of the Child*, the *International Convention on the Elimination of All Forms of Racial Discrimination*, the *European Social Charter*, and several reports of international committees; Factum of the Intervener National Association of Women and the Law in *Gosselin*, citing the *ICESCR*, the *CEDAW*; and a number of reports of international committees; Factum of the Intervener Rights and Democracy in *Gosselin v. Quebec*. See also the facta of the Charter Committee on Poverty issues, above note 33.

48   For rare examples of s. 15 arguments citing the *CEDAW*, see the facta of the Charter Committee on Poverty Issues and the National Association of Women and the Law in *Gosselin*, *ibid.* LEAF has rarely cited the *CEDAW* or international law more broadly in its s. 15 interventions. For exceptions, see LEAF's facta in *Andrews* and *Weatherall*, above Appendix 1.

49   For an article advocating the view that the *ICESCR* creates justiciable rights, see Gwen Brodsky & Shelagh Day, "Beyond the Social and Economic Rights Debate: Substantive Equality Speaks to Poverty" (2002), 14 C.J.W.L. 185. See also Martha Jackman, "From National Standards to Justiciable Rights: Enforcing International Social and Economic Guarantees Through Charter of Rights Review" (1999) 14 J.L. & Soc. Pol'y 69; Bruce Porter, "Judging Poverty: Using International Human Rights Law to Refine the Scope of Charter Rights" (2000) 15 J.L. & Soc. Pol'y 117.

50   See the *CEDAW*, above note 8, article 3. The *CEDAW* includes protection against discrimination in the areas of political and public life, education, employment, health care, economic and social life, marriage, and family relations. Women in

Canada have argued that the Canadian government has failed to live up to its obligations under the *CEDAW.* See Feminist Alliance for International Action, *Future Directions for Women's Equality: A Report from FAFIA's National Symposium* (FAFIA, 2003), online: Feminist Alliance For International Action, www.fafia-afai. org/news/NationalSymposium1103.pdf.

51 See, for example, *Gosselin, Lovelace, Walsh, NAPE, Auton,* all above Appendix 1.

52 *Miron,* above note 3, per McLachlin J. (Cory, Iacobucci, & Sopinka JJ. concurring) and L'Heureux-Dubé J. in separate judgments .

53 *Ibid.* at 450 (Lamer, C.J., La Forest, & Major JJ. concurring).

54 *Walsh,* above note 36 at para. 193. L'Heureux-Dubé J., in dissent, found a violation of s. 15, but did not refer to international law in doing so.

55 *Ibid.* at para. 101, noting "widespread international agreement that such restrictions do not implicate the essential human dignity of non-citizens to begin with." This was based on international conventions as well as a comparison with other liberal democracies. LeBel also wrote a concurring judgment, although he did not cite international law in his brief reasons (at paras. 124–25).

56 An exploration of the reasons for the Court's discomfort with substantive equality arguments is beyond the scope of this paper. For articles in this collection that deal with this issue, see the papers in Parts I and II of this collection. See also Brodsky & Day, above note 49; Porter, above note 49.

57 *Granovsky,* above note 36 at para. 34.

58 *Ibid.* at para. 35.

59 *Ibid.* at para. 81.

60 *Lovelace,* above note 33 at para. 69.

61 *McKinney,* above note 3 at 296. See also the judgment of Wilson J., in dissent, where she cited the *UDHR,* the *European Convention on Human Rights and Fundamental Freedoms,* and the *ICCPR* in examining the role of the government and its historical approach to rights and freedoms on the issue of whether there was government action under s. 32 of the *Charter* (at 355).

62 *Egan,* above note 3 at 601–2, Cory J.; McLachlin, Sopinka, & Iacobucci concurring.

63 *Ibid.* at 602.

64 Factum of the Intervener Equality for Gays And Lesbians Everywhere (EGALE) in *Egan* (at para. 7).

65 Factum of the Intervener Inter-faith Coalition on Marriage and the Family in *Egan* (at para. 41), citing the *UDHR,* the *ICCPR,* and the *European Convention for the Protection of Human Rights and Fundamental Freedoms.*

66 *Egan,* above note 3 at 540 (La Forest J.; Lamer C.J., Gonthier and Major JJ. concurring). Madam Justice L'Heureux-Dubé J. wrote concurring reasons, but did not refer to international law in her judgment.

67 *Canadian Foundation,* above note 36 at paras. 225–26.

68 Justice Binnie also wrote a dissenting judgment based on s. 15 of the *Charter,* but he did not refer to international law in his reasons. Writing in dissent under s. 7 of the *Charter,* Arbour J. referred to "Canada's international obligations" regarding the rights of children, noting that reports by the Committee on the Rights of the Child

have recommended abolishing s. 43 and similar provisions in other countries (*ibid.* at paras. 186–88). Given her finding of a s. 7 violation, Arbour J. did not consider s. 15 of the *Charter*.

69 The five-person majority in *Canadian Foundation* cited the *Convention on the Rights of the Child* and the *CEDAW* to establish that "the best interests of the child" is a legal principle for the purposes of s. 7 of the *Charter*, noting that these are international treaties to which Canada is a party. The majority went on to find that "the best interests of the child" is not a principle of fundamental justice, however. See *ibid.* at paras. 9–10. International treaties were also cited by the majority to support a reading down of s. 43 to exclude "physical correction that either harms or degrades the child," and to support the proposition that international law does not "require state parties to ban all corporal punishment of children." *Ibid.* at paras. 31–33.

70 *Lavoie*, above note 36 at para. 46.

71 *Ibid.* at para. 48. Under s. 1, Bastarache J. referred to the *ICCPR* (article 25(c)) and the *UDHR* (article 21(2)) in response to the federal government's argument that the citizenship requirement was consonant with these international documents. The plurality ultimately agreed that the citizenship requirement was justified, noting that this was in line with "international practice" (at para. 59).

72 The dissent found that "international practice" was not relevant under s. 1 either, given the different objectives at play in Canada's citizenship requirement. It did not cite international law in relation to s. 15 of the *Charter*.

73 The resolution of the debate on whether international human rights law is incorporated into Canadian law is an important aspect of the resolution of this issue. If international human rights treaties ratified by Canada are found to be implemented, and thus binding in the domestic context, the Court may be under an obligation to apply their provisions even if they narrow the scope of the *Charter*. On the other hand, the fact that s. 15 of the *Charter* permits a broader interpretation than international law may itself be evidence that international human rights treaties were not implemented *in toto* by the *Charter*.

74 See *McKinney* (in *obiter*); *Miron* (dissent); *Walsh* (concurring); *Canadian Foundation* (dissent).

75 *Canadian Foundation*, above note 36 at para. 31, where McLachlin C.J. writes, "[s]tatutes should be construed to comply with Canada's international treaty obligations." See also *Miron* above note 3, where Gonthier J. refers to the *Universal Declaration of Human Rights* as "binding" (at 449). Bayefsky notes that this is erroneous, as the *UDHR* is not a binding source of international law. See Anne Bayefsky, "International Human Rights Law in Canadian Courts" in Benedetto Conforti & Francesco Francioni, *Enforcing International Human Rights in Domestic Courts* (The Hague: Martinus Nijhoff Publishers, 1997) 295 at 327.

76 See Bayefsky, *ibid.* at 318; van Ert, above note 15 at 252; William Schabas, "Twenty-five Years of Public International Law at the Supreme Court of Canada" (2000) 79 Can. Bar Rev. 174 at 186; Stephen J. Toope, "The Uses of Metaphor: International Law and the Supreme Court of Canada" (2001) 80 Can. Bar Rev. 534 at 535;

Christof Hyns & Frans Viljoen, *The Impact of the United Nations Human Rights Treaties on the Domestic Level* (The Hague: Kluwer Law International, 2002) at 125.

77 For example, Reem Bahdi argues that there are several principles animating the Court's approach to international law: "the rule of law imperative," "the universalist impulse," "the introspection rationale," "judicial world travelling," and "globalized self-awareness." See "Litigating Social and Economic Rights in Canada in Light of International Human Rights Law: What Difference Can it Make?" (2002) 14 C.J.W.L. 158. Karen Knop critiques an over-reliance on the distinction between binding and non-binding international norms, and argues that the Court is simply using international law as an interpretive tool. Knop also notes the "blurring of international and comparative law." See "Here and There: International Law in Domestic Courts" (2000) 32 N.Y.U.J. of Int'l. L. & Pol. 501 at 525.

78 van Ert, above note 15 at 249–50.

79 See, for example, Shelley Wright, "Human Rights and Women's Rights: An Analysis of the United Nations Convention on the Elimination of All Forms of Discrimination Against Women" in Kathleen Mahoney & Paul Mahoney eds., *Human Rights in the 21st Century: A Global Challenge* (Dordrecht, Netherlands : Nijhoff, 1993) 75 at 79; Kathleen Mahoney, "Theoretical Perspectives on Women's Human Rights and Strategies for their Implementation" (1995–1996) 21 Brook. J. Int'l L. 799 at 839; Hilary Charlesworth & Christine Chinkin, *The Boundaries of International Law: A Feminist Analysis* (Manchester: Manchester University Press, 2000) at 229. Chinkin & Charlesworth note that while there is some scope for substantive equality under international law, decisions of the U.N. Human Rights Committee have dealt primarily with formal equality claims (at 215–16).

80 This explanation fits with the plurality reasons in *Lavoie*, where they refused to use international law to narrow the scope of s. 15. See also *Keegstra*, above note 26.

81 United Nations Human Rights Committee, General Comment No. 18, Non-discrimination (Thirty-seventh session, 1989), Compilation of General Comments and General Recommendations Adopted by Human Rights Treaty Bodies, U.N. Doc. HRI/GEN/Rev.1 at 26 (1994). See also United Nations Human Rights Committee, General Comment No. 28, Equality of rights between men and women (article 3), U.N. Doc. CCPR/C/21/Rev.1/Add.10 (2000).

82 Committee on the Elimination of Discrimination Against Women, General Recommendation 5, Temporary special measures, (Seventh session, 1988), U.N. Doc. A/43/38 at 109 (1988), reprinted in Compilation of General Comments and General Recommendations Adopted by Human Rights Treaty Bodies, *ibid.* at 232 (2003).

83 The Court did cite a Report of the Committee on Economic, Social and Cultural Rights in *Lovelace*, above note 33.

84 See *McKinney, Miron, Canadian Foundation.*

85 See *McKinney, Egan, Granovsky, Lovelace.*

86 See *Granovsky, Lovelace, Lavoie, Walsh, Canadian Foundation.*

87 However, the Court has failed to refer to international law in a number of recent s. 15 decisions. See *Newfoundland v. N.A.P.E., Hodge v. Canada, Auton v. B.C.,* and *Reference Re Same Sex Marriage,* all above, Appendix 1.

88 See, for example, Louis LeBel & Gloria Chao, "The Rise of International Law in Canadian Constitutional Litigation: Fugue or Fusion? Recent Developments and Challenges in Internalizing International Law" (2002) 16 Sup. Ct. L. Rev. 23; Michel Bastarache, "The Canadian Charter of Rights and Freedoms: Domestic Application of Universal Values" (2003) 19 Sup. Ct. L. Rev. 371.

89 For critiques of the *Law* test, see the papers in Parts I and II of this collection.

90 The need for a broader theory with respect to the courts' use of international law under the *Charter* has been noted by Bayefsky, above note 19 at 105, and van Ert, above note 15 at 252–53, who argues that previous attempts at such theorizing "have been rejected or ignored by the courts."

91 van Ert, *ibid.* at 270.

92 *Ibid.* at 271–72.

93 *R. v. Big M. Drug Mart*, [1985] 1 S.C.R. 295 at 344.

94 van Ert, above note 15 at 99.

95 This approach is supported by the plurality decision in *Lavoie*, above note 36. See also Justice McLachlin's judgment in *Keegstra*, above note 26.

96 van Ert, above note 15 at 274. In this volume, see Melina Buckley, "*Law v. Meiorin*: Exploring the Governmental Responsibility to Promote Equality under Section 15 of the *Charter*"; Leslie A. Reaume, "Postcards from *O'Malley*: Reinvigorating Statutory Human Rights Jurisprudence in the Age of the *Charter*"; and Andrea Wright, "Formulaic Comparisons: Stopping the *Charter* at the Statutory Human Rights Gate."

97 In "Interveners and the Supreme Court of Canada" (May 1999) 8(3) National 27, Mr. Justice Major remarked that interveners can be most useful to the Court "in presenting comparative views of other national and international courts in constitutional litigation ... particularly in private actions where litigants lack the resources to do the research necessary to provide a comprehensive comparative brief. This provides an opportunity for interveners with specialized knowledge to complement the appeal." See also LeBel and Chao, above note 88 at 60, where they note that citations of international law by parties and interveners in constitutional cases is on the increase.

Newfoundland (Treasury Board) v. N.A.P.E.

Factum of the Intervener
Women's Legal Education and Action Fund

PART I — INTERVENER LEAF'S STATEMENT OF FACTS

1. The Intervener, the Women's Legal Education and Action Fund (LEAF) accepts the Statement of Facts of the Appellant, the Newfoundland and Labrador Association of Public and Private Employees (NAPE), and also relies upon the following facts.

2. The Respondent in this case is the Newfoundland provincial government. As a government actor the Newfoundland government is subject to the *Canadian Charter of Rights and Freedoms*, and as the equality claimants' employer it is subject to the Newfoundland *Human Rights Code* — both prohibit sex-based discrimination, which includes sex-based wage discrimination.

> *Canadian Charter of Rights and Freedoms, Constitution Act, 1982*, as enacted by the *Canada Act* 1981 (UK), 1982, c. 11, sections 15 and 32(1)
>
> The Newfoundland *Human Rights Code*, 1970, c. 262, s. 9(1)(a)

3. NAPE and the Newfoundland government entered into a Pay Equity Agreement in June, 1988. The purpose of the Pay Equity Agreement was to remedy sex-based wage discrimination in the government workforce. The pay equity negotiations which resulted in this agreement were preceded by a long history of sex-based wage discrimination by the Newfoundland government. The government undertook to remedy the acknowledged wage discrimination by negotiating a remedial regime that would incrementally

achieve pay equity for the claimant employees over a five-year period beginning in April, 1988.

> Arbitration Award, April 1997, Appellant's Record, Vol. I, at 4, 6, and 30–31

4. However, payment of discriminatory wages continued for three years after the Agreement was reached, while NAPE and the government negotiated the level of redress required to remedy the identified discrimination. Prior to implementing payments under the Agreement, the government predicted a fiscal deficit. It then made deficit reduction a political priority.

5. This deficit reduction priority was largely achieved through the introduction of the *Public Sector Wage Restraint Act* (the *"Act"*). The *Act* froze the wages of all public sector employees by suspending all scheduled wage increases. Additionally, the government deprived the claimant employees of the pay equity adjustment payments owed for the period from April, 1988 through March, 1991.

> *Public Sector Wage Restraint Act*, S.N. 1991, c. 3, Appellant's Factum, Tab 2

6. In effect, the Newfoundland government knowingly persisted in discriminatory practices for three years. It relieved itself forever of its obligation to provide pay equity redress for work done between April, 1988 and March, 1991, and thus permanently confiscated the equality-promoting compensation owed to the claimant employees.

PART II — INTERVENER LEAF'S STATEMENT OF POSITION ON THE ISSUES

7. LEAF's position on the Constitutional questions in issue is that there is a violation of s. 15 of the *Charter*, which is not demonstrably justified as a reasonable limit under s. 1 of the *Charter*.

PART III — INTERVENER LEAF'S STATEMENT OF ARGUMENT

Overview of LEAF's Position on Section 15 of the *Charter*

8. This case concerns government devaluation of women's work, and related devaluation of women as citizens and members of society. LEAF's submissions on s. 15 could be presented in accordance with the three-step test articulated in *Law v. Canada*. However, LEAF submits that the *Law*

test disconnects from each other the principles underlying the substantive equality analysis, creating the potential to inadvertently undermine the *Charter*'s substantive equality guarantee. Therefore, LEAF's analysis of the s. 15 violation in this case does not match the specific *Law* steps, but instead applies a holistic, interconnected approach that focuses on the devaluing and subordinating effects of the government action. In the s. 15 submissions that follow, LEAF: (1) reviews the substantive equality principles this Court has consistently affirmed and that constitute the interconnected approach, (2) outlines the reasons why the *Law* framework operates to put the substantive equality goal in jeopardy, and (3) demonstrates that the impugned action in this case violates women's substantive equality.

> *Law v. Canada (Minister of Employment and Immigration)*, [1999] 1 S.C.R. 497

Section 15 Guarantees Substantive Equality

9. Like all the rights and freedoms guaranteed by the *Charter*, s. 15 is to be interpreted using a purposive and contextual approach.

> *Law v. Canada, supra*, at para. 40

10. Section 15 has a two-fold, remedial purpose: (1) to eliminate and prevent discrimination, *and* (2) to promote equality.

> It may be said that the purpose of s. 15(1) is *to prevent* the violation of essential human dignity and freedom through the imposition of disadvantage, stereotyping, or political or social prejudice, and *to promote* a society in which all persons enjoy equal recognition at law as human beings or as members of Canadian society, equally capable and equally deserving of concern, respect and consideration.
>
> *Law v. Canada, supra*, at para. 51 [emphasis added]
>
> Section 15 of the *Canadian Charter of Rights and Freedoms, supra*

11. Beginning with *Andrews v. Law Society of British Columbia*, this Court has consistently rejected an abstract and formalistic approach to equality rights in favour of a contextual and substantive approach.

> *Andrews v. Law Society of British Columbia*, [1989] 1 S.C.R. 143 at 164–171, per McIntyre J.
>
> *Law v. Canada, supra* at paras. 25, 38, and 81

12. The heart of the substantive equality approach is the recognition that differentiation, by itself, is not a violation of equality rights. A viola-

tion of equality rights is established by differentiations that substantively discriminate — these are grounds-based differentiations that reflect, perpetuate, reinforce, exacerbate or fail to remedy historical patterns of oppression of particular groups and individual members of these groups. The prohibited grounds of discrimination are those enumerated in s. 15, grounds analogous to the enumerated grounds, and interlocking grounds, for example, gendered disability discrimination, racialized gender discrimination and gendered age discrimination.

Andrews, supra, at 180–182 per McIntyre J.

Law, supra, at paras. 27, 63, and 81

Dianne Pothier, "Connecting Grounds of Discrimination To Real Peoples' Real Experiences" (2001) 13 Canadian Journal of Women and the Law 37

Iris Marion Young, *Justice and the Politics of Difference* (Princeton, New Jersey: Princeton University Press, 1990) at 48–65

13. The substantive equality approach is thus defined by several interconnected principles, which will be elaborated in the paragraphs that follow:

- A claimant does not need to prove discriminatory intent.
- Mere differentiation does not violate equality rights. Violations of equality rights involve discriminatory differentiation, including the failure to properly recognize and address difference.
- The focus is placed on the effect of the discrimination on the claimant(s).
- Questions of reasonableness and relevance of the challenged government action or inaction are conceptually distinct from the substantive equality analysis, and should be considered only as part of the s. 1 inquiry.

14. Substantive equality rights have a strong remedial purpose that focuses on the effects of discrimination. The purpose of equality rights is to remedy inequality; the purpose is not to assign blame or impose punishment.

Andrews, supra, at 173–174, per McIntyre J.

Law, supra at para. 80

15. Although discrimination is sometimes consciously intended, more often it unconsciously imposes the norms of the dominant group(s) so as to subordinate other norms and values. Discriminatory norms reflect and

naturalize the needs, realities and circumstances of relatively more powerful groups, relationally ignoring or devaluing the needs, realities and circumstances of relatively less powerful groups. Substantive equality claims
challenge discriminatory norms by seeking to expose the construction of
difference and the power of the dominant perspective.

Canada (Attorney General) v. Mossop, [1993] 1 S.C.R. 554 at 623–625, per
L'Heureux-Dubé J. dissenting

*British Columbia (Public Service Employee Relations Commission) v. British
Columbia Government and Service Employees' Union (B.C.G.S.E.U.)*, [1999] 3
S.C.R. 3 at paras. 39–41

Martha Minow, *Making All the Difference: Inclusion, Exclusion, and American
Law* (Ithaca, New York: Cornell University Press, 1990) at 110–112

16. Eliminating differentiation is the appropriate remedy where the
differentiation results in negative effects upon members of an oppressed
group. Conversely, differentiation is the appropriate remedy where the failure to recognize and respect different needs, realities and circumstances
results in negative effects upon members of an oppressed group. LEAF
submits that both approaches may require transformation of established
norms of social, political, economic and legal systems.

Andrews, supra at 171 per McIntyre J.

Law, supra at para. 25

B.C.G.S.E.U., supra

17. This Honourable Court has used a variety of indicia to describe
substantive discrimination, including:

"Devalued", "stigmatization", "political and social prejudice", "stereotyping", "lacking political power", "exclusion", "marginalized", "historical
disadvantage", "social, political and legal disadvantage"; "vulnerability",
"oppression", "powerlessness".

Law v. Canada, supra, at paras. 29, 34, 39, 42, 43, 44, 46, 47, 53, 63, and 64

18. These injuries of discrimination deny equal inclusion and participation in society, deny equal recognition as citizens, deny equal enjoyment of
social and economic resources, and deny equal autonomy as human beings.

19. The question as to whether a distinction is discriminatory within
the meaning of s. 15 is conceptually distinct from the question as to whether
discrimination is reasonable or justifiable. The reasonableness and justifica-

tion of discrimination are matters to be considered under s. 1 of the *Charter*, where the onus is on the party seeking to justify the infringement.

Andrews, supra, at 177–178, per McIntyre J.

Canadian Foundation for Children, Youth and the Law v. Canada (Attorney General), [2004] SCJ 6, para. 97, per Binnie J.

How the Disconnected *Law* Approach Can Undermine Substantive Equality

20. LEAF submits that the effect of the *Law* framework is to disconnect in three significant ways the substantive equality principles that are conceptually interconnected, and that therefore need to be dealt with holistically to give effect to substantive equality and to avoid an abstract, rationalizing formalism.

June Ross, "A Flawed Synthesis of the *Law*" (2000) 11:3 Constitutional Forum 74

B. Baines, "*Law v. Canada*: Formatting Equality" (2000) 11:3 Constitutional Forum 65

Sheilah Martin, "Balancing Individual Rights to Equality and Social Goals" (2001) 80 *The Canadian Bar Review* 299

Sheilah Martin, "Court Challenges: *Law*" (Winnipeg: Court Challenges Program, 2002)

Bruce Ryder, "What's *Law* Good For? Same-Sex Marriage and Other Successes" 2003 Constitutional Cases, Seventh Annual Analysis of the Constitutional Decisions of the Supreme Court of Canada; Friday, April 2, 2004; Osgoode Hall Law School, Toronto, forthcoming, (2004) Supreme Court Law Review

21. The first disconnection occurs with the three-step test. The third step of the *Law* test — where the substantive discrimination analysis takes place — is the heart of the substantive equality analysis. To isolate the question of whether there is differentiation from the substantive impact asserted by the equality rights claimant obscures what should be the focus of the discrimination analysis.

22. The second disconnection occurs with the four-factor analysis at the third step of the *Law* test. LEAF submits that the first and fourth factors lie at the core of the substantive equality approach and should guide the interconnected analysis. The first "contextual factor" examines whether the affected group has experienced or experiences oppression. The fourth "contextual factor" examines how the claimant's interest is affected by the impugned measure. However, the second and third factors should not be independent inquiries because they are corollaries of the first factor. The

second factor relates to the substantive equality principle that differential treatment can be required to properly address non-stereotypical, differential needs. If this factor is considered in isolation, however, it has the potential to import conceptions of "relevance" and "reasonableness" that fail to question the very discriminatory norms the equality claim seeks to eliminate. It also has the potential to shift the focus away from effects to look instead for discriminatory intention. Similarly, the third factor reflects the substantive equality principle that affirmative action measures are not discriminatory differentiations. This factor should be part of the analysis only where such measures are at issue, otherwise it too has the potential to shift the focus away from effects towards a search for discriminatory intention.

23. The third disconnection occurs with the separation of "dignity" from the concrete harms which are the indicia of substantive discrimination. Although *Law*'s statement of the purpose of s. 15 explicitly recognizes that injury to dignity is a harm related to "the imposition of disadvantage, stereotyping, or political or social prejudice", this fundamental connection is lost when the test is formulated to ask whether the claimant "feels" that "they are less capable, or less worthy of recognition or value". LEAF respectfully submits that this truncation treats dignity as an abstract emotive feeling, so as to trivialize and improperly individualize the concrete harms of substantive discrimination — subordination, devaluation, disenfranchisement and disempowerment, resulting in social, political, legal and economic inequality. Dignity is only relevant to a substantive equality analysis to the extent that it constitutes a value that is undermined by the harms of discrimination.

> Sheilah Martin, "Balancing Individual Rights to Equality and Social Goals" *supra*
>
> Sheilah Martin, "Court Challenges: *Law*", *supra*

24. It is important to apply a holistic, interconnected substantive equality analysis rather than a disaggregated approach to ensure that the full impact of the discrimination is exposed and addressed. In this case, an interconnected analysis demonstrates how the government's confiscation of equality-redressing pay equity adjustments designed to remedy sex-based wage discrimination violates the substantive equality rights of the claimants.

Confiscating Pay Equity Adjustments Renews, Perpetuates and Reinforces Discrimination

25. Sex-based wage discrimination refers to compensation systems and practices that devalue women and their work by paying women less than men for doing the same work as men, or for doing different work that is of equal value to work done by men. Pay equity is designed to remedy sex-based wage discrimination. Pay equity is not a wage increase.

> Pat Armstrong and Hugh Armstrong, *The Double Ghetto: Canadian Women and Their Segregated Work* (Toronto: McClelland and Stewart, 1994) at 41–45

> Nan Weiner and Morley Gunderson, *Pay Equity: Issues, Options and Experiences* (Markham, Ontario: Butterworths Canada Ltd., 1990) at 5–16

> *Canada (Attorney General) v. Public Service Alliance of Canada*, [2000] 1 F.C. 146 (T.D.) at para. 117

26. It has long been recognized that there is a significant wage gap between women's and men's paid labour. Recently, the United Nations Committee on the Elimination of Discrimination Against Women noted in its comments on Canada's conformity with the Convention on the Elimination of All Forms of Discrimination Against Women its concern with the continued failure of provincial governments to implement pay equity in practice.

> Judge Rosalie Silberman Abella, *Report of the Royal Commission on Equality in Employment* (Ottawa: Ministry of Supply and Services, 1984) at 232, 234, Appellant's Book of Authorities, Volume 1, tab 8

> Committee on the Elimination of Discrimination Against Women, Twenty-eighth Session, January 31, 2003, Draft Report on Canada's Fifth Periodic Report at paras. 49–52, available at: http://www.un.org/womenwatch/daw/cedaw/cedaw28/ConComCanada.PDF (accessed April 27, 2004)

> Submission of the Canadian Human Rights Commission to the Pay Equity Task Force, March 2003, available at: http://www.chrc-ccdp.ca/legislation_policies/equitytaskforce-en.asp at 2 (accessed April 27, 2004)

27. Sex-based wage discrimination is integrally related to other forms of employment discrimination against women — occupational segregation, barriers to advancement, sexual harassment and involuntary part-time employment — such that women's participation in the labour force is characterized by inequality. In some contexts, women's employment inequality reflects stereotypes of women as secondary participants in the workforce and secondary wage earners. Women's employment inequality may also

result from labour market oppressions of women who are already marginalized by interlocking grounds of discrimination. Aboriginal women, younger and older women, immigrant women, women with disabilities and women who experience racialized gender discrimination have the highest levels of unemployment among women and are often segregated into the lowest-valued and lowest paid jobs.

Pat Armstrong and Hugh Armstrong, *supra* at 41–49

Submission of the Canadian Human Rights Commission to the Pay Equity Task Force, *supra* at 2 and 3

Recommendations to the Pay Equity Task Force — Status of Women Canada, November, 2002, available at: http://www.payequityreview.gc.ca/4493-e.html at 2 (accessed April 27, 2004)

Women's Economic Independence and Security: A Federal / Provincial / Territorial Strategic Framework, March 2001, a joint study released by the Federal / Provincial / Territorial Ministers Responsible for the Status of Women available at: http://www.swc-cfc.gc.ca/pubs/0662655427/200103_0662655427_e.pdf at 13–16 (accessed April 27, 2004)

28. Sex-based wage discrimination results from the systemic undervaluation of women's work through the interaction of socially-constructed divisions of labour and social constructions of the value of labour. Women are occupationally segregated into low-paid and low-status jobs, which are often low-paid and low-status precisely because they are jobs women do.

Pat Armstrong and Hugh Armstrong, *supra*

Nan Weiner and Morley Gunderson, *supra*

Canada (Attorney General) v. Public Service Alliance of Canada, *supra*, para. 151

Judge Rosalie Silberman Abella, *Report of the Royal Commission on Equality in Employment*, *supra* at 245–249

29. In the context of sex-based wage discrimination, the normalization of women's subordination is reflected in the systems and practices that undervalue women's work through assumptions that stereotype and marginalize women and their work. These assumptions include:

a. Women are secondary wage earners: they are not "breadwinners" but "pin money" earners;

b. Women's work does not involve skills and expertise, but simply draws on women's "natural" or "inherent" qualities and abilities;

c. Women choose to be clustered in occupationally segregated and low-paid work;

d. Women are selfless and are willing to bear a disproportionate economic burden.

Nan Weiner and Morley Gunderson, *supra*

30. Sex-based wage discrimination tells women and men, in the most concrete of terms, that women are not worth as much as men. Unequal wages deprive women of income; contribute to the feminization of poverty; increase women's financial dependence upon men, including in situations where they are at risk of spousal abuse and violence; reduce women's pensions and disability benefits; and diminish women's ability to participate fully in society. Discriminatory wages result in discriminatory pensions and discriminatory disability benefits.

Women's Economic Independence and Security: A Federal/Provincial/Territorial Strategic Framework, *supra* at 16–19 and 23–26

Judge Rosalie Silberman Abella, *Report of the Royal Commission on Equality in Employment, supra* at 234–235

31. At the same time, sex-based wage discrimination legitimizes and reinforces men's social, political, legal and economic power in relation to women. It normalizes and rationalizes paying men more than women by sending the message that men, and men's work, are "worth more" to society than women and their work. Unequal wages for women's work increase men's power by increasing women's dependence upon men and making women vulnerable to male abuse, violence and harassment. By normalizing and rationalizing men's social, political, legal and economic advantage in relation to women, pay inequity reinforces gender hierarchy.

32. Where government perpetrates the unequal pay, it sends a message that wage equality for women is not affordable for "society". As long as government's fiscal health is subsidized by sex-based wage discrimination within its own workforce, government sends the message that women's economic inequality and social inequality are not a public responsibility, but a burden that women are expected to bear. When government devalues women's work, it devalues women's contributions to society and women's citizenship status within society. Government sends the message that women's social inequality is "affordable", while respecting women's equality rights is not. In the result, government, business, taxpayers and men are unjustly enriched at the expense of women public servants.

33. In the legal context in which this case arises, LEAF submits that the government had a legal obligation to act to remedy its own sex-based wage discrimination. This legal context consists of: (1) s. 15 of the *Charter*, (2) human rights legislation, (3) international covenants prohibiting employment discrimination generally and sex-based wage discrimination specifically, and (4) the anti-discrimination provision in the collective agreement between NAPE and the government.

> United Nations Covenants, Appellant's Book of Authorities, Volume 1, tabs 1–5

34. In *Andrews*, this Court stated: "Discrimination is unacceptable in a democratic society because it epitomizes the worst effects of the denial of equality, and discrimination reinforced by law is particularly repugnant. The worst oppression will result from discriminatory measures having the force of law."

> *Andrews v. Law Society of British Columbia, supra* at 172, per McIntyre J.

35. In this case, the impugned measure has a two-fold discriminatory impact on the claimants that violates s. 15. First, by confiscating the compensation redress payments that should have been made for work done in 1988 to 1991, the three years *prior to* the restraint period, s. 9 targeted women for a pay cut on top of the general salary freeze imposed on all government employees. Second, the three-year delay in implementing the Pay Equity Agreement meant not only that women were deprived of three years of pay equity adjustments, but also that they had to wait three more years to begin to achieve wages equal to men's.

36. By using its legislative power to renege on its pay equity obligation and commitment, the government renewed, perpetuated and reinforced the oppression and devaluation that result from sex-based wage discrimination, as described above in paragraphs 27–32. This action was in itself a s. 15 violation because it continued, condoned and exacerbated discrimination. In addition, s. 15 was violated because the government action sent a message that women's equality is a frivolous luxury that must give way to other government objectives.

37. Contrary to the conclusions of the Newfoundland Court of Appeal, the impugned government action was not merely a temporary measure. The measure had permanent effects on all of the claimants. Specifically:

a. The claimants who worked for the Newfoundland government between April 1, 1988 and March, 1991 had these three years of pay equity adjustments confiscated by the government. These women lost forever the economic effect of compounding and cumulative entitlements that would have come into play if the government had begun to make pay equity adjustment payments in April, 1988 as promised.

b. The claimants who continued to work for the government during and after the restraint period did not begin to receive the incremental pay equity adjustments until 1991, three years later than they should have. These women lost forever the economic effect of compounding and cumulative entitlements that would have come into effect if the government had begun to make pay equity adjustment payments in April, 1988 as promised.

c. Older claimants who retired between April 1, 1988 and the final implementation of the Agreement were uniquely affected because their pensions were permanently tied to discriminatory wages. These women will be at greater risk of experiencing poverty if they are forced to survive on pensions tied to unequal wages.

Monica Townson, "Reducing Poverty Among Older Women: The Potential of Retirement Income Policies", Ottawa: Status of Women Canada, 2000, chapter 3, 'The Extent of Poverty Among Older Women," available at: http://www.swc-cfc.gc.ca/pubs/0662659271/200008_0662659271_9_e.html (accessed April 27, 2004)

d. Claimants who became unable to work because of disability between April 1, 1988 and the final implementation of the Agreement are uniquely disadvantaged because their disability payments are permanently tied to discriminatory wages. Women with disabilities are also especially vulnerable to poverty.

Newfoundland Court of Appeal, Reasons for Judgement, Appellant's Record, Vol. II at 346, para. 418

Fiona Sampson, "Globalization and the Inequality of Women with Disabilities" (2003) 2 Journal of Law and Equality at 16–33

38. In conclusion, LEAF submits that s. 9 of the *Public Sector Restraint Act* infringed the s. 15 rights of the claimants, requiring their employer, the Newfoundland government, to establish that this violation was a reasonable and demonstrably justified limit on equality rights in a free and democratic society. The Newfoundland government is accountable to women public servants — as employees and as citizens — for the devaluing and disenfranchising impacts of the impugned legislative measure.

Overview of LEAF's Position on Section 1 of the *Charter*

39. The s. 1 issue in this case is whether government's discriminatory targeting of women to bear a disproportionate burden of the fiscal deficit was reasonable and demonstrably justifiable in a free and democratic society. LEAF submits below that any violation of a *Charter* right, including violations that involve resource distribution, must be justified by the government in accordance with the *Oakes* principles. LEAF submits that the government in this case failed to meet its justificatory burden.

> *R. v. Oakes*, [1986] 1 S.C.R. 103, at 137–140

Section 1 Guarantees a Substantive Free and Democratic Society

40. Section 1 has a two-fold purpose: (1) it guarantees *Charter* rights and freedoms at the outset, and (2) it sets out stringent criteria for justifying an infringement of a right or freedom.

> It is important to observe at the outset that s. 1 has two functions: first, it constitutionally guarantees the rights and freedoms set out in the provisions which follow; and, second, it states explicitly the exclusive justificatory criteria (outside of s. 33 of the Constitution Act, 1982) against which limitations on those rights and freedoms must be measured. Accordingly, any s. 1 inquiry must be premised on an understanding that the impugned limit violates constitutional rights and freedoms — rights and freedoms which are part of the supreme law of Canada.
>
> As Wilson J. stated in *Singh v. Minister of Employment and Immigration*, *supra*, at p. 218: "… it is important to remember that the courts are conducting this inquiry in light of a commitment to uphold the rights and freedoms set out in the other sections of the *Charter*".

> *R. v. Oakes, supra* at 135–136

41. Thus, although the s. 1 analysis is conducted after a finding that a right or freedom has been violated, s. 1 is not simply a "defence" to a rights violation. Moreover, the respondent must prove that they have met the exclusive justificatory criteria.

42. The s. 1 test is found in the language of s. 1 — the guaranteed *Charter* rights and freedoms are "subject only to such reasonable limits prescribed by law as can be demonstrably justified in a free and democratic society". A substantive interpretation of democracy incorporates a recognition of values and principles such as equality, inclusion, social justice, and participation, and is not a mere "majority rules" approach.

Section 1 of the *Canadian Charter of Rights and Freedoms, supra*

RJR-MacDonald Inc. v. Canada (Attorney General), [1995] 3 S.C.R. 199, at para. 126, per McLachlin J.

R. v. Oakes, supra, at 136

43. Equality is thus one of the values and principles underlying substantive freedom and substantive democracy, in addition to being guaranteed as a right under the *Charter*. Equality informs the meaning of freedom within the *Charter* and is one of the fundamental values of a democratic society.

R. v. Big M Drug Mart Ltd., [1985] 1 S.C.R. 295, at 313–314, per Dickson J.

R. v. Oakes, supra at 136

44. A substantive approach to democracy rejects majoritarianism as the defining principle of democratic governance and decision-making. Substantive democracy aspires to norms that value and promote diversity, inclusion, and belonging.

> There is also another aspect of judicial review that promotes democratic values. Although a court's invalidation of legislation usually involves negating the will of the majority, we must remember that the concept of democracy is broader than the notion of majority rule, fundamental as that may be. In this respect, we would do well to heed the words of Dickson C.J. in *Oakes*, supra, at p. 136:
>
>> The Court must be guided by the values and principles essential to a free and democratic society which I believe to embody, to name but a few, respect for the inherent dignity of the human person, commitment to social justice and equality, accommodation of a wide variety of beliefs, respect for cultural and group identity, and faith in social and political institutions which enhance the participation of individuals and groups in society.
>
> *Vriend v. Alberta*, [1998] 1 S.C.R. 493, at para. 140
>
> Donna Greschner, "The Right to Belong: The Promise of *Vriend*" (1998) 9 National Journal of Constitutional Law 417

45. A substantive approach to democracy recognizes that a formal system of representative democracy is not in and of itself enough to protect and further democratic values. Enfranchisement is more than the formal, abstract right to cast a vote in an electoral process. Under conditions of sys-

temic social, economic, political and legal inequality, a representative electoral process by majority vote is not always representative of all groups and individuals in society, and cannot by itself achieve equal representation for all citizens. Even the formal right to vote cannot be exercised equally under conditions of systemic social, economic, political and legal inequality.

46. Democracy is not a static endpoint. It is a dynamic process through which society continues to evolve and transform itself. *Charter* claims are enabled by democratic norms, are a challenge to democratic norms, and seek to expand democratic norms.

> William Connolly, *The Ethos of Pluralization* (Minneapolis: University of Minnesota Press, 1995) at xiv
>
> James Tully, *Strange Multiplicity: Constitutionalism in an Age of Diversity* (Cambridge: Cambridge University Press, 1995) at 183–187

47. Just as democracy thrives when it is informed by equality and a substantive approach, it withers when it is based on inequality and formalistic principles. Democracy can become brittle and even erode if governments are permitted to reinforce or exacerbate the oppression and disadvantage of subordinated groups. Inequality fosters conflicts, erodes the social fabric, and undermines peace.

48. LEAF submits that by treating women public servants as both second-class employees and second-class citizens, the Newfoundland government eroded the principles of substantive democratic citizenship.

49. Section 15 violations will rarely be found reasonable and demonstrably justified in a free and democratic society, because it is the right to substantive equality that has been infringed.

> In conducting the s. 1 analysis, "it must be remembered that it is the right to substantive equality and the accompanying violation of human dignity that has been infringed when a violation of s. 15(1) has been found" (*Corbiere*, supra, per L'Heureux-Dubé J., at para. 98 (emphasis deleted)). Indeed, "cases will be rare where it is found reasonable in a free and democratic society to discriminate" (see *Adler v. Ontario*, [1996] 3 S.C.R. 609, per L'Heureux-Dubé J., at para. 95 (citing *Andrews*, supra, per Wilson J., at p. 154).
>
> *Lavoie v. Canada*, [2002] 1 S.C.R. 769 at para. 6, per McLachlin C.J. dissenting
>
> Sheilah Martin, "Balancing Individual Rights to Equality and Social Goals", *supra* at 352–368

50. Applying a substantive understanding of democracy, courts should not accept rationalizations such as broad and abstract appeals to the "public good" or "the general fiscal welfare" as demonstrably justifiable limitations of equality rights, because to do so suggests that equality rights are luxuries that are separate from the democratic good, instead of rights that substantively define and enhance the public good.

51. Applying a substantive understanding of democracy, courts should not exempt government decisions involving resource allocation from the onerous review of s. 15 violations that s. 1 demands.

The Courts have a Constitutionally-Mandated Role to Protect Substantive Democracy

52. The doctrine of the "separation of powers" recognizes that each branch of government has a distinct role to play within the structures of democratic governance. All branches of government in the Canadian constitutional democracy have a duty to respect and comply with the *Charter.*

53. One role of the courts is to review the actions and inactions of the legislative and executive branches of government to ensure their compliance with the *Charter.*

> Parliament has its role: to choose the appropriate response to social problems within the limiting framework of the Constitution. But the courts also have a role: to determine, objectively and impartially, whether Parliament's choice falls within the limiting framework of the Constitution. The courts are no more permitted to abdicate their responsibility than is Parliament. To carry judicial deference to the point of accepting Parliament's view simply on the basis that the problem is serious and the solution difficult, would be to diminish the role of the courts in the constitutional process and to weaken the structure of rights upon which our constitution and our nation is founded.
>
> *RJR-MacDonald Inc. v. Canada (Attorney General)*, [1995] 3 S.C.R. 199, at para. 136, per McLachlin J.

54. The question of whether a particular rights violation is justified is to be considered on a case-specific basis, with reference to a variety of contextual factors, including, the severity of the breach and the values promoted by the government action.

> *Thomson Newspapers Co. v. Canada (Attorney General)*, [1998] 1 S.C.R. 877 at paras. 90–91

Andrews, supra at 184, per McIntyre J.

55. Government action that violates a *Charter* right or freedom must be measured against principles and values of substantive democracy to determine whether or not it is constitutional. It is essential not to conflate the constitutional requirements of democracy with government action that is taken in the name of majoritarian democracy.

> Because s. 1 serves first and foremost to protect rights, the range of constitutionally valid objectives is not unlimited. For example, the protection of competing rights might be a valid objective. However, a simple majoritarian political preference for abolishing a right altogether would not be a constitutionally valid objective.

Sauvé v. Canada (Chief Electoral Officer), supra at para. 20, per McLachlin C.J.

56. LEAF submits that the Court's institutional role is not altered by the fact that the discrimination in this case is enacted in the name of fiscal restraint. To limit the Court's role in this way would effectively make government spending decisions immune from *Charter* scrutiny and the rule of law, and would significantly undermine substantive equality.

M. v. H., [1999] 2 S.C.R. 3 at paras. 79–80

Vriend, supra at para. 54

57. LEAF submits that the Newfoundland Court of Appeal failed to require the government to justify its discrimination by allowing parliamentary democracy to trump constitutional norms, for dubious reasons such as "the *threat to North American society* so forceability [*sic*] brought to public awareness this past year" — i.e. the events of September 11, 2001.

Newfoundland Court of Appeal, Reasons for Judgment, Appellant's Record, Vol. II at 328, para. 367 [emphasis added]

58. LEAF submits that the Newfoundland Court of Appeal erred in law by misconstruing the function of the separation of powers doctrine within the Canadian constitutional democracy. The Court of Appeal then relied upon this misconstrual to relieve the Newfoundland government of its constitutional obligation to *prove* that its discrimination was reasonable and demonstrably justifiable.

The *Oakes* Principles for Government Compliance with the *Charter*

59. LEAF respectfully submits that the *Oakes* principles are designed to reinforce government accountability to its *Charter* obligations. The principles are stringent, they are intended to be applied stringently, and they are intended to be informed by the principles and values underlying a free and democratic society. As noted in para. 54 above, a s. 1 analysis is contextual, and the context of this case is a serious equality rights violation. In the case of a s. 15 breach, the burden of proof is especially onerous.

R.J.R.-MacDonald, supra at paras. 127–129 and 134, per McLachlin J.

Lavoie, supra

R. v. Oakes, supra at 137–140

60. LEAF's position is that monetary considerations should not be available as a justification in the context of equality violations.

The Supreme Court has in any event held that cost is not a constitutionally permissible justification for discrimination under s. 1: *Schachter v. Canada*, [1999] 2 S.C.R. 679, at p. 709, 10 C.R.R. (2d) 1, at p. 20, per Lamer C.J.C. Cost/benefit analyses are not readily applicable to equality violations because of the inherent incomparability of the monetary impacts involved. Remedying discrimination will always appear to be more fiscally burdensome than beneficial on a balance sheet. On one side of the budgetary ledger will be the calculable cost required to rectify the discriminatory measure; on the other side, it will likely be found that the cost to the public of discriminating is not as concretely measurable. The considerable but incalculable benefits of eliminating discrimination are therefore not visible in the equation, making the analysis an unreliable source of policy decision-making.

Rosenberg v. Canada (Attorney General) (1998), 38 O.R. (3d) 577 (C.A.) at 11

Is Expenditure Reduction a Pressing and Substantial Objective?

61. In this case, the impugned provision and the legislation share the same objective — to reduce government spending. This Court has consistently affirmed that budgetary considerations, by themselves, cannot normally constitute a pressing and substantial objective in a free and democratic society. The fact that money can be saved by disregarding *Charter* rights does not establish a reasonable and demonstrably justifiable objective in a free and democratic society. LEAF submits that this principle should again be affirmed, and should be applied in this case.

Nova Scotia (Workers' Compensation Board) v. Martin, [2003] 2 S.C.R. 504, at
para. 109

Singh v. Minister of Employment and Immigration, [1985] 1 S.C.R. 177 at 218–219

62. The monetary nature of the objective is not altered by the fact that
the cost reduction measure in this case was imposed to meet the government's deficit reduction objective. A substantive approach to democracy
challenges the very norms and assumptions informing government decisions about how to raise and spend revenues. Deficits are not naturally-oc-
curring phenomena. Nor are government revenue bases. They are produced
by governments, through complex webs of decisions about how to raise
money and how to spend money. The fact that these decisions involve questions of economic and social policy, and sometimes electoral pragmatisim,
cannot immunize them from *Charter* scrutiny if the principles of a substantive approach to democracy are to be given effect.

63. LEAF further submits that a cost reduction measure expressly
grounded in discrimination cannot be a pressing and substantial objective,
because it is contrary to the fundamental principle of equality underlying
s. 1. In this case, it is difficult to separate the objective of the impugned provision from the method by which the objective is achieved. The objective
was to reduce government spending by eliminating pay equity adjustments
owed during the first 3 years of the agreed upon implementation period.
LEAF submits that this objective is discriminatory on its face and, thus,
contrary to the equality-promoting values of substantive democracy.

64. The Newfoundland Court of Appeal accepted the government's
further characterization of the objective as fiscal restraint for the purpose
of "promoting education, heath and like social programs which are consistent with values underlying the *Charter*". The Court of Appeal also held
that in the context of a "fiscal deficit of serious enough proportions to
threaten economic security and well-being", it "can be assumed that those
'*other* values and principles' are commensurately threatened as well". In the
Court of Appeal's view, it was not appropriate to require the government
to prove the impact of alternative deficit reduction options on the other
Charter values and principles.

Newfoundland Court of Appeal, Reasons for Judgment, Appellant's Record,
Vol. II at 332 and 342, paras. 378 and 407 [emphasis in original]

65. LEAF submits that s. 1 requires the government to demonstrate a
specific and concrete objective, otherwise it will be improperly relieved of

its constitutional obligation to demonstrate how the infringing measure seeks to fulfill its objective.

> The rhetorical nature of the government objectives advanced in this case renders them suspect. The first objective, enhancing civic responsibility and respect for the law, could be asserted of virtually every criminal law and many non-criminal measures. Respect for law is undeniably import-ant. But the simple statement of this value lacks the context necessary to assist us in determining whether the infringement at issue is demonstrably justifiable in a free and democratic society. To establish justification, one needs to know what problem the government is targeting, and why it is so pressing and important that it warrants limiting a Charter right. Without this, it is difficult if not impossible to weigh whether the infringement of the right is justifiable or proportionate.

> *Sauvé, supra* at para. 20 per McLachlin C.J.

66. LEAF submits that the Newfoundland Court of Appeal's reli-ance upon vague monetary considerations exemplifies the deficiency of an approach to s. 1 that allows majoritarian democracy to trump substantive democracy. The Court of Appeal characterizes the claimants' right to "en-joyment of pay equity adjustments" as "'inimical to the realization of col-lective goals of fundamental importance'", thereby reducing women public servants as a group to an "individual" who is outside "society" and whose interests are antagonistic to society. This is an inappropriate application of *Oakes*, because in the context of an equality claim it perverts the substan-tive and equality-promoting values of a free and democratic society.

> Newfoundland Court of Appeal, Reasons for Judgment, Appellant's Record, Vol. II at 345–346, paras. 416–417

Confiscating Pay Equity Adjustments Is Not Proportionate to the Alleged Objective

67. In the alternative, if the government's alleged objective is found to be pressing and substantial, then a rational connection is conceded. How-ever, LEAF submits that the impugned measure does not minimally impair the rights in issue, and the deleterious effects of the confiscating measure far outweigh any salutary effects.

68. The minimal impairment principle requires the government to prove that it limited women's equality rights "as little as reasonably pos-

sible" in the circumstances. This standard compels the government to demonstrate that it considered, and reasonably rejected, alternative measures to confiscating women's pay equity. LEAF submits that the Newfoundland Court of Appeal wrongly disregarded these requirements in two ways: (1) by accepting the government's mere assertions that it had ruled out a limited number of alternative deficit reduction measures as *proof* of considering and reasonably rejecting alternatives to the wholesale confiscation of the pay equity monies owed, and (2) by holding that the government was not required to respond to the panoply of alternative measures raised by the government's Opposition, and acknowledged as potentially available alternatives by the Arbitration Board.

> Newfoundland Court of Appeal, Reasons for Judgment, Appellant's Record, Vol. II at 362–363, paras. 454–457
>
> Arbitration Award, April 4, 1997, Appellant's Record, Vol. 1 at 99-100
>
> *Martin, supra* at paras. 112 and 113

69. Although this Court has suggested that budgetary considerations may form part of the minimal impairment analysis, LEAF submits that they are, on their own, just as inappropriate to the proportionality inquiry as they are to the question of whether the government has established a pressing and substantial objective.

> *Reference re Remuneration of Judges of the Provincial Court of Prince Edward Island*, [1997] 3 S.C.R. 3 at para. 284

70. LEAF submits that the norms underlying government spending need to be scrutinized to reveal if and how discriminatory norms are informing resource allocation decisions. For example, the government should have to justify why reducing the deficit requires three additional years of discriminatory wages for child therapists, a class of employees covered by the Pay Equity Agreement, instead of reducing or eliminating Ministerial car allowances, one of the alternative deficit reduction options identified by the Opposition.

71. LEAF further submits that the severe discriminatory harms of the absolute and permanent confiscation of the pay equity redress, i.e. the harms caused by the renewal, perpetuation and reinforcement of sex-based wage discrimination, clearly outweigh the monetary benefit of the Newfoundland government reneging on its full pay equity obligation and promise.

Vriend, supra at para. 122

72. LEAF submits that while it is not the role of the courts to micro-manage the government's resource distribution, it is their role to hold the government accountable for discriminatory decision-making. Given the blatant nature of the violation in this case, and the government's failure to justify this breach under s. 1, the violation cannot be saved.

73. LEAF submits that the remedial purpose of s. 15, and the role of s. 1 in guaranteeing a substantive free and democratic society, are achieved only by requiring government to promote respect for and inclusion of the dis-empowered — requiring solutions that may transform established norms of social, political, economic, and legal power.

PART IV — SUBMISSIONS CONCERNING COSTS

74. LEAF is not seeking costs in this matter and submits that no order for costs should be made against it.

PART V — ORDER REQUESTED

75. LEAF respectfully requests that the appeal be allowed and that the equality rights of the claimants be recognized and respected.

All of which is respectfully submitted this 28th day of April 2004.

COUNSELS' SIGNATURES

_____   _____

Karen Schucher   Fiona Sampson

Auton (Guardian ad litem of) v. British Columbia (Attorney General)

Factum of the Intervener
Women's Legal Education and Action Fund and
Disabled Women's Network Canada

PART I — STATEMENT OF FACTS

1. The LEAF/DAWN Coalition defers to the parties for the facts related to the particular claimants.

PART II — QUESTIONS IN ISSUE

2. The Coalition's position on the questions in issue is that there is a violation of s. 15 of the *Charter*, which is not saved by s. 1. The Coalition's submissions will not address the s. 7 issue.

PART III — STATEMENT OF ARGUMENT

Introduction to Section 15 of the *Canadian Charter of Rights and Freedoms*

3. This case concerns the provision of health services benefits, and in particular the exclusion from receipt of state funding of services related to autism. The substantive equality question is whether there are marginalized segments of the population whose most pressing health services needs are disproportionately not met. The government's refusal to include, within its definition of health benefits, services with respect to autism is a denial of substantive equality because funding is arbitrarily tied to specific service providers, namely doctors and hospitals.

4. Section 15's dual purpose is to prevent discrimination *and* to promote equality. Its purpose is:

> to prevent the violation of essential human dignity and freedom through the imposition of disadvantage, stereotyping, or political or social prejudice, and to promote a society in which all persons enjoy equal recognition at law as human beings or as members of Canadian society, equally capable and equally deserving of concern, respect and consideration.

Law v. Canada (Minister of Employment and Immigration), [1999] 1 S.C.R. 497, at para. 51

Section 15 of the *Canadian Charter of Rights and Freedoms, Constitution Act, 1982*, as enacted by the *Canada Act 1981* (UK), 1982, c. 11

5. These goals are conjunctive. When the state fails to accord substantive equality based on a prohibited ground(s), this in itself should be sufficient to establish a breach of s. 15. Section 15 is aimed at preventing and remedying inequalities, ensuring that the state does not exacerbate existing inequalities. When government reinforces or ignores existing inequalities, it simultaneously disadvantages already marginalized groups, while increasing the relative advantage of dominant groups. Inequalities are measured by unequal effects, identified through a substantive equality analysis. In the present case, it is the existing inequality of the disabled that is exacerbated by the government policy respecting the definition of health benefits.

Sheilah Martin, "Balancing Individual Rights to Equality and Social Goals" (2001) 80 *The Canadian Bar Review* 299

Law Society of British Columbia v. Andrews, [1989] 1 S.C.R. 143

6. A three step test was adopted in *Law v. Canada* for the analysis of s. 15 claims, but it was emphasized that the test is not a fixed and rigid formula. The *Law* test includes a 'checklist' of factors that are often applied in a mechanistic fashion, despite the Court's direction to the contrary. The focus on formalistic rules acts to decontextualize systemic inequality analyses. Moreover, some of the factors from *Law* can be improperly used to overemphasize a focus on the purpose rather than the effects of the law or policy in question.

Law v. Canada (Minister of Employment and Immigration), *supra* at paras. 8, 88

M. v. H., [1999] 2 S.C.R. 3, at para. 46

Nova Scotia (Attorney General) v. Walsh, [2002] 4 S.C.R. 325, at para. 82 (L'Heureux-Dubé J. in dissent)

Catherine MacKinnon, "Difference and Dominance" in *Feminism Unmodified: Discourses on Life and Law* (Harvard University Press: Cambridge, 1987) 32–45

7. Although the present case can be analysed according to the three step *Law* test, the Coalition submits that it is artificial to do so because the elements of the three steps are actually substantially intertwined. A holistic substantive equality analysis, as set out below, is more appropriate especially where the differential treatment step is complex and contested, as it is here. A full analysis of inequality requires an assessment of differential treatment that incorporates the interrelated concepts of grounds and discrimination. To disaggregate the analysis potentially jeopardizes the dual purpose of s. 15 to prevent discrimination and promote equality. Disaggregation has the potential to unnecessarily complicate the analysis, and/or to obscure the actual unequal effects. In contrast, a holistic substantive equality analysis promotes equality by paying close attention to the unequal effects that are revealed when examining the interrelationships among differential treatment, grounds, and discrimination.

Law v. Canada (Minister of Employment and Immigration), supra at para. 88

8. The s. 15 analysis below will proceed in the following manner. A review of disability in general, and autism in particular, is presented to provide the necessary context for a substantive equality analysis. A holistic substantive equality analysis is set out to demonstrate that the refusal to provide autism services amounts to differential treatment constituting discrimination against the disabled. There is a breach of s. 15 because the delivery of health services primarily from doctors and hospitals is designed, for the most part, to meet the usual health concerns of the non-disabled population, typically neglecting the isolating and marginalizing effects of disability. Finally the *Law* framework is assessed and applied.

The Context for the Section 15 Analysis

9. The social perception of disability has historically determined the value placed upon the lives of persons with disabilities, and the degree of equality they enjoy within society. The characterization of disability as a negative attribute has traditionally defined the dominant social perception of disability, resulting in the isolation of the disabled from mainstream society.

Rioux, Marcia, "New Research Directions and Paradigms: Disability is Not Measles", in Rioux, Marcia and Michael Bach, eds., *Disability Is Not Measles* (North York: Roeher Institute, 1994), at 1–7

Bickenbach, Jerome E., *Physical Disability and Social Policy* (Toronto: University of Toronto Press, 1993), at 3–19

Susan Wendell, *The Rejected Body: Feminist Philosophical Reflections on Disability* (New York: Routledge, 1996), at 35–56

Granovsky v. Canada (Minister of Employment and Immigration), [2000] 1 S.C.R. 703 at para. 30

10. Historically society has understood disability as a defect rooted in the individual, and has analyzed his/her difference in bio-medical terms. Pursuant to the traditional bio-medical model of disability, the only response to disability is the modification of the individual to fit the non-disabled world, or the segregation of disabled persons from mainstream society, often through institutionalization. Although bio-medical intervention may be apt in certain circumstances (as it is for non-disabled persons), it is inappropriate to assume that it is always, in itself, an adequate or appropriate response to disability. The bio-medical model assumes that disabilities are deficits of natural assets rather than socially ascribed deficits. This model is grounded in able-bodied imperialism, as the world view of the able-bodied continues to be imposed on persons with disabilities.

Richard Devlin & Dianne Pothier, "Introduction: Towards a Critical Theory of Disitizenship" in Devlin & Pothier (eds.), *Critical Disability Theory: Essays in Philosophy, Politics, Policy and Law,* Forthcoming, UBC Press, 2004, at 14

Marcia H. Rioux and Fraser Valentine, "Does Theory Matter? Exploring the Nexus between Disability, Human Rights and Public Policy" in Devlin & Pothier (eds.), *supra* at 2–11

David Lepofsky, "*Charter*'s Guarantee of Equality: How Well Is It Working?" (1998) 16 Windsor Yearbook of Access to Justice 155 at 172

11. An excessive focus on bio-medicalization marginalizes disabled persons as the "other", and hinders societal reform that would provide for increased inclusion. The power of the dominant norm, i.e. the non-disabled norm, is further entrenched and valued by the pathologizing of difference. Because of the way in which society excludes and marginalizes persons with autism, both children and adults with autism experience extreme isolation, disadvantage and oppression if they do not receive health services support to enable their integration into society.

Auton v. British Columbia, (C.A.), Appellant's Record, Volume 2, 166–254 at paras. 2, 3, 11, 12, 15, 49, 147; *Auton v. British Columbia* (trial decision), Appellant's Record, Volume 1, 65–130 at para. 4, 147

12. It is important to recognize that not every condition requiring health services constitutes a disability. To contend otherwise, i.e. to equate any level of impairment with disability, would be to adopt a bio-medical model of disability inconsistent with a purposive interpretation of s. 15. A social model of disability, which focuses on exclusionary effects rather than just medically documented impairment, was recognized by this Honourable Court in *Eldridge* and *Granovsky*. A purposive interpretation of s. 15 must be focussed on countering such exclusionary effects. A substantial proportion of health services has nothing to do with disability because the particular conditions being treated do not result in a significant exclusion from full participation in Canadian society so as to require the protection of s. 15. Disability within s. 15 is identified based on exclusionary effects.

Eldridge v. British Columbia (Attorney General), [1997] 3 S.C.R. 624

Granovsky v. Canada (Minister of Employment and Immigration), supra

13. The stigmatization and social exclusion of disabled persons has had devastating effects. Persons with disabilities experience conditions of serious socio-economic disadvantage in Canadian society. For example, they face unemployment rates of up to 52%, are over-represented among the poor, are under-represented among those who have graduated from post-secondary educational institutions, and about 60% have incomes below the Statistics Canada Low Income Cutoff. These effects can be compounded by sexism, racism and homophobia.

M.D. Lepofsky , "Equal Access to Canada's Judicial System for Persons with Disabilities — A Time for Reform" (1995) 5 N.J.C.L. 183 at 187–188

Gail Fawcett, *Bringing Down the Barriers: The Labour Market and Women with Disabilities in Ontario* (Ottawa: Canadian Council on Social Development, 2000) at 6–7 and 26–28

14. Women with disabilities face even greater disadvantage than men with disabilities. A disproportionate percentage of disabled women in Canada live in poverty, cannot access services available to other Canadians, are unemployed, and experience exposure to the criminal justice system, either as victims or as accused. Women with disabilities face an employment rate that is about ⅓ less than the rate for non-disabled women and about 15% less than that for men with disabilities. Women with disabilities are 40% more likely than men with disabilities to be outside of the labour force. When employed, the average income of women with disabilities falls significantly

below that of non-disabled women, whose average employment income in turn falls significantly below that of men with disabilities. Women with disabilities experience violence at a rate disproportionate to that of any other group of women. The criminal law system acts to the systemic disadvantage of persons with disabilities; moreover, disabled women, in greater proportions than disabled men, are incarcerated in prisons.

> Dick Sobsey and Tanis Doe, "Patterns of Sexual Abuse and Assault" (1991) 9 Sexuality and Disability 243 at 248–9

> *In Unison: A Canadian Approach to Disability Issues* (Appendix B), released October 27, 1998 Federal, Provincial, Territorial Ministers Responsible for Social Services (except for Quebec) available at: http://socialunion.gc.ca/pwd/unison/unison_e.html

> Fiona Sampson, "Globalization and the Inequality of Women with Disabilities" (2003) 2 *Journal of Law and Equality* 16–33

> Yvonne Peters, "Federally Sentenced Women with Developmental and Mental Disabilities: A Dark Corner in Canadian Human Rights" (DAWN Canada: Ottawa 2003)

15. Although autism is more common amongst boys than girls, girls with autism, particularly as they grow older, may experience compounded and extreme discrimination because of their gendered disability. Not addressing the effects of autism will likely lead to lives of isolation and institutionalization for both male and female children. However, the negative effects will be compounded for girls with autism. For example, women with autism who are institutionalized are liable to experience one of the most serious forms of gendered disability discrimination — the physical and sexual abuse that is prevalent in institutions. Because of their gendered disability, women with certain disabilities are in some circumstances vulnerable in ways that neither non-disabled women nor disabled men would be vulnerable. Gendered disability discrimination is not the additive experience of sex plus disability discrimination; it is a distinct experience, more than the sum of its parts.

> *Auton v. British Columbia* (trial decision) *supra*, at para. 10

> Allison M. Schmidt, "Violence and Abuse in the Lives of Women with Disabilities" http://www.doug-lawson.com/dcac/ARTAbuse.htm, accessed December 24, 2003

> Laurie E. Powers et al., "Barriers and Strategies in Addressing Abuse: A Survey of Disabled Women's Experiences" Journal of Rehabilitation, Jan-March, 2002, http://www.findarticles.com/cf_dls/m0825/1_68/83910976/print.jhtml

Dick Sobsey and Tanis Doe, *supra*

16. State failure to respond to autism also produces secondary effects that are pertinent to an equality analysis. Failing to respond to autism privatizes responsibility by placing it solely on parents, increasing the challenges associated with caring for and advocating on behalf of children with autism. Privatization generally has gendered effects. Given prevailing patterns of child care responsibilities, especially with respect to children with disabilities, such privatization impacts disproportionately on women as mothers and primary care givers. Privatization also disproportionately affects those who, for reasons of class or other economically disadvantaging factors, such as race and disability, have fewer resources to draw on to care for an autistic child. Thus state failure to provide autism services creates not only an inequality for the autistic children themselves, but also differential effects on families of children with autism.

> Melanie Panitch, "Mothers of Intention: Women, Disability and Activism" in *Making Equality: History of Advocacy and Persons with Disabilities in Canada*, Deborah Stienstra and Aileen Wight-Felske, eds. (Concord, Ontario: Captus Press, 2003) at 261

17. To avoid social isolation of persons with autism, an expanded understanding of health services is required, one that is less restrictive than the traditional medical understanding. In accord with the social model of disability, the emphasis should be on removing barriers to participation rather than simply "modifying" the individual. This expanded understanding of health services must be informed by the perspective and voices of persons with autism. Moreover, it should challenge the current power and dominance of the doctors/hospitals paradigm, which defines disability as a deviation from the norm, and controls the provision of services based on medical professionals' own available skill set.

> Institute for the Study of the Neurologically Typical, Home Page and DSN-IV The Diagnostic and Statistical Manual of 'Normal' Disorders, available at: http://isnt.autistics.org/ and http://isnt.autistics.org/dsn.html

The Section 15 Breach in the Present Case

Is There Inequality?

18. It is important to appreciate the experience of inequality that constitutes a breach of s. 15. To promote equality, a substantive equality ap-

proach requires taking proper account of differential needs. In the present case, prior to the order of Allan J., the government provided no autism-related services. It thus did not respond at all to the needs of autistic children. The evidence is clear that doing nothing for autistic children will likely lead to a life of marginalization, and often institutionalisation, with the result that valuable contributions to society will be foregone.

19. The exclusionary and marginalizing effects of the state failing to respond to autism is the crux of the inequality in this case. Autistic persons who do not fit societal norms experience the stigmatization of mental disability and are banished to the margins of society. The real effect of state failure to respond to autism is to convey the message that children with autism are just not worth society's time, effort and resources. State neglect is discriminatory because it devalues the relative worth of such children, and subjects them to social isolation. Although autism is more prevalent in males, the gendered disability effects on girls and women with autism is highly relevant to an equality analysis because of the compounded impact of discrimination on females with autism, as described above in paragraph 15.

20. The Coalition submits that the s. 15 breach is the refusal to provide autism-related health services, and that compliance with s. 15 demands provision of such services in accordance with equality principles as set out below. The breach is not the refusal to fund Lovaas treatment specifically. The Coalition agrees with Allan J. at trial that this particular case does not involve a constitutional obligation to provide a specific treatment. Moreover, the nature of the record below, summary proceedings under the *Judicial Review Procedure Act*, did not permit an assessment of Lovaas treatment for its compliance with equality principles.

Auton v. British Columbia (trial decision), *supra* para. 7 and 50

Judicial Review Procedure Act, R.S.B.C. 1996, c. 241.

21. It is problematic under a substantive equality analysis to endorse a treatment that has the objective of "training" autistic "behaviour" out of the autistic child. The appropriate response to autism should be to enable full participation in society; the response should incorporate a relational approach that facilitates inclusion without forced assimilation. A non-disabled person is as different from a disabled person as a disabled person is from a non-disabled person; the difference does not explain why the non-disabled world-view is the norm. The objective of autism-related health

services should not be to rid society of autism or autistic behaviour, but to ensure that autistic persons receive the equal respect and consideration to which they are entitled.

22. This Honourable Court has emphasized that s. 15 requires a subjective/objective analysis. This poses a particular difficulty in this case because of the tender years of the infant petitioners at trial. In the lower courts there was no autistic voice in this litigation; the petitioners' voice in court has been that of the non-autistic parents. The Coalition cannot and does not purport to speak for autistic persons. The Coalition does, however, emphasize that there is a need on everyone's part to be cognizant of the perspective of persons with autism. Failure to do so risks ablist conceptions of autism and disability, and disrespect for persons with autism specifically and persons with disabilities generally. It is essential to avoid the "community prejudices", warned about in *Law*, as they apply to autism.

> *Law v. Canada (Minister of Employment and Immigration), supra* at para. 61

> Dana Baker, "Autism as Public Policy" in Devlin & Pothier (eds.), *supra* at 10

23. Parental choice on behalf of disabled children can be deferred to only with caution. Although in general parents can and should be presumed to act in the best interests of their children, as a matter of constitutional principle, there are clear limits to parental choice. Decisions must respect the equality rights of children with disabilities and must conform to equality rights principles, as elaborated in paragraph 34 below.

> *E (Mrs.) v. Eve*, [1986] 2 S.C.R. 388

> *R. v. Latimer*, [2001] 1 S.C.R. 3

24. The primary rationale for the government's exclusionary policy was that autism services are not medically insured because they are not provided by hospitals or doctors. This framework is drawn from the *Canada Health Act* which is incorporated into the B. C. *Medicare Protection Act*. The appellant relies on the statutory definition of medically insured services, which gives primacy to health services provided by hospitals and doctors. However, that very statutory framework is what is under challenge, and therefore that in itself cannot be the answer. The challenge is to the statutory framework that gives primacy to doctors and hospitals, and within that paradigm, the challenge is to the refusal to exercise the available discretion to deviate from that statutory primacy.

> *Canada Health Act*, R.S.C. 1985, c. C-6

Medicare Protection Act, R.S.B.C. 1996, c. 286, preamble

25. A critical flaw in the appellant's position lies in its narrow conception of health services. A conception of health services that is focussed on hospitals and doctors is based on the "normal" (physical) ailments of the non-disabled. The design of the health services system around doctors and hospitals is geared to the usually temporary and/or curable conditions of the non-disabled. William Lahey has commented on the "institutional asymmetry" of the primacy accorded to hospitals and doctors' services.

> [T]he legal compartmentalization of our health care system obscures the nature of the premises and assumptions on which we implicitly rely when we make choices about (for example) funding for treatments that are outside the scope of medicare. These include a premise that medicine is generally superior to other responses to illness, suffering and disability, that curing is more important than caring (as well as prevention), that dealing with the episodic illness of the healthy is more important than dealing with chronic illness and disability, and that physical health takes priority over other dimensions of health, including mental health. Seen in this broader light, the *Auton* case is a manifestation of a decision-making dynamic that cuts across the Canadian health care system.

> William Lahey, "Canada's Health Care System: The Legal Framework for Financing, Delivery and Policy-Making", in Jocelyn Downie, William MacInnis and Karen McEwen, eds., *Dental Law in Canada* (forthcoming, Butterworths) at 79–80

26. The appellant's argument takes the hospitals and doctors framework as natural and inevitable, characterizing anything outside that framework as "extra" or "special". This leaves the norm unquestioned — in defiance of this Honourable Court's direction to challenge, as part of an equality analysis, what is assumed to be natural, inevitable, or the norm.

> *British Columbia (Public Service Employee Relations Commission) v. British Columbia Government and Service Employees' Union (B.C.G.S.E.U.)*, [1999] 3 S.C.R. 3

> Shelagh Day & Gwen Brodsky, "The Duty to Accommodate: Who Will Benefit?" (1996), 75 Can. Bar Rev. 433

> Margot Young "Sameness/Difference: A Tale of Two Girls" (1997) 4 Review of Constitutional Studies 150.

> Institute for the Study of the Neurologically Typical, *supra*

27. The government's failure to provide services to autistic children means that their health services needs are substantially unmet. It is no answer to say that autistic children can receive the same services from doctors and hospitals as do other children. Such a purely formal equality analysis has been rejected as inadequate by this Court. In *Vriend* it was held that it was no answer to say that gays and lesbians were protected from, for example, race discrimination if they were in fact also vulnerable to, but not protected against, sexual orientation discrimination. That autistic children will receive treatment of, for example, broken bones is beside the point. That non-autistic children do not get autism services, which they do not need, does not nullify the inequality and discrimination of denying autistic children the autism services they do need. A substantive equality analysis requires taking account of differential need; it is not satisfied by treating everyone the same despite different circumstances. This Honourable Court in *Andrews* and in *Brooks* rejected the formal equality analysis adopted in *Bliss*.

> *Vriend v. Alberta*, [1998] 1 S.C.R. 493, para. 98
>
> *Law Society of British Columbia v. Andrews, supra*
>
> *Brooks v. Canada Safeway Ltd.*, [1989] 1 S.C.R. 1219
>
> *Bliss v. Attorney General of Canada*, [1979] 1 S.C.R. 183

28. The present case requires a distinction between the *Canada Health Act*'s principles of universality and comprehensiveness. Universality concerns the availability of insured services to all, whereas comprehensiveness concerns the list of insured services. Donna Greschner and Stephen Lewis' claim that only universality engages basic questions of citizenship is fundamentally flawed because it engages only in a formal equality analysis. Substantive equality requires an assessment of what "comprehensiveness" includes within insured services to determine if the most pressing health services needs of marginalized segments of the population are disproportionately not met, so as to amount to discrimination. The principle of comprehensiveness must be interpreted and applied in accord with the equality guarantees, and the list of insured services must be developed pursuant to the equality principles outlined in paragraph 34 below.

> Donna Greschner & Stephen Lewis, "*Auton* and Evidence-Based Decision-Making: Medicine in the Courts" (2003) 82 Can. Bar Rev. 501 at 514–5.

29. The comparative component of an equality analysis identifies reference points to illustrate the unequal effects of government policy. Care is required not to use the comparator requirement perversely to reinforce a discriminatory norm. In the present case the norm of tying insured services to hospitals and doctors must be scrutinized. That norm is not neutral, but is skewed in favour of the typical health services needs of the non-disabled. Although services from doctors and hospitals are subject to critique even in respect of the non-disabled population, persons with disabilities, and especially persons with mental disabilities such as autism, are less likely to have their disability related health needs met by such services.

> [T]he priority that is given to physician and hospital services solely *because* they are physician and hospital services is questionable, particularly from the inequity this creates for Canadians with needs that are best or at least better addressed through other kinds of treatment. ... [The current] system can produce consequences that are inconsistent with the broader objectives of the *Canada Health Act*, "to protect, promote and restore the physical and mental well-being of residents of Canada".... In the world of the twenty-first century, true fidelity to these principles would connect public funding to essentiality, not to whether or not the service was provided by doctors or in hospitals. (emphasis in original)
>
> William Lahey, *supra* at 87–88

30. State failure to fund autism services for children with autism is an example of a larger pattern. The courts below drew the comparison between autistic and non-autistic children; the Coalition suggests making the comparison between disabled and non-disabled persons more generally.

31. The difference in how health services needs of the non-disabled and disabled population are met in a system giving primacy to services from doctors and hospitals is not just a descriptive difference. The design of the current system to primarily meet the typical needs of non-disabled patients reflects the powerlessness of autistic persons in particular and the disabled more generally. The power to define the nature of insured health services lies with the dominant society, operating from a non-disabled perspective.

> Martha Minow, *Making All the Difference: Inclusion, Exclusion, and American Law* (Ithaca, New York: Cornell University Press, 1990) at 110–112
>
> Teri Hibbs & Dianne Pothier, "Post-Secondary Education and Students with Disabilities: Mining a Level Playing Field or Playing in a Mine-Field?" in Devlin & Pothier (eds.), *supra* at 6–11

32. The power of the doctors/hospitals paradigm needs to be dislodged to allow for the provision of health services for all persons with autism on an equitable basis. The failure to disrupt the norm and to provide females with autism with the necessary health services to allow for their inclusion in society risks their social isolation and stigmatisation, placing them in increased danger, over males with autism, of experiencing violence and oppression.

33. The norm of the doctors/hospitals paradigm should be disrupted by requiring that services be provided on a non-discriminatory basis, in accordance with substantive equality principles. There should be no arbitrary focus on the doctors/hospitals paradigm. Instead, a focus on essentiality of needs to further equality of outcomes is required. As with respect to minority language education rights, the role of the courts is to set the parameters of constitutional principles that must be observed, leaving the detailed implementation (subject to judicial oversight for compliance with the principles) to the executive branch of government.

Mahé v. Alberta, [1990] 1 S.C.R. 342

34. In order to avoid inequality and achieve substantive equality in accordance with the purpose of s. 15, the approach required is the application of equality rights principles to the provision of health services broadly defined. The Coalition submits that such legal principles include:

a. government policy must recognize an obligation to respond to differential needs in a contextual manner that avoids privileging of the dominant perspective, ensuring that the norm/reference is not the status quo;

b. the design of government policy must involve an authentic effort to move outside the non-disabled framework, such that government services promote inclusion without forced assimilation, i.e. there must be a commitment to non-pathologizing of difference;

c. the design of government policy must recognize an obligation to consult and consider options in good faith, listening to and taking into account the voices, lived experiences, and perspectives of the group affected (e.g: inclusion of adult autistic persons in this instance);

d. government funded services must involve a commitment to non-violent and non-coercive programs;

e. the government must commit financial and other resources in an equitable way.

35. The proceeding analysis demonstrates the utter failure of the government to apply these equality rights principles. The unequal effects of the doctors/hospital paradigm, which responds disproportionately to the needs of the non-disabled population, amounts to differential treatment that discriminates on the basis of disability. Thus autistic children are denied the ability to realize their full potential, which is a denial of substantive equality. This conclusion has been reached through an analysis that intertwines the concepts of differential treatment, grounds, and discrimination. Nevertheless, if the Court finds it necessary to disaggregate the analysis, this case meets all the requirements of the three step *Law* test, as argued below.

The *Law* Framework

(1) Differential treatment

36. As stated above, the focus on doctors/hospitals responds disproportionately to the needs of the non-disabled population instead of incorporating the equality principles set out above. The refusal to respond to the needs of autistic children fails to take into account the claimants' already disadvantaged position, including the particular oppression of females with autism, within Canadian society, resulting in substantively differential treatment between the claimants and others on the basis of disability and gendered disability. The differential treatment is grounded in the statutory framework giving primacy to hospitals and doctors, and reinforced by the administrative refusal to exercise the available statutory discretion to deviate from that primacy.

(2) Enumerated or analogous ground

37. Physical and mental disability are enumerated grounds in s. 15. Although the appellant does not concede that there is any distinction based on disability, he concedes that autism is a disability. The Coalition emphasizes that what makes autism a disability is not the neurological disorder *per se*, but how the social response to autism inhibits the participation of autistic persons in society. That is the proper focus for the social model of disability, which is necessary to give a purposive interpretation to the inclusion of disability within s. 15.

(3) Discrimination

38. The failure to cover autism-related health services, and hence the failure to provide autism services in accordance with substantive equality

principles, is discriminatory because state neglect treats autistic children as second class, thereby contributing to their oppression. State neglect further marginalizes an already marginalized group by refusing to respond to their needs. An analysis of the factors identified in *Law* support a conclusion of discrimination, incorporating an affront to human dignity.

(a) pre-existing disadvantage, stereotyping, prejudice, or vulnerability

39. This Honourable Court has previously recognized that persons with disabilities experience pre-existing disadvantage, stereotyping, prejudice, and vulnerability. There can be little doubt that persons with autism are especially subject to such experience. Moreover, as stated in paragraph 15, there are circumstances where women with autism are vulnerable to oppression and violence where non-disabled women and men with autism would not be so vulnerable.

> *Eldridge v. British Columbia (Attorney General), supra*
>
> *Granovsky v. Canada (Minister of Employment and Immigration), supra*

(b) correspondence to needs capacities and circumstances

40. The requirement that non-discriminatory legislation or policy correspond to needs, capacities and circumstances, functions as a direction against a simplistic formal equality approach. The mere fact that everyone is treated the same is not equal treatment if some have differential needs or circumstances. If government policy does not respond to differential needs, capacities and circumstances, it does not conform to the guaranteed right to substantive equality. If government policy does respond to differential needs, capacities and circumstances it conforms to the guaranteed right to substantive equality.

41. This Honourable Court has repeatedly held that discriminatory intent is not necessary to a finding of a violation of s. 15. Whatever the government's intention, the present case represents an utter failure of government policy to correspond to the needs, capacities and circumstances of children with autism. As in *Martin*, the exclusion of coverage sends a message that autistic children are not equally valued and respected so as to warrant attention to their needs. Instead their needs are totally ignored. As stated in *Martin*:

> A classification that results in depriving a class from access to certain benefits is much more likely to be discriminatory when it is not supported by the larger objectives pursued by the challenged legislation.

> *Law Society of British Columbia v. Andrews, supra*
>
> *Eldridge v. British Columbia (Attorney General), supra* at para. 62
>
> *Vriend v. Alberta, supra* at para. 93
>
> *Nova Scotia (Workers' Compensation Board) v. Martin*, [2003] S.C.J. No. 54 (QL) para. 94; 101
>
> Isabel Grant & Judith Mosoff, "Hearing Claims of Inequality: *Eldridge v. British Columbia (A.G.)*" (1998) 10 Canadian Journal of Women and the Law 229

42. It is important to note that both the preamble and the purpose section of the *Medicare Protection Act* focus on the need for necessary medical care with no reference to who provides the service. The exclusion of autism services is not in keeping with this overall purpose.

> *Medicare Protection Act*, R.S.B.C. 1996, c. 286, preamble & s. 2.
>
> William Lahey, *supra* at 87–88

43. The needs, capacities and circumstances factor emphasizes the importance of differential effects to a substantive equality analysis. The appellant seeks to obscure the differential effects of its policy by emphasizing the general beneficial purpose of medicare. To so obscure specific discriminatory effects subverts the purpose of s. 15 by importing s. 1 analyses.

> *Gosselin v. Quebec (Attorney General)*, [2002] 4 S.C.R. 429, at paras. 242–5, per Bastarache J. dissenting
>
> *Canadian Foundation for Children, Youth and the Law v. Canada (Attorney General)*, [2004] SCJ 6, para. 97, per Binnie J.

44. Similarly, to use this factor to import a relevance test into s. 15 is inappropriate because it is vulnerable to perpetuating discriminatory norms, and reintroducing formal equality.

> *Miron v. Trudel*, [1995] 2 S.C.R. 418 at para. 137, per McLachlin J.
>
> *Canadian Foundation for Children, Youth and the Law v. Canada (Attorney General), supra* at paras. 98 and 99, per Binnie J.

(c) ameliorative purpose

45. The original point of this factor was to ensure that affirmative action programs are not vulnerable to challenge. That has no possible application here. If ameliorative purpose is too broadly invoked, the balance of benefits vs. harms happens in s. 15, inappropriately increasing the burden on the claimant. As with the previous factor, this factor should not be used to ignore unequal effects and to import an analysis of intent. If the previous

factor is properly conceptualised, it subsumes the ameliorative purpose factor, since affirmative action takes into account differential needs, capacities, and circumstances. Treating ameliorative purpose as a separate factor risks misapplication and the improper importation of s. 1 justifications.

> *Canadian Foundation for Children, Youth and the Law v. Canada (Attorney General)*, *supra* at para. 227, per Deschamps J.

(d) nature of the interest affected

46. The nature of the interest affected should be a key element in a discrimination analysis. It is crucial that it be the claimant's interest that is analysed. Here, the interest affected is far-reaching. At stake is the ability of the infant claimants to participate in society as full citizens. A life with dignity requires meaningful and secure participation in society to the extent possible and desired, including such things as education, employment, social activities, political participation, voting, etc. These are things the non-disabled population typically take for granted. For autistic children, and especially girls, intervention is necessary to facilitate and enable secure participation in society, and to facilitate and enable the use of their talents and their contributions to society. Medical services to respond to autism are thus a dignity constituting benefit of substantial importance.

> Denise Réaume, "Discrimination and Dignity" (2003) 63 La. Law Rev. 645

47. To deny a response to the needs of autistic children is to strike at the core of citizenship rights of participation. For females with autism, this denial is particularly localized and severe because of their increased vulnerability to oppression and violence. Full citizenship is not a mere status category, but depends on an inclusionary society. A society that ignores the needs of disabled females and males creates second class citizens, a regime of "disitizenship" and oppression that seriously undermines human dignity. It is in the interests of both the disabled and of society as a whole to value equality and full inclusion of all members.

> *In Unison: A Canadian Approach to Disability Issues — A Canadian Approach*, *supra* at 1
>
> Richard Devlin & Dianne Pothier, "Introduction: Towards a Critical Theory of Discitizenship" in Devlin & Pothier (eds.), *supra* at 22–23
>
> Marcia H. Rioux and Fraser Valentine, "Does Theory Matter? Exploring the Nexus between Disability, Human Rights and Public Policy" in Devlin & Pothier (eds.), *supra*, at 21–23

Human Dignity and the *Law* Test

48. The s. 15 discrimination analysis, and in particular the focus on injury to dignity, must support an effective and meaningful substantive equality analysis, and must ensure that the full purpose of s. 15 is realized. The s. 15 discrimination analysis should focus on the unequal effects of systemic disadvantage to ensure that s. 15 rights are properly protected and advanced.

> June Ross, "A Flawed Synthesis of the Law" (2000) 11:3 *Constitutional Forum* 74
>
> B. Baines, "*Law* v. *Canada:* Formatting Equality" (2000) 11:3 *Constitutional Forum* 65

49. To achieve s. 15's purpose of addressing inequality, a broad understanding of human dignity is necessary. A narrow conception risks ignoring significant manifestations of inequality if it fails to incorporate the full harm of discrimination. Confining affronts to human dignity to hurt feelings ignores the structural and systemic bases of discrimination. Discrimination can include experiences of exploitation, marginalization, powerlessness, cultural imperialism, violence, historical disadvantage, and exclusion from the mainstream of society. These experiences are indicia of inequality that are pertinent to the purpose of s. 15.

> Iris Marion Young, *Justice and the Politics of Difference* (Princeton, New Jersey: Princeton University Press, 1990) at 48–65
>
> *Law Society of British Columbia* v. *Andrews, supra* per McIntyre J. at para. 43, per Wilson J. at para. 5 and per La Forest J. at para. 68

50. To fulfil the special role of s. 15, focus must be on the promotion of equality. The concrete power relations at the source of discriminatory behaviour must be examined to link more clearly the impugned law or (in)action to the relations of domination that perpetuate and rationalize the systemic inequality of oppressed groups. In this case the resulting experience of marginalization, powerlessness, non-disabled imperialism, and potential violence are all profound indicia of inequality and injury to dignity.

51. Human dignity is a malleable concept. Care needs to be taken so that it is not used to undermine substantive equality. If the inquiry is focused on individual emotive feelings, or used to import s. 1 justification questions into s. 15, or used to validate similarly situated analyses, it will indeed undermine the purposes of s. 15. What is required instead is an analysis of inequality that challenges the norm and fulfils the unique purpose of s. 15 to promote substantive equality.

Sheilah Martin, "Balancing Individual Rights to Equality and Social Goals", *supra*

Sheilah Martin, "Court Challenges: *Law*", (Winnipeg: Court Challenges Program, 2002)

Dianne Pothier, "Connecting Grounds of Discrimination To Real People's Real Experiences" (2001) 13 Canadian Journal of Women and the Law 37

Canadian Foundation for Children, Youth and the Law v. Canada (Attorney General), supra at para. 72

Denise Réaume, *supra*

Section 1 of the *Canadian Charter of Rights and Freedoms*

52. As with the *Law* framework in relation to s. 15, s. 1 should not be analysed in a formalistic manner. The s. 1 test is found in the language of s. 1, "a reasonable limit ... in a free and democratic society"; the *Oakes* analysis is merely complementary. The understanding of what constitutes a "free and democratic society" under s. 1 needs to include a broad concept of democracy that incorporates an appreciation of principles such as equality, inclusion, and participation, and not just a "majority rules" approach.

Section 1 of the *Canadian Charter of Rights and Freedoms, supra*

RJR-MacDonald Inc. v. Canada (Attorney General), [1995] 3 S.C.R. 199, at para. 126, per McLachlin J.

R. v. Oakes, [1986] 1 S.C.R. 103 at para. 64

53. In cases of under-inclusiveness, this Honourable Court has held that both the purpose of the general statutory scheme as well as the purpose of the limitation/exclusion are relevant to the s. 1 inquiry. Recently, however, Gonthier J., speaking for the entire Court in *Martin*, focused on the purpose of the limit.

Vriend v. Alberta, supra at para. 109

Nova Scotia (Workers' Compensation Board) v. Martin, supra at para. 107

54. In this case, the appellant acknowledges that financial considerations alone cannot constitute a s. 1 justification. Moreover it must be recognized that there are inherent costs of democracy and the protection of constitutional rights, e.g. the right to vote, the right to a speedy trial, etc.

Nova Scotia (Workers' Compensation Board) v. Martin, supra at para. 109

55. The appellant identifies the pressing and substantial objective as the fiscal sustainability of the health services system by focusing on core health

services. While fiscal sustainability cannot be ignored, it must be recognized that governments make choices about what resources are devoted to health services. Moreover, the appellant's conception of "core" health services cannot go unchallenged. That conception privileges the status quo distribution of health services via an "institutionalized asymmetry" that is tied not to need but to who provides the service. This cannot be a legitimate objective because it is discriminatory against persons with disabilities. Any denial of services cannot be on the backs of the disadvantaged, marginalized, and oppressed.

> The Supreme Court has in any event held that cost is not a constitutionally permissible justification for discrimination under s. 1: *Schachter v. Canada*, [1999] 2 S.C.R. 679, at p. 709, 10 C.R.R. (2d) 1, at p. 20, per Lamer C.J.C. Cost/benefit analyses are not readily applicable to equality violations because of the inherent incomparability of the monetary impacts involved. Remedying discrimination will always appear to be more fiscally burdensome than beneficial on a balance sheet. On one side of the budgetary ledger will be the calculable cost required to rectify the discriminatory measure; on the other side, it will likely be found that the cost to the public of discriminating is not as concretely measurable. The considerable but incalculable benefits of eliminating discrimination are therefore not visible in the equation, making the analysis an unreliable source of policy decision-making.
>
> *Rosenberg v. Canada (Attorney General)* (1998), 38 O.R. (3d) 577 (C.A.) at 11
>
> Shelagh Day & Gwen Brodsky, *supra*
>
> Isabel Grant & Judith Mosoff, *supra*

56. As in *Vriend*, the appellant's argument does not pass the pressing and substantial objective requirement because the objective of protecting the status quo distribution is inherently discriminatory against the disabled. This is inconsistent with the values underlying a free and democratic society.

> *Vriend v. Alberta, supra* at para. 116

57. In the alternative, the appellant's argument fails the proportionality stage of the analysis. Although, in a sense, any refusal to fund is rationally connected to fiscal sustainability, the rational connection test cannot be so empty of content. The rational connection must also be tied to the

general purpose of the statute. There is no rational connection between the provision of comprehensive health services and the exclusion of the most pressing needs of a disadvantaged and marginalized portion of the population such as persons with mental disabilities. In fact, the objective would be better achieved through their inclusion.

> *Vriend v. Alberta, supra* at para. 119
>
> *Egan v. Canada,* [1995] 2 S.C.R. 513 at para. 191, per Iacobucci J., dissenting
>
> *M. v. H., supra* at para. 116

58. In the further alternative, there is no minimal impairment in the present case. There was no attempt to prioritise health needs in accordance with *Charter* principles. The government's claim that the complex design of a health services system is not the proper role of the courts is a hollow one where, as in *Martin*, the government resorted to a simplistic and arbitrary cut-off amounting to a complete exclusion.

> However, even a brief examination of the possible alternatives, including the chronic pain regimes adopted in other provinces, clearly reveals that the wholesale exclusion of chronic pain cannot conceivably be considered a minimum impairment of the rights of injured workers suffering from this disability.
>
> *Nova Scotia (Workers' Compensation Board) v. Martin, supra* at para. 112

59. Although it is not the role of the courts to micro-manage the health services system, it is their role to hold the government accountable for inequitable practices. Where there is no transparency to government decision-making, there can be no deference to policy choices.

> *Nova Scotia (Workers' Compensation Board) v. Martin, supra* at para. 116

60. Finally, given the extreme nature of the breach, i.e. perpetuating the isolation, marginalization, and oppression of persons with autism, the deleterious effects of the exclusion far outweigh any salutary effects. What are the safeguards or assurances for the disadvantaged, marginalized, and oppressed in times of fiscal restraint if not the protection of *Charter* rights?

Remedy

61. To achieve substantive equality, the appropriate remedy is a declaration that incorporates an order that the government provide services in accordance with the principles set out above in paragraph 34. The Court's

role is to set out principles; detailed implementation is up to government, whose implementation is then subject to further *Charter* review for compliance with constitutional principles.

> *Eldridge v. British Columbia (Attorney General), supra*
>
> *Mahé v. Alberta, supra*
>
> *Doucet-Boudreau v. Nova Scotia (Attorney General)*, [2003] S.C.J. No. 63 (QL)

PART IV — SUBMISSIONS CONCERNING COSTS

62. The Coalition is not seeking costs in this matter and submits that no order for costs should be made against the Coalition.

PART V — ORDER REQUESTED

63. The Coalition respectfully requests:

(a) that the appeal should be dismissed; and
(b) that the government should be ordered to provide autism services for children in accordance with equality rights principles.

All of which is respectfully submitted this 13th day of April 2004.

COUNSELS' SIGNATURE

_____

Dianne Pothier
Counsel for the Coalition of
LEAF and DAWN Canada

_____

Fiona Sampson
Counsel for the Coalition of
LEAF and DAWN Canada

Contributors

Beverley Baines was a constitutional equality rights consultant for the Canadian Advisory Council on the Status of Women, the National Association of Women and the Law, and the *Ad Hoc* Committee of Canadian Women on the Constitution, during the fight to strengthen women's *Charter* rights in the early 1980s. With Ruth Rubio-Marin, she co-edited *The Gender of Constitutional Jurisprudence* (Cambridge University Press, 2004), examining the constitutional rights of women in twelve countries. A Professor in the Faculty of Law at Queen's University, she is currently Head of the Women's Studies Department in the Faculty of Arts & Science and teaches Law and Public Policy in the School of Policy Studies.

Dr. Gwen Brodsky is a leading national and international expert on human rights law, with graduate degrees from Harvard Law School and Osgoode Hall. She practises, teaches, and writes in the areas of human rights and constitutional law and she has acted as counsel in many *Charter* equality rights cases. An adjunct professor in the University of British Columbia Faculty of Law, she has taught a course on social and economic rights and the *Charter*. Dr. Brodsky has written extensively about equality rights theory, the *Charter*, and access to justice problems experienced by members of disadvantaged groups. She is a Director of the Poverty and Human Rights Centre and she was LEAF's first Litigation Director.

Melina Buckley is a lawyer and legal policy consultant in Vancouver, working primarily in the areas of constitutional law, human rights legislation, access to justice, and dispute resolution. She holds a Ph.D. in law from the University of British Columbia. Her doctoral research investigated mechanisms to enhance the capacity of Canadian courts and human rights commissions to enforce equality rights and centred on the development of transformative human rights practices. She has been active in equality rights litigation under the *Charter* and human rights, and has written extensively on equality and access to justice issues. Dr. Buckley has been a member of West Coast LEAF's Legal Committee and Board and served as Chair of the Board of the Court Challenges Program of Canada.

Shelagh Day is a well-known Canadian human rights expert and advocate. She is a Director of the Poverty and Human Rights Centre, whose central goal is to strengthen the human rights of the poorest women. She is also the publisher of the *Canadian Human Rights Reporter*, the leading law reporter on statutory human rights in Canada, and the co-author of two books and numerous articles on women's equality rights: *Women and the Equality Deficit* is the leading study of the impact on women of restructuring Canada's social programs, and *One Step Forward, Two Steps Back* was the first examination of how the *Charter*'s equality rights guarantee works for women. With extensive experience in the international field, Shelagh Day has appeared on behalf of Canadian women before United Nations treaty bodies examining Canada's compliance with its international human rights obligations. She is the former Director of the Saskatchewan Human Rights Commission, the first President of the Women's Legal Education and Action Fund (LEAF), and a founder of the Court Challenges Program. In addition, she was a Vice-President of the National Action Committee on the Status of Women (NAC) at the time of the Charlottetown Constitutional Talks. Currently, Shelagh Day is the Special Advisor on Human Rights to the National Association of Women and the Law (NAWL), and the Chair of the Human Rights Committee of the Canadian Feminist Alliance for International Action (FAFIA).

Margaret Denike is an Assistant Professor and Coordinator of the Program in Gender Equality and Social Justice at Nipissing University in North Bay, Ontario. On sabbatical leave in 2005–2006, she is conducting research on equality jurisprudence and international human rights law as an LLM candidate at Queen's University. She is a member and former co-chair of the National Legal Committee of LEAF.

Fay Faraday is a partner at Cavalluzzo Hayes Shilton McIntyre & Cornish LLP, a Toronto law firm specializing in labour, human rights, and public interest law. With a practice that focuses on constitutional and appellate litigation, labour, and human rights, she has extensive experience with equality rights litigation under the *Charter* at all levels of court, including the Supreme Court of Canada. She has been a member of LEAF's National Legal Committee, the National Steering Committee of the National Association of Women and the Law, and has represented and consulted with numerous social justice and labour groups with respect to *Charter* equality litigation. She has published numerous papers on equality rights.

Judith Keene joined the Clinic Resource Office of Legal Aid Ontario after practising with provincial administrative tribunals for eight years.. She provides legal advice and litigation support to Community Legal Clinics and Student Legal Aid Societies, with a focus on human rights legislation and section 15 of the *Charter of Rights* applied to issues affecting poor people. She has provided advisory support in constitutional challenges to cutbacks and restrictions in social programs (for example, *Falkiner v. Ontario (Ministry of Community and Social Services), Irshad v. Ontario (Ministry of Health), Rogers v. Ontario (Ontario Works Administrator, Sudbury), Broomer v. Ontario (Attorney General)*). Judith Keene has published a legal text on human rights and numerous articles on human rights legislation and on the *Charter of Rights*.

Jennifer Koshan is an Assistant Professor at the University of Calgary Faculty of Law. Her teaching and research interests are in the areas of constitutional law, particularly equality rights, human rights law, labour law, violence against women, and public interest advocacy. Before joining the Faculty of Law, Jennifer Koshan practised for several years in the Northwest Territories as Crown counsel, and worked as the Legal Director of West Coast LEAF. She was a member of LEAF's National Legal Committee from 1999 to 2005, and was a member of LEAF's Board of Directors from 2003 to 2005.

The Honourable Claire L'Heureux-Dubé was appointed to the Supreme Court of Canada in 1987. She retired from the Court in July 2002. Called to the Québec Bar in 1952, she served in private practice in Québec City from 1952 to 1973, and was appointed Queen's Counsel in 1969. She was appointed to the Superior Court of Québec in 1973 and to the Québec Court of Appeal in 1979. Her contributions to law and public life have been recognized with eleven honourary doctorates and numerous prestigious awards. These honours include The Yves Pélicier Award, presented by the International Academy of Law and Mental Health (2002), the Margaret Brent Women Lawyers of Achievement Award, from the American Bar Association Commission on Women in the Profession (1998), the Prix de la Justice, presented by the Canadian Institute for the Administration of Justice (1997), and The Canadian Award, presented by the Canadian Hadassah-WIZO (for An outstanding Canadian Advocate of Equality and Champion of Human Rights). On her retirement from the Supreme Court of Canada, the University of Ottawa honoured Justice L'Heureux-Dubé by establishing the Claire L'Heureux-Dubé Fund for Social Justice. She was appointed as a

Companion of the Order of Canada in 2003 and was awarded the Québec Order of Merit (l'Ordre national du Québec) in 2004.

Diana Majury is an Associate Professor in the Law Department at Carleton University in Ottawa. Her research and teaching interests include the *Charter* and equality theory, human rights, criminal law, women's health, and law and literature. She has been active in various capacities with both NAWL and LEAF since their inceptions/conceptions.

Sheila McIntyre was a member of the Faculty of Law at Queen's University from 1984 to 2003. In 2003, she became a member of the Common Law Section of the Faculty of Law at the University of Ottawa and served as the Director of the University's Human Rights Research and Education Centre until July 2005. For twenty-five years she has been a legal activist involved in education equity struggles, test case litigation, and law reform initiatives designed to reduce systemic bias in Canadian law and legal institutions and to advance the equality of disempowered groups. She was a member of the National Legal Committee of LEAF from 1990 to 1994 and has been a member of numerous LEAF sub-committees responsible for Supreme Court of Canada *facta* since 1988. She has also worked with national coalitions of women's organizations to secure equality-driven amendments to criminal sexual offence laws. The focus of her scholarship remains the analysis of systemic inequality and egalitarian change in law and the universities.

Sophia Moreau is Assistant Professor of Law and Philosophy at the University of Toronto. Her current research focuses on equality rights in the public and private sectors. She has written on the role of comparator groups in equality rights analysis (*Journal of Law and Equality*); on the relevance of philosophical analysis to constitutional argument (*Traversing Disciplinary Difference*); on practical reasoning and character (*Ethics*); and on a number of issues in normative ethics (*Ethics* and *Proceedings of the Aristotelian Society*). Prior to joining the University of Toronto, she clerked for Chief Justice Beverley McLachlin at the Supreme Court of Canada (2002–2003).

Dianne Pothier has been teaching at Dalhousie Law School since 1986 and has been a Full Professor since 2001. Her teaching and research subjects include constitutional law, conflict of laws, public law, labour law, human rights, equality rights, and disability rights. She was legal counsel to the Canada Labour Relations Board from 1984 to1986, a Supreme Court of Canada law clerk to Justice Brian Dickson in 1983, and is currently on the

Equality Rights Panel of the Court Challenges Program. In 2005, she received a Frances Fish Women Lawyers' Achievement Award from the Nova Scotia Association of Women and the Law. She was called to the Nova Scotia Bar in 1982 and her litigation experience includes being the appellant's co-counsel in the Supreme Court of Canada in *R.D.S. v. The Queen*, and being counsel for the joint intervention of LEAF and DAWN in *British Columbia v. Auton*.

Melanie Randall is an associate professor at the Faculty of Law, University of Western Ontario. She has undertaken research and educational work on issues relating to violence against women and the law. Her published work has addressed legal remedies for sexual violence, including legal constructions of "ideal victims" in domestic violence criminal cases, legal misunderstandings of women's responses to violence and abuse, comparative approaches to asylum claims based on gender persecution in refugee law, and using the law to seek state accountability for violence against women. She is co-writing the first Canadian Bench Book on domestic violence and the law for judges, which will accompany the National Judicial Institute's educational program, and is entitled "Violence and Abuse in Intimate Relationships: Enhancing Judicial Skills in Cases involving Domestic Violence."

Denise G. Réaume is Professor of Law at the University of Toronto where she has taught since 1982. She holds law degrees from Oxford University and Queen's University, as well as a degree in history from Queen's. Professor Réaume teaches in the areas of tort law, discrimination law, legal responses to a multicultural society, and feminist analysis of law. Her current research projects include work on official language rights in Canada, discrimination law, and feminist issues in tort law, all subjects on which she has published. She has also been a member of several LEAF factum writing sub-committees.

Leslie A. Reaume is counsel to the Canadian Human Rights Commission. Prior to working with the Commission, she developed an equality rights firm in London, Ontario, with a focus on statutory human rights, the *Charter*, as well as administrative and civil cases engaging human rights issues. She has argued cases in numerous administrative law forums and at all levels of Canadian Courts, including the Supreme Court of Canada. From 1997 to 2001, she was appointed part-time at the University of Western Ontario, and is currently teaching in the Faculty of Law at Queen's University. The publication of her new book, *Human Rights Law in Can-*

ada, co-authored with Philippe Dufresne, is forthcoming from Irwin Law Inc.

Fiona Sampson is the Director of Litigation at the Women's Legal Education and Action Fund (LEAF). Fiona has appeared before the Supreme Court of Canada as counsel for LEAF in the *NAPE* and *Auton* cases. Fiona has a Ph.D. in Law from Osgoode Hall Law School. The focus of her Doctoral thesis was the judicial treatment of gendered disability discrimination. Dr. Sampson was recently recognized by the Law Society of Upper Canada for her work relating to the advancement of women's equality rights in Canada.

Karen Schucher has been involved in equality and human rights litigation for many years. She was co-counsel in the Federation of Women Teachers' Associations of Ontario human rights litigation and worked on numerous equality rights issues on behalf of trade unions in her former practice with Cavalluzzo Hayes Shilton McIntyre & Cornish. Karen Schucher was counsel to LEAF in the NAPE intervention and is currently a member of LEAF's National Legal Committee. She has written on a wide range of human rights issues and is actively involved with women's organizations working on violence against women, most currently with Canadian Chiapanecas Justice for Women (CCJW), a recently-established North/South working group.

M. Kate Stephenson is a lawyer at the law firm WeirFoulds LLP in Toronto and was called to the Bar in 1996. She has a litigation practice that focuses on human rights, constitutional, and administrative law. She has been counsel in several equality cases, often involving people of low-income and people on social assistance, and often on a *pro bono* basis. For two years, she was seconded to the Clinic Resource Office of Legal Aid Ontario (2002–2004), where she was the Clinic Barrister, doing court litigation for clinics all across the province of Ontario. She was a member of the National Legal Committee of LEAF from 1999 to 2004, and she chaired that committee for two years. As a law student, she was the Director of the Centre for Spanish Speaking People's Student Legal Clinic, and presently she is a Board member of the Income Security Advocacy Centre in Toronto. In 2004 she received the first ever Advocate's Society Arleen Goss Young Advocates' Award, an award created to acknowledge a lawyer who has been called to the bar for less than 10 years, and who has demonstrated "innovative and passionate advocacy, contribution to social justice, and commitment to the community."

Andrea Wright is presently counsel to the Commission of Inquiry into the Actions of Canadian Officials in Relation to Maher Arar, specializing in national security and human rights, and the comparative study of accountability mechanisms for security intelligence in democratic countries. A graduate of the Faculty of Law, McGill University, she has practised with McCarthy Tétrault in Toronto, and has been involved in a number of public law projects and conferences. At the time of the presentation of her paper in this volume, she was counsel to the Canadian Human Rights Commission, litigating statutory human rights, *Charter*, and administrative law cases in both official languages before numerous courts and tribunals, including the Supreme Court of Canada.

Index

March 27/07